Applied Social Care

An Introduction for Students in Ireland

SECOND EDITION

Edited by

PERRY SHARE & KEVIN LALOR

GILL & MACMILLAN

Gill & Macmillan
Hume Avenue
Park West
Dublin 12
with associated companies throughout the world
www.gillmacmillan.ie

© 2009 Perry Share & Kevin Lalor

978 07171 4376 4

Index compiled by Cover to Cover
Print origination by Carrigboy Typesetting Services

The paper used in this book is made from the wood pulp of managed forests. For every tree felled, at least one is planted, thereby renewing natural resources.

A CIP catalogue record is available for this book from the British Library.

Contents

Contributors v

Part I: Introduction to Social Care Practice
1. Understanding Social Care *Kevin Lalor and Perry Share* 3
2. Social Care: A European Perspective *Pelle Hallstedt and Mats Högström* 21
3. The Practice of Child and Youth Care in North America *Grant Charles and Thom Garfat* 34
4. Social Care: A View from the UK *Claire Cameron* 46
5. Social Care and the Professional Development Project *Perry Share* 58

Part II: Theoretical Approaches to Social Care Practice
6. Psychological Theories of Child Development *Áine de Róiste* 77
7. Social Care and Social Change: Future Direction or Lost Opportunity? *Tom O'Connor* 99
8. Equality: A Challenge to Social Care *Majella Mulkeen* 110
9. Exploring the Importance of Self-awareness Training in Social Care Education *Denise Lyons* 122
10. Gender and Social Care: Mapping a Structural Analysis *Jacqueline O'Toole* 137
11. Evidence-based Practice in Social Care *Tom Farrelly* 150

Part III: Working in Social Care
12. The Social Care Practice Placement: A College Perspective *Judy Doyle and Kevin Lalor* 165
13. Using Professional Supervision in Social Care *Eileen O'Neill* 182
14. Managing Challenging Behaviour *Eleanor Fitzmaurice* 196
15. Collaborative Advantage: Interdisciplinary Teamwork in Social Care *Clare Rigg and Patrick McGarty* 211
16. Personal and Professional Development for Social Care Workers *John Byrne* 227
17. The Inspection of Children's Residential Centres *Michael McNamara* 244
18. Psychological Health Difficulties in Children and Adolescents *Mark McGranaghan* 259

19. Anti-discriminatory Practice: A New Direction for Social Care
     Majella Mulkeen   276

Part IV: Working with Specific Population Groups
20. Residential Child Care *John McHugh and Danny Meenan*   291
21. Social Care and the Older Person *Carmel Gallagher*   305
22. Social Care and Family Support Work *Colm O'Doherty*   318
23. Disability and Social Care *Karen Finnerty*   330
24. Travellers in Ireland and Issues of Social Care *Ashling Jackson*   348
25. Working with Young People *Maurice Devlin*   366
26. Exploring the Complexity of Addiction in Ireland *Joe Doyle*   382
27. Homelessness *Mairéad Seymour*   403
28. Social Care in a Multicultural Society *Celesta McCann James*   418

Endnotes   434

References   439

Index   479

Contributors

John Byrne is a social care worker and Lecturer in Personal and Professional Development, and a practice placement tutor at the Waterford Institute of Technology. He is the former co-ordinator of the Irish Association of Social Care Workers and is currently training as a person-centred psychotherapist at Dublin City University.

Claire Cameron, PhD, is Senior Researcher at the Thomas Coram Research Unit, Institute of Education, University of London, where she has been based since 1992. Her professional background is in social work and her doctorate addressed the interface of day-care services for young children and child protection policies and practices. She has conducted many studies of children's services, including cross-national studies. Her most recent book (co-authored with Peter Moss) was *Care Work in Europe: Current Understandings and Future Directions*. Her main interests are in children in care, early childhood services, and children's workforce issues, including gender.

Grant Charles, PhD, is Associate Professor in the School of Social Work at the University of British Columbia in Vancouver, Canada. He is co-editor of the Canadian journal *Relational Child and Youth Care Practice*.

Áine de Róiste, PhD, is Senior Lecturer in Social Care at Cork Institute of Technology. She is the author (with Kevin Lalor and Maurice Devlin) of *Young People in Contemporary Ireland* (Gill & Macmillan, 2007) and (with Celesta McCann James and John McHugh) *Social Care Practice in Ireland: An Integrated Perspective* (Gill & Macmillan, 2009). With her CIT colleague Joan Dinneen, she undertook commissioned research for the Office of the Minister for Children on young people's recreation and leisure. She has worked in the field of early intervention and is a registered psychologist with the Psychological Society of Ireland.

Maurice Devlin, PhD, is Senior Lecturer in Applied Social Studies at NUI Maynooth. He is a member of the National Youth Work Advisory Committee, is joint chair of the North-South Education and Standards Committee for Youth Work and Irish correspondent for the European Knowledge Centre on Youth Policy. He chairs the editorial board of the journal *Youth Studies Ireland*, is author of *Inequality and the Stereotyping of Young People* (NYCI/Equality Authority, 2006) and co-author (with Kevin Lalor and Áine de Róiste) of *Young People in Contemporary Ireland* (Gill & Macmillan, 2007).

Joe Doyle has worked at a senior level in both the community and public sectors. Currently he holds a national brief as Senior Rehabilitation Co-ordinator with the HSE. He has held positions as the HSE's National Drug Strategy Co-ordinator, Blanchardstown Local Drugs Task Force Co-ordinator and worked for 11 years with the Donnycarney Youth and Drug Projects, initially as a Community Youth Worker and then as the Projects Manager. His reporting relationship is at ministerial level as chairperson of the National Drug Rehabilitation Implementation Committee, HSE representative on the National Drug Strategy Team and board member of the National Advisory Committee on Drugs.

Judy Doyle is a Lecturer in Principles of Professional Social Care Practice, Cross-Cultural Care and Management Practice in the School of Social Sciences, Dublin Institute of Technology. She has worked in social care practice for 17 years, both as a residential care practitioner and as a manager in social care work. As a consultant to the social care sector, she has carried out independent investigations, service reviews and service evaluations and provides professional supervision to social care managers and practitioners. Areas of research include Travelling culture and care, black children in care, and inequality in the affective domain. She is a registered PhD student with the School of Social Justice, Equality Studies Centre UCD.

Tom Farrelly lectures in the areas of Sociology and Research Methods on the Social Care and Nursing programmes in the Institute of Technology Tralee, Kerry. He has had a varied career ranging from maintenance fitter in Cadbury's, to job coach working in the area of intellectual disability, to community education organiser. His research interests include adult and lifelong learning, e-learning, research methodology and medical sociology.

Karen Finnerty has been Director of the Open Training College, Dublin since 1999. Prior to taking up this post she had 15 years' experience in Ireland and the US working in the areas of general education, special education, training, services for people with disability and management development and education. Her areas of interest are quality in third-level education, life-long learning and adult education. She is a graduate of Trinity College Dublin, the Irish Management Institute and Dublin City University and is currently a doctoral student with the University of Leicester.

Eleanor Fitzmaurice, PhD, is Senior Lecturer in Applied Social Studies at Limerick Institute of Technology. She also has extensive experience as a social worker in the field of intellectual disability. Current research interests include family and community support as well as competency-based approaches to social care training.

Carmel Gallagher, PhD, is a Lecturer in Sociology and Social Policy in the School of Social Sciences and Law, Dublin Institute of Technology. She has developed and taught on professional courses in social care and has a particular research interest in older people in Irish society. She is author of *The Community Life of Older People in Ireland* (Peter Lang, 2008).

Thom Garfat, PhD, is president of TransformAction Consulting and Training. He is the co-founder and editor of *www.cyc-net.org* and Senior Editor of the Canadian journal *Relational Child and Youth Care Practice*.

Pelle Hallstedt, PhD, is Senior Lecturer at the department of Social Work, Malmö University, Sweden. He lectures in Psychology and Social Work, as well as in the programme Pedagogic Social Work with the Elderly. His doctorate in pedagogy was gained for his study (with Mats Högström) 'The recontextualisation of social pedagogy. A study of three curricula in the Netherlands, Norway and Ireland', a case study that compares three social work/social pedagogical educational programmes.

Mats Högström, PhD, is a Lecturer in Social Work in the department of Social Work, Malmö University, Sweden. His doctoral thesis from 2005, co-authored with Pelle Hallstedt, is a comparison of three social work/social pedagogical educational programmes in Ireland, Norway and the Netherlands. In recent years he has been interested in issues concerning older people and lectures mainly in the Malmö University programme Pedagogic Social Work with the Elderly.

Ashling Jackson is Senior Lecturer in Child and Social Care Studies in Athlone Institute of Technology. She lectures in the areas of sociology, community development and research methods. She is currently finishing her PhD on the topic of pre-marital co-habitation and marriage in Ireland. Her research interests include changing family patterns, gender and disadvantaged groups.

Kevin Lalor, PhD, is Head of Department of Social Sciences, Dublin Institute of Technology. He is the editor of the *Irish Journal of Applied Social Studies* and a member of the editorial board of *Child Abuse and Neglect: The International Journal*. He is secretary to the Royal Irish Academy Social Sciences Committee. Research interests include victimology, child abuse in Africa and youth. He is author (with Áine de Róiste and Maurice Devlin) of *Young People in Contemporary Ireland* (Gill & Macmillan, 2007). In 2008, he was reviewer to the WHO *Report on Violence and Health in Africa* and represented the International Society for the Prevention of Child Abuse and Neglect (ISPCAN) at the 3rd World Congress against Sexual Exploitation of Children and Adolescents.

Denise Lyons is a Lecturer in the Department of Humanities at the Institute of Technology Blanchardstown, with research interests in creative studies and the role of the self in social care practice. She has worked as a social care practitioner in residential child care, and later as a consultant trainer. She qualified in art therapy in 2003, specialising in art therapy and autism.

Celesta McCann James, PhD, is Head of Department of Humanities at the Institute of Technology Blanchardstown and former President of the Irish Association of Social Care Educators (IASCE). She is co-author of *Social Care Practice in Ireland: An Integrated Perspective* (Gill & Macmillan, 2009).

Pat McGarty is Head of the Department of Humanities and Social Studies at the Institute of Technology Tralee, Kerry. He has extensive experience of the development of social care education programmes at Athlone, Blanchardstown and Tralee Institutes of Technology. He is a founder of the Irish Association of Social Care Educators (IASCE). Research interests include the management of change and the development of leadership and teamwork in organisations.

Mark McGranaghan is a Senior Psychologist working in HSE South's Children's Residential Care Services in Cork. Work interests include developing a model of care based on promoting the psychological health and resilience of children in residential group care.

John McHugh is Co-ordinator of Social Studies at Carlow College, St. Patrick's. He has extensive social care experience in residential and community-based settings in Ireland and England. He is co-author of *Social Care Practice in Ireland: An Integrated Perspective* (Gill & Macmillan, 2009).

Michael Macnamara is an inspector with HIQA.

Danny Meenan has worked in the social care field for 21 years and is currently Social Care Manager in a residential care service for the Health Service Executive. He is formerly programme co-ordinator for the work-based degree in applied social studies for the Institute of Technology Sligo. He has an MBA in Health Services Management from UCD/RCSI.

Majella Mulkeen is Lecturer at the Department of Humanities, Institute of Technology Sligo, with teaching interests in feminist theory, sociology and egalitarian theory and practice within the social care and advocacy programmes. Her professional practice background is in youth work and community development. She is co-author of the IASCE *Practice Placement Manual* for social care students and a member of the editorial board of *Youth Studies Ireland*. Her PhD research at UCD explores discourses and practices of care among social care workers in the Irish context.

Tom O'Connor is Lecturer in Social Care, Economics and Public Policy at Cork Institute of Technology. He is co-editor of *Social Care in Ireland: Theory, Policy and Practice* (CIT Press). He is currently researching a book on the development of holistic social care plans. He has written and spoken widely in the media on the Irish economy and issues pertaining to it, in particular taxation, public spending priorities, healthcare and tackling unemployment, all of which will be developed further in a new book in 2010.

Colm O'Doherty, PhD, is Lecturer in Applied Social Studies at the Institute of Technology Tralee. He is a qualified social worker and holds a PhD from UCD. Colm has researched and published in the areas of social policy, child protection, domestic violence, social work theory and practice, social care theory and practice, and family support. He has recently published a book, *A New Agenda for Family Support – Providing Services That Create Social Capital* (Blackhall Publishing, 2007).

Eileen O'Neill is an independent trainer and consultant with a particular interest in professional practice and development. She has researched and published in the field of professional supervision and her book *Professional Supervision: Myths, Culture and Structure* was published by the Resident Managers' Association in 2004.

Jackie O'Toole is Lecturer in Social Research in the Institute of Technology Sligo. She has taught sociology and research methods to social care students in a variety of third-level institutions since 1991. She is an IRCHSS Government of Ireland Scholar, completing a PhD in Sociology at NUI Galway that explores women's stories and narratives of weight management. A committed feminist, she is interested in the implementation of equality and anti-oppressive practice in social care practice.

Clare Rigg, DBA, is Senior Lecturer in the School of Business and Social Studies at the Institute of Technology Tralee, Kerry. Early work was on urban regeneration and she previously worked at the University of Birmingham's School of Public Policy. She has worked with practitioners from all sectors, integrating action learning and action research to issues of organisation development, leadership and management development and to improving interagency working. She researches and writes on action learning, management learning and human resource development, and has co-edited the books *Action Learning for Public Leadership and Organizational Development* and *Critical Human Resource Development*. She currently leads the IT Tralee MBA, is involved with CAIPE (Centre for Advancement of Inter-Professional Education) and researches and supervises in the areas of entrepreneurial organisations, collaborative public service strategy development and management learning.

Mairéad Seymour, PhD, is Senior Lecturer at the Department of Social Sciences, Dublin Institute of Technology. She is co-ordinator of the MA Criminology programme and has researched and published in the areas of crime and social order, comparative youth crime, crime and homelessness, and alternatives to custody.

Perry Share, PhD, is Head of Department of Humanities and Lecturer in Sociology at the Institute of Technology, Sligo. He is co-author of *A Sociology of Ireland, 3rd edition* (Gill & Macmillan, 2007) and co-editor of the Institute of Public Administration's 'Sociological Chronicles' series. He is a founder member of the Irish Association of Social Care Educators (IASCE) and a Research Associate of the Irish Social Science Platform (ISSP). His research interests are in communication, professionalisation and the sociology of food and eating.

Part I

Introduction to Social Care Practice

1

Understanding Social Care

Kevin Lalor and Perry Share

OVERVIEW

There's a good chance you are reading this book because you are planning to be, or already are, a social care practitioner. Yet for many people in Irish society, even those entering the field themselves, the meaning of the term 'social care' is not self-evident. A common question directed at social care students and professionals alike is, 'What do you do?' Misconceptions abound, and in many cases practitioners are not accorded the recognition or status they deserve, at least in part as a consequence of a limited understanding of what the term means.

Some of the blame for this situation lies with the educators in the field. Although the first social care training course (in residential child care) was established in Kilkenny as far back as 1970, there has been a dearth of authoritative written material or academic research related to the area. Social care syllabi have tended to draw on elements of knowledge from social work, sociology, social policy, psychology and a broad range of other disciplines. Most of this knowledge was obtained from outside the country, largely from Britain.

When the first edition of this book was published in 2005, it was the first integrated attempt by educators and practitioners in the social care field in Ireland to define and describe the practice of social care. Inasmuch as it has been widely adopted by educators, students and practitioners of social care practice, it has represented one small step in unifying the field of social care. We hope that it will continue to stimulate debate and further research and writing by students, practitioners, academics and service users.

This opening chapter explores the notion of social care itself. It opens with an examination of some definitions, taking these apart phrase by phrase to see what is involved. Then it provides a short history of social care in Ireland, placing the current set of institutions and practices in a historical context. The remainder of the chapter describes aspects of social care practice itself: what qualities practitioners possess, what sort of work is involved, what practitioners do and where they do it, how much they get paid and what the difference between a social care practitioner and a social worker is. It is hoped that this opening chapter will answer some of the basic questions voiced by students, practitioners and others.

OVERVIEW OF THE BOOK

The chapters of the book fall into four sections. In Part I (Chapters 1 to 5), we attempt to sketch out the parameters of the field, drawing on experience in Ireland, the UK, Europe and North America. It will become clear that the practice of social care, while having many common elements across contemporary developed societies, has different nuances and emphases that reflect the different political, ideological and social systems experienced across the world. You are encouraged to view social care practice in this international context. It is always desirable to see what is happening elsewhere, in particular to draw upon international best practice, but also to be aware of national traditions, histories and particularities. The section also includes a discussion of the issue of professionalism in social care, an important and pertinent theme that you will no doubt encounter at every stage of studying in or working in this field.

Part II of the book (Chapters 6 to 11) identifies some of the theoretical bases of social care practice. These include ideas drawn from psychology and sociology and an examination of gender and sexuality in social care. There is also an examination of the fundamental role of the 'self' in social care practice and of the key discourse of equality. The theory base of social care practice is an evolving one and has developed through the interplay of theory-building, evidence-gathering, policy development and polemical debate. The years to come will see the emergence in Ireland of an ever more distinctive body of knowledge and thought in relation to social care practice that will be inextricably linked to the development of professionalism.

Part III (Chapters 12 to 19) focuses on practice issues. These range from broadly based practices such as student placement, workplace supervision, multidisciplinary teamworking and the role of the Social Services Inspectorate to specific aspects of practice such as responding to challenging behaviour and mental heath issues. This part of the text does not claim to address every aspect of the dynamic and expanding field of social care, but rather to provide some knowledge about and insight into the realities of social care practice, as well as linking that practice to theory.

Part IV (Chapters 20 to 28) examines social care practice with particular social groups, from young people to older people, the homeless and those with addictions, and from Travellers to new immigrant communities. You will see that there are common themes that span social care practice, such as respect for the people social care practitioners work with or a close relationship to the life-worlds of others, but also particular skills and approaches associated with working with people within specific social structures and circumstances. Social care practice is becoming an ever more complex mosaic, and this section tries to illuminate some of the pieces that comprise it.

DEFINITIONS

It is difficult to define social care for a number of reasons. Undeniably, it has suited governments and some agencies *not* to have a standard definition; as a consequence, salary and career structures remained vague for some time, and at the time of writing (early 2009) there remains much to be done. For example, the full implementation of the Health and Social Care Professionals Act 2005, the key legislative basis for defining social care practice, has yet to occur.

A further, and linked, problem is the contested notion of social care as a profession, which we discuss in far greater detail in Chapter 5. There is something of a chicken-and-egg situation here: it is hard to define social care because of the lack of a clear professional grouping we can point to as 'practising social care', which in turn makes it hard to pin down what social care practice might be.

We hope that by the time you have read this book, and certainly – if you are a student – by the time you qualify as a social care practitioner, you will have formed a clearer idea of what social care practice means. Inevitably, though, this understanding will be complex. You will have become aware of social care's flexible nature; its contested position vis-à-vis other practices and occupations (such as nursing, social work, counselling, occupational therapy and so on) and, above all, its dynamism. Social care is a rapidly changing and developing field, in Ireland as elsewhere. We hope that you will pick up something of this dynamism from this book, from your studies, from your interpretation of the world around you and from your own practical experience.

Below we offer a variety of definitions of social care practice that have emerged from attempts by a number of key bodies in the field in Ireland to clarify what social care practice is. These attempts at clarification have largely emerged for pragmatic reasons: the bodies concerned are closely involved in the provision, management or funding of social care or in the education and training of its practitioners, so they have a strong stake in attempting to define it. As a possible future (or current) practitioner, you will also have a strong interest in how to define the field you are entering.

A basic definition agreed by the Irish Association of Social Care Educators (IASCE), the body that represents the educators in the field, runs as follows:

> [Social care is] a profession committed to the planning and delivery of quality care and other support services for individuals and groups with identified needs.

The following are key terms that help to mark out the territory of social care practice.

- *A profession*
  Social care practice is not just an ordinary job, nor is it something done on a voluntary or amateur basis. This distinguishes it from the vast bulk of (equally

valuable) care that is carried out informally in our society by family and community members. The notion of 'professionalism' also implies that this is an occupation with some status and one that requires access to a specific body of skills and knowledge. The complex issue of professionalism is discussed in detail in Chapter 5 of this book.

- *Planning and delivery*
  Social care is not just about providing services, but also about devising and planning them. It thus requires at least two types of skill and understanding: the ability to provide hands-on care and support to people as well as the ability to identify what people require and the ability to be able to plan accordingly, preferably drawing on available evidence and policy guidance. This dual role makes social care practice difficult and challenging, yet also rewarding.

- *Quality care and other support services*
  Social care is indeed about care and it requires qualities of compassion, empathy, patience and resilience. Yet it is also about providing other supports, which may include advocating on behalf of another, turning up in court to speak before a judge or knowing where to refer a person who has particular problems.

- *Individuals and groups*
  Social care can be, and often is, provided in a one-to-one situation, but it can also mean working with small or large groups of people. As a result, both well-developed interpersonal communication skills and a good knowledge of group dynamics are required.

- *With identified needs*
  The traditional 'client group' of social care practitioners in Ireland (and many other countries) has been children in the care of state or voluntary organisations. While caring for this group remains an important task, social care practitioners may now find work with a broad range of groups of all ages that have had special 'needs' or vulnerabilities identified, or indeed with individuals and groups in what we might think of as 'mainstream' society, such as young people in suburban housing estates. The needs and the groups are various, as we will see.

There may also be people whose needs have *not* previously been identified or have been identified only recently, such as survivors of clerical sexual abuse or children with hyperactivity disorders. Our society has only recently recognised and identified the needs that such people have and sought to respond to them. New sets of identified needs may emerge at any time: for example, it is quite likely that there will be a need for ethnically appropriate care of older people in Ireland in the future. The dynamic nature of society helps to explain why social care is a constantly changing field of practice.

We can see that even a single sentence can constitute quite a complex definition. Two further definitions cast a little extra light on what social care might be and what social care practitioners might do. The following definition comes from the IASCE brochure 'What Is Social Care?', which is distributed to guidance teachers, potential students and other members of the public:

> Social care is an (emerging) profession characterised by working in partnership with people who experience marginalisation or disadvantage or who have 'special needs'. Social care practitioners may work, for example, with children and adolescents in residential care; people with learning or physical disabilities; people who are homeless; people with alcohol/drug dependency; families in the community; older people; recent immigrants to Ireland; and others. Typically, though not always, social care practitioners work with children, youth and their families.

While this definition shares much with the more basic definition discussed earlier, there are some additional terms here that are significant.

- *Working in partnership*
  The notion of partnership is important. Social care aims to be not a 'top down' practice, but one that respects the position of the 'client' or 'service user'. In other words, all are equal, working together to find solutions to various challenges. In practice, this aim may not be attained, and the extent to which it is provides much debate in social care.

- *Marginalisation or disadvantage*
  These terms draw attention to the 'social' aspect of social care. They refer to the structures of society that help to create the problems that people face. A 'blame the victim' approach is rejected; rather, social care practice seeks answers to problems, at least partially, in the unequal and discriminatory areas of our society, such as poverty, racism, sexism or violence.

- *People with learning or physical disabilities, people who are homeless, people with alcohol/drug dependency, families in the community, older people, recent immigrants to Ireland*
  This list illustrates some of the people social care practitioners work with. Generally what they have in common is that they are less powerful in Irish society, experience various forms of disadvantage and often suffer through discrimination. It is not an exhaustive list, as will become clear in the course of this book.

- *Children, youth and their families*
  This draws attention to the *holistic* nature of social care practice. It often involves working not just with an individual, but with a network of people, whether a couple, a family or a group. This is another way of emphasising the 'social' in social care.

A third definition of social care is offered by the Joint Committee on Social Care Professionals. This committee, representing the Department of Health and Children, social care employers and the IMPACT trade union, was set up in 2001 in the wake of a number of Labour Court recommendations that followed a period of industrial unrest in the social care sector. Part of the Joint Committee's task was to agree a definition of a social care practitioner so that the government and employers would be better able to decide on what they did, what their status was vis-à-vis other occupations and, ultimately, how much to pay them. The Joint Committee defined social care as:

> the professional provision of care, protection, support, welfare and advocacy for vulnerable or dependent clients, individually or in groups. This is achieved through the planning and evaluation of individualised and group programmes of care, which are based on needs, identified where possible in consultation with the client and delivered through day-to-day shared life experiences. All interventions are based on established best practice and in-depth knowledge of lifespan development. (JCSCP nd.: 13)[1]

We can see that many of the terms used here are similar to those in the other definitions, but there are some additional important features.

- *Day-to-day shared life experiences*
  This refers to an important aspect of social care practice, one that for many practitioners is a key defining element of their work: that they interact with those they are working with in a relatively informal, extended and intimate way. This can be contrasted, for example, with a doctor who may see a patient for just as long as it takes to provide a diagnosis or carry out a procedure. Social care practitioners sometimes (though not always) live for a period of time in the same space as those they work with, interact with them in normal daily activities and get to know them on a much deeper level. A number of chapters in Part IV of this book draw attention to this crucial dimension of social care practice.

- *Established best practice*
  Social care practice is not dreamed up in response to a given problem. Rather, it should draw on established models and evidence about how to work in given situations. Much of the education of social care practitioners concentrates on

helping them to develop their knowledge and expertise regarding what to do in given situations; this is learned at both a theoretical and an experiential level. Both are vital.

- *In-depth knowledge of lifespan development*
  Much of the expertise of social care is in knowing how people change and develop over time and how that development is interlinked with the actions and attitudes of others, particularly families and communities. This knowledge has psychological, sociological, physiological and philosophical dimensions.

At this stage, we have discussed several elements that you could assemble to create a 'perfect' definition of social care practice. To some extent, this will help you to understand what social care practice is, but it is also the case that the reality of social care practice does not always adhere tightly to the definition. Sometimes the elements outlined above are ideals that may never be attained. Often, particular elements are favoured in specific situations. There are also quite political debates and disagreements over what social care practice *should* be. We suggest that you make use of these ideas to carefully examine and think about any examples of social care practice that you encounter, either directly or through reading and research. Ask yourself: Which aspects are brought to the foreground? How could things be done differently? How could they be done better?

In the broader European context, social care practice is usually referred to as *social pedagogy* and social care practitioners as *social pedagogues*. In the United States, Canada and South Africa, the term 'child and youth care' (abbreviated as CYC) is commonly used with the derivation child and youth care worker. The social care contexts of Europe, North America and the UK are explored in some detail in the next three chapters of this book.

HOW DOES SOCIAL PRACTICE WORK DIFFER FROM SOCIAL WORK?

A frequently asked question, especially from potential students of social care practice, is how does it differ from the profession of social work? This can be difficult to answer, as 'social work' has different meanings in different countries, and also because social work is equally as complex to define and describe as social care practice. Thus, Sarah Banks, a leading British writer in the field of social work and the so-called 'social professions', notes the following (2006: 1):

> Social work has always been a difficult occupation to define. It is located within and profoundly affected by diverse cultural, economic and policy contexts in different countries of the world. Social work embraces work in a number of sectors (public, private, independent, voluntary); it takes place in a multiplicity of settings (residential homes, area offices, community

development projects); practitioners perform a range of tasks (caring, controlling, empowering, campaigning, assessing, managing); and the work has a variety of purposes (redistribution of resources to those in need, social control and rehabilitation of the deviant, prevention or reduction of social problems). This diversity, or 'fragmentation' as some have called it, is increasing, which raises the question of whether the occupation can retain the rather tenuous identity it was seeking to develop in the 1970s and 1980s.

Although social work practice varies from country to country, the International Federation of Social Workers (IFSW) uses the following definition to seek to unite all social workers:

> The social work profession promotes social change, problem solving in human relationships and the empowerment and liberation of people to enhance well-being. Utilising theories of human behaviour and social systems, social work intervenes at points where people interact with their environments. Principles of human rights and social justice are fundamental to social work. (www.ifsw.org)

What is interesting from our perspective is how broad this definition is, and how it could similarly apply to social care practice. That is, it shares key points with some of the social care definitions we have considered earlier. For example:

- The assertion that the discipline is a profession.
- The emphasis on 'problem solving', providing services to people with needs.
- The use of theories of human behaviour and social systems to inform practice.
- The goal of empowerment and liberation of service users. This aspect of the professional's work is perhaps less explicitly stated in definitions of social care work (notwithstanding references to advocacy), compared to social work, where the definition also contains a commitment to principles of human rights and social justice.

Thus, there are considerable areas of commonality between social care practice and social work, and in other countries (such as the UK) the two professions overlap to a much greater degree. That being said, there are considerable differences in their roles. In the Irish context, the statutory child protection guidelines (*Children First*) (Department of Health and Children 1999), 'while acknowledging the need for multi-disciplinary and inter-professional responsibility, clearly locate primary responsibility for child protection with community care social work teams' (Skehill 2003: 146). This gives priority to the social work profession – yet such teams also typically contain social care practitioners!

It is probably fair to say that in Ireland, social care practice and social work have developed on parallel yet separate paths. The historical development of Irish social work has been comprehensively outlined by Caroline Skehill and others (Kearney and Skehill 2005; Skehill 1999, 2003). It is the story of an occupational group seeking to develop a coherent professional identity, largely shaped by contemporaneous processes in the United Kingdom. This process has resulted in a recognition by the Irish state that social workers have key, legally defined roles in relation to areas such as child protection and adoption, and also have a specific location in the health services (e.g. in hospitals) and in the justice services (e.g. in probation). Social work education and training are confined to the university sector, often at postgraduate level, and the number of places is strictly limited and controlled.

In the Irish context, a major difference between social care practice and social work lies in the work orientation (Table 1.1). Social care practitioners typically work in a direct person-to-person capacity with the users of services, sometimes called 'clients' and other times called 'service users'. They seek to provide a caring, stable environment in which various social, educational and relationship interventions can take place in the service user's day-to-day living space. An emphasis is on therapeutic work, but not in the context of more formal structured counselling.

The social worker's role is typically to manage the 'case', for example, by arranging the residential placement setting a child is placed in, co-ordinating case review meetings and negotiating the termination of a placement.

Table 1.1. Social Work and Social Care Practice

Social work focuses more on:	*Social care practice* focuses more on:
• Social and community networks. • Social problems. • Organisations and policies. • Knowing about children and families. • A wide variety of societal groups and issues. • Problem-solving. • Gaining power and societal influence.	• Individual and interpersonal dynamics. • Human development. • People and relationships. • Living and working with children and families. • Specific needs of particular groups. • Helping and growth process. • Gaining self-awareness and personal growth.

Source: Anglin (2001: 2).

Social care practice is in many ways a 'newer' professional area, and as we will see in Chapter 5, it has yet to unambiguously attain 'professional status'. Its origins lie in a range of areas, but most specifically in the residential care of young people and the disability sectors. It does not have a legal definition or regulation, though this will change with the enactment of the Health and Social Care Professionals Act 2005. The education and training of social care practitioners are carried out in the main in the Institute of Technology sector, with elements in the further education and private sectors. It is largely confined to the undergraduate area, though postgraduate programmes are emerging. The number of entrants is not controlled by any overarching body and the number of students of social care practice has increased rapidly and substantially over the last decade (Lalor 2009).

So while there is much similarity on paper in the nature of social work and social care practice, we can see that the pathways into practice are quite different, as is the status of the profession in relation to the state. The social position of social work is more favourable, with greater public influence and recognition, and consequently the profession is more open to public scrutiny and criticism. Social care practitioners are much greater in number, may potentially have a much greater impact on the day-to-day delivery of social services and are to be found in a much broader spectrum of activities. Increasingly, both groups are to be found in multidisciplinary teams along with others such as nurses and psychologists, so it will be interesting to see how the different yet overlapping occupational and professional identities are played out and developed in the future.

A BRIEF HISTORY OF SOCIAL CARE IN IRELAND

In order to understand what social care is, it is important to understand where it has come from. In Chapter 2, Hallsted and Högström stress the strong link between social care practice in Ireland and the role of particular organisations and institutions. Thus, any attempt to sketch out a history of social care practice in Ireland inevitably results in a strong emphasis on this institutional context.

Modern social care practice in Ireland was born out of 'serious deficiencies in the running of children's centres … and the recognition of the need for pro-fessionally trained staff' (Kennedy and Gallagher 1997). In independent Ireland, social care was historically provided on behalf of the state by the Catholic and other churches (Fanning and Rush 2006: 12–13) and, until very recently, was largely unregulated or, perhaps more accurately, regulated in a very fragmentary way. For example, pre-school regulations were introduced only in 1996, after decades of both public and private provision. In relation to the care of children, a piece of UK legislation, the 1908 Children's Act, provided the legislative framework in Ireland for the greater part of the twentieth century. But by 1991, the social and political situation with regard to children 'at risk' had changed significantly, reflecting a greater consciousness of the centrality of the rights of the child (Buckley et al. 1997; Focus Ireland 1996; O'Higgins 1996).

The Child Care Act 1991 is in total contrast to the 1908 Act, which simply imposed negative duties to rescue children who had criminal offences committed against them or who were being cruelly treated. Specifically, the 1991 Act recog-nises that the welfare of the child is the first and paramount consideration. The rights and duties of parents are important (and indeed are endorsed in the Constitution), but due consideration must be given to the child's wishes. The Children Act 2001 governs the administration of juvenile justice and, as such, impacts on the work of social care professionals in the children's detention schools (formerly industrial schools and reformatory schools). More recently, the Criminal Justice Act 2006 contains a number of provisions for juvenile justice (Lalor et al. 2007: Chapter 9).

Several influential reports have been published that have helped to shape the development of social care practice. Reflecting broader international trends, they aimed to fundamentally reorient the direction of social care provision away from care in large institutional settings and towards care in small-scale units and in the community. They also emphasised the rights of the 'cared for' and criticised many aspects of institutional practice. These reports have been extensively reviewed and described by a range of writers (Buckley et al. 1997; Ferguson and Kenny 1995; Focus Ireland 1996; Gilligan 1991; O'Higgins 1996; Skehill 2005), so we will not outline them here. The most significant reports were arguably the Tuairim Report (1966), the Kennedy Report (Department of Education 1970), the *Task Force Report on Child Care Services* (1980) and the *Report of the Kilkenny Incest Investigation* (McGuinness 1993). There has also been a succession of influential reports in the disability sector (see Chapter 23), the most important of which has been A *Strategy for Equality* (Commission on the Status of People with Disabilities 1996), while in the education and training sector, the *Report on Caring and Social Studies* (NCEA 1992) laid the basis for today's range of degree programmes in social care and applied social studies.

All of these documents commented on aspects of social care provision and, amongst other things, were influential in shaping the type of education and training that social care practitioners should receive. In turn, this has led to changes in the skill sets of practitioners, with less emphasis on some 'practical' skills (such as home-making and health care) and a greater emphasis on research, policy issues and academic knowledge. There has been, and still is, much debate about the virtues or otherwise of such a shift.

Social care practice has long been associated with residential child care. This emphasis has changed dramatically, especially with the decline of large institutions (such as children's homes) and the emergence of alternatives such as foster care, community-based projects and community child care. In recent years, the field of social care has expanded greatly, in Ireland as elsewhere. It has been acknowledged that the types of skills and knowledge that social care practitioners exhibit can be constructively applied in other areas, such as in the care of those with disabilities, in working with older people and in responding to the needs of a broad range of people, from drug users to victims of domestic violence to asylum seekers.

Inevitably, this brings social care practitioners into contact with other professions, including medical professionals, social workers and An Garda Síochána. Social care practitioners' participation in multidisciplinary professional teams is now quite common, which also means that there are challenges to how people work in these fields. For example, the introduction of models of social care practice to the care of older people will involve a challenge to the highly medicalised practices in this field, where nurses and other medical practitioners have been dominant (see Chapter 21). This will lead to debate and perhaps even conflict between professional groups.

WHAT PERSONAL QUALITIES DOES A SOCIAL CARE PRACTITIONER REQUIRE?

We can see from the definitions explored earlier that a social care practitioner must have a broad range of personal and intellectual attributes. 'Academic' qualities include a broad knowledge base in their field, the ability to work both independently and as part of a team, research skills and a problem-solving approach. Much social care education and training aim to assist students in developing these skills. The models from other parts of the world outlined in the next three chapters suggest that different attributes are seen as more important in different societies. In Ireland, for example, it is suggested that the ability to work as part of a team and to fit into an organisation is seen as important, while in the Netherlands there is much more focus on the practitioner as an independent but accountable professional. It may be interesting to discuss why these differences in emphasis exist.

In addition, certain personal attributes tend to characterise practitioners, such as reliability and trustworthiness, altruism, empathy and compassion and maturity. Social care practitioners must be open minded and prepared to examine and perhaps even change their own attitudes towards others. It can be debated whether these qualities can be taught or are somehow 'innate' in people who are attracted to social care practice as an occupation. Again, education and training may seek to emphasise and develop these qualities, but we can legitimately ask whether good social care practitioners are born, not made. Chapter 9 examines this and related questions.

How a social care practitioner develops as a person and as a professional depends on a number of things:

- The quality of the practice environment.
- The quality of undergraduate education and training available and, after graduation, the quality and accessibility of continuing professional development (CPD) training.
- The quality and consistency of professional supervision.
- The philosophy of one's work peers towards the work, service users and their families.
- The ability to be self-reflective in one's work.

- The ability to take constructive criticism and turn it into 'best practice'.
- A determination to keep up to date in reading, in seeking out evidence-based solutions and in considering and evaluating new approaches to work.
- A willingness to be an advocate for the profession.

This constitutes a comprehensive and demanding set of challenges for the professional social care practitioner.

WHAT QUALIFICATIONS DOES A SOCIAL CARE PRACTITIONER NEED?

In Ireland, the basic professional qualification for social care practice is a BA (Ordinary) Degree in Applied Social Studies/Social Care. The recognised qualifications are detailed in Schedule 3 of the Health and Social Care Professionals Act 2005. The Act uses the old terms of 'Diploma' and 'National Diploma', even though these qualifications were reconfigured as the BA (Ord.), Level 7 by the National Qualifications Authority of Ireland (NQAI), which was established in 2001. Many qualified practitioners go on to complete an Honours Degree (NQAI Level 8) in the field, and an increasing number progress to postgraduate qualifications. Professional-level courses in social care are now offered at all the Institutes of Technology, with the exception of Dún Laoghaire, as well as at Carlow College and the Open Training College (based in Goatstown, Co. Dublin, and specialising in the field of intellectual disability). Significant numbers of students are also enrolled on FETAC Level 5 social care/applied social studies programmes in Colleges of Further Education (FE), such as Ballyfermot College of Further Education, Coláiste Dhúlaigh College of FE, Inchicore College of FE and Cavan Institute.

A course of study in social care typically includes subjects such as sociology, psychology, social administration and policy, principles of professional practice, law, creative skills (art, drama, music, dance, recreation) and research methods. Many courses offer specialised modules in particular areas, such as community, youth or disability studies. A key element of studying to be a professional social care practitioner is involvement in a number of supervised work practice placements of several months' duration. Some students already working in the field ('in-service' or 'work-based-learning' students) may undertake their placements at work, closely supervised (see Chapter 12 for more on the placement experience).

Students of social care practice are challenged to develop academically by deepening their knowledge, to develop professionally by learning and practising social care skills and to develop personally by developing a capacity to look at their own strengths and weaknesses in relation to the work.

In the first edition of this book (2005: 13), it was argued that:

> In the new millennium, there has been a surge in the number of students applying for social care courses, paralleled by a dramatic expansion in the number of colleges that offer such an education. There is a danger of saturation at ordinary degree level and it is likely that this will ultimately lead to the development of more specialised courses in the future, with individual educational courses focusing on different aspects of care. Similarly, students will probably elect to study for more specialised programmes at Higher Diploma and masters levels.

This process continues apace, with many colleges now offering part-time, flexible programmes to allow graduates of the Ordinary Level 7 BA to progress to the Level 8 Honours degree. Similarly, there has been a growth in masters and continuous professional development programmes in a number of specialised areas. It is likely that these types of programmes will continue to develop in the next five years.

The pathways towards a social care education are diverse and include school leavers entering courses through the CAO, those with other qualifications seeking credit for prior learning and experienced workers already in the field undertaking work-based learning programmes. Most social care courses actively recruit mature students (23+ years) and those who have completed relevant FETAC and BTEC/Edexcel (a UK further education accrediting body) courses within the further education sector.

The question of 'oversupply' of social care graduates is difficult to assess. As indicated earlier, there is no national system to monitor the education of social care practitioners. Colleges survey their graduates regarding their employment and further education experiences through graduate destination surveys, and though response rates to such surveys are generally poor, they do provide some indications of graduates' success in securing relevant employment. Thus, as an example, the social care practice class of 2006 from the Dublin Institute of Technology appears to have had little difficulty in sourcing employment in the sector. Respondents who graduated from the BA in Social Care Practice in 2006 reported that 82 per cent were in employment (80 per cent of these were in social care positions), 13 per cent were in further study and 5 per cent were not available for employment. Similarly, respondents who graduated from the Honours Degree in Social Care reported that 86 per cent were in employment (all in social care positions) and 14 per cent were in further study. Since then there has been a significant change in the economic situation, so such trends are not necessarily a guide to current or future outcomes. Overall, there is a strong argument for the ongoing monitoring of graduate output by individual colleges, by the Irish Association of Social Care Educators (IASCE) and by the Higher Education Authority (HEA).

WHAT DO SOCIAL CARE PRACTITIONERS DO?

What do social care practitioners actually do? Anglin (1992) has observed that they work in two main areas, with a very broad range of practices, as listed below.

Direct service to clients:
- Individual intervention.
- Group intervention.
- In-home family intervention.
- Office-based family intervention.
- Assessment of child.
- Assessment of family.
- Child management.
- Child abuse interventions.
- Employment counselling or assistance.
- Life skills training.
- Health management.
- Education remediation.
- Recreational leadership.
- Arts and crafts leadership.
- Counselling on death and dying.
- Therapeutic play.
- Parenting skill training.
- Sexuality counselling.
- Marriage counselling.
- Stress management.
- Lifestyle modification.

Organisational activities:
- Case management.
- Client contracting.
- Report writing and formal recording.
- Court appearances/legal documentation.
- Programme planning and development.
- Use and interpretation of policy.
- Individual consultation with other professionals.
- Participation in professional teams.
- Co-ordination of professional teams.
- Contracting for services.
- Supervision of staff, students or volunteers.
- Staff training and development.
- Public relations/community education.
- Organisational analysis and development.
- Policy analysis and development.
- Financial analysis/budgeting.

A scan of the above lists will reveal the diversity of a social care practitioner's role. Many of the individual chapters in this book expand on some of the different types of work that social care practitioners carry out. If we were to prioritise, we might suggest that the main role of the practitioner is to work *alongside* service users to maximise their growth and development. The social care practitioner is also, crucially, an advocate for change.

WHERE DO SOCIAL CARE PRACTITIONERS WORK?

In Ireland, social care practitioners may be employed in the state (statutory) sector (for example, the Departments of Health and Children; Education and Science; or Justice, Equality and Law Reform); in what is termed the non-governmental sector (in organisations such as Barnardos, the Brothers of Charity, Enable Ireland and Focus Ireland, among others, many of which are fully or partially funded by government); or in community-based organisations (such as community development projects or Garda youth diversion projects).

In the early 2000s, the Joint Committee on Social Care Professionals (JCSCP nd.) enumerated some 2,904 social care practitioners working across various sectors, including community child care (71), staff in children's residential centres (1,214) and staff in intellectual disability services (1,619). Of these, just over 55 per cent held what might be termed a professional qualification, with 14 per cent holding no qualifications at all. Today, the Health and Social Care Professionals Council estimates that up to 8,000 people will be eligible to register as 'social care workers' when the relevant Registration Board is established.

Social care practitioners make valuable contributions in emergent and developing areas such as community development, family support, Garda and community youth projects, women's refuges, County Childcare Committees, care of older persons and research and policy work. The breadth of chapters in this book reflects some of this diversity, though again, statistics for the numbers working in such areas are hard to come by.

SALARY SCALES

The late 1990s saw a period of considerable activity by social care practitioners and their trade union representatives for an improvement in salaries and career pathways. This led to a significant increase in 2001, by as much as 33 per cent for some grades. Figure 1.1 shows the salary scale (in euro) for social care workers relative to nurses and primary teachers as of March 2008.

Figure 1.1. Social Care Worker Salary Scales, Relative to Staff Nurses and Primary School Teachers (March 2008)

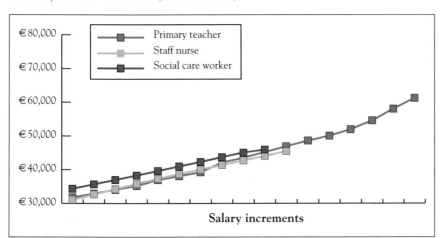

Source: Based on information from relevant trade union websites (IMPACT, the Irish Nurses' Organisation and the Irish National Teachers' Organisation).

As we can see, the three professions share similar salary scales for the first 10 points. Thereafter, the teachers' scale progresses considerably, reflecting the position that teachers do not have a 'Senior' or 'Leader' scale to progress to, as do nurses and social care practitioners, respectively.

SOCIAL CARE PRACTICE: A CHALLENGING OCCUPATION

Social care work can be very challenging, emotionally and physically, and can mean working in some very difficult environments. It can also be uniquely rewarding. For example, the profile of children in residential care may often include multiple loss, rejection, deprivation, neglect and abuse. As a consequence, there can be a large gulf between desires, expectations and reality. An example of this might be working with young offenders in a custodial setting (such as a secure unit) where those in the service user group (a) do not want to be there in the first instance; (b) have been removed from their place of origin and their families; (c) are locked up for a good part of the day; (d) are distrustful and resentful of perceived authority figures; and (e) are facing lengthy sentences. Here, the work of the social care practitioner calls for a unique mix of skills and personal attributes. *Risk* is now synonymous with child protection and welfare (Bessant 2004). Attention is increasingly directed at what are variously termed 'high risk', 'high challenge' and 'at risk' children, with a child protection service concentrated on an even smaller number of cases at the heavy end of the (perceived) spectrum of risk.

Unfortunately, it is not uncommon for social care practitioners to fail to receive formal supervision on a regular basis; to receive verbal and sometimes physical abuse from service users; to work in under-resourced areas; and to work unsocial hours. With increasing professionalisation and regulation of the field, there is a hope that many of these issues will be addressed in the future.

CONCLUSION

Social care has been a growth area in Ireland. It is demanding but rewarding, as social care practitioners make a real difference in the lives of others. Formal social care had humble beginnings, located within a largely clerical or philanthropic context, but has now expanded to include the statutory, community and voluntary sectors. Social care practitioners are now trained and educated to degree level and increasingly to postgraduate level. Salaries and career structures have seen an immense improvement in recent times. A statutory registration system is being established that will oversee future professional development in the field. The management and reporting structures in social care practice are moving towards an acceptance of the social care practitioner as an independent, autonomous professional. There is no better time to enter the social care profession in Ireland.

2

Social Care: A European Perspective

Pelle Hallstedt & Mats Högström

OVERVIEW

European curricula in social care have been designed in many different ways. Personal development has at times been given much space. Organisation and leadership are other fields that have been considered important. Some courses have tended to focus on the best way to be a proficient social care practitioner. In recent years, there has been a strong tendency to raise the academic or theoretical level of the curricula – the contents of study programmes have been changed. But what factors influence the content and design of social care curricula? Why do study programmes in social care vary in different countries? What is the impact of the content and design of the curricula on social care as it is carried out in the work field?

In this chapter, based on our recent research (Hallstedt and Högström 2005), we inquire into these questions. There are many possible answers. It is quite likely that the predominant model of social care practice in a country will influence the content of social care curricula, but this is not the only factor to influence what is included in the educational programmes. Other factors also contribute to decisions about what it is possible to insert into or erase from curricula – factors such as discourses of education and the academy, of professionalisation and of marketisation. The following examination of the experience in a number of European countries aims to provide an insight into such interconnections. This may help you to place your own experience of social care education and practice in a broader context.

We first focus on the relationship between the social political system and the curriculum. Second, we refer to current discussions about social care practice as a disciplinarian and/or emancipative project. The reason for highlighting the first issue is that social care is part of national social policy. Social policies are dependent on how the responsibilities of welfare are distributed between the state, civil society and the market. Social policy, according to an influential categorisation by Esping-Andersen (1990), falls into three different regime types: the liberal welfare state, the conservative-corporatist welfare state and the social democratic welfare state (also called the 'Scandinavian model').

We relate these different regime types to curricula in social care in the Netherlands, Norway and Ireland, and also make some references to the Swedish

curriculum. Each programme for the study of social care is constructed in a particular social political system. Current discussions about professionalisation, options for social care workers in the market or about academic demands influence the design of social care courses. We discuss the interplay between the different factors, both theoretically and through an analysis of a range of European curricula in social care.

By way of conclusion, we argue that the content and design of a curriculum will have a substantial impact on the practice of social care practitioners. We locate these outcomes in relation to the two traditions that have dominated the debate about social care: discipline and emancipation. The discussion about discipline and emancipation raises problematic issues regarding *power*.

THE DESIGN OF STUDY PROGRAMMES

What are the aims of social care work or – as it commonly termed in Continental Europe – social pedagogy or social educational work? How should social pedagogy be planned and carried out? There are numerous views on this matter, held by different groups such as politicians, social administrators, social educational workers and many others. Differences in views are as common within groups as between them. Different views on the content and aims are separated and developed into a number of homogenous ideas of social pedagogy. Ideas vary depending on the client or service user; the role of the client's social network; methods of work; the use of force or restraint; and other issues.

A central theme is the balance between the use of force or restraint and a therapeutic, care-giving kind of work. Each model of social educational work promotes its views in contrast to the others. This is how different discourses are built which become engaged in a power struggle over the definition of social educational work. The struggle for a central position occurs on different levels and employs different means: research findings, ethical discussions and logical reasoning on the relationships between aspects like emancipation, autonomy and safety for the individual, and the use of force or restraint from an organisational perspective.

In this struggle, any one model strives to be considered the only reasonable one – beyond discussion. However, that position is only a temporary one, because the struggle for dominance in the discourse of social pedagogy will continue. The discussion about what is relevant – even what is allowed to enter into the discussion and who is allowed to take part in it – continues. There is a dialectic, or two-way, relationship between this ongoing discussion and debate and the practice in the field – the content and structure of the work that is carried out under the label 'social care work'.

The discourse of social pedagogy is one departure point for an analysis of the content and structure of study programmes. Another is the qualitative level of education. The traditional academic discourse, with its emphasis on a research basis for education, has become an important source of influence, reflecting the

trend towards a higher average level of formal education in society. Other important discourses are a professional discourse that stresses the uniqueness of the position as social care practitioner; the 'employability' discourse of vocational education; the emphasis on direct practical preparation for work; and the market discourse, with its emphasis on a marketable and competitive product. The following sections examine social care/social education curricula in a variety of European countries, including Ireland, in relation to broader socio-political issues. The discussion will show that there is no single model of what social care or social pedagogy does or should embrace. This also impacts on how it is taught and learned.

EXAMPLES OF CURRICULA IN SOCIAL CARE/SOCIAL PEDAGOGY

Nijmegen, the Netherlands

In the Netherlands, there is a social profession known as *sociaal pedagogische hulpverlening* – literally, social educational work. Social pedagogy in the Netherlands is a mixture of youth work, residential work with a variety of target groups, and occupational therapy. Traditionally, social educational work emphasises 'doing things' together with people in need.

As outlined above, each particular exercise of a profession, as well as the supporting curricula, has to be seen in context. The welfare discourse prevalent in Dutch society can be categorised as a mixture between the conservative–corporatist and the social democratic welfare state, though welfare researchers differ about where exactly to place the Netherlands. Esping-Andersen (1990) refers to it as a conservative–corporatist welfare state, but there are significant features of its welfare policies that bring it closer to the social democratic welfare state. Other researchers are more inclined to categorise the Netherlands as a social democratic welfare state; these include Goodin et al. (1999), who contrast the Netherlands with the United States (a liberal welfare state), and Germany (a conservative–corporatist welfare state).

A significant feature of the conservative–corporatist welfare state is its variety of different types and sources of social service. Thus, the family, the Church and voluntary organisations have traditionally been amongst the providers of social and economic assistance. Another significant feature of Dutch society is its 'pillarisation': there are numerous sub-cultures, such as religious (e.g. Catholic) and other social groupings that have had a substantial influence on Dutch society. Distinctive features of Dutch social provision are a huge number of voluntary social workers and organisations together with a society characterised by cultural diversity and a liberal view on social issues such as prostitution and drugs.

The Nijmegen study programme in social educational work is one of 20 in the Netherlands. The duration of the course is four years. The content and the form of the curriculum produce a certain kind of social educational worker. A student who is educated at the college in Nijmegen has achieved a 'professional identity'. This is gained through a focus on the individual student and the promotion of his/her self-awareness. Achievement of a professional identity means that Nijmegen graduates should be able to create a distinctive image of themselves in relation to other professional groups.

A discourse of professionalisation is here mixed with discourses of marketisation. A traditional academic discourse is not very visible in the curriculum – rather, students' personal growth and self-awareness are emphasised. The consolidation of knowledge about oneself and self-awareness is accomplished through experiencing diverse situations. Artistic means (drama, music, sports and play, arts, audiovisual and dance and movement) are used to help the potential social educational worker to encounter the client or service user in an appropriate way.

An important aspect of the professional identity of the care worker is the ability to decipher clients' needs, as well as how their requests for changes are to be met. The identity construction also enables the practitioner to dissociate him/herself from the client; it is important not to be too close but yet to be 'on the same side as the client'. The fostering/disciplining elements are balanced in that the social educational worker takes the client's 'request for help' as a starting point for actions. How the client's request for help is dealt with by the social educational worker is the starting point in achieving an emancipating outcome.

Lillehammer, Norway

In Norway, the term 'social pedagogy' is used to describe two different professions: child welfare workers (*barnevernspedagoger*) and welfare nurses (*vernepleier*). The welfare nurses traditionally work with people with disabilities of various kinds, in particular those with learning difficulties. Recently, the target groups were expanded to include older people with dementia, people with psychiatric problems, those with substance abuse problems and so on. This work takes place in many different institutional and, more commonly, community-based settings. The occupation of welfare nurse is licensed, which means that the curriculum is externally regulated to a certain extent. The child welfare worker works primarily with children and youth but also with other target groups, such as refugees, substance abusers and the mentally ill. This work also takes place in a variety of different settings, such as residential homes, youth clubs, after-school centres and so on.

Child welfare workers, welfare nurses and social workers are all educated to the same academic level, according to a common national curriculum, in 17 institutes of higher education across Norway. The study programmes are three years long. They are similar for the three groups and, to a certain extent, they are taught together in a common study programme (with a common first year).

The first national curricula for the two social professions were established in 1991 and replaced shorter, in-service training programmes linked to the large care institutions. Welfare nursing and child welfare are therefore quite well established as professional groups in Norway: training programmes for welfare nurses date from 1961 and from 1968 for child welfare workers.

The context of the Norwegian curricula is the Norwegian welfare society, with its own distinct qualities. According to Esping-Andersen (1990), the Norwegian welfare state belongs to the social democratic regime type. In short, this means that social rights are universal – they encompass all citizens without any prior means testing. This approach can be contrasted to the liberal model, where the state is responsible for assistance only to those proven to be in a needy situation. The social democratic welfare type encompasses the middle class as well as the working class, whereas the liberal model is primarily directed towards the latter.

It is possible to detect some salient discourses in the curricula. One of them is what we may call a social political discourse. Its aim is that students should learn that all members of society have the same rights, independent of disability or any other impeding factors. Integration into society of those on the margins should proceed guided by the 'principle of normalisation' (Askheim 1998; see also Chapter 23). On graduation, Norwegian students have achieved an identity as 'welfare navigator'; they are practitioners who can find a proper balance between clients' needs and society's demands. The welfare worker's mission is to guide the clients into societal norms as well as to be the initiator of changes in individual behaviour and of societal structures.

However, the principle of normalisation is not uncomplicated. There are tensions in the framework and legislation that make the principle of normalisation possible. One of the tensions is that there is a special legal framework for some groups of people, which states that the 'abnormal' should be given the same rights as the 'normal'. The aim of the legal framework is that when the aims are fulfilled, the framework should be erased. On the other hand, the aims are of a utopian quality, which means that special treatment of some groups of people will always be necessary. It has been a matter of debate whether the principle of normalisation had any positive effects towards integration in the last decade of the twentieth century.

In order to counteract the totalitarian, paternalistic and homogenising tendencies within the principle of normalisation, the Lillehammer students are also taught about empowerment, an ideology that aims to tilt the division of power in favour of the client.

The second salient discourse in the Norwegian system is the academic. The studies at Lillehammer College are characterised by the traditional division of subjects – into sociology, psychology and law, for example. Many of the lecturers are researchers, and students write academic theses that give access to further education.

There are further discourses that compete with the social political and the academic. In one of the curricula – welfare nursing – a medical discourse intrudes, which makes it compulsory for the study programme to include certain elements that are not compatible with social political discourse. Divergent legislation and frameworks prevent the amalgamation of the two study programmes for welfare nursing and child welfare, though this has been on the agenda among staff and administrators at the college for a long time.

Another factor that influences the study programmes is the discourse of professionalisation. The workers' trade union brings pressure upon the college to educate one category of social workers, not three. From the point of view of the professional in the work field, this is a logical step, as the three groups of social workers (social workers, welfare nurses and child welfare workers) are united in one union. But there are strong forces amongst the different categories of workers themselves which seek to preserve their separate professional identities.

Sligo, Ireland

In Ireland, the most important area of work for social care practitioners is with children and youth, for example, in residential homes and special institutions, and work with people with intellectual disabilities. The work takes place in close relationship with clients; this, together with the typical client groups, places social care work in the tradition of social pedagogy.

The context for social care work, the social political environment, has a number of original features. The Irish history of the twentieth century had an impact on virtually all sections of society. Where the material interests of social classes have been the basis for political action in most European states, nationalism has overshadowed class interest in Ireland. Catholic and nationalist ideologies presented Ireland as a classless society with a culturally homogenous population (McLaughlin 2001). Politics, including welfare politics, was naturally very influenced by this.

Welfare policies in Ireland do not fit easily into the Esping-Andersen classification system. On the one hand, Ireland has certain features of the conservative–corporatist welfare state, where a comparatively large part of social work is fulfilled by the family, the Church and private organisations. At the same time, on one of the central properties in the Esping-Andersen system, de-commodification, Ireland scored low. The conclusion was drawn that Ireland belongs to the category of the liberal welfare state, key features of which are means-tested aid, modest universal transfer and modest social insurance.

Social care practitioners in Ireland are educated mainly in regional Institutes of Technology. In the Institute of Technology, Sligo, students follow a three-year ordinary degree programme with an optional additional honours degree year.

Sligo students are commonly inspired to see themselves as agents of organisations that foster people. In the terminology of the discourse of social pedagogy, the disciplinary side of the discipline–emancipation continuum is stressed. This is seen in the way adherence to the workings of organisations is emphasised. It is also present in the way theories of behavioural science are used. The relationship between practitioners and clients is presented in the curriculum as a tool of social educational work rather than, as is the case in some other traditions and approaches in social pedagogy, a central means or end in itself.

The curriculum has a tendency to form a special category for people referred to as 'clients'. Moreover, the student is on a different level from the client. The potential relation between the two is mostly asymmetrical.

Students are being 'coached' or inspired to take care of themselves. Self-awareness is an essential aim in the curriculum. This focus in assignments on students' self-monitoring – of their own progress, for example – is also present in Nijmegen. This is an example of how social control has moved to people themselves (Foucault 1991). Another fundamental aim is to motivate students to adjust to the functioning of the workplace/placement. In many parts of the curriculum, the starting point for assignments or activities is the working of the organisation, not the client. In explaining what social care work is about, the curriculum repeatedly refers to 'transferring help to people in need'. Assignments tend to focus on the delivery of a service in an organisational framework.

Sligo can be placed in the orbit of discourses on different levels. One is the academic discourse that sets the limits for what is to be considered as an acceptable programme. Another is the professional discourse of social care that will be a basis for considerations of what the field (in terms of its unions, professional organisations and publications) will accept. The academic discourse could be seen as a means to advance the status of social care, not as an origin for fundamental changes in the profession.

Malmö, Sweden

A fourth curriculum to serve as an example is the social work programme at Malmö University. In the first decade of the twentieth century, the Swedish Poor Relief Association launched a vocational training programme for the principals of poor relief institutions. In the beginning of the 1950s, the programme was divided into two separate training programmes: one for adults and one for children and youth. In 1959, the name of the certificate was changed from 'manager of orphanages' to 'social pedagogue'. In 1970, the curriculum in Social Pedagogy was launched.

The programme was three years long and was intended to cover the need for qualified staff in institutions and activity centres for children and youth with social, psychiatric, psychological and physical disabilities. Students were also trained to become managers of such units. In 1983, the educational programme in social pedagogy was changed at the same time as new educational directions emerged. The educational programmes were given full academic status at that time. One of the new study programmes was directed towards people with learning disabilities, and another was directed towards the elderly. The core subject for all programmes was called Social Care; social pedagogy became a separate specialisation under this umbrella term.

Since 1983, the educational programmes have been changed several times (in Sweden – unlike Norway – there is no national curriculum, which results in great variety in the organisation and content of study programmes). In 2001, there was a major change. The core subject is now Social Work. The Department of Social Work in Malmö is divided into four specialisations: social work specialising in multicultural aspects; social work specialising in social education (social pedagogy); social work specialising in social care (the elderly and functional impairments); and social work – administrative specialisation. All specialisations are three and a half years long. In four of the seven semesters, the content is the same for all four specialisations. It can be said that in Malmö, the academic discourse has become more and more salient at the expense of vocational and professional discourses; this in turn affects the identity construction of the students.

We have earlier proposed that there are discernible identity constructions as a result of the curricula in Lillehammer and Nijmegen. We called them 'welfare navigator' and 'professional identity', respectively. In Sligo, no particular identity is promoted in the curriculum. Rather, the curriculum is characterised by an effort to give students an adequate academic education and to make them 'employable'. This suggests that the potential employers set the standard for social care work.

What sort of identity do the Malmö students develop? We find this difficult to answer unambiguously. The students have been exposed to considerable changes; these have modified an identity that was not very clear from the beginning. The students have been moulded in different ways through vocational and professional ideas about the profession. Now, because of recent changes (since 2001), students and lecturers are to be acclimatised into an 'academic' social work discourse, but this has not yet been fully established in educational practice.

SOCIAL PEDAGOGY, SOCIAL CARE AND SOCIAL WORK

There has been a long-running debate about the demarcation between social pedagogy/social care on the one hand and social work on the other. A notable contributor to the debate is Professor Sven Hessle. At a conference in Stockholm in 2002, he asked: 'What happens when social pedagogy becomes a part of the academic university discipline social work?' This question was particularly pertinent for the situation at the University of Stockholm, where the study of social pedagogy has been subsumed within the school of social studies. The situation is different in Malmö, as the department of social work was recently established alongside the long-established school of social studies at the nearby University of Lund.

In spite of different organisational conditions, similar issues arise. Curricula in social pedagogy and social care have traditionally had a strong vocational orientation. It is now obvious (in Sweden and elsewhere) that this vocational discourse is increasingly being replaced by an academic discourse related to social work. Another question arises: 'Are the centres for children, youth, the elderly and the disabled in need of academically educated social educational workers?' This is a question that is often raised by both educational representatives and professional workers.

For us, it is obvious that Hessle's question is relevant. He implies that the theoretical core that upholds social pedagogy, and that for a long time formed the demarcation line with social work, has vanished in the traditional academic settings. This theoretical core, according to Hessle (derived from Lorenz 1994), could be found in 'self-directed learning processes' (Hessle 2002: 2). This means that clients themselves are the ones who formulate needs and learn how to cope with and change life situations. The social pedagogical intervention is in the use of theoretical knowledge, combined with a communicative and reflective capability in the encounter with the client.

According to Lorenz (1994), this reflective and communicative competence, developed through the situation of living with people in need, is the foundation of social pedagogy. This is fundamental to social pedagogy as distinct from a social work discourse, with its specific roots in many different disciplines with their own point of departures (Hessle 2002).

This theme is elaborated by Eriksson and Markström (2003), who have strongly endeavoured to make the core of social pedagogy visible. They have carried out a sort of restoration of the forgotten roots of the social pedagogical approach. Other contributions, for example by the Norwegian Roger Mathiesen (2000) and the Danish Bent Madsen (1995), have contributed to revitalised discussions about the nature of social pedagogy.

From the descriptions in the literature, it is easy to get an impression of a highly emancipating attitude inherent in social pedagogy, compared to social work, which is seen as more system oriented. Nevertheless, in social pedagogy as well as in social work theory and practice, disciplining as well as emancipating actions are to be found. Careful micro-studies are required to find arguments to support the contention that social pedagogy is more emancipating than social work, or vice versa.

However, Hessle's point, which we can agree on, is that it is not possible to teach students to act in a 'social pedagogical way' solely through academic studies. Hessle consequently has a very pessimistic view on courses in social pedagogy – at least on those in Stockholm. There are reasons to take Hessle's worries on board and to give serious consideration to the question of how to make it possible to emphasise the core of social pedagogy in social work education without diminishing academic demands.

To conclude this section, we find that the Nijmegen curriculum aims for the construction of social pedagogues able to assert themselves in an open work field without a limiting framework. The thrust of the course in Lillehammer and of the curriculum in Sligo is rather to contribute to the creation of a corps of academi-cally well-prepared welfare workers. Similar tendencies are seen in the Malmö curriculum, but also tendencies to adjust the education to changes of the welfare society such as privatisation, complexity and an increasing number of alternative ways to organise welfare.

DISCIPLINE AND EMANCIPATION

As we have seen, different study programmes can put the emphasis on various parts of the programme. Does this mean that the resultant social educational work carried out by graduates will vary accordingly? This does not have to be the case, since many factors will influence the development of the actions of the social educational worker, not least socialisation into the workplace. Still, the course will probably be an important factor, especially when it comes to how the social educational worker will relate to clients or service users. This brings us to the question of how a study programme will prepare the students for meeting the client.

In the discourse of social pedagogy, there are two main positions: discipline and emancipation. The former puts the emphasis on helping clients to create a viable situation in life, with the assumption that they need a certain amount of guidance. In contrast to this, emancipation has as its principal goals helping the client to come out of precarious situations and to remove the obstacles for an autonomous life.

The concepts of *discipline* and *emancipation* seem like the extremes of a continuum. Let us look at the situation, assuming that the most important aspect of social pedagogy is the relationship between the client and the social educational worker. What are the properties of this relationship? One vantage point is to investigate *power* in the relationship.

One way of investigating power is to see who has the power and who is subject to it. The pattern is obvious: the social educational worker has the tools of power; the client is in the lowest position. An example is the situation in a treatment institution where sanctions are multifarious, with dismissal as the ultimate threat. The predicament for the client is to adjust to the social educational worker, or else life will be unpleasant. Structural power is with the social educational worker.

Another way to examine power is to look at the use of power. This emphasis on the properties of power is a central theme in Foucault's (1991) writings on the subject, in which power is underlined as a movable instrument. People and organisations make the necessary adjustments in order to bring about changes in their environment. Foucault has shown how power has developed and changed its appearance over the centuries. It has changed from being clear and transparent to appearing in guises that are hard to detect. Open sanctions and threats of violence were replaced by surveillance and, ultimately, control moved to people themselves. This new form of control works through the influence on people of social standards for appearance, clothing, aspirations, expression and thinking. There is not just one standard, though. Discourses are constantly struggling for dominance. As noted above, the most effective form of dominance is that which does not appear as dominance. If we conceive of something as taken for granted and 'normal', we will not have the sense of being dominated at all.

In what way can this shed light on the relationship between the client and the social educational worker? First, both parties are subjected to influence from dominating discourses in society. These discourses and the power relation between them are in constant flux. The particular 'subject' (the client or the social educational worker) will act individually within the domain of the discourses, but may, even against their own will, be the conduit for dominating norms in society. Second, stressing the movable property of power, it might be the case that the client occasionally dominates the social educational worker, and not the reverse. One way of describing the relationship is to begin by investigating the resistance that the client could use in order to block the intentions of the social educational worker.

Let us return to the treatment institution. Usually the social educational worker holds the tools of power, but power always operates in a limited range. The client cannot be *forced* to recover! However, resistance from the client does not have to mean that they have a certain intention – they may simply reject what has been offered. This takes us to another aspect of power: that change can be accomplished through the use of power. It is common to conceive of power as something negative, but Foucault (1980) argues that it is possible to look at power without deciding whether it is in itself good or bad, rather just to consider what is accomplished through the use of power.

There are many channels of power. In the social care field, knowledge can be seen as a powerful tool. Most study programmes in the field contain the study of clients – of special target groups like people with learning difficulties, substance abusers and elderly people. Indirectly, clients can be reviewed in themes like communication, ethics and developmental psychology. To describe people through the use of classification systems, a regular procedure in social educational work, is a form of power in use. As Foucault (1980) suggests, there is a close connection between power and knowledge.

Another important channel for power is the power over thoughts. They are organised in discourses, hard to detect for clients as well as for social care practitioners. For social care, 'the right way of thinking' and what is 'reasonable' must always be objects of scrutiny. For instance, is the liberal complementary form of social policy a suitable basis for care work intended for the emancipation of people? To leave people to themselves – is that the only way to support their emancipation? Could the extensive Scandinavian welfare system really be designed for the advancement of autonomy and independence? Or will emancipation turn out to be no more than attractive phrases contradicted by a practice more correctly described as discipline? How could the different study programmes be analysed in light of the interplay between emancipation and discipline in the discourse of social pedagogy?

CONCLUSION

In this chapter, we have discussed four different curricula and their social political environment. The discussion can be summarised as follows.

• The Dutch curriculum has been developed in a social political environment characterised by great diversity and a modest governmental structure. The most representative property of the Nijmegen curriculum is the strong emphasis on the self-reliant and independent social educational worker. Artistic subjects, so central in the curriculum, serve two different aims – to expand the practitioner's self-awareness and to be used as a means in the communication with the client. Organisational matters form another important part of the curriculum. The student is prepared to function in a variety of workplaces. A general aim is to promote a strong profession.

- The Norwegian curriculum is located in a different social political environment. The course can be conceived of as part of the normalisation strategy of the Norwegian welfare state. It is more oriented to academic education than the Dutch course. Social law constitutes an important framework for the curriculum. Empowerment is an important concept and students are trained to work together with the client in order to find an appropriate position in the welfare system.

- Sligo students are trained to use different means to analyse the client and the communication relationship between the client and themselves. Social, cultural and, in particular, psychological aspects are studied. Self-awareness is an important part of the study programme, but it is apparent that the aim is to make the student function in a position as social care practitioner in an asymmetrical relation to the client. This impression is accentuated by another observation in our study of the Sligo curriculum – that the organisation of social care work is the most common starting point. We find this to be compatible with the Irish social political environment, with its mixture of government and privately organised welfare production.

The study of organisations is important in all the different curricula. The main difference between how the curricula consider the organisational environment is that in Lillehammer, government organisations are the most important, while in the other colleges, organisations in general are the objects of study.

The client's interest is central in all the curricula. The difference between the curricula as to how this is treated is that in Lillehammer and Sligo, clients are approached top down; in Nijmegen the approach is bottom up.

Is it reasonable to impose education on a person? Is it reasonable to take part in the emancipation of a person? The answers are not obvious, certainly not if they must be produced without reference to criteria based on a set of values, values that will probably be parts of dominating discourses. To work for emancipation will, in this view, mean to promote discussions on related matters, such as: What are the properties of dominating discourses? What are the properties of the main channels of power? What are reasonable aims for social educational work? Is it justifiable to use force or restraint in order to reach those aims?

These matters have been discussed extensively (see Kelly 1994). Questions have been raised about what is right and wrong in social care, about values and criteria. The manner in which these questions have been presented has often been criticised for not showing any criteria for decisions. This reluctance to point to something *outside* the discussion on the future of the client, their network, demands from the public and other concrete problems takes us to the following conclusion on the central discourses in the field of social care: concepts like discipline and emancipation must always be objects of examination; they are open concepts and should always be examined in a concrete context.

3

The Practice of Child and Youth Care in North America

Grant Charles and Thom Garfat

OVERVIEW

Child and youth care work (CYC) in North America refers to social care work that focuses primarily upon the well-being and treatment, as the name implies, of children and youth and, increasingly, their families. It has existed for well over 150 years, although not always in a form that would be recognisable today. Indeed, the term itself is relatively recent. This chapter provides an overview of CYC in North America. It defines and describes child and youth care; traces the historical roots of the discipline; provides an overview of education and training programmes and opportunities; and discusses current trends and challenges that affect North American practitioners.

INTRODUCTION

The delivery systems for child and family services in which most CYC practitioners work are quite often philosophically and instrumentally distinct from each other in Canada and the United States. This is a reflection of the value differences between the two countries as well as how services to children and families are organised and funded. As a result, there has not been an equal development of CYC in the two countries. Nevertheless, there is enough common ground to be able to provide an overview of CYC work across the continent. While there has been a great deal of debate – even as far back as the early 1960s – as to whether CYC in North America is a 'profession', 'discipline' or a 'field' (Beker 2001; Burmeister 1960; Jull 2001; Kreuger 2002; Stuart 2003), for the purposes of this chapter, the terms will be used interchangeably.

HISTORICAL ROOTS

It is hard to locate the exact origins of CYC in North America with certainty. There are four paths along which the historical roots can be traced. The first is from the orphanages that were established in the 1700s in a number of communities across the continent. The original orphanages were run by religious orders (Charles and Gabor 2006). By the mid-1800s, as they expanded, they began to hire lay staff, though often remaining under the auspices of religious orders. The lay staff tended to work directly with the children in the institutions.

Many of those who entered these orphanages were not orphans in the true sense of the word in that their parents were not dead. Rather, it was often the case that the parents were unable to provide adequately for their children due to poverty or illness. It was not unusual, for example, for men to be away from home for extended periods of time, working in the forests or fisheries or fighting in wars and unable to provide adequate support for their families. In these cases, children were placed in orphanages, usually on a short-term basis, until the financial situation of the family improved or the absent parent returned to the family home.

Child and youth care in North America can also trace its roots to the recreational and 'fresh air' movements that occurred across the continent during the big waves of immigration of the mid-1800s to early 1900s. Millions of people immigrated to North America, primarily from European countries, but also from other parts of the world. Organisations such as the Young Men's Christian Association (YMCA), the Young Women's Christian Association (YWCA) and the Boys' and Girls' Clubs were founded, in part to provide services to young people who came from backgrounds of poverty common in the greater immigrant population. While these organisations were not established to work exclusively with 'troubled' youth, they were among the first to do so in North America. They set up community-based recreational and social service programmes and residential youth homes as a means to help those young people who would nowadays be termed 'at risk' to become productive members of society. As with the orphanages, these services were generally set up within the context of a Christian orientation, though 'Ys' (YMCAs and YWCAs) and Boys' and Girls' Clubs tended to be run by laypeople rather than members of religious orders.

A third historical foundation of child and youth care was within the 'correction' movement, within which the industrial and training schools for juvenile delinquents, as well as the hospitals for the 'mentally or physically deficient', were found (Charles and Gabor 2006). These facilities were usually, though not exclusively, run by state or provincial governments. Many of the programmes were set up as a part of, or in conjunction with, adult services. By the beginning of the 1900s, separate services for adults and children had been established. Though frequently serving children from urban centres, many of these facilities were built in rural communities or on the outskirts of cities so as to hide these 'deficient' children from the eyes of society or to remove them from the corrupting influence of urban life. Even though North America was becoming increasingly urban during this period, rural life was still idealised.

A parallel movement occurred with the establishment of residential schools for aboriginal youth in the latter part of the 1800s (Charles and Gabor 1990, 2006; Chrisjohn and Young 1997; Fournier and Crey 1997). These residential schools, while funded, for example, by the federal government in Canada, were run by religious personnel from amongst the Roman Catholic and Anglican Churches. As with the orphanages, the facilities tended to be managed by members of religious orders such as the Oblates while being staffed by laypeople. The purpose of the schools was to assimilate aboriginal youth into mainstream society (Charles and Gabor 2006). While it could be argued that the goal of each of the previously mentioned services was to assimilate children and youth into 'society', the residential schools were a deliberate attempt to destroy aboriginal culture. They separated young people from their families, in essence creating cultural orphans. The aim was to replace traditional indigenous socialisation processes with what have become known as Eurocentric values and beliefs.

It was within these programmes that CYC was born in North America.

Child and youth care is not the only professional group that evolved from these services: recreational therapy, psychiatric nursing, rehabilitation services, correctional services and social work can also locate their origins within all or part of the above-mentioned types of programmes. It is important to note that the roots of the CYC profession were highly ethnocentric in that the organisations from which it grew tended to reflect the values and beliefs of the Anglo-Saxon elites of North America. Non-Anglo-Saxon people, whether they were, for example, aboriginal, Irish, Italian or Asian, were seen by the elite to be inferior and in need of assistance to become contributing members of society. The poor, regardless of their ethnic origins, were also seen to be in need of proper socialisation and corrective intervention.

The organisations in which the 'original' CYC workers worked were reflections of their times, and those times tended to be moralistic and exclusionary. As such, they were often oppressive. This is not to say that some good work was not done. Indeed, many children owed their lives to the work of these original workers. But we cannot deny that assimilation, with all of the associated negative consequences, was a goal and that the original workers were agents of these assimilation policies. It should also be noted that with the exception of some of the programming by the 'Ys' and the Boys' and Girls' Clubs, the origins of CYC were in residential programmes of one sort or another.

It was not until the 1950s, with the beginning of the deinstitutionalisation movement, that North America saw the beginning of the professionalisation of CYC. Before this, people in the institutions worked in positions that, while reflecting the later work of CYC practitioners, were not recognised as a distinct profession, discipline or field. As governments across North America began to close the large, supposedly impersonal institutions, they replaced them with specialised treatment facilities. This is not to say that there were not treatment centres prior to this time. Rather, there was a rapid expansion of such programmes (Charles and Gabor 2006). Many of the treatment facilities were administered by the same organisations, albeit revamped, that had run the old institutions, although there was a significant decrease in the number with formal religious affiliations. These institutions did not disappear overnight; indeed, it was a 30-year process, with closures peaking in the late 1960s and early 1970s. Some of the correctional and hospital facilities are still in existence, though often on a much smaller scale than they were in their 'glory days'.

The new treatment facilities were smaller, more focused and more likely to be located in urban areas, as opposed to the rural location of the old institutions. They tended to be managed by professional rather than lay staff. It was within these programmes that CYC first began to be acknowledged as a discipline with specialised skills and knowledge. With this acknowledgment came a realisation that staff needed specific rather than generalised training and education.

DEFINITION AND DIFFERENCES

Definitions of child and youth care have evolved as the field has changed over the years. Ferguson (1993) suggests that as a field, CYC had its beginnings in residential care. Early definitions made little distinction between child and youth care and residential work. Since then, the field has expanded to include school and community-based care, infant development, child life in hospital settings, juvenile justice, rehabilitation and recreation. Though we should record that the roots of CYC were not found only in residential care, it is also important to note that CYC has moved into new areas in the past two decades, especially into community-based programming. As such, the definition of CYC has broadened in recent years to take into account the skills and competencies needed to work in these areas (Krueger 2002; Stuart et al. 2007).

There has been much debate over the past 20 years as to whether CYC is a profession or a discipline. Those who would argue that it is a profession, or at least a developing profession, make their case based on the uniqueness of the work performed with clients. Anglin (2001) believes that CYC is unique in that it focuses primarily on the growth and development of children, is concerned with the totality of a child's functioning, has a social competency base, is based upon, but not restricted to, day-to-day work with children and involves the development of therapeutic relationships with children.

On the other hand, Gaughan and Gharabaghi (1999) argue that while the ability of CYC staff to work in the daily life of children distinguishes CYC workers from other professions such as psychology or social work, this in itself is not enough to make CYC a profession. They suggest that CYC lacks a disciplinary epistemology whereby unique knowledge is produced by the field. Rather, they argue, CYC 'knowledge' is borrowed from other disciplines. They also suggest that there is a lack of role distinction with other professional disciplines. These points suggest that CYC does not have control over a specialised or specific knowledge base and therefore is not really a profession.

Overlap also remains between CYC and other professions and disciplines. In some jurisdictions, for example, child protection work is conducted by social workers and CYC workers. There can be overlap in hospital settings between CYC, social work, occupational therapy and rehabilitation workers. This adds to the confusion over whether CYC is a distinct profession or discipline. This debate has not been resolved and is likely to continue for some years to come (see Chapter 5 for a more extended discussion of the concept of professionalism).

EDUCATION AND TRAINING

It is interesting that the 30-year span in which many of the old institutions were closed or downsized saw a blossoming in the establishment and later expansion of formal higher educational programmes in child and youth care. In Canada, the provinces of Ontario and Quebec were leaders in this area, with the establishment of two-year (later expanded in Ontario to three years) specialised educational programmes at the community college equivalent level (similar to Irish Higher Certificates and Ordinary Degrees). Similar diploma-level programmes were set up in a number of states and provinces, although, even 30 years later, there are many jurisdictions that do not have college-level training programmes. Despite a number of openings in recent years, university-level programmes in CYC are still rare in North America and educational opportunities beyond the undergraduate level are almost non-existent. Among the exceptions are the School of Child and Youth Care in Victoria, British Columbia and Nova/Southwestern University in Florida, which offer graduate and postgraduate education programmes. Canada is more developed than the US in terms of formal CYC educational programmes. Neither country has a formal accreditation process to ensure minimal quality for post-secondary programmes (Stuart 2001).

While several institutions of higher learning offer formal educational training for CYC professionals, the majority of staff members come to the workplace without professional training in the area. Anglin (2002), in a study of residential programmes for young people in the province of British Columbia, notes that a significant number of staff do not have specialised tertiary-level training in CYC. Others may come from a number of post-secondary programmes that may or may not have any relationship to CYC, while some have little or no education past high school. For example, in the province of Ontario, only half of the workers employed in the field have formal training (Gaughan and Gharabaghi 1999). This is the case even though Ontario has a long history of providing post-secondary education opportunities in child and youth care. It also has the oldest and largest CYC association on the continent.

Also to be noted is an unfortunate recent trend whereby agencies, unable to attract sufficient numbers of men to work in their programmes, have shown a tendency to lower their formal hiring criteria so as to attract men to the field. This has come about as a result of the limited number of men within the 'helping disciplines' in educational programmes. A concurrent problem with regard to the education and training of CYC workers in North America is the limited funds available to agencies to provide professional development for their current staff. While some funds are always available, they tend to be spent on mandatory or legislated training, such as violence management, with the result that few agencies are able to provide training that would, in effect, enhance the workers' abilities to provide effective services to young people and their families. The end result is that with the exception of those agencies able or willing to hire graduates of academic programmes, many programmes stagnate at their current level of service.

CERTIFICATION AND REGISTRATION

To address the disparity in staff qualifications, some jurisdictions have begun to develop a certification process for CYC workers. The most successful has been the province of Alberta, which has provided a certification process for government workers since 1979 and for all other CYC workers since 1985 (Berube 1984; Phelan 1988). The province of British Columbia has developed a certification plan, but it has yet to be implemented (Stuart 2001). Certification programmes tend to be replacement programmes rather than supplementary programmes to formal education. For example, while it recognises formal education, the Alberta certification process has a grandfather clause for individuals who do not have formal qualifications (CYCAA 2000; Stuart 2001).

In other words, the certificate programmes are developed as a way to ensure a minimal training standard for frontline staff. They have not been developed as a means of professional registration, as would be the case in some other disciplines in the caring fields. This ability to regulate educational expectations, entry qualifications and the use of the name of the profession is a central consideration in determining in North America whether a profession is 'truly a profession', both legally and in the eyes of other professions. The Association for Child and Youth Care Practice has recently established the North American Certification Project, designed to 'provide a framework for beginning the process of unifying the many existing credentialing efforts currently underway' (ACYCP 2007).

PROFESSIONAL ASSOCIATIONS

While the first CYC state or provincial association was established in the province of Ontario in 1959 (MacKenna 1994), there has never been a time when all of the provinces and states have had active associations. At the peak in the 1980s, fewer than half of the US states had CYC associations (Krueger 2002). Nevertheless, CYC workers in the two countries are represented by national organisations. In the US, the Association for Child and Youth Care Practice (ACYCP) provides national leadership, while in Canada, the same function is carried out by the Council of Canadian Child and Youth Care Associations (CCCYCA). While separate organisations, the two do co-operate on matters of common interest: they jointly sponsor an international CYC conference that is offered on alternating sites between the two countries and they have also co-operated in the development of standards for certification.

Neither association has a high national profile, unlike their counterparts in professions such as social work, nursing, psychology or medicine. The CYC associations tend to have a much lower profile in terms of government lobbying, partly a result of a comparative lack of funds, but also related to the low profile of the profession in the minds of the general public. Few people in either country are aware that CYC is a separate professional grouping under the general umbrella of the caring professions. This is partly an outcome of the failure of the associations to formulate a strategy that will raise CYC's profile.

A lack of public profile is not the only difficulty facing the Canadian and American associations. A disturbing trend over the past few years has been a significant decrease in the membership levels in many state and provincial organisations. This has corresponded with the disappearance or weakening of a number of the associations themselves. Unlike other professional or discipline-specific bodies, many of the CYC associations are dependent on a small group of dedicated people for their survival or at least effective functioning. As these people move on, the associations often go into a period of stagnation or, in some cases, disappear altogether. A number of state associations have shut down in recent years (Krueger 2002). The end result is a constant ebb and flow of associations, which makes such activities as effective long-term planning and lobbying difficult, if not impossible.

Several other groups have been founded to contribute to the development of the profession in North America.

- The International Leadership Coalition for Professional Child and Youth Care Workers (ILCFPCYCW) was founded in 1992 to support the work of the associations (Krueger 2002).
- CYC leaders came together to promote the field through helping the ACYCP to develop a national code of ethics and certification standards. The code of ethics was developed so as to create a common guide for workers in their interactions with clients by addressing such areas as responsibility for self, clients, employers and society (Krueger 2002).
- The North American Certification Project (NACP) was initiated by ILCFPCYCW in conjunction with the two national associations to develop common certification standards for both countries.
- Two other CYC organisations worth mentioning are the Academy of Professional Child and Youth Care and the North American Consortium of Child and Youth Care Education Programmes (Krueger 2002; Ricks et al. 1991). The first consists of selected leaders in the profession, while the second represents educators from the college and university CYC programmes. Both have been active in promoting issues relevant to the field.

CONFERENCES

Though the roots of child and youth care go back many years, the first dedicated CYC conferences date only from the period of rapid expansion of the treatment centres. The Thisletown Conference in Toronto and the Valley Forge Conference in Pennsylvania were among the first forums at which CYC practitioners came together to discuss issues common to people in the field. From these early beginnings have grown a number of state, provincial, national and international conferences. The first national CYC conference in Canada was organised at the University of Victoria in Victoria, British Columbia, in 1981. The first international conference was held in Vancouver, British Columbia, in 1985. The international conferences are a co-operative endeavour between the ACYCP and the CCCYCA. While there has been a decrease in the number of provincial and state conferences in recent years, the attendance at the Canadian national and the international conferences continues to be strong.

JOURNALS AND ASSOCIATED WRITINGS

There are four major journals that promote CYC in North America. The journal *Relational Child and Youth Care Practice* (formerly the *Journal of Child and Youth Care*) is a Canadian publication currently originating from Ryerson University in Toronto. *The Child and Youth Care Forum* and the *Journal of Child and Youth Care Work* are both published in the US. The subscription base for these journals is relatively small, although they tend to be highly influential in the field. *CYC-OnLine* is a web-based journal, published monthly. Though published in South Africa, many of its contributors and readers are based in North America and it has a significant impact on Canadian and American workers. As of mid-2008 there had been over 900,000 distinct visits to *CYC-net* in the previous year, with a strong representation from Canada and the US (www.cyc-net.org). Many of the individual CYC associations also publish newsletters that contribute to their local memberships. There has also been an increase in the number of books being published that are directly related to child and youth care practice (Charles and Gabor 1988; Fewster 1990a; Garfat 2004; Krueger 1998).

CHALLENGES

CYC practitioners in North America face many challenges, including the lack of a recognised professional identity, with a corresponding lack of respect from other allied professions. It is not as if the other professions are deliberately disrespectful towards CYC, rather, it is that they are not aware of its specific role. The same tends to apply for governments across the spectrum of services. Few acknowledge that CYC is anything but a job description, even in programmes that they run directly. In Canada, CYC is not recognised as a profession in the various provincial health discipline Acts under which most of the caring professions are governed, although the provinces of Ontario and Alberta have recently made tentative steps to address this issue.

This lack of recognition is reflected in the low membership of CYC workers in their professional associations: the vast majority of CYC workers do not belong to a provincial or state association. This creates a circular problem, as the low numbers of members mean that the associations have to survive on minimal budgets, which significantly handicaps their ability to lobby their respective governments for official recognition. This lack of recognition also means that, unlike most other professions in the caring fields, CYC cannot demand mandatory registration, which in turn means that there is no money to assist in the lobbying efforts. Mandatory registration would go a long way to ultimately solving the whole issue of whether or not CYC is a profession.

One of the reasons why governments in Canada have not recognised CYC under the health services or related categories is that such recognition would result in an increase in pay for workers. While most governments have not even considered such recognition, those that have done so may have pulled back because of the increased costs related to such a decision. While this stance does not create a new problem for CYC practitioners, it does reinforce an existing one. The caring fields tend to be poorly paid in North America, and CYC is one of the poorest of the poor. This creates a high turnover in workers, as people are forced to look for other means of making a living.

In many ways, child and youth care is a young person's profession. Many people, regardless of where their hearts lie, leave CYC for other professions that have higher profiles and therefore more status and pay. It is not unusual for social workers, teachers and psychologists to have begun their careers in CYC but then to have moved on to their new profession. It is often these very people who have either contributed in some way to the leadership of the profession or who would have been likely to have taken a leadership role in the future – the very people the profession cannot afford to lose. CYC is seen as a stepping-stone profession where one can acquire excellent skills and knowledge that can then be used to be successful in other fields. This is beneficial to the individual worker but hurts the long-term development of the field.

Not only is there a high turnover in the field, but there is also a lack of men. Male staff members are both hard to recruit and hard to retain, especially when the economy is healthy. This is a problem in many of the caring fields, but is particularly acute in CYC. The vast majority of students in the college and university programmes are female. This means that it is not only difficult to hire men, but also that the ones who are hired tend to be the least qualified in terms of education and training. This difficulty in hiring and retaining male staff is compounded by the fear that many men have of residents making false allegations of abuse. In North America, as in many jurisdictions, allegations of abuse have come from past residents of some of the institutions. Some of these are founded and some unfounded. There have been some situations where government investigations of abuse have been inappropriately conducted, with the result that quite innocent staff members have been branded as abusers. This has created an atmosphere of fear that contributes to the turnover of male staff.

The high turnover of staff is not, however, restricted to males. Both males and females leave child and youth care because of non-pay working conditions or the fear of allegations of abuse. An increasing problem, especially in the residential programmes, is the apparent changing nature of the behaviours of the young people themselves, as it would appear that there has been an increase in the amount of violent behaviour exhibited by young people in recent years. There is some debate about whether this is actually the case, but the perception remains. The result is the creation of working environments that are tense and sometimes dangerous. This also contributes to staff turnover, especially in the smaller programmes or in remote or rural areas where there may not be access to the same level of support that may be found in larger programmes.

There is no doubt that the working environments are potentially more dangerous, but this may not be related to an increase in violent youth – it may actually be a reflection of the numerous cutbacks that have occurred in recent years in many states and provinces. This has caused the closure or downsizing of programmes, with the result that many young people are referred to services that are not equipped to meet their needs. This is compounded by cuts in staffing levels and training budgets. Such cuts contribute to people leaving the field as it becomes increasingly difficult to do one's job. As people leave, so does their collective wisdom. This causes a vicious circle that contributes to a downgrading of the quality of programmes. As experienced people leave, the knowledge of how to work with troubled youth also leaves, causing interventions to become more behavioural than relationship focused. This in turn creates more situations that are about control rather than change, with a greater consequent likelihood of violent rather than growth responses from young people. Unfortunately, there does not seem to be an end to the cuts in children's services. At a time when there has been an explosion in the number of young people coming into care across the continent, governments have been either freezing children services budgets or actively cutting them. This is having a significant impact on the field, as people are being asked to do ever more with less.

The cutbacks are also having an impact on hiring practices. Lack of funds is forcing many programmes to hire inexperienced or untrained staff in order to meet budget quotas. Even though CYC is not a high-paying field, experienced and higher-educated staff tend to be paid more than uneducated or inexperienced people. The issue is compounded by a decrease in training and staff-development budgets, which are often the first to be cut in times of restraint. This is bad enough when staff members are experienced and well trained, but potentially deadly when dealing with poorly trained or inexperienced people. Children have died in care in recent years in Canada during physical restraints because staff had apparently not been properly trained in the appropriate use of such interventions. For example, two cases under review in the province of Ontario involve staff allegedly restraining children for inappropriate periods of time, using what have long been considered dangerous forms of holding. In both cases, the holds allegedly contributed to the death of children.

While the financial cutbacks are having the most significant impact on CYC, there are also several other issues influencing the direction of services, and therefore people, in our profession. There is an increase in the demand by governments and funding agencies for proof that the money being spent on children's services is having an impact (Stuart et al. 2007). This demand for programme and intervention accountability is primarily being dealt with through the development of service standards. Organisations such as the Child Welfare League of America and the Alberta Association of Services for Children and Families have long had standards of services that are used by many of the organisations that hire CYC staff. What is new is that funders are expecting agencies and facilities to become accredited while there is not a uniform accreditation process in North America. Instead, there are accreditation bodies that are local, national or continental. The funders often dictate which accreditation body an individual organisation accesses. The aim of accreditation is to improve service delivery, but at a time of staff cuts, the energy it takes for an organisation to become accredited often takes away from the work being done with clients. Few jurisdictions provide funding for agencies to go through what is often a lengthy and time-consuming process. Thus, the desire to increase standards often results in a lessening of service quality.

Related to the development of standards is the corresponding development of outcome measures. As with the development of standards and accreditation processes, the goal of outcome measures is service improvement. This long-needed initiative requires that interventions be performed on a planned and measured basis, rather than in the intuitive manner in which many interactions occur. Organisations such as the Canadian Outcome Research Institute and the Child Welfare League of Canada are active in the development of outcome measures and the corresponding measurement support systems for children's services programmes. As can be expected, there is some resistance by CYC workers to the development of outcome measures: although many support this initiative, not everyone wants to have their work examined or analysed. Similar resistance is evident among some people towards service standards and accreditation. But it is unlikely that governments and other funding bodies will back away from their demands in these areas. Accountability will be a strong force in children's services, and in CYC, for the foreseeable future.

Finally, it must be recognised that one of the leading challenges to the field is the development of a common definition of the field itself in a way that articulates the purpose, role and value of child and youth care. While writings within the field, as noted, have increased significantly in the past 10 years, there is still a general misunderstanding of what it means to practise CYC. Various models drawn from the behavioural sciences, for example, compete for position with those founded in a more phenomenological orientation. This can lead to confusion as to what is meant by a child and youth care approach. This lack of an agreed-upon definition creates confusion within other professions (some of which still think of CYC as a simple supplement to their own work) and limits the ability of the field to promote itself. Added to this is the current debate, at least in Canada, regarding the societal mandate of child and youth care, which is seen by some as oppressive and supportive of the limited discourse of capitalism. 'Radical child and youth care practice' (Skott-Myhre 2004; Skott-Myhre and Skott-Myhre 2007), for example, challenges some of these basic assumptions, thus contributing further to the potential confusion over the meaning of CYC practice.

CONCLUSION

The key challenge that faces child and youth care in North America is that of change. At the core of this process is the debate about the professional status of CYC. This is in some ways a false issue. What ultimately matters is whether the mandate of child and youth care is being met. CYC's current mandate is to promote the healthy growth of children and youth and to help them to become contributing members of society. This is not to say that the work to promote CYC as a profession is a wasted effort. Anything that contributes to the growth of CYC as a viable force within the caring fields will contribute to the well-being of children. Such initiatives help us to deal with changes demanded of us and are clearly influenced by the massive change occurring in children's services and in North American societies as a whole. Perhaps this is fitting. A profession that has at its core the responsibility to promote change in young people is in itself inextricably involved in the process of change.

4

Social Care: A View from the UK

Claire Cameron

OVERVIEW

In the UK,[1] 'social care' is an umbrella term used to define provisions for individuals, families and communities that meet needs for support and assistance with everyday life. It aims to improve a person's quality of life and promote independent living through enhancing his/her resources and capabilities. In this chapter, we will outline the development of social care and refer briefly to the related field of social work; establish the values and principles of social care; describe the characteristics of the social care workforce; and discuss what social care workers actually do, drawing on a study of care work in Europe. The chapter will conclude by considering the relationship between social care and the Continental European understanding of social pedagogy.

DEFINITION AND DEVELOPMENT

In the UK, the term 'social care' came into being in the late 1970s in order to represent an overarching idea 'of the ways people look after each other … and the ways they can be helped to do so by or through official or unofficial caring agencies' (Barnes and Connolly 1978: iii, cited in Higham 2006). A more recent comparative study of social care in Europe similarly concluded that social care had a capacity to straddle established boundaries of service provision:

> social care is assistance that is provided in order to help children or adult people with the activities of their daily lives and it can be provided as paid or unpaid work, by professional or non-professionals and it can take place in the public as well as in the private sphere. In particular, social care is unique in that it transcends the conceptual dichotomies between the public and the private, the professional and the non-professional, the paid and the unpaid. (Kröger 2001: 4)

Social care thus refers to the direct, hands-on care and support of people, usually (but not always) older people or people with disabilities, who need physical and social help, rather than strictly medical help, with everyday life. It grew out of what was called 'personal social services'. Personal social services included residential, day and home-based or domiciliary care and mostly developed during and after the Second World War. Home helps, for example, were provided in people's homes for reasonably fit older people who were unable to cope with the austere conditions associated with rationing. Help was seen as cleaning, shopping, collecting pensions and laundry on weekly visits and was greatly appreciated (Sinclair et al. 2000).

Residential care, however, has a long-standing tradition in the UK (as in Ireland) in the form of the Poor Law workhouses that were organised by parishes and only available to people who were destitute. In 1948, the Poor Law was abolished and responsibility for residential care was passed to local authorities. During the post-war era, a wider range of services developed through local authority departments and voluntary organisations aimed at the support needs of various groups.

In 1971, new legislation applicable in England and Wales meant that these support services came under the jurisdiction of one local authority social services department, which became responsible for 'the welfare of deprived children, the elderly, families in difficulties and the mentally and physically handicapped' (Brown 1971). The vision was that social services would be a 'community based and family oriented service, which will be available to all ... [and] enable the greatest possible number of individuals to act reciprocally, giving and receiving services for the well-being of the whole community' (Seebohm Report 1968: paragraph 2). This organisation meant that personal social services covered people's needs for support from birth to death in one department, with a reoriented approach away from rescue and towards the promotion of a more positive image for services, centred on well-being (Brown 1971), arguably a far vaguer and more ambitious agenda. What was critical here was a generic approach that combined assessment of needs and provision of services to individuals, families and communities.

At this point it is useful to consider the role of social workers in relation to social care. Social workers began to be employed by local authorities after the Second World War as part of the expansion of the welfare state. In this employment context, social workers had, and retain today, a role that is largely based on meeting the needs of individuals and families, although they can also have social justice roles or reflexive therapeutic roles (Payne 1996). Social work is distinct from social care in that social work's methods are more about case work, counselling and assessment, rather than about hands-on caring work. It is also distinctive in that social work has achieved professional recognition through having a distinctive research-based body of knowledge, a code of ethics, recognised practice expertise through post-qualifying training, and entry is restricted to those meeting qualification standards. In 2003, protected status was given to social work so that only those qualified could call themselves social workers and, in 2005, registration of social workers on a social care register was made compulsory. Social care, on the other hand, does not have professional recognition, although it is growing in influence (Higham 2006).

Despite distinct roles and traditions, social care is now the overarching label used to refer to social work, and is 'recognised as the broad domain of interventions operating within community projects, day care, residential care, and home based care organisations' (Higham 2006: 19). Alongside this, social care also refers to the local authority systems to do with enabling personal and social care to be provided by the private and voluntary sectors, and the administration of finance, known as direct payments, to enable clients to organise their own care services (Wistow 2005: vi).

Two further points are worth mentioning in relation to the definition and development of social care. First, although there has always been a role for the voluntary sector in the provision of care services for all client groups, this has significantly expanded, as has the growth of the private sector, since the early 1990s. Now, much of the residential care for both older people and children and home care services (note the changed title from 'home help'), is located in the private and voluntary sector. Simon et al. (2008) report that in England, 46 per cent of residential workers and 56 per cent of home carers and care assistants are employed in the private for-profit sector. The implication of this shift is that local authorities are commissioning and regulating services as well as providing services, and that clients, or service users, as they are often now known, are negotiating a more diverse and potentially more fragmented and complex social care field.

The second point is that the development of social care, and social work, has been influenced by the rise of the consumer-orientated, rights-based, active citizen model in which the idea of 'independence' takes centre stage. As we have seen, the idea of promoting independent living through service provision is a long-standing one, but the emphasis has changed in the context of shifts in how the relationship between the state and the individual is conceptualised. State services no longer exist simply to supplement or replace what the individual cannot do, such as shopping or cleaning. The individual is now seen as an autonomous consumer of services who is expected to make calculated choices about quality and investment and with whom contracts are drawn up. Individuals are seen not as dependent on or obliged to the state, but as citizens who take responsibility for themselves and their care by exercising choices about services. Independence is often expressed in care services for older people as 'not doing for', but in terms of 'keeping people at home for as long as possible'.

Associated concepts for giving meaning to independence are empowerment and enabling, again supporting the idea that individuals choose services for themselves (Cameron and Moss 2007). One clear example of individuals exercising choice is the introduction of 'direct payments', referred to above, whereby older or disabled people, or carers of disabled children who are assessed by the local authority as in need of services, are given a budget and can organise their own care and support rather than receive the services available through their local authority. In this case, 'service users' can become employers of personal assistants and fulfil the obligations of employers.

Finally, the development of social care was further affected by the reorganisations of the early 2000s. In 2003, the English government launched a White Paper,

Table 4.1. The Organisation of Social Care in England, 2008

National government department	Department of Children, Schools and Families	Department of Health
Purpose (from relevant government department website)	To make England the best place in the world for children and young people to grow up. We want to: • Make children and young people happy and healthy. • Keep them safe and sound. • Give them a top-class education. • Help them stay on track.	To define policy and guidance for delivering a social care system that provides care equally for all, while enabling people to retain their independence, control and dignity.
Local authority responsibility	Director of Children's Services and overseen by Children's Services Committee.	Director of Adult Social Services in partnership with health agencies through Care Trusts, overseen by Health and Social Care Committee (or similar title).
Service provision (may be provided directly or in conjunction with, or directly by, private and voluntary providers)	• Social workers for children and families; child protection, adoption and fostering; leaving care teams; foster carers; residential care; family support services. • Early childhood care and education services, including children's centres, childminders, nurseries and pre-school playgroups, after-school and holiday provision (not social care, but some social care responsibilities and staff). • Schools (not social care, but some social care responsibilities and staff).	Social workers/care managers for adults; adult protection; residential care; day care; domiciliary (home) care for older people, people with disabilities or impairments; some mental health hospitals; and primary health care (not social care, but some social care responsibilities and staff).

Every Child Matters, which was followed by the Children Act 2004. This legislation united local authority education departments and those parts of social services that were concerned with children into Children's Services departments. This meant that children's social care, such as foster care, residential care, child protection and family support, was relocated within the new department. A similar move to unite health and social services for adults, including older people and people with disabilities and their carers, had begun in 2000 when the government introduced Care Trusts, which aimed to ensure that the National Health Service and local social services had pooled budgets and worked 'together for the good of the patient' (House of Commons 2001). These developments encouraged a return to specialisation by age group, with children's social care in one local authority department and adult social care in another.

One way of viewing the approach to service provision in England is 'targeted within a universal context'. Social care represents the *targeted* services for those who need assistance beyond that available within their family networks, while *universal* represents the services defined as a social good, such as health and education. Table 4.1 sets out the current position for social care in England (although variations between local authorities exist, so this table will not represent social care in every area) and shows how the idea of targeted services (social care) is contained within universal (children's services, health) administrative spheres.

Summary

Social care is a relatively new occupational field and one subject to rapid change in scope and definition. It is the umbrella term used to refer to both professional social work, with its assessment and case work responsibilities, and direct, hands-on, everyday care work with individuals, families and communities. Social care can cover professional and non-professional work. It also includes informal care by relatives as well as formal, paid care, and it includes attention to the private sphere of the family and the public world of service provision according to national policies. The problem with overarching definitions combined with a new and evolving field is that there is relatively little consensus about what is actually contained within social care.

THE VALUES AND PRINCIPLES OF SOCIAL CARE

One way of trying to establish the unique and distinctive contribution of a field is to identify its values and principles. Wistow (2005), drawing on a wide range of evidence about the development of and prospects for social care, identified a number of emergent key values:

- Choice and independence.
- Citizenship and empowerment.

- Social inclusion and respect for diversity.
- Care and protection for vulnerable adults, children and young people and the community.

Wistow (2005) argues that while the values and principles appear to be straightforward and their meaning assumed, there is often considerable ambiguity about underlying definitions. For example, as alluded to earlier, citizenship refers to the 'active citizen' with social obligations rather than the rights of citizens. In terms of principles, Wistow (2005) refers to the following:

- The social model of disability, which sees incapacity coming from social processes that exclude people and not just individual failings, is applicable to all people. This has implications for society as a whole in terms of human rights, social inclusion and community capacity and not just social care work practices.
- Services should be configured around the needs of individuals within their own circumstances and environments. This has implications for flexible community-based and home-based services; residential services often have the effect of taking people away from their immediate environment.
- Services should be organised in a collaborative way between statutory and voluntary and private providers to ensure a 'seamless' delivery of care to individuals.
- Controlling expenditure and ensuring value for money.

Arguably, these values and principles are not unique to social care and could also apply to other fields of work with people, such as education. But they form a foundation from which more clearly distinctive values may emerge in time. As well as field-specific values, social care is also currently shaped by wider government reforms of the public sector and related local government reforms. For example, contemporary public sector reforms are focused on 'putting people at the centre of public services', with a focus on national standards to encourage uniformity of the quality of services, local delivery responding flexibly to local needs and aspirations, and offering choice to service users.

Similarly, local government reforms have been focused on the idea of 'sustainable communities' that offer people affordable homes, desirable communities, and the opportunities to develop skills and interests, access jobs and services and engage in community life. Wistow (2005: 14–15) argues that there is an overlap between the aspirations of public sector and local government reforms and that of social care service users, with a focus on greater equity of access, improving social inclusion and working to an agenda defined by service users, especially that of securing relationships with care workers based on continuity and trust. It can be seen that the principles discussed here are very much time and policy context specific; they may change with a change of governmental policy direction. Social care is in a fledgling state of development.

SIZE AND CHARACTERISTICS OF THE SOCIAL CARE WORKFORCE

Estimating the size of the social care workforce is difficult (Cameron and Moss 2007; Eborall 2003). Statistics are collected in different ways for different service sectors within formal care work and there are also many unpaid carers who could be counted as part of the social care workforce, as well as variations in which services are included within social care. Prior to the *Every Child Matters* reforms, the day nursery, playgroup and childminding workforce was commonly counted within social care, but since these reforms, this workforce is now usually considered as part of the children's workforce. On the other hand, even though the school workforce clearly works with children, it is not covered by the Children's Workforce Development Council.

Eborall (2003) estimates that there are 929,000 people working in social care in local authority social services, local authority and private and voluntary sector home-based and daycare provision, and some health services employed staff with mainly care work duties. This estimate grows to 1.55 million if early childhood care and education staff, additional health services staff and foster carers are included. Using a national survey of the labour force and standard occupational classifications, Simon et al. (2008) report that for the period 2001–2005, there were 732,000 social care workers, including social workers, youth and community workers, housing and welfare officers, houseparents and residential wardens and care assistants/home carers. If the child care workforce is included, such as nursery nurses, childminders and related occupations and playgroup workers, this grows to 1.01 million. Neither of these estimates includes the unpaid carer workforce or those who are paid by cash through direct payment schemes or work as private foster carers, such as unregistered childminders, nannies, au pairs or domestic care workers. According to the 2001 census, there are 5.2 million unpaid carers and the number of non-declared care workers has been estimated as more than 10,000 (Van Ewijk et al. 2001).

Whichever estimate is used, the social care workforce is evidently sizeable. The proportion of the total workforce engaged in paid care work was estimated as 5–6 per cent for the period 1999–2001, with many in part-time work. This compares with Sweden and Denmark, where the equivalent workforce is 9–10 per cent, with most in full-time work, and the Netherlands, where it is 7 per cent, again with many in part-time work (Cameron and Moss 2007: 38).

Most social care workers are female (84 per cent), aged over 35 years (average age 41 years), and 90 per cent are ethnically white, compared to 93 per cent in the entire female workforce (Simon et al. 2008). Within the social care occupations, the most divergence is over qualifications. Over four-fifths (86 per cent) of social workers have qualifications at A levels (equivalent to Irish Leaving Certificate) or above, with 50 per cent having a university degree. On the other hand, fewer than half (46 per cent) of care assistants have qualifications at A levels or above, with only 4 per cent having a degree (Simon et al. 2008). This difference in qualification is reflected in pay reported by social care workers. Social workers reported mean annual gross pay of £21,886 (€24,500 as of May 2009), while care assistants earned £9,424 (€10,500) on average. This compares to £13,893 (€15,600) for all women workers.

WHAT DO SOCIAL CARE WORKERS DO?

Discussions of social care often neglect actual practice. We have seen that social care is about practical help to older and disabled people, but also children and families, designed to support and sustain independent living and making choices. But this is not the whole picture. One area of debate in social care is the extent to which care replicates, consciously or unconsciously, care that is carried out within families, and more specifically by women who are mothers or carers (Cameron and Moss 2007). In relation to care of children, such a replication, or a 'substitute mothers' approach, has been viewed as problematic (Dahlberg et al. 1999), but in relation to care of older people, replication has been viewed as potentially valuable. A role as an informal or unpaid carer develops capacities and skills that should be used in paid services (Waerness 1995).

Cameron and Moss (2007), reporting a European study of care work, compared actual care practice with older people, people with severe disabilities and with young children across six countries. Using reports from care workers[2] themselves, the authors found that work with older people was interpreted as 'working closely with the older person's active consent and negotiating with them' (2007: 68). In residential care for older people, it included practical tasks interspersed with organised activities and of routine interrupted with flexibility about what happens when and to whom. The day's work consisted of assisting older people according to their needs and desires, and requires knowing each person as an individual. An English residential worker said, 'You have to literally do everything for them up to what they require or what they'd like basically' (ibid.: 69). Knowing people as individuals also led to emotional support – 'if they want to talk or are worried about something' – and enabled workers to assess their abilities by careful observation of older people completing everyday tasks such as making breakfast or getting dressed (ibid.). Care workers' roles were also about providing social activities such as reading groups, coffee mornings or celebration dinners, and therapeutic activities such as reality orientation or mobilisation classes.

In home care work, the main work was, according to one English home care worker in a rural area, about 'looking after their personal welfare ... shopping, pension collecting, meals, putting to bed, everything really that we do personally every day for ourselves we do for the clients'. As with residential work, home care workers, who often worked to very tightly controlled timescales and conditions of work, went beyond their contracted hours and duties in order to offer emotional support to older people. As one home care organiser said, 'We have got a good bunch of carers working out in the community. We are not just there to do the job. The girls listen, they are there for the clients ... to talk to, to confide in sometimes' (Cameron and Moss 2007: 72).

These three elements – practical tasks, emotional support and support for social or leisure activities – were also reported in similar work in Sweden and Spain and in work with people with severe disabilities in the Netherlands, Denmark and Sweden. Work with young children in the countries studied (Hungary, Spain and Denmark) tended to be conceptualised as 'education' in its broadest sense, and to be about free play, organised activities and supporting individual children. But there were distinct similarities with care work with older and disabled people. Work with young children was also a combination of routine and spontaneous activities interspersed with judgements about flexibility and change to routines according to the need and expressed desire of those worked with.

Overall, the study found that the broad purposes of care work were to provide support and assistance with everyday life and to provide an interface between the individual and the society within which they lived. These commonalities were evident despite the different ways that care work was organised and conceptualised in the six countries. The person-centred element of care work – developing a relationship with each individual in order to judge their support and social needs more finely – was more clearly present among work with young children in countries with a broad educational, or pedagogic, focus and in work with people with disabilities, where such relational work was seen as advocacy, friendship or as a 'significant other' (Cameron and Moss 2007: 78). Among work with older people, the relational or person-centred element was weaker, in part because care workers were not given as much responsibility or autonomy around identifying need and developing plans.

In terms of the second key role, all care workers in all the countries reported acting as an intermediary, advocate or adviser for or with the clients or service users. The wider community could be parents, carers, social networks, other professionals or institutions. Such representational work could take the form of working on behalf of a disabled person to achieve an objective set by that person, or talking to parents or carers about the cared-for person's day or referring that person to other services. Variations in the breadth and depth of this work occurred according to the level of training of care workers and the mandate given to the type of work. For example, advocacy work with people with disabilities was designated as appropriate for highly trained pedagogues in Denmark, while similar work organised via a direct payments scheme in England could employ an untrained personal assistant.

There are, of course, many differences across countries and types of care work, or human services work, as well as similarities. The differences can be explained by the wider societal approaches to, resources invested in, and disciplinary traditions in providing services (see also Chapter 2). Stark differences emerged in the *Care Work in Europe* study, particularly between the educational or pedagogic focus within a social democratic welfare state for services with young children and people with disabilities, and the social care focus within what is often called an advanced liberal or neo-liberal welfare state for residential and home care services for older people. In the former, a relational, goal-oriented approach was predominant, while in the latter, care workers with older people were often operating in a more restricted environment with little opportunity for developing a relational approach within their contracted duties (Cameron and Moss 2007).

However, similarities are often overlooked. The *Care Work in Europe* study concluded that in optimum conditions, all care workers are:

- Fulfilling physiological needs among care recipients, including needs for protection.
- Investing in a relational approach, practising communication and empathetic skills, and spending meaningful time with clients, being curious about them as individuals and developing solidarity with them.
- Supporting development and autonomy in the individuals and groups they work with.
- Supporting integrative relationships between the person cared for and his/her wider networks, supporting inclusion and citizenship.
- Networking on behalf of service users, and teamworking with other workers and in other services.
- Renewing their knowledge and their identity values over their career.
- Responding to changing societal images of 'cared for' people, from passive recipients to active subjects with rights.
- Working with diversity in terms of gender, ethnicity, age and sexuality.

CONCLUSION

Social care in England is an emergent field being created from a 'space' between and overlapping with familial care and professional care, referring to hands-on provision for older people, people with disabilities and children and their carers and families. Aspirations for social care are that it ensures that people who are not able to manage their own lives are able to manage with help. As we saw earlier, UK government ambitions for children are that social care helps children to grow up in the best possible place, while ambitions for adults indicate a rather non-interventionist approach, with a focus on services that do not interrupt independence or impair dignity or control over one's own life. These ambitions indicate a somewhat different approach to the state's role in everyday lives than that advocated by Seebohm in 1971, which was more about reciprocity and ensuring community well-being. Although the universal vision has been renewed in some respects, social care services have come to be seen in the intervening decades as clearly targeted provision, in an era of ever-tightening financial resources, that families cannot provide for themselves.

Arguably, the fledging state of social care, despite the advent of government-sponsored organisations to register and regulate social care (General Social Care Council), to inspect and report on social care (Commission for Social Care Inspection) and to document and disseminate social care practice (Social Care Institute for Excellence) is already under threat.

This threat comes from three directions. First, there is a substantial lack, and uneven spread, of resources to meet people's support needs (Commission for Social Care Inspection 2008). For example, it is estimated that about 60 per cent of all older people with any kind of disability or impairment have some shortfall in their care, if it is assumed that families do not provide care for their kin. Problems such as variable local political commitment to social care for adults, use of unqualified social workers to make discretionary decisions about who should receive care services and uneven use of information services to direct potential clients to other service providers meant the social care system was not only inadequately resourced, but highly variable in its performance (Commission for Social Care Inspection 2008).

A second threat to the field of social care comes from a lack of articulation of its distinctive underlying principles, values and concepts. In comparison with other European countries, particularly those where the concept of 'pedagogy' or 'social pedagogy'[3] is employed to refer to work with people in residential and day services, social care is an 'empty' concept. As we have seen in this chapter, if we disregard social work, where there has been a theoretical base, there is little that is distinctive about social care itself. In England, the everyday life of work in a care capacity, outside 'health' and 'education', has not been theorised to an extent where one can easily identify what it is trying to do and with what aim in a way that transcends current policy directions. Having a clear disciplinary base is important to acquiring professional status (Higham 2006).

This is related to the third threat, which is to do with the qualification base of the social care workforce, which, apart from social work, is generally low. National expectations on qualifications for staff in social care are not high relative to other European countries, and attempts to ensure that staff hold relevant qualifications have not been universally achieved. Eborall (2003: 241) found that by 2002–2003, only 35 per cent of local councils had completed all aspects of their training needs, and only one-third of residential child care workers had achieved the expected Level 3 award in caring for children and young people. Compared to their Danish and German colleagues, English residential care workers are unlikely to hold a high-level qualification. Ninety-four per cent of residential workers in Denmark (pedagogues) held a degree-level qualification, compared with 20 per cent in England and 51 per cent in Germany (Petrie et al. 2006). Data on qualifications held by staff in the independent sector, where many care workers are located, is difficult to obtain, although once the sector is subject to registration requirements through the General Social Care Council, this data may become available (Eborall 2003). Simon et al. (2008) found that 15 per cent of care assistants have no qualifications at all.

The educational qualifications held, and training completed, within a staff group enable an occupation to develop critical thinking and confident responses to new situations and apply them to current workplace specifics (Balloch et al. 1999). Qualifications that are cross-sectoral enable an occupational area to develop common discourses underpinned by common understandings that feed into the debates that give rise to common concepts – the field itself. This is yet to be achieved within social care in the UK, and what is more, the location of social care as the 'targeted' work within the universal of health on the one hand, and children's services on the other, may paradoxically work against the achievement of a distinctive arena for social care.

5

Social Care and the Professional Development Project

Perry Share

'Professions … are all conspiracies against the laity.'

George Bernard Shaw,
preface to *The Doctor's Dilemma* (1906)

OVERVIEW

This chapter addresses the question of professionalisation and social care. It is likely that you have thought about yourself, now or potentially, as a 'social care professional'. Indeed, this term has been used a number of times in this text. Yet what does it mean to be a professional? Is social care practice a profession? The term is not as simple or straightforward as it might first appear.

In this chapter, we explore the concept of professionalism, pointing to how sociologists in particular have interrogated it. They have drawn attention to *power* as a key aspect of the creation and maintenance of professional groups. To say you are a professional gives you power in our society, but you also need access to power to be able to make this claim.

We examine the 'professional development project': the complex process by which those in the occupation of social care practice, or other interested stakeholders, have sought its recognition as a profession. The analysis of this project points to the importance of language, or 'discourse': what are the key terms and arguments needed to convince the broader society that social care practitioners merit the label of 'professional'?

The chapter also looks at the content of social care practice, particularly how it is coming into increasing tension with the demands for 'accountability' from a managerial state. The chapter concludes with a suggested typology of professionalisms for social care – not as a way to divide up the existing workforce, but rather as a set of suggested strategies that aspiring social care practitioners may adopt in the future. Inevitably, the graduates and practitioners of the early twenty-first century will be the ones to shape this ongoing process.

THE NATURE OF PROFESSIONALISM

Fundamental to an assessment of the professional status of social care is a critical analysis of the term 'profession' itself. Professionalisation is a process whereby an occupational group can claim special status and power for itself. We recognise that certain occupational groups – in particular doctors, lawyers and priests – have traditionally enjoyed high *status* in society and also considerable *power*, both over their own lives and over the lives of others. This is generally reflected in significant levels of influence, income and wealth. But how can we critically understand this process? How do certain activities, individuals or occupations become associated with the label of 'profession'? How does this change over time, and why is it that professionals tend to be highly favoured in our society?

There have been many attempts to provide a checklist of *traits* or qualities that constitute a professional. Scottish residential care expert Margaret Lindsay (2002: 76) bases her own definition of the term on a series of interviews that she undertook with 'a few people from the general public'. Her interviewees came up with a set of defining characteristics (see Table 5.1); the criteria produced by these 'ordinary people' reflect those identified by academic analysts of the topic. We return to these themes later in this chapter, but also point to some other approaches that might help us to understand professionalism.

Table 5.1. Defining Features of a 'Professional'

Feature	What it means	What does this mean in relation to social care?
Learning	Professionals have specific expert skills and knowledge; training is long and demanding and it requires hard work to build up the expertise required.	What specific knowledge, skills and knowhow do social care practitioners have?
Attitude	Professionals have a calling or a vocation; there is a moral dimension and a sense of duty to others. This requires an active role in society.	Do social care practitioners exhibit a vocation? Do they act in society to further their profession?
Responsibility and autonomy	Professionals have responsibility for what they do and are personally accountable for their work; they have a high degree of autonomy and have to exercise judgement.	Are social care practitioners autonomous? Are they accountable to society as a whole?
Public image	Professionals are highly regarded and trusted by the public; they command trust, respect, even awe.	Are social care practitioners held in high regard by others in society? Do they enjoy status and respect?

Source: Lindsay (2002: 76–7).

Sociologists have long been interested in the professions. An early analyst of the phenomenon, pioneer sociologist Émile Durkheim (1858–1917), saw the development of professionalism as a way that the personal power and status of certain individuals and groups could be balanced against the needs of society. Professionalism was a trade-off: certain individuals could enjoy the status of being a professional, but they also agreed to be bound by certain *ethical principles* and a measure of accountability to society (Aldridge and Evetts 2003: 548).

A later major sociologist, Max Weber (1864–1920), argued for a more critical approach. He saw professionalisation as a way that those with power and status could *limit the ability of others* to access these. Professionalism is thus a form of 'social closure'. Those who enjoy membership of a professional group can make it very difficult for others to join them, for example through establishing long and expensive courses of study; limiting the numbers admitted; discriminating against certain categories of poeple (women or members of particular religious groups); or through the creation of difficult and complex bodies of knowledge that people must master (e.g. having to learn Latin or complex mathematics). This model of professionalism reflects the Western experience of the traditional 'learned professions' of religious ministry, medicine and law.

The American writer Eliot Freidson (1923–2005) was the dominant socio-logical analyst of the professions for over 40 years. His primary work, *Profession of Medicine* (1970), was followed by further discussions of the topic (1990, 1994, 2001) that responded to criticisms of his initial analysis and amended his theoretical and empirical approach. Another major contributor to the field (especially concerning the medical profession) has been the British sociologist Robert Dingwall, who in 2008 published a collection spanning over three decades of his writings in the field. Anyone wishing to explore the sociology of professionalism should start with the work of these writers.

A common approach to the analysis of the professions is to compile a list of key *attributes*, such as the following (Williams and Lalor 2001: 77):

- Ownership of a recognised body of knowledge exclusive to that profession, with development of new knowledge through research.
- Self-government through a body that sets and monitors its own standards of practice.
- Control of training and recruitment.
- Monopoly of practice in its own field of work, with registration by the state.
- Conformity to moral and disciplinary codes of behaviour.
- Autonomy of practice and greater individual accountability.
- A public ideology of service to a client group.

Criteria similar to these have been widely used by many writers to assess and judge the extent to which an occupation can be said to be a profession. They are useful in pointing to some of the strategies that occupational groups have undertaken.

They all relate in different ways to the exercise of *power*: the power to define, to act, to manage, to control, to admit or to exclude.

Contemporary analyses of professionalisation have argued against this 'checklist' approach to the analysis of professionalism. They stress the importance of seeing professionalisation as a dynamic and complex *process* or even as a form of social 'game'. Professionalism must be viewed as a result of *interaction* between groups in society (Craig 2006: 15–16). Whether or not nurses can call themselves professional, for example, is an outcome of their interaction, as an occupational group, with other groups such as medical doctors, legislators and hospital managers. Similarly, if Irish social care practitioners are to attain professional status, it will be as much as a result of their interaction with senior civil servants, social workers, HSE line managers and – crucially – the broader public as it will be due to the content of social care practice itself.

CONSTRUCTING PROFESSIONALISM

What might this more dynamic analysis of professionalisation look like? Initially, it must focus on the strategic activities that an occupational group can engage in to increase its social standing and power. These activities may involve claims by a group to possess particular types or levels of *commitment* and *skills* or knowhow. In a brief paper prepared in 1990, Freidson (1990: 3) suggests that professionalism has two key meanings. First, it 'represents a more than ordinary commitment to performing a particular kind of activity' – the notion of 'vocation' voiced by Lindsay's interviewees. Second, it refers to 'the productive labor by which one makes a living, a full-time occupation that entails the use of some sort of specialized skill' – Lindsay's 'learning'. Only when these two attributes are combined, suggests Freidson, do we find a distinctive 'profession'. To apply this analysis, a person might be very skilled at hairdressing, but we do not think of this occupation as a 'vocation'. Similarly, a person might be a very dedicated carer, but we may not define them as 'professional' unless they have a particular type and level of training and education.

Freidson makes the further important point that in the contemporary world, a particular profession cannot be thought of outside of the specific and distinctive *institutions* of our society. Thus, one cannot be an intensive-care nurse without the institution of the modern hospital or a lawyer without the system of legislation, courts, tribunals and so on. Thus, it can be argued by extension, it is impossible to be a social care professional unless you are connected in some way (perhaps as an employee or as a consultant) to an institution that provides social care services.

We can see that any occupational group that claims professional status must be able to demonstrate access to a specialised area of skills or knowhow; must be able to link into an institutional basis in society; and must be able to appeal to some higher-level concept of altruism, service or 'vocation'. Clearly, this is quite a challenge.

The institutional dimension of professionalisation leads Freidson to stress the connection between professions and *work* – professions should be understood as particular types of *occupations*. But what is distinctive about these occupations is that, compared to most others, the workers have a very high level of *control* over the terms, conditions and goals of the work they do:

> The occupational group determines whom it recruits, how they shall be trained, and what tasks they shall perform. It has a monopoly in the labor market over a specific set of tasks, an exclusive jurisdiction. Furthermore, members of the occupation have the exclusive right to evaluate the way their tasks are performed and the adequacy of the goods or services their work produces. Neither lay executives in work organizations nor individual consumers have authority over the performance and evaluation of professional work. (Freidson 1990: 14)

Freidson argues that it is this level of control and *autonomy* in relation to work that distinguishes professionals from other types of occupations.

Another important commentary that relates to issues of power comes from feminist writers. They have stressed the *gendered* aspect of professionalisation (see also Chapter 10). The profession of medicine, for example, was at least partially founded on a process of replacing 'folk' knowledge about healing, largely maintained and used by women, with 'professional' knowledge that was exclusively the property of men. Thus, the female occupation of midwife has come to be dominated by the male-centred practices of obstetrics and gynaecology (Ehrenreich and English 1974).

Overall, Freidson (1990: 9) sees professionalism as a *positive* force in contemporary society, particularly inasmuch as it provides a 'third way' between government regulation on the one hand and the unfettered free market on the other. A crucial dimension that professionalism supports, according to Freidson, is a strong element of *trust*. Neither the free market nor a system of bureaucratic control, he suggests, can produce the unique relationship of trust that exists between a professional and his/her client. Yet recent years have seen these trust relations coming under threat, as a number of professional areas have been riven by scandals of abuse, incompetence and dishonesty. In Ireland, we can think of the problems in relation to the blood transfusion service (O'Carroll 1998), the so-called Neary case in the Drogheda hospital (Inglis 2008) and cases of child sexual abuse within the religious and teaching professions. A key element of the maintenance of professional status is about repairing such trust relationships; any 'new' profession will have to actively build trust from a more sceptical public.

We can see, then, that any occupational group aiming to pursue a profession-alisation project faces a complex task. As well as defining a specific field of knowledge and gaining a high level of autonomy, it must also link to key institutional sites of power in society. In addition, it must develop and sustain more ephemeral and intangible sets of relationships and values related to vocational commitment and trust with clients or users as well as the broader public. This is where language – or *discourse* – becomes crucial.

DISCOURSES OF PROFESSIONALISM

Aldridge and Evetts (2003) suggest that professionalism has become a way that both workers and their managers *talk about* work practices, a process that can have benefits – and drawbacks – for each. They argue that 'professional' has entered the English language as a generic term that represents something *good*:

> The discourse of professionalism is now used as a marketing slogan in advertising to appeal to customers, in recruitment campaigns and company mission statements, in organizational aims and objectives to motivate employees, and has entered the managerial literature and been embodied in training manuals. (Aldridge and Evetts 2003: 555)

As Freidson (1990: 2) had earlier pointed out, 'professional' is 'an ambiguous [term], used more often symbolically and globally than precisely and concretely'. As a term, it is highly desirable – it makes workers feel better about what they do – but it may also be used by employers and managers to exercise *control* over employees' behaviour. Professional workers can be encouraged to work harder and longer, to 'self-exploit' themselves. They may be told that 'as professionals' they have obligations to the wider society that override normal work demands – for example, they should stay at work until a job is finished instead of knocking off at five o'clock, or they can be expected to bring work home at the weekends.

Following the work of French writer Michel Foucault (1926–84), Aldridge and Evetts (2003: 556) argue that professionalism today has much to do with self-discipline and *self-management*. The successful employee today is one that self-consciously fits into an occupational hierarchy, where:

> the community of fellow workers and the hierarchy of positions in organisations and other workplaces (such as peers, superiors and juniors) constantly reiterate and reinforce this sense of self and position as well as appropriate behaviours and work decisions and choices.

Much of 'being a professional' is to become accepted, by one's peers and the broader public, as working within a distinctive occupational community and having and expressing a professional self-identity (Costello 2005). There is much talk now of the professional 'role'. This suggests that issues of personal and professional identity are becoming increasingly linked in contemporary society. This has important implications for professionals' self-management, but also for their well-being. As Craig (2006: 21) notes, 'when professionals identify so intimately with their work, it can be almost impossible to "switch off" when it is time to go home'. This can result in high levels of work-related stress and potential burnout.

The discourse of professionalisation is sometimes used to effect *change* in organisations and occupations. This is often linked to new forms of organisation; to legislation and regulation; to a greater emphasis on formal education and accreditation; and to new forms of technology, such as computerisation. Change can be a difficult and conflictual process: 'an occupational identity crisis may follow, emerging as discontent particularly on the part of older and more experienced groups of workers' (Aldridge and Evetts 2003: 556). This may become a major issue in the professionalisation of social care in Ireland and elsewhere.

In all these examples, professionalisation is constituted through language – in how people use the term. But this use of language is always social; it involves negotiation and a struggle for power between different groups. The concept can be said to be *deployed* towards particular strategic ends. When a group embarks on such a strategy, it is involved in a 'professional development project'.

THE PROFESSIONAL DEVELOPMENT PROJECT IN IRISH SOCIAL CARE PRACTICE

Swedish writers Hallstedt and Högström (2005: 18) suggest that all occupations in the field of welfare 'are fighting for the right to call themselves professions'. In the Irish context, Farrell and O'Doherty (2005: 81) refer to the 'slow and tortuous process' of the professional development project in social care. In the early 1990s, it was suggested by sociologist Pat O'Connor (1992) that, in Ireland, the prospects for professionalisation in the 'child care' field were not high. By 1998, Crimmens (1998: 314) could refer to the training of social care workers in Ireland as a 'professional qualification'. At the end of the 1990s, Gallagher and O'Toole (1999: 78) identified the issue of professionalisation as 'central to the development of social care work' but argued that development of a 'coherent professional identity' was stymied by:

> a lack of internal unity, fragmentation across qualification level, diverse client and administrative settings, a changing role and exclusion from key policy-making structures within the bureaucratic professional hierarchy of state welfare services. (Gallagher and O'Toole 1999: 83)

In 2001, Williams and Lalor (p. 73) saw that 'the profession [of residential child care] is presently at a young stage in its development', while by 2005, Farrelly and O'Doherty (p. 81) concluded that 'the promise of official and public definition and acceptance of social care work has [now] become a reality'. Does this mean that the professional development project in Irish social care has been finalised?

Hallstedt and Högström (2005: 18) argue that the three main sets of actors in the professionalisation project are *practitioners* themselves, *academic institutions* and the state. In Ireland, the emergence of a professional discourse has not been the result of organisational activity within the occupation itself. The representative body for social care practitioners (formerly the Irish Association of Care Workers (IACW), now the Irish Association of Social Care Workers (IASCW)) has tended to be fragmented, unrepresentative and relatively ineffective as an organisation (Byrne 2005) and has not yet been able to generate a sustained push towards professional status. The social care managers' organisation (the Resident Managers' Association (RMA)) has been better organised and more reflective of its membership base. Through its conferences, publications and involvement in state-sponsored consultative groups, it has had a greater impact on the profes-sionalisation process. Arguably the most influential occupational groups have been the major unions that represent social care practitioners (IMPACT and SIPTU, which have been successful in significantly enhancing the salaries and conditions of their members) and major employers (such as the HSE and some in the non-governmental sector), which have established minimum standards of qualification (at degree level) for practitioners.

In the educational field, there has been little input into the accreditation process. Nevertheless, in May 2009 HETAC convened a representative expert group to develop national social care education standards. Much responsibility has tended to devolve to the educators themselves through their representative body, the Irish Association of Social Care Educators (IASCE). Members of IASCE have carried out research on topics related to professional development, have facilitated discussion on the issue at its conferences and have supported the production of the first textbook in the field – this one. The *Irish Journal of Applied Social Studies*, now under the control of the IASCE, has also carried a number of articles related to the academic and professional development of social care. In addition, develop-ment has occurred in social care curricula, spurred by the emergence of new and revised degree programmes at a number of institutions.

These developments are largely internal to the educational institutions concerned, sometimes informed by local state actors such as the HSE or other organisations that employ social care practitioners. Nevertheless, the education sector has not been able to exert any significant pressure on either employers, in terms of restriction of jobs to those with specific qualifications, or the state, which has largely excluded educators from proposed regulatory mechanisms.

The strongest influence on the social care professionalisation project has come from the state itself. On 30 November 2005, Dáil Éireann signed into law the most significant piece of legislation yet in relation to the professionalisation of social care practice: the Health and Social Care Professionals Act 2005. The background to this legislation, and its possible implications, are explored in detail in Farrelly and O'Doherty (2005). Nevertheless, at the time of writing (early 2009), the legislation has yet to be enacted in relation to social care practitioners and there are no indications that this is imminent.

Thus, we see that in Ireland, the professionalisation project in social care has been relatively weak. Those in the occupation itself have not coherently pursued professionalisation and it has largely been left to employers and unions to shape the occupational landscape. The education sector has been influential to a limited degree, but has been structurally excluded from the principal institutional sites. The main impetus has come from the state, in the form of proposed registration, but this may have stalled and does not appear to be a major government priority. In light of these factors, it could be said that the professionalisation project in social care has been less than successful, though it remains the case that social care practitioners in Ireland are better educated, more generously paid and have superior career structures to those in many other Western countries.

The remainder of this chapter examines some key issues in relation to the professionalisation project in more detail. These include the problem of defining 'social care practice'; the content of such practice; the relationship between the professionalisation project and broader issues of institutional change; and the counter-discourses that express themselves as resistances to professionalism. The chapter closes with a suggested typology of ways that social care professionalism may be developing.

THE PROBLEM OF DEFINITION

Social care work has been defined in the British (Banks 2004) and European (Lorenz 1994) contexts as one of the 'social professions'. In the Irish context, however, it has become an increasingly difficult field to define. From a clear point of departure in the provision of care in defined institutional contexts (reformatories and industrial schools), 'social care' has evolved into a loosely linked set of practices that spans youth work, residential child care, community child care, project work, educational work, community development and aspects of therapeutic practice.

As Farrelly and O'Doherty (2005: 84) point out (referring to the relationship between social care practice and social work), there is a blurring of boundaries, as 'traditional points of demarcation are less credible as a result of the changing circumstances surrounding the education, training and deployment of qualified social work and social care practitioners'. Petrie et al. (2005: 2) note, in the English context, that 'borders and relations between different types of services are changing, workforce issues are to the fore, and there is a desire to find new approaches'. There is a convergence between social work, social care practice and youth and community work, but at the same time a fragmentation of roles as new job titles and occupational identities are created (such as various types of project and community-based work). Interprofessional and interagency work may be on the increase (Pollard et al. 2005), but at the same time, the nature of the individual 'professions' involved is less clear.

In the European context (and in particular in Scandinavia, Germany and the Netherlands), the term 'social pedagogy' points to a certain set of traditions, practices and professions (Eriksson and Markström 2003; Petrie et al. 2005). It is itself a somewhat amoebic term, having 'joint contents with many other occupational groups such as educational workers, social care workers, youth workers, child welfare nurses, welfare nurses, and animators' (Hallstedt and Högström 2005: 29). The history of the term varies in different societies, and the divisions between social pedagogy/care practice and social work, and the relations between them, vary in different countries. But again, these divisions may be breaking down, as suggested by Van Ewijk (2008: 10): 'the time of defending territories and insecure professionals appears to be over and replaced by a more positive attitude towards ... a common identity of social professionals'.

As we have seen in Chapter 3, in the US and Canada the field is commonly referred to as child and youth care (CYC). This tends to focus on the welfare of children and young people – other professional groupings direct their efforts at the disabled or other client categories. The basis of CYC can be found in a multiplicity of locations: in religious-run orphanages, in the 'fresh air' movement of the nineteenth century, in the state correctional facilities for deviant and criminalised youth and in residential centres for indigenous young people, especially in Canada. Since the 1950s, CYC has seen the emergence of professionalising strategies. The CYC approach tends to be individualistic, therapeutic and case based. As with social care practice in Ireland, CYC has extended from its residential base into community-based activities and strategies.

In Ireland, Farrelly and O'Doherty (2005: 84) suggest that:

> the necessary expansion of education and training routes ... has in turn generated a professional social care project concerned with determining the combination of theories, practices, methods, organisations, responsibilities and other features that characterise ... social care work.

This refers to the internal activities that are helping to coalesce the discursive constructions of social care practice. But there has been little external discussion: for example, there has been no forum where the relationship between social care practice and social work can even be named, let alone debated.

THE CONTENT OF CARE PROFESSIONALISM

In Ireland, social care practice developed as a range of activities that people carried out within and for institutions, such as residential centres, regional Health Boards (now the HSE) and voluntary bodies. With professionalisation has come a breaking of the nexus with specific organisations. The professional care practitioner can now be a 'free agent' who can offer a portfolio of experience and who can lay claim to a certain range of competencies. The *content* of social care practice then becomes a much bigger issue. It is no longer a question of 'who do you work for?' but 'what do you *do*?' and 'what *can* you do?'

In a study of social care in a number of European countries (see Chapter 2 for more information on this research), Hallstedt and Högström (2005) review some of the key aspects of social care practice, which they alternatively term 'social pedagogy' and 'social educational work'. We can debate the extent to which these characterise social care work in the Irish context.

Hallstedt and Högström (2005: 33; 47) identify 'living in' (sharing life space) and 'close work with people in difficult situations' as key elements of social pedagogy. This has also been described as the process of 'being with another' and even 'keeping an eye out' (Collander-Brown 2005). Typically, 'the relations between the social educational worker and the clients generally are long lasting and intense'. Social pedagogy is about social relationships 'because a functioning relation is a necessary condition for a dedicated and unbiased search for optional actions' (Hallstedt and Högström 2005: 48). Thus, the work of social pedagogy embraces sets of relationships, goals of action, particular methods, specific competencies and personal qualities. Overall, the work is related in some way to the question of *integration* in society.

Drawing on the work of Danish writer Madsen (1995), Hallstedt and Högström (2005: 48) suggest that 'social educational work can be described as an exploration of the possibilities to change critical life situations and at the same time not to deprive the client of his autonomy'. This points to the tensions engendered by the asymmetrical power relationships between practitioner and client. Navigating this tension is one of the skills of social care work and may thus be an element of professionalism (see also Chapter 8).

Hallstedt and Högström (2005: 50), again drawing on Madsen, suggest that this gives rise to two requirements for social care practice. First, there is 'an ethical structure to minimise or delay the administrative structure of the relationship'. This refers to a professional ethics and a stance characterised by trust and a general will to meet the client on the same level. This is termed 'the relational competence of the social educational worker'. Second, the social care practitioner requires the competence to 'lead a critical discussion on life conditions' in contemporary society, leading to a constructive pedagogical goal. This is termed 'goal-directed social education work'.

At the root of this practice is an ability to communicate in an emancipatory manner ('to side with the underdog'). This means operating at the client's level and engaging in open communication on the client's situation from that position (Hallstedt and Högström 2005: 53). The content of social care practice then can be broadly summarised as follows:

- The ability to recognise and deal with the *asymmetrical relationship* between practitioner and client and to turn that imbalance of power into a working relationship.
- The ability to make use of broad social, cultural and theoretical knowledge to *interpret* another's life. ·

- The formulation of a *constructive pedagogical goal* or goals with reference to the actual client's resources and the potentials for action.
- Citing Madsen (1995), 'the synthesis of the communication should include an *evaluation* of the content of the client's life aspirations and resources, the culture and ultimately of the potentials for action'.
- To *reflect* on the behaviour, to be aware of the quality of the current relationship and to act in accordance with *ethical principles*.

Ultimately, a feature of care work is that it is replete with uncertainty, ambiguity and unresolved (and perhaps irresolvable) tensions. Schön (1991a) argues that this is in fact a feature of all professional practice: it eludes the attempts of technocratic rationality to 'pin it down'. He says (1991a: 19) that:

> professionals have been disturbed to find that they cannot account for the processes they have come to see as central to professional competence. It is difficult for them to describe and teach what might be meant by making sense of uncertainty, performing artistically, setting problems, and choosing among competing professional paradigms.

This raises challenges when the arena of professional practice encounters the powerful discourses of managerialism and performativity.

PERFORMATIVITY AND INSTITUTIONAL REFORM

The 'content' of social care practice is just one part of the complex factors that shape the professionalism discourse. Such practice takes place in a range of institutional contexts. The social professions in general are very much determined by the activities and structures of the contemporary welfare state; indeed, the 'social professions' are an important link between civil society and the state.

'Traditional' notions of professionalism are increasingly open to challenge. Part of this is due to the increased climate of 'risk' that pervades aspects of contemporary society. Dent and Whitehead (2002: 1) suggest that part of the social pressure that is helping to shape professionalism is a 'loss of faith, trust and sense of order, an increased perception of risk'. This may particularly be the case in Ireland, as suggested earlier, with a succession of high-profile 'failures' of professionalism in, for example, the religious, political, medical, planning, judicial and business arenas.

The state is neither a monolith nor a static entity. In recent times, there have been major shifts in how contemporary states conduct their business. There has been a powerful emergent discourse, derived at least in part from the globalised business sector, that refers to concepts such as the 'new accountability', 'joined-up thinking' and 'modern management' (Banks 2007; Dewe et al. 2005). The ideologies of 'efficiency' and 'accountability' have been reinforced in Ireland by the perception of 'rip-off Ireland' and most recently by the emergent global economic and fiscal crisis.

In Ireland, the penetration of business and managerialist discourse has been explicitly expressed through the Strategic Management Initiative (SMI) of the Irish government, as this has been translated into the activities of a wide range of state departments (such as the Department of Health and Children) and agencies (such as the Social Services Inspectorate). This has led Farrelly and O'Doherty (2005: 87) to suggest that 'managerialist practices and thinking' are impacting in a negative way on social work practice in Ireland.

Such state initiatives, found in all developed economies, impinge on and help to shape definitions of 'professionalism'. The effects are contradictory, as Banks (2004: 34–5) points out:

> On the one hand these moves towards standardising practice can be seen as advancing the professional project insofar as they have resulted in clear definitions of the purpose and nature of the work of the occupations … regulation of entry and standards of conduct. This could be seen to advance the credibility, status and public trust in the occupational groups. On the other hand the standards and controls have been initiated by the state, and although practitioners have had a role in their development, their room for manoeuvre has been somewhat limited.

For Dent and Whitehead, accountability is now all-pervasive. Thus 'the professional has no escape from being managed nor, indeed, from managing others' (2002: 1). The consequence is a 'culture of performativity', where the rewards go to those who can demonstrate that they can perform in relation to a range of discourses: flexibility, reflexivity, teamwork, lifelong learning, market orientation, managerialism and entrepreneurialism. Such attributes are often couched in the language of 'competencies' ('the ability to do something well using necessary skills and knowledge') that can often be quite narrowly and instrumentally expressed (Miller 2008). The successful professional must be able to live and perform within these discourses. Within this world, the professional must be prepared to be subjected to performance measurement and competitive assessment according to various modes of calculation – often administered by their peers.

An emergent pattern is not a sharp conflict between managerialism and professional autonomy, though this may be expressed symbolically and strategically at moments of tension. Rather, we see the emergence of strategies of 'soft bureaucracy' and 'soft coercion' (Sheaff et al. 2003) whereby professional groupings are dominated through 'sophisticated management strategies' that operate on the basis that 'experts' accept limitations on their autonomy. 'Soft coercion' is often based on responses to perceived threats to an organisation from the state, competitors or the legal system. It involves 'technically legitimated rules of professional practice which regulate the individual professional's work' (Sheaff et al. 2003: 421).

Ideally, 'control is exercised by a supervisory stratum from within the ranks of the profession itself'.

RESISTANCES TO PROFESSIONALISATION

The powerful discourses of accountability and efficiency give rise, of course, to discourses of resistance. There are tensions here. Part of the notion of 'social profession' expresses a relationship, indeed perhaps an obligation, to 'society' – a relationship of accountability. Many social professionals are quite literally described as 'public servants'. Yet for many, to quote Banks (2004: 154) again:

> the demands of employers seem to be taking precedence over the welfare, needs and respect of service users; agency values, translated into detailed procedures, are dominating professional activity at the expense of professional values relating to respect for service users, confidentiality and so on; and the scope for professional judgement based on expertise and professional values seems to be seriously constrained by the new accountability requirements.

Banks points out that there is 'an identifiable strand of reluctance towards moves to professionalise' in the social professions, as this involves the creation of *distance* between practitioners and their clients. This connects back to the issues of asymmetry of power mentioned earlier. As Banks (2004: 140) suggests, 'professional culture' can be a way that distinguishes 'us' from 'them', marking out 'our ways of doing things' (based on our values, language and methods of working) from 'their way of doing things'. This conflict may run counter to more egalitarian and inclusive occupational discourses.

Another important strand of resistance focuses on what is termed the *deprofessionalisation* of social care practice (Clark 2005). Here, the processes of regulation and managerial control serve to remove professional discretion from practitioners, replacing it with adherence to more abstract rules and procedures defined by external bodies. At worst, this may require practitioners to act in ways they would not want or that may not be in the best interests of those they work with. There is considerable debate as to whether deprofessionalisation has taken place within the social professions. While it is clear that they may be more subject to regulation, especially by the state, it can also be argued that this is at least partly a consequence of the greatly increased power of social professionals, including social care practitioners, to determine others' lives. In other words, if social care practice is closely regulated, this is indicative of the greater power of social care practitioners, not a sign of their weakness.

THE NEW PROFESSIONALISMS?

Based on the discussion in this chapter, I would like to propose a fivefold typology of professionalising strategies that may be adopted by social care practitioners. It is not suggested that any single professional care practitioner falls easily into one category or another – rather, these strategies or styles may be adopted by or may be reflected in the actions and attitudes of those who define themselves as professionals.

- *The manager/practitioner*: Buys into the 'new accountability' and the 'audit culture'. Relates closely to state and organisational projects for change, restructuring and reform. Endorses concepts of accountability, self-management, competition and performativity. May also favour 'evidence-based practice' (see Chapter 11).
- *The 'traditional professional'*: Tends to be modelled on the established professions, in particular medicine and social work. Focuses on content of knowledge, especially in terms of academic material. Endorses technical rationality in Schön's (1991a) sense; endorses the boundaries that surround, contain and 'protect' the professional group; is collegial and group focused. Anti-managerial and sees accountability as an unwarranted intrusion into personal and professional autonomy.
- *The reflexive professional*: Person and client centred rather than group focused. Sees the 'self' and work on selves as the basis of professional work. Has a therapeutic and individualistic bias. Favours flexibility, indeterminancy. Opposed to rigid structures, externally mandated competencies or checklists.
- *The 'democratic professional'*: Community focused and consultative, 'works with collectivities, is participatory and acknowledges a primary responsibility to users' (Banks, 2004: 44). Leadbetter (2006) refers to the professional who works within 'postindustrial public services, which are more collaborative, networked and distributed'.
- *The entrepreneurial professional*: Opportunistic, network focused, project focused. Non-organisational but can use organisation as resource. Individualistic and eclectic. Strategic, flexible, portfolio worker.

Further research in the field of social care practice is required to establish the extent to which this categorisation is justified, and whether it helps us to better understand the self-definitions of care practitioners. It is hoped that the outline suggested here will contribute in some way to the emergent discussion on the professionalisation of social care, in Ireland and elsewhere.

CONCLUSION

The issue of professionalisation has been around in Irish social care for a long time. It has begun to attract the attention of government, which is now, however slowly, beginning to pay more strategic attention to the range of social care occupations and settings. The trade unions that represent many social care practitioners have begun to use the concept in order to improve the pay and conditions of their members. Employers have also started to use the term in recruitment advertisements.

But it is crucial to the future of social care in Ireland that practitioners themselves engage seriously with the concept of professionalism and begin to discuss what it might mean. Are social care practitioners seeking to become another type of social worker, nurse or some other favoured 'professional' group, or are there other models that can provide a more liberating and – dare we say it – empowering form of professionalism? How might this be achieved? The social care practitioners of the future will be the ones to help determine the future of social care.

Part II

Theoretical Approaches to Social Care Practice

6

Psychological Theories of Child Development

Áine de Róiste

OVERVIEW

Developmental psychological theories offer the social care professional a rich repository of different perspectives with which to consider and support human development. This chapter examines three main sets of theories: theories of cognitive and language development (Piaget, Vygotsky), learning theory (Skinner, Bandura) and theories of socio-emotional development (Maslow, Erikson, Bowlby). In the closing section, Bronfenbrenner's ecological theory will be introduced as a model that enables the integration of psychological along with sociological and other theories to understand human development and behaviour from a holistic, multidisciplinary standpoint.

THEORIES OF COGNITIVE AND LANGUAGE DEVELOPMENT

Cognitive development refers to the advance in thought processes across childhood, while the specific process through which children come to understand and express language is described as language development. These processes will now be described in the theories outlined below.

PIAGET'S CONSTRUCTIVIST THEORY

Jean Piaget's (1896–1980) theory of cognitive development is a 'domain-general' theory in that advances in one area of cognitive ability are associated with progress in other cognitive abilities. This contrasts with 'domain-specific' theories (for example, Fodor 1992), where development is seen to vary across different cognitive abilities and areas of the brain.

For Piaget (1959), cognitive development is a series of stages, each with distinct qualitative differences in thinking. This development is underpinned by genetic maturation and thus is more rooted in 'nature' than 'nurture'. Piaget was a 'constructivist', seeing children as actively 'constructing' their own development. Mental schema (representations, sets of perceptions, ideas and/or actions which go together) initially develop through sensori-motor activity (thought being seen to develop from action) and are the building blocks of cognitive development. The processes of *assimilation* (taking material into the relevant mental schema in the mind from the environment) and *accommodation* (an alteration or difference made to mental schema to fit in the new information acquired via assimilation) contribute to the further development of these mental schema and are central to the advance of all cognitive abilities.

Across the stages, thinking becomes more logical and abstract with the achievement of key milestones, including object permanence, conservation, decentering, diminished egocentrism, increased symbolic representation and metacognitive understanding (these will be explained below). Research into object and spatial categorisation (how we categorise objects and spatial relations such as above/below) supports this developmental trend towards increasing abstraction (Quinn and Eimas 1997).

PIAGET'S STAGES OF COGNITIVE DEVELOPMENT

1. Sensori-Motor Stage (Birth–2 Years)

This stage is divided into six sub-stages:

1. *Reflexive stage (0–2 months):* Simple reflex activity such as grasping, sucking.
2. *Primary circular reactions (2–4 months):* Reflexive behaviours occur in stereotyped repetition, e.g. opening and closing fingers repetitively.
3. *Secondary circular reactions (4–8 months):* Repetition of interesting change actions, e.g. kicking feet to move a mobile.
4. *Co-ordination of secondary reactions (8–12 months):* Responses become co-ordinated into more complex sequences with intention. Achieves object permanence (realising things exist even when no longer visible).
5. *Tertiary circular reactions (12–18 months):* Discovery of new ways to achieve the same consequence, e.g. pulling a cloth to get a toy on it.
6. *Invention of new means through mental combination (18–24 months):* Greater symbolic thought by symbolising action sequences before real actions are shown. Responses now arise to symbols, such as a parent putting on a coat (this symbolising the parent's imminent departure).

2. Pre-operational Stage (2–7 Years)

Language (verbal representation) is now used to represent objects (thinking about an object without the object being present). However, understanding is still not 'firm', as the appearance or perceptions of objects (how they look) dominate a child's judgement of them. This is apparent in how children classify objects, for example a child grouping together all the green blocks regardless of shape or all the square blocks regardless of colour. The child grasps some logical concepts but still does not 'decentre', focusing attention on one aspect of an object while ignoring others (centration). They are still not able to see situations from the perspectives of others. Play becomes more symbolic and imaginative rather than being just simple motor play.

3. Concrete Operational Stage (7–11 Years)

The child now thinks in a logical, concrete way but is still concerned with the manipulation of objects as opposed to ideas. Thinking shows conservation (realisation that objects remain the same even when they are changed about or made to look different) and classification (the child can classify objects and can order them in series along a single dimension such as size). Thinking is less egocentric than before, with the child showing a greater capacity to see the world as others do and to empathise. In play, co-operation and the understanding of games with rules are more evident.

4. Formal Operational Stage (11+ years)

In this stage, thinking is more flexible and creative, with irony and sarcasm now shown. Scientific thought incorporating the systematic testing of hypotheses and logical thought about abstract propositions are shown. Thinking becomes more abstract and greater ability to reason is shown, with greater attention to the hypothetical and to the future. A child is now less likely to immediately accept one answer to any given question as true and is more likely to see other possible answers (Glaser 1984). Symbolically, the child can think in terms of proportions, abstract processes, propositional logic and can do algebraic manipulation. Metacognitive understanding (reflection on one's own thinking) is shown in terms of greater self-awareness and self-reflection.

Piaget's theory has made a momentous contribution to our understanding of the development of children's thinking. It has provided a frame of reference, a body of concepts and a series of research experiments with which to examine intellectual development. At a practical level, Piaget's theory influenced teaching, emphasising 'discovery learning' and a child's 'readiness to learn' in class planning.

Criticism of Piaget's theory has been levied at its narrow focus on reasoning and logic and lack of attention to other facets of thinking, such as creativity and intuition, which may develop at different rates (indicative of domain-specific theories of cognitive development). Still others oppose the principle of the stage-based progression in cognition and criticise Piaget's theory for neglecting the role of individual differences (thinking styles, IQ) between children, as well as social (instruction), cultural (social values, the mass media) and contextual factors

(Goswami 2001; Kuhn et al. 1988; Vygotsky 1978). For example, propositional logic (based on propositions, i.e. true or false statements), indicative of formal operations thinking, is lacking in cultures where there is no formal schooling, implying that some features of this stage are not universal but are dependent upon culture (Case and Okamoto 1996; Suizzo 2000).

The methodology of Piaget's research has also been criticised in that most of his research was based solely on observations of his own children and his research experiments were not easily understood by children. More 'meaningful', 'real-life' versions of his experiments have found children to show cognitive abilities much earlier than Piaget's research (Keating 2004).

VYGOTSKY'S SOCIAL-CONSTRUCTIVIST THEORY

Lev Vygotsky's (1896–1934) theory emphasised social interaction and cultural tools, as opposed to Piaget's emphasis on the child's independent constructive actions. According to Vygotsky (1978: 57):

> Every function in the child's cultural development appears twice: first, on the social level, and later, on the individual level; first, between people (interpsychological) and then inside the child (intrapsychological) … All the higher functions originate as actual relationships between individuals.

The key role of social interaction in Vygotsky's theory can be seen in his concept of the 'zone of proximal development' (ZPD), a level of development attained when children engage in social behaviour. Full development of the ZPD depends on social interaction as the range of skills developed with adult/peer guidance surpasses what can be attained alone. Instruction, guidance and encouragement are features of the ZPD. For example, a child who cannot solve a jigsaw puzzle on her own masters it following interaction with a parent/sibling or peer. According to Vygotsky, more experienced others play a crucial role in cognitive development. They show a child what to do, discuss activities and help to 'make sense' of what is going on. They also create 'cognitive conflict', challenging children to progress in their thinking (Tolmie et al. 2005). Bruner's (1993) concept of 'scaffolding', whereby someone provides structured support to help a child resolve a problem in how he/she thinks about or approaches a task, relates to this. Vygotsky's emphasis on the value of peer collaboration can be seen in 'peer tutoring' and group-based activities in the classroom (Littleton et al. 2004).

In contrast to Piaget, Vygotsky also saw 'culture' as a powerful influence on development. Through social interaction, children internalise or 'take in' cultural tools (language, social rules, writing and number systems, computers) and use them in their thinking. Cultural developments, such as information technology, lead to changes in how people relate to the world. Thus, to comprehend the development of children in different cultures, we need to understand development in its cultural context. We should not expect all children to be computer literate or good swimmers by a certain age, but see development in all abilities, including these, as anchored in a child's cultural context.

LANGUAGE DEVELOPMENT

Piaget and Vygotsky also differed on language development. For Piaget (1959), language developed as a consequence of symbolic development, an inner constructed capacity dependent upon maturation and based on genetics. Vygotsky (1978), in contrast, saw language as being developed primarily through meaningful social interaction. This is assisted by 'motherese' (also now called parentese), that is, features of caregiver talk adopted in talking to an infant such as higher vocal pitch, simpler speech content and attention strategies such as gestures.

Much debate exists over whether language development is genetically or environmentally determined. Chomsky (1968), Pinker (1994) and others argue for the innateness of language, based on, first of all, the universality of language (language being found in all human groups across different environments), and secondly on the fact that children can produce language they have never heard before, meaning that they could not have imitated or learned it. In the words of Pinker (1994: 32), 'Children actually reinvent language, generation after generation – not because they are taught to, not because they are generally smart, not because it's useful to them, but because they just can't help it.'

Finally, research on brain structure and function shows that language is genetically based in the left temporal lobe. Neuropsychological studies of brain damage do, however, show that other regions of the brain can support language development, implying that environmental factors can lead to alterations in brain, and language, functioning (Neville et al. 1998). This suggests that the brain's ability to process language is more anchored in general brain structure and shaped by the environment than it just being genetically pre-wired in a specific brain region.

Milestones of Language Development

The first three years of life are particularly important for language development, as it is a period when the brain is developing and maturing. A language-stimulating environment at this time is one that is rich with sounds, sights and plenty of exposure to speech.

The newborn communicates by vocalising and crying for food, comfort and companionship. Soon after birth, newborns show a preference for the human voice over other sounds and recognise the sound of the maternal heartbeat, and by four weeks prefer their mother's voice to other female voices (DeCasper and Fifer 1980; Mehler and Dupoux 1994). This suggests that humans are born prepared for communication and language. As they grow, infants sort out the speech sounds (phonemes) that compose words and by six months recognise the basic sounds of their native language. Infants also quickly develop a preference for language familiar to them, probably based on the prosody of the language (intonation, stress, rhythm). Head turning, looking/not looking and sucking are some of the behaviours used by researchers as indicators of infant preference, as they are controlled by infants from birth. For example, infants will adapt their sucking on a 'dummy' to hear their 'preferred' language, that is, the language they are familiar with (Christophe and Morton 1998).

As the jaw, lips, tongue and vocal tract mature, an infant is able to make controlled vocalisations (Harris 2004). Word comprehension begins at about seven months, with the child's own name, family members' names (including Mummy and Daddy) and names of familiar objects, e.g. 'bottle' and 'teddy', being amongst the first words to be understood (Harris et al. 1995). By 12 months, most children say a few simple words, with girls being typically ahead of boys (possibly because they are spoken to more, though the reason is not conclusive (Fenson et al. 1994). Children are probably unaware of the meaning of their first words, but soon learn these from the responses of others. Bruner stressed that children associate words with people, objects and steps of a routine, so words acquire a social meaning. There is a strong correspondence between what a parent says and what is happening with gaze direction, head turning and pointing used by adults as 'cues' to refer to something being spoken about (Harris et al. 1983).

Table 6.1 below provides an approximate guideline to the typical milestones of language development. Caution needs to be exercised, though, in applying these to children, as many factors are known to influence language development. Poor health, sensory problems, birth order and communication patterns in the home all influence the language milestones exhibited by any child.

Cognitive, language and physical developmental milestones are used by psychologists and other professionals in child assessment to determine whether a child is showing 'normal' development. A child's progress is compared to standardised norms reflecting what is typical for a child at a given age. For example, babbling milestones are used as indicators of delay if not shown at the approximate time listed. Developmental milestones also underpin interventions to assist developmental progress. In parenting programmes, developmental milestones help inform parents about what to expect of a child at a given age and what to do to help optimise a child's development.

LEARNING THEORY

Learning theory arises from the school of psychology called behaviourism, which emphasises the study of what is observable in people, i.e. behaviour. Behavioural psychologists identified different ways in which people (and animals) learn, which are the core of learning theory.

Table 6.1. Language Milestones

Birth to 6 months	2–3 years
• Vocalises sounds of pleasure and displeasure (giggles/fusses). • Makes noise when talked to. • Sounds begin to be used communicatively. • Watches a face when it speaks.	• Knows about fifty words. • Knows pronouns, e.g. 'you', 'me', her', 'him'. • Knows adjectives, e.g. 'happy', 'sad', 'big'. • Answers simple questions. • Begins to use plurals, e.g. 'shoes', and verbs in past tense ('ed'). • Speaks in two- or three-word phrases.
6–11 months • Babbles (ba, ma, da) with syllables (canonical babbling). • Understands no-no. • Tries to communicate by actions/gestures. • Reduplicated babbling (8 months). • Tries to repeat sounds spoken to him/her. • Variegated babbling (ba-da, da-de).	**3–4 years** • Identifies primary colours. • Uses verbs ending in 'ing'. • Can describe use of simple objects, e.g. 'ball', 'fork'. • Expresses ideas and feelings. • Enjoys rhyme and language absurdities. • Uses consonants in sentences.
12–17 months • Points to objects, pictures, people. • Says two to three words to label a person/object. • Follows simple directions given with gestures. • Answers simple questions non-verbally.	**4–5 years** • Says about 200–300 different words. • Understands spatial concepts, e.g. 'behind'. • Answers why questions. • Understands complex questions. • Uses irregular past tense verbs, e.g. 'ran', 'fell'. • Describes how to do activities, e.g. painting.
18–23 months • Points to simple body parts, e.g. nose. • Says eight to 10 words. • Asks for common foods by name. • Makes animal sounds, e.g. moo. • Pronounces most vowels and begins to combine words. • Understands simple verbs, e.g. 'eat', 'sleep'.	**5–6 years** • Engages in conversation. • Sentences can be eight or more words. • Understands time sequences (what happened first, next). • Uses imagination to create stories. • Describes objects. • Names opposites and days of the week.

Source: Interpreted from www.nidcd.nihgov/health/voice.

The first of these is called 'classical conditioning', where learning arises through association. Pavlov (1849–1936) identified classical conditioning from his experimental work with salivating dogs. Pavlov (1927) found that dogs automatically salivated to food and he called this an 'unconditioned response' reflecting an 'unconditional reflex'. The unconditional stimulus (food) automatically elicits an unconditional response (salivation); the term 'unconditional' is used as the response to the stimulus happens naturally. Pavlov then looked at what happens if something is associated with the presentation of food. Pavlov rang a bell (a neutral stimulus) just before presenting an unconditional stimulus (UCS) such as food, which unconditionally evoked a response (salivation). After a number of times, the neutral stimulus (now termed the conditioned stimulus (CS)) came to

Figure 6.1. Classical Conditioning

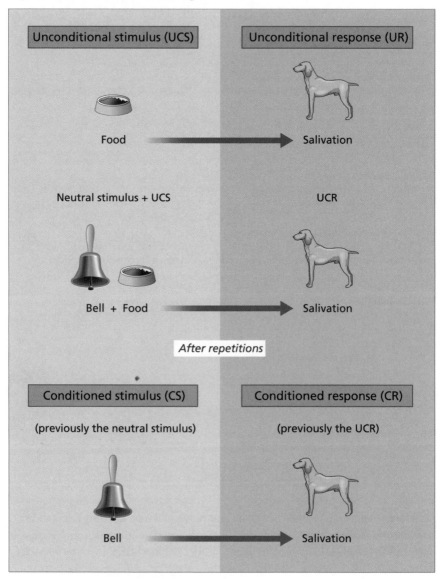

Source: www.nidcd.nihgov/health/voice.

evoke the same response (salivation) on its own without the UCS. Thus, the dog came to associate the bell ring with food, reacting in the same way (salivating), after repeated exposure to the bell and food combination, to the bell on its own as to the food. The dog had learned to salivate in response to the bell. Pavlov called this a 'conditioned response' (CR). When the CS (bell) is presented without food following it, the dog learns over time that the bell is no longer associated with food and stops displaying the conditioned response (salivation). Pavlov referred to this as 'extinction', the conditioned response having become 'extinguished' (see Figure 6.1).

These observations were then extended to explain how humans learn, even including the learning of fears and phobias. Watson (Watson and Rayner 1920), another learning theorist, in his infamous study with an 11-month-old boy called 'Little Albert', found that objects become feared through their association with something unpleasant (Watson and Rayner 1920). In this study, a rat that previously did not induce fear in Albert was shown to Albert in conjunction with a loud banging noise, and after a number of pairings the rat alone induced fear in Albert. This showed that emotional responses could be conditioned, or learned.

Another type of learning is operant conditioning. Operant conditioning is where an association is formed between a behaviour and a consequence. Skinner (1904–90) coined the term 'operant conditioning' as a type of learning in which behaviour is influenced by its consequences. Consequences have to be immediate or clearly linked to the behaviour for the learning to occur. Anything that increases a behaviour is a 'reinforcer', while anything that decreases it is a 'punisher'. Four possible consequences follow on from any behaviour:

- Something good can start or be presented, resulting in an increase in the behaviour (positive reinforcement).
- Something good can end or be taken away, resulting in a drop in or reduction of the behaviour (negative punishment).
- Something bad can start or be presented, resulting in a drop in or decrease in the behaviour (positive punishment).
- Something bad can end or be taken away, resulting in an increase in the behaviour (negative reinforcement) (Skinner 1953).

In positive reinforcement, a behaviour is strengthened by the consequence of experiencing something positive, e.g. a child receiving a chocolate as a reward for doing some household job. The child's behaviour of doing household work is increased. Another example is providing positive reinforcement (rewards) once certain behavioural goals (not showing inappropriate behaviour) are achieved, e.g. a trip to the cinema once X number of inappropriate behaviours are not shown in a set time period.

In negative reinforcement, or 'avoidance learning', a particular behaviour is strengthened by the consequence of stopping or avoiding a negative condition. For example, someone driving a car too fast and receiving a speeding fine learns that to stop this negative consequence from happening again, they must not drive so fast. Negative reinforcement increases a behaviour by ending or removing something bad or aversive. Someone is rewarded by feeling better, increasing the likelihood that they will repeat the behaviour that was occurring when the 'bad event' ended or was avoided. When something bad is removed or avoided, relief is often felt, so another way to think of negative reinforcement is that you are providing relief, which makes it an example of *positive* reinforcement – thus positive and negative reinforcement can be confused. This highlights 'internal reinforcers', which are difficult to identify and assess, yet also play a role in learning. These may often lead to a behaviour becoming 'self-reinforcing' in that the unobservable, internal consequence of the behaviour positively or negatively reinforces that behaviour, e.g. stress or boredom relief gained from screaming can reinforce the behaviour of screaming. Guilt, on the other hand, is an internal punisher, reducing the likelihood of the behaviour that elicited the guilt from occurring again.

In punishment, a behaviour is reduced by the consequence of experiencing something negative. Negative punishment reduces a behaviour by removing something good, while positive punishment (positive in the sense that is presented, as opposed to it being pleasant or nice) is something that is presented that reduces a behaviour. When used effectively, punishment is one of the most effective ways to end unwanted behaviours. However, it does not teach what behaviour is appropriate (Baum 2005).

Shaping is another contribution from learning theory seen in social care practice. Shaping (also known as successive approximation) is where a behaviour is encouraged by rewarding incremental improvements in that behaviour. For this to happen, the target behaviour is broken down into small steps that are rewarded as they become progressively closer to the target behavioural goal. This is often used in behavioural charts or reward systems and in teaching particular skills (Baum 2005).

OBSERVATIONAL LEARNING

Another type of learning is where a person learns through observation, i.e. by seeing something done and seeing the consequences of that action. This has been called 'observational learning' or 'modelling'. Through observation, a person learns not only what to do, but also what actions produce positive or negative consequences and what distinguishes situations requiring different behaviours. Albert Bandura (1965) drew attention to the significance of observational learning and stressed that it has four steps:

- *Attention:* Paying attention to a model's behaviour.
- *Retention:* Remembering the model's behaviour.
- *Reproduction:* The physical ability to reproduce the behaviour.

- *Motivation:* The desire to reproduce the behaviour, which is strongly based on what we expect to arise from doing the behaviour (Bandura 1977).

Bandura's (Bandura et al. 1961; Bandura 1965) seminal 'Bobo doll' experiments showed the role of observational learning in aggression. Children who were exposed to a model acting aggressively towards a 'Bobo doll' were more likely to act aggressively towards the doll afterwards. When children viewed the aggressive behaviour being rewarded, ignored or punished, those children who saw the model being punished were less likely to display aggressive behaviour than the other children. These experiments stimulated much research into the impact of seeing violence. In general, research suggests that viewing media violence increases the likelihood of aggression while also reducing human concern about the suffering of others and their sensitivity to the violence itself (Eron 2000; Huesmmann 1997).

The significance of observational learning for understanding learning and the importance of modelling good behaviour in social care practice cannot be overemphasised. Observational learning can also be used in peer tutoring as a way for some service users to show others what to do. This then means that it is not always the professional, but sometimes the service users themselves who become the 'teachers', which is empowering. An example of the use of learning principles, including observational learning, is the Irish 'Parents Plus' parenting programme, which uses video modelling and other principles from learning theory (Quinn et al. 2007).

One of the primary limitations of learning theory is that it neglects the role of consciousness (expectations and interpretations) in learning. Cognitive behavioural therapy, however, explores the role of a person's thinking in various conditions such as depression and eating disorders, applying learning principles to their amelioration (an interesting reading on this is the chapter on cognitive behaviour therapy by Carr and McNulty (2006) in their book *Handbook of Adult Clinical Psychology: An Evidence Based Practice Approach*).

A recent development in the field of learning theory is 'relational frame theory', which takes a behavioural analysis approach to explaining language and cognitive development in terms of relational frames, networks and rules (Barnes-Holmes et al. 2004; Hayes et al. 2001). This theory focuses on how humans learn language through interactions with the environment and show relational responding, reflecting new generalisations of learned behaviour. However, research support for this theory is still in its infancy.

APPLIED BEHAVIOUR ANALYSIS

Applied behaviour analysis (ABA) is the application of learning theory to establish a structured environment to enable children to communicate, learn and behave better. It is used in particular with children with autism spectrum disorders, conduct disorder and attention deficit hyperactivity disorder (Baer et al. 1987;

Emerson 2001; Snyder et al. 2006). In Ireland, a number of schools for children with autism spectrum disorders run a CABAS (combined applied behavioural analysis) programme.

In ABA, the child and the instructor are observed and functional assessments of behaviours (what the child is trying to achieve or communicate in the behaviour) are undertaken to help understand the child's behaviour. Intensive individualised programmes are developed, focusing on areas such as literacy, problem-solving, self-management and the teaching of individual behavioural repertoires (see Cooper et al. 2007).

THEORIES OF SOCIO-EMOTIONAL DEVELOPMENT

Socio-emotional development refers to how children develop in how they relate to others, and how they express, understand and regulate their emotions. Many theorists emphasise the critical role that others play in children's growing ability to relate to others and to themselves and their own feelings. Consequently, social and emotional development are often considered in combination by theorists. The theories described below also highlight the integral role played by other people in socio-emotional development.

MASLOW'S HIERARCHY OF NEEDS

Maslow's (1908–70) theory of motivation from a developmental perspective emphasises personal growth, with a person intentionally growing towards 'self-actualisation', or personal fulfilment. He proposed a hierarchy of needs (see Figure 6.2), with individuals motivated to progress from basic to higher needs. According to Maslow (1970), the lower needs in the hierarchy are the most fundamental, so a person needs to address these before moving on to higher needs.

Through research involving the biographical analysis of people who Maslow had felt were self-actualisers, such as Abraham Lincoln (as well as people who were not famous), Maslow identified qualities characteristic of self-actualisers. These include humility and respect, creativity, self-acceptance (being as you are rather than being pretentious or artificial), acceptance of others (taking people as they are, not wanting to change them), differentiating what is fake from what is real and comfort with autonomy while also enjoying deep personal relations with a few close people (rather than more shallow relationships with many). Self-actualisers also tend to have more 'peak experiences' (where a person feels out of themselves, a feeling of being a part of the infinite and the eternal) than the average person.

Maslow's theory is not without criticism. There is little evidence to support the exact hierarchy. Some theorists contend that esteem needs occur before love needs, in keeping with Erikson's theory that people progress through identification to intimacy with a need to form a strong sense of self and identity prior to being able to form a loving relationship (Goebel and Brown 1981). Many people show

Figure 6.2. Maslow's Hierarchy of Needs (1970)

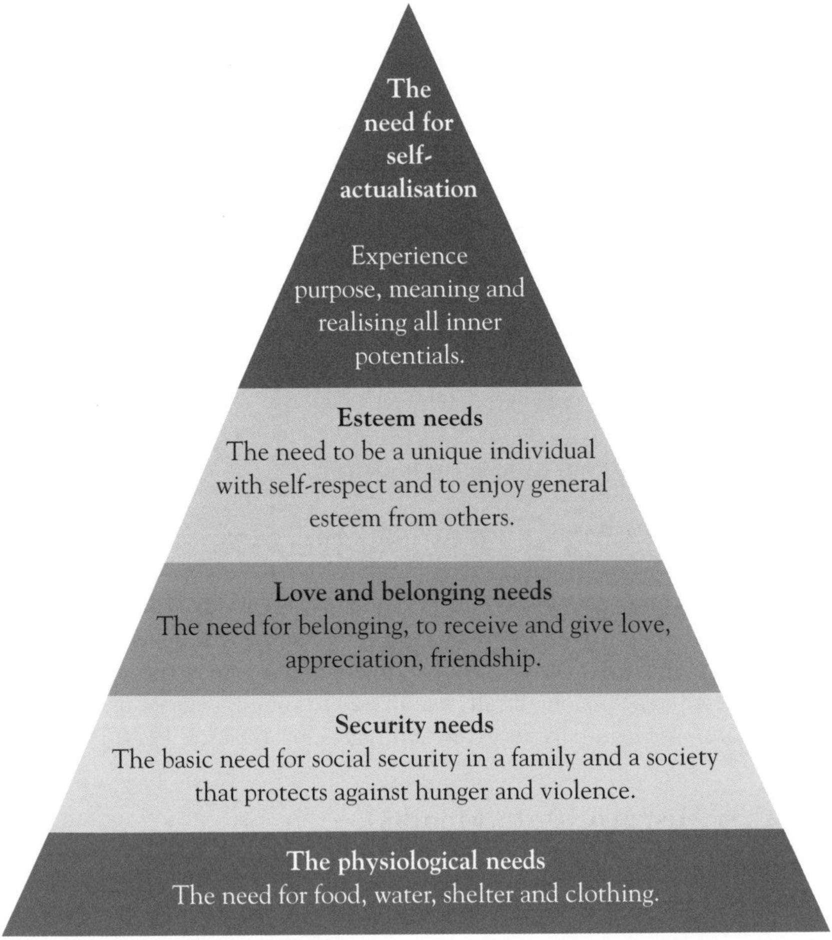

qualities of self-actualisation yet have more primary needs unmet. For example, many famous novelists, artists and scientists, such as Rembrandt, Galileo and Beethoven, lived in poverty without their basic needs being met. Others reach fulfilment but then turn their back on their ability, thereby apparently putting a stop to their self-actualisation. Much criticism has also been levied at how Maslow developed his theory. He selected a small number of people that he himself identified as self-actualising, using his reading and interviews to determine what self-actualisation was, all of which is scientifically very poor as it is open to bias and lacks reliability and generalisability.

For social care practice, this theory highlights the importance of addressing lower needs, such as reducing physical discomfort, tiredness or hunger, first before trying to work on higher needs. Safety and security needs can be met by making people feel safe, having routines, protection from danger (perceived or actual) and by building up a relationship of trust. The concept of a 'secure base' from attachment theory is related to this – the idea that having a trusted person one can go to enhances a child's sense of safety and nurtures her independence. Love and belonging needs can be enhanced by developing social skills, a social network and sense of belonging, for example to a group, place or organisation. Relationship-building can take place by supporting a child's relationships. Problems from past relationships also need to be addressed, such as a fear of abandonment or intimacy. Esteem needs can be addressed by acknowledging a person's qualities and helping her/him to identify and develop self competencies. This might take the form of displaying their creative work of art or going to a concert/match they are participating in. Respect can be shown by allowing children to make choices and by facilitating their involvement in decision-making pertaining to them. This is applied in 'person-centred planning' in care work.

ERIKSON'S PSYCHOSOCIAL THEORY

Erik Erikson (1902–94) was a neo-Freudian who developed a theory of psycho-social stages in personality development. Each stage is focused on a particular issue (a 'crisis') to be resolved and has a basic virtue or strength and a secondary virtue attained by a helpful balance between the extremes in each stage. Maladaptive tendencies and malignancies represent extremes in response to the 'crisis' of each stage, reflected in behavioural traits manifested to various degrees, as opposed to being clinical problems. His stages are outlined below (Erikson 1970, 1980).

Trust vs. Mistrust (0–18 Months)

The infant forms a first loving, trusting relationship with the caregiver or deals with feelings of mistrust. The task of this stage is to develop trust without completely eliminating the capacity for mistrust. Through the parents' responses, the child learns to trust his or her own body and biological urges. Trust is lost and mistrust arises with abuse or neglect, while a false sense of trust arises if an infant is overprotected or overindulged, with no feelings of surprise and a lack of ordinary reality. With a proper balance between trust and mistrust, the child develops the virtue and inner strength of hope, the belief that things, even if not going well, will work out well in the end, a trust in life, the self and others. However, if an infant is too trusting, the maladaptive tendency of 'sensory maladjustment' arises, whereby the child becomes overly trusting, gullible and naïve. Excessive mistrust results in withdrawal, characterised by fear, depression and paranoia.

Autonomy vs. Shame/Doubt (18 Months–3 Years)

The child focuses on developing physical skills (walking, grasping and rectal and sphincter control) but may feel shame and doubt. Autonomy refers to self-reliance and self-confidence, whereas shame and doubt refer to the emotions that undermine independence and self-confidence. Parental responses and encouragement of a child's growing independence enable a child to become autonomous. Parental behaviour that is too discouraging or pushy leads a child to doubt her own abilities and feel shame about her efforts at independence. Additionally, if a child is given too much freedom or helped to do what they should do for themselves, they will feel that they are not good for much. A little shame and doubt, though, are useful, as otherwise 'impulsiveness' occurs, that is, excessive wilfulness and recklessness. Too much shame and doubt leads to 'compulsiveness', where a child obsesses about everything for fear of making a mistake. A good balance between autonomy and shame/doubt leads to the virtue of 'willpower', including self-efficacy, or what has been called a 'can do' attitude.

Initiative vs. Guilt (3–6 Years)

In becoming more assertive, the child takes more initiative, but this may lead to guilt. Initiative refers to feeling purposeful and the capability to devise actions with a self-belief that it is okay to do so, even if there is risk of failure or being seen as stupid. Guilt, on the other hand, refers to feeling that it is wrong or inappropriate to initiate something oneself. Being encouraged to take a risk or chance and to engage in experimentation or adventure supports the development of initiative, as does curiosity and imaginative activities.

Guilt arises when children are given out to, told that they are a disappointment or that their actions are disapproved of. A good balance is thus needed between encouraging children to try things out while simultaneously protecting them from danger. If there is too much initiative and too little guilt, 'ruthlessness' arises, where a child becomes exploitative and uncaring. Too much guilt and too little initiative results in 'inhibition' – a lack of adventurousness. A good balance leads to the psychosocial strength of purpose, where a child is willing to take action and achieve meaningful goals.

Industry vs. Inferiority (6–12 Years)

In dealing with learning new skills, the child risks feelings of inferiority and failure. By 'industry', Erikson meant the development of competence, a sense of self-efficacy in abilities, which is integral to the school experience. This refers to the ability 'to do', to be productive, to apply oneself and to feel valued for one's actions, skills or abilities. Children must learn that there is pleasure not only in devising actions, but also in carrying these out, working by rules and towards goals.

They must learn the feeling of success, in school or elsewhere. Experiences of accomplishment lead a child to resolve this stage. However, if children experience nothing but failure with no development of their own capabilities, they experience feelings of inferiority with low self-worth. Racism and sexism also contribute to this, since if a child believes success is related to who you are rather than to how hard you try, then why try?

According to Erikson, too much industry results in 'narrow virtuosity', whereby children, such as child prodigies, spend all their energy and time on one ability, associated with obsession. On the opposite side, too much inferiority leads to 'inertia', apathy and low self-worth. A good balance between industry and inferiority, where a child develops and applies her abilities but has enough inferiority to feel humble, leads to the virtue of competency.

Identity vs. Role Confusion (12–18 Years)

In trying to forge an identity, a young person must reconcile individuality with a desire to belong to a peer group. This stage coincides with the Freudian genital stage (puberty) and is the stage that Erikson wrote most about, as he had a particular interest in identity formation.

Identity refers to a sense of self or individuality, how one sees oneself in relation to the world and to others in it. In adolescence, young people strive to be part of a peer group, to 'belong', yet at the same time seek to be individuals, distinctive in their own way.

Role confusion (an absence of identity and uncertainty about one's place in society and the world) is where someone does not have a distinctive sense of who they are, their beliefs, opinions, values and individuality. If a person has 'too much identity', she will be too self-important and narrow minded, unable to recognise the perspectives of others, which is indicative of 'fanaticism'. A fanatic believes that his or her way is the only way. Too much role confusion leads to 'repudiation' – a person repudiates her need for an identity, cutting herself off and becoming 'lost' in a group that provides a ready identity. The virtue of fidelity (integrity to yourself) is achieved if this stage is successfully negotiated.

Intimacy vs. Isolation (19–40 Years)

The person tries to become closer to others but may feel isolated. The focus of this stage is the forging of close relationships with family and a marital or sexual partner. Intimacy involves the ability to be close to others, as a lover, a friend and so forth. To be intimate involves both the reception and expression of love and the honesty and capacity to commit with others for mutual satisfaction. Conversely, isolation means feeling excluded from the usual life experiences of mutually loving relationships with feelings of loneliness.

Too much intimacy results in 'promiscuity', being sexually needy and becoming intimate too freely without any emotional involvement. Too much isolation results in 'exclusion', i.e. self-containment and the tendency to distance oneself and withdraw from love, friendship and community. 'Fear of commitment' is an example of immaturity in this stage.

Successful negotiation of this stage results in the virtue of love, being able to set aside differences and conflicts through 'mutuality of devotion'. It includes not only the love in a good marriage, but the love between friends and the love of one's neighbour.

Generativity vs. Stagnation (40–65 Years)

The adult strives to give something to future generations but may become self-absorbed. Generativity refers to being productive, in work and other areas, as well as the unconditional giving of parental love for a child and generativity towards future generations. It is a concern for the next generation and future generations and thus is less 'selfish' than the love present in the intimacy of the previous stage. It is giving without the expectation of reciprocation. While raising children is one way of being productive, other ways include social activism, teaching, writing, invention, the arts and sciences – anything, in fact, that satisfies that old 'need to be needed'. Stagnation is where intimacy turns inward in the form of self-interest and self-absorption, representing feelings of selfishness, self-indulgence and a lack of interest in future generations and the wider world.

Too much generativity results in 'overextension', where people are so extreme that they become over-involved in something with no time for themselves, which ultimately undermines their generativity or contribution to the world, such as someone who takes on so many causes that he/she cannot effectively contribute to any particular one. Too much stagnation, on the other hand, results in 'rejectivity', characterised by cynicism. Successful negotiation of this stage results in the virtue of 'caring'.

Ego Integrity vs. Despair (65+ Years)

A sense of oneself as one 'is', feeling fulfilment or despair. In this last stage, the task is to develop integrity and feelings of contentment with oneself and the world, with a minimal amount of despair and regrets. Integrity means coming to terms with your life, and thereby coming to terms with the end of life. If one is able to look back and accept the course of events, the choices made and the life as one lived it, then death is not feared.

Most people in late adulthood experience a detachment from society through retirement or reduced participation, which can be associated with feelings of uselessness. Poor health and illness may compound such feelings, along with bereavement for the loss of spouse, friends and family, which understandably contributes to despair. Despair also includes regrets and wishing to be able to turn back the clock and have a second chance. In response to despair, some people become preoccupied with the past, when life was better, while others become preoccupied with regrets.

Successful negotiation of this stage leads to the virtue of wisdom, a generosity of spirit characterised by a nonjudgmental acceptance, tolerance and calmness of mind.

Assuming too much integrity results in 'presumption', characterised by conceit and pomposity, which is superficial and blocks the attainment of true insight and acceptance. Too much despair blocks acceptance and integrity, resulting in 'disdain', a lack of fulfilment and a contempt of life (one's own or anyone else's).

In considering Erikson's theory, it is worth noting that his research relied heavily on biographical case studies which lack scientific credibility. Critics also suggest that the theory fails to accommodate individual change in, for example, identity across the lifespan. However, this theory is widely applied in the social care sector in a variety of ways, such as personal development groups, therapeutic work and even supervisory relationships (Ruch 2005). Along with other socio-emotional theories, these theories are also drawn upon in experiential group work and personal and professional development modules in social care degrees.

ATTACHMENT THEORY

John Bowlby's (1907–90) attachment theory was based on ethological and psychoanalytic ideas and emphasised the immense role of primary attachment relationships upon psychological development and social relationships across the lifespan. According to Bowlby (1951), attachment is a biologically based 'behavioural system' and is a need as fundamental as the need for food and water. It is visible in proximity-seeking and separation-protest behaviour. Attachment formation develops from six months to three years and is not dependent upon physical care, but rather develops through interaction with the primary caregiver(s), typically the parents. Warmth, responsiveness, sensitivity and consistency are critical features of parenting that enhance attachment formation. Comforting interactions that involve relaxation after raised arousal, such as comforting a crying infant (the arousal-relaxation cycle) and pleasurable interactions, such as face-to-face games and cuddling (positive interaction cycle), also contribute to attachment formation (Bowlby 1969, 1978; Holmes 1993).

A person's social and emotional development are anchored in the early attachment relationships because experiences of responses from significant others are the foundations of a child's 'model' of relationships and how the self and relationship behaviour are thought and felt about (Lewis et al. 2000). How a child expresses and interprets relationships is shaped by her early attachments. For example, is the relationship experienced as positive, involving trust and love, or negative, involving the fear of rejection or abandonment? This inner organisation of attitudes, feelings and expectations about the self, others and relationships was called an 'internal working model' (IWM) by Bowlby (1973). More recent theoretical developments on this involve 'scripts' (typical action sequences and expectations associated with various events, activities and places) (Fivush 2006; Waters and Waters 2006).

According to Bowlby, an insecure primary attachment is characterised by a lack of trust, consistency and sensitivity, so the child comes to view others as hostile and untrustworthy and to see the self as inadequate and unworthy. Consequently, the child is likely to show poor social skills and to be distrustful. In contrast, a child with a secure attachment is more likely to be optimistic, positive and trusting in relationships, with good social skills (Lewis et al. 2000).

Any significant disruption in an attachment leads to feelings of grief and loss. However, Rutter (1981) argued that Bowlby had confused maternal *privation* (children who had never received maternal care) with *deprivation* (children who had experienced a relationship with their mother but who had then lost it) and neglected attachment *distortion* (where the relationship is altered, e.g. through separation or divorce). While cases of maternal privation tend to show more problems, the consequences are more difficult to predict for cases of maternal deprivation and attachment distortion, as care from substitute others may ameliorate the effects (Howes and Hamilton 1992). Thus, Bowlby may have overstated the case that it is not any and every separation from the primary caregiver that is harmful, but rather only certain *types* of separation and how they are handled (Rutter 1995).

Maria Ainsworth and colleagues (1978) developed 'the Strange Situation', an observational procedure of mother–child and stranger–child interaction, classifying one-year-old children into different types of 'attachment strategies'. The procedure involves a series of episodes in which the mother and child are together, the child is left alone by the mother, a stranger enters and approaches the child and the mother returns and is reunited with her child. Attachment classification is based primarily on the child's observed proximity and responses to the mother during the reunion episodes. The 'secure' attachment strategy is the most prevalent form of attachment. These children show a distinct preference for their attachment figure over strangers and trust their attachment figure's availability and responsiveness. They show better emotional expression and regulation, fewer behavioural problems and better social skills than their insecure counterparts (Ainsworth et al. 1978; Kochanska 2001).

The second type of attachment strategy is 'insecure ambivalent-resistant', characteristic of 'chaotic parenting'. These children and their attachment figures tend to have a fractious relationship, tinged with anger and resentment. They are unable to predict the response to their attachment behaviours and so experience anxiety about their own safety and comfort. They show poor emotional regulation and tend to seek out, yet simultaneously resist, their attachment figures, which is indicative of emotional ambivalence (Graham 2006; Kochanska 2001).

The third type is 'insecure-avoidant', characteristic of cold, rejecting parenting. These children are emotionally self-contained, with little emotional expression while aggressively independent. They have learned to suppress their emotions and see intimacy as threatening (ibid.).

The fourth type is 'insecure-disorganised', where children show marked and pervasive fear in the presence of their attachment figure. It is fright but without a solution for the fright and these children often display a 'freezing' response. These children are at high risk for behaviour problems and this attachment strategy is characteristic of maltreatment and unpredictable early care (Ainsworth et al. 1978; Dozier et al. 2001; Main 1995).

Caution must be exercised in the interpretation of these types, as every child is unique with a distinctive relationship context. These attachment types should thus be considered as a light to illuminate behaviour as opposed to rigid fact. 'The Strange Situation' is also problematic, as it is culturally biased with questionable validity. Rather than labelling someone as (in)secure, it may be more appropriate to label the particular relationship (McMahan-True et al. 2001; Rutter 1995). Children have different relationships with each parent and vice versa (Dunn 1993), and adverse environments that predispose to insecurity usually include risk factors for later psychopathology. Thus it may be these factors, as opposed to an insecure attachment per se, that underpin later problems (Dunn 1993; Rutter 1995).

In reviewing attachment theory, it is important to note that many of Bowlby's original ideas were reformulated by him and others. Rather than emphasising one primary attachment figure, contemporary attachment research sees children as having a hierarchy of attachment figures or an 'attachment network' of whom the mother is usually (but not necessarily) the most important (Holmes 1993). After the mother may follow (in varying orders of importance) the father, grandparents, siblings, care minders and possibly pets or transitional objects. In the absence of the most preferred, the child will turn to the next most preferred. Children may also have different types of attachment relationship with different people (Kosonen 1996).

Attachment theory has many important implications for social care practice, some of which were outlined in the first edition of this book (de Róiste 2005). Attachment theory emphasises the significance of early relationships for psychological development and for understanding why children (and adults) behave as they do in relating to others; the importance of supporting a child's sense of continuity in belonging to a family to which she feels attached and identified with; the role of grief and loss in how children respond to attachment disruption; and the significance of considering attachment history in therapeutic work with children who have any problematic attachment histories.

Graham (2006) outlined how a social care professional might work with children showing different attachment strategies in the family context. For a child with an avoidant strategy, this focuses on building up a child's sense of safety and comfort, while for the child displaying an ambivalent-resistant strategy, it involves supporting the attachment figure to respond in reliable, consistent ways. With the child showing a disorganised strategy, professional work should focus on modelling parenting practices and helping the attachment figure(s) to control their own emotions when with their child.

Other psychological theories that relate to socio-emotional development and social care practice include Klein's object relations theory and the theories of Freud and Winnicott (see Dennehy 2006).

ECOLOGICAL THEORY

Bronfenbrenner's (1979) ecological model (see Figure 6.3) (or in its most recent inception, Bronfenbrenner and Evans's (2000) 'bioecological' model) provides a systemic framework within which to consider various psychological and sociological theories in respect of human behaviour and social events. From a developmental contextual perspective, child development is placed within a multi-layered socio-cultural context, with development seen as the culmination

Figure 6.3. Bronfenbrenner's Ecological Model

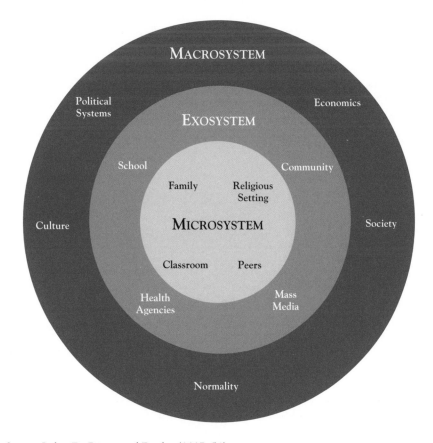

Source: Lalor, De Róiste and Devlin (2007: 54).

of many direct (genetic) and indirect influences (including culture) mediated through various 'layers' or systemic levels in the child's ecology. Children both act 'in' and 'on' their world and are influenced by the timeframe in which they live (chronosystem); general cultural and social structures, such as economic conditions and cultural values (macrosystem); contextual factors influencing the child via others, such as the local neighbourhood (exosystem); and immediate relationships (such as parent– child and child–peer) (microsystems), as well as the relations between these (for example, how a relationship with a parent affects a child's relationship with their sibling (mesosystems)).

This model recognises that contextual variables may combine additively or multiplicatively to explain individual differences in child development, vulnerabilities and resilience. It helps in designing interventions with children, whether at a one-to-one level (microsystem) or at the broader systemic levels of the community and culture. It also ensures attention is paid to what makes childhood a unique as well as a shared experience for each individual. Sociologically, it is useful as it facilitates links to be made between social institutions, structures, changes and events and childhood experience (a useful reading on this in an Irish context is Greene's (1994) article, 'Growing Up Irish').

CONCLUSION

In sum, this chapter provided an introduction to some of the most widely used psychological theories that inform and guide social care practice. In conjunction with theories from other disciplines, they provide a reservoir of knowledge to understand behaviour, guide interventions and evaluate practice.

7

Social Care and Social Change: Future Direction or Lost Opportunity?

Tom O'Connor

OVERVIEW

This chapter critically examines the current social care project in Ireland and seeks to explore the underlying value base that informs social care education and practice. It also develops theoretical insights from the sociological and political economy perspectives into the ongoing development of social care practice and looks at how the field might forge a stronger professional identity and so become an agent of social change.

THE REALM OF SOCIAL CARE

The realm of social care is a new profession and is undefined, but this does not adequately explain the ambiguity and lack of clarity in the public mindset as to what social care is or what its practitioners do. I would suggest that 80 per cent of career guidance teachers and students who attend college open days do not know the difference between social care and social work. One might suggest that they would want to do their homework, get the course outlines, read the blurbs and know what they were talking about! But if it was as simple as that, there would not be any real issue. In fact, the problem is more deeply rooted – the ambiguity extends to social care educators and practitioners themselves. Research is needed to test my hypothesis, based on discussions with students working in social care practice over the past decade, that for a majority of educators and practitioners, social care is all about helping the client on a day-to-day basis – but no more.

This popular view of social care holds that in addition to the provision of shelter, food and other items (residential care) or comfortable facilities (community care), the major task for the social care practitioner is to promote the personal development of the client in a broadly therapeutic way: through organising outings, recreation, sport or other activities. In a more narrowly therapeutic way, there may be the offer of counselling, anger management, circle time, life space intervention or, in difficult situations, therapeutic crisis intervention (TCI).

The major contemporary perceived departure from 'natural' caring practice and, arguably, from the practice of older care workers is that newly trained 'switched-on' social care practitioners operate from clearly defined principles that may include empowering the client; giving the client choice in his/her everyday life; collaborating with the client and/or the client's family in drawing up care plans; promoting independent living; moving away from institutional and residential care to community care; adopting the principle of normalisation; and adopting a client-centred approach (Beresford and Trevillion 1995; Department of Health and Children 2001b; Kennefick 1998; Means et al. 2008).

IMAGINING A SWOT ANALYSIS

Thus, we have the 'caring imperative' in the main, augmented with a set of strong principles and values that inform a strongly ethical social care practice with clients. Indeed, writers such as Beresford and Trevillion (1995) and O'Shea (2005) point to contemporary best practice in social care as being collaborative, offering choice to clients and sharing power between the professional and service user. O'Shea (2005) applies these principles to the needs of geriatric patients, particularly those in residential care. He argues that equality of respect between the professional and client is part of the new practice and pays attention to the need for 'personhood'. For a professionalised social care practitioner to treat all clients as homogenous just because they are 'clients' negates such 'personhood'. Thus, each client is seen as a person with specific choice sets and a singular identity, reflecting his/her own unique personality, foibles and idiosyncrasies. To take one ordinary example from O'Shea's research, each older client may have a particular preference for a newspaper that must be respected. Consequently, the practice of social care in the evolving 'higher spec' professional form is expected to produce well-educated and trained social care practitioners in all the areas mentioned. This ultimately results in a sharing of power, responsibility and respect between the professional care practitioner and each client as an individual person, stakeholder and service user (Finlay 2000).

This is a great improvement on what went before, where the value base of largely unqualified care workers was often to treat clients as 'unfortunates' or as subordinates, where empowering the client was not an objective and where the client was often viewed as lucky to be receiving care, largely based on charitable interventions. This was the mindset and institutional structure that facilitated the neglect and abusive treatment witnessed for many years in Ireland and highlighted in books and films such as Paddy Galvin's *Song for a Raggy Boy* (Galvin 2002) and Mary Raftery's *Suffer the Little Children* (Raftery and O'Sullivan 1999). The Kennedy Report (Government of Ireland 1970) and subsequent legislation and policy have revolutionised social care in Ireland, largely for the better, but significant internal challenges remain for the profession. If we could imagine engaging in a SWOT analysis (strengths, weaknesses, opportunities, threats) of the social care profession at the moment, what might it look like?

Strengths and Opportunities

- Social care educators provide in-depth courses that contain a professional body of knowledge and produce well-rounded and well-meaning social care practitioners.
- Social care offers enriching and diversified education and training from a broad range of disciplines.
- Social care is now recognised as a profession under the Health and Social Care Professionals Act 2005.
- Social care practitioners are better trained and work from clear principles of best practice that respect the client as a person, as distinct from him or her as an 'unfortunate' needing charity.
- Social care training is flexible and practitioners can work with varied client groups in areas such as homelessness, intellectual disability, physical disability, old age, care of children and mental illness.
- Social care provides a service that has been and will be in huge demand.

Threats and Weaknesses

- Social care education is fragmented.
- Social care educators have widely disparate positions on what constitutes the professional project of the social care practitioner.
- Social care is viewed as inferior by other 'caring professions'.
- Social care practitioners do not have a strong representative body or union.
- The social care profession is ignored as a profession in plans to develop primary care teams (Department of Health and Children 2001b) and community-based mental health teams (Mental Health Commission 2006).
- The number of varying client groups is so large that specialised training for all the client groups is not realistic.

Having acknowledged the strengths and opportunities outlined above, I do not propose to focus to any great extent on discussing them. Instead, the urgent tasks outlined in the weaknesses and threats section above will be addressed here.

THE LACK OF A CLEAR SOCIAL CARE PROJECT

Social care courses contain inputs from a broad variety of other disciplines and professions. They may draw on psychologists, sociologists, counsellors, public policy analysts, economists, political scientists, social care practitioners, leisure and health educators, art and drama therapists, management lecturers and others. This is a strength that can be stimulating and enriching for learners, yet it may also be argued that the breadth of disciplines, if pursued without a clear social care project, is a significant stumbling block for the profession.

Some might argue that the medical profession similarly embraces a variety of different disciplines, such as surgery, haematology, psychiatry, endocrinology and so on, but medicine has a singular focus on the human body and in attempting to make the patient well in body and mind. It works with treatments that have a proven effect and are subject to rigorous analytical research and prior testing. In addition, medicine has been established for many centuries and has a clear professional identity. Social care, by contrast, is relatively new. Furthermore, it has no single focus, but a wide remit and a multiplicity of client groups. For this reason, social care, in terms of integration, may be said to resemble a large 'V', with activity going in opposite directions.

The older profession of social work, which draws on similar professional discourses to social care, has long been attempting to integrate as a profession (Skehill 1999). Writing of the UK experience, Clarke (1993: 60) notes that:

> a core part of any professional practice is its ability to lay claim to a distinctive knowledge in advancing a field of expertise. Social work students … were confronted with a legacy of three distinct approaches: casework, groupwork and community work. Each sought to incorporate psychological and sociological theories from relevant academic disciplines to demarcate a sphere of knowledge and expertise.

This outcome was a relatively unified and distinct 'social work' body of knowledge. This enabled social work to 'overcome the fragmentation of … the "tri-method" approach … integrating all the ways of understanding social work into a single model' (Clarke 1993: 61).

This process, still only partially successful, has yet to start in the area of social care. There is as yet no blueprint for the unification of the social care profession. Neither is government nor the profession calling for such a move. Mulcahy (2007) reports that most social care students perceived that theoretically based courses were taught separately and were largely unconnected to their therapeutic and social care practice subjects. Most also stated that in their experience, much of their theoretical knowledge was ignored in the field. This separation within teaching was also noted by O'Connor (2008).

The difficulty of formulating a social care project with a unified focus should not detract us from attempting to do so. If we fail, the profession is likely to maintain a blurred identity, ultimately detrimental to practitioners, clients and society as a whole. The challenge of forging a sense of common purpose has to start with the value base of the educators and their own vision for the social care profession.

THE SOCIAL CARE PROJECT: NEW DIRECTIONS

The 'popular practice of social care' outlined above is arguably a 'paternalistic and protective' practice (Braye and Preston-Shoot 1995), albeit embellished with new principles such as choice and empowerment. It involves little more than looking after the day-to-day needs of the client and utilising strategies to improve his or her level of personal development. This is a hugely important job, but is essentially short term in nature. For the most part, it deals with the symptoms of the challenges that face the client: occupational therapy for mentally ill clients, speech and language therapy for autistic clients and so on.

This is critically important to the client's welfare, but societal challenges are often more deeply rooted and require other interventions and strategies. Social care practitioners generally do not try to address these. Failure in this respect is due to a failure to integrate critical knowledge. Thus, the legal, economic and sociological education that students have experienced, and that might empower their clients and themselves as joint advocates, is ignored in the field of practice due to a lack of integration of these component elements. The dominant methodologies and values in social care practice tend to derive from the counselling and therapeutic profession, which focus almost entirely on the individual (Kennefick 2006) and fail to address the deep-seated problems in society that strongly impact on clients' lives. These two deficiencies, resulting in a one-dimensional practice, do not address the totality of clients' needs in the longer term, as is illustrated in the following section.

Mental Health

The Irish mental health system offers little choice other than medication. The physical infrastructure is appalling and it is almost impossible to access cognitive behavioural therapy (CBT) or other necessary therapy from the public health system (O'Connor 2007). The cost of providing adequate infrastructure and services would be less than €900 million (Mental Health Commission 2006), yet the Irish government has stalled on allocating these resources, despite giving tax breaks to the well-off of over €12 billion during the period 1999 to 2005 (Goodbody Economic Consultants 2006; Indecon 2006). Notwithstanding the goodwill and hard work of the social care practitioner, this economic imbalance strongly militates against an increase in clients' health and well-being.

Children

In the summer of 2008, the Health Service Executive (HSE) confirmed that it did not have the resources to commit to an out-of-hours social work service that could deal with emergencies after 5:00 p.m. and at the weekends. This is still the case despite several recent tragic cases that might have been avoided if there were appropriate after-hours services.

The Irish government continues to refuse to recognise the needs of disability service providers who have established applied behavioural analysis (ABA) projects to provide a more effective treatment for children with autism. The government has spent €18 million defending its position through the courts, using money that could have provided for the ABA treatment in the first instance.

Older Persons

An embargo on the hiring of staff by the HSE since October 2007, coupled with the emergent financial cutbacks, has resulted in hours being removed from elderly people needing home help services as well as a chronic shortage of speech and language therapists and occupational therapists, despite the crucial nature of these interventions to clients.

These three examples highlight the centrality of the state's response in the context of the wider economy as a critical determinant of the quality and type of social care delivery that professionals can carry out. Students and practitioners of social care need to bring such insights, encountered in the theoretical modules of their educational programmes, into ongoing social care practice development. Having been thus 'conscientised' (Friere 1972) towards the need for social justice, they should apply this approach within their social care practice and also bring it to their ongoing professional development as 'reflective practitioners' (O'Doherty 2008). This process is intrinsic to the new directions for social care suggested later in this chapter.

IMPLICATIONS FOR EDUCATORS AND PRACTITIONERS

There is a failure to build in the knowledge from non-therapeutic subjects (economics, sociology, law) into social care practice, which is then reflected in the day-to-day practice of social care. Thus, for example, only a small number of social care organisations actively engage in advocacy and campaigning. These are largely national umbrella organisations such as ISPCC, Age Action Ireland and the Disability Federation of Ireland. At the level of local organisations, this is not part of the day-to-day work (Mulcahy 2007). Social care practitioners often do not have the responsibility to advocate on behalf of clients and liaise with state agencies, for example in the areas of housing need, non-availability of suitable mental health services or of ABA education. While students' exposure to discourses of sociology and social policy should sustain an ongoing focus in social care practice towards the collective needs of clients, in effect, social care practice remains an individual act between the practitioner and the client (Kennefick 2006). In this context 'client centredness' is often used as a justification for focusing entirely on the individual client's needs, thus ignoring the deeper social causes of the client's problem (McVerry 2008).

As a result, training in this area that might promote advocacy and campaigning strategies eventually dissipates and deeper-seated societal problems are rarely considered. This situation is often legitimated by a value base in the therapeutic 'reflexive professional' model (see Chapter 5) that does not regard these issues as part of the practice of social care in the first instance.

The failure by therapeutic practitioners to see the relevance of a critical approach means that they, perhaps unwittingly, may succumb to an exercise of power by wider social and economic forces. In addition, though well intentioned, they may deflect the infusion of social care practice with campaigning and advocacy strategies.

How can this be the case? The answer starts with a short discussion of Lukes's work on power (1974). For Lukes, there are three 'faces' of power, the most obvious being where someone's issue is shouted down or ignored. This is the first face of power. The second face of power is where a person or group's grievances are prevented from becoming issues; the most common way this is done is through keeping certain matters 'off the agenda'. The third face of power is the most insidious of all: it involves deliberate attempts by people, groups, governments and others to fool people into believing, largely by way of ideological means, that they do not have any grievance or problem in the first place. Government 'spindoctoring' is an example of this practice.

The issues identified above reflect structural problems that result from a failure by the state, strongly influenced by its dominant view on the economy. The social structure also contains other elements, such as the class structure, disability, race and gender. For example, the failure to adopt the social model of disability (see Chapter 23) is also a structural failure.

If practitioners fail to appreciate that these structural failures need to be dealt with by an integrated response, are they not being duped through the third face of power? If practitioners choose to exclude strategies that might work against these structural problems, are they then not setting the agenda for what is included and excluded from social care practice? Is this not the second face of power?

WHAT NEEDS TO BE DONE?

Disabled people's movements have been beacons in transforming the social world. Up to the 1960s, the biomedical model of disability was uncontested. The rise of disabled people's movements since then, starting with the Campaign for Independent Living in the US (Casey 2005; Toolan 2006) and the success of its message, has resulted in the fact that the 'social model' of disability is now almost universally accepted as being the appropriate one.

Crucially, the success of disabled people's movements was based on the fundamental recognition that 'the personal is the political'. In order to change the dominant biomedical view, to improve the resources and facilities allocated by governments and to achieve independence through society taking responsibility for disabling them, disabled groups had to challenge the exercise of power over them. This was intrinsically a political act. It required a new mindset that went beyond the day-to-day issues of clients' welfare. As Braye and Preston-Shoot (1995: 47) point out:

understanding how an individual's experience of disability is created in interactions with a physical and social world designed for non-disabled living … and recognizing the assumptions that inform dominant orthodoxy about the identity and ability of disabled people … lead to a value position which sees disability as a human rights issue requiring political action rather than a social problem requiring welfare provision.

Consequently, the theoretical positions and strategies of new social movements (NSMs), such as the environmental or women's movements, have a lot to offer in terms of suggesting new ways to address the absence of social structure in social care practice. Most European NSMs offer emancipatory potential to people in civil society who have issues, whether in the realm of social care or not. With the decline in the numbers of people joining political parties and the individualisation of social problems through clientelism and brokerage (Coakley and Gallagher 2005), more and more people are joining pressure groups that seek social change. Such movements are varied and may include single issue movements, such as those protesting against a phone mast, or women's movements that argue for equality, child care provision or other services (Connolly and Hourigan 2006; Share et al. 2007: 491–519).

In Ireland, there has been an explosion of NSMs that seek to improve the position of various client groups. In the field of disability, there are People with Disabilities in Ireland, the Disability Federation of Ireland and others; in mental health, there is the Mental Health Coalition and others. In the area of homelessness, there is the Simon Community and Focus Ireland; the Fr. Peter McVerry Trust campaigns for young offenders, drug abusers and homeless people; while Age Action Ireland campaigns for the rights and interests of elderly people. In the area of poverty, numerous organisations campaign, including Saint Vincent de Paul and CORI, whereas the Irish Society for the Prevention of Cruelty to Children and Barnardos advocate on behalf of children.

These groups share a common view of the world: that without political action, the rights and lives of those in need of social care will at best stand still or even deteriorate. The dominant ideological mindset of Irish governments is increasingly wedded to neo-liberal values. The resulting paradigm and policies are not committed to a strong welfare state or caring for the less able or less well-off. The statistical evidence shows that Ireland's tax take, at 29 per cent of GDP (O'Connor 2008), is, within the OECD, the second lowest only to the US. The overall level of government spending in Ireland, at 35 per cent of GDP, is, together with the US, the lowest in the OECD. Ireland's spending on public social expenditure, which includes many areas of social care, is, at 16 per cent of GDP, amongst the lowest of all the 27 EU member states.

The manifestations of these figures are obvious within the fields of social care mentioned above. Dozens of others could also be provided to illustrate the indifference of neo-liberal governments in Ireland to those in need of social care. This means that strategies to deal with the deep-seated neglect of social care clients need to become intrinsic to social care practice, something that has become obvious even to the medical profession: at its 2008 conference, the Irish Medical Organisation banner read 'Advocacy is a duty, not a responsibility'.

In recent years, probably the most significant principle for the delivery of social care is that it should happen in the *community* (Kennefick 1998; Means et al. 2008). Community care is now the ideologically dominant mode of delivery and it will continue to grow in importance in the coming years. Community care can be considered, along with related practices such as community development and youth work, as a 'model' of community work. The site of such practices is the local community, the point of closest access to clients and one that contributes to the normalisation of their care. Practitioners in these fields aim to improve the quality of life of individuals, and if we accept the necessity for an emancipatory focus for social care workers, share a common purpose to argue for social change outcomes, often through political means, for the benefit of citizens and clients alike.

The wellspring of values from which all could draw emanates from what could be termed 'critical social education' (Hurley 1992). This model is most popularly associated with the work of the Brazilian educator Paulo Freire. In his work with poor and marginalised people in South America, Freire emphasised that people need to be educated about the economic, political and social structures that disempower them. That the poor in Latin America continued to live in poverty, remain illiterate and had poor health services was all due to *political* decisions. Through facilitating the poor to think this through with the aid of 'critical reflection' and talking to each other – a process Freire termed 'dialogical education' – disempowered and marginalised people can be armed with the knowledge to struggle and work for change. In this 'popular education' model, 'knowledge is power' and potentially emancipatory. When people can see the structural powers that disempower them, be it corrupt governments or other forces, they are then 'concientised' into campaigning and engaging in community action to change their plight (Shor 1992).

It is this value base and model that must infuse social care practice. This has already happened in the disabled people's movement and needs to become part of the everyday practice of social care. Given that 'community care' is often co-located with 'community development', for example in family resource centres and community development agencies, there are opportunities for a symbiotic relationship or alliance between the two professions. This unified focus could improve the ability of each in achieving its aims and prevent possible divisions between 'service providers' and 'community development workers'.

HOW?

The disabled people's movement has revolutionised how we view disability. In Ireland, it has been instrumental in achieving the introduction of the Disability Act 2005. The strategies that were employed to achieve this outcome included:

- Protest.
- Lobbying government.
- Written submissions.
- Organisational campaigns.
- Working with representative groupings, including unions.
- Legal challenges to government.
- Media campaigning.
- Setting up alternative services.
- Threat of running electoral candidates.
- Introduction of new practices at the organisational level.

In formulating care plans for clients, the political, campaigning, change-orientated and advocacy focus of what Share (Chapter 5) terms the 'democratic professional' needs to now be urgently integrated at the level of social care practice delivery and in training and education by social care educators. This view is echoed by many now writing in the area of social care. For example, for Sarah Banks (2006) it is now a duty of social (care) workers to 'recognise the need for and seek to promote policies and practices which are non-discriminatory and anti-oppressive'. Similarly, O'Doherty (2008), in arguing for a 'critical social care practice', posits the values of this type of practitioner: 'It entails operating from a foundation of values and assumptions. These include a fundamental commitment to social justice which leads to forms of practice which are empowering and anti-oppressive.' This needs to result in 'critical action':

> Fashioning a convincing and concrete vision and agenda for change, in a way that makes real how things could be other than they are. This is best achieved through an incremental action learning process, which involves addressing change across a broad range of policy and practice. (O'Doherty 2008)

In the face of restricted staffing levels, poor resources and organisational practices that result in inferior outcomes for clients, social care practitioners have an obligation and a duty to engage in the strategies outlined above, as has been pursued by the disability movement. When designing or implementing care plans, where there are deficiencies or omissions, strategies to overcome these need to be written in as legitimate objectives to be pursued.

For example, a written submission may need to be made to the line manager and ultimately to the middle/upper managers. In the absence of a satisfactory result, the care plan should stipulate other courses of action, which might include bringing in the representative body or union to discuss the matter. Teachers' unions, farmers' groups and business groups have all secured state interventions through lobbying and campaigning in the past 40 years that have mainly benefitted their own members. Social care unions and representative bodies can engage in similar practices. While the pay and working conditions of the social care practitioner may improve, an equality of focus must be on improving the care available to the client. For example, the Irish Nurses Organisation has successfully advocated for clients of the health system as well as their own working conditions in recent years.

Social care practitioners can also learn from established advocacy groups that work on behalf of their clients. Yet it would be a mistake to think that advocating is only the job of such bodies: it is equally part of the role of the social care practitioner him or herself. Suitable strategies for action to ameliorate challenges to quality care outcomes can be adopted in care plans drawn up by care practitioners in partnership with relevant advocacy groups, such as those mentioned.

An invigorated and integrated social care professional can also be instrumental in injecting lifeblood into a strong representative body for the sector. At present, many social care educators and practitioners view themselves as counsellors who work within the social care profession but are members of a counselling representative body. Other social care educators may view themselves solely as legal experts who happen to teach in social care. Many managers in social care may view themselves as managers who happen to work in this particular sector.

A unified and integrated social care practice and education would provide a vision and blueprint that would firmly locate these varied professionals as *social care professionals* in the first instance. This unity can help to grow a strong representative group for social care, which is now urgently needed.

There are added benefits: the weakness in terms of a blurred professional identity, which results in social care practitioners' exclusion from government plans on community-based mental health teams and primary care teams, can be ameliorated to a large extent by the above strategies. Social care practitioners would now have a unified and clear identity. In addition, a stronger representative body that espouses a clear vision would strengthen the position of the social care field when in negotiation with government, state agencies and other providers.

CONCLUSION

This chapter is based on the contention that social care practice excludes an adequate appreciation of the impact of the social structure on the lives of clients. This stems from a failure to fully appreciate the links between the different elements of social care education. Contemporary examples from social policy and practice point to the need to incorporate structure, campaigning and advocacy into social care practice. Lessons on how this might be successfully achieved are taken from the disabled people's movement and a range of other advocacy movements. Finally, it is suggested that a move to an integrated social care practice and education would strengthen the identity of the profession and its professional organisations. This could ultimately place the profession in a stronger position in taking its place as an autonomous profession as part of government plans for the future in various areas. Ultimately, this will lead to a social care practice that can address the root cause of the persistent social care challenges that face clients, rather than focusing only on day-to-day care needs.

8

Equality: A Challenge to Social Care

Majella Mulkeen

OVERVIEW

This chapter considers the challenge posed to social care by the concept of equality. The space occupied by social care practitioners in Irish society offers a unique opportunity to challenge inequalities as they are experienced by the people they work with. By virtue of their role and the social groups they engage with, social care practitioners witness the impact of inequality on the everyday lived experience of people affected.

Nevertheless, it cannot be taken for granted that social care as a profession has a commitment to promoting equality. Evidence from the experiences of people with intellectual disability (Ryan 1999), children placed in industrial and reformatory schools (Raftery and O'Sullivan 1999), families living in poverty (McKay 2007), people with mental illness (Crowley 2003) and Travellers (Kenny and McNeela 2006) demonstrates that high levels of inequality persist. Furthermore, a variety of social professions charged with responsibility for the delivery of services can operate in a manner that amplifies the exclusion and oppression of the people they are there to 'serve'. The power of professionals to act as 'gatekeepers', influencing the life chances of those they are engaged with, alongside the potential of the social professions to act as a site of resistance and empowerment, have been articulated by a number of writers (Adams et al. 2002; Duyvendak et al. 2007; Garfat 1998; Knorth et al. 2002; Lindsay 2002; Thompson 2006) and are examined in other chapters in this book.

This chapter seeks to engage social care students and practitioners in a consideration of the issues related to equality and inequality in Irish society. It outlines the persistence of inequality in Irish society alongside a framework of analysis that can inform equality objectives for social care practitioners. It examines contested definitions of equality, the role of the state in generating inequality and the response of civil society. A critique of current definitions of social care is provided in order to challenge educators and practitioners to develop models of emancipatory practice.

DEFINING EQUALITY

What does equality mean, who is entitled to be treated equally and what goods or opportunities in life should be equally distributed? While many attest to a belief in equality, differences arise about how to define equality, who should be equal to whom and in what circumstances. The concept of equality is hotly contested. Many believe that *inequality* is natural and good for society. For example, in 2005, the then Minister for Justice, Equality and Law Reform, Michael McDowell, argued that inequality is necessary in a capitalist society (specifically Ireland) because it provides an essential incentive to work harder and achieve (Wilson 2005). Of course, the strongest advocates of this perspective themselves rarely experience the brunt of inequality.

In 1962, Douglas Jay asked:

> Why should I have more right to happiness than you? ... If we believe that all human beings have an equal right to happiness and a civilised life, then it is for this reason that we should seek to establish a society in which these rights are embodied. The ultimate ground for condemning inequality is that it is unjust, not that it causes resentment or envy. (Jay 1962: 5)

This belief remains evocative today. Equality is a traditional idea. It has been one of the guiding principles behind political, economic and social reform in European and other countries for over two centuries. Revolutions and wars of independence have been fought to banish centuries of privilege and inequality in the name of equality, e.g. the French Revolution. The cornerstones of democratic systems of government are often couched in terms of 'equality for all'. Political ideologies such as liberalism and socialism have also placed equality at their core, even if the concept is interpreted quite differently. The Irish Constitution states in Article 40.1: 'All citizens shall, as human persons, be held equal before the law.' Furthermore, the Universal Declaration of Human Rights (1948) states: 'All human beings are born free and equal in dignity and rights' (Article 1).

To begin conceptualising equality, it can be argued that:

> basic equality is the cornerstone of all egalitarian thinking: the idea that at some very basic level all human beings have equal worth and importance and as such, equally deserve concern and respect. (Baker et al. 2004: 23)

Because concepts such as 'worth', 'respect' and 'concern' are open to a wide range of interpretations, definitions of basic equality specify what kind of minimum standards should be expected in terms of equal treatment, respect and concern for people on the basis of their humanity. Such minimum standards are generally found in documents such as the Universal Declaration of Human Rights and in preambles to relevant legislation. A broad range of United Nations conventions on civil and political rights, social and economic rights, the elimination of discrimination against women and the elimination of all forms of racial discrimination identify the value base of equality as a global phenomenon. They are critically important as they include, for example, prohibitions against cruel and degrading treatment, protection against violence and at least some commitment to providing for people's most basic needs (Crowley 2006: 2–3).

When discussion about the meaning of equality moves beyond the provision of minimum standards, different views exist about who should be equal to whom and what should be equalised. We will examine two different perspectives on these questions: the *liberal*, or equality of opportunity, perspective and the *radical*, or equality of outcomes, perspective.

The *liberal* perspective is primarily concerned with equality between individuals. As individuals are different in their aptitudes, interests and abilities, liberal egalitarians assume that inequalities between people are unavoidable and inevitable. For liberal egalitarians, equality strategies in any society should aim to manage these inequalities in a fair manner by strengthening the minimum everyone is entitled to and by providing fair and equal opportunity to access valued social goods. In practical terms, this means that the state should provide a safety net through various provisions of the welfare state and that opportunities to compete for advantage in an unequal world should be governed by the principle of equal opportunity.

Liberal equality takes the view that merit or advancement in life is gained through individual effort alone. For example, success in the Leaving Certificate is often attributed to the hard work and 'ability' of the individual and failure is associated with inadequate preparation or less 'ability'. 'Ability' is considered to be innate, with no reference to the social context learning takes place in (such as class size) or the supports and opportunities available (such as access to the internet).

This *individualistic* approach neglects disparities between social groups in their access to valued social goods such as health, housing, education and employment. For example, access to education or employment is more difficult for people with disabilities because they experience barriers and unfair treatment in their access to such opportunities (see Chapter 23). These barriers and exclusion impact on the efforts of individuals to achieve, no matter how talented they may be. In this way, equality of opportunity is limited in its ability to address deeply entrenched experiences of discrimination and inequality.

A second tenet of the liberal egalitarian perspective is respect for difference. Individuals are different in their customs and beliefs and tolerance of individual and group differences (as long as they respect basic rights) is embedded in freedom of conscience and opinion. Liberal equality holds that the basic arrangements of our society should be impartial among such different beliefs, cultural customs, sexual preferences and so on (Baker et al. 2004: 26).

The dominance of liberal perspectives on equality in Western democracies has contributed to strategies to prohibit discrimination and remove formal barriers to access for social groups that have historically been denied opportunities. This represents a significant achievement for many historically excluded groups. For example, women were allowed to register as students in Trinity College, Dublin in 1904 but with restrictions on their access and movements up until the 1960s. The marriage ban, abolished in 1973, meant that women working in the public and civil service had to resign upon marriage. Prohibitions on discrimination and the legal requirement to implement equality of opportunity have contributed to greater equality in our society. Nevertheless, significant inequalities persist both globally and in Ireland and liberal definitions of equality have failed to make significant inroads in this regard.

The notion of *equality of outcomes* is a more radical perspective and challenges liberal ideas about the inevitably of inequality. It points to the fact that inequalities are generated by social structures that have been amenable to change in the past and can be shaped in an egalitarian manner again in the future. For example, during the first half of the twentieth century in Ireland, women who gave birth to a child outside marriage were routinely sent to Magdalene laundries and their children placed for adoption. This approach would be unthinkable today because such inequality in the treatment of women would be unacceptable in Irish society.

This perspective on equality has outcomes rather than just opportunities as its focus. The provision of equal opportunities must lead to roughly equal outcomes for individuals within different social groups. From a radical perspective, when there are persistent and significantly unequal outcomes for some social groups when compared with other groups in the benefits accruing from income, education, health, housing, employment and so on, this points to the need for a change in how power and privilege are distributed.

Central to a radical perspective is an emphasis on how *social structures* serve to privilege some groups and disadvantage others. This perspective emphasises the influence of social factors on people's choices and actions, rather than treating individuals as solely responsible for their successes and failures (Baker et al. 2004). Strategies for equality within this perspective focus on a world in which people's overall resources are much more equal than they are now so that their prospects for a good life are roughly similar. This perspective seeks to massively reduce the current scale of inequalities. This does not mean a demand for sameness or mathematical equality, but rather a society where the enormous inequalities between social groups are altered to ensure all people have genuine opportunities to develop their talents and abilities, regardless of their family background, ethnicity or gender. It would involve a dramatic change in the distribution of income and wealth and in access to public services (Baker et al. 2004: 36–7).

Those who support this perspective accept that people are different in their talents and motivations and should be rewarded accordingly, but suggest that the privileges that accrue to some social groups are at the expense of other groups and cannot adequately be explained by the different talents and abilities of individuals. This is not a new idea. In 1931, Tawney put it succinctly:

To criticise inequality and to desire equality is not, as is sometimes suggested, to cherish the romantic illusion that men are equal in character and intelligence. It is to hold that while natural endowments may differ profoundly, it is the mark of a civilised society to aim at eliminating such inequalities as have their source, not in individual differences, but in its own organisation. (Tawney 1952: 57)

The equality of outcome approach is critical of the liberal view that tolerating difference is sufficient. Tolerance is viewed as problematic, as it sits easily with ignorance and contempt for difference and can be viewed by the dominant groups as a badge of superiority (Phillips 1999). A radical perspective demands that difference and diversity be accommodated and celebrated rather than just tolerated. This does not mean that it is wrong to criticise beliefs we disagree with. Since all cultures include oppressive traditions, none are above criticism, and this includes the dominant culture in any society (Baker et al. 2004: 35).

In comparing the liberal and radical perspectives on equality, I have focused on who should be equal to whom (equality between individuals or equality between social groups); how each perspective views society (unavoidably unequal or open to change); how resources should be distributed (the provision of a basic minimum for all or a dramatic reduction in inequalities between social groups); how difference is viewed (tolerance or accommodation and celebration); and how equality is conceived (equality of opportunity or equality of outcome). In many respects, equality of outcome is a logical extension of the liberal perspective – it builds on its achievements but also seeks to address its shortcomings.

EQUALITY AND 'DIFFERENCE'

Phillips (1999: 20) states that 'for much of the twentieth century inequality was associated with the distribution of income and wealth ... equality was conceived as a substantially economic affair'. The rise of the feminist and anti-racist movements modified this significantly, and in more recent years the relationships between equality and difference have moved centre stage in Western societies.

This move points to the complex nature of equality. Those who believe in a more equal society seek to have resources distributed more equally among social groups and individuals. Those who have least access to a fair share of income and wealth are among those social groups viewed as 'different' and they share the experience of exclusion: people with disabilities, women, Travellers, black and ethnic minorities, people who are gay, lesbian or bisexual, very young and older people. For many, poverty exacerbates their exclusion (Combat Poverty Authority and Equality Authority 2003).

Phillips (1999: 25) states that:

the notion that we make people equal by ignoring or suppressing their differences easily turns into a statement of inequality ... the resulting emphasis on equality through difference is probably the most distinctive feature of contemporary thinking on democracy.

Calls for the recognition of difference have informed the provision of maternity leave for women and reasonable accommodation of people with disabilities. Recent Irish campaigns seek to establish legal recognition for same-sex marriages and an end to the discrimination experienced by same-sex and co-habiting couples in matters such as tax and inheritance. The decision of An Garda Síochána to ban the wearing of turbans by Sikh members of the force while on duty (O'Brien 2007) and the legal requirement on employers and service providers to reasonably accommodate people with disabilities signify different opinions on how diversity should or should not be accommodated.

Parekh (2002: 240) notes that:

> Equality involves equal freedom or opportunity to be different, and treating human beings equally requires us to take account both of their similarities and their differences. When the latter are not relevant equality entails uniform or identical treatment, when they are, it requires differential treatment ... Essentially equality involves full recognition of legitimate and relevant differences.

This way of thinking about what constitutes 'equal treatment' is useful in highlighting the wide range of inequalities experienced by a broad and diverse range of groups in Irish society. It highlights how factors such as gender, disability, ethnicity and/or sexual orientation can undermine equal citizenship. While our society remains a highly unequal one, it is the duty of those committed to changing this situation to envisage a new alternative in the sense of a picture of a better society. This means identifying sites where resistance can be mobilised and concrete actions taken to generate equality (Baker et al. 2004; O'Connor 2005).

EQUALITY AND INEQUALITY: THE ROLE OF THE STATE

The dominant understanding of inequality in a society will shape action to address it and the extent to which equality can be realised. In the period after the Second World War, many Western societies began to address the persistence of economic inequality. This led to the development of welfare states that aimed to ensure a more egalitarian distribution of resources. There was a marked decline in socio-economic inequality during the period up to the late 1970s. Inequality of household incomes fell in countries such as the US, France, Sweden, the UK, Germany and Japan (Corry and Glyn 1994, cited in Kirby 2001: 5). In this era, equality was the pervasive value of many such societies. Then, from the late 1970s, an emphasis on market-led approaches to economic development and the slimming down of government – widely termed neo-liberalism – resulted in policy approaches characterised by targeting resources on the poorest and programmes to integrate marginalised groups into the paid labour market. A *poverty reduction* approach gradually replaced socio-economic equality as the main distributional goal of public policy (Kirby 2006).

Sen (1992, cited in Kirby 2001: 9) identifies 'two implicit programmes' that inform discussions about how the state provides for its citizens: one based on the *social welfare* model and the other on *social justice*. The former is concerned with poverty reduction and selectively targets resources on the poorest sections of the society. The social justice view is concerned with how to reduce inequalities in the society as a whole and focuses on the universal provision of high-quality public services. The English welfare state up until the 1980s was an exemplar of the latter. It has its fullest expression in the development of social democratic welfare states such as Sweden, where:

> states pursue an equality of the highest standard, not an equality of minimal needs ... services and benefits are at levels commensurate with even the most discriminating tastes of the new middle classes ... workers have full participation in the quality of rights enjoyed by the better off. (Esping-Andersen 1990, cited in Kirby 2001: 13)

Ireland is a country with a serious problem of socio-economic inequality, operating as it does from a social welfare view of provision. It can be characterised as a country with declining levels of consistent poverty alongside growing inequality. Between 1973 and 1994, the gap between the incomes of poorer and richer households was narrowing. The decrease in inequality was slow and modest, but the trend was nonetheless positive. Then, as the boom took off, that trend halted. Over all the boom years, inequality was maintained at relatively high levels (O'Toole 2008).

According to the Central Statistics Office (2007e), almost 7 per cent of the population lives in consistent poverty, that is, almost 300,000 people living on incomes of less than €11,000 for a single person and unable to afford two pairs of strong shoes, a meal with meat or chicken or fish every second day or a waterproof coat. Ireland lags behind not only other wealthy EU states, but also poorer states in its spending on social provision such as 'benefits for sickness and disability, old age, survivors of deceased persons, family and children, unemployment, housing and other forms of social benefit' (Eurostat 2005, cited in Kirby 2006: 119).

The above evidence suggests that greater equality in the distribution of resources is important given the level of economic inequality in Irish society. Certain social groups have higher poverty rates than the rest of the population and experience higher levels of discrimination in their efforts to access employment and services. Poverty, economic inequality and discrimination are inextricably linked for many individuals within such groups. The position of women, black and minority ethnic groups, lone parents, people with disabilities and children are very much bound up with the above economic indicators. The women's movement, the disability movement, anti-racism movements and, more recently, children's rights campaigns have highlighted issues of poverty, unemployment, low pay and lack of participation as critical in achieving greater equality in Irish society. Thus, a focus on particular disadvantaged or privileged social groups is useful because individuals usually experience inequality or privilege as a consequence of their membership of these groups (Baker et al. 2004: 43).

THE RESPONSE OF CIVIL SOCIETY

The challenge to address the levels of poverty and exclusion experienced by sections of Irish society outlined above was met by agencies and campaigning groups emerging during the 1990s with unprecedented vigour and exerted a powerful influence on the direction of government policy.

Organisations such as the Irish National Organisation of the Unemployed (INOU), the National Women's Council of Ireland, Forum of People with Disabilities, Pavee Point, the Irish Traveller Movement, Age Action Ireland, OPEN (Network of Lone Parent Groups) and Barnardos, among others, have worked for many years to provide services and to campaign for material improvements and greater equality for specific social groups. Such work has been supported by the state, which itself has been a pioneer internationally in establishing such agencies as the (now abolished) Combat Poverty Agency, the Equality Authority and the Human Rights Commission, all devoted to addressing these major problems in Irish society (Kirby 2006: 112). It is in this intersection of sometimes contradictory and different emphases in government policy and commitments that a space emerges for action to promote equality by exposing contradictions and developing alliances for positive change.

The state is itself a site of oppressive practices, but it also contains sites of resistance where strategies to build a more egalitarian society exist alongside policies that perpetuate inequality. Several developments during the 1990s helped provide the impetus for a more strategic focus on equality for such groups and they were successful in negotiating with the state as a partner in bringing about change. Given the policy shift away from addressing socio-economic equality, such groups set about lobbying the government to develop a more strategic approach to addressing a range of inequalities relevant to their identity. A key focus remained the reduction and elimination of socio-economic inequality as it intersected with groups experiencing discrimination.

Three significant policy documents emerged at this time that enabled the advancement of an equality agenda for significant segments of the population. A key strategy for organisations and groups campaigning for equality during this period was the targeting of resources to the constituent group and the enactment of anti-discrimination legislation.

- The Commission on the Status of People with Disabilities was set up in 1993 with the active involvement and support of a broad representative body of disability bodies and state agencies. It published its report, *Strategy for Equality*, in 1996.

- The Task Force on the Travelling Community published its report in 1995, setting out the policy agenda in relation to Travellers. The monitoring committee published its first progress report in 2001.
- The Second Commission on the Status of Women published its report in 1995. The Fourth World Conference on Women took place in Beijing in 1996 and Ireland signed up to a Platform for Action and set up the Gender Equality Monitoring Committee to monitor the implementation and recommendations of the Second Commission.

For many groups, the lack of legal recourse in situations of discrimination was a significant barrier to establishing their right to be treated equally. This was particularly so as *institutional discrimination* excluded such groups from access to and more equal outcomes from both employment opportunities and public or private service agencies.

PATTERNS OF INEQUALITY

Discrimination and inequality follow clear patterns: economic, political, cultural and affective. *Economic inequality* arises from the unequal division of a society's resources between different social groups and ultimately between individuals. It takes the form of inequalities of income and wealth as well as other income-related resources such as education, health and housing. Economic inequalities shape social class formations, where privileged classes have more resources, greater power, better working conditions and better access to education (Baker et al. 2004).

The virtual lack of political representation from many marginalised groups signals the existence of a significant degree of *political inequality*. This occurs where groups and individuals have little or no representation in institutions charged with making or implementing decisions that impact on their lives either at local or national levels. In a statement that reveals the real impact of inequalities of representation and power in Irish society, the Minister for Finance stated in 2004 that his decision to grant substantial funding to the disability sector 'was based on his experience that for many years the disability programme was at the end of the queue for resources. It did not benefit from the type of professional lobbying and support which acute hospitals and primary care programmes got from traditionally strong organised interests in the health services' (Brian Cowen 2004, cited in Crowley 2006: 121).

At the level of *cultural representation*, there are inequalities in how 'difference' is understood and accommodated within Irish society. The status and respect accorded to different groups in a society are often manifest in the language used to describe groups that are constructed as 'different', whether this is on gender, disability, class, sexual orientation or ethnic grounds. How difference is understood impacts on how such groups and individuals within them are represented or misrepresented in media and education discourses.

At the level of *affective relations*, it is a critical element of all human existence that people have access to relations of love, care and solidarity. Individuals and groups who experience hostility, isolation and a removal of opportunities for caring relations are subjected to this kind of inequality, as are those who carry a disproportionate burden of the work that providing such care involves.

Social care practitioners are witness to all these patterns of inequality in their daily work with individuals and families who struggle against poverty and discrimination. The face of inequality is familiar to them in their work within family resource centres; neighbourhood youth projects; with people with intellectual impairments living independently, in group homes or attending day centres; with people with physical disabilities struggling to establish or maintain independence; with children and young people looked after away from their family; migrant workers; or women as lone parents struggling to access support in their care roles. The question for social care practitioners is how they can promote a more egalitarian society with the people they work with. Clarifying what a more equal society might look like is a critical first step in a transformative approach among social care practitioners (Chapter 19 examines more specific models of anti-oppressive practice).

WHAT WOULD A MORE EQUAL SOCIETY LOOK LIKE?

A more equal society is likely to be shaped by pursuing a radical perspective of equality with an emphasis on equality of outcomes for all social groups. At the level of economic resources, there is clearly a need to promote a more egalitarian sharing of economic resources in Irish society, particularly in light of the links established earlier between group membership, inequality and poverty. As spending on social protection decreases, there is an increasing challenge for civil society to highlight this and lobby for change (Kirby 2006). Social care practitioners have a particularly important role here, given their work with groups who have the least access to society's economic resources.

Access to the power to influence decisions that impact on one's life is critical to a sense of belonging and to 'having a say'. It is particularly important if one is a member of a group routinely excluded from decisions impacting on one's life. Phillips (1999: 31) states that:

> empowerment of the currently disadvantaged is often a prerequisite for rather than a consequence of more equitable social policies. For until people become active participants in the policy process, the policies adopted cannot be expected to reflect their needs.

There is a rich opportunity for social care practitioners in all arenas of professional practice to ensure that service user partnership and participation is not tokenistic, but is committed to sharing power and knowledge so as to better address needs as defined by those who experience them. Current developments in self-advocacy among people with intellectual disabilities is a welcome development and one in which many social care practitioners have taken the initiative.

A culture of respect and recognition is necessary so that the diverse social groups in our society and the individuals who make up these groups can 'live their lives without the burden of contempt and enmity from the dominant culture' (Baker et al. 2004: 34). Cultural equality is about how a society accommodates and celebrates the cultural and social differences between individual and social groups, evident in how structures such as health services, schools and the media engage with difference, whether in sexual orientation, ethnicity, age, disability or other grounds. In a more equal society, diversity would be accommodated in all service provision and respect for difference would be a hallmark of institutions such as the media and education.

Affective equality seeks to generate greater equality in how caring work – whether for children, for older dependent people or those with significant disabilities – is shared out between women and men in particular. Many groups who have little access to power over decisions affecting them experience significant neglect, such as some older people in residential nursing homes, unaccompanied minors living in hostels unsuitable for their care, prisoners, people who are homeless, children in secure residential care and adults with intellectual/ physical disabilities living in institutions or group homes. Greater equality in respect of care would involve providing a structure for the care of those who are dependent that values the care provided and enhances the opportunities for relationships among those in receipt of such care (National Women's Council to Ireland 2003).

THE ROLE OF THE SOCIAL CARE PROFESSIONAL

As outlined in Chapter 1, social care practitioners operate to provide a range of supports to families, children, Travellers and migrant groups, young people and to adults with intellectual, physical or mental disabilities in a variety of settings. The contribution of social care to challenging inequalities must be considered in this context. Given that social care professionals work at the intersection between marginalised and subordinated groups and the state, there is significant potential to challenge exclusion and build a more equality-focused practice.

The role of the social care practitioner has been defined specifically by the Joint Committee on Social Care Professionals as 'the professional provision of care, protection, support, welfare and advocacy for vulnerable or dependent clients, individually or in groups'. Such a definition does point to varied roles and places them in the context of 'established best practice and an in-depth knowledge of lifespan development' (Joint Committee of Social Care Professionals nd.: 13). Its focus on 'vulnerable or dependent clients' neglects any analysis of the context in which people become and/or remain dependent or vulnerable. Nor does this definition identify the role that social divisions play in the maintenance of dependency and vulnerability. Clearly, factors such as gender, social class, ethnicity, disability, sexual orientation and age are some of the recurring factors that shape inequalities and the resultant dependencies (Baker et al. 2004: 8–10).

Furthermore, the definition makes no reference to what constitutes 'established best practice' in the field of care, support, protection, welfare and advocacy. While an elucidation of the skill and knowledge base required is outside the scope of a definition, an explicit acknowledgement of the impact of social inequality on the lives of those at the receiving end of social care services is missing, as is a professional commitment to effect change in such situations. While the provision of care, protection, support and welfare may be necessary roles for a social care professional, they are all deeply contested concepts and can easily be considered paternalistic and disempowering (Preston-Shoot and Braye 1995). The inclusion of an advocacy role holds the best chance of developing an empowerment approach within social care work (Leadbetter 2002). An understanding of the structural nature of inequality and its impact on the lives of individuals is essential to enable the social care professional to develop the skills and the commitment to bring about greater equality in life chances for those they work with. According to O'Connor (Chapter 7), current social care programmes overly focus on the symptoms of social systems' failure rather than consider the root cause; as such, they are an inadequate response to complex social problems. For O'Connor, a structural understanding of society must be integrated into social care practice courses.

CONCLUSION

This chapter has sought to engage social care students and practitioners with questions of equality and how they can develop emancipatory practice. The chapter has addressed contested definitions of equality and the sometimes contradictory role of the state in challenging and generating inequality in Irish society. A model for understanding patterns of inequality has been outlined alongside a vision for a more equal society. Finally, social care practitioners are challenged to contribute to the creation of such a society.

I believe it is time to revisit how we define our work as social care practitioners and bring to it a renewed commitment to egalitarian change where the potential for oppression is replaced with empowerment and social care moves towards the development of a transformative project for itself.

9

Exploring the Importance of Self-awareness Training in Social Care Education

Denise Lyons

OVERVIEW

This chapter defines 'self' and presents a rationale to the social care student or worker for engaging in the challenging process of becoming more 'self-aware'. Central to the student's ability to develop as a competent practitioner is his or her knowledge of self and of how their upbringing, experiences, values and beliefs affect their ability to work with vulnerable people. Social care workers are judged by their ability to perform a variety of duties 'on the floor', irrespective of their theoretical knowledge or education. Becoming self-aware can help eliminate the fear of being labelled a 'bad worker' by the staff team. Self-awareness teaches us more about ourselves, which also impacts on the relationships we have with others. Within the working relationship, we need to learn about our use of power and the impact our own values and needs have on the decisions we make.

This chapter presents methods to learn about the self and introduces 'self-awareness snapshots', developed from my personal experience of becoming self-aware. Irrespective of the way you choose to learn about your 'self', there is always room for further discussion on the importance of 'self training' in your preparation for the diverse and challenging job ahead.

DEFINING SELF

Self, or the 'individuality or essence of a person' (Jenkins 1996a: 29), is not a new area of study, as it has interested many philosophers and psychologists throughout history. The 'self', a multi-dimensional entity, contains the self-concept, self-image, ideal self and self-esteem, to name a few aspects (London 2002).

Learning about the self, or becoming aware of aspects of the self, is referred to as 'self-awareness' and 'self-development' (Taylor 2002). The 'self' develops naturally through the impact of life experiences, growth and maturity. This chapter focuses on a conscious process of awareness and development. For this conscious 'self-development' to occur, a person needs to become aware of his/her internal processes (thoughts, feelings, moods, beliefs and actions) and have an awareness of how these internal processes impact on others as an external process (Day et al. 2004).

Attitudes, Beliefs and Values

Central to the discussion of self is the acknowledgment that becoming self-aware includes exploring personally held attitudes, beliefs and values.

- *Attitudes* are thoughts that develop towards people and experiences; they may be neutral, positive or negative (Alderson 2000; Hayden 1997).
- A *belief* is a perception about a person, experience or situation (Open University 1975), and although perceptions are developed through an internal filtering system, they are believed to be true in the person's own mind (Alderson 2000).
- *Values* are attitudes or feelings about the worth of people, objects or activities. Individual values can be conflicting and are contained within a value system, the adopted set of values influenced by culture, family, religion and society.

WHY LEARN ABOUT THE SELF?

This section offers a rationale to you, the reader, for learning about the self. The self is introduced as 'the principal tool of the social care worker' (Kennefick 2006: 213). We should learn about this 'tool' to enable us to face the fear of being considered a 'bad worker'; to learn about the impact of our needs and our hidden characteristics; to become more reflective and aware in our relationships with others; and to not hide behind our 'professional cloak'. The discussion on why we should learn about the self begins with a description of the self as a toolbox, and continues to examine our fear of being labelled a 'bad worker'.

Unlike many professions that use a toolbox to aid them in their work, in social care, the worker is the toolbox. Academic training and practice experience can only be used as a guide for practice, as each practice situation encountered is unique. Therefore, the worker needs to integrate theory and practice into the self to encourage the creation of an ethical and informed decision-maker (Garfat and Ricks 1995; Ricks and Charlesworth 2003). Patti MacKenna, an experienced child and youth care worker, wrote a paper in 1999 entitled 'Self – It All Starts Here'. One of the key themes to emerge from the study was the issue of self. As one participant in her study said, 'We don't have any other instrument. We are the total instrument. It is a hell of a responsibility' (MacKenna 1999: 76). Tools are not useful if you do not know how they work, and in the same respect, the social care worker is not practising to his or her full potential if they are not engaged in awareness and development of the self.

Facing the Fear of Being the 'Bad Worker'

Social care is a unique profession in that the skills required vary, depending on the aims of the specific service (elderly care, disability, secure care) and the individual needs of those using the service. Fear of not being a competent worker is experienced by both the qualified professional and the practising unqualified worker. There is a fear that the social care worker has to appear all-knowing and that asking for support may be deemed as demonstrating a lack of confidence, incompetence and failure. This fear is based on an acknowledgement that workers will be judged by their colleagues and the service users on their performance. This judgement is based on individual perceptions, both internal and external. Thus, social care workers may potentially be judged on their ability to:

- Form and maintain relationships.
- Adhere to the policies and working practices of the agency.
- Uphold the cleaning standards of their colleagues.
- Handle a crisis appropriately.
- Communicate well, both verbally and on record.
- Be a consistent team member.
- Be on the floor (performing direct care tasks) at the right time.
- Do the office work without appearing to hide from a crisis on the floor.
- Avoid making mistakes.

Competency in all the tasks of social care is difficult but achievable, primarily when the worker is willing to be open about what he/she feels is expected from self and others.

This fear of being a 'bad worker' does not disappear after graduation, as success in college is not viewed as an indication of ability to do the job. Therefore, the social care graduate is reliant on the feedback of work colleagues for reassurance. To eliminate this fear, regardless of training and experience, the worker needs to recognise that he/she has the right to make a mistake and to acknowledge this mistake publicly, without fear of the internal or external judge. This requires the self-awareness to know that acknowledging weakness or mistakes is not a sign that you are a 'bad worker', but a reflective practitioner and someone who accepts that there is an opportunity for self-learning in every experience.

Awareness of Needs, Values and Feelings

The student or worker, by the very nature of the work, is likely to encounter experiences that challenge his/her own values, views and potential prejudices. Social care practice is about making decisions for and on behalf of others, and decisions are based on values, views and beliefs. If workers are unaware of their own issues, they will continue to work without regard to people's feelings, deeming that they know exactly what the other is feeling. In addition, they will ignore the effects that the other person's feelings, behaviour and experiences are having on themselves (Burnard 1992). 'In order to become attuned to other people's feelings, we need to be in touch with our own feelings, and aware of how situations are affecting us emotionally' (Thompson 2002b: 4).

Getting to know 'self' enables workers to question why they entered the social care profession in the first place, as the answers given can influence future practice. It is not enough to enter the field because you want to help without first asking why you are motivated to help others. Fewster (1999) states that people may enter the helping professions for 'selfish' reasons, which may include fulfilling your own needs rather than others', needing approval, having low self-esteem and, lastly, working out your own problems by focusing on someone else's troubles rather than your own. Layder (2004) argues that people may not be consciously meeting their own needs over the needs of others, as most people in the helping professions are well motivated, but sometimes their effort to do well may be misguided. Examples might include indirectly persuading the service users to go to 'your choice' of movie or concert, or planning your 'social life' while in work, right up to the worker who fulfils a need for affection by unconsciously spending more time with the affectionate service users.

Social care workers study the needs of others and apply their education and practice experience towards deciding on the right course of action. This is a powerful position to hold in someone's life. A 'lust for power' was a term utilised by Hawkins and Shohet (2000) to define the student's wish to 'help' or 'care for', 'cure' or 'heal' others. Workers may be attracted to work with vulnerable people because, in comparison, they feel cured, right, well, fortunate and powerful over others. According to Maier (1990), increased self-awareness arms workers with an understanding of their ability to handle power. Needs are not all negative; they are also necessary for social care workers to remain motivated and committed to the helping profession (Hawkins and Shohet 2000).

> Needs in themselves are not harmful, but when they are denied they join the shadows of counselling and work from behind as demands ... Demands ask for fulfilment, needs require only expression. (Hillman 1979: 16)

The Relationship

The core practice skills of providing direct care, therapeutic practice and key-working are performed through the relationship between the worker and others (Cashdan 1988; Eraut 1994; Fewster 1990b; Garfat 1999; Krueger 1999; Maier 1990). According to Kennefick (2003), if children are taken from their family of origin, the alternative care provided for them must be better. This is achieved through 'the quality and texture of the relationships they are offered with their carers' (Kennefick 2003: 91). The professional relationship was identified by

Clarke (2003) as the catalyst through which tasks are performed, defined as the professional 'giving of the self' (Byrne and McHugh 2005; Maier 1990). As the relationship is defined as the giving of self, students need to learn how to use the self within all their relationships.

Garfat (2003) defined the social care worker as being in a 'process of becoming'. He defined the characteristics of this 'becoming worker' as including the ability to be 'actively self-aware and be able to distinguish self from other, and be able to utilise self and the aspects of self in relationships with youth' (Garfat 2003: 10). Part of this becoming involves 'being present' (Fewster 1999), and according to Krueger (1999), presence cannot be faked. When a worker is 'real', it will be sensed by others. The worker must not think of being present as a technique to be learned, but as a 'way of being, that one senses while trying to be in tune with self and other' (Krueger 1999: 70). Ricks (1989) states that when workers are present and engaging with others during daily life events, both their behaviour and 'self' changes, influenced by the other. Being present means that you are not daydreaming or thinking about what theory you can apply – it is about listening, observing and 'being' with the other in the moment. Stuart (1999) suggests that the key to becoming more present in your practice is to begin with your own personal development.

The Professional Cloak

Fewster (1990b) stated that there is a real danger that the social care worker will sacrifice the use of self in favour of a 'learned professionalism', which can manifest itself as extreme professional distance, with no use of touch, and in the over-reliance of organisational policies and procedures.

According to Hawkins and Shohet (2000), workers in the helping professions develop through stages, which reflect their experience, maturity and ability to practise effectively. According to Phelan (2003), recently qualified workers are at stage one (0–24 months in the field) and are primarily concerned with personal safety, evident in their dependence on supervision for appraisal and on their over-reliance on learning the rules in order to feel safe. Therefore, it is difficult for level one workers to avoid hiding behind 'the cloak' when they are centrally concerned with feeling safe. Through effective supervision and an awareness of the impor-tance of being self-aware, they will gradually develop through the stages, relying more on the relationship rather than the enforcement of rules (see Figure 9.1). It is essential for workers to use professional boundaries while being personal, i.e. to wear the cloak, but not to hide behind it. This may prove more difficult for workers in care environments where concern for physical safety is a reality, or where the culture of the organisation is procedurally driven.

Figure 9.1. Developmental Stages of Workers in Helping Professions

Level 1: Capable Caregiver
- Relies on rules to feel safe.
- Rushes in to give consequences to the service users for 'bad' behaviour.

Level 2: Client Centred/Treatment Planner/Change Agent
- Bouncing between dependence and independence and feeling overconfident and overwhelmed.
- Finding the balance between uncontrolled emotional involvement and over-clinical avoidance.
- Giving power back to service users.
- Thinking long term and trusting own judgement.

Level 3: Process-Centred Worker
- Uses helicopter skills to view situation from objective stance.
- Conscious use of self.
- Focus on 'what I can change in myself first'.

Level 4: Integrated (Master)
- The knowledge of theory and experience is integrated into practice and becomes wisdom.

Impact of Levels on Management of Team
Many social care workers are promoted to a leadership role within the profession. The ability to lead effectively depends on the developmental level of workers when promoted.

Level one staff will not have the capacity to supervise staff at higher levels of development. They are concerned with rules, rather than reflection. Workers at levels three and four make better leaders.

Source: Hawkins and Shohet (2000), Phelan (2003).

Hidden Self

William James, the philosopher, wrote an essay in 1890 entitled 'The Hidden Self' where he defined the 'self' as being unknown and hidden (Lapsley and Narvaez 2004). The term 'hidden self' emerged again within counselling psychology and is regularly used to define the place where the unknown human emotions reside (Hawkins and Shohet 2000). The hidden self is also defined as 'the shadow', prevalent in the work of Carl Jung, who considered it to be the negative side of the personality and all the qualities that we like to hide (Hawkins and Shohet 2000; Rogers 1993). The process of learning about self encourages workers to become aware of their shadow characteristics. The difficulty for a social care worker is not in having a shadow side, but in ignoring or dismissing the existence of the shadow side (Byrne 2000; Wosket 1999). According to MacKenna (1999), social care practitioners wished they had explored their issues and values prior to practice in order to help them become aware of their shadow characteristics and the needs they may have met through others (see Figure 9.2). Page (1999) stated that people can become aware of the shadow side through reflective self training.

Figure 9.2. Meeting the Shadow: The Two Sacks Story

Imagine that as a child we are born carrying two sacks. One is filled with all the positive comments, acceptable behaviours and traits, obvious talents and skills and any quality deemed desirable by parents, teachers and peers. The second sack becomes filled alongside the first, only this sack contains all the dismissed behaviours, the unacceptable thoughts, feelings and actions and any quality that is deemed unacceptable by parents, teachers and peers. Due to the nature of the social care profession, social care workers need to know what both sacks contain, as both may affect the worker's relationship with others.

SELF TRAINING WITHIN IRISH SOCIAL CARE EDUCATION

Social care workers do not need a fully developed sense of self, but they must begin their own process of awareness and self-development prior to practice (Fewster 1999). Clarke (2003) stated that social care workers need to be open to learning about the self, and that initial self training begins within the worker's formal education, before they replace good practice with a professional ego. According to Liberatore (1981), training programmes should not ask students to do any more than they require from the children in their care – namely, the challenge to look internally and promote change and growth, where this is required. Byrne (2000) highlighted the need to include self-awareness and self-development training as part of social care education, as students were being assessed on their self-awareness while on placement by the placement supervisor.

Tsang (1993: 63) writes that 'the multidimensional nature of professional practice, that is the involvement of the practitioner's feelings, conceptualisation, reflecting and doing, must all be the concern of the professional education'. Therefore, educators should be aware that the development of the 'self' is not to be undertaken alone, and that this important and difficult learning requires support. The students need to learn that 'support' is a life skill – the skill of knowing what supports they need, and from whom.

Existence of Self Training

Self training does exist within Irish social care education in many forms. In Dundalk IT and Limerick IT, for example, self training is provided within a designated subject entitled Personal Development, and within Cork IT as Communications and Personal Development (College Prospectus 2007–2008). One example of self training within Irish social care education was documented by Patricia Kennefick, formerly a lecturer at the Cork Institute of Technology.

Kennefick (2003) described the Personal Development (PD) programme in Cork as consisting of safe groups, meeting for 90 minutes per week during each academic year. The aim of the PD programme is awareness, both intrapersonally and interpersonally. In relation to intrapersonal awareness, the 'training attempts to identify, examine, and deconstruct the underlying external demands' on the self, from early socialisation (Kennefick 2006: 218). The experiential session begins with a 'check-in', and warm-up exercises aimed at relaxing the participants. As the participants gain confidence and experience within the group, they are expected to further engage in the training exercises and in 'bringing [current] issues to the group' (Kennefick 2003: 93). Being able to express and identify feelings is also a learning outcome of the programme.

To assist the sharing of current feelings, Kennefick (2006) uses 'mind maps' (developed by Tony Buzan as visual learning aids), frameworks and questioning, acquired primarily from the psychological disciplines of person-centred therapy, psychoanalysis and behavioural therapy. This directed learning within the group includes the following: use of feeling language, listening, the Satir Model (placater, blamer, preacher and avoider) (Wheelan 1990), and some psychological processes, e.g. 'projection, introjection, confluence, retroflection, avoidance, and denial' (Kennefick 2003: 94). Students are provided with learning opportunities to explore their own introjection, thus enabling them to learn how they can project their feelings onto others, called 'aware projection'. 'The process of disentangling the projection – seen in someone else – from the introject – which is our own – is an integral part of personal development' (Kennefick 2006: 222). The students receive academic theory, also on a weekly basis, to support the experiential learning.

In Limerick Institute of Technology (LIT), self training is provided in a designated subject also called Personal Development (PD), which is a core subject over the four-year honours degree programme. Students receive theory within the larger class group, and weekly experiential learning through a smaller group of 10 participants (Lyons 2007). The design of the experiential programme was influenced by Kennefick (2003), where the students are encouraged to focus on current issues and informed of the support services (college counsellor) available to them if personal issues arise. The experiential group incorporates a similar methodology to the model within CIT, having the check-in and utilising psychological training frameworks. The LIT programme has three main learning objectives: listening skills, group process and ethics and values awareness training.

The programme is assessed by a reflective journal, a creative presentation to the group and a final exam.

According to Kennefick (2003), personal therapy is not part of the social care personal development programme. However, personal therapy is considered to be a necessity within counselling training. Kennefick (2006) stated she is unclear why social care workers are not encouraged to engage in personal therapy, especially in light of the intensely personal and therapeutic relationship created, and the long hours of contact involved in social care practice.

> Counsellors and therapists in training do hundreds of hours of personal therapy before they can be registered and unleashed on the public. But when we consider it – care workers have more ongoing and intimate contact with [others] than counsellors do in the traditional hour a week. (Kennefick 2003: 91)

According to Kennefick (2006: 216), personal therapy provided a safety net for therapists, preventing them from 'becoming entangled, or in some way personally invested, in the outcome of the [others'] work'. If social care workers do not learn about the self prior to practice, they also have the potential to become entangled or invested in the outcome of others.

Institute of Technology, Tralee highlighted four key subject areas where the self is trained: Communications in Professional Practice, Health and Leisure/Creative Practice, the Skills Lab and Placement. Support for the training of self is included in the following extracts:

> Students will be required to look at factors which can cause problems for communications – such as; *differences in perception, jumping to conclusions, stereotyping, lack of knowledge, lack of interest, difficulties with self-expressions, emotions, personality* – and identify a professional set of values, attitudes, assumptions and beliefs which can support and sustain effective interpersonal communication. (Institute of Technology, Tralee 2006)

> Through the media of sport, drama, music and dance students will be encouraged to develop awareness of their own unique qualities and strengths which they can bring to helping relationships. (Institute of Technology, Tralee 2006)

> In the skills lab in second and third year, the exploration of the practical and personal implications of theoretical material is actively encouraged and facilitated through some form of activity (role play/exercise). Theory can raise very different issues for different students, in acknowledging this, the skills laboratory attempts to achieve the delicate balance between the development of self, skills and theory. In this regard, it contributes to the holistic development of students through its facilitation of their personal and professional development. (Institute of Technology, Tralee 2006)

In a study of 185 graduates of the Degree in Applied Social Studies (Social Care) (Lyons 2007), 76 per cent reported that they had received self-development training within their education. The social care graduates were invited to identify where in their education they received training on the self (see Table 9.1).

Table 9.1. Self-training in Social Care Education

	Per cent
Group work	77
On placement	59
Creative studies	42
Counselling classes	38
Journal	29
Other	9

Of the respondents who reported they had received training on the self, 77 per cent located this training in 'group work', followed by 'placement' (59 per cent) and 'creative studies' (42 per cent). The level of 'self' training within either group work or creative studies depends on the ability and willingness of the student to engage in the process, and the interest and specific training of the lecturers. The self training on placement depends on the awareness of the supervisor and/or practice teacher. Therefore, the self training experience of social care students varies from college to college and student to student. Irrespective of the training or practice experience you received, if willing, you can learn how to become more self-aware.

HOW TO LEARN ABOUT THE SELF

The ability to develop or train the self depends on our motivation to aspire towards the ideal and the freedom to do so (Gould 1995). This freedom depends on the contexts to which the person is exposed. Thus, all friendships, family, work and learning contexts need to be favourable to the self-development process. In addition, we are not motivated to change the self unless we have fulfilled our basic physical and safety needs (Layder 2004). This may be relevant to the age of the students engaged in social care training. Eighteen- to 21-year-olds may be more interested in relationship development and leaving the family home than the mature student who is settled and secure and seeking a new challenge. Engaging in self-development requires the ability to accept less desirable personal qualities. However, this is only possible for people with a healthy self-esteem and a secure sense of self (Cross and Papadopoulos 2001).

According to Layder (2004), the self can be viewed as a 'project' that can be worked on, but never completed. Johns (1996) concurs by describing self-awareness as a lifelong journey that extends until retirement or death. Not all information obtained by the self develops the self. Sometimes focus or training is required to direct this awareness towards change or development, and self-awareness tools can aid this process.

Use of Self-awareness Tools

According to Kelly (1991) and Day et al. (2004), self-awareness can occur unconsciously, but for any self-awareness to promote change and have a positive effect on development, conscious rituals, environments and models are needed. Learning about the self is a personal process, and there are a variety of ways to engage in this learning, such as counselling, reflective journaling and meditation. The method is not particularly relevant, as all require willing participation and acceptance of the lessons that emerge. Two examples of how to learn about the self are presented here, which may be useful tools to begin this journey into the self.

Emergent Practice Planning

According to Ricks and Charlesworth (2003), the self is 'emergent' – a changing self is influenced by experiences and purposeful awareness. 'The challenge is to know the self at any point, because not only is your practice emergent, but you are too' (Ricks and Charlesworth 2003: 23). According to Ricks (1989), the worker has two sides: the internal 'life position', which encompasses values, ethics and beliefs, and the external behaviours, thoughts and feelings, defined as 'styles' or 'postures'. It is easy to go through the motions within the working environment, but sometimes an experience will occur that leaves a residue in your mind. This, according to Ricks and Charlesworth, is a glimpse of the internal life position. The worker can use this opportunity to check in with the possible reasons for these feelings. If a social care worker is surprised by a thought or feeling they have experienced within work, they can trace this feeling back to the source – the internal value or belief. According to Ricks and Charlesworth (2003: 23), it is not enough for the worker just to be personal – they need an 'intentional use of self'. Eckstein (1969, cited in Hawkins and Shohet 2000) described dumb spots, blind spots and deaf spots as possible blocks to becoming aware of the emergent self (see Figure 9.3).

Figure 9.3. The Three Blind Spots

BLIND SPOT
- The worker's values, attitudes, and beliefs that get in the way of seeing the service user clearly.

DEAF SPOT
- When the worker does not hear what the service user is saying. It can also refer to an inability to hear constructive criticism due to defensiveness.

DUMB SPOT
- Believing you fully understand what it is like from the perspective of the service user, without asking.

Source: Ecksteins (1969).

Self-development Using Self-awareness Snapshots

This model is how I made sense of my personal therapy and group therapy during a three-year Art Therapy training programme. Self-awareness processes present 'snapshots' of your hidden self, which you can either look at and learn from or choose to ignore. If you examine the snapshots of your hidden self, then self-development and change is the outcome. The process of change outlined in this model involves five stages – the experience, reflecting on feelings raised, action stage, self-learning snapshots and the development of self (change stage) – and is illustrated in Figure 9.4.

Figure 9.4. Self-development through Learning Snapshots

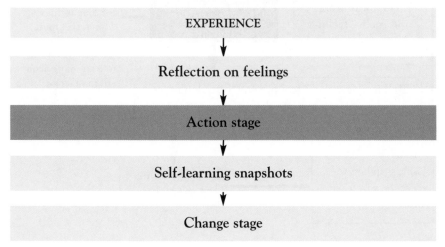

Similar to Ricks and Charlesworth (2003), here workers are encouraged to use the feelings that emerge from experiences in practice as an opportunity for self-learning. Workers are presented with a choice to either take action and learn, or to do nothing and continue as before. The choice to take action provides the workers with a self-learning snapshot and a new piece of knowledge about themselves. The learning is defined as a 'snapshot' because it is one image of the self, not the full self. This knowledge has the potential to create change, but one needs to constantly check in with the self to create a more permanent awareness and development of self. An example of how this learning tool can be used in a practice situation is illustrated in Figure 9.5.

Figure 9.5. Using the 'Self-development through Snapshots' Model in Practice

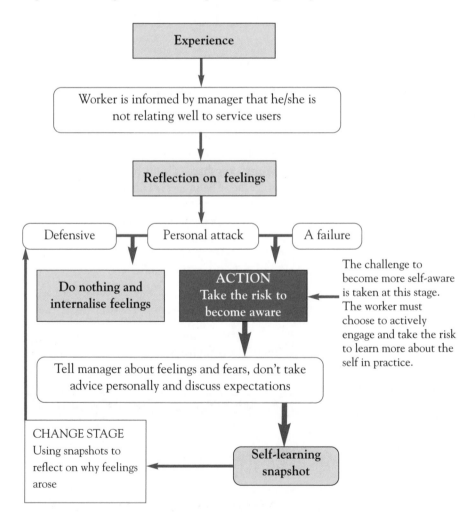

Cross and Papadopoulos (2001) and Thompson (2002b) suggest ways to enhance the development of the self by using reflective techniques, including role play, journaling and audio and video recordings. Day et al. (2004) also recommend incorporating formal ritual and the use of personal and practical experiences. All are useful; you just need to take action and begin to learn about the self.

Taking the risk to discuss your feelings and fears requires maturity, a belief in self-awareness as a process and the knowledge of how to support this learning, either using supervision within work or through the use of external consultation or therapy. Brehm et al. (1999) state that people become self-critical if they fall short of the expectations they have of themselves or the perceived expectations of others, and the outcome of critical self-awareness is a low feeling about self. Self-awareness is challenging, as this process may initially raise uneasy feelings about your strengths and weaknesses, your confidence or your overall sense of your self, so find a support system that works for you.

CONCLUSION

Recent Irish literature on the self (Garfat et al. 2005: 109) argued against 'returning to the annals of philosophy' to understand the current use of this phrase. However, the evolution of the term 'self' throughout history has an impact on how the term is viewed and used today. Self within this chapter was presented as multifaceted: our 'known' thoughts, feelings, values and beliefs and an 'unknown' or hidden self influenced by internal and external views. Both are important, as the social care worker or student must be aware of how the self influences and is affected by relationships with others.

According to Courtney (2003), in the closing line of his welcome address to the Irish Association of Social Care Educators (IASCE) conference, 'social care education and training is a journey, not a destination'. This chapter argues that both are relevant. Social care education is a journey of personal, practice and academic learning, directed towards a clear destination – employment within social care. As social care practice is a specialised profession, a specific type of worker is required. Increased self-awareness will encourage social care workers to become aware of their negative characteristics (Byrne 2000; Wosket 1999), thus enabling them to do the best that they can in full awareness of their emerging self. Having an awareness of shadow characteristics is also essential because negative traits emerge unconsciously when triggered, especially within the worker's relationship with others.

According to Fewster (1990b), Kreuger (1999) and Stuart (1999), workers need to be personal and real and be present when they are with others. Tsang (1993) wrote that it is important to be aware of how you may affect the people you are working with. Many inexperienced workers hide behind a 'professional cloak' to protect themselves from becoming involved in the work, thus maintaining a distance from others. This may not be problematic for workers, but it will certainly inhibit the experiences of the service user. By exploring the hidden self, students will encounter the way they use power and will gain an awareness of how power can be abused within social care. Through engaging in this process, students will also gain awareness of their other needs, such as their need for approval or need to be loved, and will then be able to assess if they are trying to inappropriately fulfil their own needs through vulnerable others.

All is not lost, as learning about the self can begin within social care education with self-awareness models and rituals. Unfortunately, this is not a theory that can be learned, but a process that requires the courage to take action and a belief in the benefits of knowing the self.

10

Gender and Social Care: Mapping a Structural Analysis

Jacqueline O'Toole

OVERVIEW

This chapter provides an overview of gender issues as they permeate social care. It maps debates on gender and social care that are becoming central in the academic literature and in social care practice. We require a clear understanding of the contexts 'social care' is performed in and the multiple meanings that exist amongst practitioners, educators, policy makers and employers (Gallagher and O'Toole 1999: 70). We must also consider the relative weight of the family, state, market and voluntary sectors in care work and the interconnections between them. In turn, this will generate an account of the social organisation of care work in Ireland (Lyon and Glucksman 2008).

The dominant discourse of social care work in Ireland suggests it involves a broad spectrum of specialised and professional/professionalised interventions in people's lives and that it is:

> pivotal in the delivery of a range of residential, day and community social services, particularly child care services for children at risk, services for children and adults with disabilities and other support services for marginalised groups. (Gallagher and O'Toole 1999: 71)

But as O'Connor suggests (see Chapter 7), what is missing in the debate on social care practice in Ireland is a structural analysis of its practice and delivery. In other words, it is not enough to embed an individualistic, therapeutic and 'professionalised' framework in the teaching and delivery of social care practice. Rather, in light of increasing evidence of social inequalities of race, age, education, ethnicity, gender, sexuality and disability, social care practice must embrace a radical agenda that emphasises the structural context in which problems are produced and reproduced (Rojek et al. 1988, cited in O'Connor and Murphy 2006: 89). Practitioners and social care client groups possess an economic, political and social existence *in addition* to having day-to-day needs.

Gender is one aspect of a structural analysis. Share et al. (2007: 242) suggest that the topic of gender is open to discussion from any number of vantage points. This chapter takes one such vantage point, a feminist sociological approach that sees gender inequality as an underlying feature of contemporary global societies. Such inequality needs to be analysed, explained and challenged. The chapter examines a number of gender issues that have implications for the contexts, meanings and practices of social care in Ireland. Social care practitioners can play a crucial role in the reproduction of these inequalities, but also, importantly, in the challenge to gender-based oppressions.

Three important themes will be addressed:

- The concept of gender.
- Gender processes in social care.
- The concept of sexuality, particularly as it pertains to social care practice.

WHAT IS GENDER?

Sociologists have conceptualised the relationships between women and men through a distinction between *sex* and *gender*. Sex is seen as a biological category that refers to the different physical and biological features that women and men possess, including genitals, chromosomal structures, reproductive systems and secondary sexual characteristics such as the distribution of body hair and breast development (Macionis and Plummer 2008: 367). Sex is rooted in nature and gives rise to two categories: female and male.

Gender is viewed as a social category that refers to the socially constructed and variable notions of femininity and masculinity (Oakley 1972). It is concerned with the socially ascribed characteristics associated with being female and male and with dominant ideas about what women and men should be like. At any time in any society, there may be much variation in understandings and expectations associated with the biological categories of females and males and the social categories of femininity and masculinity. Table 10.1 captures some traditional notions of these understandings found in Western societies, including Ireland.

While there have been many recent changes vis-à-vis feminine and masculine traits and gender identities, this table illustrates the idea that in many societies there exists a hierarchal gender order. In other words, this list is not just one of specific characteristics: those listed for males are often seen as positive, while those for females are negative. A gender order refers to how societies shape notions of femininity and masculinity into power relationships. When we discuss smaller groups such as a residential care home, a day-care centre or a crèche, we can investigate the workings of a *gender regime*. This refers to the gender order as it works through in smaller settings.

The simplistic distinction between sex (nature) and gender (culture) has begun to be challenged. Cross-cultural evidence suggests that simple binary oppositions

Table 10.1. Traditional Notions of a Polarised Gender Identity

Female/feminine	Male/masculine
Submissive	Dominant
Dependent	Independent
Unintelligent/incapable	Intelligent/competent
Emotional	Rational
Receptive	Assertive
Intuitive	Analytical
Weak	Strong
Timid	Brave
Content	Ambitious
Passive	Active
Co-operative	Competitive
Sensitive	Insensitive
Sex object	Sexually aggressive
Attractive because of physical appearance	Attractive because of achievement

Source: Macionis and Plummer (2008: 369).

of female/male and femininity/masculinity may not capture the complexities of gender in people's lives. Indeed, the divisions that are drawn in Table 10.1 are also social constructions. The process of gender attribution, whereby we assign ideas about gender to females and males, is itself a social process that varies from one social setting to another: witness drag and transsexualism, for example. Each involves a transgression of historically given boundaries and notions of female/male and femininity/masculinity.

A final consideration concerns the *acquisition* of gendered identities. A range of sociological theories suggests that some form of socialisation is a key part of this process. From an early age, girls and boys are exposed to their society's under-standings of gender; indeed, the process of learning about gender roles and identity begins even at birth. Clear messages about gender differences emanate from parents, caregivers, the media, peers, the education system and culture.

The socialisation thesis, while interesting, is limited. A passive conception of the person is invoked, where the child is viewed as a sponge waiting to be 'filled up' by society and culture. There is a deterministic slant to socialisation that ignores the capacity of individuals to change, resist and alter dominant meanings in society. In addition, there is a sense in which gender identity becomes the central feature of a person's identity. Thus, although women may be differentiated according to social class, ethnicity and sexual preference, in socialisation theory, the fact that they are women appears to be the overwhelming constituent of their identity. Black, lesbian and postmodernist feminists have all questioned the validity of this assumption. Other identity indicators, such as social class, ethnicity and sexual preference, heavily influence the experience of being a woman or a man and mediate femininity and masculinity.

HOW DO PERCEIVED GENDER DIFFERENCES LEAD TO GENDER INEQUALITY?

From the late 1960s onwards, gender began to appear as an organising concept in sociology and elsewhere. Inspired by the women's and civil rights movements, academics and activists started to examine how almost all societies appeared to be organised in ways that benefited men more than women. It seemed to many social observers that women's and men's lives were radically different in various ways in relation to quality of life; experience of poverty; social status; access to income, education and employment; and participation in politics and economic life.

Women were perceived as second-class citizens whose main focus in life was the reproductive sphere, through maintaining and rearing a family, while men were viewed as somehow more important citizens as they concerned themselves with life in the public sphere of politics, culture and economics. Further, relations between women and men were conducted within these types of divisions. In Ireland, various movements and organisations, including the Irish women's rights movement, began to actively challenge these assumptions and realities of everyday life and sought at both a policy and interpersonal level to overhaul what they saw as an unequal society that disproportionately benefited men (Connolly 2002). A key question that surfaced was: why? Why did these unequal relations between women and men exist?

One of the main approaches sees gender inequality as socially constructed, as made in society and as linked to an understanding of power. In the 1970s, feminists focused attention on the *patriarchal* nature of Western societies and on gender stratification to help explain continued unequal relations between women and men (Walby 1990). Patriarchy is conceptualised as the systematic patterning of society in ways that men dominate, exploit and oppress women (O'Connor 1998: 7; Walby 1990). In an Irish context, O'Connor (1998) enunciates an understanding of patriarchy as a system made up of six key structures of social relations that enable men to dominate women: paid work; the family and household; culture; sexuality; male violence; and state violence.

There are difficulties with the notion of patriarchy. It can be presented as a descriptive and universal category rather than one that is explanatory and historically specific. It suggests that *all* societies have always been patriarchal in nature and organisation. This may tell us very little about the variation in gender relations that exists within and between societies or about the subjective experiences of women and men as they seek in their everyday lives to challenge the existence of structures that dominate them. While some degree of patriarchy is universal, Macionis and Plummer (2008: 369) suggest that there is significant variation in the relative power and privilege of males and females around the world. Notwithstanding these conceptual difficulties, Share et al. (2007: 45) state that 'it is certainly the case that all societies are differentiated by gender and have been dominated in various ways by men'.

Thus, it may be a fallacy to ignore the important contribution that the concept of patriarchy offers as a descriptive and partial explanatory concept (Moane 1999). Indeed, both Walby (1990) and O'Connor (1998) articulate accounts of British and Irish society, respectively, that clearly demonstrate the many ways in which each society is organised at an overall level to benefit men. Of course, every individual man may not benefit from this system and not all women experience exploitation within such social arrangements.

To develop a more sophisticated understanding of gender differences and inequality, we can usefully turn to the work of Australian sociologist Connell (1987, 1995). Connell is concerned with the perpetuation of patriarchal social relations in the everyday lives of women and men. He argues that although gender is typically thought of as a property of individuals, it is necessary to move beyond this and conceptualise it as a property of institutions (Connell 1987: 139–41). Gender, he argues, is a fundamental feature of capitalist societies that are run mainly by, and to the benefit of, men. Every society has a gender order comprising attendant hierarchies. This is made up of a historically specific division of labour; a structure of desire; and a structure of power, authority and control. Processes and practices of patriarchal control exist at each of these levels.

A variety of masculinities (some dominant and some not) and femininities are generated within the gender order. One such form of masculinity is *hegemonic* masculinity. According to Connell (1995: 76–86), only a minority of men practise this type of masculinity, which involves active subordination of women and other men such as gay men, but he believes that most men gain an advantage from the subordination of women in terms of honour, prestige and the right to command: this is termed the 'patriarchal dividend'. The form of masculinity associated with this is *complicit* masculinity. Connell suggests that although the majority of men may not actively seek to dominate women, it is in their wider interests that traditional gendered ways of 'doing things' remain constant. Other forms of masculinity include *marginalised* (black men, working-class men), *subordinated* (gay men) and *resistant* (pro-feminist men) masculinities.

Some men view certain changes in society as an attack on their patriarchal privilege. In Irish and other Western societies, many other men are challenging and changing notions of hegemonic and complicit masculinity. Overall, I suggest that the concept of gender needs to be contextualised within a complex and sophisticated understanding of patriarchal social relations as they exist in particular societies at particular times.

GENDER PROCESSES AND SOCIAL CARE: THE LANGUAGE OF CARE

Gender is implicated in all social processes. Social care work is a gendered sphere. Following O'Connor's argument (see Chapter 7), a dearth of structural analysis in social care practice is evident in the Irish social care literature. This has by and large ignored a theoretical and applied analysis of gender (see Gallagher and O'Toole (1999) and O'Connor (1992) for initial attempts at such an analysis). If gender is included, it tends to act as a synonym for either 'women' (usually) or 'men' instead of addressing the social relations between them. But to explore aspects of the gender-related issues in social care, we first need to understand the 'language of care'. What exactly does 'care' mean?

Care is difficult to define and has been strongly contested as a concept. Unpacking the meaning of care, Fink (2004) suggests that there are inconsistencies in how the term is understood, with variables including who undertakes the care, who receives it, the relationship between the two and the social domain within which the caring takes place. One of the difficulties when teasing out the meaning of care relates to the distinctions routinely drawn between paid and unpaid caring work (Gallagher and O'Toole 1999: 78), between formal and informal care work (Feder Kittay 1999; Lynch and McLaughlin 1995) and between the public and private spheres. Moss and Cameron (2004: 224) suggest that the distinctiveness of social care is that it can transcend these dualisms and has enormous scope to reach across the life course, encompassing work with children, young people and adults of all ages (see also Kröger 2001). Lyon and Glucksman (2008) suggest that the distinction between paid and unpaid is not coterminous with that of formal and informal. There is no one-to-one pairing of paid with formal, or of unpaid with informal, evidencing yet again the need to understand contemporary transformations of (care) work across the full range of socio-economic sectors of activity.

In Ireland, at a social policy and state level, paid care work has come to refer to the provision of facilities and carrying out of tasks for those unable to do so for themselves. Carers are those *paid* to do this task (Orme 2001: 93). Although Bubeck (1995: 127) defines care as both an activity and an emotional state, in the context of formal care work, emotions may not necessarily be involved, nor indeed encouraged, in doing this work (Ungerson 1997). Some of the debates on professionalism maintain that a critical and emotional distance is necessary for social care as a profession. This is an interesting argument, as what may actually occur is the careful management of emotions in the performance of the work (see Chapter 9). More research is needed in this area in Ireland.

An understanding of care must also recognise those who receive care and the definitions they hold of the activities, tasks and relationships that unfold in the caring sphere. It is mostly women who provide and receive care in the informal sector (Gerstel and Gallagher 2001; Herd and Meyer 2002). This is largely a result of constructions of femininity that see caring as an innate female quality. This has repercussions for the formal/paid/public sector, as assumptions exist that it is only 'natural' that women will enter the caring field. In the caring marketplace, different values are placed on similar skills according to who is using them, the criteria frequently being the gender and power of the worker.

WOMEN AND MEN AS SOCIAL CARE PRACTITIONERS

In some ways, social care practice can be seen as a non-traditional occupation for men. It is seen as a 'caring' profession, and while some aspects of the work involve control and surveillance, the emphasis on care positions it as a feminised profession (Christie 1998, 2001). Orme (2001: 14) believes that the connections between social care and gender are evident in that practitioners in this sphere work, in the first instance, within gender-constructed social relationships. She suggests that the combination of social relations and power makes the concept of gender useful when analysing social care.

Furthermore, understandings and constructions of femininity and masculinity explicitly and implicitly permeate the provision of care. Lyon and Glucksman (2008) believe that all forms of care work are predominantly undertaken by women. Despite a slight increase in the proportion of men employed in care, the high proportion of women in paid employment in care work remains entrenched, making formal, paid care work more gendered than unpaid, informal care.

An emerging debate in social care concerns the small proportion of men amongst those entering the profession. It is interesting to note that an exploration of the meaning of both masculinity *and* femininity in caring contexts is at an early stage here. Key initial questions relate to the number of men working in the field, the role of men in social care and the necessity of attracting more men into care. This requires ongoing research in an Irish context. Interesting work elsewhere suggests that a structural analysis of gender and attendant links with the notion of power provides a framework in which to analyse the roles women and men enact in the social care arena, both as carers and service users (Adams et al. 2002; Cavanagh and Cree 1996; Dominelli 1997; Hanmer and Statham 1999; Hearn 1999).

Women dominate the membership of full-time programmes in social care practice courses in Ireland. The consequences are manifold, an important one being that stakeholders are only now, in an Irish context, beginning to debate some of the issues, including 'making care work attractive to men', men as carers and the possible outcomes of care provision, service use and receipt.

As social care work involves the sharing of life-space and encompasses management, therapeutic and personal care tasks (Graham 1995), gender social relations are paramount. Anecdotal evidence from the profession indicates that women and men perform quite different roles when providing and using care and, further, that such roles are rooted in a particular construction of femininity and masculinity. In relation to men, Dominelli (1997: 111–12) argues that:

feminists have been crucial in raising the problematic nature of masculinity for both men and women and revealed how men are limited in expressing the full range of their emotions and organisational skills because certain characteristics have been defined as 'feminine' and out of bounds to them.

Research indicates that when men enter non-traditional occupations such as care work, masculinity may turn out to be a boon for them, as qualities associated with men become more highly regarded than those associated with women, even in predominantly female jobs (Cree 2001: 153). Cree (2001) also observes that there are other advantages for men in non-traditional occupations: these include greater access to promotion, achieving more attention because of their small numbers and being rewarded for an ability to express feelings and emotions which, it would seem, are taken for granted in women. More research is required in an Irish context that can interrogate masculinity and the potential impact of male privileging in the social care environment.

What it means to be a male in social care is an important question, but a gendered analysis demands that this question be critically linked to a number of other questions, including:

- What does it mean to be a woman in social care?
- How are gendered social relations enacted in the social care arena?
- What discourses of femininity and masculinity exist in the training of social care practitioners and in the social care work environment? What is the impact of these discourses on individual and collective social practices?
- How can men begin to address their positions in social care in a way that takes account of their privileged positioning as men in the wider society? For instance, how is it that men, although considerably fewer in number than women in the education and training of social care practitioners, dominate the management positions in the educational institutions?
- An interrogation of femininity is also required.

There is little published material in Ireland that explores the gendered social relations that permeate interactions and interventions between social care practitioners and service users. A main goal of social care work is to empower those who use services to reach their full potential as human beings. As reflective practitioners, care practitioners must be aware of how their interactions might be underpinned by sexism and be connected to gender and power. To ensure non-oppressive practice, the generation of knowledge about gender and power, both in society and in social care, is necessary. Moreover, interactions and interventions between practitioners and users of a service must also be understood in the context of social class, sexuality, 'race' and ethnicity and attendant power relations.

THE SOCIAL CONSTRUCTION OF SEXUALITY

Sexuality, like gender, is a social construction. There is no one 'true' sexuality or way of expressing desires; rather, there exists a variety of sexualities in all societies. Sexuality is thus 'a diverse field of experience and behaviour that is brought together at certain times through a common body of language or discourse' (Share et al. 2007: 269–70).

At different times in the history of societies, different meanings and practices emerge that guide our understanding and expression of sexuality. For instance, in many Western societies, expressions of homosexual and lesbian sexuality have been negated and denied as they do not fit into dominant meanings of sexuality that emphasise heterosexuality as the norm.

Inglis (1998a, 1998b) suggests that there are powerful discourses moulding sexuality in Irish society. Discourses refer to dominant ideas and understandings about a topic that define how people experience and behave in their everyday lives. Such ideas become established as a knowledge or way of looking at the world. There may be a number of different and competing discourses at play at any one time, such as hegemonic and resistant masculinity. Discourses are linked to discipline. This means that individuals tend to be positioned in particular ways according to discourses and may be forced to behave in particular ways through self-imposed or externally imposed discipline. Importantly, within any discourse, there is always the potential to *resist* the demands placed on individual experience and behaviour.

According to Inglis (1998b), some of the more powerful discourses that mould sexuality in Irish society are generated within the family, the education system, medicine, popular culture, religion and the legal and political systems. He argues (1998a) that from the nineteenth century until the 1960s, the social construction of sexuality was immersed within discourses of sexuality promulgated by the Catholic Church, through the words and actions of bishops and priests. Sexuality was not so much hidden or repressed as talked about and enacted in a different sort of way from today. In particular, sexuality was viewed as a powerful force that needed to be regulated within the institution of marriage. The discourses linked sexuality to notions of sin, control, danger, guilt, suspicion, celibacy, purity, innocence, virginity, humility, piety and regulation that emphasised Catholic moral and social teaching (Inglis 1998b).

The Catholic Church imposed a strict discipline of sexual morality where both men and women were encouraged to feel ashamed of their bodies. This imposition may have been experienced differently by women and men. Condron (1989) and Inglis (1998b) state that women were expected to embody Catholic morality by being virtuous, chaste and virginal. If women contravened the conventions, strict sanctions were imposed.

O'Connor (1998) suggests that historically, women's sexuality was constructed around notions of reputation, marriage, childbirth/rearing and family. Since the foundation of the Irish state, women have grown up within a dominant understanding (discourse) of sexuality that specifies the woman as mother, carer and wife. O'Connor asserts that female sexuality continues to possess the following attributes: active heterosexuality; difficulties with contraception; an emphasis on the complex notion of 'love'; the experiences of sexual harassment; the stigmatising of abortion; powerful and contradictory messages around body image; sex being viewed as a consumer product; and pressures against saying 'no'.

Dominant understandings of male sexuality were constructed around the notions of the uncontrollable and insatiable nature of sexual expression for men. Historically in Ireland, male sexual expression was deemed powerful and a man's right to express himself sexually was, within reason, inalienable. Up until 1990, for instance, a man, upon marriage, had the right to demand sex from his wife, even if she resisted. In 1990, legislation was passed to criminalise rape within marriage and effectively remove the notion of wife/woman as male property. It must be noted here that the experiences of many men in Irish society did not and do not conform to these dominant discourses.

Great change has taken place in the past 30 years with regard to sexual attitudes and practices. Sexuality has become public in Irish society: a new way of speaking by a variety of commentators has emerged to directly challenge and contest Catholic discourses of sexuality. Diversity, pleasures, preferences and choices have become the concepts that underpin the deployment of sexuality in contemporary Ireland (Layte et al. 2006). Freely available contraception; the decriminalisation of male homosexuality; the equalisation of age of consent between lesbians, gay men and heterosexuals; co-habitation; and the public celebration of sex in and outside marriage have all been part of the new discourses of sexuality.

Sexuality is 'out there' and 'in here': in the media, in the school playground, in the nightclub, in the minds and bodies of Irish people. Inglis (1998a) believes that what we now require is an analysis of Irish sexuality that describes and analyses how sexuality was and is seen, understood and embodied by participants in Irish social life. There are still substantial gaps in our knowledge about sexual attitudes and behaviour in Ireland (see Layte et al. 2006 for the first attempt at a systematic sociological analysis of sexuality in Ireland). Much has changed in terms of sexual expression, including greater acceptance of the multifarious ways in which people live their sexual lives, but sexuality must be understood as linked to particular understandings of femininity and masculinity in society and to gender social relations and power.

SEXUALITY AND SOCIAL CARE

We have seen that it is important to reach a better understanding of gender social relations in the social care environment. It is also important to explore the links between gender, power and sexuality in social care environments. Social care work is characterised by the sharing of life-space. Expressions of sexuality thus permeate the everyday interactions of social care practitioners and service users in a variety of ways that include touch, looking, physical stance, clothes and language. Within the social care setting, this can have major consequences for the level and type of interactions; concerns with and about behaviour; planning and controlling activities; developing care plans; specifying interventions; and general day-to-day living. As Irish academic studies of sexuality are limited, it is no surprise to find no published text or piece of research that deals with its impact in the social care environment in an Irish context.

This is not to say that sexuality has never been talked about in relation to social care. The topic has been addressed in the development of 'good' models of practice in the disability sector and within children's and youth centres. Organisations are developing in-house programmes and policies with regard to people with learning difficulties and sexuality. Topics such as self-advocacy in terms of sexual expression; protection of vulnerable people against sexual exploitation; age-appropriate sexual behaviour; development of relevant sex education programmes; and responsibility in sexual behaviour are inherent in such programmes and policies. Such programmes may become particularly relevant in an Irish context with the many revelations of sexual abuse in institutional care.

Many such programmes and policies operate within a discourse of sexuality that has placed issues of *regulation* and control at the forefront. There is a need for ongoing research to tease out the implications of regulation and control for both the care practitioner and the service user. The increasing emphasis in wider society on liberal attitudes to sexuality suggests that issues of self-advocacy and the role of appointed advocates are central to the debates on sexuality, especially as service users demand greater control over their sexual selves.

Managing sexuality and sex in human relationships is difficult. Humans have developed complex ways to manage and deal with their feelings in all kinds of relationships (Cavanagh and Cree 2001). Since the mid-1990s in Ireland, *protection* has become a key element of the practice of social care work. The numerous accounts of sexual abuse have left social care practitioners and service users with a legacy so powerful it now guides the types of physical and intimate interactions that occur.

It is necessary to develop good practice models that protect all actors in these kinds of social relationships. The issues are complex. On the one hand, the protection of service users and practitioners is paramount. On the other hand, a crying child, missing its parents, sometimes needs the security and intimacy of human touch. The fear attached to expressions of affection between practitioner and service user must be unpacked to uncover what this fear is about and where it comes from. Sex and sexuality are sometimes viewed as sensitive areas that are too difficult to discuss with service users. Yet as many social care practitioners act *in loco parentis*, it will be necessary at some stage to deal with sexuality with clients.

As in all social relationships, it is imperative that social care practitioners develop an awareness of their own sexuality. Increasing awareness will help social care practitioners to acknowledge their own feelings and desires and how these affect their professional relationships with their clients. Social care practitioners must understand and acknowledge their own sexuality in order to work effectively and safely with others.

An important dimension of any discussion on sexuality is language. How people speak about sexuality and sex and the terms they use impact on social behaviour. Language usage is connected to power and the ability of certain people to speak for and about others. For instance, terms like 'slag' and 'slut' may have particular consequences for women's feelings and actions in their everyday lives (Lees 1993; O'Toole 1998). Terms like 'sissy', 'cunt', 'faggot' and 'queer' are currently employed as terms of abuse that, if used in the social care context (or indeed any social context), contribute to oppressive practices. Words for sexual behaviour and genitals carry considerable power. Social care practitioners must examine their own use of language and the use of language in the social care context to avoid perpetuating oppressive behaviours.

A final issue to consider with regard to sexuality and social care is the link between sexual preference, particularly homosexuality, and anti-oppressive practice. Share et al. (2007) suggest that one of the more rapidly changing discussions around sexuality in Ireland relates to the experiences of lesbians and gay men. In 1993, sexual relations between men were decriminalised. Women had never been covered by the Victorian legislation that had criminalised sexual relations between men. Although equality legislation has been enacted to protect gay people, amongst others, this has not necessarily meant that the everyday lives of gay people in Ireland are left untouched by anti-gay feeling and outright discrimination.

O'Carroll and Collins (1995) and O'Brien (2003) document aspects of the many and varied lives of gay people in Ireland, including their experiences of coming out, relationships, discrimination, national identity and sense of self. Despite significant changes in Irish society with regard to sexuality, there is still considerable work to be done to achieve an egalitarian existence for gay people. Further, the inequalities of gender that permeate wider society also infuse the lives of gay men and lesbians. Their experiences as gay are not symmetrical. Lesbians can experience discrimination on the basis of being women, just as gay men may benefit from being men within a patriarchal gender order.

Within care work, cognisance must be taken of the issues that affect gay men and lesbians as practitioners and client service groups. It is useful if social care practitioners develop an increased awareness of their own sexuality and attitudes to sexuality. Anti-oppressive practice – part of social care work training and practice in many countries, including Britain – demands that the lives of gay people be both protected and celebrated within the social care environment (Department of Health and Children 2007; Thompson 2006). Social care training in Ireland makes limited use of anti-oppressive practice in its training and education programmes. Modules on equality are part of some social care programmes.

Anti-oppressive practices refer not only to the need to challenge attitudes and practices towards gay people, but also to challenge other ways in which people are discriminated against, including ethnicity, 'race', gender, social class, age, disability, education, marital status, family status and religion (see Chapter 19).

It is imperative that social care – in theory, policy and practice – revisits its values base to assess its relevance and contribution to anti-oppressive practice. It is only in recent decades that learning about homosexuality has been removed from 'abnormal' psychology modules. Labelling anything 'abnormal' is questionable in the context of the need to explore the value of anti-oppressive practice.

In summary, this section has explored some of the sexuality issues that pervade the social care environment and which facilitate the mapping of a structural analysis of social care. Sexuality is a complex feature of all human relationships and developing an awareness of how it impacts on social care is crucial. Further, increased awareness of sexuality will facilitate the discipline in developing anti-oppressive practices in relation to sexuality, racism, social class, ethnicity, age and disability.

CONCLUSION

This chapter has introduced an array of gender processes that are central to an understanding of social care work in Ireland in order to initiate mapping a structural analysis. I have argued that gender is a complex concept, the meaning of which must be contextualised within an understanding of patriarchal social relations in the wider society. Forms of femininity and masculinity vary within and between societies. Their constructions within care work may provide an insight into how gender is understood within society generally. Social care would benefit from a structural analysis to interrogate the relational categories of both femininity and masculinity as they are enacted by relevant social actors in the various social care arenas.

11

Evidence-based Practice in Social Care

Tom Farrelly

OVERVIEW

This chapter introduces the concept of evidence-based practice and how it might be used in social care. As a current or future professional practitioner, you need to be mindful of adopting a critical and inquisitorial approach to research or, more importantly, evidence. You are encouraged to develop a 'research-minded' approach to your practice.

If you have asked or have been asked 'How did you do that?' or 'Why did you do it that way?', you have engaged in research. We often think of research as a ponderous calling pursued by serious-minded people removed from the hustle and bustle of 'real life'. Research is often seen as a remote activity, particularly by those at the coalface of practice. Yet many practitioners are engaged in the research process, even if they do not realise it. Every time you read a study, report, journal article or review document, you are consuming research. If there were no readers, there would be no research, thus you are an invaluable link in the research chain. But as well as being *consumers* of research, practitioners can and should be *producers* of research.

WHAT IS EVIDENCE-BASED PRACTICE?

There is nothing new about the idea that policy and practice should be informed by the best available evidence. Evidence-based practice (EBP) was first introduced in medicine and allied health professions. More recently it has been advocated in social work as an alternative to 'authority-based practice' or practice based solely on the expertise and experience of practitioners (Edmond et al. 2006). Gibbs and Gambrill (2002: 452) define evidence-based practice as 'the conscientious, explicit, and judicious use of current best evidence in making decisions about the care of clients'.

Evidence-based practice has become a byword for better, more appropriate and efficient practice. In essence, an evidence-based approach asks that practitioners use the best available evidence to guide and inform their practice. We need to ask ourselves what constitutes best evidence and how we choose one source of evidence over another (Sheppard 2004). In addition, we need to unpack the term 'evidence-based practice', particularly as it relates to the area of social care.

Appleby et al.'s (1995) definition of EBP reveals its medical origins, noting that it represents a shift in health care decision-making. Evidence-based practice represents a move away from opinion, past practice and precedent towards a decision-making framework that relies on greater use of research and evidence. The basic principles underlying the EBP movement are that there is a hierarchy of evidence and that modern information systems can make the evidence available to practitioners at the point of care.

WHY AN EVIDENCE-BASED APPROACH TO SOCIAL CARE?

The Department of Health and Children policy document, *Working for Children and Families: Exploring Good Practice*, outlines seven management principles that should underpin child and family services, including the need for practitioners and their managers to 'ensure that their practice and its supervision are grounded in the most up-to-date knowledge' (Department of Health and Children 2004c: 15). In addition to making use of relevant research, the report suggests, practitioners should draw evidence from local statistical data, national policies, evaluations and audits and the lessons learned from case reviews.

Williams (2000) argues that the benefits of an evidence-based approach for social care work are:

1. More effective social care interventions.
2. Improved resource efficiency.
3. Improved analytical practice.
4. Raising the status of social care professionals.
5. Improved public confidence in social care.

Marsh and Fisher (2005: 3–4) make some strong arguments for the adoption of a research evidence-based approach and these are summarised in Table 11.1.

Few would argue that social care interventions should not be as effective as possible: the argument is that the use and application of new or existing interventions should be informed by evidence. While the arguments for the adoption of an evidence-based approach may be convincing, it should be noted that finding and using research, particularly of high relevance and good quality, is not always easy.

Table 11.1. Arguments for the Adoption of Evidence-based Practice

Reason	Argument
Impact on the immediate life chances of service users	In extreme cases, such as child protection, decisions may influence life-or-death situations; practitioners should be as informed as possible.
Impact on the long-term life chances of service users	Decisions made may well affect long-term life chances such as educational outcomes or mental health; practitioners should be as informed as possible.
Challenge to fundamental assumptions about social care	Evidence may produce a shift in the way practitioners, service users, the public and other allied professions see social care work.
Providing safeguards to service users	There are substantial areas of social care where professionals have strong powers or where the courts may make decisions regarding major aspects of people's lives ... best available evidence is an important component of processes of control of this power.
Encourage and facilitate a more informed public	An informed public can better engage with relevant debates about services ... it is right that citizens have access to the best evidence.
Informed service user and carer communities, and individuals	Direct involvement in services and engagement with the development of services requires access to the best evidence.

Source: Marsh and Fisher (2005).

ISSUES IN ADOPTING AN EVIDENCE-BASED APPROACH TO SOCIAL CARE PRACTICE

Stevens et al. (2007) have reviewed the research priorities of UK practitioners working with children in social care. They highlight a number of important issues with regard to the expansion of the use of EBP. They found that social care practitioners make limited use of research findings in practice. The barriers to using research included a lack of time, lack of research skills and research resources and, in many organisations, an underdeveloped culture of research use. Another problem highlighted was the range of target groups in social care: practitioners work with a wide range of clients, thus making it more difficult to adopt a unified approach to research.

Rosen (2003: 199) identifies five factors that impede implementation of evidence-based practice:

1. Characteristics of the knowledge to be used.
2. Characteristics of the practice situation and setting.
3. Attributes of the medium through which the knowledge is communicated.
4. Characteristics of the practitioner.
5. The social-cultural context in which utilisation takes place.

Some aspects of these are explored in the remainder of this chapter.

WHAT CONSTITUTES EVIDENCE?

Using research in social care requires the integration of different types of *knowledge*. Pawson et al. (2003) have usefully produced a system for the classification of the sources of social care knowledge (Table 11.2).

Table 11.2. Sources of Social Care Knowledge

Type	Source
Organisational	Knowledge gained from organising social care, through governance and regulation activities.
Practitioner	Knowledge gained from doing social care, which tends to be tacit, personal and context specific.
User	Knowledge gained from experience of and reflection on using social care services, which again is often tacit.
Research	Knowledge gathered systematically within a planned strategy, which is mostly explicit and provided in reports, evaluations and so forth.
Policy community	Knowledge gained from the wider policy context and residing in the civil service, ministries, think tanks and agencies.

Source: Pawson et al. (2003: 22).

This system does not imply that all sources of knowledge are equally regarded: research or empirical knowledge generally appears to be held in the highest esteem. Furthermore, not all research is regarded equally; health care, for example, has a well-established 'hierarchy of evidence'. At the top of this hierarchy are randomised controlled experiments and systematic reviews; conversely, studies employing observation are regarded as having less rigour and credibility (Davies and Nutley 1999). This dichotomy in sources of evidence is frequently characterised by the conceptual shorthand of *quantitative* and *qualitative* for different approaches to research.

Qualitative research is a generic term for a range of different methodologies (Flick et al. 2004). While these vary in their object of investigation and methodological focus, they share a number of defining characteristics. For Bryman (2004: 19–20), the qualitative approach is a 'research strategy that usually emphasises words rather than quantification in the collection and analysis of data'. It rejects the practices and understandings of the natural scientific model that is *positivism* and instead emphasises how individuals interpret and construct reality. From this perspective, the social world is not the same as the natural world: human beings can react differently in similar situations. Research methods or tools associated with this approach include observation, diaries and interviews.

Quantitative research, as its name suggests, 'is a research strategy that emphasises quantification and analysis of data' (Bryman 2004: 19). It reflects the practices and norms of the scientific or positivist model with its understanding that social reality is an external, objective and measurable reality (Sarantakos 2005). This type of research is characterised by the tight control of the variables under investigation, protocols for measurement and intervention and the use of statistical testing to establish levels of confidence in the results (Houser 2008). Research methodologies associated with this approach often include quasi and natural experiments and surveys and sophisticated statistical analysis.

The two research approaches are not necessarily regarded as being of equal value. With its presumed adherence to superior procedural rigour and validity, it is argued that quantitative studies 'produce some of the strongest evidence for the benefits of an intervention' (Houser 2008: 38). Conversely, qualitative research is sometimes accused of being too impressionistic and subjective and it may be difficult to generalise findings (Bryman 2004).

This either/or dichotomy should be treated with some degree of caution and scepticism. Layder (1993) argues that this debate is no longer useful, going so far as to suggest that it is a false distinction with no real merit. Punch (1998) argues that being at loggerheads about which approach is better misses the point – the question should simply be what is the most appropriate method to answer the research question posed? Plath (2006: 64) argues that judging research 'becomes more complex than deciding between qualitative and quantitative approaches'. Regardless of the research approach used, the knowledge produced by empirical studies is frequently regarded as superior to the knowledge produced by users and practitioners.

HOW DO I CRITIQUE EVIDENCE?

There is sometimes a tendency to overestimate the quality of a piece of research, particularly if the reader is less than familiar with the topic in question or inexperienced in evaluating research. Just because a study has been published does not necessarily mean it is good-quality research. The informed practitioner not only knows what the research says about the topic, he/she is also able to judge the quality and the relevance of the research (Sheppard 2004). Becoming an evidence-based practitioner requires adopting a critical stance to research. Being critical does not mean *criticising* by simply pointing out the limitations of the study (Burns and Grove 1997). Rather, it is about *critiquing* a piece of research through a methodical appraisal of the strengths and weaknesses of a study in order to determine its credibility (Coughlan et al. 2007).

The key word in this instance is *methodical*: we need to adopt a step-by-step process that will enable us to make an informed judgement about the quality of the evidence offered. The framework outlined in Table 11.3 uses the questions a journalist might ask in order to understand a story: who, what, why, when and where? As noted earlier, there are two broad types of research: qualitative and quantitative. While each has its own theoretical and methodological approaches and considerations, a number of common questions can be applied.

Table 11.3. Critiquing Research: An Introductory Framework

Who?	• Who are the authors: are they practitioners and/or academics? What qualifications and experience do they have? Are they noted in their field of expertise? • Who commissioned the study? There may be an issue of funding bias; he who pays the piper may call the tune. • Who was the target population of the study? Are they so dissimilar to the group that you work with that lessons may be difficult to apply? • Who is the study aimed at? Is it meant for general readership, academics, policy makers and/or practitioners?
Where?	• Where is the study published? A peer-reviewed journal? A government report? Peer-reviewed journals generally adopt a more rigorous approach and consequently the study's integrity and reliability may be greater. • Where was the study conducted? If the location is very different, can the findings be applied to your own workplace?
Why?	• Why was the study undertaken? Is it part of a postgraduate programme? Was it undertaken to evaluate an intervention or initiative? • Why did the author adopt one research method in preference to another? Is this justified and consistent with the overall research approach, whether qualitative or quantitative? Do the methods chosen add to the general credibility and reliability of the study and were they carried out in an appropriate manner?

When?	• When was the study carried out? How recent is the publication? Has the context changed much over time?
What?	• What operational definitions were employed? For example, if the study is about investigating poverty, what definition of poverty is being employed? • What ethical safeguards were put in place? Were participants fully informed about their rights, such as confidentiality and anonymity, and were they able to withdraw at any time? • What was the timeframe? Was it a longitudinal or a cross-sectional study? A cross-sectional study simply provides a once-off 'snapshot' of a phenomenon or event, which is useful but limited. • What is the research question? Is it clearly stated? Qualitative-type studies are interested in understanding, not testing, thus they will simply have a question, while quantitative-type studies employ testable hypotheses to either be proven or disproven. • What size was the sample and how was the sample selected? In quantitative studies, sample sizes are required to be at least 30 in order to be considered statistically significant. In addition, probability or randomly selected samples are considered to be more appropriate. Qualitative studies are less concerned with probability and minimum sizes and more with providing a deep and rich understanding of the topic. • What is the strength of the link between the evidence and the conclusions and recommendations? Has the author made a logical and believable argument?

This framework is not intended to be comprehensive; what it offers is a useful toolbox you can use to begin the process of critiquing articles, reports and studies.

UTILISING THE INTERNET AS A SOURCE OF RESEARCH

The majority of searches for evidence are now undertaken using electronic sources; in practice, this means using the internet. It is important to realise and understand the range of search facilities open to the practitioner and researcher. Students or practitioners who have access to an online library facility can remotely retrieve a vast range of journals through databases such as EBSCO, Ingenta, ERIC, CINAHL and MEDLINE.

For the hard-pressed practitioner or student, the internet is a powerful research tool, providing remote access to a wealth of material. Search engines have become an increasingly important part of the online experience for the majority of internet users. Well-known providers such as Google and Yahoo! dominate the market, providing a quick and easy-to-use search tool. A useful part of the Google service is the Scholar option, which allows users to access a wide range of academic papers. It is limited in that it often links only to a title and abstract rather than full text; nonetheless, it provides a relatively quick way to search a wide range of academic sources and can provide a starting point in the search for evidence.

Another recent phenomenon that has provided a source of reference for count-less students throughout the world is the world's leading online encyclopaedia, Wikipedia. As with all sources of evidence, it is important to exercise caution and judgement. The problem with judging the trustworthiness of information 'on the World Wide Web is becoming increasingly acute as new tools such as wikis and blogs simplify and democratise publications' (Dondio et al. 2006: 362). On Wikipedia, topics are edited by the users, allowing any user to contribute information on a topic, but the sites also rely on other users to correct errors found on the site. While a number of stories have highlighted the vulnerability of Wikipedia to hoaxes (Parfitt, T. 2006), there have also been studies that argue that Wikipedia is generally reliable. As a source of information to help clarify or introduce a topic, Wikipedia is useful, but as a source of definitive evidence upon which to base practice, the best advice is the Latin phrase 'caveat emptor' ('buyer beware').

Whichever source is used, it is vital that clear search terms are used. Gossett and Weinman (2007: 147) provide a useful step-by-step guide to using electronic sources for locating evidence:

- *Step 1:* Convert client needs into answerable questions. Questions that lend themselves to searching for the best evidence must be specific enough to generate an answer in an electronic search.
- *Step 2:* Locate the best external evidence to answer the question. This step requires access to bibliographic databases such as the Cochrane Database or Campbell Collaboration. In addition to database access, the skills to effectively navigate the various sources are important.
- *Step 3:* Critically evaluate the evidence. The framework in Table 11.3 can be employed as a useful starting tool. When critically evaluating the evidence, Gibbs (2003) recommends the use of a rating form, such as the Quality of Study Rating Form, which can be located in his book *Evidence-based Practice for the Helping Professions.*[1] Whichever framework or analysis tool is employed, the important feature is that it is a systematic approach.

WHERE CAN I FIND CRITIQUED RESEARCH?

No framework can be considered exhaustive and this one is no exception. Nonetheless, it provides the novice researcher with a useful way to begin the process of evaluating empirical evidence. As you become more adept at evaluating research, you may wish to enhance your range of research sources.

Sifting through a series of research documents can be very time consuming. What the hard-pressed student or practitioner needs is a clearinghouse for research. Luckily, there is such an organisation: the Campbell Collaboration. This resource is based on a well-established facility, the Cochrane Collaboration, which contains systematic reviews of randomised control trials in the biomedical arena. The Campbell Collaboration has adopted the protocols developed by its older sister organisation: it maintains a large group of members, reviewers and contributors who undertake systematic reviews in the areas of crime and justice, social welfare and education. The Cochrane Collaboration, with its medical focus, may be of less use to social care practitioners; nonetheless, it can provide useful material on topics such as mental health and health promotion.

A *systematic review* is an extensive and rigorous literature review that focuses on a single question with the aim of identifying, appraising and summarising existing research studies in order to derive guidelines that can inform practice (Houser 2008). From the student or practitioner's perspective, a systematic review can take a lot of the drudgery and guesswork out of finding and evaluating a wide range of studies. The following scenario provides an example of how using a systematic review can aid evidence-based practice.

SCENARIO

You are a social care practitioner in a children's residential unit. One of the children (a 13-year-old girl) has a history of being sexually abused. In preparation for her next case review meeting, the unit manager has asked that you investigate possible interventions to be included as part of the forthcoming discussions.

In addition to your own and co-workers' knowledge and experience and some locally sourced research, you are keen to explore the range of available interventions. Thus you undertake the following search:

1. Access the Campbell Collaboration (C2) website at http://campbell collaboration.org.
2. You now have two options:
    (a) Access the 'social welfare' tab; click on the sidebar menu for protocols, reviews and related papers and scroll down the webpage looking for possible suitable reviews; or
    (b) Click on the link for the C2-RIPE's Report Generator. This method has the advantage of doing the search for you, provided you specify the criteria.
3. Through the search, a promising review is identified: *Cognitive-behavioural Interventions for Children Who Have Been Sexually Abused* (Macdonald et al. 2006). In investigating the efficacy of cognitive behavioural approaches (CBT), this review synthesises 10 studies involving 847 children into one accessible and comprehensible document.
4. The reviewers note that CBT offers some positive possible outcomes but that the evidence offered only enables a tentative conclusion to be drawn.

In reality, you would need to undertake a more comprehensive search; nonetheless, this example demonstrates how you might access a wide range of well-reviewed research material that in turn can be used to inform your study or practice.

It is important to note that despite the huge advantages that the internet presents to the student, researcher and practitioner, other media continue to be of great importance. Traditional sources of evidence such as books, theses, print journals and conference proceedings can inform practice. A systematic and critical approach should be employed regardless of the source of evidence (Tremblay and Downey 2004).

PRACTITIONERS AS RESEARCHERS

Social care is a practice-based discipline, so there remains a potential difficulty in reconciling empirical scientific knowledge with that derived from experience and practice. As noted above, the former have taken precedence over the latter (Brechin and Siddell 2000): this reflects what Schön (1991a) has termed 'technical rationality'. The philosopher Gilbert Ryle (1963) suggests that prepositional or 'knowing that' knowledge 'precedes and informs "knowing how" – that we must first learn the theory before applying it to practice' (cited in Rolfe et al. 2001: 6). If this is the case, then it can be appreciated how scientific theories or the 'knowing that' knowledge came to be seen as having pre-eminence over experiential 'knowing how'.

The former Director of Research at the Joseph Rowntree Foundation, Janet Lewis (2001), offers a more balanced view of the knowledge base for social care:

knowledge = evidence + practice wisdom + service user and
carer experiences and wishes

As you can see from this formula, there is no hierarchy. Knowledge is the equal combination of all three components: evidence (empirical research), the practice wisdom or practitioner knowledge and the users' and carers' experiences and wishes. This formula posits that practitioners as well as researchers can be the producers of knowledge and evidence. From this perspective, it can be argued that as well as *using* knowledge to become evidence-based practitioners, these same practitioners can *produce* knowledge and so inform others in their practice.

Engaging in research is widely accepted as being one of the defining characteristics of a profession. For Tripodi (1974), many of the processes and skills used in professional practice transfer easily and support the tasks required to undertake research. For example, in social work, practitioners are required to make an initial assessment while the researcher is required to formulate a question. The social worker is then required to design an implementation plan, while the researcher is required to design a strategy that will enable the collection of the data, and so on. In essence, research and practice are about applying a methodical approach to solving a problem. You may have begun the process of becoming research-minded already without necessarily being aware of it.

When starting a research project, where do you begin? Table 11.4 provides some suggested entry points for beginning research (adapted from the Research Mindedness Virtual Learning Resource at www.resmind.swap.ac.uk).

Table 11.4. Entry Points for Beginning Research

A problem in practice – an idea to test	A number of social care practitioners have reported that the effectiveness of therapeutic crisis intervention (TCI) with children in residential care appears to drop markedly after two years of use. Why might this be so?
A gap in the available data	The child protection team has produced local guidelines to help indicate whether an injury to a child might be non-accidental, but there appears to be no such guidelines to draw upon for the elder care team. Surely such guidelines must exist: could these be sourced and presented to the team?
Service evaluation	Your family support unit has introduced summer camps as a pilot project. Anecdotal evidence seems to indicate success, but you need to evaluate the effectiveness if you are to seek continued funding.

Source: www.resmind.swap.ac.uk.

Research can involve a large team with plenty of resources and the focusing on a large number of people. It can also focus on one or two people and be carried out by a lone researcher. Just because the focus of a piece of research may be small and it may have little widespread applicability does not mean that undertaking that study is not worthwhile.

THE RELATIONSHIP BETWEEN RESEARCH, POLICY AND PRACTICE

Although the need to translate research messages into policy and practice has been recognised and improved, this tripartite relationship continues to be complex. Policymakers often want research messages that are unequivocal and relevant to current and impending issues.

Gaffney and Harmon (2007), in an overview of the proceedings of the National Economic and Social Forum (NESF) conference on evidence-based policy-making, note that while it is not the role of the research community to design policy, it does have a role to 'assist in the design of policy, evaluation of its effectiveness and perhaps challenging the policymaker … based on the available evidence' (2007: 8). At the same conference, the then Taoiseach, Bertie Ahern, noted the importance of an evidenced-based approach, stating that 'the better quality information we have, the better founded our beliefs and working models will be' (Ahern 2007: 13).

A CAUTIONARY NOTE

While there are apparent benefits to the adoption of EBP, it should be noted that there have been a number of concerns raised. These can be summarised as:

- Questions about the appropriateness and validity of the scientific or positivist approach to the generation of evidence.
- Questions about the genuineness of the motives behind the adoption of an evidence-based approach, notably if the move is really about a managerialist push for efficiencies.

Plath (2006: 57) argues that:

> the association of evidence-based practice with a scientific or positivist paradigm can produce tension for social workers who recognise the importance of reflective, interpretive and humanist responses to the personal and social conditions encountered in practice.

This tension can result in the marginalisation of the esoteric and aesthetic elements of care work, such as intuition and reflection. These cannot easily be reduced to quantifiable, measurable constructs and hence do not lend themselves easily to positivistic reductionism.

As previously noted, one of the arguments for introducing an EBP approach is that it should bring improved resource efficiencies. But the pursuit of greater efficiencies can only be carried so far; agencies do need adequate resources. Adoption of an EPB approach to practice requires an honest appraisal of a number of issues, not least an agency's ability to implement new regimes or ways of operating. Fundamental issues such as staff workload, physical resources and staff qualifications also need to be considered. However attractive it may be to adopt a more evidence-based approach to practice, the mundane issues also need to be attended to: 'EBP will not overcome structural issues like caseload size' (Blome and Steib 2004: 612).

CONCLUSION

A formalised evidence-based approach to social care practice remains largely underdeveloped. Nonetheless, it should be acknowledged that many practitioners are engaged in practice that is informed and reflective. There is much research available that focuses on the topics of interest to social care practitioners, such as childhood, addiction, intellectual disability and so on. The amount of this research that constitutes 'quality evidence' remains debatable. Social services are by their very nature fluid and dynamic, and practitioners need to be mindful of adopting a dogmatic approach. Sheppard (2004: 23) argues that practitioners should be 'looking at information that can help provide *guidance* and *better-informed judgements* but not certainty' (italics in original). Perhaps, ultimately, the term 'research-informed practice' might be more applicable than 'evidence-based practice'.

Part III

Working in Social Care

12

The Social Care Practice Placement: A College Perspective

Judy Doyle and Kevin Lalor

OVERVIEW

The aim of this chapter is to examine the supervision, management and operation of social care students' practice placements and to outline the roles of the student, the placement supervisor and the college tutor. Social care students may be placed in a wide variety of statutory and non-statutory agencies, such as residential care homes, special schools, high-support care, community work, homeless agencies, drug treatment centres, disability services and care of the elderly. Placements are an integral component of all courses in social care. The student, the college tutor and the placement supervisor are central to the student's placement experience and form a triad in practical and academic communication.

Figure 12.1. The Tripartite Relationship between Student, Supervisor and Tutor

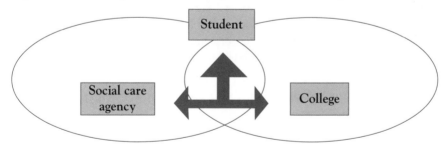

The triad of placement supervisor (also referred to as practice teacher), college tutor and student (Figure 12.1) is central to the 'learning by doing' model adopted by social care courses. The practice placement is the interface between theoretical knowledge and practical experience of hands-on work. Individual thresholds of stress, strengths and weaknesses are explored and tested at the coalface of social care practice. Coping mechanisms are enhanced and developed. The *Practice Placement Manual* for IASCE (the Irish Association of Social Care Educators) states:

On placement, the students experience the world of work, with its ups and downs. They see the impact of dedicated staff in difficult situations. They encounter the teamwork that goes on behind the scenes in meetings and networking. They get to know how organisations work and relate to each other. (IASCE 2009: 7)

Hence, the student placement should offer a secure and supportive environment for learning and imparting knowledge.

KEY PLAYERS

The placement supervisor is generally an experienced, qualified social care practitioner who has undertaken to supervise the student's work practice in the particular agency. The college tutor is generally a member of the lecturing staff who monitors the student's progress with regard to course requirements. Finally, and most importantly, the student is registered on a programme of study and is committed to becoming an effective social care practitioner.

In this chapter, we will examine:

- The purpose of the practice placement.
- Key events before the practice placement.
- Key events during the practice placement.
- Key events after the practice placement.

The chapter is illustrated with:

- Placement experiences of two social care students in Dublin Institute of Technology (DIT), which provide valuable insight into the challenges and complexities of social care practice placements.
- A particular focus on coping with challenging behaviour.

THE PURPOSE OF SOCIAL CARE STUDENTS' PRACTICE PLACEMENTS

The purpose of practice placement is to expose the student to the practical world of social care work in a controlled manner in order to facilitate the acquisition of practice skills. The goals are to link theory to practice and to aid learning through the acquisition of practice skills. Consequently, placements are designed to encourage the development of a professional social care practitioner who is:

- Able to work therapeutically with clients.
- Reliable, responsible, intuitive and observant.
- Capable of problem-solving.

- Competent in effective, efficient decision-making.
- Able to implement and evaluate the effectiveness of treatment programmes.
- Sensitive in communication with vulnerable people.
- Able to understand a client's value system.
- Aware of the needs and rights of various client groups.
- Able to respond appropriately to collective and individual needs.
- Skilled in forming relationships.
- A constructive team worker.
- Respectful of confidentiality.
- Able to keep records and case files.

Initially, placement may prove a daunting prospect. It may be the student's first experience of the world of work; it may be their first exposure to a client group of which they have various misconceptions, apprehensions and stereotypes; they will almost certainly find the work physically tiring; and finally, it may trigger a host of unexpected emotional responses. We will examine these issues in further detail later in the chapter.

Accordingly, the practice placement is an aspect of social care education that must be carefully managed. Though fortunately rare, negative placement experiences can lead to profound student discouragement, even to the extent of leaving the social care area altogether. This chapter examines issues that must be considered before, during and after the practice placement so that we maximise the number of students who find their placement to be a positive, rewarding experience.

KEY EVENTS BEFORE THE PRACTICE PLACEMENT

Supervision of students by college tutors begins on their first day in college. It should involve individual and class tutorials, the development of relationships with lecturers and monitoring of pastoral and academic well-being. Students are requested to read and familiarise themselves with IASCE (the Irish Association of Social Care Educators) and college student placement handbooks, where common standards on student placements are documented. A number of important factors for tutors to consider before a student is allocated a social care placement are noted in the following section.

Quality of Fit

An early consideration for the college tutor is the compatibility of the student's abilities with the requirements of the agency. While a majority of students will adjust well to most working environments, there are exceptions. Occasionally, a placement will be terminated because of gross unsuitability. Whether it is as a result of the particular demands of an agency or because of the personality of a given student, student placement 'fit' must be given serious thought. Tutor familiarity with the demands and expectations of agencies is essential. A college tutor will strive to build up knowledge of care agencies that can provide high-quality supervision of students. In certain circumstances, a student might present certain traits that are particularly demanding of supervisors. For example, a student may have failed practice placements in the past or shown resistance to instruction. Some supervisors pride themselves on being able to provide a positive learning experience for students who have previously had unhappy experiences.

The student's preferences must also be considered. Ideally, a student should experience a wide range of social care agencies and client groups, which provides him/her with an overview of the range of social care work situations. Students should have the opportunity to express preferences for particular client groups. Occasionally, a student will have overwhelming apprehensions about a particular client group, often as a result of circumstances in his or her own background. Such fears must be respected, and students should not be placed in a position where they are fearful on work placement. Of course, confronting mild apprehensions is an important aspect of practice placement and is usually resolved satisfactorily. Indeed, there is a strong sense of empowerment in overcoming initial apprehensions and learning to be comfortable with, and work effectively with, a particular client group.

Garda Vetting

Following intense lobbying by IASCE, individual colleges and other relevant associations such as the ISPCC, Garda vetting of all social care students became operational in 2007. This vetting is processed through a designated person in each Institute of Technology or college who liaises with the Garda authorities. The Garda Central Vetting Unit (CVU) conducts the search of Garda records and returns the findings to the college's designated officer (often the admissions officer). In the vast majority of cases, the vetting shows no recorded conviction against the student. In the small number of cases where a student is shown to have a criminal conviction, it is then the decision of the college authorities to determine whether the nature of the conviction makes the student unsuitable to register or re-register on a social care programme. Such judgements will be made according to a policy document in operation in each college. Many colleges use a template developed in University College Cork and approved by the Irish University Association.

It is important that all applicants to social care programmes who have a criminal conviction declare this to the appropriate college authorities before undergoing Garda vetting. Failure to disclose a conviction (even an apparently minor conviction unrelated to working with social care clients) is considered to be a serious deception by college authorities.

Of course, having a criminal conviction does not make one automatically unsuited to social care work. As noted above, college authorities will judge whether an individual should be allowed to register on a course of study. In turn, where a minor criminal conviction is recorded against a student, managers in practice placement agencies will determine whether they will accept the student on placement.

Pre-placement Visit

Placement supervisors will be concerned that the student is mature, committed, amenable to instruction and reasonably comfortable with the client group. In order to determine this, a pre-placement visit should be arranged. In addition to allowing the supervisor to screen students, it also plays an important role in allowing the student to determine whether a placement is workable. Students should arrange this pre-placement visit themselves so that they can begin to take control of, and responsibility for, the placement. It should be impressed upon students that it is *their* placement and *their* responsibility to ensure that it is as rich and rewarding an experience as possible.

Students should bring a CV to this meeting so that supervisors can keep on file a record of the student's relevant previous experience. Supervisors may wish to contact character references for the student.

Pre-placement Seminar

When students have been matched with suitable agencies, it is useful to hold a seminar to discuss the roles and expectations of supervisors, students and tutors alike. Such a seminar is an opportunity to consider a range of important issues.

Professionalism

The minimum standards of behaviour expected of students on placement must be made clear, such as professional boundaries, ethical obligations, punctuality, reliability and confidentiality. As we have already mentioned, practice placement may be the student's first experience of the world of work and they may need clear guidelines. For example:

- *Punctuality and attendance*: Student's working week should be that of the social care staff in that agency.
- *Dress*: The majority of agencies take a relaxed, informal stance on the issue of dress. However, supervisors do not always approve of typical student garb.
- *Smoking*: It is not acceptable in the presence of most clients and generally is not permitted in agencies.

Students should adopt a kind, sympathetic approach to clients and ensure that organisational rules are consistently applied. Students must appreciate the importance of treating clients with respect. In residential care, the student is working in a home-from-home environment.

Recognising Your Limits

A desire to 'make a difference' is a natural and commendable aspiration of many social care students. However, such an aspiration is sometimes the product of an insufficient grasp of the complexities of the cases they are likely to encounter. A more realistic understanding of the nature of care work will decrease the likelihood of disillusionment and disappointment in not achieving the elusive 'breakthrough' after a matter of weeks.

The emotional aspect of care work should be recognised. Students will come from a variety of backgrounds and will be varied in their maturity and ability to deal with upsetting cases. It helps to acknowledge that social care staff work with vulnerable people. Strategies for dealing with upsetting incidents at work include having outside interests, such as sports and hobbies, informal support through discussion with others in the field and the formal support of tutors and supervisors.

Befriending Clients

Another natural tendency for students is to strive to be popular and well liked. Of course, the primary goal of social care practitioners is to be effective in their interaction with their client rather than to be liked. A common pitfall is that a student may become so friendly with clients that he or she loses the separateness necessary to function professionally. A common example is where a student becomes drawn into 'slagging' and overt criticism of staff, thus undermining their own position as a student on placement.

Evaluation

Ultimately, a judgement will be made as to the student's performance. Particular colleges' procedures for such an evaluation must be made clear to students. Sometimes students fail a placement or the placement breaks down. The alternative arrangements that may or may not be made in these circumstances should be made clear.

Altruism

Does altruism really exist? The pre-placement seminar is a useful opportunity to question our motives for becoming involved in social care work. Jungian psychologists suggest that there is a strong link between our impulses to help people and our own need for power. As Hawkins and Shohet (2007) explain:

> The role of helper carries with it certain expectations. Sometimes clinging to our role makes it difficult to see the strengths in our clients, the vulnerability in ourselves as helpers, and our interdependence … [we must] face the good and bad, pure and impure motives in ourselves before we can help others.

Students' Pre-placement Checklist

- Be professional in your dealings with agencies. Remember, you are an ambassador for your college and your course.
- Be aware of the legal framework, national standards and guidelines on child protection and welfare that govern social care practice.
- Recognise your limitations.
- Mind your own feelings and emotions.
- Do not befriend clients.
- Be aware of your duty to care.
- Be aware that Garda clearance is required.
- Be open to advice and constructive criticism. Ultimately, your performance will be formally assessed.

PRACTICE PLACEMENT KEY EVENTS

Once the placement begins, the day-to-day management of the placement shifts to the student and supervisor, although the college tutor retains an important role. Let us consider the roles of each part of this triumvirate.

Role of the Supervisor

Supervisors who agree to monitor students' practical learning have undertaken to provide an appropriate induction programme for students. At a minimum, this should involve introducing the student to staff and clients, familiarising the student with the aims and objectives, work practices and roles of different personnel, guiding the student through the physical layout of the agency and clarifying the agency's rules and ethos. The supervisor should:

- Establish mutually agreed goals and learning objectives towards which the student will work during the placement. These goals should be formalised in a written document that can be reviewed periodically.
- Develop a relationship of trust and confidence with the student.
- Encourage the student to identify his or her learning needs and target his or her related goals.

- Set aside time for an agreed regular meeting with the student to give feedback on progress and discuss issues arising out of placement.
- Facilitate the student in applied academic projects, portfolios, assignments or interventions.
- Make an end-of-placement report. Students should be involved in this process and be aware of the content of the report.

Student–supervisor meetings should be predictable, i.e. at a set time each week. Some agencies claim to be habitually 'tearing busy' or 'in a crisis' and find difficulty in providing students with adequate supervision. The suitability of such an agency for further student placement should be carefully considered.

Writing of social care staff supervision, Skinner highlights the important link between supervision, good practice and integration of learning in residential care:

> Residential staff should always receive supervision from their line manager, covering both their day to day work and their professional development. Such supervision is not a luxury; it is a prerequisite for good practice and sound management. Regular individual supervision is always difficult to achieve with the constraints of a staff rota, and is extremely vulnerable to any kind of crisis large or small. But it is the means by which staff can integrate learning and experience. (Skinner 1994: 76)

Weekly student–supervisor meetings should be held in order to facilitate feedback to the student and to provide an opportunity for students to discuss their learning. Students and supervisors should keep a written record of the salient points discussed at such meetings and future learning needs should be identified.

The Irish Association of Social Care Educators (IASCE) *Practice Placement Manual* states: 'It is important that supervision is part of the training experience of the potential caring professional. As well as learning the "what" and "how" of the social care profession, the student must develop self-awareness and an ability to explore new practice challenges in a safe way. It is a central role of the supervisor to facilitate this process' (IASCE 2009: 15). Student–supervisor interaction should be an exercise in constructive criticism. It is not a forum for 'showing off' or 'nagging'. Nor should students perceive comments as a 'put-down' or an affront to their ability. Rather, it is an opportunity for the student to benefit from the guidance of an experienced professional. This requires openness, honesty and a degree of humility on the part of both student and supervisor (see Chapter 13 for further discussion of supervision in social care).

Role of the Student

Students have two primary roles while on practice placement: first, to strive to make the placement as rich a learning experience as possible – to seek and heed guidance and instruction, where necessary, and to bring a positive attitude to dealings with colleagues, clients and families. A second role is to monitor the quality of the placement. For various reasons, the student–supervisor relationship may become unsatisfactory. Students may feel that they are not being given adequate opportunities, or they may find that a supervisor leaves because of holidays, illness or maternity leave. In such instances, it is primarily the student's responsibility to communicate such developments to the college tutor so that a solution can be arranged.

A further role of students is as an ambassador for their college. While each student should be taken on his or her own merits, the reality is that agencies will build an impression of a particular college and its courses based on its previous experiences with the college's students.

Role of the Tutor

During the placement, the college tutor will continue to monitor the student's placement experience. This may be by way of small group discussions around relevant issues or by one-to-one tutorials. The tutor must be alert to issues that might require his or her intervention and be available to students to deal promptly with any such issues.

A further function of the tutor is to arrange placement visits where the student, supervisor and tutor will meet formally to discuss the student's placement experience and decide on future targets and placement objectives. While the visit shall be arranged between the supervisor and tutor, the supervisor should ensure that the student is informed and adequately prepared for the visit. It should be stressed to students that they should be open, honest and straightforward in their dealings with supervisors and tutors. It is only in this way that emerging difficulties can be identified and managed. In the words of the IASCE placement manual (2009: 11), students must 'work through' rather than 'get through' the placement.

Justin and Danielle's Placement Experiences

Having examined the role of each of the actors, two case studies are presented below, which typify students' experiences of practice placement.

JUSTIN'S EXPERIENCES

My social care placement experiences have been very positive and valuable. In my view, it has been the most important part of the course, as without it the academic knowledge acquired would not have had a clear applied link to practice. Being able to use what has been learned in lectures while also observing the practical skills needed to work in social care is what makes the practice placement so important.

My first practice placement was in the learning disabilities sector, and while I was not given a huge amount of responsibility, I did learn a lot about myself. It gave me the confidence that I could actually do this type of work, and also that I did actually enjoy it and it was something I wished to continue in. It is only through reflection that I also realise that I used classroom learning subconsciously during this placement.

The level of support from the staff was essential to this practical learning. While there are invariably some staff members who you may not see eye to eye with, having the support of most of the team can make or break a student's experience and confidence on placement.

How the staff and supervisor handle certain situations is also crucial – having someone who will not let a student be in a situation they cannot handle, but will also let certain situations develop to facilitate the student's learning is a valuable and insightful tool for a student. This was exactly the type of supervisor that I experienced in youth and community work. The project workload was often hectic, but my supervisor was brilliant in her role as supervisor, making sure to fit my academic work with the placement plan we had set out at the start. The supervisor trusted me and gave me appropriate responsibilities, and explained why she was getting me to do certain tasks and the importance of such tasks. During our supervision meetings she set out what I was doing well and not so well, and how to improve in certain areas of practice. One of her supervision techniques that impressed me was if I was making mistakes, she would let them run their course, as long as it was not putting anyone in danger physically, psychologically or emotionally. On occasions when this happened it made me realise the importance of shift planning and the need to be astutely aware of what is occurring in my work environment. Everyone makes mistakes, but not everyone will be fortunate enough to have a supervisor who will let certain mistakes happen and then teach you what you should or should not have done. It is learning that has remained with me, and will influence my future practice.

As most students on social care courses are female, my placements, other agencies I visited and clients were always surprised to meet a male social care student. The lack of males in some agencies can affect the quality of care, for instance on outings. Not having a male carer for toilets and changing rooms can cause difficulties and embarrassment. As a male social care student, I may have been slightly more cautious at times in some circumstances. Clients put me in some awkward situations, but this was not a problem due to having strong staff to support me. Whether this is because I am a male or purely because I was a new member of staff and the clients wanted to test out boundaries with me, I'm not sure, but I was made to feel uncomfortable due to being a male. Social care needs to attract more males, and if it is done correctly, with appropriate safety measures in place, the benefits of having a gender-balanced social care team will enhance the level of care and provide appropriate role models for vulnerable people.

Practice placement has augmented my strengths and made me aware of my weaknesses. With the support of supervision, my knowledge from class and the type of experience one can only get from working in a social care agency, I feel that leaving college I will be a more capable and confident social care worker because of my academic learning applied to experiences in practice placements.

DANIELLE'S EXPERIENCE

My first placement was in a special needs school for children with mild to profound learning disabilities. When I applied to do the BA social care course, I was unaware that I would be doing a placement in this area, so I was very anxious as I had no idea what to expect. On the first day of my placement, I sat in the hallway watching the children coming into school. Most of them were in wheelchairs, some could not speak and others had very little body movement. I met with the school principal, who described the range of disabilities that the children suffered with and how it affected their lives. The principal also explained how the school operated and gave me a copy of their mission statement before bringing me to meet the class where I would work during my placement.

Initially I was unsure of my role in this area of learning disabilities, as I did not have the specialised training of the special needs teacher. I felt useless, as I could not help with feeding or lifting the children, but as I observed the care practices it did not take long for me to adjust to the routines. The disability sector is very hands-on work and although I could not do certain aspects of the work, I could spend quality time listening and doing art and drama activities with the children. At the end of my placement I did not want to leave; because the children had disabilities they were more vulnerable, so leaving them was distressful. The children loved to be cared for and to get hugs; spending time with them and seeing their faces light up gave me great job satisfaction. Working in the disability sector has given me such insight into self-awareness. It has also put perspective on my own life and shown me how easily I can take things for granted, for example walking and talking. Furthermore, seeing how much these children love their lives and how resilient they are is a very humbling experience.

My third year placement was with children and adolescents between the ages of six to 16 living in residential care. I met my supervisor in the residential home prior to starting my placement. At this meeting, my supervisor provided me with information on their service provision, my role on placement and specifics of work in a residential care setting. Meeting my supervisor before starting my placement gave me great confidence. During the first week in the residential home, I received induction and external training, which helped me feel like part of the team. My supervisor met me every second week and talked through my placement experiences. I felt supported, as supervision was carried out professionally. Before I started this placement, I thought I would spend my time caring for children at risk and out of control. I prepared myself for children who would be challenging to care for because they had experienced many difficulties in their lives. However, I met children who liked to laugh and play and who needed affection. They did have times when they were stressed and challenging, but because I had seen their vulnerable side, it made it much easier to understand and support them. Studying challenging behaviour, principles of professional practice, psychology, communications and child protection gave me direction during placement. Learning about working in the life-space of others helped me to assist the young people feel self-worth by reflecting good times from their day. Principles of professional practice taught me self-awareness, to be professional and not to become overly emotionally involved, and to keep perspective on the heartbreaking life stories of the young people. I learned that while I cannot change their past lives, I can make the time that I am with them memorable for good reasons, therefore on placement I began to understand what empathy really means.

In the disabilities sector, the social care worker's role is very hands-on as the young people need physical and emotional care and are dependent on you for day-to-day routines. In residential care, the young people are more independent and even though you are needed to cook and clean with them, your role is more observational and involves active listening. You need to be an emotional rock that will be strong and will not break, because at times they may need to break down or act out in their behaviours. Psychology plays an important part in both the disability sector and in residential child care, as you must be aware of the young people's psychological development in order to monitor how the young people are coping and to determine how much help they need.

At the end of the placement, the supervisor completes an assessment form that details how well you did during your placement. It emphasises your strengths and weaknesses that you brought to the placement. During the year, your college tutor visits you on placement. This visit can be daunting, as you might be very good in the classroom but it is very different when you work in the field of social care. However, placement is a time to put theory into practice. You are still learning and you can be unsure at times, so it is essential to have guidance and support from an effective supervisor. Seeing how valuable supervision was during my placement in residential care made me realise how much supervision was lacking in my previous placement. This may have been because it was my first placement and I was not sure what to expect of supervision or even understood what adequate supervision was meant to be. I believe that dedicated supervision is essential to making a social care student placement a beneficial experience. My ability was lacking in the disability sector, but in residential care I was an equal part of the team and I believe that this was due to the confidence and support I felt and received from my supervisor.

Discussion on Justin and Danielle's Placement Experience

Justin and Danielle have presented insightful views of the placement experience in social care work from the student's perspective. It is interesting to note the differences that they have demonstrated, both in the diversity of placement types, their individual experiences from a male and female perspective and the influences that each placement had on them as students in their self-awareness development, on their life perspectives and appreciation of their quality of life. The significant learning curve provided in the learning-by-doing model on practice placement clearly incorporates the social care worker's required core competency skills, as we note later in Table 12.1. The importance of the practice teacher's delivery of supervision to a student is crucial on several levels of learning and in understanding the application of theory to practice. Justin and Danielle refer to the significance of formal, structured, consistent supervision and to the empowering role that the practice teacher plays in developing young practitioners' confidence in their ability to understand professional boundaries. Induction to placement and in-house training are noted as informative tools that help to abate student anxiety. College tutors are also informed of key times where students require support, such as the initial engaging process with the placement agency and at the tripartite meetings between the student, practice teacher and the college tutor. Danielle notes her experience of weak supervision in the disability sector, while Justin highlights the male perspective and the learning challenges that his supervisor posed for him in allowing certain situations to develop.

Coping Strategies for Challenging Behaviour

Finally, let us examine the issue of challenging behaviour (see Chapter 14). Behaviours that cause most difficulty for social care students and experienced practitioners can be the areas of violence, self-inflicted injuries and child sexual abuse. Violence can pose a personal threat, while sexual abuse and working with the manifestation of very challenging behaviours in the aftermath of sexual abuse can be daunting. Often as a result of biological family and foster care breakdown, multiple challenging behaviours may be manifested. Experienced social care practitioners are highly skilled in addressing such behaviours in a firm but kind manner. They are equally skilled at imparting such knowledge to students in a role-modelling manner. Consequently, the student learns to:

- Observe offensive behaviours.
- Stand back from the manifesting behaviour and put the action into context.
- Avoid reacting to or escalating the behaviours.
- Become aware of verbal and non-verbal body language that presages such behaviours.
- Become aware of triggers that provoked such behaviours.
- Respond in a calm manner that de-escalates the impending crisis.
- Lower their voice tone.
- Use slow body movements.
- Remove peers who may be inciting behaviours.
- Take responsibility and action that restores calm to the environment.
- Talk to the child/young person following the incident to help resolve conflict.
- Aid the person in looking at alternative methods of dealing with strong feelings and actions.

Student and practitioners alike must remember that the young person may re-enact their past life experiences, whether they are living in residential care or are on a supervision order at home. Consequently, it is usually learned patterns of behaviour that we are observing. Often, such patterns have been a way for the child to survive past life experiences or are a reaction to the trauma, rejection, abuse, hurt and pain that they are experiencing. By projecting their anger, emotional turmoil, sadness, anxiety and confusion on their caregivers, the child's expectation is that we can handle these horrible feelings for them. That is, the challenging behaviour is often a cry for help. Although difficult to deal with or to comprehend at times, it is far healthier in terms of outcomes if the child is supported in expressing such feelings as opposed to suppressing them. It is also an opportunity to form attachment with a child/adolescent at the de-escalation point in the arousal-relaxation cycle, where the child is often emotionally drained from the outburst, relieved of their tension and open to forming attachment and bonding to the person who has stayed with them through this frightening cycle.

Consider the example of a child in residential care who has been promised a visit by her mother on her birthday. On the day, the mother rings to cancel the visit. The girl becomes very upset. She smashes a window, scratches her arms, breaks dishes, bites her key-worker and kicks furniture. Eventually, with gentle and persistent persuasion, she falls asleep in her key-worker's arms and, upon awakening, sighs, groans loudly and says so sadly, 'Oh, I wish you were my mammy.'

A young person who has experienced sexual abuse can experience flashbacks at any time, where incidents are recalled in explicit detail; such painful memories prove very difficult for the person to cope with. A range of behaviours may manifest for such individuals, such as inappropriate touch, sexualised play, offensive language and overt aggressive behaviour. The experienced social care supervisor will engage the social care student in understanding the background to these behaviours in a safe environment. Consequently, when the student encounters the reality of these behaviours, there will be an enlightened understanding of the reasons why the person is acting in this manner.

Challenging behaviour may also be manifested by clients who have psychiatric illnesses, addictions or intellectual disabilities. Social care practitioners may be shouted at, lashed out at or even hit. There are no easy responses, theoretical words or magic wands that can eradicate other people's pain or teach us how to cope and work with such case scenarios. College can prepare the nurse for her first experience of a patient dying; the doctor for her first experience of having to inform family that a loved one has died; the social worker for his first experience of having to remove a child from its family. Similarly, challenging behaviour will be covered in college for social care practitioners, but it is not until the student has actual hands-on experience of such behaviours that they will truly understand the meaning of what they have learned or can have an understanding of how they are expected to respond so that they can establish coping mechanisms for the future. This is where knowledge and practice truly intertwine and become embedded in the mindset of the social care graduates of the future. Supervision and shift hand-over meetings that provide debriefing sessions are essential to staff support and staff retention where challenging behaviour is an ongoing part of a work and placement environment.

KEY EVENTS AFTER PRACTICE PLACEMENT

The evaluation of a student's performance as 'satisfactory' normally concludes the practice placement. A student assessment form will be completed by the supervisor, in the presence of the student, and should be countersigned by the student. Generally speaking, placements are assessed on a pass/fail, rather than on a graded, basis. Each student should be assessed at his or her own level – that is, a mark of 'satisfactory' does not indicate that performance is that of a 'satisfactory' care practitioner, but that it is of a 'satisfactory' student of social care work at a particular stage of development.

The student evaluation is primarily the role of the supervisor, but it is the college tutor who will present this result for ratification to the college examination board. Thus, the tutor must be satisfied that it is a fair assessment of the student's performance.

Two further tasks remain for the college tutor. The first is to elicit feedback from students on the quality of supervision that they received on placement and the overall quality of learning experienced. This helps to ensure that the agencies in which students are placed offer high-quality supervision and learning experiences. The second task is to co-ordinate a supervisors' meeting. This will generally involve inviting supervisors to attend a seminar where feedback on the management of student placement can be discussed. It is a useful opportunity to invite a guest speaker to speak on a topic related to supervision in social care.

END RESULT

The staff team in an effective practice placement agency will collectively support and be inclusive of the student on placement, while the supervisor will support the student in this steep learning curve. This is a dual process that should result in the student blossoming in the following areas:

- Self-knowledge and open accountability.
- Proficiency in client advocacy.
- Confident competency skills.
- Critical incident analysis.
- Interpersonal skills.
- Clarity of role, role expectation and task acquisition.
- Reduced anxiety with awareness of potential stressors.
- Effective and efficient aspiration towards standards of excellence in their duty of care towards others.
- Team player awareness.
- Moral and ethical awareness of the use of power with vulnerable people.
- Ability to handle fear.
- Awareness of professional obligations in role-modelling; respectful behaviour to service users and colleagues.
- Awareness of the unpredictable nature of the work and the need to look towards positive solutions based on consultation and participation.
- Being child centred, with an awareness of the relevant legislation, child protection and welfare guidelines and the United Nations Conventions on Human Rights and on the Rights of the Child.
- Promoting equality by opposing oppression, discrimination and racism and by acknowledging ethnicity.

A checklist of core competency skills is detailed below (Table 12.1).

CONCLUSION

In conclusion, one of the most important attributes that students of social care can have is a sense of humour, for while social care work can find practitioners working with some of the most vulnerable people in society, where sadness and poverty abound, there will also be good times with positive outcomes. Such good humour can prove invaluable and has often been used appropriately to ease tense situations.

Table 12.1. Core Competency Skills of the Social Care Worker

Communication	Assessment	Planning	Intervention	Self-awareness
• Empathy • Observation • Culture awareness • Behaviour triggers • Empowering • Active listening • Love and care • Questioning • Clarifying • Validating • Summarising • Evaluating • Monitoring • Report writing • Sensitivity to literacy • Teamwork • Links to other professionals • Networking with family and significant others	• Needs of service users • Cultural norms • Relationships • Family dynamics • Sensory deprivation • Prioritising essential needs • Identifying long-term needs • Risk analysis • Monitoring work climate	• Situation analysis • Strategic plans • Objective setting • Prioritising goals • Key work management • Time management • Policy knowledge • Procedures and laws • Care plans • Aftercare plans • Reunification • Role of family • Action plans	• Immediate needs • Long-term needs • Attachment issues • Self-harm/abuse • Health care • Identity • Cultural context • Education • Confidence building • Self-esteem issues • Positive identity • Social skills • Life skills • Aftercare • Independent living skills • Impulse control • Anger management	• Self-management • Professional judgement • Stress management • Objectivity • Empathy • Calm in crisis • Reflective judgement • Appropriate power • Emotional control • Externalising abuse/stressors • Identification of coping strategies • Collusion avoidance • Ongoing up-skilling • Consistency

When working with crisis, it can be easy to be wise in hindsight. Sometimes there is a sense that all the experience or learning in the world will not prepare us adequately for certain work-related circumstances. However, one can often look back and feel a sense of achievement when, finally, that child happily returns home or is doing well in foster care, or an adolescent is successful in her exams, or Mum succeeds in giving up alcohol. Truly, such rewards are the essence of social care work.

ACKNOWLEDGEMENT

We would like to acknowledge the significant and insightful contributions of Danielle McKenna and Justin McCarthy, graduates of the BA (Hons.) in Social Care at DIT, for their valuable contributions to this chapter. Danielle and Justin have openly described their placement experiences; this information will serve to enlighten academic tutors and practice teachers in their support to social care students.

13

Using Professional Supervision in Social Care

Eileen O'Neill

OVERVIEW

Professional supervision is an integral part of effective practice for many social care practitioners, while for others it can remain an irregular and confused experience. To ensure that supervision is used as a positive resource, it is necessary to fully understand its purpose and functions. It is necessary to accept that both supervisor and supervisee share responsibility with the organisation for its effectiveness.

As far back as 1950, Bettelheim identified the need for supervisory support for staff who worked in residential child care settings. Exactly 50 years later, the National Standards for Children's Residential Centres (Department of Health and Children 2001a) in Ireland echoed this by identifying the standard that:

- All staff members receive regular and formal supervision, the details of which must be recorded. (2.13)
- There is an effective link between supervision and the implementation of individual placement plans. (2.14)

The inclusion of these criteria as a standard has led to supervision becoming a reality for those working in residential child care services, although how participants experience supervision can differ considerably. Those working in community-based services or those employed in the disability sector do not have such a mandated requirement for their supervision although, in recognition of best practice, some such organisations ensure that supervision is available.

This chapter focuses on how to use supervision to ensure that it is a positive resource that benefits staff at all stages of their career while contributing to the ongoing development of the organisation. This facilitates practice that is accountable and relevant to the needs of those who use the services at times of need in their lives.

Attention is paid in this chapter to the following:

- Professional supervision – why have it? What is it?
- Three functions of supervision and a *dual-focus approach*.

- Using professional supervision as a student.
- Using professional supervision as a staff member.
- Using supervision as a supervisor.

WHY DO WE NEED PROFESSIONAL SUPERVISION?

Society in general has become more demanding of service provision, with an increased expectation for quality and standards. Legislation has placed a higher requirement for accountability in all areas of working and public life. Key statutes in the area include the Safety, Health and Welfare at Work Act 1989, the Freedom of Information Act 1997 and the Protection for Persons Reporting Child Abuse Act 1998. Coupled with these, a number of scandals that emerged in the 1990s in political life, in the business world and in professional services have highlighted the need for a recognised framework for accountable practice and for the ongoing development of practitioners in a supportive environment. Professional supervision, when provided and used effectively, contributes to this.

In summary, the following factors indicate why professional supervision is deemed necessary.

- *Professional task:* The professional dimension to a discipline requires recognition, structure and monitoring. Supervision is part of accepted practice in a number of disciplines: psychology, occupational therapy and social work as well as social care.
- *Inquiry reports:* Inquiries into service deficits and abuse in the past identify the absence of regular, formal supervision for a range of staff in the health sector (Laming 2003; Leavy and Kahan 1991; McGuinness 1993). The recommendations of these reports strongly advocate the availability and use of regular, structured supervision, particularly for those working in the areas of child care and protection. Evidence of learning from the gaps and mistakes of the past must be integrated into responsible practice.
- *Accountability:* Practitioners must be accountable for what they do and for how they do it. Employers need to have established structures that facilitate this process.
- *Workers are recognised as a vital resource:* Investment in the human resources of services can aid staff retention and is recognised as beneficial for effective and improved delivery of services. Research (Sinclair and Gibbs 1998) suggests that supervision is important for staff morale. This is particularly important at times of high staff turnover. People are more likely to stay in a job where they feel valued and good about what they do.
- *Continuing professional development (CPD)* is perceived now more than ever as a necessary component for practitioners at all stages of their career. Qualification is an entry requirement and it is necessary to develop skills and self-awareness further in order to become a truly competent worker.

- *Duty of care and recognition of demanding work:* Supports and structures to enable staff to work in demanding and potentially stressful working environments are recognised and accepted as necessary.

What Is Professional Supervision?

Professional supervision is a partnership process of ongoing reflection and feedback between a named supervisor and supervisee(s) to ensure and enhance effective practice. Provided in a supportive manner, it offers a structured opportunity to discuss work, to reflect on practice and progress and to plan for future development.

In describing supervision as a *partnership*, it is implied that both participants have responsibilities. When entering any partnership, it is necessary for both people to be aware of what is expected of them and of what they can reasonably expect from the other. The partnership of supervision requires that there are clearly identified expectations on both sides. Coupled with expectations come responsibilities.

Examples of responsibilities shared by both supervisor and supervisee include:

- Preparation for supervision.
- Contributing to the agenda.
- Starting on time.
- Using the allocated time fully.
- Honest two-way feedback and communication.
- No interruptions.
- Ensuring that postponement is rare.

Describing supervision as a *process* indicates that the functions of supervision need to permeate beyond the supervision meeting and become integrated into practice. This process of supervision is evident when the supervisee leaves supervision with something to think about as well as identified objectives for his/her practice. Experiencing supervision as a process is more likely to contribute to the ongoing development of the participants and, potentially, of the service.

Reflection and *feedback* are recognised as key components in all supervision. Reflective practice is regarded as a means to develop self-aware professionals who possess the maturity and insight to learn from their experiences – the positive experiences as well as those that require improvement. Participating in supervision provides the opportunity for reflection on the detail of day-to-day practice as well as on any significant events that may have occurred. Reflecting on practice with another can lead to greater objectivity through exploration and feedback. Feedback in supervision is a two-way process – both supervisor and supervisee share responsibility for its effective use.

The core process of supervision takes place in regular, planned, structured time, between a named supervisor and supervisee(s). This time provides an opportunity to ensure the standard of service and care to those who use the services, and facilitates the practitioner's development in a supportive manner. Some circumstances may require additional supervision – for example, in response to a particular change or difficulty. At such times, it is important that responsive supervision is available.

While supervision in social care generally takes place on a one-to-one basis, it is useful if attention is also paid to the supervision of the team as a whole. Service delivery is dependent on the manner in which the team functions, and teams can benefit greatly from the opportunity to reflect in a structured way on their practice, with a view to identifying the strengths of the team and the areas that need further development.

Confusion has existed for some people regarding supervision. One reason for this has been the many and varied ways in which supervision has been experienced by practitioners. On the one hand, it has often been experienced solely as a response to a concern or crisis, thereby becoming associated with problems only. This is a limited view of supervision and has contributed to negative interpretations and uses of what can be a positive and proactive resource. On the other hand, many practitioners have found supervision to be nothing more than 'checklisting' to make sure that they have carried out certain tasks. This can lead supervisees to feel that they are back at school, having their homework corrected – not very empowering for adults with responsible workloads!

Supervision will be used effectively only if its functions are identified and understood from the beginning of one's career and if supervisor, supervisee and organisations share common and realistic expectations regarding its implementation. To this end, it is necessary to know what supervision is *not* as well as what it *is*.

Supervision is *not*:

- A casual activity that takes place over a cup of coffee.
- A chat.
- An optional extra.
- Counselling.
- Appraisal.
- A grievance session.
- A telling-off.
- Something that happens only when there is a problem.
- Something that happens only when there is nothing else to do.

Supervision *is* a regular opportunity to:

- Reflect on the daily work – the process as well as the content.
- Discuss any particular responsibilities of the supervisee.
- Monitor and ensure the quality of practice.
- Identify and further develop understanding and skills.
- Seek and receive support and feedback.

- Consider the impact of the work.
- Keep up to date with agency changes and requirements.
- Be constructively challenged.
- Identify areas for further professional development and implement a professional development plan.

Three Functions of Professional Supervision

Accountability, support and learning are the three main functions of professional supervision.

- *Accountability* for effective practice and service delivery. It is important that practitioners are accountable and are held accountable for their work.
- *Support* for the individual staff member to carry out their work in a demanding work environment.
- *Learning* and ongoing development and self-awareness of the participants.

Each of these three functions needs to be present in a balanced way over time if supervision is to meet its objectives. The skilled supervisor is aware of this and has the ability to hone in on a particular need the supervisee may present while remaining focused on the overall functions. The overlap between the three functions is apparent in the majority of situations brought into supervision (see Figure 13.1).

Figure 13.1. Balance of the Functions in Supervision

Source: Based on Kadushin (1976).

Regular overemphasis on any one or two components will not lead to the best use of supervision.

- If the main focus is on *accountability* to the exclusion of the other two functions, there is a risk of 'checklist' supervision becoming the norm. This will monitor the content of the practice of the individual to a certain extent, but fails to pay due attention to the wider picture. Some managers may overemphasise this function, as ensuring accountable practice of others is the remit of the manager. But the supervisor must be aware of the fit between accountability and the other functions if supervision is to be truly effective.

- If *support* is the primary objective of supervision, there is a likelihood that such support may become a crutch for the individual while they move from one difficulty to another. Recently appointed supervisors or those who supervise colleagues can overemphasise the support function at times, at the expense of the other two. Professional supervision must facilitate the supervisee in a supportive manner, but must also be about more than support if it is to ensure the ongoing development of accountable practice.

- When *learning* is regularly the main objective in supervision, there is a risk of it being viewed as a teacher/pupil interaction. In such situations, the supervisor is expected to be the source of all knowledge and the supervisee the receiver of the information. This can eventually lead to the supervisee, although well informed, having limited opportunity to develop through self-reflection and responsibility. Ongoing and lifelong learning are recognised as necessary in today's workplace. Supervision provides a regular and structured opportunity to integrate the learning from everyday work experiences.

DUAL-FOCUS APPROACH

In the past, supervision has frequently had a single focus for many practitioners. It focused either on their responsibilities, with particular attention paid to checking up on the work, or it provided a forum to focus solely on themselves, with little, if any, attention paid to the details of the work. Neither of these approaches on their own leads to effective supervision. Rather, a combination of both promotes the best use of the supervision.

Maintaining a *dual-focus approach* (Figure 13.2) ensures an operational and a developmental focus. The operational aspect considers the task of the work: the detail of practice with attention to the particular responsibilities of the individual in the context of his/her job description. The developmental aspect considers the person who carries out the job: the person him/herself as a practitioner.

Figure 13.2. Dual-Focus Approach

Operational focus is on the task of the job and the tasks of the work	Development focus is on the person who carries out the job
Examples include: • The purpose and function of the service.	Examples include: • The impact of the work on the person.
• Job description and responsibilities.	• The skills and strengths of the supervisee. • Areas for further development.
• Policies and procedures.	• Reflection on practice, ideas.
• The client group – assessing needs, direct care.	• Working as part of a team.
• Care plans, key work, recording and report writing, time management.	• Formulating, implementing and evaluating a professional development plan.

Source: O'Neill (2004).

Professional supervision is an effective resource at all stages of one's working life, from student days to experienced professionals in senior positions. The next part of this chapter introduces Maria at three different stages of her career and considers her use of supervision at each stage.

MARIA – USING SUPERVISION AS A STUDENT

Maria is a student on an Applied Social Studies course. So far, she has enjoyed her studies, particularly the varied nature of the programme, with its mix of theoretical and practical subjects. She knew that practice placements were part of the course and was looking forward to this new experience with a mixture of anticipation and apprehension.

Preparation for placement had taken place throughout the year in lectures that had considered the purpose and function of placements and the roles of the college, the student and the workplace (see Chapter 12). Maria had visited the workplace, as required, in preparation for the placement. She had met the manager of the service and the staff member who was to be her direct supervisor for the next 12 weeks.

She was aware that regular, structured supervision was a requirement of all placements, but despite all she had been told in class about what this would entail, she was not sure what she thought about it. This was not helped by the mixed messages she was getting from fellow students and friends.

- One person had experienced supervision as a friendly chat with her supervisor, with whom she worked daily. The supervisor was herself less than a year out of college. After the first few weeks, this chat began to be more and more casual and less and less focused on the work. The student found this enjoyable at a personal and social level, but not helpful in using the placement as the learning opportunity it was meant to be.
- Others had very limited contact with their supervisor, whom they met only for periodic, brief supervision meetings because of frequently cancelled appointments. The students felt that the meetings were rushed and only went through the motions of what supervision should be – there was little investment by either in making them work. In fact, the students felt they did not need to make any effort at all, as the supervisor did most of the talking anyway.
- Supervision was experienced differently again by others who worked with an experienced member of staff as their supervisor. Although working together most days provided the opportunity to discuss aspects of the work as they arose, they also met, uninterrupted, once a week to reflect on themselves and on the work and to plan for the coming week. These students felt they had been challenged to do better and therefore supervision was a worthwhile experience, though not always easy.

With all of this in mind, Maria was curious as to how she would experience supervision in her placement. Although she had been told that the agency had a clear supervision policy for staff as well as students, she was also aware that policy and practice did not always match.

Remembering from her placement class that both supervisor and supervisee are together responsible for how supervision is experienced, Maria realised that she had a part to play in making sure that she got what she wanted and needed from it.

On the first morning of her placement, Jane, who was to be her supervisor for the next 12 weeks, met Maria. Jane, who had been working in the centre for almost three years, explained that she had set aside an hour later in the morning for them both to sit down together and consider the details of how the placement would be structured. Maria was given a copy of the centre policy on student placements and on professional supervision, for consideration later. In the meantime, Maria was shown around and introduced to members of staff and to three adolescent boys who were residing in the centre at the time. So began her placement.

From the beginning, there was an expectation that all those working in the service, regardless of their experience or position, would participate in regular structured supervision at least every four weeks. The policy and practice matched perfectly in this regard, as supervision was incorporated into the working day for all.

Maria was told in the first meeting with her supervisor that they would meet weekly unless one or other were sick or there was an immediate crisis; in the latter case, supervision would be rescheduled for later in the day. The purpose of these meetings, as outlined in the policy and identified by the supervisor, was to enhance the placement experience through regular reflection and feedback in order to ensure that Maria began to look behind what she was seeing and experiencing and develop her understanding and self-awareness in the process.

In the early weeks and based on the experiences of her friends, Maria was somewhat sceptical about what she was told concerning the frequency and expectations regarding supervision. She also experienced more than a little apprehension, as she feared that supervision might turn into nothing more than a litany of her mistakes and transgressions.

Maria and her supervisor did, in fact, meet weekly throughout the 12-week placement and also had two extra meetings to ensure that the support and direction she needed were available to her when a particular crisis occurred.

Because supervision happened regularly and frequently, as planned, Maria quickly became comfortable with meeting her supervisor and discussing all aspects of her placement experience. Her supervisor helped Maria to consider the range of things that were included on the agenda. Examples of these were:

- The policies of the particular service and how they impacted on direct practice.
- The needs of adolescents in general and how such needs can be met in a group care setting, while also taking into account the specific needs of each young person and the reasons for their admission to care, as well as care plans, key work and working with families.
- The value of undertaking ordinary, everyday tasks for and with young people.
- Identifying her own strengths and skills and the areas she needed to develop further for professional practice. Maria received regular, balanced feedback throughout her placement. Her supervisor spoke honestly to her, highlighting areas of concern or difficulty and how she could improve while also affirming, with specific examples, Maria's strengths and skills, as appropriate.

There was a clear focus on integrating reflection on practice at all stages of her placement experience. This introduced Maria to the practice and process of reflective practice, which was to stand to her in her future career.

MARIA – USING SUPERVISION AS A STAFF MEMBER

Having qualified 18 months ago, Maria now works as a social care practitioner in a residential child care service, with young people aged 12 to 16 years. She is one of a team of eight staff who work closely with teachers, psychologists and social workers to ensure wide-ranging services to the young people and their families.

Maria finds her work satisfying and challenging in equal measures. Working with young people who present with such acute needs and individual behaviours ensures that every day is different, with no likelihood of boredom. Although in her second year out of college, Maria finds that she is still constantly developing new skills and gaining new insights.

When Maria arrived in the service, her induction highlighted that she, like all staff, would participate in structured supervision every four weeks. Again, this information brought up a mixed response in her. It reminded her of her previous experiences of supervision as a student and she wondered what would be expected of her by her new supervisor. She was somewhat apprehensive, as she could not imagine what she would use supervision for once she became familiar with the work. In chatting to other staff, she began to pick up that some staff used supervision to discuss the key work they were involved in or to look at a report they had to prepare – this sounded straightforward enough; others used it, they said, as a 'sounding board' – this sounded rather vague to Maria, who could not fully imagine what that meant.

Molly, who worked as one of two child care leaders on the team, was Maria's supervisor from the outset. The first supervision meeting explored their previous experiences and ideas of supervision and examined its purpose and function within the service. They discussed the possible uses of supervision and examined the service policy regarding how the details would work between them. The meeting concluded with both of them signing a brief contract of commitment to the supervision process.

Before they finished, Maria was asked to consider what she had taken from the meeting and realised that she was more relaxed and clearer about supervision.

- They would meet once every four weeks for one hour – this was outlined in the policy and was in keeping with residential services generally.
- The meeting would be recorded on the agency recording form at the end of each meeting. They would both be involved in the recording, which they would sign. The form would be kept by Molly and Maria could access it through her or through the line manager at any time.
- The agenda, to which they would both contribute, would be decided at the start of each meeting.
- Information shared between them would not be discussed with the rest of the team members. Both had a responsibility to highlight with their line manager any difficulties that might arise if they were unable to resolve them together.
- Although supervision received a high priority within the service, it was acknowledged that there might be some circumstances that might require postponement of an occasional meeting. In such an event, they shared responsibility for rescheduling the meeting as soon as possible.

- Supervision would be reviewed between them at least twice a year. This would give them both an opportunity to give and receive feedback on how each of them was experiencing supervision, what was working and what needed to improve.

On reflection, Maria also felt that she had begun to get to know a little about her supervisor from some of the discussions they had shared. By now, she was surprised to find herself looking forward to the supervision to come, her apprehension somewhat lessened but not gone.

In the early days of supervision, Maria used the time to ask questions concerning the policies of the organisation and to find out more about what to do in certain situations with the young people and when working with their families. Her supervisor responded at times with very specific information and direction. At other times, Maria was asked her opinion on a situation, and then her response was further discussed relating to a specific area of the work.

Maria always arrived to supervision with a list of items for the agenda. At times, this was drawn up in a panic just prior to supervision, with little thought given to preparation in between the meetings. But Maria was happy that she could think of things to talk about. Molly was careful to facilitate her in reflecting on her actual practice and the rationale behind this last-minute approach. Through supervision, Maria became more self-aware. She realised that she had a responsibility to plan for the meeting in order to get the most from it. This would benefit her in a realistic manner within her practice.

Her supervisor helped Maria to identify the skills that she was using and to further develop her ability to cope with all the new experiences she was meeting in day-to-day practice. Through reflecting on events within her area of work, Maria was guided to recognise alternative strategies for managing both young people and her reactions and interactions.

Using speculation, with her supervisor asking 'what if' questions, helped her to explore new approaches to practice in the safety of supervision. She no longer felt afraid to voice suggestions and opinions and grew in her ability to participate in team meetings as a result. Her skill in advocating for young people was also developed through supervision. As she grew more self-aware, her supervisor was better able to challenge her around scenarios and thus encourage her to move out of her 'comfort zone' to consider new ways of working.

At one of their regular review sessions, her supervisor used feedback to identify changes in Maria and her practice. Through a mutual exchange of reflections on her practice, they were able to create a picture of Maria's development to date. She was both surprised and delighted by some of these changes. This helped her to recognise that her confidence had improved significantly, although she also acknowledged her need to continue to develop. Using this information, they focused on identifying areas for Maria's ongoing development in the coming year. Her supervisor assisted Maria in formulating a personal development plan (PDP).

Maria's main objective was to become more competent in understanding the 'bigger picture' so that she could avoid her tendency to get bogged down in one aspect of a situation. They broke this overall objective into specific tasks that related to her daily practice and current workload. These included:

- Considering the children in her care within the context of their families.
- Examining the wider regional and national policies and legislation that inform practice.
- Looking at her skills and how transferable they were to other client groups and areas of work.
- Reflecting on her own attitudes and how they impacted on decision-making.

These were incorporated into the process of supervision over the coming months. This gave Maria a particular focus for her work and contributed to her increased motivation. She also began to use supervision in a more responsible way.

MARIA – USING SUPERVISION AS A SUPERVISOR

It is now three years since Maria first qualified. She has recently successfully competed for and been appointed to the post of Child Care Leader within the unit. She is aware of the wider organisational issues associated with working in the service and is familiar through her practice with the policies and procedures and their implication for effective service delivery.

Her experience in supervision has helped her to progress to this stage. In recent months, she has reflected on the skills necessary to achieve promotion to this senior post. She was encouraged by her supervisor to examine her motivation for seeking more responsibility and to identify areas she would have to do further work on to be effective in the role. This ensured that Maria continued to work within a context of awareness around her ongoing development achievements and needs. As part of her new role, she has supervisory responsibilities for a number of other social care practitioners. Although looking forward to the post in general, this is one aspect she has some apprehension about.

She has learned to use her supervision consistently to deal with the realities of her experiences. In this way, she is able to voice her concerns and anxieties about her new role within supervision. Together with her supervisor, she identifies skills necessary for her to become an effective supervisor for other staff. These include:

- Listening.
- Reflecting.
- Supporting.
- Prompting.
- Questioning.
- Guiding.

- Problem-solving.
- Time management.
- Feedback.

Through discussion and prompting, Maria becomes aware that she already uses these skills in her everyday work. To be an effective supervisor, she now needs to focus on her use of these skills and to develop a methodology for transferring these into her role as a supervisor. Attending the forthcoming training for new supervisors within the organisation will help this. In addition, Maria's ongoing supervision with her own supervisor will play a crucial part in her ability to become a good supervisor.

Working with her supervisor, Maria realises that one of her main anxieties as a new supervisor is that she will be expected to supervise staff members with whom she previously worked on a peer level. Her supervisor helps her to recognise that maintaining the balance between the three key aspects of supervision – namely, support, learning and accountability – is the priority at this stage. She knows that it would be all too easy to slip into the supportive, empathetic role and fail to question, challenge or direct practice.

It is here that remembering the principles of the *dual-focus approach* will inform her own practice as the supervisor. The important point to keep in focus is that the two facets of practice – namely, the task and the person *in* the task – must both be examined and reflected upon.

In discussing her concerns with her supervisor, Maria is challenged to consider her own first impressions of supervision, subsequent actual experiences and their impact on her attitudes to being a supervisor. Through her reflection, the importance of developing a clear framework within which she can commence and continue the process of supervision with her new supervisees is highlighted.

As she prepares for her first supervision meeting, she establishes a plan for this framework, identifying certain areas for inclusion. She discusses this with her supervisor as follows:

- The need for both supervisor and supervisee to tune in to each other's expectations and experiences of the supervision process.
- The need to identify what is meant by professional supervision to ensure a shared understanding from the outset.
- The need to clearly explain and establish the ground rules and practicalities and policies relating to meeting for supervision.
- The drafting and signing of an agreed contract for supervision.
- The process and practice of recording a summary of the supervision together.
- The need to provide the proper environment for effective supervision. This includes an interruption-free zone with no external pressures to distract either party – no phones or mobiles, no emails, no callers.

In keeping with the principles of supervision, Maria feels secure enough to discuss with her supervisor, on an ongoing basis, any concerns she may have regarding her own role as a supervisor. Through continuous reflection and challenge, Maria develops her knowledge, awareness and confidence as a supervisor in her new role. This is not always easy and at times she becomes aware of just how skilled her supervisors have been throughout her career to date:

- She was facilitated to develop at her own pace.
- She was encouraged to question and also to consider her own opinions.
- She was supported and did not feel judged at times of doubt and confusion.
- She was challenged to improve in specific areas.
- She received regular feedback as a matter of course. This feedback was always presented clearly and was relevant to her practice – at times it was affirming and at other times it was corrective.
- She received direction and guidance.

Maria realises that good supervision did not happen by chance. It required sustained, focused effort on behalf of the supervisor, realistic commitment by the organisation and active, responsible engagement by the supervisee. Both supervisor and supervisee have a responsibility to make sure that the supervision they engage in is good supervision. To achieve this, they have to commit responsibly to honest, respectful communication, feedback and reflection.

CONCLUSION

Working with people at times of vulnerability or need in their lives demands self-aware practitioners of the highest calibre who are in touch with their own strengths and limitations. Active and responsible participation in regular, structured supervision can contribute to this at all stages of professional life.

14
Managing Challenging Behaviour
Eleanor Fitzmaurice

OVERVIEW

This chapter explores what is meant by 'challenging behaviour' in social care contexts and outlines strategies for managing such behaviour. Definitions of challenging behaviour and their implications for social care practice, including the importance of observing the duty of care, will be outlined and a brief overview of issues of workplace health and safety will be given. Employers must comply with legislation to ensure that both employees and clients are kept safe from harm. Working with vulnerable clients entails an increased risk of verbal or physical aggression, with consequent effects on the social care practitioner's well-being. Appropriate support and training in the management of challenging behaviour is a priority to ensure positive outcomes for clients in social care placements.

It is important to state at the outset that people who use social care services are not a homogenous group. For different reasons, they have different needs, and the behaviours they manifest are different. It is not possible to devise a set of instructions for the management of challenging behaviour that would apply to all social care settings. What this chapter aims to do is to point out universally and generally applicable strategies for the management of care situations where there is the risk of upset or injury to staff or clients due to challenging behaviour.

Most of the available guidelines on managing challenging behaviour have been issued in response to an expressed need of practitioners in different settings, such as teachers, nurses, health care workers and social care practitioners in direct daily contact with clients. General principles may be identified that will assist in understanding the kind of approach most likely to lead to the successful management of volatile situations.

Agencies that support clients with particularly challenging behaviours have tended to train all their frontline staff in one chosen behaviour management approach. Generally, the approach chosen is in line with the ethos of the service; the ethical and legal implications of managing behaviour amongst the client groups that the agency supports; and the limits the agency sets out on the extent to which staff may intervene in violent situations. The adoption of one particular approach in an agency has the benefit of ensuring that all staff members have an acceptable level of insight and competence in maintaining a consistent, therapeutic approach to clients. Students on placement need to become familiar with the particular approach used by their placement agency, through observation of workers and through asking pertinent questions in supervision.

SAFETY AND HEALTH AT WORK: THE NATIONAL AND INTERNATIONAL CONTEXT

The Safety, Health and Welfare at Work Act 2005 covers safety, health and welfare matters in all workplaces. It places obligations on employers, employees and the self-employed to contribute to ensuring that their workplace and systems of work are safe. It is the employer's responsibility to assess risks and take reasonable but rigorous steps to avoid or control any that arise. Employers should ensure that instruction and training are given to workers in appropriate behaviour and risk management strategies. A precise system of incident reporting must also be in place. Employees at risk of threatening or violent behaviour from clients should be able to avail of health checks and counselling should be provided if needed.

While the Act relates to all workplaces, it is particularly important to pay attention to its content in the case of professions where the risk of injury is high. Health and social care practitioners have been identified as being at high risk of injury from clients. The risks associated with working in health care settings are well documented, largely because of the long history of health care in institutional and community settings. Social care is often coupled with health care in the statistics and it is difficult to separate out the specific aspects of the social care role, and the characteristics of social care settings, that lend themselves to high risk of injury. However, it can be inferred that the levels of risk for staff who deal with certain members of the public are similar. Clients with emotional and behavioural difficulties (due to factors such as unstable family histories, psychiatric disturbances, conduct disorders and exacerbating environmental influences) pose significant risks for carers. Balancing therapeutic interventions with the need to maintain a safe workplace is a complex task.

The Health and Safety Authority (HSA) (2007) provides data on reported workplace injuries which indicates that health professionals rank within the top five most dangerous occupations, along with mining, construction, manufacturing and transport. Manual handling incidents continue to cause most workplace injuries, followed by 'slip, trip and fall' incidents. Violent incidents also feature in the top five categories: 'shock, fright and violence of others' triggered 4 per cent of all reported injuries in 2006. The public administration (17 per cent) and health/social work (16 per cent) sectors reported particularly high percentages of incidents described as 'injured by person – violent' (HSA 2007).

The HSA identifies the most common causes associated with workplace injury as 'loads – handled by hand' (7 per cent), followed by 'humans' (6 per cent) and 'surfaces – at ground level' (5 per cent). What is interesting is the breakdown of the 'humans' category by sector: the proportion of incidents associated with humans in health and social work (29 per cent) and public administration (18 per cent) far exceeds that in any other sector (HSA 2007).

Concern about risks to workers in vulnerable roles is not confined to Ireland. Across Europe, Cooper et al. (2003: 3) point out the concentration of reported physical violence among 'certain occupations such as health care, police, social services, taxi drivers and drivers of public transport, hotel and catering employees, security personnel and teachers'. Chappell and Di Martino (2006) include health care, education, community services and social services in their listing of the occupational groups at highest risk.

Efforts to highlight internationally the risk of workplace violence are part of the International Labour Organization's (ILO) commitment to promoting 'decent work'. Decent work, as the ILO (2003) defines it, is work that:

- Is productive and safe.
- Ensures respect of labour rights.
- Provides an adequate income.
- Offers social protection.
- Includes social dialogue, union freedom, collective bargaining and participation.

Historically, ILO interventions in the area of workplace violence were primarily focused on preventing gender discrimination in the form of sexual harassment. More recently, the organisation has focused on other forms of workplace violence as an aspect of its 'decent work' agenda, in particular calling for the preservation of human dignity in the workplace.

Difficulties associated with accurate definition have hampered attempts to identify the extent of work-related violence. Some clarity has emerged with the adoption by the European Commission of Wynne et al.'s (1997) definition of such events as 'incidents where staff are abused, threatened or assaulted in circumstances related to their work, involving an explicit or implicit challenge to their safety, well-being or health'. Similarly, accurate international measurement of the incidence and severity of workplace violence is difficult, as different countries and agencies measure different aspects of risk and violence. For Beech and Leather (2006: 29), 'the safest conclusion that can be drawn on the basis of officially reported incidents is that the numbers are a gross underestimate of the actual numbers of incidents'.

The European Foundation for the Improvement of Living and Working Conditions (2004) has identified the following key factors in the effective reduction of work-related stress and injury:

- Adequate risk analysis.
- Thorough planning and a stepwise approach.
- Combination of work-directed and worker-directed measures.
- Context-specific solutions.
- Experienced practitioners and evidence-based interventions.
- Social dialogue, partnership and workers' involvement.
- Sustained prevention and top management support.

It is important to note that challenging behaviour is not confined to violent or aggressive behaviour (see Table 14.1). The HSA defines workplace violence and aggression as occurring where 'persons are verbally abused, threatened or assaulted in circumstances related to their work'. Verbal abuse can often be as intimidating and upsetting as the risk of violence, and more protracted. Non-physical aggression can have an even more pervasive impact on the social care practitioner and the agency, as staff may not report incidents due to uncertainty and embarrassment. Inappropriate behaviour may continue unchecked, and the resulting impact on the client and the worker remain unacknowledged. The client does not learn alternative and appropriate ways of acknowledging and managing anger, while the worker may be reluctant to report the offending behaviour for fear that they may be accused of overreacting, exaggerating or in some way contributing to the inappropriate behaviour.

Table 14.1. Types of Physical and Non-physical Violence

Physical Violence	Non-physical Violence
Assault causing death	Verbal abuse
Assault causing serious physical injury	Racial or sexual abuse
Minor injuries	Threats (with or without weapons)
Kicking	Physical posturing
Biting	Threatening gestures
Punching	Abusive phone calls
Use of weapons	Threatening use of dogs
Use of missiles	Harassment
Spitting	Swearing
Scratching	Shouting
Sexual assault	Name-calling
	Bullying
	Insults
	Innuendo
	Deliberate silence

Source: Bibby (1994).

THE COSTS OF WORKPLACE VIOLENCE

Beech and Leather (2006: 29) point out:

> Among those intrinsic work features which put an occupational group 'at risk' is the need to interact with members of the public who are in pain, frustrated, receiving bad news that confirms their worst fears, or who may have poor impulse or anger control as part of their problem, or who are in hospital against their wishes.

While this statement refers to workers in the health care sector, it is clear that many of the features identified correlate strongly with the characteristics of certain groups of social care clients. Working closely with certain client groups poses risks to personal safety that need to be assessed and managed for the safety of social care practitioners, other clients, members of the general public and the client displaying the challenging behaviour. Installing appropriate and responsive procedures for assessing and managing risks in the workplace is likely to assist practitioners in maintaining a positive, therapeutic and client-centred approach in their work.

Any behaviour that is aggressive or violent will have negative consequences for individuals, agencies and for the broader society. Stress and injury caused by such behaviour also has a financial consequence in terms of absenteeism, premature retirement, frequent staff turnover, low morale and its consequent effect on team membership, productivity and the potential effectiveness of client placements. According to Cooper et al. (2003: 5):

> both physical and psychological violence have serious implications for health and well-being, with post-traumatic stress disorders and suicidal thoughts relatively common in the most serious cases. Fear of violence in its own right may also have an adverse effect, involving a much larger proportion of the population than those who are directly affected by the violence. Exposure to violence manifests itself behaviourally, with negative implications for job satisfaction, productivity and group dynamics.

Cooper et al. (2003) also make the point that third parties may be affected by workplace violence, most notably the families and friends of practitioners injured while at work, whose relationships suffer as a result of the stress experienced.

THE DUTY OF CARE

It is important to bear in mind that all attempts to manage challenging behaviour in social care settings must take cognisance of the 'duty of care' towards clients. This means taking reasonable care to avoid acts (or omissions) that could expose people, for whom there is an acknowledged responsibility, to a foreseeable risk of injury. Duty of care does not only apply to the helping professions. All employers must ensure that they provide and maintain a safe workplace, safe plant and machinery and safe operating systems. Workers have a duty of care to each other, while agencies must take reasonable care to ensure the welfare of both staff and clients. In social care settings, however, an equal reciprocal responsibility for the maintenance of the duty of care may not reasonably pertain. Vulnerable clients cannot always be expected to understand or agree to the maintenance of a code of conduct that is based on equal levels of knowledge, understanding and commitment.

Social care practitioners thus have an undeniable duty of care to their clients, many of whom are vulnerable to exploitation and harm. Special attention needs to be paid to the potential for aggressive behaviour in vulnerable or distressed clients and the adoption of particular approaches to the management of such behaviour that respect the right to the safety and dignity of all.

DEFINING 'CHALLENGING BEHAVIOUR'

Emerson (1995) defines challenging behaviour as:

> behaviour of such intensity, frequency and duration that the physical safety of the person or others is likely to be placed in serious jeopardy or behaviour which is likely to seriously limit or delay access to, and use of ordinary facilities.

This definition was developed in the context of the needs of people with intellectual disabilities, but subsequently extended to cover a wide range of social and health care client groups. It is interesting to note that interpretation of this definition has altered over time. Challenging behaviour was initially assessed as the degree to which it impeded a person's access to the ordinary, everyday settings that constitute normal social life. The 'challenge', therefore, was not interpreted as a hostile and aggressive attempt by the client to provoke a reaction from the staff member, but referred to how the service should respond to the needs of a client. The service was being 'challenged' to devise approaches that would reduce or remove altogether the client's need to behave inappropriately. Over time, the term has come to be used to mean 'problem' behaviour, indicating disruption, hostility and potential violence.

CAUSES OF CHALLENGING BEHAVIOUR

There are obvious dangers to attributing a general set of causes to the behaviours demonstrated by heterogeneous groups of people. It may safely be stated that there are personal, social and cultural factors associated with any individual's challenging behaviour. Specific conditions, for example, may predispose individuals to display challenging behaviour. Within the intellectual disability sector, certain biological syndromes, such as Prader-Willi Syndrome, are generally associated with challenging behaviour. People with severe intellectual disability may display aggressive behaviour, as they are unable to indicate that they are in pain or distressed. Older people with dementia may find it difficult to deal with a change of carer, routine or environment. Children with Attention Deficit Hyperactivity Disorder (ADHD) may have serious difficulty accepting the limits to their behaviour imposed by a structured classroom setting. None of the above examples indicates an intractable predisposition towards challenging behaviour. With careful observation and assessment, conditions may generally be treatable or manageable, with a consequent improvement in the quality of the therapeutic relationship enjoyed by the client and the carer.

On a social level, adverse family experiences may result in out-of-home placements for children and young people. Recovering from these experiences is a painful and complex matter. Young people often manifest a range of challenging behaviours in attempts to express fear, anger and anxiety. The development of models of care that focus on offering normalised, individualised and personalised support to clients has brought about significant insights into how episodes of challenging behaviour can be understood and managed. These insights, originating in the disability services, have been extended to service design and delivery across a range of personal and social needs. The gradual replacement of the medical model of care with a greater understanding of the social construction of ageing, disability, deviance and delinquency has led to more humane and responsive delivery of social care services to all client groups. A result of this has been that clients can now expect greater tolerance and respect for their individual needs and increased opportunities for higher levels of individual attention, in itself likely to reduce the need to engage in challenging behaviour in order to seek attention or reassurance.

On a cultural level, it is apparent that societal expectations have a key role to play in the behaviours manifested by those who are marginalised and subject to negative criticism. The pervasive effects of stigma (Goffman 1963) may be manifested by clients in ways that are self-injurious and also threatening to others.

The UK Mansell Report (1992) was a key driver in the attempt to respond to clients in a proactive and supportive manner. Mansell identified four essential aspects of service response to challenging behaviour:

1. *Prevention*, which includes an enriched and stimulating environment as well as the promotion of adaptive behaviour.
2. *Early detection*, including the observation and management of emergent problems.
3. *Crisis management*, involving contingency planning and skilled intervention.
4. Specialised *long-term support*, which emphasises individualised help for clients and high levels of support for staff.

Service developments have increasingly taken account of the disempowering effects of institutional care. The move away from large institutions – in all aspects of care, including elder care and residential child care as well as services for people with disabilities – towards community-based services has resulted in more responsive, person-centred approaches based on strong therapeutic relationships. A recognition that many behaviours are a response to social and environmental factors has led to increased efforts to assess those factors in care environments that contribute towards or hinder the attainment of a good quality of life. It is widely recognised that this may best be assured through the adoption of empowering approaches to delivering social care. *Empowerment* is a central theme in the design and delivery of social care services. Gibson (cited in Heumann et al. 2001: 9) defines empowerment as 'a process of recognizing, promoting and enhancing people's ability to meet their own needs, solve their own problems and mobilize necessary resources in order to feel in control of their own lives'.

Braye and Preston-Shoot (1995) express concern that service provision in itself may be oppressive. Services should value and build on people's strengths rather than focus on their deficits. Attempts to manage challenging behaviour within a culture of blame and power imbalance are more likely to reinforce the conditions and attitudes that caused the behaviours than to assist in their management. Some authors hold that empowerment is easier to define in terms of its absence. Rappaport (1984), for example, identified certain key factors as indicative outcomes of disempowerment – a state of powerlessness, whether real or imagined, learned helplessness, alienation and the loss of a sense of control over one's own life. In situations of perceived powerlessness, the client may engage in behaviours that guarantee personal attention, even if the consequences are negative or unpleasant.

Braye and Preston-Shoot (1995) stress the impact that collective endeavour has had on the development of a strong and active user movement in several social care fields. The principles of respect, tolerance and self-direction are exemplified in the participation of clients in their own service design and delivery. Such participation is likely to assist individuals and their families in articulating their preferences, feelings and fears and thus reduce the likelihood of resorting to challenging behaviour to have their needs and wants met.

While the Mansell Report (1992) offered insights into the roots of challenging behaviour and appropriate service responses, it also highlighted the important issue of whether it is appropriate to use *restraint* in care settings for people with intellectual disabilities. The debate extends to other social care settings where the effective and ethical management of challenging behaviour is a key factor in the development of positive therapeutic relationships with clients. Stirling and McHugh (1997: 1) point toward the professional drive to find non-aversive management strategies for managing challenging behaviour. They identify the main professional and ethical criticisms of control and restraint as the fact that 'the techniques used inflict some degree of pain or discomfort to the client, and the fact that it remains a reactive strategy with no theoretical framework for professional practice. On this basis, alternatives should be sought which seek to address these issues.'

Since the publication of the Mansell Report, agencies have used a variety of approaches to the management of challenging behaviour, most of which require the training and accreditation of practitioners. These approaches share similarities, tending to use combined strategies gleaned from the behaviourist perspective in psychology and counselling approaches. The behavioural interpretation understands challenging behaviour as a learned response to environmental stimuli. Managing the environment so as to carefully increase those stimuli that result in appropriate behaviour and reduce those that have negative outcomes is at the root of behaviour management strategies. Helping clients, through empathic support, to deal more appropriately with situations that trigger their negative responses is an intrinsic part of this approach.

Examples of popular behavioural management approaches include the following.

- *TCI (therapeutic crisis intervention)* is used exclusively in the residential care facilities under the aegis of the HSE. All residential care staff in HSE centres must be certified TCI practitioners and require regular recertification of their credentials.
- *CPI (the Crisis Prevention Institute)* provides a practical behaviour management programme, known as Non-violent Crisis Intervention, used extensively in services for people with intellectual disabilities. It is also practised in settings where clients tend to be confrontational, disruptive and/or aggressive.
- *MEBS (multi-element behaviour support)* is a non-aversive, supportive approach to working with challenging behaviour. It is primarily used in services that support people with intellectual disabilities and with autism spectrum disorders. The model is founded on a human rights-based approach and within a model that stresses person-centred planning.
- *A-B-C (antecedent-behaviour-consequence)* is based on functional behavioural assessment (FBA). This is a process primarily used to develop an understanding of a child's challenging behaviour and is used mainly in educational settings. The goal of FBA is to identify the function of the child's behaviour – the reason or purpose why a child behaves as they do in specific situations. This approach is also used by many child and family support agencies, where observation and assessment of the child's behaviour are central features of treatment strategies.

Other models also exist, designed to suit the requirements of specific care settings and clients, using insights, theories and approaches tried and tested by various professional groups such as nursing, psychology, social work and social care. These various models share certain common characteristics.

CHARACTERISTICS OF BEHAVIOUR MANAGEMENT MODELS

Any response to challenging behaviour should be consistent, fair and considered. The adoption of a particular approach to behaviour management by an agency is an attempt to ensure that the safest possible work practices are followed, with positive implications for the continued emotional and physical well-being of all the members of the agency community. While it is apparent that some behaviour may best be dealt with by the simple expedient of ignoring or redirecting it, it is not appropriate to ignore behaviour that is potentially abusive, destructive, threatening or dangerous.

All models that address the management of challenging behaviour emphasise the following 10 key characteristics.

1. *An ethos of respect for all members of the service community, including management, team leaders, staff and clients*
This is the essence of the duty of care, involving mutual responsibility for the maintenance of a respectful, supportive and therapeutic milieu.

2. *Endorsement and support of the behaviour management system by management*
This involves a full undertaking by management of the responsibility to ensure that the workplace is as safe as it can reasonably be. Management needs to acknowledge the need of staff and service users for full availability of resources – including adequate staffing levels, physical and technical resources, time to plan, implement and evaluate appropriate procedures, relevant training and professional supervision – necessary to deliver a professional, client-centred service.

3. *Effective risk assessment procedures*
The main aim is to attain a clear understanding of the specific behaviours that cause concern, to identify the environmental triggers and to measure the frequency and intensity with which the behaviour occurs. Measuring the behaviour involves questions such as how often and where does it occur? How long does it last? How do people in the vicinity normally react to it? How successful are current interventions? According to Scott (2008), 90 per cent of problematic behaviours in dementia care settings occur as a response to care practices or environmental factors. Identification and measurement of such factors in the care environment would appear to be essential to the assessment and management of risk.

Highly developed observational skills are necessary for accurate risk assessment. Even apparently minor factors in a client's environment can contribute to a build-up of tension that can spill over into inappropriate and aggressive behaviour. Practitioners need to be aware that even when situations are calm, there is a need to be alert to triggers that might cause an outburst. A sudden change in a client's behaviour, indicated perhaps through restlessness or extreme stillness, raised tone of voice or moody silence, can signal the onset of a challenge that may be verbal or physical, minor or extreme. It is at this point that the effective practitioner is considering appropriate responses, assessing risks, scanning the environment for objects that could become weapons, locating the presence of other staff and clients and generally engaging in mental and physical preparation for avoiding or dealing with a violent confrontation.

4. An individualised approach to understanding and relating to clients with challenging behaviour

Every client is unique, with a history of experiences different from everyone else. Clients who feel their individual concerns are being minimised or overlooked will tend to feel unhappy and possibly resentful. Such resentment can gradually build up to become a source of anger and frustration. Being acknowledged as an individual within a group setting is a reminder to clients of the special relationship that exists between themselves and those around them. Generally, this relationship is valued by clients, who may have experienced disappointment, neglect and abuse in the past.

If the practitioner calmly communicates empathy and understanding to the client, it may defuse a potentially aggressive situation. It is always necessary to emphasise the behaviour rather than the personality of the client. In this way, disapproval is directed away from the client and onto the unacceptable behaviour. The client and the practitioner are able to be clear and specific about the issue at hand. This clarity enables the client to accept the possibility that a change of behaviour is possible and preferable to an aggressive outburst. The relational aspect of client/practitioner interactions, which emphasises trust and respect, is central to effective behaviour management.

5. Self-awareness of staff

Reflective practice is the cornerstone of effective social care. Practitioners need to be willing to constantly scrutinise their practice and its relevance and effectiveness for clients. Each challenge brings with it a plethora of reactions. Practitioners need to be aware of their own responses to the challenging behaviours and acknowledge vulnerabilities, counterproductive reactions, tendencies to blame clients, reluctance to seek support and guidance and ineffective use of supervision. In particular, the management of challenging behaviour warrants continuous examination of the effect such behaviour has on the team members. All interactions with clients have emotional implications for practitioners, none more so than those in which the situation is highly charged and risk laden.

6. Clear incident and response plans and reporting procedures

Reporting and recording systems are essential for identifying the type of challenging behaviour encountered in specific workplaces or associated with particular clients. Such identification assists in the preparation and implementation of timely and effective interventions. In particular, all incidents involving physical and/or psychological aggression should be accurately and promptly reported and recorded.

The ILO (2002: 26) recommends that report forms include the following information.

- Where the incident occurred, including a description of the physical environment.
- The date and time of day.
- Activity at the time of the incident.
- Details of the victim.
- Details of the alleged perpetrator.
- Relationship between the victim and the alleged perpetrator.
- Account of what happened.
- Names of witnesses.
- Outcome of the incident.
- Measures taken after the incident.
- Effectiveness of such measures.
- Recommendations to prevent a similar incident from happening in the future.

The ILO also recommends that workers should be encouraged to report incidents where they are subjected to unnecessary or unacceptable levels of risk, regardless of whether a violent or dangerous incident has occurred.

7. Staff training

Effective models of behaviour management specify clear methods and rationales for intervention. Whatever model of behaviour management is used in a service, relevant staff training is a key factor in improving the quality of care offered to clients who demonstrate challenging behaviour. Allen and Tynan (2000) found trained staff to be more knowledgeable and confident than untrained staff when it came to managing challenging behaviour. McDonnell et al. (2008) noted increases in carer confidence in managing challenging behaviour after training.

The type of training undergone seems to be significant. Shore et al. (1995) found that an in-service training course that gave verbal instructions and explanations to staff was not effective at persuading staff to implement certain advocated approaches to managing challenging behaviour. Similarly, McDonnell et al. (2008) make the point that training workshops may not be sufficient for behavioural change in clients to occur. They recommend follow-up support and supervision in the workplace to increase the effect of the training. Scott (2008) also advocates a combination of teaching, supervision and intense support for workers who regularly have to manage challenging behaviour.

8. An *effective and relevant behaviour management approach*
It is essential that practitioners are able to:

- Identify the stages of a client's gradual build-up (or 'escalation') to a crisis.
- Quickly make use of individual and team responses that will assist the client to de-escalate.
- Use verbal and sometimes non-verbal interventions to manage behaviour that is in danger of becoming out of control.
- Use debriefing techniques appropriate to the client's level of understanding and self-awareness and to the needs of practitioners.
- Document the incident honestly, thoroughly, dispassionately and fairly.

McDonnell (1997) recommends three elements in a behaviour management approach: simple preventative strategies, a low-arousal approach to reducing aggressive behaviours and, if necessary, socially validated physical interventions designed to avoid pain. These should be underpinned by an understanding of thenature and causes of aggressive behaviour. Staff, therefore, need a strong contextualised knowledge base as well as practical training in behaviour management strategies.

Simple *preventive strategies* rely heavily on practical management of the environment. Reducing excessive heat and noise, ensuring adequate physical space and removing objects that might become weapons are sensible attempts to reduce situational factors that might lead to an escalation of tension and violence. Strategies to promote positive behaviour are also part of the management of challenging behaviour. Praising clients for good and helpful behaviour, increasing self-esteem by recognising talents and skills and creating opportunities for praise and encouragement are all strategies for reinforcing the therapeutic relationship and supporting respectful communication.

It is also necessary to have a behaviour management plan for each individual who displays challenging behaviour. This is to ensure that practitioners do not simply react to isolated incidents, but regard each episode as part of an overall management strategy, with clear goals and observable outcomes. Precise identification of which behaviours are to be managed, and how, is essential, as most clients will exhibit a range of behaviours and it is counterproductive to attempt to change all of them at once.

The *low-arousal approach* is an essential feature of effective situational management. Direct confrontation, featuring a raised tone of voice and a potentially threatening stance, is likely to lead to an escalation of the tension and anxiety that prompted the challenging behaviour in the first place. Effective communication skills, including assertiveness, are crucial components of the low-arousal approach. The ability to establish personal contact and maintain the therapeutic relationship with the client, even when under considerable pressure, is a key feature of professionalism in social care. The quality of the rapport between the practitioner and client needs to be sustained purposively by the former from the moment that tension and anxiety are noted, through the entire episode and during the outcomes phase.

The use of *physical interventions* to prevent or control aggressive behaviour has long been a contentious issue in health and social care. Discussion and elaboration of the legal situation of agencies and practitioners in relation to the care of vulnerable children and adults is outside the remit of this chapter. It should be acknowledged that the law recognises the need to take action using the minimum possible restraint to prevent injury to the individual or to others and to prevent damage to property. Minimal force should be used when restraining clients whose behaviour has escalated to the point where they are a danger to themselves or to others. Apart from the danger of inflicting injury on a client, there is also the ethical question of whether using aggressive responses to challenging behaviour is appropriate, just or therapeutic. The decision to restrain a client should never be taken by a sole individual, but taken jointly by team members and should always be the last resort of staff members in a critical incident. All other strategies for managing the behaviour must have been tried before a decision to restrain is taken. It is also essential that only those trained and certified as competent to use restraint engage in holding clients, due to the real risk of injury to the client and to the practitioner. Not all agencies advocate the use of physical restraint; many prefer to use situation management techniques consistently and repeatedly in order to engage therapeutically with challenging clients.

9. A team approach
This is necessary to ensure the consistency, transparency, efficiency and effectiveness of interventions. The practitioner also needs to feel supported by colleagues in order to ensure that levels of personal effectiveness are not undermined by lack of confidence in each other's capabilities. The practitioner needs to be able to maintain rapport not only with the client, but also with other workers. High levels of tension can interfere with the ability to offer unconditional support to the client, and the fear and anger often generated in critical incidents can prevent practitioners from supporting each other. Failure to deal with this aspect of the situation can lead to the breakdown of trust between team members, with negative implications for future team work.

10. Debriefing
According to the ILO (2002: 26), debriefing should be made available to all who experience workplace violence and should include:

- Sharing personal experience with others to defuse the impact of violence.
- Helping those who have been affected by workplace violence to understand and come to terms with what has happened.
- Offering reassurance and support.

- Getting people to focus on the facts and give information.
- Explaining the subsequent help available.

Ideally, debriefing after a violent or threatening episode should take place within the relationship of professional supervision. Within a pre-existing relationship of trust and support, a practitioner will be facilitated to come to terms with the conflicting emotions emanating from the personal experience of violence in the workplace. Many practitioners feel angry with the client, with the agency and with the management. There can also be feelings of guilt that such an incident happened while the client was in their care. Fear of a repeat incident or of appearing to be incompetent can also feature in the practitioner's personal response. All these emotions contribute to feelings of vulnerability. This makes it difficult to achieve a reasonable level of understanding of why the incident happened, the part that the practitioner had to play in handling the situation and how more positive outcomes could be achieved in the future. Effective debriefing is essential for the practitioner's continued psychological well-being. It is also an important part of the risk assessment strategy of the agency, as vulnerabilities are clarified and patterns of interaction explored.

CONCLUSION

This chapter has attempted to clarify certain key aspects of the management of challenging behaviour in social care settings. The balance between maintaining a therapeutic relationship with the client while also keeping the client, other clients and practitioners safe is a serious challenge in social care. Agencies attempt to address their responsibilities towards clients and practitioners by adopting certain behaviour management approaches and training all staff to use them competently. For successful outcomes, such approaches need to be practised within a team situation where mutual responsibilities are acknowledged. Professional supervision is a primary safeguard for practitioners' health and well-being. By paying attention to the continuous development of self-awareness and professional skills within a respectful team ethos, practitioners can engage meaningfully with the attempt to place the client's well-being firmly at the centre of all interventions. It is apparent, therefore, that safe and competent management of challenging behaviour can be a catalyst for clients to develop positive strategies for seeking reassurance and support during their social care placements.

15

Collaborative Advantage: Interdisciplinary Teamwork in Social Care

Clare Rigg and Patrick McGarty

OVERVIEW

Social care is a broad field of work, and social care graduates can find themselves working in a wide range of jobs and services. Whichever direction they take, however, one thing is certain – social care practice invariably involves collaborating in teams with other professions and disciplines, because it is increasingly recognised that service needs, social issues and societal problems cannot be resolved by single agencies or individual professions alone. Service users often have multiple needs that benefit from integrated service provision, rather than a fragmented series of encounters with disparate agencies. A teenager arriving on the door of a homeless shelter, for instance, may well not only need accommodation, but also have mental health problems and need money advice. In addition, the underlying issues that result in service needs, whether it be, for example, domestic violence, substance abuse or homelessness, typically have complex causes, leading them to be termed 'wicked problems' (Conklin 2006; Rittel and Webber 1973).

One of the defining characteristics of wicked problems is that the different people involved (the stakeholders) have radically different worldviews as well as different values and perspectives for understanding the problem (Conklin 2006). This means that getting teams to work effectively is an even greater challenge than teamwork within a single organisation. Collaboration between professions and disciplines potentially offers advantages to social care provision – the 'collaborative advantage' of interdisciplinary team-working – but there are pitfalls. The aim of this chapter is therefore to address some of the issues related to interdisciplinary[1] teamwork in social care practice arising from the complex context described above. The chapter will cover the following:

- What is a team and what is an interdisciplinary team?
- When to use teams and when not to.

- Creating a team – getting off to a good start.
- What makes teams high performing?
- Why teams can be dysfunctional and what can be done about them.
- Leadership behaviours that make the most of team-working.

INTRODUCTION

In recent times, the pace of change in social care services in Ireland has been rapid and has affected everyone from managers, to frontline staff, to end-users. Ongoing restructuring in relation to planning, organisation, funding and delivery of services has presented new challenges for social care practitioners, and the expectations placed on managers are now many and varied. Government policies now emphasise accountability, quality, performance, value for money, an emphasis on outcomes and the integration of health and social care services in a dynamic work environment. Health and social care services are not a conventional service industry, yet managers face the normal dilemmas of any industry in relation to staffing, resourcing and budgeting. The fact that social care managers operate within a legal and increasingly structured framework means that they need to be not only supervisors of professional good practice, but also monitors of compliance of agreed care procedures. In this context, the importance of human relationships in the workplace should never be taken for granted (Henderson and Atkinson 2003). In particular, organising service delivery through teams and teamwork is most important. Strategic planning in health and social care recognises the contribution of teams in the sector – multidisciplinary teams rather than individuals will become the building blocks of organisations pursuing health gains (Doherty 1998).

One of the consequences of the growth of such teams is the potential for tensions based on the different values and norms that often arise from diverse professional backgrounds, conflicting allegiances, contrasting performance management regimes or differing financial and information management systems. While education and training in social care and social work now emphasise teamwork, many professionals still have only a limited understanding of the implications of team-working, particularly when the team is interdisciplinary.

WHAT IS A TEAM?

In its broadest sense, 'team' is an everyday concept familiar to everyone, but the term is often confused with other groupings. When asked, many people will define a team as a group of people, but if asked to list a range of groups they themselves are members of, only some of these will be a team. The list of groups is likely to include family, friends, church or other religious group, sports team, band, hobby group, fundraising committee, class cohort, work colleagues, etc. However, these are only a team if they have most or all of the following characteristics (Adair 1983; Kazenbuch and Smith 1993):

- A *definable membership:* A collection of three or more people identifiable by name or type.
- A *group consciousness or identity:* The members think of themselves as a group.
- *Committed to a common purpose:* The members share some common task or performance goals.
- *Interdependence:* The members rely on each another to accomplish this purpose and hold each other mutually accountable.
- *Interaction:* The members communicate with one another, influence one another and react to one another.
- *Sustainability:* The team members periodically review the team's effectiveness.
- An *ability to act together,* as one.

Usually, the tasks and goals set by teams cannot be achieved by individuals working alone because of limited time and resources, and because few individuals possess all the relevant skills and expertise. Sports teams or orchestras clearly fit these criteria. Families, class cohorts and hobby groups generally do not.

Just because a group has the title 'team' does not mean it is a team if it does not show most of the characteristics above. Every workplace has groups that are called a team (e.g. senior management teams, project teams), but in reality the members do not share a common purpose, they communicate poorly and do not work interdependently. The entire workforce of any large and complex organisation is rarely a genuine team, but is often described as such. In summary, if a group of people are accurately to call themselves a team, they will be a small group with a mixture of skills, sharing a common purpose to achieve some specific outcomes for which they see themselves as mutually accountable.

WHAT IS AN INTERDISCIPLINARY TEAM?

In social care work, teams are regularly used to bring people with different expertise together to try to address difficult problems and improve services. Teams may be assembled to carry out a variety of roles on a short-, medium- or long-term basis. In a social care environment, effective teamwork will ultimately shape the quality of service delivered to client groups. Some examples of interdisciplinary teams are as follows.

- An *Intercultural Strategy for Youth Work* is being developed through collaboration between youth work policy-makers, practitioners such as youth and community workers, and representatives from minority ethnic communities and organisations.
- *Domestic violence* is typically addressed through collaborative approaches involving local refuges, women's aid, Gardaí, community medical and health professionals, accident and emergency unit staff, legal professionals and community workers.

- The *National Youth Health Programme* is a partnership between the National Youth Council of Ireland, the Health Service Executive and the Youth Affairs Section of the Department of Education and Science, for the purpose of providing a broadly based, flexible health promotion, support and training service to youth organisations and to ensure that young people's health is on the policy agenda.
- The *Central Remedial Clinic* is a non-residential national centre for the care, treatment and development of children and adults with physical disabilities. Services provided involve professionals in clinical assessment, physiotherapy, hydrotherapy, speech therapy, occupational therapy, social work, psychology, nursing, dietetics, orthotics, technical services, orthopaedics, paediatrics, parent support, vision and hearing specialists, transport and catering.
- *Primary care centres* aim for a more integrated and comprehensive care service by bringing together in a single centre such professionals as GPs, public health nurses, social workers, child protection workers, chiropody, speech and language therapy, opthalmics and physiotherapy.

These are all examples of interdisciplinary teams in that they unite people of diverse professional skills (that is, from differing disciplines) for a shared purpose of making a bigger difference in tackling complex issues such as domestic violence, racism, young people's health or enabling people with disabilities to develop their potential. It is the extra dimension of teamwork that makes performance levels greater than the sum of the individual bests of team members possible. Simply stated, a team is more than the sum of its parts (Kazenbuch and Smith 1993). In social care environments, some of the strongest teams have developed vision, direction, momentum and common purpose, working with the most difficult of client groups.

Teamwork is, of course, used within single organisations, e.g. senior management teams, area social worker teams or teams of play-workers on a summer play scheme. The key distinction of an interdisciplinary team is that the members have diverse professional backgrounds, giving them quite distinct training, skills and roles, as well as (typically) differing values, norms, social status and ways of talking about and understanding the causes of the issues they are working on. Herein lies both the potential for mixed teams, but also the challenge in how to form them effectively. But first a caution – for all the enthusiasm about team-working, there are times when they are best not used.

WHEN, AND WHEN NOT, TO USE TEAMS

We have discussed why interdisciplinary teams can benefit service delivery and also instances when the term 'team' is applied to groupings that actually do not function as a true team. In addition, it is important to acknowledge that not all situations require a team or in fact benefit from teamwork. If a task is fairly simple and there is little need for co-operation amongst different people to complete the task, a team is not necessary (Pedler et al. 2004). For example, if all that is needed is regular progress updates of what other people are doing on their respective tasks, and if completing these tasks does not need other people's expertise or ideas, there is no need for teamwork. In fact, to try and force teamwork in such circumstances may well be detrimental, in that people can feel it is a waste of their time and it can overcomplicate a simple issue.

CREATING A TEAM – GETTING OFF TO A GOOD START

While the benefits of working together are well known, building teams and achieving effective teamwork are often difficult. Often, a group of people is thrown together and it is assumed they will naturally make a team. This is not the case and teamwork will not result in every instance.

Various models of team formation recognise that a group has to mature to reach the point of mature team-working. Tuckman and Jensen's version, for example, suggests stages of formation, including the following.

- *Forming*: When people come together and tend to be guarded and often excessively polite.
- *Storming*: Where personal differences begin to emerge as individuals conflict over such issues as how to work and whose ideas will dominate.
- *Norming*: Where ground rules and ways of working are established and trust begins to develop.
- *Performing*: Being able to work at a high level, making decisions, openly disagreeing and valuing members' diverse ways of thinking and operating, even if this is frustratingly different from your own (adapted from Tuckman and Jensen 1977).

Getting a group off to a good start means allowing time to work through these stages and taking steps to deliberately take a group through them. This can mean using an external facilitator to guide the team through some initial structured discussions that explicitly explore the following.

- The purpose of the team, its primary task and the intended outcomes – it is amazing how often people come together thinking they have a shared purpose, but then find they have quite different views on what they want the team to achieve.
- How to organise – what will be the working processes, such as making decisions or voicing disagreement, and ground rules for how members will act towards each other.
- What role individual members will play and who will formally take the lead in the team.

These points are important for any team, but they are heightened for inter-disciplinary teams. Among the barriers often highlighted are intra- and inter-professional rivalries that can occur. Interpersonal differences, lack of teamwork training and competing priorities of members' employing organisations will also risk fragmenting an interdisciplinary team. So what can be done to help a team become high performing and really fulfil its promise of being more than the sum of its parts?

WHAT MAKES A TEAM HIGH PERFORMING?

High-performing teams are those that work extremely effectively, deliver strong results and also continue to be significant for the individual members. Some key features are as follows.

- A well-defined purpose that is seen as significant by all team members.
- The expertise and characteristics of members of the team are complementary.
- The team initially allowed itself time to go through the stages of development – forming, storming, norming and performing – with the result that there is good trust and valuing of personal differences amongst members.
- Good habits for making decisions and taking action.
- Regularly takes time out to review how it is working and is open to self-criticism.
- Effective ways have been developed for individuals and the team itself to continue to learn.
- Combines both support and challenge – has a good balance between being supportive of individuals and encouraging questioning, challenging and experimentation.
- Individuals feel the team is making an impact and achieving results.

In addition, the high-performing team avoids what are termed the 'trappings of success' (Pedler et al. 2004), such as becoming complacent, keeping others out or being condescending to clients.

Thus, we can see that teamwork requires behaviours such as listening and responding constructively to views expressed by others; providing support and feedback; recognising the interests and achievements of others; and being open to challenging questioning.

TEAM ROLES

Teams work well when everyone has a role that complements the others. Ideally, the composition and skill set of a team should ensure that there is appropriate diversity to undertake the necessary team roles. There are two different ways of categorising these roles: *task roles* and *process roles*.

Table 15.1. Useful Roles to Have in a Team

Team Role	Team Contribution Strengths	Allowable Weaknesses
Plant	Creative, imaginative, unorthodox, solves difficult problems. Team's source of original ideas.	Ignores incidents. Can dwell on 'interesting ideas' and be too preoccupied to communicate well.
Implementer	Disciplined, reliable, conservative and efficient. Turns ideas into practical actions. Turns decisions into manageable tasks. Brings method to the team's activities.	Somewhat inflexible. Slow to respond to new possibilities. Upset by frequent changes of plan.
Completer-finisher	Painstaking and conscientious. Searches out errors and omissions. Delivers on time.	Anxious introvert; inclined to worry unduly. Reluctant to delegate. Dislikes casual approach by others.
Monitor-evaluator	Sober, strategic and discerning. Offers dispassionate, critical analysis. Sees all options. Judges accurately.	Lacks drive and ability to inspire others. Lacks warmth and imagination. Can lower morale by being a dampener.
Resource investigator	Extrovert, enthusiastic and communicative. Explores opportunities. Diplomat with many contacts.	Over-optimistic. Loses interest as enthusiasm wanes. Jumps from one task to another.
Shaper	Challenging, dynamic, thrives on pressure. Brings drive and courage to overcome obstacles. Task minded; makes things happen.	Easily provoked or frustrated. Impulsive and impatient. Offends others' feelings. Intolerant of vagueness.
Teamworker	Promotes team harmony; diffuses friction. Listens. Co-operative, mild, perceptive and diplomatic. Sensitive but gently assertive.	Indecisive in crunch situations. May avoid confrontation situations.
Co-ordinator	Clarifies goals; good chairperson; promotes decision-making; good communicator; social leader; delegates well.	Can be seen as manipulative. Inclined to let others do the work. May take credit for the team's work.
Specialist	Provides rare skills and knowledge. Single-minded and focused. Self-starting and dedicated.	Contributes only on a narrow front. Communication skills are often weak. Often cannot see the 'big picture' and dwells on technicalities.

Source: Adapted from Belbin (1993).

Task roles are those to do with the content of the work and the functional expertise an individual brings. For example, a youth justice project might involve Gardaí, a family social worker, probation officer, teacher and community worker. Each will contribute their professional view and their particular expertise, for example, knowledge of the law, education resources, sources of income.

Process roles are to do with the part each member contributes to help the team function and get the work done. One useful way of thinking about these roles comes from Belbin's work on teams (Belbin 1993). He defines a team role as a tendency to behave, contribute and interrelate with others in a particular way. The behavioural-based model of team roles he developed suggests that effective teams need to have a range of participants who play nine very different roles within the team structure (see Table 15.1). No one person can have all the attributes, but individuals will tend to be stronger in two or three areas. Each role has particular strengths a team needs, but also particular 'allowable' weaknesses that can be compensated by a well-balanced team.

WHY TEAMS CAN BE DYSFUNCTIONAL AND WHAT CAN BE DONE ABOUT THEM

It is not uncommon for teams to struggle and even for what were once high-performing teams to slide into difficulty. Such dysfunctional groups are often teams in name only, but in reality are splintered into sub-groups with one or two individuals feeling left out. A common cause is behaviours by some individuals that damage trust and weaken communication, such as:

- Avoiding disagreements or voicing true opinions.
- Simmering, unresolved conflicts.
- Going along with decisions to avoid argument.
- Competing for control of the group.
- Putting up a front to avoid looking bad.
- Constantly drawing attention to themselves.
- Insufficient leadership.
- Losing sight of any common purpose.

Turning a dysfunctional team around is not easy. It has to start with acknowledging the unhelpful behaviours and a reminder that the team exists to deliver certain outcomes to a particular set of clients. This is often best done with external facilitation. If members remind themselves of the common purpose they share – that the reason they came together was to make a specific difference to users – this can sometimes help them move on (for further reading on working with groups, see Bion 1961; Obholzer and Roberts 1994; Rigg with Richards 2006).

It is often said that a strong team is one with good leadership. However, this begs the question: what is leadership and where might you find it in a team? These questions are discussed in the next section.

EXAMPLE OF A DYSFUNCTIONAL TEAM

A child care group has eight members and is chaired by the county council service director. Two of the members of the group are candidates for an important promotion and are keen to impress the director, whose opinion is crucial to their chances. Group meetings are generally argumentative, with these two members interrupting each other and 'getting at' each other personally. The meetings also seem to go on for ages without getting anywhere, because with strong, undeclared hidden agendas, people argue about issues without being honest about the reasons for their disagreements. Outside the group, people express a sense of frustration and alienation from the main issues, but they never voice their feelings or views inside meetings.

LEADERSHIP AND FOLLOWERSHIP

Leadership has traditionally been defined as the process of influencing others to work willingly towards the objectives and goals of a group, team or organisation. 'Leadership' is a term that is much used and can seem very familiar and yet be much misunderstood. If we say we want more and better leadership, what do we mean – where and from whom? If asked to name three significant leaders, most people will pick quite remote, often historical figures (such as Mother Theresa, Nelson Mandela, Ghandi or Hitler). Yet if asked to name three people who have had the most influence on them, they generally pick close-by individuals, such as a teacher, parent, employer or sports coach. The two lists rarely overlap. This makes it very difficult to pin down a set of traits that define good leadership, though many have tried (see below).

It is helpful to think of leadership in three ways:

1. *Leadership as position*: The formal position of authority – sports team captain, project leader, service director. The hope is that the position holder can influence others because he/she has formal authority.
2. *Leadership as function*: The broad activity of directing the organisation, recognising key challenges and mobilising action.
3. *Leadership as practice*: This refers to what leaders do – the everyday actions they carry out in response to challenges, for example, how they use power, how they challenge or whether they work with a clear purpose. This is a useful distinction, because it opens up the space for thinking about what leaders do, rather than getting overly concerned with a person's position.

Good leadership of teams is important for social care clients and organisations. One of the leading writers on leadership, Beverley Alimo-Metcalfe (2002), suggests there are three rationales for leadership: a performance case, a business case and a moral case (Alimo-Metcalfe and Nyfield 2002).

The *performance case* sees leadership as 'helping unremarkable people to do remarkable things'. The hope is that in a complex world, leadership helps people focus their effort. This means providing direction for their work, stimulating problem-solving, getting things done and dealing with multiple priorities. Leadership is about imagining ambitious, better futures, rallying followers' energies and developing their capacity for higher levels of performance. This case for leadership is reinforced by the view taken by Mike Pedler et al. (2004), that leadership is about action in the face of challenge – that is, without leadership, less gets done and difficult issues go unaddressed. Individuals certainly benefit from leadership in that it has been found that without having their motivation and self-confidence nurtured, then after 18 months in a new job, people's performance level tends to flatten.

The *business case* for leadership is backed up by evidence of the cost of poor leadership. Through poor leadership, organisations waste money and staff. Job changes are frequently provoked by the desire to get away from a poor boss – people leave their managers rather than their job. It is known that organisations lose money from absenteeism, but it is also likely there is a connection with poor leadership. A recent Confederation of British Industry study (CBI 2007) found that 72 per cent of absenteeism is attributed to stress. Two-thirds of this is put down by staff to their boss. Poor leaders fail to help their staff deal with the stresses of work and indeed exacerbate stress through their behaviours.

We know the potential of power to corrupt, but Rosabeth Moss Kanter suggests also that 'powerlessness corrupts and absolute powerlessness corrupts absolutely' (1977: 166). This recognition of the inhumane consequences of poor leadership is the basis for the *moral case* for leadership. Bad leadership, whether in the form of bullying, inequity or inconsistency, can contribute to a poor working environment that is damaging for people. Yet just as bad is poor leadership that takes the shape of inaction, or abdication of responsibility. In fact, some would argue that leaders are servants and leadership is a service to others which there is a moral responsibility not to decline.

The arguments above suggest why social care staff might benefit from good leadership and that, likewise, clients benefit from the improved services that better leadership should produce. But what exactly is a good leader? This is a question that has preoccupied many people for many years.

WHAT MAKES A GOOD LEADER?

Reflecting on leadership qualities, Dixon (1994) concluded:

> One comes to the simple truth that leadership is no more than exercising such an influence upon others that they tend to act in concert towards

achieving a goal which they might not have achieved so readily had they been left to their own devices. The ingredients which bring about this state of affairs are many and varied. At the most superficial level they are believed to include such factors as voice, stature and appearance, an impression of omniscience, trustworthiness, sincerity and bravery. At a deeper and rather more important level, leadership depends on a proper understanding of the needs and opinions of those one hopes to lead, and the context in which the leadership occurs. It also depends on good timing. Hitler, who was neither omniscient, trustworthy nor sincere, whose stature was repellent, understood these rules and exploited them to full advantage. The same may be said of many good comedians. (Dixon 1994: 214–5)

Thinking about leadership can be divided into four approaches, each of which is expanded in the box below.

1. Trait.
2. Style.
3. Contingency.
4. New transformational.

The important trend to notice is that thinking about leadership has moved away from the belief that good leaders are born with certain traits to the belief that leadership concerns actions and relationships between leaders and followers.

A SHORT HISTORY OF LEADERSHIP THEORY

Trait Theory

The time during the 1930s to 1950s was dominated by beliefs that good leaders were those that had core heroic personality traits, such as initiative, self-assurance, appearance, imagination, sociability and decisiveness; that leaders are born, not made. These 'Great Man' theories foundered because there was never any consistent agreement on what the essential traits of leadership were and many of the attributes outlined describe patterns of human behaviour rather than personality traits. Despite trait theory being discredited in many academic quarters, many managerial selection schemes and testing procedures still operate on a trait basis in identifying potential managers.

Style Theory

In contrast to trait theorists, style leadership theorists argue that employees will work harder for managers who employ certain *styles* of leadership.

Organisation psychologists in Michigan and Ohio State universities in the 1950s identified two pillars of leadership behaviour: employee-centred behaviour that focuses on relationships and employee needs, and job-centred behaviour that focuses on getting the job done. This led to the development of the notion of democratic and autocratic leadership styles, with two types of leadership behaviour – consideration and initiating. Consideration is leadership behaviour that involves participation in decision-making and involves trust and support for the workforce. In contrast, initiating behaviour emphasises performance and goal attainment and expects workers to follow instructions. Likert (1961) elaborated a further model with four different styles of leadership: dictatorial, autocratic, democratic and laissez-faire.

Contingency

While it is recognised that an employee-centred, participative and democratic style of leadership is favoured by most employees, proponents of contingency theory argue that one leadership style may not be effective in all circumstances, but is contingent on the particular situation. According to Fielder (1967), the style a leader should choose to be effective is dependent on a number of factors, including the leader's personality, whether the leader is motivated by relationships or task completion, whether the leader has control and influence in the workplace, and by wider environmental factors, such as organisation structure, characteristics of employees, the nature and complexity of the group's task, reward structure, nature of work contracts and external environment, all of which contribute to unique situations that ultimately influence leadership style.

New Transformational

Since the 1990s, thinking about leadership has changed to focus on activities and relations: on what leaders actually do across all levels of a hierarchy and on the inter-relationships between them and others. A differentiation is made between *transactional* and *transformational* leadership behaviours (Alimo-Metcalfe and Nyfield 2002). Both are necessary for organisation performance, but it is transformational leadership that most influences followership. Transactional leadership is the familiar management, whereby the manager makes transactions, exchanges resources, plans and monitors systematically. A core principle of transformational leadership is that people follow when they can see connections between their own sense of purpose and identity and the wider organisation vision or purpose. Transformational leaders are those who help make those connections. However, people also follow leaders whose values and actions they respect, so transformational leadership qualities include integrity, consistency and equity, or *modelling the way* as well as decisiveness and willingness to take risks. It is well summarised by Jim Collins (2001: 36) when he describes great leaders as 'a paradoxical blend of intense professional will and personal humility'.

Before going back to discuss leadership of social care teams, there is one other area of debate that is worth introducing. It was suggested above why social care clients might benefit from good leadership, but it is too simplistic to say that what a team therefore needs is someone in charge, like a team manager. This is partly because, as we have said before, the idea of leadership going with position is only one of three aspects of leading. However, it is also because to lead is not the same as to manage, as we now discuss.

LEADING AND MANAGING – HOW DO THEY COMPARE?

Good leadership overlaps with good management, but many would argue it differs in a number of key respects. It is not new to look to manage efficiency and effectiveness to deliver successful organisational performance, but this is no longer sufficient. As discussed above, the social care world presents increasingly complex challenges, which need more than efficient procedural responses: 'Managing is more about bringing order and control and implies systems and procedures ... leading is more concerned with finding direction and purpose in the face of critical challenges' (Pedler et al. 2004: 3).

Pedler et al. clearly see leadership as distinct from management, but this is a much-debated question. Academic debate has centred on arguments in relation to the difference, if any, between leadership and management. Some would see these terms as synonymous, as leadership is part of the management role. Mintzberg (1979) contends that the distinction between leadership and management is blurred, as the roles overlap. He asserts that leadership is but one dimension of a multifaceted management role. Many other commentators would argue that leaders and managers play different roles and make different contributions to organisation development and direction. They contend that leaders have followers, while managers have subordinates.

Those who make a clear distinction portray the leader as someone who develops visions and drives new initiatives, and the manager as someone who monitors progress towards objectives to achieve order and reliability (Huczynski and Buchanan 2001). The leader is prophet, catalyst and mover-shaker, focused on strategy, while the manager is operator, technician and problem-solver, concerned with the routine here-and-now of goal attainment (Bryman 1986). The leader establishes vision and direction, motivates and inspires, while the manager establishes plans, designs and staffs the organisation structure, controls perform-ance and produces order. Consistency and predictability are the hallmarks of a manager, while passion and energising are the very different words that often describe a leader. Kotter (1990) contends that there are clear distinguishing factors between both functions (see Table 15.2).

Table 15.2. Leadership and Management Compared

	Leadership Functions	Management Functions
Creating an Agenda	Establishes direction: vision of the future, develops strategies for change to achieve goals.	Plans and budgets: decides actions and timetables, allocates resources.
Developing People	Aligning people, organising and staffing: communicates vision and strategy, influences creation of teams that accept validity of goals.	Decides structure and allocates staff, develops policies, procedures and monitoring.
Execution	Motivating and inspiring: energises people to overcome obstacles, satisfies human needs.	Controlling, problem-solving: monitors results against plan and takes corrective action.
Outcomes	Produces positive and sometimes dramatic change.	Produces order, consistency and predictability.

Source: Kotter (1990).

Thus, there is strong evidence for a clear distinction between the process of managing and the process of leading, what Kouzes and Posner (1987) summarise as the difference between getting others to do and getting others to *want to do*. Leaders do this by being credible; they establish this credibility by their actions – by challenging, inspiring, enabling, modelling and encouraging. Thinking of leadership as practice like this (the third domain above) is useful because it also does not imply that leadership is only shown by people in charge of an organisation or team.

LEADERSHIP IN INTERDISCIPLINARY TEAMS

Now we want to highlight some implications for interdisciplinary teams. A feature of interdisciplinary teams is that they often comprise a group of people from different professions with equal authority in their own particular areas of competence. Decisions about clients' care and treatment are arrived at by consensus; no single member is able to override others. In this kind of team, there is typically no single senior individual in the formal position of team leader. There may well be a designated leader selected from within the team, but they will not have greater status than others and will perform more of a role of co-ordinator or chairperson. It may be a self-managed team that rotates the role of co-ordinator.

Thinking of leadership as practice helps us recognise that what is important for team effectiveness is less the question of who has the formal role, than who engages in leadership practices. An effective team is one where leadership is *distributed* across the team and not confined to those with formal leadership roles and titles. This is termed *distributed leadership* (Spillane 2006). What this means in practice is that there will be actions from many, if not all, team members that help to create and sustain effective team relationships. For example, these leadership practices might include asking questions that help the team develop and keep its sense of purpose, such as, 'What is this team for?', 'What is our work?', 'What will we do?' and 'What impact do we want to have?' Other 'distributive leadership' practices would contribute to helping people build relationships.

In summary, effective and high-performing teams will have extensive leadership practices distributed throughout the team. As Gerard Egan has said, 'If your organisation has only one leader then it is almost certainly short of leadership' (cited in Peddler et al. 2004: vii).

CONCLUSION

Social care work aims to make a difference to people's lives, often through tackling some of the most difficult or 'wicked' problems. Teams are not always the best way of organising in all situations, but they have an increasing role to play both within organisations and drawing from multiple organisations into interdisciplinary teams. These bring a wider range of skills together into more integrated service delivery and more comprehensive problem-solving than any single agency or profession can achieve alone.

When it works well, an interdisciplinary team is more than the sum of its parts. But alongside the potential benefits of diverse professional backgrounds are the challenges that are posed by the mix of values, norms, social status and ways of talking about and understanding the causes of the issues they are working on. There is a danger of interdisciplinary groups punching below their weight and not fulfilling their potential as a high-performing team. To make the most of their potential and to avoid such dysfunctional pitfalls as splintering or being a mere talking shop, teams can take the following steps.

1. Invest time in initial *team formation* and do not just assume a collection of individuals thrown together will naturally form a team.
2. Pay attention to achieving a balance of *team roles* to aid the *process* of working as well as the mix of professional skills.
3. Encourage *distributed leadership* so that leadership actions are taken by many (or all) of the team members.

16

Personal and Professional Development for Social Care Workers

John Byrne

OVERVIEW

Social care in Ireland is changing faster than ever before. It is widely accepted that while having a kind, caring disposition is a prerequisite to work in the profession, by itself it is not enough. Social care service users present with a wide range of complex issues. They may be homeless and/or have addiction difficulties; they may have physical, sensory or intellectual disabilities; they may have experienced, or be experiencing, extreme disadvantage; and they may be victims or perpetrators of various forms of abuse, neglect and maltreatment. Irrespective of the service user or the presenting issue, the task for the social care worker is the same: to help clients to identify their needs and to ensure that those needs are met.

This chapter explores the task of social care practice and identifies why it is necessary for students and workers to engage in an ongoing process of both personal and professional development. The training requirements for practice are identified with reference to a bio-psycho-social model of needs assessment from residential child care. An emphasis is placed throughout on the concepts of reflective practice and continuing professional development.

INTRODUCTION

In 1997, an expert group was established as a result of a Labour Court recommendation to report on issues affecting 10 health and social care-related professional disciplines. The report recommended the development of a joint committee to explore and report on issues affecting the residential child care sector. The committee was to consist of representatives of IMPACT, the Health Services Employment Agency (HSEA), the Resident Managers' Association, the Department of Health and Children, the Social Services Inspectorate and employers. A subsequent Labour Court recommendation expanded the terms of reference of that joint committee to include the intellectual disability sector.

The report of this Joint Committee for Social Care Professionals (JCSCP) defined social care as being 'the professional provision of care, protection, support, welfare and advocacy to vulnerable or dependant people individually or in groups' (JCSCP nd: 3). The committee states at the outset that social care is professional care. The extent to which this is the case is the focus of ongoing debate within academic discourse (see Chapters 1 and 5). For the purposes of this chapter, it is assumed to be true. In order to identify the developmental needs of professional social care workers, it is first necessary to take a closer look at the Joint Committee's definition and explore the individual tasks/expectations that are placed on a social care worker in practice. Below, we shall look in more detail at the various components of the social care worker's role, that is, care, protection, support, welfare and advocacy.

CARE

Depending on the nature and context of the agency, the role of a social care worker is to provide care to people who are defined as being vulnerable or dependant. This essentially means that the service user is at risk of getting into some form of difficulty if he is left to look after himself, or that he is clearly unable to meet one or all of his needs by himself.

Abraham Maslow and others identified people's needs as falling into five broad categories: social, emotional, intellectual, physical and spiritual (Ward and Rose 2002). While some service users may be able to meet some of these needs by themselves, they may also require some form of help or 'intervention' with some aspects of their lives. Having conducted an assessment of need (Palmer and McMahon 1997), social care workers deliver care through the implementation of individual care/placement plans. While these terms are used interchangeably here, care and placement plans are technically not the same thing, as care plans tend to outline the general long-term goals for the placement, while placement plans relate more specifically to day-to-day care issues. Wherever possible, care plans aim to enable/empower people to help themselves (Thompson 2009). This approach looks to enhance dignity, confidence, self-respect and ultimately independence for the service user.

Development of the placement plan is the responsibility of the care staff in consultation with other professionals such as the client's doctor, social worker, therapist or teacher. While care-related assessment models exist (such as those presented in Ward and Rose (2002)), there is no standard assessment template for the development of placement plans, either in published literature or in Irish social care practice.

There follows below a proposed model of the type of assessment/information-gathering a social care worker engages in prior to developing a placement plan for a young person in residential care. It consists of pertinent questions to consider when developing a placement plan. This list is not exhaustive and may be adapted to suit the needs of individual clients or agencies. Having conducted the assessment of need, issues that require attention are prioritised and become the basis for short-, medium- and long-term interventions.

ASSESSMENT MODEL FOR YOUNG PEOPLE IN CARE

Social

1. How does the child interact with adults inside and outside the home?
2. How does the child interact with children inside and outside the home?
3. Does the child maintain age-appropriate eye contact when communicating?
4. Does the child present with an age-appropriate command of language?
5. How does the child cope with group care?
6. Does the child display an age-appropriate ability to negotiate?
7. If playing with other children, does the child display an age-appropriate ability to take turns?
8. If playing with other children, does the child display an age-appropriate ability to assert himself?
9. How does the child present during mealtimes?
10. Identify the child's social network (friends, clubs).
11. Does the child have any hobbies or interests?
12. Does the child present with any sexualised behaviours?
13. Does the child have a history of damage to property and/or fire setting?
14. Is the child known to the police?
15. Does the child present with any behaviour that could be considered to be culturally antisocial?
16. What is the child's perception of people in authority?

Emotional

1. How does the child feel about his placement in care?
2. Can the child differentiate between feelings and behaviours (e.g. anger and violence)?
3. How does the child usually express emotion?
4. How would you (and the child, where appropriate) rate the child's level of self-esteem?
5. How would you (and the child, where appropriate) rate the child's level of confidence?
6. Would you consider the child to be impulsive?
7. Does the child have an age-appropriate understanding of gender and related issues (relationships, sexuality, gender identity)?
8. How does the child perceive himself physically?

9. Does the child have a history of self-injury?
10. Does the child present with any issues of concern in relation to food?
11. Does the child seem emotionally connected to his physical self (can he identify hunger, cold, pain)?
12. Is the child aware at an age-appropriate level of issues related to personal hygiene?
13. Does the child seem emotionally connected to his physical space (does he display claiming behaviours)?
14. Does the child seem emotionally connected to any particular possessions (toys, photos, jewellery)?
15. Are there any issues related to enuresis or encopresis?
16. How does the child negotiate issues related to control?
17. Does the child display an ability to form attached relationships?
18. How is the child's relationship with his natural family and/or significant others?
19. Does the child have an age-appropriate understanding of his cultural identity?
20. Does the child display an ability to empathise with others?
21. Does the child have any fears or phobias?
22. How is the child's sleep pattern?
23. How would you describe the child's level of concentration?
24. Does the child present with any issues of concern related to physical touch?
25. Does the child have any interest in animals?
26. Has the child ever been diagnosed with a psychiatric illness or developmental disorder?
27. How often does the child smile/laugh?
28. Is the child (where appropriate) engaged in a life skills development or independent living programme?

Intellectual

1. Does the child attend the required amount of school?
2. How does the child perceive his own academic ability?
3. Can the child tell the time?
4. Can the child read and write to an age-appropriate level?
5. Does the child present as having an age-appropriate level of general knowledge?
6. Is the child preparing for any state exams?
7. Are there any concerns from the staff relating to the child's academic ability or attainment?
8. Identify the child's interests and explore how these interests could be used as educative tools.

Physical

1. Has the child had a medical and dental examination upon admission to the home?
2. Is the child the recommended height and weight for his age?
3. Does the child engage in regular physical activity?
4. Is the child taking any prescribed medication?
5. Does the child have any allergies?
6. Does the child have any injuries or disabilities?
7. Does the child have asthma or any breathing difficulties?
8. Are there any sensory issues (hearing, taste, touch, smell, sight)?
9. Is the child keeping to a daily physical care routine (shower, hair, teeth, nails, etc.)?
10. How is the child's diet?
11. Is there any evidence of the child smoking or taking any other legal or illegal mood-altering substances?
12. Does the child have any birthmarks, tattoos, piercings or other distinguishing features?
13. Does the child (where relevant) have a normal menstrual cycle?

Spiritual

1. Is the child part of any religious group or organisation?
2. What is the child's understanding of spirituality?
3. Would you consider the child to be creative?
4. What are the wishes of the child's parents in relation to the child's spiritual development?

It is clear from the range of biological, psychological and social issues that may present in this assessment form that the professional social care worker requires comprehensive knowledge of a range of issues related to human development. The training requirements for care practice will be discussed in more detail later in this chapter.

PROTECTION

Social care service users may present with a variety of social, emotional, behavioural and psychiatric difficulties that require them to be protected from either themselves or others (Ward and Rose 2002). The legal mechanisms for such protection are outlined by Conneely (2005) and include the Children Act 2001, the Domestic Violence Act 1996 and the Child Care Act 1991. The Disability

Act 2005 and the Equal Status Act 2000 are also important legislative frameworks for the protection of social care service users.

In law, the standard of care and protection expected from a professionally trained social care worker is judged by the 'standard of the reasonable professional' (Van Doccum 2004). It is important, therefore, that social care workers are aware of their legal responsibilities as they relate to their 'duty of care' and the possible implications of providing a standard of care/protection that is less than adequate or even negligent.

SUPPORT

Depending on the outcome of the needs assessment, service users may require anything from minimal to intensive support in order to meet their needs. This usually requires a multidisciplinary approach, with input from teachers, social workers, doctors, therapists, psychiatrists and religious/spiritual representatives. Sutton (1997: 169) outlines the cyclical nature of the assessment and intervention process with the ASPIRE model: assess, plan, implement, review and evaluate.

WELFARE

Social care service users are, by definition, in receipt of a social service. While no national statistics are available, it is generally the case that the majority of service users are either in receipt of, or are eligible for, a range of social welfare benefits. The role of a social care worker in consultation with the social worker is to ensure that the service user receives all of his or her rights and entitlements in this regard (Howe 1987).

ADVOCACY

An advocate is defined as 'one who pleads the case of another'. In all areas of social care practice, the role of the worker may involve acting or speaking on behalf of an individual or group of service users in order to ensure that their needs are met. Professional advocacy often requires the worker to possess an understanding of social policy and political philosophy. Women's Aid, Enable Ireland, Barnardos and the Irish Traveller Movement are some of the better-known examples of professional advocacy groups in Irish social care, though at a local level workers advocate on behalf of individual clients at team meetings and to external agencies on an ongoing basis.

We have seen that the role of a professional social care worker is complex and multifaceted. The following section explores the relationship between the social care worker and the client and explains why workers need to engage in an ongoing process of personal and professional development.

PERSONAL DEVELOPMENT

The task of social care occurs in the context of a relationship between two people, the worker and client, where the worker facilitates the client through a process of growth or change.

While there is no doubt that being a professional 'anything' requires knowledge (Mills 2002), knowledge by itself will not achieve success in relationships. The term 'bedside manner' is often used in the medical profession to describe the doctor's ability to connect and communicate with patients. In social care practice, the relationship is more intimate, prolonged and intense than that of the doctor–patient relationship and therefore the worker's ability to form and be in a relationship with another human being is an absolute prerequisite to an effective intervention (Thompson 2009).

It seems reasonable, then, that if we are to be effective in relationships, we must know something of how we relate to other people. This conscious bringing into awareness of a greater understanding of both who, and how, we are in the world is known as the process of personal development (Parfitt, W. 2006) (see also Chapter 9).

In social care education, personal development is encouraged through the student's participation in small practice-based process groups. These groups are usually informed by some school of counselling thought and aim to improve the student's general level of self-awareness (Kennefick 2006). Students are also often taught practical counselling skills to enable them to provide emotional support to their clients and to develop their ability to be 'present' in the helping relationship. The concept of remaining 'present' in practice involves staying focused in the 'here and now' on the work with the client. This can be difficult, as it requires the worker to be aware of what is going on, both in his own personal life and in the relationship with the client, and not allow either to distract him from the work he is doing with the client.

While developing our general awareness of self can enhance the quality of all our relationships, in social care education the purpose of personal development is primarily to enable the student to become a reflective practitioner. The concept of reflective practice refers not only to who and how we are in relationships, but to how and why we make decisions that affect our clients (Graham and Megarry 2005; Thompson 2009). By critically analysing our practice on an ongoing basis, we minimise the likelihood of poor judgement and the potential of further harm to our clients. We also reduce the likelihood of placing ourselves at unnecessary risk in our work.

The use of self in a relationship with another, for the sole purpose of helping the other to change, grow or heal, is essentially therapy (the term 'therapy' being derived from the Greek 'therapeia', meaning healing (Corry and Tubridy 2001)). Yet social care workers are not therapists, and despite the unquestionable benefits of their interventions for the service users, the extent to which social care could be described as a 'therapeutic intervention' has never quite been defined in any consistent way, either in practice or academia. For example, 8 per cent of a sample of social care workers described their role as being 'to provide therapeutic intervention' (Byrne 2008).

The significance of identifying the therapeutic role of the care worker is that it has implications, in both training and practice, for the extent to which the worker should be required to engage in a process of personal development. Depending on the therapeutic orientation, psychotherapists in Ireland are required to engage in up to 100 hours of personal therapy across their three years of training (O'Farrell 1999). It is interesting to note that a recent study identified that 75 per cent of social care workers felt that they should also be required to attend ongoing personal therapy in order to train and practise social care (Byrne 2008), a notion that has yet to be explored in social care education.

At this point, it is perhaps important to identify that the therapeutic orientation of this chapter is 'integrative' (it draws from several therapeutic traditions), with an emphasis on the person-centred approach founded by Carl Rogers (1951, 1967) and developed by Mearns and Thorne (2007). Rogers (1967) argued that in order for client healing to take place in the therapeutic relationship, the therapist needs to provide three core conditions: empathetic understanding, genuineness/congruence and unconditional positive regard (UPR/acceptance). Each of these are considered in some detail below.

Empathetic Understanding

> It is only as I understand the feelings and thoughts which seem so horrible to you, or so weak, or so sentimental, or so bizarre – it is only as I see them as you see them, and accept them and you, that you feel free to explore all the hidden nooks and frightening crannies of your inner and often buried experience. (Rogers 1967: 34)

O'Farrell (1999) describes empathy as the process by which the therapist attempts to understand the client's world without becoming enmeshed in it. The skill is to try to see the client's world from the client's perspective as if it were your own, while remaining detached enough to remember that it is not your own. O'Farrell goes on to highlight that this empathetic understanding must be conveyed to the client, but highlights that we can never feel someone else's experience because we are not them, thus feeding back our understanding requires sensitivity and careful wording.

Genuineness/Congruence

> I have found that the more genuine I can be in the relationship the more helpful it will be. This means that I need to be aware of my own feelings in

so far as possible rather than presenting an outward façade of one attitude while actually holding another attitude at a deeper or unconscious level. (Rogers 1967: 33)

According to O'Farrell (1999), in order to be genuine with clients, the therapist requires an in-depth knowledge of him/herself, which can only be obtained through ongoing personal development. In a social care context, being 'real' in relationships can be misunderstood by both students and practitioners and can lead to situations where workers relate to clients as they would with friends or family. This potential blurring of the boundary in relationships, if left unchecked, can cause problems for both worker and client and is best addressed by engaging in formal professional supervision (Hawkins and Shohet 2007). It is not easy to be real, yet professional, in relationships, but it is the worker's responsibility to maintain the boundary and be aware of both how he/she interacts with clients and whose needs are being met in that interaction. It is important for workers to remember that friendship is a two-way street where an individual gives and receives support, but a professional helping relationship is where workers give support to the client while getting their own emotional needs met elsewhere.

Unconditional Positive Regard/Acceptance

By acceptance I mean a warm regard for him as a person of unconditional self worth, of value no matter what his condition, his behaviour or his feelings. It means a respect and liking for him as a separate person, a willingness for him to possess his own feelings in his own way. (Rogers 1967: 34)

Also referred to as non-possessive warmth, or non-judgemental attitude, this principle is at the core of both person-centred therapy and social care practice. It essentially means the ability to separate people from behaviour and accept that, by nature of the fact that you are a human being, you deserve to be treated with dignity and respect. The principle of UPR relies absolutely on unconditionality (Mearns and Thorne 2007). UPR is the closest thing in therapy to love (in its broadest sense) for another human being and its effectiveness relies on the consistency of its application by the therapist. Rogers (1967) states that it is only when the client sees that the therapist accepts him as he is that he can really begin to accept himself. Unconditional positive regard does not mean that the worker condones unacceptable behaviours in a client, but simply sees past them and values the client fundamentally as a human being (Biestek 1961).

While the ability to be congruent and empathetic can be difficult to internalise for both students and practitioners, it is usually the case that unconditional positive regard is the most challenging of Roger's core conditions to put into practice. This is because in order to be truly non-judgemental (if indeed that is even possible), the worker needs to attain a heightened level of self-awareness that explores and challenges his entire belief system, which often includes varying levels of prejudice and preconceived judgements.

There follows a number of practice examples that highlight the application of Roger's core conditions in a social care context.

Practice Example 1

Mary was raised with a strong sense of social justice. She always believed that violent criminals should be severely punished and that people who choose to take heroin don't deserve any state support. When Mary completed her practice placement in the treatment centre for people with addiction difficulties, she quickly became aware that things are not always that black and white. Mary realised that the service users were ordinary people who may have done dreadful things, but in many cases had been deeply wounded in relationships in the past. Some had also been failed on many levels by the range of services with which they had been involved. In supervision, Mary reflected on how surprised she was that she had begun to see past the addictive behaviours and developed a real empathetic understanding of her clients.

Practice Example 2

Joe worked in a residential children's home. One day, the parents of one of the children came to visit the house and the child's mother had a very badly bruised face and bandaged arm. Despite being told that the injuries were sustained in a fall, it became apparent that there had been an incident of domestic violence. In supervision, Joe reflected on how difficult he found it to continue to treat the child's father, who was the perpetrator of the abuse, with dignity and respect.

It is important to remember that personal development is an ongoing process and one cannot (nor would it be helpful to) simply flick a switch and undo a lifetime of deeply held opinions or beliefs. It is, however, important to be aware of how we impact on others and how they impact on us. The term 'trigger' refers to an issue or action that evokes an emotional response in the worker (Thompson 2009). This response can be positive or negative and may help or hinder the task at hand. In the case of Joe above, the domestic incident became the trigger that blocked his ability to provide unconditional positive regard to the child's father.

Practice Example 3

Frank was working in a homeless advice service when a client presented under the influence of alcohol. When Frank asked him to leave, the client became threatening and abusive. Frank's immediate response to the threat was to forcibly remove the client from the premises. In supervision, Frank reflected on how he had responded. While he had achieved the desired outcome, he accepted that physical intervention should have been the last rather than the first response. He became aware through exploration of the issue that threats of violence were a trigger that evoked a particular emotional response in him.

In this example, Frank was unable to convey his real/genuine response to the situation, as he was unaware of it himself. His first reaction was to contain and control the situation rather than to be in touch with his own feelings around the threat of violence. When a worker is even temporarily blinded by his emotional response to a situation, he limits the options available to him and increases the likelihood of an error of judgement. These types of situations are very challenging, as sometimes containment and control are required for health and safety reasons.

People internalise their experience of the world through a filter that is largely based on past life experiences. Therefore, how we view the world may be influenced by our culture, gender, class, religion, ethnic origin or family make-up. Applying Roger's core conditions in the helping relationship can be complicated when the worker's value system is not consistent with that of the client or agency, or when practice presents a moral dilemma for the worker.

Practice Example 4

Susan believed that interventions with homeless people who had alcohol problems should prioritise abstinence, and she could not understand why a hostel would allow a service user to drink on the premises. Having worked in a 'wet hostel', Susan's values changed when she became aware that sometimes people are not ready to stop drinking, and while she may have been technically correct in her view, applying that value in practice would mean that some service users simply would not access the service and could therefore be at greater risk of harm through street drinking.

We can see from the above examples that applying Roger's core conditions in practice require the worker to possess a heightened level of awareness of her values, prejudices and emotional responses.

RAISING AWARENESS

Personal development is an ongoing process. As we experience the world, we re-evaluate our views and opinions and therefore we never really get to know ourselves, as some aspects of the self are changing all the time. There are, however, a number of tools, such as raja yoga or meditation, that we can use to help bring aspects of ourselves that we may not be fully aware of into consciousness. At a more basic level, though, it is surprising how much we can learn by simply stopping and reflecting on who and how we are in the world. Journaling or keeping a diary can also be a helpful aid to this process.

A commonly used tool for developing self-awareness is the Johari window (see Figure 16.1). The window is a sort of map of consciousness and the aim is to reduce the unknown area through a careful balance of self-disclosure and receipt of feedback from others (this is also the theory behind the process groups in social care education). It is important to remember, however, that disclosure can create vulnerability, and sometimes there is a value in being appropriately selective about how much of ourselves we disclose and to whom we disclose it.

Figure 16.1. The Johari Window

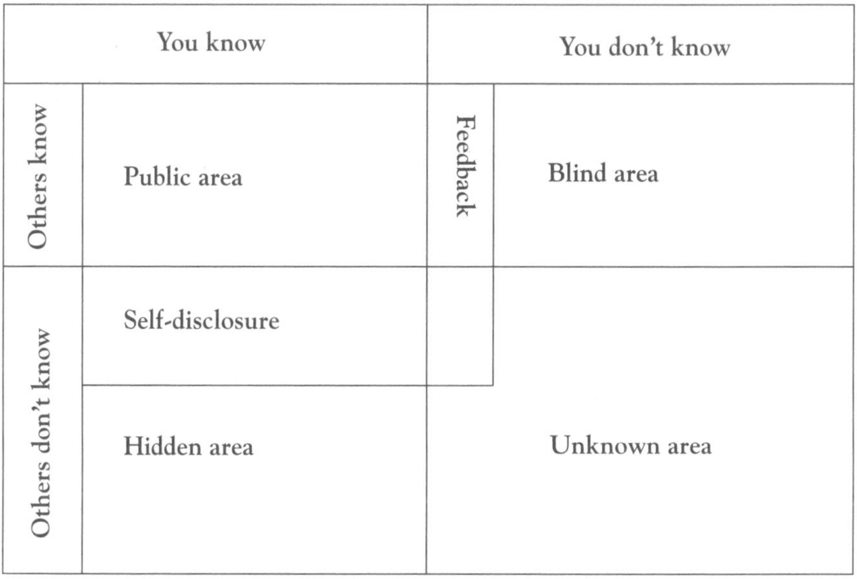

	You know		You don't know
Others know	Public area	**Feedback**	Blind area
Others don't know	Self-disclosure		
	Hidden area		Unknown area

Source: Adapted from O'Farrell (1999: 91).

PROFESSIONAL DEVELOPMENT

This section explores the concept of the professional development of the individual social care worker, rather than the professional status of social care generally, which is explored in Chapter 5.

According to Laurence (1999: 53), professional conduct is 'a particular form of human conduct which is claimed to be of special significance for human well being in modern society'. It was accepted earlier in this chapter that social care is professional care, but simply calling oneself a professional does not make it so.

Whatever the discipline, a key characteristic of professional status is education and training (Mills 2002).

It is not uncommon for social care workers without qualifications to refer to themselves as 'professionals' based on their often lengthy experience of working in practice. Proponents for the employment into social care of unqualified people correctly argue that sometimes the gardener or cleaner in a care setting can possess a greater ability to form relationships with clients than the most highly qualified practitioner. However, relationship is only the foundation for professional social care practice. The bio-psycho-social model of needs assessment of young people identified earlier requires the worker to possess a general knowledge of both developmental and abnormal psychology. The concepts of empowerment and social integration that are central to care practice also require the worker to possess an understanding of sociology, social policy and political philosophy, while the complex nature of many of the presenting issues requires an understanding of legal aspects of care. Professional social care workers also need to possess an awareness of counselling skills and have an ability to draw from a range of creative tools (drama, art, dance and music) that facilitate communication and expression with the more hard-to-reach clients.

Whether or not people should be allowed to gain access to the profession without formal education remains a contentious issue. In 2005, a proposal for two grades of practitioner (as with a nurse and nurse's aid) was proposed for social care. This model would have acknowledged the benefit of having unqualified people as part of a care team, but it was flatly rejected by both social care workers and students. Ironically, the majority of workers who rejected it were themselves unqualified (Byrne 2005). Whatever the answer, there is little doubt that in practice, common sense and a kind disposition will only take you only so far; after that, there is a requirement for formal training.

EDUCATION AND TRAINING

> It is a fallacy to think that any motherly woman with common sense can undertake such work. This is an unrealistic and misleading over-simplification, which ignores the understanding and the skills required to care for other people's emotionally unsettled if not disturbed and unhappy children. Neither affection nor common sense is sufficient by themselves. (Department of Education 1970: 13)

The complexities of the role of the social care worker with children in residential care were highlighted as far back as 1970. The Kennedy Report (quoted above) is clear that social care work in residential child care requires more than a caring disposition. The Kennedy Report was the impetus for the first training course for social care workers in Kilkenny in 1970.

In 2005, the Irish government signed into law the Health and Social Care Professionals Act, which stipulates that in order to call oneself a professional social care worker, one must possess a minimum HETAC or DIT Level 7 BA (Ord.) degree (formerly Diploma) in Child/Social Care or Applied Social Studies. However, this piece of legislation is not fully implemented (as of May 2009) and the Social Care Registration Board is yet to be established. The anomaly exists that even when the registration board is operational, individuals without social care training can still be employed in practice, but they will not be able to register or call themselves social care workers.

The difficulty with employing practitioners from a range of professional backgrounds, including nursing, teaching and social work, is that it undermines the professional credibility of social care education by suggesting that anyone qualified in these areas can automatically practise social care. It also leads to significant inconsistencies in the approach to practise within the profession. A random survey of delegates at the IASCW conference in 2008 identified that 45 per cent did not hold the minimum diploma or BA (Ord.) in social care (Byrne 2008).

It would seem, then, that if social care is to attain professional status with any credibility, there is a significant task ahead to train all those in practice to the same basic minimum standard.

CONTINUING PROFESSIONAL DEVELOPMENT (CPD)

Once qualified, just as doctors and nurses are required to update their training in accordance with the most recent developments in their field, social care workers have a moral, if not yet legal, obligation to themselves and their clients to continually develop their knowledge and skills throughout their career. In recent years, the publication of texts (such as this volume) and the development of postgraduate programmes in social care have led to an ever-expanding body of knowledge informing care practice.

The extent to which there is a culture of investing time, energy and money in one's professional development remains unclear in social care. It is worth noting that 52 per cent of social care workers surveyed said that they spend nothing at all on their professional development (Byrne 2008). This suggests that if employers ceased funding staff training, there could be significant implications for the ongoing staff development and subsequent care practice. Whether the financial responsibility rests with the individual worker or the employer, professional social care is presently defining itself faster than ever before and workers need to be aware of those developments if they are to optimise the quality of care to their service users.

The implementation of the Health and Social Care Professionals Act 2005 will result in the development of a Social Care Registration Board. The responsibility of such a board will be not only to 'ring-fence' social care and stipulate the entry requirement for the profession, but also the requirement for any ongoing training for workers wishing to renew their registration.

SUPERVISION

The concept of continuing professional development often refers to ongoing reading or attendance at conferences and courses. However, formal professional supervision is also a useful tool to enable workers to enhance their learning and practice (see Chapter 13).

Professional supervision is often misunderstood in social care, with only 40 per cent of workers reporting it as being a positive or useful experience, while 43 per cent report it as being inconsistent in both frequency and usefulness and 17 per cent stating that they don't receive professional supervision at all (Byrne 2008). Supervision is not simply working alongside your supervisor or having an informal chat about work over a cup of tea. Supervision is a formal meeting between supervisor and supervisee for the purpose of enabling the latter to be more effective at helping people. It should occur in an undisturbed environment, and while regularity and duration will depend on the nature of the agency, generally supervision should take up to one hour about once every two weeks and should explore all aspects of work practice.

According to Hawkins and Shohet (2007: 59), the primary foci of supervision are to:

1. Provide a regular space for the supervisees to reflect on the content and process of their work.
2. Develop understanding and skills within the work.
3. Receive information and another perspective concerning one's work.
4. Receive both content and process feedback.
5. Be validated and supported both as a person and as a worker.
6. Ensure that as a person and as a worker, one is not left to unnecessarily carry difficulties, problems and projections alone.
7. Have space to explore and express personal distress, restimulation, transference or counter-transference that may be brought up by the work.
8. Plan and utilise their professional and personal resources better.
9. Be proactive rather than reactive.
10. Ensure quality of work.

These foci can be categorised into three main groups: they are to provide a supportive, educative and managerial function to the worker. For supervision to be effective, there needs to be a willingness from both parties to engage in the process, rather than simply going through the motions for the purpose of policies and procedures. It is also helpful for the supervisor to receive formal supervision training, though this is not yet a requirement in social care practice.

There are various types of supervision other than the traditional one-to-one meeting and these include group, peer and self supervision. It is important for the worker/student to remember that where adequate supervision is not available to them in their work, or where they feel inhibited in the relationship with their supervisor, there is always the option of sourcing external supervision. While this has cost implications for the worker, the benefits of receiving feedback from someone who is independent of the agency will result in the worker receiving a completely fresh perspective and can enable him to engage in a much more open and meaningful way in the process.

MEMBERSHIP OF IASCW

The Irish Association of Social Care Workers (IASCW) was formed in 1972 to provide professional representation to social care workers and students. Its primary functions are to:

1. Provide a support network to it members.
2. Establish and maintain a professional culture within social care.
3. Represent its members at public and policy-making level.

The IASCW has undergone various transformations over the intervening period. It is entirely voluntary and remains in existence almost solely as a result of the unquestionable commitment of a small number of dedicated members.

Unfortunately, the association is relatively stagnant and virtually ineffective. This is not necessarily a reflection of the association itself, but rather a result of the lack of commitment from the 15,000 potential full and associate members to join and become involved in the association (Byrne 2005).

The Irish Farmers Association (IFA) has approximately 80,000 members and the Irish Nurses Organisation (INO) has 32,000 members, but the IASCW has approximately 120 members. This is arguably why the IFA and INO are in a position to assert political influence and effect real change on issues relevant to their members while the IASCW did not manage to attract even a junior minister to attend their annual conference in 2008, which was attended by fewer than 90 delegates.

In April 2008, an RTÉ documentary identified a crisis in homeless services in Ireland on the same day that the IMPACT trade union threatened strike action on behalf of its health and social care members (RTÉ 2008). The IASCW had no media presence on either of these core issues despite the obvious relevance for its members, the main reason being the lack of a paid employee who is available to engage with the media as and when issues arise.

The existence of a professional association is central to the development of professional social care. If the IASCW is to survive, it is incumbent on social care workers and students to become the driving force for its re-emergence, and to support the association through active membership.

In May 2008, the IASCW agreed a subsidisation package with a private residential child care provider which saw a dramatic reduction in the cost of membership to both students and practitioners, with a subsequent increase in membership.

CONCLUSION

While there are many excellent and highly professional staff working throughout social care, the profession itself remains in a state of flux, evolving toward professionalisation (see Chapter 5). There are still people being appointed in practice who do not hold formal social care qualifications. Investment in professional development is inconsistent and the quality of supervision often inadequate. The state is only just beginning to implement the most important piece of legislation ever to affect social care, and our professional association, through lack of members, is not in a position to do anything to further that process.

If any of this is to change and if we are ever to be taken seriously as professionals, workers need to make a commitment in the first instance to training to a basic entry level, but also to continually develop and update their knowledge and skills when new information becomes available.

Social care workers provide intensive therapeutic interventions to some of the country's most vulnerable people, yet our potential is being hampered by a relative lack of recognition for the complex nature of our work.

Social care service users deserve the best-quality care that we can provide and the only way that will happen is if we take individual responsibility for our own personal and professional development, while collectively endorsing our professional association so that it has the resources to create the climate that will enable us to become all that we can be.

The Inspection of Children's Residential Centres

Michael McNamara

OVERVIEW

Children living in the care of the state deserve the highest possible standards of care. The structures and procedures in place to ensure this are detailed in this chapter.

RESIDENTIAL CHILD CARE

Residential child care in Ireland has undergone a period of enormous change in recent years: there are far fewer children in residential settings than previously, placements are likely to be of shorter duration, fewer children aged 12 and under are in residential centres and there is likely to be a greater concentration of children and young people who have experienced abuse and/or present with severe emotional and behavioural problems. The children often have a poor sense of self-worth, poor educational attainments and frequently have little hope for their future.

Table 17.1 shows the percentage of children in different types of care placement. The number in residential care is 400 (7 per cent) out of a national total of 5,449.

The trend to use residential care only for the most needy of children in care has continued for several years. In the UK, Warner (1992) concluded that as well as dealing with children who were increasingly difficult to manage, residential care itself had historically suffered from a number of problems, chief amongst which were the lack of attention from senior managers, poor management, deficient employment practice, inadequate knowledge and training and a deficient policy and planning framework. A taskforce set up after the Warner Report to deal with some of these problems reported that the overall outcome of a period of residential care would either be helpful or unhelpful for the child concerned, but was unlikely to have a merely neutral effect; in other words, it will either help or hinder his/her progress towards becoming mature adults. This places a serious responsibility on those who work in residential care.

Table 17.1. Children in Care by Placement Type, November 2008

Placement Type	Number of Children (Per Cent of Total)
Foster care	3,296 (60)
Foster care with relatives	1,555 (29)
Residential care	400 (7)
'Other', including separated children seeking asylum, support lodgings, B&B and at home under care order	198 (4)
Total	5,449 (100)

Source: HSE, personal communciation.[1]

William Utting, in *Children in the Public Care* (1991), offers the following suggestion as to what the purpose of residential care should be.

The purpose of residential care should be to provide a home for children who:
- Have decided that they do not wish to be fostered.
- Have had bad experiences of foster care.
- Have been so abused within their family that another family placement is inappropriate.
- Are from the same family and cannot otherwise be kept together.
- Need expert multidisciplinary help with social and personal problems in a residential setting.
- Require containment and help in conditions of security.

Residential homes fulfil a specialist role as partners in a range of preventive and rehabilitative services designed to meet specific needs: observation and assessment, permanent family placement, juvenile justice projects, respite care for disabled children and preparation for independent living. In *People Like Us* (1997), Utting wrote: 'There is no doubt that the safeguards for some children living away from home should be strengthened. Every organisation must make their safety its principal objective.'

THE AIMS AND OBJECTIVES OF RESIDENTIAL CHILD CARE

It is essential that there is absolute clarity about the aims and objectives of residential care. It should be a positive choice of placement, provide a positive experience and have positive outcomes for the child. It should be operated by skilled staff with high esteem who are valued for the important job they do, and who are well managed, well trained and well motivated to offer the best possible care to children. It must be part of an organisation with strengths in ongoing policy and planning development and be fully integrated into the full range of other children's services. It must offer children protection. Children must have available to them the skilled help they require in a setting that is safe, caring and well organised and which respects and promotes their right to grow, develop and recover from experiences that have caused them to be looked after. To achieve this, it must be adequately resourced.

It must also be a quality service, responsive to those in its care. Factors associated with quality from the service user's perspective are as follows.

- Staff behaviour towards the service users is characterised by respect, helpfulness and approachability.
- Staff responsiveness to service users is evidenced by ease of access, listening, consulting and taking views into consideration.
- Service users are able to understand the complaints procedure and experience it as effective.
- The centre is responsive to individual difference and different individual needs.
- Discrimination and bullying are appropriately challenged.
- Service users are given information in an accessible format about the care provided to them and about their rights.
- Service users have access to records about them and are sure of their confidentiality.
- Service users are secure and confident of being protected.
- Parents and others with an interest in their care are assured that children are well looked after and protected.
- The service is well managed and operates to the highest possible standards, which are explicit and adhered to.

These expectations are embedded in the National Standards for Children's Residential Centres (Department of Health and Children 2001a).

The National Standards for Children's Residential Centres were launched by the Minister for Children on 10 September 2001 and are a revision of standards issued in 1996. The current standards can be found at:

www.hiqa.ie/media/pdfs/standards_children_crc.pdf.

Simplified versions for children and young people, respectively, can be found at:

www.hiqa.ie/media/pdfs/standards_children_rc.pdf
www.hiqa.ie/media/pdfs/standards_children_yp_rc.pdf

BACKGROUND: INSPECTION

The inspection of children's services in Ireland is a relatively recent development. While inspection was considered and provision made for it in the Child Care Act 1991, the relevant section of the Act (s.69) was not implemented until April 1999, when the Social Services Inspectorate (SSI) was established as an independent agency under the aegis of the Department of Health and Children, with plans in place for it to become a statutory body.

Initially, inspections focused on children's residential centres in response to major public concerns about the state of residential care following revelations of widespread institutional abuse that came to light in the 1980s and 1990s.

The purpose of inspection is twofold. First, inspections are conducted in order to independently check and verify that the care provided to children in residential centres is safe, that it fully meets the needs of the children for growth and development, promotes their well-being and complies with legislation and nationally agreed standards.

Second, inspections provide a public account of the service provided to children by or on behalf of the state. All SSI inspection reports are published.[2] In several instances, the account entails the identification of deficits and makes recommendations to bring services up to standard, but it also means acknowledging best practice where it is found and promulgating information about what works and constitutes good quality in the residential care of children.

THE ROLE OF THE SOCIAL CARE PRACTITIONER

The role of social care staff in residential children's centres is highly important in terms of the children's experience of day-to-day care and the implementation of the placement plan. Inspectors give the performance of social care practitioners due weight in inspections because the success of plans and the delivery of care depend so much on the quality of daily interactions. Where there is a high standard in residential care, it is because ordinary things are done extraordinarily well. In preparing for inspection, care staff should essentially be themselves, but in the course of their work inspectors would expect that they have:

- A good knowledge of the policies of the centre.
- Familiarity with procedures for dealing with children's complaints.
- Familiarity with safeguarding principles and procedures for reporting child protection concerns.
- A well-informed consciousness of children's needs and children's rights.
- Clear knowledge of the centre's health and safety policies and procedures.
- Professionalism in their role in contributing to the team's co-ordination of care.
- Knowledge of the regulations and standards the service is provided under.
- Ability to show appropriate care for the children entrusted to them.

The legal authority to inspect is granted by Section 69 of the Child Care Act 1991, which affirms that an inspector, in the course of inspection, may interview whichever persons and see whichever documents he or she sees fit.

Until May 2007, the SSI functioned within the administrative structure of the Department of Health and Children but maintained its operational independence. From May 2007, the SSI became a component of the Health Information and Quality Authority (HIQA), a statutory body established by the Health Act 2007.

THE HEALTH INFORMATION AND QUALITY AUTHORITY

HIQA was established on 15 May 2007 as an independent statutory body reporting to the Minister for Health and Children. It incorporated two other organisations, the Social Services Inspectorate (SSI) and the Irish Hospital Services Accreditation Board. Although it is an autonomous body, its remit is to work closely with the health system and engage with stakeholders, establishing work programmes and priorities aimed at achieving an overall improvement in the standard and quality of services throughout the state.

Its objective is described in Section 7 of the Act: 'to promote safety and quality in the provision of health and personal social services for the benefit of the health and welfare of the public'. Further, its key functions are described in Section 8 of the Act:

> setting standards on safety and quality, setting standards on data and information held by the HSE and other providers, monitoring compliance with standards, health care quality assurance and audit, operating service accreditation programmes, social care quality assurance, social care inspection and registration, assessing the clinical and cost effectiveness of health tech-nologies, the establishment and evaluation of national health information systems, and undertaking investigations.

Where HIQA SSI Fits in the Health Service Structure

With the establishment of the Health Service Executive (HSE) in January 2005, the Department of Health and Children took a step back from involvement in the provision of services, maintaining emphasis on its role in formulating the policies that shape health and social services.

The HSE is a national autonomous organisation established by law in the Health Act 2004. Since January 2005, the provision of all health and social services, whether directly by the HSE itself or through other agencies it has made arrangements with in accordance with Section 38 of the Health Act 2004, are the responsibility of the HSE.

The Health Information and Quality Authority was established as a statutory body independent of both the Department of Health and Children and HSE. Its primary role within the structure is to manage information systems that will accurately inform health policy and to set standards against which to measure the safety and quality of services. The SSI is a component part of HIQA, maintaining its inspectorial independence within the overall structure.

The three elements are interdependent in so far as a partnership is necessary to ensure that the service users' best interests are met within the functions of each and that there is clarity about their different purposes in the structure.

THE OFFICE OF THE CHIEF INSPECTOR OF SOCIAL SERVICES

The Office of the Chief Inspector of Social Services is a key provision of the Health Act 2007. The overall objective of the office is detailed in Part 7 of the Act, with its functions described in Section 41:

- To set standards for the care of children and older and disabled people being cared for in designated residential centres.
- To inspect and register all *designated* residential services, both the statutory services of the Health Service Executive (HSE) and non-statutory services provided by private and voluntary providers. A *designated centre* is defined in Section 2 of the Health Act 2007 as:

  > An institution at which residential services are provided by the HSE, a service provider or a person receiving assistance under section 39 of the Health Act 2004, or in accordance with the Child Care Act 1991, or to persons with disabilities in relation to their disabilities, or to other dependent persons.

  The term does not include special care units, children's detention schools, centres registered by the Mental Health Commission, institutions for acute illness or palliative care or recreational/educational centres.
- To inspect foster care services. Inspections of fostering services are conducted according to the Child Care (Placement of Children in Foster Care) Regulations 1995 and the National Standards for Foster Care 2003. Within the limits of the resources available to it, the inspectorate has carried out a pilot inspection as well as two inspections of private fostering agencies and two of HSE local health area fostering services.[3]
- To inspect special care units annually. *Special care units* are the only children's residential centres children may be detained in for their own safety under an order from the High Court. There are three in the state, in Cork, Dublin and Limerick. When the Children Act 2001 is fully implemented, special care units will be have to be certified by the Minister for Children and Youth Affairs in order to operate and children will be placed in them under Special Care Orders granted by the District Court.[4]

- To inspect children's detention schools annually. *Children's detention schools* were previously operated under the aegis of the Department of Education and Science. Since March 2007, they have become the responsibility of the Irish Youth Justice Service, which is an operational arm of the Department of Justice, Equality and Law Reform. Inspection of the schools has transferred from the Department of Education and Science to the Office of the Chief Inspector of Social Services.
- To maintain registers of designated centres in accordance with Section 49 of the Act.
- To monitor a range of social services including day care, support services to people living at home and child protection.
- To monitor the HSE's inspections of pre-schools and crèches.
- To undertake investigations.

The Act empowers the District Court to play a role in the inspection process; for example, it may issue a warrant enabling an inspector to enter premises in the company of Gardaí. Also, proprietors who want to appeal against a registration decision may do so to the court. The legislation includes a 'fit person assessment', which is a means by which the suitability of a person to provide or run a service for children, older people or people with disability can be determined.

HOW THE NEW LEGISLATION WILL CHANGE WHAT THE SSI DOES

HIQA SSI's remit extends well beyond its previous scope of children's services and includes services for older persons and people with disabilities. The standards for these have been produced, and under the Health Act 2007, HIQA SSI will register and inspect services for older people from 2009 and follow this with registration of services for people with disability. While these two areas are initially being registered under the new Act, children's services will continue to be inspected as before under the Child Care Act.

The principal change under the new legislation will be the registration of HSE-provided residential care services. The Act gives the Office of the Chief Inspector of Social Services considerable powers to ensure that all services are compliant with regulations and standards. Regulations necessary for the fulfilment of the Chief Inspector's functions are being developed by the Department of Health and Children, and standards, policies, methodology, an inspector's code of conduct and procedures for investigation and enforcement are being prepared by HIQA alongside the recruitment of the number of inspectors necessary to register all centres within the three-year timescale. It is estimated that HIQA SSI will have over 1,600 residential services to register every three years and that inspections will be carried out by 170 inspectors.

THE CURRENT SITUATION: WHAT IS INSPECTED

HIQA SSI inspects children's centres and special care units run by the HSE throughout Ireland. The inspectorate also inspects foster care services run by the HSE and private organisations. Since 2008, the inspectorate also inspects children's detention schools. For children's services, particularly residential care, inspections are currently carried out under Section 69 of the Child Care Act 1991, as they have been since the SSI was established. The process of these inspections is described in detail below. This will continue until HIQA is in a position to introduce registration of all designated children's residential services, both statutory and non-statutory.

Registration

The HSE has local registration and inspection units (R&I). Their inspectors register and inspect private and voluntary children's centres under Section 63 (2g) of the Child Care Act 1991. R&I inspectors will continue to inspect as before until the full range of HIQA SSI registration inspections under the Health Act 2007, which covers centres run by the private and voluntary sector as well as by the HSE, commences. Registration is for three years and follows inspections carried out by local HSE inspectors. At present it applies only to private and voluntary centres. In the greater Dublin area, registration and inspection are carried out by a registration team based in the Northern Area. In other parts of the country, there are regionally based registration inspectors. Currently, the SSI has the authority to inspect but not to register centres run by the HSE. However, under the Health Act 2007, the SSI will have the authority to register all centres and services, and appeals against registration decisions will be through the District Courts.

Monitoring

The monitoring of children's residential centres is carried out by monitoring officers under Article 17 of the Child Care Regulations 1995, which requires the HSE to appoint a person to inspect centres regularly to satisfy itself that regulations and standards are being met. All centres, both statutory and non-statutory, are monitored, and Standard Three of the National Standards for Children's Residential Centres describes the monitoring officer's duties. In parts of the country outside Dublin, registration inspectors also act as monitoring officers in HSE centres. In the greater Dublin area, there are three monitoring officers. The monitoring officer's duties are described in the National Standards.

Regulations and Standards

Inspections are carried out according to regulations and standards. Regulations are statutory requirements issued by the minister. Standards are a set of principles and criteria for providing care against which inspectors inspect the service provided in the centre. They are underpinned by the Child Care (Children in Residential Care) Regulations 1995, which stipulate basic requirements for the care of children. Other standards are for special care (2001) and foster care (2003). The minister issued regulations for special care in 2004. These, as well as special care legislation and standards, are currently under review.

In the context of residential care, the word 'standard' means the quality of performance required in the management and delivery of a service. Standards are derived from legislation, regulation and guidance and current professional understanding and are based on research and professional experience of what constitutes best care practice.

In inspection, standards are criteria for judging quality, worth or value. Since its establishment, HIQA SSI has produced standards for residential care of older people, and at the time of writing (late 2008), standards for people with disabilities are in draft form. In time, HIQA SSI will revise the standards on children's residential centres and foster care.

There are two main types of standard: the majority, which represent current good practice and as such should reflect what service providers are either doing or aiming to do, and a smaller group of standards which are aspirational and represent practice that all service providers should be aiming to achieve but are not currently achieving.

Why Have Standards?

It is necessary to have standards to make explicit to everybody what services should be doing to protect and promote the welfare of the children they are designed for and to help make explicit who is responsible for which functions and tasks. They also provide a means by which service providers and others, such as inspectors, can assess the impact of outcomes of their interventions. They also help ensure that children in need throughout the state experience equality of access to quality services.

THE INSPECTION PROCESS

The overall plan is to inspect centres regularly. Special care units are inspected annually, and the objective for other centres is to inspect them at a minimum of every three years. This timescale will be the period of registration when the Health Act 2007 is fully implemented.

Centres are chosen for inspection through a series of criteria: for example, length of time since the last inspection, information of concern about standards of a particular aspect of child care practice being brought to the attention of the inspectorate through the HSE monitoring officer's reports or through concerns directly communicated to the inspectorate.

Before the Inspection

An inspection may be announced or unannounced. In announced inspections, the centre manager is informed of the inspection six weeks before fieldwork. The announcement is made by letter and includes a request for a range of information that will be required by inspectors prior to visiting the centre. This includes details of current residents, their social workers and other significant people who will be contacted in the course of the inspection; census data on staff and children; policies and procedures; details of significant events, such as unauthorised absences and the use of physical restraint; and copies of statutorily required documentation on insurance, fire safety and health and safety.

Fieldwork

'Fieldwork' is the term used for the inspectors' visit to the centre. Most inspections are carried out by two inspectors. One is the lead inspector and the other, who has a particular role in maintaining a record of the inspection fieldwork, is the support or co-inspector.

All centres are inspected against the relevant standards rather than through comparisons between one centre and another. The overall objective is to determine whether and to what extent each standard is met.

The following principles apply when gathering evidence during inspection.

- The process is fair and open throughout the inspection.
- Children's confidentiality and identity are protected.
- Evidence is based on information from more than one source.
- The inspection is of the service provided in the centre, not case management or the child's care history.
- Each centre is inspected against relevant standards, but where some comparisons in standards are made, such as in a themed inspection, the identity of individual centres is protected.

While at the centre, the inspectors gather evidence to support their judgements in a variety of ways: examination of documentation, observation and interviews.

Documentation

Section 69 (4b) of the Child Care Act 1991 states that the inspector may 'examine such records ... as he thinks fit'. Before and during the inspection, a wide range of documentation is examined, including:

1. Requirements of the regulations (the regulation is referenced in brackets):
- Written confirmation re: fire safety and building control (12(1)).
- Evidence of fire drills and evacuation procedures (12(3)).

- Records of accidents and injuries (13(2)).
- Evidence of insurance (14).
- Evidence of notification of significant events (15).
- Administrative records (including daily logs) (16).
- Evidence of medical examination (20).
- The centre's register (21).
- Care records (22).
- Each child's care plan (23).

2. Requirements of the standards:
- Health and safety risk assessment.
- Health and safety statement.
- Evidence of the roadworthiness of centre vehicles.
- Medication records.
- Fire safety statement.
- Evidence of the maintenance of fire safety equipment.

3. Inspection documentation:
- Census data on children.
- Census data on staff.
- Details of the management structure.
- Questionnaires completed by children, parents, social workers and teachers.
- Letters from GPs and other professionals.
- Details of the following in the year prior to the inspection: complaints, unauthorised absences, the use of physical restraint, child protection concerns and the use of single separation in a special care unit.
- Notes taken during the inspection.

4. Other documentation:
- HSE policies and procedures.
- The centre's policies and procedures.
- Personnel files.
- Staff supervision records.
- Relevant records held on the centre's computer.

Observation

The inspectors observe a number of aspects of the centre.

- *Physical:* This entails a formal inspection of all of the premises to assess compliance with the recommendations of the centre's health and safety assessment and the suitability and standard of the accommodation used by the children in the centre.

- *Care*: The inspectors observe how children are looked after and treated in the centre in general terms.
- *Ambience*: The inspectors assess the degree to which a centre is homely, open, child centred, outward looking, welcoming to parents and families and has an ethos suitable for promoting the development and emotional well-being of the children.
- *Management*: Observations about how the centre is run.
- *Dynamic*: How those in the centre get on with each other.
- *Interactive*: How those in the centre get on with inspectors, parents, social workers and others who have a bona fide interest in the children.

Interviews

Section 69(4b) of the Child Care Act 1991 states that the inspector may 'interview such members of the staff of the board [since amended to HSE] as he thinks fit'.

During the inspection, inspectors interview a series of people: children, the centre manager, care staff, parents, supervising social workers, HSE monitoring officers and external managers. In some centres and special care units, they interview other professionals such as psychiatrists, psychologists and guardians *ad litem*.

All interviews are formal. Inspections are open, transparent processes carried out within the Freedom of Information and Data Protection legislation, so nothing is 'off the record'. Most interviews are face to face, but occasionally they are conducted over the phone.

Interviews enable the inspectors to clarify the role of the person interviewed, assess their understanding of the purpose and function of the centre's policies, ascertain their account or views of aspects of the centre's functions and the care it provides and cross-check and verify information already found through observation, in documentation or other interviews. The overall objective is to make a sound judgement about the quality of care received by the children in the centre and to determine whether it is in compliance with the regulations and standards.

After Fieldwork

At the end of the fieldwork, inspectors give preliminary verbal feedback to the centre manager and sometimes to external managers as well, indicating initial provisional findings. Inspectors then analyse all the evidence gathered and write a report of their findings on each standard. Inspectors use a range of terms of reference as a framework for analysis, including the following:

1. Statutory requirements:
- Child Care Act 1991.
- Children Act 2001.
- Child Care Regulations 1995.
- Child Care (Standards in Children's Residential Centres) 1996.
- Special Care Regulations 2004.

2. National standards:
- National Standards for Children's Residential Centres 2001.
- Special Care Standards 2001.

3. Circular letters from the Department of Health and Children on staff vetting procedures, 1994 and 1995.

4. National policy:
- Children First: National Guidelines for the Welfare and Protection of Children 1999.
- National Guidelines on the Use of Single Separation in Special Care Units 2003.
- The National Children's Strategy.
- The United Nations Convention on the Rights of the Child.

5. Other:
- Academic research.
- Relevant policy reports.
- Enquiries – for example, the Madonna House enquiry (Department of Health 1996).

This and other relevant knowledge and experience of the inspector are factors in making judgements and presenting findings, evidence and analysis in inspection reports and making recommendations for action.

Inspection Reports

Inspection reports contain a brief description of the centre and an analysis of findings. Inspectors report their findings independently, 'without fear or favour'. The report presents them under all the standards relevant to the centre, in three categories: practice that met the required standard, practice that met the standard in some respects and practice that did not meet the required standard. Where practice did not meet or only partly met the standards, specific recommendations are made. Where inspectors have serious concerns about the standard of care in the centre, they have an option to reinspect after a specified time. A recommendation of closure of the centre is also an option, albeit rarely used.

The draft report is sent to the HSE local health manager, who ensures that the centre manager and others the recommendations are relevant to (for example, a recommendation on preparing care plans within statutory timescales would be relevant to social workers) check it for factual accuracy and anything that might identify an individual child. The local health manager returns the draft to the inspectors after any amendments have been made.

The inspection report is then published and is sent to the service managers in the HSE. A copy of the report is sent to the Department of Health and Children for the attention of the Minister for Children and Youth Affairs. Between seven and 10 days after publication, the report is put on the HIQA website.[5]

Along with the inspection report, the HSE local health manager is also sent the recommendations in a template for an action plan. The local health manager co-ordinates the response to the report and returns an action plan to the inspectorate in three weeks. The plan gives details of actions and timescales and names persons responsible for meeting each recommendation.

After Inspection

In most cases, the progress made in meeting recommendations is assessed and verified by the lead inspector during a return visit to the centre three months after the publication of the report. The inspectorate's response is added to the action plan template and is published on the HIQA website alongside the inspection report. Where the responses to the recommendations are seriously inadequate, the SSI will inform the Minister for Children and Youth Affairs.

KEY FINDINGS OF INSPECTIONS TO DATE

In the course of inspections generally, there have been some key positive findings.

- Some children's residential services are excellent.
- Standards on primary care and health are generally well met.
- Most centres provide good emotional support to children, have a good system of keyworking and easy access to specialist services.
- Relationships with staff are very good in the majority of centres.
- Centres are visited regularly by HSE monitoring officers.
- Most supervising social workers visit children regularly in accordance with regulations.
- Contact between children and their families is good in many centres and is a key indicator of the quality of care in those centres where the standards were very well met.
- Generally, the standards on safeguarding and child protection were well met.
- Children's rights to be consulted and make complaints were well met.

CONCLUSION

Despite these broadly positive trends, instances of poor practice and unacceptable standards have been reported and centres have been closed as a result. The inspection process must continue to be a well-resourced function at the centre of child care provision to ensure the best quality of care for some of the most vulnerable children in our society.

18

Psychological Health Difficulties in Children and Adolescents

Mark McGranaghan

OVERVIEW

Social care practitioners may often be well positioned in their various roles to notice potential difficulties in the psychological health and development of children and young people, and to provide support in terms of awareness-raising, prevention, appropriate referral direction, assessment and direct intervention. Awareness of such difficulties is therefore required from the social care practitioner. This chapter presents an overview of the issues relating to psychological problems and mental health difficulties that apply to children and adolescents. Issues of definition will be addressed and possible guidelines to determining the presence of psychological problems will be presented. Typology and prevalence of psychological difficulties in children and adolescents will be discussed. Some of the more influential factors which contribute to the development of psychological problems for children and adolescents will be reviewed and approaches to assessment and intervention will be discussed.

WHAT CONSTITUTES A PSYCHOLOGICAL PROBLEM?

Most children will show isolated and transitory emotional disturbance and/or behaviour difficulties while growing up, and to do so is within expectations in the course of normal development. Some children show levels of the above that may *interfere* with development and therefore indicate a need for some influence or intervention to redress these difficulties and allow normal development to progress. How to discriminate what is psychologically healthy and unhealthy is therefore an important question to answer if we are to make decisions about whether to intervene or not.

The Mental Health Foundation (1999) in the UK defines emotionally healthy children as having the ability to:

- Develop psychologically, emotionally, creatively, intellectually and spiritually.
- Initiate, develop and sustain mutually satisfying personal relationships.

- Use and enjoy solitude.
- Become aware of others and empathise with them.
- Play and learn.
- Develop a sense of right and wrong.
- Resolve and face up to setbacks and learn from them.

Such a definition of emotional healthiness is similar to the personal characteristics associated with the concept of childhood resilience (for example, Daniel et al. 1999). Resilience may be viewed as the ability to thrive, mature and increase competence in the face of adverse circumstances. Characteristics associated with resilient children include cognitive proficiency (especially intellectual curiosity and problem-solving), autonomy (the ability and desire to accomplish things on one's own), good social skills (for example, comfort and confidence in interacting with others, sensitivity to others' emotions) and internal locus of control (that is, the belief that we have control over what happens to us rather than that events are outside our ability to control).

The World Health Organization (WHO 2001) describes mental health as an integral component of health through which an individual realises his or her cognitive (intellectual), affective (emotional) and relational (social) abilities. With 'good' mental health, a person is more effective at coping with life stresses, can work productively and fruitfully and is able to make a positive contribution to his or her community.

While such conceptions may be a useful starting point in determining what it is that a psychologically healthy child should be able to do *should they so choose*, it must also be accepted that good psychological health is not a static state (Dogra et al. 2002). Psychological health may be influenced by individual characteristics and environmental events (as we will consider later) and changes in these factors may determine changes in psychological health status.

It is also useful to consider psychological health status as existing on a continuum between well-being and severe mental health problems. Trying to determine the cut-off between what is 'normal' and 'abnormal' may be difficult – we must not just pay attention to the presence of symptoms, but also to the impact on a particular individual's functioning. Some of the issues that compound difficulties in this regard include the following (Dogra et al. 2002).

- Sometimes symptoms can be severe but manageable (for example, a spider phobia may be just as distressing as a needle phobia, but the latter may have a more detrimental effect on being able to function normally).
- Some experiences/behaviours that may be associated with psychological problems may also be indicators of problems not associated with mental health (for example, agitation and mood change may be indicative of thyroid dysfunction).
- Distress is a component of human experience and does not necessarily indicate psychological problems.

For the most part, psychological problems do not constitute conditions that are qualitatively very different from normality. They often differ quantitatively (that is, in frequency, duration or intensity) and in terms of impairment, but minor variations of the same symptoms are found in otherwise psychologically healthy children.

Isolated symptoms are very common. Psychological difficulties are often identified, not on the presence of singular behavioural or distress symptoms, but on the basis of patterns of multiple symptomology that are persistent and socially handicapping.

Psychological difficulties should be perceived and approached in terms of their interactional nature – namely, that the problem is most usually located in the interaction between a young person and his or her environment, and not usually within the child.

Rutter (1975) asserts that the severity of difficulties is what will determine the presence of psychological problems but that this severity must be gauged on the basis of two evaluations – evaluation of abnormality (in terms of quantitative difference from the normal or expected) and impairment (in terms of limitations imposed on social functioning and development). Rutter offers the following guide to what to consider when making a judgement regarding the presence of psychological problems.

Abnormality

- *Age and sex appropriateness*: Bedwetting may be quite common in five-year-olds, but worthy of more attention in a 13-year-old. Similarly, separation anxiety can be a feature of normal development in the pre-school years, but can be viewed as unusual in a 12-year-old. While there is overlap in the exhibition of male and female traits in boys and girls even in later childhood, it would be rare for a boy to show all feminine traits (and vice versa) and so this might be seen as statistically abnormal.
- *Persistence*: As has been mentioned, it is quite common for behavioural or emotional disturbance to be exhibited in a transitory manner in childhood. Difficulties that persist over time, however, can be more likely to warrant concern in terms of needing intervention.
- *Life circumstances*: Development rarely follows a smooth trajectory. Plateaux in development and even periods of regression are not unusual. These are more likely to occur at certain times and in response to certain kinds of event than others (for example, starting a new school, bereavement, relocation, new baby in the home, parental separation). Attending to the unique life circumstances of any child is important in trying to evaluate the abnormality of his or her presenting difficulty.
- *Socio-cultural setting*: Different socio-cultural settings may have different expectations and norms regarding children's behaviour and may involve different child-rearing practices and priorities. Such differences need to be

taken into account when coming to decisions regarding what is normal and abnormal.

- *Extent of disturbance:* Isolated symptoms are more common than the simultaneous presence of many symptoms. Greater consideration to possible disturbance should apply when a child presents with multiple manifestations of emotional or behavioural difficulty, especially if these extend across different areas of psychological functioning.

- *Severity and frequency:* Mild and infrequent difficulties are more common than severe or infrequent ones. The difference between symptoms that may require intervention and those that may not is often associated with the degree of manifestation of the difficulty rather than the presence of the difficulty (that is, how frequent, intense or long-lasting the problematic symptom is).

- *Type of symptom:* How the problem manifests itself may influence the degree of concern raised regarding possible psychological difficulties in that certain symptoms are sometimes associated more with psychological dysfunction (Rutter et al. 1970). Nail biting, for example, is often associated with stress but is just as common in children who are psychologically healthy as those who are not – stress affects everyone sometimes and is not equated with psychological disturbance. Disturbed peer relationships, on the other hand, are more often associated with psychological problems.

- *Change in behaviour:* If the problematic symptom represents an alteration in behaviour for a particular child and is not a change related to normal maturation and development, then it may have more significance.

- *Situation specificity:* In general, problematic symptoms that manifest themselves in a number of contexts and settings are more significant than those that are only observed in a specific context – much will depend, however, on the type and severity of the problem.

Impairment

- *Suffering:* Even where presenting difficulties may be evaluated as abnormal according to the above, we must also ascertain if the difficulty is impacting on the subjective experience of the child. We may be concerned, for example, that a child is not joining with others for play. How significant this is in terms of disturbance may vary according to whether the child is highly self-sufficient and perfectly content in choosing to not engage or is miserable and anxious because he does not know how to join in.

- *Social restriction:* If the identified problem prevents or restricts the child from doing things that he or she wants to do, or results in a limitation of the opportunities for social engagement and interaction, then this represents impairment and may require action.

- *Interference with development:* Normal development in any area of psychological functioning usually follows a sequential path where later developmental targets are achieved on the basis of previous developmental attainments. Presenting problems must be viewed in terms of their potential impact on slowing down or interfering with normal developmental trajectories.

- *Effects on others:* We function in a social environment and our interactions and relationships with others are central to our psychological health. This is particularly pertinent for the developing child, as primary family relationships and later peer relationships are influential in determining healthy social and emotional functioning. Accordingly, problematic symptoms need to be considered in an interpersonal context. The impact of a young person's behaviour on others, in terms of undermining relationships with them or causing stress or psychological damage to them, is important to consider. This is most important when such an impact affects those with whom the child needs to have a healthy relationship.

MANIFESTATIONS OF PSYCHOLOGICAL PROBLEMS

It is far beyond the scope of this chapter to provide more than a summary consideration of the range and configurations of psychological problems affecting children and adolescents. Two major classification systems exist to try to organise how psychological problems are grouped and organised in a useful way. These are the *International Classification of Diseases*, 10th edition (ICD–10, WHO 1992) and the *Diagnostic and Statistical Manual of the Mental Disorders*, 4th edition (American Psychiatric Association 1994). Such classification has some useful functions (Carr 1999). It allows information such as problem description, aetiological factors, maintenance and course of the problem, and even possible interventions and management plans, to be organised in a way that might be useful for clinical practice. It also provides a structure for the gathering of information about incidence and prevalence of particular problems. Such classification also allows a common language whereby clinicians can communicate about psychological problems. Difficulties exist, however, with regard to low reliability and validity, difficulties attributing presenting cases to clearly defined categories, an over-emphasis on pathology as opposed to consideration of personal strengths and resources, and limitations in failing to take account of the sophisticated interactional characteristics of most childhood problems – information that is crucial in developing intervention plans (Carr 1999).

Rutter (1975) also refers to the fact that such classifications focus on the lowest common denominators when trying to group disorders and disregard uniqueness. Diagnostic formulation should emphasise what is different and distinctive about a particular child and offer suggestions, for example, regarding what psychological mechanisms might be operating, what the underlying causes and precipitants for this child are, what protective factors might be harnessed to intervene in this instance and, on the basis of these considerations, what interventions are most likely to be effective.

A different approach to categorising children's difficulties is to measure the 'amount' of symptomology displayed by the child and to interpret this according to a particular set of dimensions that statistically relate the symptoms as being associated with each other. Achenbach (1991), for example, has shown that the majority of the behavioural difficulties that lead to referral can be considered as reflecting clusters of symptoms along two dimensions – emotional behaviours (such as crying, withdrawing, fretting), which he terms internalising behaviours, and aggressive and delinquent conduct problems (such as fighting, disobedience, stealing, destructiveness), which he terms externalising behaviours. Smaller categories of clustered behaviours that seemed to represent mixed syndromes (including, for example, sleep problems, social problems and attention problems) were also identified.

Some of the main manifestations of psychological difficulties in childhood and adolescence are summarised below. These are organised, after Carr (1999), according to the developmental stage at which they are most likely to initially present.

PRIMARY PSYCHOLOGICAL DIFFICULTIES IN CHILDHOOD AND ADOLESCENCE

Early childhood:

- *Sleeping problems*, including difficulties settling, waking at night, nightmares, night terrors, sleepwalking.
- *Toileting problems*, including enuresis and encopresis.
- *Learning and communication difficulties*, including intellectual disabilities, specific language delay, specific learning difficulty.

AUTISM AND PERVASIVE DEVELOPMENTAL DISORDERS

Middle childhood:

- *Conduct problems*, including oppositional defiant disorder and conduct disorder, the main features of which include defiance, aggression, anger, family relationship difficulties, educational difficulties, peer problems and difficulties with social interpretation and problem solving.
- *Problems with attention and overactivity*, characterised by persistent over-activity, impulsivity and difficulties sustaining attention, i.e. ADHD.
- *Fear and anxiety problems*, for example, generalised anxiety disorder, panic disorder, specific phobias, agoraphobia, social phobia, post-traumatic stress disorder.
- *Repetition problems*, for example, obsessive compulsive disorder, Tourette's Syndrome, tics.

- *Somatic complaints*, that is, the expression of distress via physical or illness-related symptoms.

Adolescence:

- *Habitual drug abuse.*
- Mood *disorders*, for example, depression, bipolar disorder, substance-induced mood disorder, adjustment disorder affecting mood, bereavement sequelae.
- *Anorexia and bulimia nervosa.*
- *Schizophrenia.*

Source: Carr (1999).

In addition, there are a number of problem presentations that are less well associated with onset at a particular developmental stage and are better organised in terms of being associated with major forms of stress. These include problems associated with physical abuse, emotional abuse and neglect and sexual abuse (for example, emotional regulation problems, development of negative self-evaluative beliefs, attachment problems, non-organic failure to thrive, intellectual impairment and developmental delay, externalised and internalised behaviour difficulties, sexualised behaviour) and problems associated with adjustment to major life transitions, such as reactions to admission to care, separation and divorce and bereavement.

PREVALENCE

The recorded prevalence rates for psychological problems vary across different studies, most likely as a function of differences such as the measures used and difficulties considered, the cultural context in which they were used or the size, sex or age range of the targeted population.

The World Health Organization (WHO 2001) reported that 20 per cent of 15-year-olds or younger in the world experience mild to severe mental health difficulties, but that many of these remain untreated because of lack of services. The National Institute of Mental Health (2000) in the US reports prevalence rates for mental health problems in young people of 10 per cent, but notes that less than one in five of those needing intervention actually get it. Rates of mental health problems in young people for the UK have been reported by the Office for National Statistics (2000) as 10 per cent.

Carr (1999) reports a number of prevalence studies in various countries (all using the same measurement instrument) that indicated differences in rates from 4 per cent to 23 per cent depending on geographical location. Higher rates were associated with urban rather than rural locations and Western rather than Eastern culture. Cohen et al. (1993) and Bird (1996) have both reported findings that suggest that psychological problems are more prevalent among boys than girls, that conduct and 'externalising' difficulties (expressed in behaviour that impacts on the environment) are more prevalent in boys and that there are higher prevalence rates for emotional and 'internalising' difficulties (expressed in internally focused disturbance) in girls.

A useful recent study in the Irish context has been that by Martin and Carr (2007). This study screened 3,374 children and adolescents up to age 18 years in the Clonmel area (74 per cent of all under-18s in the area) using the Achenbach Child Behaviour Checklist or Achenbach Youth Self Report Form. Those that screened positively, and a random sample of those that screened negatively, were further interviewed using the Diagnostic Interview Schedule. Of the total sample, 18.71 per cent met the criteria for at least one psychological disorder (14.9 per cent of under-five-year-olds, 18.53 per cent of six- to 11-year-olds, and 21.11 per cent of 12- to 18-year-olds). A breakdown of rates of various disorders is summarised in Table 18.1. ADHD was more common in children and conduct disorder was more common in adolescents. Separation anxiety disorder was more prevalent in primary school children than adolescents. Anxiety disorders were more common in girls, disruptive behaviour difficulties in boys. Approximately 20 per cent of identified cases with a psychological disorder had problems associated with clinical risk (for example, thoughts of death or dying, suspension/expulsion from school). Those with identified disorders had associated profiles of social disadvantage, increased behavioural difficulties and adaptive behaviour problems, more physical health problems, more family problems, more life stress and poorer coping skills.

Table 18.1. Rates of Different Psychological Disorders Reported in Clonmel Project

Type of Disorder	As a Percentage of All Identified Disorders
Anxiety disorders	43%
Oppositional defiant disorder	25%
ADHD	Just over 20%
Conduct disorder	Just over 10%
Mood disorder Alcohol abuse Intellectual disability	10%
Nicotine dependence Specific reading disorder Tic disorders Marijuana abuse Substance abuse Eating disorders	Under 10%

Source: Martin and Carr (2007).

In summary, prevalence rates seem to suggest that significant numbers of children and teenagers (approximately one in five) have psychological difficulties and that services need to be organised accordingly to provide appropriate levels of treatment and intervention.

FACTORS CONTRIBUTING TO THE DEVELOPMENT OF PSYCHOLOGICAL PROBLEMS

Cooper (1985), following on the work of Kellmer-Pringle (1974), has described the range of needs that children have if they are to achieve and maintain psychological health and well-being (Table 18.2). Factors and events that interfere with responding to and meeting these needs are therefore likely to increase risk with regard to the possible development of psychological problems.

Table 18.2. The Needs of Children

Basic physical care	Warmth, shelter, adequate food, rest, hygiene, protection from danger.
Affection	Physical contact, holding, stroking, cuddling, kissing, comforting, admiration, delight, tenderness, patience, time, making allowances, approval.
Security	Continuity of care, expectation of continuing stability, predictable environment, consistent patterns of care and routine, simple rules, harmonious relationships.
Stimulation of innate potential	Praise, encouraging curiosity, learning and play opportunities, responsiveness to questions.
Guidance and control	Teaching of adequate social behaviour within child's capacity, authoritative parenting.
Responsibility	Progressively encouraging decision-making that the child needs to have to function adequately according to age, gaining experience via success and mistakes, reinforcement for striving to do better.
Independence	Progressive encouragement of making own decisions within structure of family and society rules, balancing protection with overprotection.

Source: Cooper (1985).

Herbert (1981) has presented a 10-factor formulation regarding the interacting contributory variables to any presenting emotional and behavioural disturbance.

- *Genetic constitution*, e.g. temperament, IQ.
- *Home atmosphere and child rearing*, e.g. reinforcement history, attachments and parent-child relationships, discipline, consistency, disharmony.
- *Early development*, e.g. pregnancy, birth, postnatal depression.
- *Personality factors*, e.g. extraversion/introversion, self-esteem, locus of control.
- *Milestones*, e.g. health, identity, schooling, skills.
- *Developmental stage/developmental crisis*, e.g. puberty, starting school.
- *Current life circumstances*, e.g. housing, neighbourhood, friendships, activities, achievements.
- *Socio-economic demographic variables*, e.g. race, class, income level, socially disadvantaged environment.
- *Person variables*, e.g. cognitive and perceptual processing, expectancies, motivation.
- *Situation ABCs*, e.g. people, time, circumstances.

Consideration of all the variables associated with increasing the risk of psychological difficulties for children and adolescents, particularly as there are highly interactive relationships between variables, is a complicated task. Brief consideration, however, will be given here to selected risk factors, including early attachment experiences, family stress and adversity in childhood, parenting style and discipline and temperamental factors.

Attachment

Attachment (see Chapter 6) refers to the earliest relationships that a child forms with his or her main caregivers. Fahlberg (1994: 14) defines an attachment, quoting Klaus and Kennell (1976), as 'an affectionate bond between two individuals that endures through space and time and serves to join them emotionally'.

The concept was first utilised by Bowlby (1969) to refer to the cluster of behavioural and emotional sequences shown by infants towards their caregivers in situations of stress. Bowlby stresses a biological need to seek and maintain contact with others, an impulse to maintain closeness, to restore it if repaired and the need for a *particular* person if distressed. Klaus and Kennell (1976), in summary, note that attachment *behaviours* (the distress behaviours exhibited by children when anxious or discomforted) are rooted in instinct and have evolved to increase the chances of survival. More than physical care is needed for attachments to form. Sensitivity to a baby's signals, warmth and responsiveness are required – it is the nature of the social interaction that seems to be important.

The purpose of attachment behaviours is to achieve proximity to the caregiver, while the function is to achieve a subjective state of 'felt security'. Felt security contributes to the establishment of the caregiver as an emotional 'secure base', enabling interaction with the outside world and learning (interaction is blocked in states of anxiety). Felt security also contributes to the establishment and progressive development of an 'internal working model' of relationships, which includes predictions about the predictability/trustworthiness of others and a basic self-concept as 'worthy' or 'unworthy' that is influential in determining future emotional and social development.

Fahlberg (1994) notes that having a secure attachment history is related to higher measured self-esteem, better relationships with caregivers, better relationships with peers, better ability to control impulses and emotions, better levels of co-operation, more sophisticated development of compassion, empathy and other 'social' emotions, greater independence and autonomy, more positive core belief systems, a solid and positive sense of self, pro-social values and maturity in morality and conscience development, and overall greater resilience (the ability to handle stress and adversity). Conversely, children who have a significantly compromised attachment history may be more at risk of difficulties with conscience development, impulse control, self-esteem, interpersonal interactions, emotional regulation and cognitive skills.

Both Ainsworth et al. (1978) and Main and Solomon (1990) have identified different patterns of attachment relationships that seem to be associated with different parenting characteristics, particularly the consistency, level and focus of responsiveness to the child. Howe et al. (1999) describe characteristics of each of these identified patterns.

- *Secure attachment* is associated with positive, sensitive carer behaviour that is encouraging of close physical contact. Securely attached children show stress when they feel it and respond positively to the carer. They are more curious and interested in the world around them. As toddlers, they learn more easily to deal with emotions via language and cognitive processes and can more easily begin to use shame for self-regulation. As older children, they are more flexible in dealing with social encounters and are more resilient.
- *Insecure anxious-avoidant attachment* is associated with carers who are dismissive of emotions, restricted in the range of emotional expression and who may be uncomfortable with close physical contact. Children with this pattern may experience that their proximity-seeking behaviour in terms of distress is not responded to and they may learn to disconnect from feelings of anxiety and from their emotional world. As older children, they may be emotionally inhibited, anxious to please and lack social competence and sensitivity.
- *Insecure anxious-ambivalent attachment* is associated with carers who are preoccupied with their own emotional needs and who may be inconsistently emotionally available and responsive to their child. Such children seem to have internal models that view adults as not to be relied on to respond. Emotionality may govern the behaviour of such children and exploratory behaviour may be limited, with possible impacts on cognitive development. Demandingness, poor frustration tolerance, poor regulation of emotion via reflection, coercive behaviour and attention-seeking behaviour may be more likely.

- *Disorganised attachment* is the least frequent pattern observed and represents the most severely dysfunctional relationship pattern. Carers may be characterised as frightened or frightening, emotionally unavailable or toxically available. They are often not able to respond to any of the other organised attachment behaviour patterns in their child. Such children cannot organise their behaviour into a consistent strategy to achieve soothing proximity. Behaviour and emotional response are often contradictory and confused. Such children often show signs of traumatic experience.

Attachments develop as a result of interactions between the carer and the child and two mechanisms have been commonly described (for example, Daniel et al. 1999; Fahlberg 1994). The Arousal Relaxation Cycle describes a sequence where the child develops a need that results in discomfort. This is expressed in distress and proximity-seeking. Carer attention to the need reduces anxiety and the child re-establishes a state of contentment. Interactions of this nature are felt to encourage the development of trust and security. The Positive Interaction Cycle describes situations where interaction is initiated by the carer, which evokes a positive response from the child, which in turn modifies or reinforces the carer response in a cyclical manner. Such interactions are believed to encourage the development of self-worth and self-esteem. Reciprocity is a feature of both mechanisms.

Obviously, factors that interfere *consistently* with the sensitivity and responsiveness of the carer to the child may impact negatively on attachment formation. Such factors can include the carer's own childhood attachment experience, temperamental/constitutional difficulties in the child that may make the child's signals difficult to interpret, stress for the carer, lack of social support for the carer, lack of emotional availability of the carer due to substance influence, and some mental health difficulties.

Family Stress and Childhood Adversity

Children who belong to families who are struggling to cope with social disadvantage are more likely to experience emotional and behavioural difficulties (Sutton 2000). This may be related to the possibility that isolation, low levels of educational opportunity and attainment, poor housing and lack of support from family members are often associated with social disadvantage, and such stressors may lead to difficulties in delivering consistency in parenting and providing appropriate levels of stimulation. Blanz et al. (1991) have found that early onset serious behaviour problems (that is, those commencing at eight years or younger) were associated with chronic family adversity and stress. Carer stress and lack of support have also been identified as potentially harmful to the formation of secure attachment relationships.

Children who have faced adversity (that is, life events that may strongly threaten psychological well-being) are at greater risk of developing psychological difficulties (Dogra et al. 2002). Confusion about events and lack of explanation of what is happening can compound distress. The vulnerability of any young person to adversity may vary according to individual strengths and resilience. Adverse events associated with increased risk of psychological dysfunction include:

- Marital discord.
- Parental separation, divorce and/or remarriage.
- Domestic violence.
- Death of a parent.
- Neglect.
- Emotional abuse.
- Physical abuse.
- Sexual abuse.
- Care upbringing (particularly institutional care).
- Homelessness.

Parenting Style and Discipline

A further variable that impacts on psychological well-being is the child's experiences of parenting style. Kazdin (1995) reports that problem-maintaining interactions between parents and children can emerge when the rules governing acceptable behaviour are not linked to the logical or other consequences associated with keeping or breaking them, either because these links are unclear to the child, or because they are inconsistently applied. A result is that the child has difficulty internalising the rules and appropriately regulating his or her social behaviour.

Reviews of literature on parenting reveal a consistency in the usefulness of viewing different parenting styles along two dimensions: the amount of responsiveness or warmth shown by parents, and the amount of demandingness or control exerted by parents (Baumrind 1972; Darling and Steinberg 1993; Maccoby and Martin 1983). Four configurations or styles of parenting can result from combining these dimensions and each parenting style has been related to characteristic consequences for children (Maccoby and Martin 1983).

- High warmth with high control (*authoritative parenting*) involves affectionate but firm parenting. Behavioural expectations are clear but developmentally appropriate. Discipline is rational, with explanation and discussion. This style is associated with children who are socially competent, affectionate, responsible, successful in school and possessing high self-esteem.
- Low warmth with high control (*authoritarian parenting*) emphasises obedience and conformity and discipline is punitive and not open to discussion.

Independence and autonomy are discouraged and this style is associated with children who are more dependent, less socially competent and low in self-confidence.

- High warmth with low control (*indulgent parenting*) involves few demands being placed on the child, passive or little discipline and few boundaries around inappropriate behaviour. Exerting parental control is viewed as interfering with the child's freedom and rights and this style is associated with children who are more socially irresponsible and prone to conforming to peer pressure and demands.

- Low warmth with low control (*indifferent parenting*) is characterised by parents who are concerned with meeting their own needs and who discipline on the basis of responding to their own needs being infringed. This style is quite neglectful and the child's interest is not considered. Inconsistent discipline, often including physical punishment and anger, often result. This style is associated with children who are impulsive, aggressive and anti-social in behaviour.

Temperamental Factors

As has been suggested earlier, the psychological make-up of an individual may impact on how susceptible he or she is to developing psychological difficulties. Temperament refers to those components of personality for which there is an implied underlying genetic contribution but which may be further influenced by parental attitude, child-rearing and experience. Thomas and Chess (1977) identified nine temperamental attributes in young children, which they grouped into three temperament types. 'Easy' children were adaptable, easy to manage, established eating and sleeping routines quickly, and were generally responsive and contented. 'Difficult' children were less adaptable, found it more difficult to establish routines and were more irritable in response to new situations. 'Slow to warm up' children fell somewhere between these two, finding it difficult to establish routines, but once these were established were otherwise easy to manage. 'Difficult' children were found to be at higher risk for developing psychological problems. Such children had more conflict with others, elicited negative reactions from carers more often and tended to gravitate towards a more deviant peer group. They were more prone to developing conduct difficulties and adjustment problems. 'Difficult' children adjust better if there is a 'goodness of fit' between their temperament and parental expectations and parenting approach (Chess and Thomas 1995).

ASSESSMENT AND INTERVENTION

The way that services in Ireland are delivered to children with psychological problems may be conceptualised as occurring at different levels.

- The first level is provided by those working in frontline services to the public and with whom the public make direct contact. Such practitioners will include GPs, public health nurses, teachers, youth and community workers. Responses may include promotion of psychological good health, information-giving and education, identification of problems early in their development or referral on to more specialised services.
- At level two, responses are provided by specialised practitioners from a variety of disciplines who conduct activities in a uni-disciplinary way, for example, psychiatrists, psychologists, counsellors, social workers. Activities include consultation, assessment, intervention and the identification of more severe/complex needs that might need referral to more specialised services.
- At level three, practitioners usually work in multidisciplinary team activity providing services for children with more severe, complex or persistent difficulties. The same practitioners may work at level two and three depending on their activity with a particular case. Level three may include more detailed multidisciplinary assessment over a longer time period than level two.
- Level four responses are essentially highly specialised and intensive interventions and care for relatively few, but the most troubled, young people who present with the most complex difficulties. Such services are usually the most invasive and are often regionally or nationally provided.

Effective intervention requires appropriate assessment and identification of needs and should lead to a formulation of the problem that suggests appropriate action.

Assessment is informed by data from a number of possible sources. These may include:

- Child-centred interviews/testing.
- Interviews with parents.
- Interviews with the nuclear family.
- Interviews with extended family.
- School interviews.
- Direct observation of the child in different contexts.
- Measurement and recording of aspects of behaviour/experience and environmental events (for example, diary keeping).
- Interviews with other professionals/practitioners involved.
- Clinical team meetings.
- Professional network meetings.
- Attendance at statutory case conferences.
- Information gathered from tests and other psychological evaluation instruments.

The focus of information gathering may include building an evidence-based understanding of the following:

- Current presenting problems and measurement of severity of same.
- History of the presenting problem.

- Child's developmental history.
- Current family relationships and functioning.
- Family history.
- School and education functioning.
- Current psychological functioning of child, including strengths and deficits, resiliencies and vulnerabilities.
- Motivation for change of child and parents.
- Parenting skills and deficits, and parental capacity.
- Family/community resources and supports.

Assessment needs to be viewed as a recursive process of hypothesis generation and testing, and progressive refinement of a formulation in the light of each new assessment activity.

Formulation needs to communicate an understanding of the presenting problems and their genesis, maintenance and function; identify protective factors; and suggest interventions that might be indicated. The formulation should be consistent with the assessment evidence, resonate with others' experience of the child and be consistent with the available knowledge base about similar problems (Carr 1999).

Interventions may include:

- Information-giving/psycho-education.
- Ongoing supportive consultation.
- Direct therapeutic work with the child (individual or group).
- Indirect therapeutic work with the child.
- Direct therapeutic work with parents/family.
- Parent training.
- Medication.
- Changes to care/schooling arrangements.
- Referral to specialised treatment.

Effective interventions are often multi-modal and/or multi-systemic – that is, more than one intervention strategy may be used simultaneously and intervention may need to focus across different systems in a child's life.

Children are part of families and interventions need to include, involve and/or focus on the family system. Engagement of parents and family can sometimes be difficult, but efforts to establish a collaborative partnership are likely to lead to better outcomes.

Interventions should be chosen and delivered in a responsible and accountable way. Any intervention should be empirically supported as appropriate and relevant to the presenting difficulty. Direct interventions should be delivered by practitioners with proven competence in the field. Interventions should be related to outcome goals and monitored for their effectiveness in moving towards achieving the same.

Realistic expectations should be communicated regarding the possible costs/ benefits of any interventions proposed. While there is compelling evidence that psychological treatment, either alone or as part of treatment programmes involving psychotropic medication, can be effective with a wide range of psychological problems of childhood and adolescence (Martin and Carr 2007), it should be realised that for children and adolescents with all types of psychological problems, the best available treatment may not work for up to one-third of cases (Carr 2000).

CONCLUSION

This chapter has reviewed a number of issues regarding the psychological health difficulties experienced by young people, which social care practitioners may encounter in the course of their work.

In reviewing what might constitute a psychological difficulty, it is useful to conceive of children's psychological health as not being a static state, but as something that may vary with changing personal characteristics or environmental events. It is also important to view psychological health status as lying on a continuum between good psychological health and serious mental health difficulties. Further, in attempting to assess psychological problems, we need to pay attention not only to the nature of the presenting symptoms in terms of evaluating 'abnormality', but also to the impact of the child's presenting difficulties on her own development and on her own (and others') happiness and well-being before concluding that a certain presentation represents a psychological health problem.

The range of psychological difficulties that may present in children and adolescents has been described and we have also discussed the prevalence of such difficulties with reference to a number of studies. An implication from recent Irish-based work is that we should be planning services to be able to intervene at some level with as many as one in five young people, though this does not presume that such intervention is required only from specialised mental health services.

In reviewing how children's psychological health difficulties may develop, it is evident that the development of many difficulties is associated with the interaction between multiple factors. Implications are that effective intervention will often require attention not to the individual young person alone, but also to the other social systems within which he or she functions.

The different levels of possible service intervention for children presenting with psychological health difficulties were briefly described. Effective intervention for identified psychological problems requires appropriate assessment and identification of needs and should lead to a formulation of the problem that presents an understanding of the problem and its development and suggests appropriate action. Interventions should be empirically rooted, be delivered by people competent in their use, should be systematically monitored and evaluated, should in most cases include and involve the child's family, and will likely be more effective if they are multi-systemic.

19

Anti-discriminatory Practice: A New Direction for Social Care

Majella Mulkeen

OVERVIEW

This chapter examines why social care practitioners should be concerned with inequality and discrimination and explores the potential of social care practice to directly address these issues. The chapter is best read in conjunction with Chapter 8, which discusses broader issues of equality and inequality. In particular, this chapter sets out a rationale for the inclusion of anti-discriminatory practice as a core element in social care practice and education, linking this to the role of values in professional practice.

This chapter focuses on discrimination as a deep and pervasive experience for many of the people social care practitioners engage with. It examines three levels discrimination occurs at and the varied ways discrimination takes place, linking these to social care practice. Specific strategies to challenge discrimination and inequality are then examined in the light of Irish equality legislation and new directions in the role of the social care professional. The chapter also focuses on concepts that can influence discourses of care, such as user-led initiatives, rights, partnership and empowerment, which are used to develop an egalitarian perspective in social care. The chapter concludes with a model of emancipatory and anti-discriminatory practice that has the potential to engage social care in a transformative project.

Why should social care practitioners be concerned about discrimination? Following Thompson (2002a: 89–93), we can outline a number of reasons why a concern with discrimination is central to best practice in the social professions.

1. If we are to understand the people we work with, it is essential to *understand how inequality and discrimination have played a part in their lives to date and continue to do so.* Allen and Langford (2008: 21) are of the view that it is important to be aware of the structures of society that contribute to people feeling powerless to change their situation and why people may sometimes act in a helpless manner and feel they have no influence over their own lives.

2. To work effectively and ethically as a social care practitioner, *it is essential that our own actions or inactions do not contribute to discrimination and inequality* in the lives of those we work with (Thompson 2007). The emotional aspects of dealing with discrimination mean that it is virtually impossible not to be subjectively involved to some degree in how we interact with people different to ourselves, reflecting as it does our own expectations and socialisation.

3. Allen and Langford (2008: 22) state that discrimination will inevitably be an issue for care practitioners and the individuals they work with in their transactions with powerful institutions, such as state bureaucracy. Such transactions often demonstrate the existence of *institutional discrimination*. The Macpherson Report, produced in Britain in the aftermath of the murder of black teenager Stephen Lawrence, offers the following definition of one form of institutional discrimination, institutional racism, as:

> The collective failure of an organisation to provide an appropriate and professional service to people, because of their colour, culture, or ethnic origin. It can be seen or detected in processes, attitudes and behaviour which amount to discrimination through unwitting prejudice, ignorance, thought-lessness and racist stereotyping which disadvantage minority ethnic people. (Macpherson Report 1999: para. 6.34)

For Barnes (1991: 1), in writing about the experiences of people with dis-abilities:

> institutional discrimination ... is apparent when services are ignoring or meeting inadequately the needs of disabled people. It is also present when these agencies are regularly interfering unnecessarily in the lives of disabled people in ways and or to an extent not experienced by non-disabled people.

Where institutional discrimination occurs, awareness means we may be more skilled at recognising its existence and can develop our own capacity to challenge it. Challenging the institutional practices that oppress and system-atically disempower those with whom we work is the task of the social care practitioner in these contexts (Dalrymple and Burke 2007).

4. Treating people equally must *take into account their differences* and respond to their needs, circumstances and background accordingly. The relationship between the social care practitioner and those they work with is a double edged one, according to Thompson, consisting of elements of care and control. It is also double edged in the sense that it can lead to either potential empowerment or potential oppression (2006: 14). Openness, empowerment and partnership are therefore central in addressing these real and apparent power differentials. Allen and Langford (2008: 24) note that social care practitioners are often in positions of power where they may gate-keep resources, or where reports they

write will have a significant impact on a person's life. Thus, to promote greater equality, it is necessary to tackle discrimination. The challenge for social care practitioners is not to act as mere functionaries of the agency, following policy and procedure without any questioning or reflection as to the impact of decisions and actions on those with whom they work (Thompson 2002a).

WHERE DOES DISCRIMINATION OCCUR?

Thompson (2006) identifies three levels discrimination operates at: the personal, the cultural and the structural level.

Discrimination occurs at the level of *personal prejudice*, where it can take the form of verbal and physical attacks and individual exclusions. It is manifest in individual practitioner's interaction with individual clients where prejudice and inflexibility of mind can stand in the way of fair and non-judgemental practice in social care (2006: 26).

Discrimination at a personal level is embedded in the *culture* of the society. Individuals, while being unique, owe a great deal of their beliefs and attitudes to the prevailing norms and expectations of the society in which they live. Cultural practices in a society can operate to privilege dominant lifestyles, values and identities while labelling others in a manner that encourages hostility, discrimination and exclusion at the level of access to resources, recognition and representation. Privileged groups tend to have greater access to the resources of the society (Baker et al. 2004), thus discrimination also occurs at a cultural level.

The third level discrimination occurs at is the *structural* level: the network of social divisions and the power relations so closely associated with them. It relates to how inequality and discrimination are institutionalised and thus sewn into the fabric of society (Thompson 2006: 29).

HOW IS DISCRIMINATION ENACTED?

Thompson (2003: 82–92) highlights how discriminatory practice occurs in social care settings. While the most damaging act of discrimination is exclusion, other processes tend to interact, combine and reinforce each other, such as stereotyping, marginalisation, infantilisation and welfarism.

1. *Stereotyping* is frequently closely associated with oppressed groups and is often a vehicle for maintaining oppression. Stereotypes are oversimplified, generalised, biased and inflexible conceptualisations of a social group. For example, individuals with an intellectual disability are often referred to by their condition: 'He's a Downs.'
2. *Marginalisation* refers to how certain groups are pushed to the margins of society and excluded from the mainstream, for example, the provision of segregated education for Traveller children and children with disabilities in Irish society.

3. *Infantilisation* involves ascribing a childlike status to an adult and is used as a form of disempowerment. The use of terms such as the 'girls in the office' to describe women serves to reinforce power differentials. A female director of services is unlikely to be referred to as a girl. Forms of talk often used by nurses and care practitioners with older people or with adults with an intellectual disability testifies to a way of regarding people as dependent, childlike and unable to communicate or engage in their own right.

4. *Welfarism* refers to the tendency to regard certain groups as being necessarily in need of welfare services by virtue of their membership of such groups. Lone parents, people with disabilities and older people have been subject to this kind of discriminatory behaviour. Disability rights organisations have been critical of the overemphasis on disabled people's care needs at the expense of their rights.

The above examples of discriminatory processes represent an often unwitting misuse of power and are often used in a routine, unthinking way with damaging consequences for those at the receiving end. Social care practitioners need to recognise such processes and consider their personal value systems and how they impact on their professional role. Such reflection will support them in challenging discrimination appropriately in their work.

A discussion of *values* is pertinent to professional development in social care and is part of the training and education programmes offered throughout the country. Many of our values are internalised, arising from our family background, the community we grew up within, our class position, our gender and so on. We will reject some as incompatible with social care practice, but others come with us into our encounters in social care and impact on our work. While many social care students experience a transformation in their values, outlook and commitments as a result of their practice learning and education, it can be a personal and professional challenge to appreciate that one is not completely free of prejudice (Thompson 2002a).

A lack of sensitivity and an unwillingness to change dearly held views are likely to result in unconscious, unintentional but nevertheless damaging discriminatory behaviour. A concern with *outcomes* rather than intentions can help social care practitioners to focus on what is happening in any situation. Clearly, a focus on the personal level is important, but recognising how values impact on the professional role is central to understanding how discrimination is institutionalised. We will examine these issues further when we discuss new directions for social care below.

As we have seen, a useful starting point in developing strategies to counter discrimination and promote equality is an awareness of how our own values impact on our professional practice. A second strategy is an understanding of equality legislation and its relevance to groups that are marginalised and/or discriminated against.

EQUALITY LEGISLATION

Social care practitioners can use their knowledge of equality legislation to support the development of anti-discriminatory practice by being aware of the legal protections available to themselves as workers and by being able to advocate on behalf of those less powerful, where necessary. Crowley (2006: 4–5) notes that Irish equality legislation reflects an emphasis on difference and diversity, addressing as it does nine separate grounds for the prohibition of discrimination: age, gender, sexual orientation, marital status, family status, race, religion, membership of the Traveller community and disability. Identity is significantly determined by one's gender, sexual orientation, skin colour, national identity, religion and so on, and can in part be shaped by experiences of discrimination and exclusion, such as sexism, racism, homophobia and ageism.

The use of legislation to underpin rights and to prohibit discrimination is an important part of any strategic action to promote equality in a society. Two pieces of legislation are relevant to our current discussion: the Employment Equality Acts 1998 and 2004 and the Equal Status Acts 2000 and 2004. The provisions of this legislation are important, as they affirm diversity, prohibit discrimination against particular groups experiencing inequality and encourage a more positive approach to the promotion of equality.

The Employment Equality Acts 1998 and 2004 cover all aspects of employment. The Equal Status Acts 2000 and 2004 prohibit discrimination in the provision of goods and services, with particular reference to educational institutions, accommodation providers and registered clubs. In this section, we will give a brief overview of the legislation and examine definitions of discrimination, harassment, reasonable accommodation and positive action. In addition, we will offer a critique of the legislation and briefly look at the work of the Equality Tribunal.[1]

- *Discrimination:* Discrimination is defined under both Acts as occurring if a person is treated less favourably than another person is treated, has been treated or would be treated on the basis of membership of any of the nine grounds.
- *Indirect discrimination:* This is defined as discrimination by impact or effect. It occurs where an apparently neutral provision puts a person belonging to one of the discriminatory grounds at a particular disadvantage. For example, in a case taken by the Psychiatric Nurses Association on behalf of a number of female claimants in 2006 (*O'Donnell and Others v Health Services Executive NW Area: DEC-E2006-023*), the Equality Officer concluded that the roster, which required the claimants to work six or seven consecutive days and on occasion 13 to 16 days, impacted more heavily on them as women and primary carers and was indirectly discriminatory on the gender ground (Equality Authority 2006b: 32).
- *Harassment:* Both Acts prohibit harassment and sexual harassment. Sexual harassment is any form of unwanted verbal, non-verbal or physical conduct of a sexual nature. In the case of sexual harassment and harassment on any of the

nine grounds, it is conduct that has the purpose or effect of violating a person's dignity and creating an intimidating, hostile, degrading, humiliating or offensive environment for the person.

- *Reasonable accommodation*: Both Acts include a significant positive duty on employers and service providers to reasonably accommodate the needs of people with disabilities. This obligation ceases where the costs involved are more than a nominal cost. In 2005, the Labour Court (Determination EED051: *A worker v A company*) made an award of €57,900 in respect of an employee who was found to have been discriminated against on the ground of his disability. The court found the company failed to do all that was reasonable to accommodate the complainant so as to enable him to return to work on a phased basis after he suffered from a psychiatric illness (O'Leary 2005).

- *Positive action*: The Acts allow employers and service providers to put in place positive action measures to promote equal opportunities and full equality in practice across all nine grounds, with a view to removing existing inequalities that affect opportunity. It recognises that individual effort alone will not address the inequalities in access to employment experienced by members of the discriminated group. They may need additional training and to be provided with resources and opportunities specifically geared to their needs to enable them to 'catch up'.

While this legislation has played a significant role in highlighting how pervasive discrimination is in Irish society and has supported individuals to protect their right to equal treatment, it does have a number of drawbacks that hinder its effectiveness. Two aspects are briefly addressed here.

1. Both Acts are retrospective in their application and depend on an individual to enforce the rights therein. An incidence of discrimination must first occur and then an individual must take a civil case challenging this discrimination to the Equality Tribunal. This means that rights are generally enforced on a case-by-case basis. As such, this approach provides a limited response to the persistence of inequality and discrimination. According to Crowley (2006: 108–109), the development of a legally based statutory duty on the private and the public sector to promote equality alongside the individual enforcement model would be of enormous significance to the groups who experience discrimination and inequality.

2. The positive action provision in the legislation at present is voluntary in nature. Crowley (2006: 113) recommends that 'requirements on employers and service providers to take positive action where significant imbalances in equality outcomes are identified, would underpin and ensure a targeting of resources and initiatives to address and eliminate existing inequalities'.

The Equality Tribunal is an independent and quasi-judicial body that investigates or mediates complaints of unlawful discrimination. Its decisions and mediated settlements are legally binding. Figures from the Tribunal show that the race, gender, age and disability grounds comprise the main categories of discrimination cases taken under the equality legislation. Gender cases, mostly taken by women, continue to feature highly. The race ground features significantly since 2003, with cases relating to migrant workers and the inability of employers to accommodate diversity and promote equality. Disability continues to feature prominently in case files. Age remains one of the four highest categories, consistently demonstrating a strong strain of ageism in Irish society (Crowley 2006: 79). Under the Equal Status Acts, two arenas have emerged in case law where persistent discrimination occurs: licensed premises and educational establishments.

In summary, equality legislation provides a legal framework that prohibits discrimination and promotes equality of opportunity in the workplace and in the provision of services. The legislation has been successful in raising awareness of the pervasive nature of discrimination and it has given people who experience discrimination a means of legal redress. In addition, cases can be brought to the Equality Tribunal without the costs or anxiety often associated with vindicating one's rights in the courts. The process is accessible and social care practitioners can act as advocates in supporting people to vindicate their rights, either informally or through the Tribunal. Further information on taking a case to the Equality Tribunal can be accessed on the Equality Tribunal's website at www.equalitytribunal.ie.

A NEW DIRECTION FOR SOCIAL CARE

In many jurisdictions with a tradition of anti-discriminatory practice, such as the UK and US, legislation provides guidance to employers and service providers and supports the development of more emancipatory practice among the social professions. In the Irish context, there has been little attention to anti-discriminatory or anti-oppressive practice among the social professions. As a result, many of the theoretical models derive from the UK experience. In this final section we will draw on some of this theoretical work to inform our discussion of the possibilities for new directions within social care while being mindful of the distinctiveness of the Irish context. We will examine the emancipatory model of social care practice and the influence of user-led initiatives, partnership and participation models and rights on the potential for social care to develop as a transformative project.

Dominelli (2002) identifies three broad approaches in social work that can be usefully considered as the basis for a discussion of approaches to social care work: the therapeutic approach, the maintenance approach and the emancipatory approach.

- Interventions based on a *therapeutic* approach focus on the individual and his/her psychological functioning. Such approaches are best exemplified by counselling theories where a better understanding of oneself can enable the person to be more effective in dealing with his/her situation.

- *Maintenance* approaches seek to enable people in difficult and vulnerable situations to cope adequately with their lives. Social care practitioners working in this model tend to be pragmatic in their approach, passing on information, accessing resources and using the authority vested in them appropriately. Any change effected in both these approaches is in the individual, who learns how to deal with situations more effectively.
- The *emancipatory* approach seeks change at a personal and a societal level. While therapeutic and maintenance approaches provide essential support to individuals to change and to cope, the emancipatory approach challenges systems that thwart the rights of marginalised groups. With a focus on empowering practice, people are supported to gain greater control over the effects of discrimination on their life chances, with an emphasis on collective action to bring about change. The practitioner identifies the resilience of people in managing oppressive situations and builds on their strengths while acknowledging that this process is slow, requiring as it does capacity-building among those whose self-confidence and skills may have been shaped by exclusion and discrimination.

Working with particular social divisions is a form of emancipatory practice and social care practitioners may focus their professional commitment to women, to people with disabilities, migrants and others where they can support and lead change. Thompson (2002a: 94) suggests that reworking the strengths of social care to include new insights and approaches informed by user-led initiatives, participation and partnership and the concept of rights will generate opportunities for social care practitioners to challenge unequal power relations. We will briefly examine these developments in the Irish context, as they have influenced the work of social care practitioners and provide a space to support a more equal distribution of power and resources.

USER-LED INITIATIVES AND MOVEMENTS

The growth of user-led initiatives and movements in recent years has brought about new perspectives in understanding the experiences of marginalised groups. Traditionally, charity- or 'expert'-led models of care were the basis of social provision, where experiences were invariably oppressive and practices exclusionary. The challenge of user-led movements arises from an analysis of power and oppression by the people directly affected by discrimination and inequality. According to Dominelli (2007: 1), as marginalised groups:

> organised in 'new' social movements to challenge their unequal treatment, they found their own voices and used these to begin influencing prevailing

practice, especially ... in the fields of professional practice including social work, health and education. These voices from below became significant forces for change in the theories used to understand the world and the practices utilised to intervene in people's lives.

For example, Irish Travellers have been represented by settled people for many decades using a model of assimilation that sought to ensure Travellers became settled and that ignored cultural practices central to this group's identity. Since the 1980s, the growth of Traveller-led organisations such as the Irish Traveller Movement and the development of a partnership approach between settled people and Travellers in organisations such as Pavee Point have challenged established ways of thinking and acting towards Travellers. Emancipatory work with Travellers is premised on the belief that real improvement in Travellers' living circumstances and social situation requires the active involvement of Travellers themselves and that non-Travellers have a responsibility to address the various processes that serve to exclude Travellers from participating as equals in society (Kenny and McNeela 2006).

The disabled people's movement can best be defined by distinguishing between organisations for and organisations of people with a disability. Organisations for people with disabilities are concerned with disability issues but are largely staffed by able-bodied people working in partnership with national and local government, such as the National Disability Authority and the Brothers of Charity Services. In contrast, organisations of disabled people are run exclusively by and on behalf of people with impairments and are informed by the social mode of disability, which places emphasis on the disabling environment as a barrier to participation and the exercise of one's rights rather than solely on individual impairments (Barnes 1991). Examples of these are the Centre for Independent Living and the Federation of People with Disabilities. The challenge to the charity module of service provision for people with disabilities has been a significant force in bringing about change for people with disabilities in Irish society over the past decade (see Chapter 23).

Women with experiences of unequal pay, of exclusion from the labour market, of rape, sexual abuse and violence and many other discriminatory and oppressive practices have long led campaigns and initiatives to challenge such inequalities (O'Connor 1998).

Mental health services users have also organised to challenge inappropriate and oppressive institutional practices that carry the power to control and contain distress and apply chemical and legal straitjackets to people whose behaviour is alarming, bizarre or frightening (Braye and Preston-Shoot 1995: 106). Demands to be treated as people, not 'cases'; to information about and choices in treatment; and access to safe environments are all part of new analyses seeking change in the way the law defines them and how professionals exercise power over them, demanding greater influence over decisions and access to resources.

PARTNERSHIP AND EMPOWERMENT

Partnership is a process whereby provider and user define how the services should be designed and delivered. As such, it attempts to alter the balance of power within such relationships. For social care practitioners who question their own power base and their right as professionals to impose their own opinions on people's lives, partnership is a vehicle that values and respects the rights of those who use services and seeks to promote greater equality in decision-making.

Empowerment reminds professionals of the essential contribution to be made to the quality of services by the people receiving them. It is crucial to guard against the dilution of empowerment practices by professionals and social care managers, for example where power remains in the hands of professionals to decide how empowered they will allow people to be and control is delegated over matters of little import, such as a non-negotiable budget within which the service user must make decisions (Leadbetter 2002: 206–207).

While partnership may not mean that participants always have equal power, it does imply recognition and open discussion about how power will be distributed and used. It will result in the redistribution of some of the power held by the more powerful group and the employment of external resources to support the capacity of the less powerful group to participate as equal partners.

RIGHTS

Social care practitioners are aware that *rights* are more readily enacted by some groups in our society than others. The concept of rights entails an acceptance that society is diverse and that such diversity may require protection in order to flourish. For many decades, subordinated minority groups in our society were placed in a position of going 'cap in hand' to government or to charitable organisations looking for what other groups were able to access as a right.

Such an approach involves working to ensure rights are translated into material improvements for people in everyday life. Social care practitioners committed to supporting people to enact their rights will seek accountability for how decisions are made, how resources are deployed, how difference is accommodated and how relations of love and care are supported. This is a significant challenge in social care practice. Braye and Preston-Shoot (1995) point out that in the social care context, rights are often uncertain and difficult to enforce, even when they are known. The language of rights is often greeted with anxiety about undermining professional authority; there is a lack of clarity about addressing conflicts of rights (such as between autonomy and protection); and there is often reliance on custom alongside restrictive and protective attitudes.

Yet there are sites of resistance in many situations where oppressive practices operate, and it is social care practitioners' responsibility to support and develop such resistance to inequality. Gardener's (2008) reflections of the complexity of this work are insightful. She warns that a desire to treat service users equally should not lead to an idealisation of practice and a refusal to face up to the use of power and authority. Further, she states that 'when we root our practice in individual lives we cannot preclude politics: treating others as equals is itself a political as well as a personal stance' (2008: 52).

Social care practitioners have a significant contribution to make to the broader egalitarian project. This potential has not been fully realised. User-led initiatives, models of partnership and empowerment and the concept of rights have helped to shape discourses of care over the past decade in Ireland and have directly impacted on social care practitioners working in the residential child care, community development and disability sectors in particular. The challenge now is to incorporate the discourse of equality into the education of social care practitioners and into professional practice.

The strategies outlined below are not definitive but are first steps in developing an emancipatory practice among students and professionals working in social care practice. They draw on the work of Thompson (2003) and Braye and Preston-Shoot (1995).

- *Developing and owning a personal commitment to empowerment*. The process of unlearning prejudice and assumptions and relearning understanding is essential for competent practice and requires active consideration of personal value assumptions in all professional interactions (Braye and Preston-Shoot 1995: 114).
- *Professionals are personally responsible for ensuring that good practice prevails* and cannot cite a lack of policy, procedure or resources as an excuse.
- *Social care organisations must recognise that staff who are not empowered cannot empower others* and so must be committed to 'doing something different' and be willing to discuss how need is defined and how services are negotiated and offered.
- *Letting go of the culture of 'knowing best'*, speaking for others, gate-keeping resources and deriving role security from such actions is an essential starting point in establishing emancipatory professional practice.
- *Recognition of the impact of internalised oppression* is necessary, requiring a willingness to ensure that people who partnerships are operating with have the support to be equals in such an arrangement.
- *Critically reflective practice*, developed from the work of Donald Schön (1991a, 1991b), places an emphasis on reflecting on the typically 'messy' human situations in which social professionals engage. It requires skill and discrete action on the part of the professional, unlikely to be found in textbooks. Critical reflection helps to check assumptions that can be discriminatory, avoids reliance on 'common sense' and supports one's commitment to challenging oppression and reducing power inequalities in professional practice. Being open and critical in relation to one's own practice is defined

by Thompson (2006: 178) as perhaps the most fundamental step towards anti-discriminatory practice.

- *Challenging the actions of others* where it is discriminatory or oppressive in its outcome is necessary as part of a broader promotion of equality. While attending to one's own behaviour is essential in this regard, discriminatory behaviour by others cannot be condoned but must be challenged in a way that is tactful and constructive and avoids a personal attack.
- *Being sensitive to language and images* is critical because language plays a pivotal role in constructing reality. It subtly incorporates discriminatory practices such as the use of unnecessary derogatory, negative and dehumanising words to describe groups that are oppressed.
- *Openness and demystification* ensure decisions are taken in an open and transparent manner. Where events, decision and planning take place behind closed doors, the scope for oppressive practices is significant.
- *Humility* is required, as discrimination and inequality are complex and ever-changing, with new challenges to our understanding and practice arising all the time.

CONCLUSION

This chapter has sought to engage with questions of equality and in particular with how social care students and practitioners can develop an emancipatory model of practice. It has drawn on Ireland's existing infrastructure of equality legislation and suggested how practitioners may build on such legislation to develop a more critical approach to care practice, including their own. Such a process can inform personal and professional strategies to challenge inequality and discrimination and help to develop a new direction for social care practice in Ireland.

Part IV

Working with Specific Population Groups

Residential Child Care

John McHugh and Danny Meenan

OVERVIEW

This chapter has two aims: first, to outline the residential child care system in Ireland, and second, to identify and discuss some aspects of working in residential care settings. The chapter outlines some of the key features of residential care as a sector, emphasising the vulnerable nature of the young people that enter the system and the challenges posed for those who practise in this area. The skills required of practitioners are outlined, as are some of the key personal attributes that contribute to effective care practice. The complex and challenging – yet ultimately rewarding – nature of the day-to-day work is explored and the importance of self-care is emphasised.

The discussion is by no means exhaustive, but should act as a stimulus to further reading and research. Working with children in residential care is challenging but rewarding. It may be beyond an individual, group, agency or government to provide perfect care in perfect settings, but all involved in residential care provision must strive to develop and maintain the best possible care.

TOWARDS AN UNDERSTANDING OF RESIDENTIAL CHILD CARE

The Constitution of Ireland (Bunreacht na hÉireann) is the basis of Irish law. Article 42.5 clearly pledges the government to provide care for children who, for whatever reason, cannot be cared for by their parents:

> in exceptional cases, where parents for physical or moral reasons fail in their duty towards their children, the state as guardian of the common good, by appropriate means shall endeavour to supply the place of the parents, but always with due regard for the natural and imprescriptible rights of the child.

This commitment has been elaborated on and further consolidated through the implementation of the Child Care Act of 1991, the Irish government's ratification in 1992 of the United Nations Convention on the Rights of the Child and the publication of the *National Children's Strategy* in 2000. The government implements its commitment through the Office of the Minister for Children and Youth Affairs within the Department of Health and Children.

Ferguson and O'Reilly (2001) explain that social service intervention in a case of child protection is a result of concern being raised by an interested party. Upon notification to the Department of Health and Children, an investigation is carried out by a social worker in consultation with a social work team. Where further investigation or intervention is necessary, the primary focus is always on attempting to maintain the child within his or her family. The Health Service Executive (HSE) may do this by providing a 'family support worker' to work with the family on issues of concern in their own home. The family support worker is answerable to the social worker, who maintains regular contact with the family (Ferguson and O'Reilly 2001: 101). Where it is deemed impossible to maintain the child in the family, they may be taken into the care of the HSE ('alternative care') under the provisions of the Child Care Act 1991. A child taken into care may be placed either in foster care (possibly with his or her extended family) or in a residential child care service.

The purpose of residential care is to provide a safe, nurturing environment for children and young people who cannot live at home or in an alternative family at that time. The environment aims to meet, in a planned way, the physical, educational, spiritual and social needs of each child.

The responsibility for residential child care services in Ireland is divided amongst three government departments. While overall responsibility for services rests with the Department of Health and Children, the Department of Justice, Equality and Law Reform is responsible for the 'special school sector', which consists of five residential schools that range from fully open facilities (Ferry House, Clonmel) to fully secure centres (Trinity House School, Dublin). The Department of Justice is also responsible for St Patrick's Institution, the juvenile wing of Mountjoy Prison (situated in the same grounds), which caters for children aged 16–18 years.

As of June 2007, there were 5,477 children in care. Of these, 4,731 were in foster care and 423 (7.5 per cent) were in residential care. This is an overall increase on 2004, when there were 5,060 children in care, with 4,243 (84 per cent) in foster care and 442 (9 per cent) in residential care. See Chapter 17 for further details on the number of children in care.

In 2007, there were 116 residential children's centres in the country, 81 run by the HSE, 27 by voluntary bodies and eight that were privately run. The number of operational units tends to vary from year to year. The average number of children per unit is three to five and the cost of residential care is high. Unpublished figures from the HSE reported in *The Irish Times* on 5 February 2009 indicate that €135 million was expended on the residential care of about 400 children and young people, an average of €337,500 per child per annum, with private care costing up to €420,000. By contrast, the cost of foster placements in 2007 was €98 million, or about €21,000 per child per annum.

It is generally accepted that all children in care have experienced a degree of life trauma by virtue of the fact that they have been separated from their birth families (Fahlberg 1994). Many have also experienced varying degrees of emotional and/or physical abuse or neglect. These findings were reflected in an Irish context by Richards's (2003) study of residential child care in the South Eastern Health Board region (Table 20.1).

Table 20.1. Reasons for Children Being in Residential Care

Reason Given	Number
Foster care breakdown	20
Sexual abuse by parents or foster parents	14
Severe alcohol problems at home	8
Abandoned/neglected	8
Chaotic home environment, inability to cope	8
Unintegrated children	7
Out of control behaviour	7
Sexualised behaviour in child	6
Psychological disturbance of child	6
Physical cruelty to child	6
Young people themselves sexually abusive	4
School exclusion	4
Suicidal tendencies	2

Source: Richards (2003: 24).

The emotional impact of early life trauma on children is well documented. Fahlberg (1994) suggests that children who have experienced early life trauma may present with particular emotional or behavioural difficulties. Children with such difficulties often find it hard to cope with the necessary structures in place in residential services. The Eastern Health Board (EHB 1998) found that some children may run away from residential care or be removed for presenting with chaotic violent behaviours or drug misuse. These children often end up as homeless and are deemed to require a more secure form of accommodation. A number of cases have been before the courts in relation to the lack of facilities available for such children.

The difficulties experienced by the health service in finding 'suitable' placements for homeless children with behavioural difficulties has led to the development of the 'special care' and 'high-support' services. While there is no accepted national definition of such services (SRSB 2003), they generally consist of residential children's homes designed to meet the needs of children deemed to pose a danger to themselves or to someone else or who may be frequent absconders from non-secure placements. While both special care and high-support services work with similar children, there is a higher level of general security in special care services; increased staff–child ratios are the main feature of high-support services.

YOUNG PEOPLE IN RESIDENTIAL CARE

Children and young people enter into residential care for a number of reasons, such as abuse, neglect or foster care breakdown, or they may live in unsafe environments where their protection cannot be guaranteed.

Many young people in residential care can experience deep-seated feelings of loss, separation and abandonment. They may carry the baggage and scars of multiple placements and transfers of bases where they have not had opportunities to build trusting relationships or invest in emotional security. Fahlberg (1994: 160) discusses how unresolved separations can interfere with the development of future attachments. She suggests that the new attachments that young people make are not meant to replace the old attachments – they can co-exist.

This is also true for young people in residential care. For a number of young people, prior negative experiences with adults and other caregivers have led them to develop their own coping mechanisms. These may prevent the development of further attachments, either out of loyalty to birth parents or as a means of self-preservation.

The role that residential workers play in the lives of young people in care is of vital importance. The smallest aspects of everyday caring can make a difference and have a great impact. In this process, the residential worker adopts many guises, such as teacher, mentor, role model, friend and advocate, to name just a few. It is incumbent on every social care practitioner to remain professional, to be efficient and to carry work through to all the various agencies that they make contact with.

The role the residential worker plays may be a far cry from the other adults these young people have known throughout their short lives. Some may have had to learn to be self-reliant due to extended periods of neglect or being left alone and tend not to trust adults readily. For many, the apparent containment of a mainstream residential centre, with its rules and responsibilities, may prove difficult to adhere to and can lead to potential areas of conflict. For some young people, residential care may be the best option, as living within a foster care placement may constantly remind them of the dysfunctionality of their own families, adding to their pain and frustration. Residential care can also be seen by the young person as a temporary base, away from their home, where they can explore specific issues that caused their family to break down.

While there are many common factors that lead to young people coming into care, everyone in residential care has their own unique set of circumstances. Each young person is an individual and should be treated accordingly. Residential workers often find it difficult to come to terms with the fact that some young people will present particular behaviour as a way to avoid an exploration of the reasons for their admission into care. The presenting behaviour is what is dealt with and the underlying reason is not disclosed. This can lead the practitioner to feel frustrated and may sometimes lead to feelings of self-doubt.

It is essential that where the social care practitioner is unable to identify or explore the core reason for behavioural problems, they recommend referral to an appropriate discipline such as psychology or child and adolescent mental health. All residential workers must understand that some young people in residential care may *never* fully discuss their true feelings or how the emotional impact of their past experiences has affected them. The simplest triggers – a song on the radio, a phrase someone uses, the smell of a particular perfume or cologne – may bring memories flooding back. These can be the precursor to a violent outburst or a retreat into their inner space. The important thing is to let these young people know that there is someone who will be there for them when they feel that they are ready to talk. This is a personal journey which, for some young people, may take many years to travel.

RESIDENTIAL CHILD CARE SKILLS

So what are the skills that are needed to equip residential practitioners in their role? For Clough (2000: 23), one of the challenges of working in residential child care is to define what is specific and distinctive about it. He suggests that in residential houses there is a mix of physical care, holding and the development of self. Residential care should provide a good place to live, where residential workers can respond in everyday activities in ways that are therapeutic and life enhancing.

From research that involved talking to social care practitioners in residential care about the key skills and attributes for working with young people (Meenan 2002), the following were identified:

- Non-judgemental.
- Team member.
- Good communicator (oral and written).
- Good listener.
- Problem-solving.
- Patient – remaining calm in crisis.
- Awareness of self.
- Caring nature.
- Assertive.
- Open to learning new things.

- Understanding.
- Creative and imaginative.
- Sense of humour.

Key words such as 'rewarding', 'demanding' and 'challenging' were used to describe working with young people in residential care. Some people see their work in residential care as more of a vocation than employment. They emphasise staying focused and being consistent and dedicated, even in the most difficult times, to help make a difference in young people's lives, rather than just coming to work as a means to an end.

Residential care can be a mind-opening experience for many residential workers. Many initially find it difficult to comprehend what some children and young people have already experienced in their short lives – more than many other adults, including staff themselves, will experience in a lifetime. Practitioners have talked about how, in the beginning, it was difficult to rationalise how adults could treat children and young people with such contempt and cause so much pain. Residential care 'opened their eyes' to personal trauma and behaviour that they never knew existed.

So how do we prepare ourselves to work in this environment? Many residential workers would support the development of the theory related to this work. A professional entering residential child care experiences a very sharp learning curve that requires quick thinking and ingenuity on a daily – sometimes hourly – basis. For many, the theory studied at college does not always match the reality of working in a residential centre, but it can provide insights into why some young people behave the way they do. Professional training also provides opportunities to practise skills and heighten self-awareness. These attributes, coupled with relevant theory, promote a reflective approach to social care practice. It is the responsibility of the individual practitioner and of the service provider to ensure that all staff are both aware of and equipped for their professional role.

We, as adults and staff, need to afford young people, including those in residential care, the opportunities to explore issues and learn from life experiences and, indeed, to make mistakes. Sadly, we also have to realise that as a consequence of their experiences prior to admission, some young people in residential care may never change their behaviour or break the spiral of negative or offending behaviour, no matter how many safety nets we provide.

Social care ethics direct us to support and be proactive in young people's development, safety and journey to adulthood. It is an integral part of the job to network with other agencies while still being fully cognisant of confidentiality and of children's right to privacy. It is imperative that we document and accurately record any information that will help and enable the choices and opportunities for the young person.

WORKING IN RESIDENTIAL CHILD CARE SETTINGS

'The needs and problems of many children in care are complex and difficult to serve appropriately. Or more correctly, their needs are deceptively simple, but delivering the right response is deceptively complex' (Gilligan 2001: 1). This section examines life and work across the range of residential care settings. Children and young people who live in residential care have faced, and bring with them, exceptional problems and difficulties. These may include neglect, abuse (physical, emotional, sexual), family breakdown, separation and loss or betrayal of trust. This may be their first care placement or they may have moved several times from one care setting to another. They may have a clear understanding and acceptance of what is happening in their life or may be confused, anxious or angry. The young person may be open to talking about her situation or may not yet be able to express what she is feeling. They may have an ability to quickly form relationships with new people or they may prefer to cut themselves off from any kind of relationship that involves trusting others. Their behaviour may be 'normal' and stable or unpredictable and even dangerous.

According to Chakrabarti and Hill (2000: 9), 'it is the responsibility of residential staff and carers, acting on behalf of society at large, to promote these children's well-being and to minimise the negative consequences of separation'. This overall aim is usually broken down into a number of professional tasks that permeate all aspects of life in residential care. They include:

- Developing and working with care plans and placement plans.
- Relationship building.
- Keyworking.

The next sections expand on these key elements of residential care.

CARE PLAN AND PLACEMENT PLAN

The Child Care (Placement of Children in Residential Care) Regulations 1995 require that a written care plan is in place either before or immediately after a young person is placed in residential care. A distinction is made between the overall long-term plan for the care of the young person and the more immediate plan with regard to the time he or she is in the centre. The overall care plan takes account of the young person's educational, social, emotional, behavioural and health requirements, whereas the placement plan focuses on how the residential care setting plans to meet these needs.

The social care practitioner must have a clear understanding of the needs of young people generally. Knowledge of developmental psychology, attachment, behaviour management and health and safety will help in responding to the needs of particular children and young people. Practitioners need to have:

skills and knowledge ... drawn from a number of different disciplines, ranging from the directly practical – nutrition, recreation and health care, for example – to personal, people centred skills – such as care and control, communicating with children, counselling and family work, backed by in-depth and detailed knowledge of child development. (Residential Forum 1998: 11)

It should be noted that life in care for the young person may be far less clear than that reflected in the care or placement plan. Their unique story may have a lot of pain, hurt and confusion. Success of the placement largely depends on the trusting relationships built with those with whom they share this part of their life. But the care plan can be a useful tool to assess progress and bring some overall clarity to the complex task of working with children in care.

RELATIONSHIP BUILDING

The caring relationship is at the heart of good and effective professional social care. But relationships, in residential care settings or in life generally, are often complex. They change and develop over time and involve sharing ourselves with others at various levels – emotionally, physically and professionally. Relationships are entered into rather than created. While there is no easy formula for creating an effective relationship with positive outcomes, Rogers (cited in Murgatroyd 1996: 15) suggests that professional caring relationships have three basic qualities that the worker needs to be able to communicate if the relationship is to be successful: empathy, warmth and genuineness.

> *Empathy*: the ability to experience another person's world as if it were one's own without ever losing that 'as if' quality.
> *Warmth*: accepting people as they are, without conditions, and helping them to feel safe.
> *Genuineness*: a way of being with other people built on open communication and respect.

In residential care settings, working with children and young people who have not experienced positive, trusting relationships can make the task of relationship-building even more challenging. Trying to define and analyse relationships may not be of much help in developing skills in relationship-building. Think of important relationships in your own life: they are usually described in terms of actions and feelings rather than defined through words or terminology. Thus, 'relationships are developed through the most mundane and routine of tasks from reading a story at bedtime, to repairing a puncture in a pushbike, or providing hugs or reassurance when a child falls over, as well as through sharing critical episodes and crises' (Residential Forum 1998: 9).

Professional social care work in residential child care settings is about creating and maintaining meaningful relationships through everyday activities. As Gilligan (2001: 56) suggests, 'it is often the little things that carers do that register with and reassure children. It seems that, through these little things, the carers somehow communicate interest and concern and help the child feel connected to the carer.'

The social care practitioner must be equipped for this kind of work. A thorough knowledge of the procedures, politics and legislation that provide the framework the caring agency operates in is necessary. The practitioner also needs to have a theory base that gives his/her an understanding of people, systems and practices: 'The nature of relationship-based work is that it gives rise to many questions. The purpose of theorising is to promote thinking so that practice is improved' (Residential Forum 1998: 12). Perhaps the most challenging aspect of working with young people in residential care is sharing life: sharing experiences, perspectives, feelings, emotions and beliefs. This aspect of professional practice demands a high level of self-knowledge through personal development.

KEYWORKING

Keyworking is a system for providing individualised social care through named persons. The keyworker is the person who has responsibility and accountability for the care of the service user and for decisions relating to their situation.

Keyworking involves (Social Care Association 1991):

- Mutual trust and respect.
- The social, physical, intellectual, cultural, emotional and spiritual aspects of the service user's development and well-being.
- Creating a sense of purpose and change.
- Partnership between the keyworker, other service providers and those who are the users of their services.
- Planning (utilising the abilities of individuals and groups in the arena of problem-solving).
- Changing social environments (including, for example, challenging racist, sexist and ageist attitudes and behaviours).

The residential care centre is a busy place, with all the activity of daily living: breakfast, school, games, clubs, TV, internet, homework, cleaning and cooking. There is the added complication that it is not a family unit, with a team of social care practitioners taking on a parenting role. As Burton (1993: 48) puts it, 'I am not saying that the worker is a parent to the child ... the worker remains a worker throughout, but we are using inner resources and knowledge – the most personal and tender and vulnerable areas of our inner selves – to do the work.' In the context of the residential care centre, the relationship between practitioner and the young person is clearly of vital importance. However, it can be difficult to develop and maintain significant relationships in an environment interrupted by shiftwork patterns, or where high staff turnover puts an end to developing attachments and relationships.

Another factor that may impact negatively on quality personalised care and relationship-building is the sheer amount of activity within and around the residential centre. This may include official business regarding the care and related issues of the children and young people; staff meetings; new admissions; aftercare; and daily living tasks and issues, for example, school, hobbies and interests, shopping, eating and so on. The primary role of the keyworker is to help make sense of this experience of living for the individual child or young person. Keyworking has been found to 'improve personalised care, relationships, the clarity of the residential tasks and helped to improve other aspects of life in the establishment ... for the staff as well as for the resident' (Clarke 1998: 31).

The keyworker is usually given particular responsibility in relation to a child, for example to accompany him/her to appointments or to liaise with relevant professionals, agencies, school and family. For this to take place, emphasis is placed on developing a positive, professional caring relationship between the young person and the keyworker. The keyworker needs to have a clear understanding of theory that underpins the work, for example, attachment theory, the hierarchy of need, developmental psychology and so on. They must also develop competency in a range of skills relating to communication, active listening, advocacy, boundary maintenance and confidentiality. A practitioner who takes on a keyworker role should receive and use supervision and may need further training depending on the specific needs of the child. It is expected that the keyworker attend reviews of children for whom they are responsible.

Times of transition or change in a young person's life often bring with them anxiety, insecurity and feelings of vulnerability. The keyworker can have an important role at these times. In preparing to leave a care setting, the young person may be supported, empowered and gain confidence through clear guidelines around moving on and outreach. The keyworker plays a vital role at this time and can provide further support through planned aftercare.

It is clear from this section that the role of keyworker within the residential care centre is central to the quality and effectiveness of care experienced by the young person: 'enduring relationships with committed people become very important for young people growing up in care. It is from these relationships that their "secure base" may emerge' (Gilligan 2001). Enduring relationships are important in enabling any of us to negotiate our way through difficult periods of our lives. Young people in care have a special need for experiencing such relationships, as their home base is at best fragile and perhaps disintegrated. Developing a trusting, mutually respectful relationship with an adult can give the young person some of the tools to begin building that secure platform for future life experience.

RESIDENTIAL STAFF

The issues of self-awareness and professional boundaries are always contentious for those who work in residential care. There is always a need to remain safe, but provision of a high quality of care can sometimes leave individual staff in vulnerable situations. Communication among the team is a very important aspect in residential work. Sharing ideas, consulting with others and ensuring a consistent and continuous approach, with all staff following agreed protocols and policies, cannot be emphasised enough.

Practitioners in residential care must be aware of what they bring as individuals to residential work – their own prejudices, beliefs and values. They feel they have something to offer the young people they work with; why else would they be there? But practitioners' own experiences and life events should not colour their vision or lead them to make particular judgements just because they feel they know better or have experienced a similar emotional trauma. Practitioners in residential care must always retain an open outlook and see each young person as an individual who will react differently in a variety of similar situations. Practitioners must work at an appropriate pace and level of understanding to help children and young people to deal with their issues.

Many residential staff are faced with situations that challenge their thinking and force them to think more laterally and constructively. Residential teams are usually made up of a variety of individuals who have stories to tell and experiences to share. There should always be opportunities to grow and develop, both personally and professionally. There need to be strong elements of trust and open communication between team members, as each individual social care practitioner needs to feel a sense of support and security from others at times of heightened anxiety or aggression within a centre. Knowing that someone is there to assist you through particularly difficult situations can be the factor that gives residential staff the impetus to continue with a particular course of action. Structures, routines, consistency and clarity of actions are all important aspects of team cohesion.

The shift system, if not organised properly, can allow different staff members to work in significantly different ways. If the same rules are not applied by all staff in a consistent manner, this can potentially lead to confusion and frustration for the young people, as well as difficulties in staff relations. Failure to maintain equilibrium of approach can be reminiscent of the previous experiences of some young people. They may quite naturally play off one set of staff against the other. Communication is vital and properly structured handover meetings between shifts reduce the opportunities for manipulation and potential conflict. Some centres that have a high staff turnover may reflect the previous turmoil in some young people's lives and reinforce the inconsistency and lack of constancy in their lives.

Throughout our social care practice we have worked with many residential staff who were at different points in their careers: students on placement, new young unqualified staff, people with many years of life experience, recent graduates and others with years of work experience. They all agree that you have to actually work in residential care to experience the emotional rollercoaster that it can be, but they also stress how rewarding, worthwhile and enjoyable it is to make a positive contribution to the lives of children and young people.

SELF-CARE

One of the most important issues about working in residential care is the issue of self-care. Of course, this is an issue not solely for social care practitioners in residential settings, but given the pressure and stress that this type of work creates, it can be an area that some people can neglect.

Self-care means that every individual must take responsibility for his/her own safety and well-being. We cannot provide adequate and appropriate care for others, particularly troubled children and young people, if we do not make time to look after ourselves. It could be said that as we are the only person who is constantly with us, we must always be the one to care for ourselves.

Self-care in this environment is closely linked to self-awareness. Individuals must remain acutely aware of their own limitations and levels of tolerance and anxiety. The ability to recognise incidents of high anxiety in ourselves may take some time to actually master, but if we are not careful and continue to work, oblivious to our mood and ignoring the indicators, this may lead, in time, to feelings of complete exhaustion and occupational burnout.

Many people do not recognise that they are suffering from stress. They think that these feelings of rushing adrenalin and high anxiety are part of the job, and in some circumstances are the stimulus that keeps them going. Failure to recognise that you are under pressure can often lead to additional issues in the workplace. For some people, this could mean making rash decisions or reacting in an unaccustomed manner that may lead to the further deterioration of a situation that can spiral out of control. The young person can end up feeling, and reacting, defensively and neither side is willing to back down due to the fear of losing face.

Everyone wants to do their best for the young people and can become quite attached, even to the young people who constantly challenge them and stretch their patience to the limit. People generally get support and guidance from other team members and the longer-serving members of the team often find themselves in the position of mentor and emotional supporter during times of upset and frustration.

Good support through supervision is vitally important for all residential staff (see Chapter 13). Supervision should not be a place that just evaluates your plan of work for your key child and organises your next time off. It is an opportunity to explore the impact of particular situations and events and how they have affected you on all levels as well as a chance to plan how you will deal with similar situations better. At times, people will avoid exploring specific issues in supervision, as they often fear letting their guard down. They wonder how their manager will view them if they really say what they are feeling or thinking.

It is healthy to explore all the emotions that negative situations may generate; individuals can remain emotionally stunted if they do not fully express the issues that contribute to their frustrations and distress. In meeting the needs of residential staff, it may be useful to make use of the services of an external clinical supervisor who can provide a place where the safety valve can be opened and personal issues can be released and explored. Many staff have found this method of self-exploration in a non-work environment very therapeutic and have stated that it gives them the opportunity to explore specific issues and frustrations in a freer manner, without the fear of feeling professionally vulnerable. We all need to have this opportunity to explore the specific issues that residential care can throw at us, since without it, our vision may be clouded, our opinions misjudged and our work with young people tinged with misunderstanding.

These feelings are often stronger after an aggressive outburst, where a lot of anger is displayed and even physical assaults take place. No one comes to work to be assaulted or verbally abused, but the fact remains that in residential care, it can be an occupational hazard that cannot always be prevented, but must never be condoned.

When children and young people have been traumatised, they can act out in aggressive and unpredictable ways. For many young people, it is an open expression of the inner turmoil that one manager described as being akin to a 'volcano' before it erupts. It is unhealthy for anyone, particularly troubled young people, to repress anger and hurt, as they will often erupt at times when you least expect it.

Children and young people are naturally active and boredom can often lead to frustration and an inappropriate response to the simplest of requests. Residential staff need to be proactive in promoting ways that allow and facilitate young people to let off steam. Social care practitioners in residential care have the responsibility to ensure that this happens in a safe environment and that a steady stream of activities facilitates this.

As in all professions, people have a certain working style or forte that leads them to work in particular environments. Some prefer to work with younger children, others with adolescents. Some enjoy the revolving door of a short-stay or assessment centre as opposed to the longer commitment of medium- to long-term care. No matter which environment you choose to work in, be it mainstream, high-support or secure care, remember that you are not working in a vacuum – other professionals are there to support and help you, both inside and outside the service. Do not feel undervalued or intimidated by the seniority of other professionals. Residential child care practitioners have the best knowledge of the young people in their care; after all, they are with them almost every day, experiencing the variety of emotions that are displayed. It is important that you share your knowledge clearly and confidently, as you are also an important contributor in the decision-making process and can influence the development of plans for the young people under your care.

CONCLUSION

This short introduction to the world of residential child care has attempted to outline a context for this area of service delivery, to provide some basic facts and figures and to reflect something of the experience of working in this field. It can be easy to be overwhelmed by the raft of legislation, reports, enquiries and guidelines in this area, but it is important to have an understanding of the framework within which residential care is provided in order to be able to focus on the quality of the professional caring relationship between practitioner and young people.

In using this chapter, you should try to relate the issues to your own practice experience and/or further reading with a view to developing your own ability to work with children and young people in residential care settings. The challenge must surely be to move from learning *about* to learning *with* children in care in order that this sometimes necessary response can be of the best possible quality.

21

Social Care and the Older Person

Carmel Gallagher

OVERVIEW

This chapter examines policy, services and issues related to social care for older people in Ireland. The chapter begins with a brief discussion of population ageing in Ireland and the implications of an ageing population for service provision. The chapter goes on to outline the welfare model for social care services for older people in Ireland and describes the principal policy developments in care services for older people from the 1960s to date. The provision of residential care for incapacitated older people is examined and recent legislative initiatives to improve quality of care are discussed. Different types of residential care are described – public, private and voluntary – and an example is given of a residential home in the voluntary sector. The chapter then discusses day care service provision, outlining aims, examining policy issues and describing day centres. The chapter highlights the issue of improving quality in care settings and examples are given of good practice and innovative projects. Quality initiatives are analysed in the context of a social care model of service provision, which is contrasted with a medical model. Consideration is given to the implications of a social care model for education and training of staff. The chapter concludes by advocating a positive vision of the possibilities for living a full life in later years and the challenges involved for social care practitioners in achieving this.

INTRODUCTION

When social care is discussed in relation to older people, it is often associated with tailored services that aim to meet personal and social needs of frail, chronically ill or confused older people. Ageing or senescence is associated with a decline in physiological effectiveness that affects us all sooner or later and is an intrinsic part of growing old. While disease affects only certain members of the older population, many diseases are age related. The combination of senescent changes, such as hearing loss or deteriorating eyesight, and a greater risk of illnesses such as stroke or heart disease makes the older person more vulnerable and dependent.

The realities of old age have come to be seen by contemporary governments as presenting problems that require solutions. There has been an increase in the proportion of older people in the populations of many Western countries. Ireland has been an exception to this trend and is, in fact, a young country in comparison to its European neighbours (O'Shea 2006). In 2006, Ireland had the lowest proportion of older people in its population among EU countries: 11 per cent of the population was aged 65 or over, compared to an EU 27 average of 16.8 per cent (Central Statistics Office 2007f: 10). However, projected population estimates predict a substantial increase in the absolute and proportionate number of people aged over 65 in Ireland to a level of 15 per cent of the total population in 2021 (Connell and Pringle 2004).

This projected increase in the number of older people in the population will give rise to additional demands for formal social care in both non-residential and residential institutions for the dependent elderly (Fahey and FitzGerald 1997: 95). Given the preference of older people to be cared for at home and the central role accorded to the family in the provision of day-to-day care, policy has been focused on support and advice for carers, the development of domiciliary services such as home help and on improving the range of services and quality of care provided in day and residential centres. Traditionally, many social care services for older people were provided by voluntary organisations, with nuns from religious orders providing much of the expertise. With the decline in the number of religious, these services are increasingly coming under the remit of the Health Service Executive. Notwithstanding this, the voluntary sector continues to play an important role at the local level in the provision of many day care services and supported housing projects. In the development of these services, the health and housing authorities seek to work in partnership with voluntary bodies where possible. In residential care, the private sector has played an expanded role within a framework of legislative regulations and state subvention. Thus, a mixed economy of welfare model is evident in the provision of social care services for older people.

However, it has been argued that the services and supports necessary to give effect to such principles of 'ageing in place' have been slow to develop. Specific policy areas that have remained underdeveloped include the home help service, rural public transport and sheltered housing for semi-dependent older people (Layte et al. 1999: 22). For example, a study of the use of health and social services by older adults in the community found that among a sample of 937 older people in two Health Board areas, a substantial proportion (37 per cent) of those found to be severely impaired in carrying out activities of daily living had not received any home-based services in the previous year (Garavan et al. 2001: 23). Important community care services are thinly spread and have no legal basis. For example, meals on wheels are provided almost entirely by voluntary groups to less than 1 per cent of the elderly population, there is an acute shortage of paramedical and therapeutic services and there are very few day care places available across the country (O'Shea 2006: 16).

It is increasingly acknowledged that the older population is a more heterogeneous group than is often suggested. Most 'young elderly' are fit and active and the vast majority of older people live independent lives. Decline in physical function may be of little consequence to an older person until they cross some threshold that prevents them from carrying out necessary activities. Indeed, older people contribute to the quality of life of family and kin through being involved in a long-term chain of support, including emotional support and care for ill and dependent relatives. There is evidence of older people giving considerable amounts of practical and emotional support in daily living, mainly to family but also to friends and neighbours (Gallagher 2008; Phillipson et al. 2001).

POLICY DEVELOPMENT SINCE THE 1960s

Until the 1960s, social service provision for older people in Ireland was limited to a number of core income maintenance schemes and a rather stigmatised system of residential care for infirm and chronically ill elderly people with limited means. Since the 1960s, a number of key government reports have shaped policy and services for older people in Ireland.

The 1968 *Care of the Aged* report (Inter-departmental Committee on the Care of the Aged 1968) was a seminal document that addressed the needs of older people as a distinct group in a coherent way. The *Care of the Aged* report signalled a move away from institutionalised care to care in the community, based on the belief that 'it is better, and probably much cheaper, to help the aged to live in the community than to provide for them in hospitals or other institutions' (Inter-departmental Committee on the Care of the Aged 1968: 13).

Twenty years later, *The Years Ahead: A Policy for the Elderly* report (1988) was published and this report has been the basis of official policy for older people in Ireland (Department of Health 1988). *The Years Ahead* report advocated a strong service-delivery model relating to health and social care services for older people at home, in the community, in hospitals and in long-term care. The role of key health professionals and social care providers was emphasised and reflected the growth in professional health and welfare services since the *Care of the Aged* report.

The Department of Health 1994 report, *Shaping a Healthier Future: A Strategy for Effective Healthcare in the 1990s*, represented a challenge to this service-oriented approach. It made two key points: first, one cannot assume that services have an inherent value – it is necessary to evaluate the health and social gain they produce; and second, it is essential to have consumer participation in the planning of services and in ensuring the accountability of service providers.

A health promotion strategy for older people – *Adding Years to Life and Life to Years* (Department of Health and Children 1998a) – was launched in 1998. The strategy addresses health for older people, in its broadest sense, acknowledging the impact of environmental and social factors on the quality of life of older people, and the contribution that many sectors outside the health sector make.

The Department of Health and Children (2001b) health strategy, *Quality and Fairness – A Health System for You*, highlighted quality of life as one of its central objectives and proposed a number of comprehensive actions to meet the needs of older people into the future. These included health promotion, dementia services, clarification on eligibility and subvention arrangements for long-term care, provision of additional community nursing unit places, extension of the remit of the Social Services Inspectorate to include residential care for older people, and preparation of national standards for community and long-term residential care (O'Shea 2006: 16).

As a result of these and other policy developments, the range of social care services now provided for today's older population – covering income maintenance, health care, domiciliary care, housing and residential care – is wider than any previous generation of older people could have visualised.

RESIDENTIAL CARE

The provision of long-stay care for older people who can no longer be cared for at home for social and medical reasons gives insight into perceptions of the life course and, in particular, the needs of, and possibilities for, very frail and incapacitated older people. We will examine the different types of long-term care available before considering the quality of care that infirm older people receive.

Care of the Aged (Interdepartmental Committee on the Care of the Aged 1968) had differentiated between different types of institutions providing extended care for older persons. The County Home model of institutional care was to be replaced by a number of different types of geriatric/welfare facilities: general hospitals, geriatric assessment units, long-stay units and welfare homes. Despite the trend for new facilities to be much smaller in size and part of a continuum of care, the legacy of the policies of the 1950s and 1960s – where all dependent older people were gathered together in one County Home – can still be seen in the considerable number of large, institutional geriatric hospitals and homes in all parts of the country.

The Years Ahead report (Department of Health 1988) recommended a wider range of facilities to meet the low- to medium-dependency needs of frail older people. These included sheltered housing with back-up day care facilities, boarding out of older people under the supervision of the Health Boards, multi-purpose homes (as developed in Donegal) and community hospitals with a range of services to include assessment and rehabilitation, respite, day care, short-term care and long-term care. However, there was little reflection on what type of life might be aspired to in extended care facilities. Furthermore, while *The Years Ahead* clearly recognised the role that private nursing homes play in caring for older people, and the right of older people to avail of such care as a matter of choice, its recommendations were confined to a licensing and inspection system with minimalist standards. The report also recommended that Health Boards would provide subvention for patients assessed as being in need of continuing care. Criticism of the operation of the subvention scheme has led to the development of a new scheme for assessing and charging for long-term care in Ireland. The

Nursing Homes Support Scheme Bill 2008 was published in October 2008 and the new scheme will be implemented in 2009 (Department of Health and Children 2008).

LEGISLATION AND IMPROVED QUALITY OF CARE

Introduction of a regulation and inspection system under the Health (Nursing Homes) Act 1990 resulted in improved levels of care in private nursing homes (EHB 1999: 86). Since the introduction of this legislation, the role of the private sector in particular has been expanding, with the HSE contracting private nursing home beds to meet their obligations. However, recent scandals have focused attention on quality issues in residential care. An RTÉ documentary, *Prime Time Investigates*, screened on 30 May 2005, highlighted substandard conditions and patient neglect at Leas Cross, a private nursing home in Swords, Co. Dublin, where the HSE had contracted beds. A subsequent report by Geriatrician Professor Des O'Neill concluded that there had been systematic abuse and failures at many levels, including management, clinical leadership, policy, administrative and legislative shortcomings in delivering quality care to incapacitated older people. While, as discussed, care and welfare regulations have been in place since 1993, under the Health (Nursing Homes) Act 1990, these are largely concerned with medical, nursing and health and safety standards. There were no requirements in relation to the social, recreational, creative or spiritual needs of older people, and no participative role envisaged for the residents themselves. Furthermore, the statutory sector has been exempt from the quality controls and inspections that apply only to the private and voluntary sectors.

Draft National Standards for Residential Care Settings for Older People was published in January 2007 by the Minister for Health and Children, Mary Harney, TD (Department of Health and Children 2007). The standards will apply to all residential settings (public, private and voluntary) where older people are cared for and for which registration is required. The standards are based on legislation, research findings and best practice.

The proposed regulatory framework reflects current expectations and ideas about quality of care and quality of life and was underpinned by research that examined the views of service providers and service users. Key quality of life domains were identified based on what residents in long-stay care themselves valued (Murphy et al. 2006). These included the following.

- Independence, privacy, and self-expression.
- Confirmation that their life contains meaning and hope in the same measures as before.
- A homely atmosphere and person-centred routines that emphasise choice and empowerment.

- Aesthetically pleasing physical environment.
- To be connected to other people and to be able to maintain relationships with family and friends.
- To have meaningful and purposeful activity that they themselves are involved in planning and arranging.

The new standards include requirements in relation to consultation and participation, civil, social and political rights, care plans and autonomy and independence. For example, Standard 18.2 of the Regulations states: 'The resident is given opportunities for participation in meaningful and purposeful activity, occupation or leisure activities, both inside and outside the residential care setting, that suit his/her needs, preferences and capacities' (Department of Health and Children 2007).

The importance attached to these aspects of care is highlighted in two care settings described later in the chapter.

SOCIAL CARE SETTINGS

There are approximately 20,000 residents aged 65 or over in long-stay residential care in Ireland, representing just under 4.6 per cent of the total elderly population. It is estimated that 31,000 (or 7 per cent) of the elderly population living at home need high or continuous care (O'Shea 2006: 12–13). Statistics from the Department of Health and Children indicate that 72 per cent of residents are in the high or maximum dependency category. Chronic physical illness (33 per cent) and mental infirmity or dementia (24 per cent) are the main reasons for admission into long-stay care (O'Shea 2006: 13). However, just over 12 per cent of older people in long-stay care have been admitted for 'social reasons'.[1]

Private nursing homes are the main provider of long-stay care for older people, followed by HSE geriatric homes and hospitals. Other settings are voluntary geriatric homes and hospitals managed by religious orders and charitable groups, district or community hospitals and welfare homes (Department of Health 1997). A recent survey of long-stay care settings showed that the vast majority of residents are aged 75 years or more, while just over 40 per cent are aged over 85 years (Murphy et al. 2006: 114). In general, residents of private and voluntary nursing homes are not as dependent as residents of public long-stay geriatric hospitals and homes. The survey also showed that the largest units are the public geriatric homes/hospitals, which have a mean capacity of 92 beds. Private nursing homes have the lowest mean number of beds at 39 (Murphy et al. 2006: 113).

Two models of public residential care that have become increasingly popular since *The Years Ahead* report was published are community hospitals and community nursing units. They provide a contrast to the old-style geriatric hospital/home in size, range of services and emphasis on health and social gain. Community hospitals are designed to provide a broad range of services, including long-stay care; assessment and rehabilitation; convalescent care; day hospital and/or day care services; respite care; and information, advice and support for those caring for older persons at home. Community units are small nursing units catering for up to 50 people and have a day care centre attached. They differ from the traditional model in many respects, including location (less isolated), architectural style, provision of individualised programmes of animation, a wider range of recreational activities on offer and more emphasis on being part of the community. Of particular significance was the employment of a full-time Activities Nurse in each unit. However, the development of community hospitals and community units has been slow and uneven around the country (Ruddle et al. 1997). In the Eastern region, despite ambitious plans to build more community units and to replace/refurbish existing units (as outlined in the *10 Year Action Plan* (EHB 1999), progress has been very slow (Eastern Regional Health Authority 2001: 3).

Many nursing homes built or refurbished in recent decades incorporate good design and strive to enhance health and social gain for all residents. A brief description is given below of a voluntary nursing home in Dublin.

St Gabriel's is a voluntary nursing home in Raheny in Dublin. Purpose built and opened in 1991 by a religious order of nuns, the Poor Servants of the Mother of God, it replaced an older residential home in the inner city. It does not have a specific catchment area and admissions are determined by the management, but most residents come from the adjoining areas. It has 52 individual en-suite rooms on two storeys. Residents on the first floor are reasonably mobile, while those on the ground floor are more incapacitated. Each room is individually arranged by the resident with memorabilia, including photographs, pictures on the wall and items of personal furniture. The day rooms are spacious and bright and there is a central conservatory. The use of glass creates a bright and sometimes sunny interior. In addition to a dining room, there are small kitchens attached to the sitting rooms, where residents may make a cup of tea. There is an oratory where daily mass is said, which is attended by both residents and day care users. An activity programme, run by a part-time Activities Co-ordinator, is posted up each week. Activities include Sonas,[2] bingo, a reminiscence programme, quizzes, pampering sessions and computers. St Gabriel's relies on volunteers to provide some of its activities, including reception staff, fundraising and visitation of residents who have limited mobility and few visitors. St Gabriel's also provides respite and day care.

DAY CARE SERVICES

The main objectives of day centres, as set out in *The Years Ahead* report (Department of Health 1988), are to:

- Provide services such as a midday meal, a bath, physiotherapy and a variety of other social services.
- Promote social contact among older people and prevent loneliness.
- Relieve caring relatives, particularly those who have to go to work, of the responsibility of caring for older people during the day.
- Provide social stimulation in a safe environment for older people.

A report by the National Council on Ageing and Older People on the development of day services classified them in the following way: day care centre, day centre, social club and dementia-specific day care (Haslett 2003). Like the home help service, provision of day care is also a discretionary service and involves a mix of public and voluntary input and different models of service provision. Day care centres provide a range of medical, therapeutic and social services, such as nursing, physiotherapy, bathing and chiropody. These are important in the continuum of care, particularly for those with reduced mobility. They are funded by the HSE and are usually attached to HSE geriatric hospitals, community hospitals/units or voluntary nursing homes. They are staffed by health care professionals and are designed to support independent living and to give respite to carers. Referrals are usually made by public health nurses, GPs or on discharge from hospital.

Day centres are mainly managed by locally based voluntary/parish groups and are grant aided by the HSE. Their focus is mainly social and recreational and they usually provide a meal. However, while many day centres/social clubs may have started out only having a social mandate, due to a chronic lack of day care centres many of these have ended up providing services to a wide spectrum of older people:

> The social club/day centres are providing increasing levels of service in the areas of personal care, paramedical treatments and even nursing. They are providing relief to family carers and the safe environments needed to avail of these services. They are, in fact, fulfilling many of the classic day care objectives while, at the same time, catering for a constant flow of more active people. (Haslett 2003: 175)

There are also dementia-specific day care centres designed to give stimulation and care to the person and to provide a break for the primary carer. Clubs for older people are primarily voluntary social groups and include Senior Citizens' clubs and Active Retirement groups.

While the number of day centres and clubs for older people has expanded in recent years,[3] there is a shortage of day care places, particularly in the Eastern region. It has been estimated that there are approximately 2,000 day care places in the Eastern region, but many of these places are only available to individuals for one or two days a week (Eastern Regional Health Authority 2001: 11). The unevenness of day care provision around the country is illustrated by the availability of five-day day care in some facilities and one-day-a-week day care in others.

On the basis of consultations with day service providers, older people themselves and their family carers, Haslett found that day services are hugely beneficial to the many different categories of older people attending a variety of day care environments:

> Apart from the tangible health and social benefits conferred by the delivery of services in all categories of centres, these older people and their family carers become part of a wider network of caring. They are known to, and looked out for by, not only a range of service providers (e.g. members of voluntary committees, managers, care attendants, drivers and volunteers), but by each other. The social capital gains achieved through mutual support, co-operation, empathy and trust are very real. (Haslett 2003: 167)

While Haslett comments that the concept of a social club or active retirement group is not very well developed in social policy, she argues that 'the social club extends limits and challenges the usual stereotypes of what older people can, will and want to do' (Haslett 2003: 179). There is evidence that many clubs and day centres are adopting principles of empowerment and encouraging more active participation by service users in the choice and running of activities (Gallagher 2008: 97).

In terms of the future development of day services, Haslett has identified the following issues and challenges:

- Insufficient numbers of centres, long waiting lists and unsuitability of day care centres for some categories of older people.
- Understaffing and difficulties in providing quality services, particularly physiotherapy.
- Motivational issues and the reluctance of older men to attend.
- A need for greater support for family carers.

A brief description is given below of a day care centre in Dublin that strives to enhance health and social gain for participants.

Clareville Day Care Centre was opened in Glasnevin in 2000. It is a purpose-built centre in the grounds of the Clareville Court sheltered housing complex. The centre involved co-operation between Dublin City Council, responsible for social housing for older people, the HSE and the local community. Service users come from both Clareville Court and the general community and the centre can cater for about 80 people every day. The manager and public health nurse decide on admissions and people are allocated a set number of days and collected by bus. Those who can come independently can use the centre five days a week if they wish. There are eight staff (three full-time and five part-time) and 12 volunteers.

Facilities include treatment, assisted bathing and a laundry service. The public health nurse and chiropodist attend regularly. There is a full meals service and a wide range of activities to suit what residents themselves want. Activities on offer include relaxation and self-development, bingo, computer classes, art, table quiz and bridge. There is a music session and mass every month and a weekly bus trip to a local shopping centre. The staff makes a special effort to mark the seasonal festivals of Christmas, Easter, Halloween and St Valentine's Day. Every year there are outings organised, an art exhibition of work done in the centre and a community week held in the summer. The ethos of the centre is that the service users are encouraged to be involved in decisions about the running of the centre and help out themselves in small daily tasks.

QUALITY INITIATIVES IN RESIDENTIAL CARE

Recognising that older people have a capacity for continuing learning and activation of their creativity, many initiatives have been undertaken to provide meaningful activity programmes in care settings. Activities such as drama, art, storytelling, craft work and creative writing have been introduced successfully in day and residential settings and have challenged perceptions that passive leisure and entertainment such as bingo or sing-songs are sufficient to satisfy older people (Gallagher 2008: 96).

Projects involving the introduction of arts activities in care settings have been undertaken in recent years. One such training initiative, 'Arts for Older People in Care Settings', was undertaken by a partnership involving the Midland Health Board, Laois County Council and Age and Opportunity. The initiative was designed to enhance the quality of life of long-stay residents by providing stimulation that was regular, reliable and part of the normal routine. This was to be achieved by developing the necessary facilitation skills in the staff themselves to bring art and drama to residential care settings in the course of the daily routines.

An evaluation report (Midland Health Board 2002) gave positive feedback from participants, facilitators, residents and directors of nursing. Among the benefits reported by the staff were increased confidence, discovery of their own creativity, new ideas, greater empathy with residents and raised awareness of the residents' abilities and talents. Feedback from residents included an expanded range of activities open to them, an increase in communication and interaction with one another and with staff, discovery/rediscovery of their talents and skills, higher levels of morale and a new sense of social inclusion/community. One of the challenges identified in the evaluation report was that of including the most dependent residents in arts activities.

Healthy ageing initiatives that involve an emphasis on maintaining physical and mental fitness have been introduced to many residential and day centres. The *Go for Life* campaign is a joint initiative of Age and Opportunity and the Irish Sports Council. It promotes physical exercise and sport activity to suit all ages and levels of fitness.

In a recent survey of 322 long-stay facilities, a wide range of organised activities was found to be available. Listed in order of highest to lowest availability, they included visits from schools, music, physical exercise, bingo/cards/board games, arts, complementary therapies, Sonas, dancing, gardening and Snoezelan. In addition, library facilities were available in most of the facilities surveyed (Murphy et al. 2006: 128–9). However, the authors commented that while there is a significant amount of activity taking place, the opportunity to participate in meaningful activity is much more circumscribed (Murphy et al. 2006: 138). For example, only one-third of community/district hospitals allowed residents to participate in household tasks (Murphy et al. 2006: 138).

A study that compared community-dwelling older people with nursing home residents (largely concentrated in private nursing homes) in terms of their cognitive, sensory and sensorimotor abilities found a high degree of idleness among residents of nursing homes typified by long periods spent in the television room and little conversation (Walsh 2004). The author was critical of the institutional environment, which he argued encouraged dependency and discouraged the activation of self-care and independent skills and induced a norm of 'batch living'. He also examined the availability of four different activities in 17 nursing homes: exercise, painting, parish activities and Sonas. He found that each of these activities was available only in one nursing home out of the 17. These research reports suggest that there is considerable variation in the quality of the social and recreational environment in different types of facilities.

SOCIAL CARE MODEL

There is a growing recognition that services for the dependent elderly should follow other services, such as those for people with intellectual and physical disabilities, in adopting a social care model in preference to a medical one in meeting their needs (see Chapter 23 on social care and disability). Unlike other services, residential and day services for older people have developed and expanded in recent decades with little input from the emergent social care profession (Gallagher and Kennedy 2003). The largest group of employees in residential care settings are nurses and care attendants and a medical model could be said to dominate, rather than a social care approach. The characteristics of a medical model are a focus on problems and deficits and institutional provision of care, with routines designed for efficiency and little attention to individuality, autonomy or normal daily living.

A social care model would aim to:

- Explore attitudes and expectations within a value framework that stresses individualisation and normalisation.
- Develop effective communication techniques and use of creative activities.
- Foster a more lively atmosphere by bringing residents out and bringing activities and groups in.
- Use older people themselves as a resource and involve them in decision-making.
- See social, emotional and spiritual needs as on a par with physical needs.

A social care model can be observed in the move away from large institutional settings with a hospital atmosphere to smaller homely units, and the increasing emphasis on purposeful activity and links with the community. But the implications for training have not been fully worked out, given the traditional staffing structures of such services (Gallagher and Kennedy 2003). In response to concerns about a lack of appropriate training opportunities, a training initiative was undertaken in the School of Social Sciences and Law, Dublin Institute of Technology. This involved the development of a part-time course: Developing a Social Care Value Based Activities Programme for Older People. The course is designed for social care and nursing staff who have responsibility for planning and providing activities for older people in both day and long-stay residential facilities.[4] The programme commenced in 2004 and has had approximately 100 participants to date.

CONCLUSION

Services for dependent older people have developed from the institutional model of the County Home – still dominant up to the 1960s – to smaller, more homely units where routines are designed to be more normal, where stimulating recreation is provided and where links with the outside community are cultivated. Expectations in relation to what a dependent older person might want in a residential unit have changed from an emphasis on physical care to meeting psycho-social, spiritual and emotional needs. In the future, achieving quality and high standards will be supported by legislation. There are many innovative examples of good practice involving the arts in care settings, participation by service users themselves in the programmes provided in care centres and more inter-agency co-operation in creating healthy ageing opportunities for older people in the community.

It is clear that positive ageing is enhanced by attention to suitable housing, a safe environment and amenities and facilities for social and recreational activities. The contribution that older people make and can make in their own communities is increasingly being recognised. Traditional ideas about older people as 'good causes', while worthy and helpful in past decades in eliciting a humane response to deprivation, have been challenged by groups representing older people, who rightly aspire to a more participative role in society. In a report on volunteering in Ireland, a recommendation was that older people be targeted as recruits: 'There is great potential in older people given their accumulated skills and experience. They may benefit with a healthier lifestyle and more enjoyable life, while society benefits from greater social cohesion and intergenerational solidarity' (National Committee on Volunteering 2002: 72).

Underpinning all these developments must be a vision of what the possibilities are for living a full life during the latter stages of the life course, or of what constitutes good human functioning for older people, whatever degree of dependency they may experience. Challenges remain in relation to how best practice can be introduced, whether in private nursing homes or the old-style geriatric institutions and in providing acceptable and dependable community services. A key issue is that of education and training in relation to how best to promote a social care model in work with older people.

Social Care and Family Support Work

Colm O'Doherty

OVERVIEW

This chapter focuses on social care as a form of community practice directed towards the promotion of well-being and the prevention of negative outcomes for children and families. According to Butcher et al. (2007: 4), community practice is concerned with processes that 'are about stimulating, engaging and achieving active community'. In order to achieve 'active community', social care practitioners must nourish the glue of collective support alongside the solvent of individuality and self-esteem. The purpose of this chapter, therefore, is twofold: to provide a framework for social care practice that delivers a range of services meeting the needs of parents and their children in their local communities and to identify a new agenda for practice that promotes generalised well-being and social cohesion.

Beginning with an account of changing family types and practices in contemporary Ireland, the reader is then introduced to models of family support and social care practice responses aimed directly at promoting the well-being of children, parental capacity-building and wider society.

UNDERSTANDING FAMILY

The grand narrative of traditional family life, espoused by the 1937 Constitution, has been increasingly replaced by the construction of many different truths, produced by many different actors, reflecting the social identity of family life in contemporary Ireland. I have suggested elsewhere (O'Doherty 2007: 39) that the family unit now operates as a social franchise under whose auspices individuals are free to live for themselves.

To be successful, any franchised venture must appeal on some level to potential customers. Membership of a social franchise, such as the family, is more likely to be encouraged if individuals see the franchise as operating on principles that are responsive to their needs. The challenges of this changed operating environment and principles affecting this new franchise are detailed in Table 22.1.

Table 22.1. A New Social Franchise: The Changing Irish Family

Drivers for Change	Challenges	Principles
1. The number of traditional families in the state (477,705) is declining in all the main cities. 2. The number of one-person households grew by 18.7% (up 51,877) between 2002 and 2006. 3. Co-habiting couples represented the fastest-growing type of family unit at 121,800 in 2006 (11.6% of all family units), compared to 77,600 in 2002 (8.4% of all family units). 4. The number of divorced persons has increased by 70% (from 35,000 to 59,500) between 2002 and 2006. 5. The average number of children per family declined from 2.2 in 1986 to 1.4 in 2006. 6. 419,733 (10% of the overall population) indicated that they had a nationality other than Irish.	1. Changing work practices – one's geographical location, employment status, range of skills and self-identity are now open to change in the flexible new economy. 2. Changes in intimate life – increased availability of birth control, visibility of gay and lesbian relationships, divorce and global development of feminism. 3. Challenges in parenting – parents must earn their authority over their children while facing an uncertain future.	Relationships set up under this franchise must be capable of the following. 1. Promoting emotional and sexual equality. 2. Acknowledging mutual rights and responsibilities in relationships. 3. Facilitating co-parenting. 4. Accepting lifelong parental contracts. 5. Negotiating authority with children. 6. Fulfilling obligations towards older family members.

Source: Census 2006 – Volume 3, Household composition, family units and fertility.

UNDERSTANDING SUPPORT

A major UK government-funded research initiative inquiring into the informal and formal supports parents need to help them look after their children effectively found that:

> 'Support' is a very general term. It is easy to respond to a problem by saying that we should 'put in more support', without being at all clear what we mean or what we want to achieve. Support for parenting is complex to assess, to get right and to deliver because of the balance between the neglect of family problems and intrusion into family life, not to mention ideas of what satisfactory parenting is, how and when this needs support and who should decide that. (Quinton 2005: 156)

Families and children can benefit from different types of family support, some of which are detailed in Table 22.2.

Table 22.2. Types of Family Support

Categories	Types of Support	Integration of Family Support Services
Formal Personal social services delivered by social care/work personnel. Structured individual or group support from a family or resource or health centre (Springboard). Structured support from health personnel such as public health nurses.	**Basic practical support** Help with child care arrangements, e.g. a neighbour who is not working might provide after-school care for a working neighbour.	Provision of commissioned/ collaborative services: family support centre provides services on behalf of another agency. This might also include purposive mixing of family centre staff with professionals from other agencies to provide a specific service in order to run a group, with shared input and responsibility.
Semi-formal Groups geared towards particular parenting activities, such as nutrition. Personal development groups. Parenting programmes. Luncheon clubs. Groups for parents of children with specific needs, e.g. disability.	**Emotional support** Listening and communicating. Listening is a skill that requires cultural awareness and understanding.	Provision of complementary services: family centres and other agencies might provide separate services to the same families to meet different needs. This could include commissioned working (by the HSE) and family centres acting as a venue for other service providers (e.g. public health nurses) to work with the family.
Informal Cultural activities (music classes, drama groups, literary groups, sport/outdoor pursuits) that are accessible to parents and children in their locality.	**Esteem support** Communicating to a person that they have value. The person may be valued for their being kind or fair, brave or bold, a good parent or a good friend in their dealings with me or others.	Provision of an integrated service: this would mean family centres and other agencies had an explicit joint plan of work for the provision of family support services where they could call on each other to provide their respective inputs to the family.

Source: Jack and Gill (2003).

UNDERSTANDING PARENTING

Parenting is a difficult but essential and rewarding social task that carries a range of formidable responsibilities. In the twenty-first century, men and women who are parents frequently negotiate their parenting role. Approaches to parenting are variable and open to debate. Factors affecting contemporary parenting endeavours include the following.

- *The influence of experts*: So-called 'expert advice' on parenting may complement and in some instances replace the advice and practical support previously offered by extended family members. The expert advice can be offered by psychologists, doctors, feminists, economists, academics, nurturant fathers and government agencies through different media pathways. Along with the more traditional parenting advice columns of the print media, there has also been a growing popularity of parenting websites. *The Irish Times* newspaper has a parenting section in its weekly Health Plus supplement and websites such as netmums.com, mumsnet.com, raisingkids.co.uk, magicmum.com and roller-coaster.ie are dispensing advice and offering support networks to parents (mainly mothers) who are feeling overwhelmed, stressed or isolated by the demands of raising children. According to a founder of one of the websites (netmums.com):

> Mothers either don't know how to find experts themselves or don't want to go to an institution with their problems because they fear official procedures that could lead to the situation spiralling out of their control. Asking for advice from other mothers on a website is different; you're anonymous, everyone comes up with their own solutions so no one judges you and if one piece of advice doesn't work, you can try another. (Hill 2008)

  For example, a pregnant woman living in Kimmage, Dublin, says she doesn't know her neighbours but through Magicmum she has been able to meet up with mothers living in the area and looks forward to their company and support once the baby is born (Wayman 2008).

- *Parenting and finding oneself*: An observable feature of life in the twenty-first century is the 'project of the self'. Individualisation, the process whereby a person maps out an identity and life plan for themselves rather than for the wider community or family, may not be harmonious with the self-denying responsibilities of parenting.
- *Parenting and risk*: Parenting now involves managing the risks generated by natural hazards, the effects of social change, economic forces, scientific development and technological change.
- *Parenting and inequality*: Child poverty is a serious problem in Ireland. According to the EU *Survey of Income and Living Conditions* (Central Statistics

Office 2007f; European Anti-Poverty Network Ireland 2008b), one in five people in Ireland is at risk of poverty, while one in nine children in Ireland is at risk of poverty. Those who fall into the 'at risk of poverty' or 'relative poverty' category are people whose income is below 60 per cent of the national median (middle range) income. One in three of those in consistent poverty[1] are children, while 17 per cent of those in consistent poverty are members of lone-parent households. Almost 9 per cent of people in Ireland experience debt problems and the income of the top 20 per cent of the population is five times greater than that of the lowest 20 per cent.

- *Parenting and children's rights*: Current constitutional provision in Ireland is imbalanced in so far as it favours the rights of parents over the rights of children. The state's overreliance on parents to vindicate the rights of children has also led to under-investment by the state in family support services.

UNDERSTANDING FAMILY WELL-BEING

Family well-being is promoted when the relationship between families and wider society is characterised by respect for the family as a social asset and an essential social welfare organisation.

> The idea that parents and carers need support should not be seen as strange – a stranger idea is that parents and carers do *not* need support. But what kind of support? When and why might support be needed? How should it be provided? By whom? (Braun 2001: 243)

All families benefit from being supported and esteemed by their immediate community and wider society. What weaves all family types together is the thread of relationships. The quality and tone of internal and external relationships are at the heart of family life and family well-being is influenced by the interplay between children's developmental needs, parenting capacity and wider family and environmental factors. In order to fully understand the dynamics of these interrelationships, it is necessary to draw on specific lines of reasoning that refer to the mutual interdependence of people and their environments (ecological theory), the role of formal and informal social support networks and the importance of social capital in promoting social cohesion.

Table 22.3. Factors Influencing Family Well-being

Ecological Perspective on Family Well-being	The ecological understanding is 'borrowed' from biology and usually refers to the mutual interdependence of plants, animals, people and their physical environments. Within the ecological perspective, the child, the child's family and the environment in which they live influence one another in a constant process of reciprocal interaction. The ecological perspective links the well-being of parents and children to the characteristics of the environment that they inhabit.
Role of Formal and Informal Networks in Promoting Well-being	Gilchrist (2004) sets out the benefits of community and social networks: they provide an alternative user-friendly source of help during crisis points for those seeking help with risky or embarrassing problems who do not wish to resort to professional (sometimes stigmatised) service provision. Social networks supply informal care over and above the care provided by family and friends. In addition to these practical benefits, social networks provide their members with opportunities for positive emotional engagement: community networks foster informal modes of communication and co-operation between people. Community networks underpin collective action strategies that are focused on people working together to achieve or defend shared interests.
Importance of Social Capital Generation for Family Well-being	Social capital (O'Doherty 2007) is a community resource, the 'social glue' that creates social cohesion. It is formed by creating opportunities for people to develop trusting relationships through participation and engagement in mutual support organisations such as family support services and community development projects. Participation in cultural, recreational and sporting activities with other people helps to overcome barriers of mistrust and build social capital. Day-to-day experience, backed up by international research, tells us that social capital is an essential factor in the development of healthy communities. The benefits of social capital in promoting health and well-being, reducing levels of crime and improving economic prospects have been well established through academic research. Investment in social capital will, however, also necessitate a new approach to the organisation and delivery of key services, which impacts on the relationships between families and wider society. In this regard, services for children, young people and their families must be directed towards promoting trust and engagement between professionals and service users.

UNDERSTANDING FAMILY SUPPORT SERVICES

Broadly speaking, family support services in Ireland can be categorised according to their function and governance structures.

Family Centres

Family resource centres provide focused but flexible programmes that enhance individuals' self-esteem and potential and actively increase the capacity of local communities to become self-reliant and self-directed. Typically, such centres deliver a mix of services to meet child and family needs at different life stages. Operating under a voluntary management committee structure, generally comprised of representatives from target groups within the community, these centres provide open access to members of a community or neighbourhood. This open access or universal framework approach means that information and support can be seen as everyone's entitlement, thus taking away the stigma of asking for it. Family resource centres were first established in the early 1990s on a pilot basis under the Department of Social Welfare. An evaluation of the pilot programme (Kelleher and Kelleher 1997) crucially recommended that funding be mainstreamed for the centres by the Department of Social Welfare and not the Department of Health, which carried the main responsibility for personal social services. This decision meant that family support services were not integrated with health and personal social services. In 2003, a Family Support Agency was set up and given responsibility for the Family and Community Services Resource Centre Programme. By 2006, 70 centres were established and funded by the Family Support Agency. The overarching objectives of these centres, expressed through their mission statements, are focused on building social capacity and social capital formation.

> The mission of the centre is to create an environment that welcomes, supports, empowers and encourages people to belong and participate in their own community's development and to develop services and facilities that will improve the quality of life and respond to the needs of all ages. (South and Mid-West Community Development Support Agency 2006: 69)

Family centres provide a framework for the development of an interpersonal economy that fosters skills, competencies, capacities and connections, leading to the establishment of social networks. The interpersonal economy assigns value to relationships and emotions rather than material goods (see Jordan 2007 for a full account of this relationship model). Supports and services typically provided by family centres include the following.

- *Support for individuals:* Women's groups, men's groups, immigrants, luncheon clubs for elderly citizens.

- *Child care*: Pre-schools, playschools, summer camps, homework/breakfast clubs, youth clubs/drop-in centres.
- *Counselling for individuals and families*: Relationships, separation, bereavement, stress, bullying, domestic violence, debt, substance abuse.
- *Community and adult education*: Parenting programmes, IT skills, preparation for interviews, return to work programmes, personal development work, committee skills, employment law, cookery.
- *Cultural and artistic opportunities*: Arts and crafts, musical tuition, dramatics.
- *Sports and recreational activities*: Athletics, football, basketball, snooker/pool, outdoor pursuits.

In addition to the direct provision of supports and services, family centres act as gateways for individuals and groups to access formal services from public health nurses, social workers, local authorities, youth justice and crime agencies, chiropodists, speech therapists, physiotherapists, legal aid, meals on wheels, GPs, education providers, money advice and budgeting services. In this way, each family centre can act as a *one-stop shop*. Their location and integrity help to maximise access to centres and underpin links and partnerships with other agencies. Open access family centres providing universal services (available to everyone) have the dual advantage of reducing stigma and increasing the acceptability of specialised mainstream helping services.

Furthermore, the gateway function of family centres can enhance the co-ordination of local services. An evaluation of the Shanakill Family Resource Centre Tralee (O'Doherty 2003) established that the centre operates as a gateway to outside agencies/organisations dealing with problems and difficulties that require a response or a resource that is beyond the scope or expertise of the centre's staff. Similarly, Tunstill et al.'s study (2007) of family centres in the UK found that:

> First, centres acted as a gateway for families to access other services, which could be alternative, supplementary or subsequent to those on offer in the family centre. A second aspect of co-ordination was the provision of a gateway for professionals in other agencies to access families using the family centres who might need the service of other agencies. (2007: 87)

The Springboard Programme

Springboard is a community-based programme that aims to support vulnerable families in the home, school and community. Springboard projects are located in high-stress neighbourhoods where there is a marked incidence of factors contributing to the reception of children into care. Each Springboard project has its own history and developmental pathway. Fourteen Springboard family support projects were launched by the government in 1998. The expectation of the Department of Health and Children in overseeing the development of Springboard was that the projects would achieve the following:

- Identify the needs of parents and children in a specific area and focus on safeguarding children in families where child protection concerns exist.
- Target the most disadvantaged and vulnerable families in an area and focus on improving their parenting skills and child–parent relationships.
- Develop programmes of family support services in partnership with different agencies in an area, key groups, individuals in the community and families.
- Provide direct services through a structured package of care, intervention, support and counselling to targeted families and children, and to families within the wider community.

Since 2001, 13 new Springboard projects have been established. There are now 22 projects operating across the country and another five have been commissioned.

Specialised Family Support Services

Enable Ireland 'provide a wide range of services for families with children/adolescents with physical disabilities. The aim of the service is to provide a fun, child centred environment in which each child is facilitated to participate in activities that enhance their social, physical and personal development' (Enable Ireland 2008). Family support services currently provided in Kerry by Enable Ireland include an after-school programme, a summer programme, a sport and recreation programme and trips away.

Schizophrenia Ireland provides support to families with mental health problems. The organisation 'hosts family support groups, support courses and education courses for caring relatives in Ireland' (O'Doherty et al. 2006: 26).

Home-Start

Home-Start is a voluntary organisation committed to promoting the welfare of families with at least one child under five years of age. Volunteers offer regular support, friendship and practical help to young families in their own homes, helping to prevent family crisis and breakdown. Home-Start projects are currently operating in Athenry in Co. Galway and Lucan and Blanchardstown in Co. Dublin.

Health Service Executive Family Support Services

The Health Service Executive (HSE) is obliged under Section 3 of the 1991 Child Care Act to provide family support services to promote the welfare of children not receiving adequate care and attention. However, despite this obligation, child protection, and not family support, has dominated and continues to dominate the practice activity of Irish social workers, leaving statutory family support services underdeveloped and patchy.

While the philosophy of the 1991 Child Care Act is that families and children should be supported and that children should be brought up within their own families, the Health Service Executive has no dedicated family support programme. A new organisational platform that could deliver a range of services, targeted at different levels of need, within a framework of prevention is vitally necessary to ensure that HSE family support services are developed and are adequately resourced.

The issue of different priorities is a major factor in the differing perspectives of social workers and family support practitioners. Social work services in the Health Boards and latterly the HSE are, in the main, characterised by a style of practice that is legalistic, formal, procedural and managerial. Research carried out by O'Doherty (2004) into the national statutory child care system highlighted the ways in which key stakeholders in the system (social workers, child care managers) privilege child protection work over family support initiatives. Social work is locked into a power-laden investigative approach that struggles to meet the complex needs of families.

While family support is underdeveloped within the HSE overall, some service development has taken place. For example, a successful, if limited (in terms of staffing), Kerry Family Support service has been operated by the HSE's Southern region since 2004. The service, which is circumscribed by its low staffing level, dealt with 205 families between 2004 and 2007 and aims to 'improve the quality of family life by broadening parents' knowledge, skills and confidence so that they are better equipped to manage behavioural, emotional and developmental problems as presented by their children' (Health Service Executive Kerry Family Support Team 2007). Community child care workers are also employed across the HSE.

SOCIAL CARE AS COMMUNITY PRACTICE

What kind of education and training are required for family support work? Social care professionals are increasingly making the link between service delivery work and social intervention in communities (see O'Doherty 2007, 2008). This translates into a holistic practice model where social care practitioners engage with the whole person, the whole system and the whole community. A holistic social care practice model that can be employed in family centres, Springboard projects and specialised family support services comprises three interlocking components: values, practice strategies and working methods.

Social care practitioners who are interested in becoming policy/practice pioneers in family support interventions will need to embrace a professional value system that promotes social justice, participation, equality, learning and co-operation. Social justice requires that people be enabled to claim their human rights, meet their needs and have greater control over the decision-making processes that affect their lives, while participation involves the facilitation of people in issues that affect their lives. Family support practitioners manifest the value of equality by challenging and resisting discrimination against and marginalisation of individuals and communities. The learning that results from people taking action to tackle social, economic, political and environmental problems should be acknowledged and practitioners should adopt a co-operative approach to working with service users and other professionals.

In turn, the practice strategies through which these values are manifested are focused on enabling, encouraging, empowering and educating people. The working methods that social care professionals engaging in family support work employ are dictated by a broad range of tasks implicit in the process of strengthening and assisting families. The range of tasks includes providing resources, providing information, helping groups, education and training, establishing groups, establishing networks, policy work and community-based art work.

The very essence of social care practice is its focus on promoting well-being by enabling full participation in work and mainstream society. Levels of well-being are related to health, relationships and work-role satisfaction. This practice approach draws on a human rights-based approach to family support.

A Human Rights Approach to Family Support Work

The United Nations (1994) states that 'the family is the basic unit of society'. Social care as community practice should focus on rights rather than on need. The principles underpinning a human rights-based approach are:

- *Legitimacy*: Human rights-based solutions are based on the human rights recognised in international law.
- *Accountability*: An accountability procedure is a mechanism or device whereby governments and public institutions are answerable for their acts or omissions in relation to their duties.
- *Empowerment*: Human rights-based development serves to empower communities and individuals to know, claim and defend their rights and to know their responsibilities.
- *Participation*: Human rights-based solutions maximise the participation of the community. Participation must be active, free and meaningful.
- *Equality*: Non-discrimination and prioritisation of vulnerable groups. The prioritisation of vulnerable groups and the principle of non-discrimination are expressly included in all human rights theories. This reflects the fact that equality is a fundamental issue central to all human rights: social, economic, cultural and political (European Anti-Poverty Network Ireland 2008a: 10).

In human rights terms, the professional activity of social care practitioners is directed towards maximising opportunities for people to determine the conditions of their own lives so that they can fully develop their capacities. Capacity-building involves a great deal more than priming individuals to contribute to the material economy through the labour market. There is mounting evidence to suggest that, in an overall sense, citizens have not benefited from the high priority afforded to the material economy here in Ireland and other similarly affluent countries (Cullen 2006; Halpern 2005; Helliwell and Putnam 2005; Layard 2005). Riley (2008), in his study of 12 middle- and low-income countries, has found that such countries build social capital in a different way.

> Through the pursuit of what is called *social growth or social development*, rather than economic development, low-income countries found ways to build their own forms of social capital even though their people had little capacity for spending on things other than the basic necessities of life and their governments lacked the revenues to fund costly programs. (Riley 2008: 3)

Jordan (2007) makes a strong argument for social care practice to reassert the value of the interpersonal economy, that is, the value produced in relationships. Such an approach would focus on boosting the interpersonal economy, which creates value through relationships of empathy, equality and justice. The value of the interpersonal economy is realised through its role in the creation of higher levels of social capital in communities and wider society. Social capital, an intangible resource generated through collective interaction, builds greater community cohesion and social integration. Put simply, it improves people's lives by engaging them in mutually supportive activities that are beneficial to them and their communities. This kind of service development is vitally important in an Ireland where social cohesion is being undermined by growing inequality, the challenges of diversity, increasing crime, substance abuse and mental ill health.

CONCLUSION

This chapter began by highlighting the challenges facing families and the support available to them in contemporary Ireland. It moved on to explore family support provision and concludes by making the case for social care practice that safeguards and promotes the well-being of children, communities and families.

23

Disability and Social Care

Karen Finnerty

OVERVIEW

This chapter introduces current issues and approaches in relation to people with disabilities in Ireland. All disabilities are included – intellectual, physical, sensory and mental health – since the issues discussed pertain to all. The chapter aims to provide an understanding and appreciation of the key issues. You may find some of the content challenging and contrary to what you have previously learned or experienced about disability. It is hoped that this chapter will help you to develop a broader understanding of the area and help you to see disability as fitting within a human context that applies to *all* people.

The chapter opens by discussing what we mean by 'disability' and how it is defined. Understanding of definitions is important, as they continue to influence attitudes and decisions made in relation to people with disability and the design and delivery of services. How services developed in Ireland influences how disability is viewed, so their historical development is outlined. This lays the groundwork for an understanding of the two models of service response, the medical/traditional model and the social model, both of which are presented.

The chapter concludes with a discussion of the role of the social care practitioner in the context of disability, with a particular emphasis of working from the perspective of advocacy and person-centred planning.

WHAT IS DISABILITY?

Defining what we mean when we speak of 'disability' is challenging. The word suggests a person in a wheelchair, a person with a guide dog or a child with Down Syndrome. Rarely do we consider that disability operates on a continuum, and therefore any of us who experience difficulties could be considered 'disabled'. For example, we tend not to think of people with chronic or long-term illness as disabled. Even more rarely do we consider how people labelled as 'disabled' or 'handicapped' feel about the use of terms that can impact significantly on their quality of life. The National Disability Authority (NDA 2005a: 1) has noted that how disability is defined and understood 'has implications for how people with disabilities are treated, the nature of service provision, and the extent and type of legislation and policy that includes a disability focus'.

This, then, is the first big challenge we face in this chapter: when speaking of 'disability', what exactly do we mean and of whom exactly do we speak? More significantly, what has created the situation where we believe it is acceptable to speak of 'the disabled' as a distinct and homogenous subset of Irish society, separate and different to the rest of us?

Different countries use different definitions, and even within countries different definitions are used in different contexts. Furthermore, people with disabilities have taken issue with the definitions used and have proposed their own. So let us start there – with the views of people with disabilities themselves. In Ireland, the 1996 Report of the Commission on the Status of People with Disabilities (*A Strategy for Equality*), probably the most significant document in relation to disability to emerge in Ireland in the last century, defined the term 'people with disabilities' to include:

> [C]hildren and adults who experience any restriction in their capacity to participate in economic, social or cultural life on account of a physical, sensory, learning, mental health or emotional impairment. (Commission on the Status of People with Disabilities 1996: 11)

Very often, the terms 'disability', 'handicap' and 'impairment' are used interchangeably, with no real consideration of what the terms mean or how they are defined. The emergence of the general use of these terms has a long history (that we will explore later), but a definite influencing factor was the World Health Organization (WHO), which in 1980 developed a three-tier definition that refers to impairment, disability and handicap:

> An *impairment* is any loss or abnormality of psychological, physiological or anatomical structure or function; a *disability* is any restriction or lack (resulting from an impairment) of ability to perform an activity in the manner or within the range considered normal for a human being; a *handicap* is a disadvantage for a given individual resulting from an impairment or a disability, that prevents the fulfilment of a role that is considered normal (depending on age, sex and social and cultural factors) for that individual. (WHO 1980, s27.29.14) (Italics added)

There are strong medical overtones in the language used in this definition, focusing as it did on the cognitive, emotional and physical aspects of the person. The concepts of abnormality and normality are difficult to define and, more importantly, they created a 'them and us mentality', which ensured that people with disability were viewed as different to the rest of the population. While this WHO definition had wide acceptance amongst health bodies and governments and was used for many years, disability activists rejected it. They argued that disability is not caused by chance, nor is it limited to the impairment experienced by the person. They acknowledged the impairment but argued that the arising *disability* was a social construct, created through society's response to the impairment and by its failure to put sufficient supports in place to ensure that the person with the impairment achieved the same quality of life as other members of society. Applying this thinking, the original WHO definition (above) is aligned largely to what is now known as the *medical model of disability*.

On the other hand, the approach proposed by disability activists is more closely aligned to what is termed the *social model of disability*. The social model defines disability as the barriers created by how society, governments and health agencies respond to impairments experienced by a person. The social model requires a political response, since the problem is based in society and its attitudes and in how people respond to those with disability.

Debates on these definitions raged in many countries during the 1990s, informed by the concept of human rights and the belief that all people have the right to be treated equally. The either/or position of the medical/social approaches found some common ground during the 1990s in what is known as the *biopsychosocial model*, developed in 1977 by American psychiatrist George Engel. He developed the model to incorporate the biological, psychological and sociological systems of the body (Engel 1977). In essence, the model sought to view the person as a whole.

In 2002, incorporating the thinking of the biopsychosocial model, the WHO revised its earlier definition. It published the *International Classification of Functioning, Disability and Health* (ICF), which outlines a standard language and framework for the description of health and health-related states. It expresses a universal classification of disability and health and is a significant development on the previous definition:

> [U]nlike the previous definitions ICF puts the notions of health and disability in a new light. It acknowledges that **every** human being can experience a decrement in health and thereby experience some disability. ICF mainstreams the experience of disability and recognises it as a universal human experience. (WHO 2002: 3)

The ICF provides a framework for defining disability. Notwithstanding this, differences of definition can and do emerge and the legal definition of disability has posed problems for many countries and has generated much debate around the globe (Bickenback 1992). Despite the ICF framework, currently there is no universal legal definition of disability, nor is there one in any European country. Definitions vary depending on the area under discussion, e.g. employment, social welfare entitlement and income matters (Degener 2004).

In Ireland, we have progressed a great deal in the approach to and understanding of how disability is defined – evidenced in recent Acts and policy documents (see Box 23.1). However, we too have varying definitions. For example, the Employment Equality Act 1998 defined disability much in line with the original 1980 WHO three-tier definition, with a focus on medical issues and language grounded in the medical model. The 1998 Act was an anti-discrimination Act and was in line with how other countries were approaching disability legislation at that time. By 2005, the focus had shifted somewhat:

> [D]isability in relation to a person, means a substantial restriction in the capacity of the person to carry on a profession, business or occupation in the State or to participate in social or cultural life in the State by reason of an enduring physical, sensory, mental health or intellectual impairment. (Disability Act 2005)

This definition is closely aligned to the definition used in *A Strategy for Equality* (Commission on the Status of People with Disabilities 1996), but still defines disability in terms of impairment. This Act also used two definitions: one relating to the assessment of need (Part 2 of the Act) and the one above relating to the remainder of the Act.

Thus, while significant progress has been made in our understanding and definition of disability, and notwithstanding efforts of services to move toward the social and biopsychosocial models, organisations that provide services to people with disabilities and the staff who work in them still deal with the legacy of the original medical model and its associated definitions and attitudes. To understand this legacy, an exploration of how services developed in an Irish context is important. The picture was further coloured by the involvement of religious organisations that moved to address significant societal needs from a charitable standpoint where, at that time, the state was failing to do so.

HISTORY OF SERVICES FOR PEOPLE WITH DISABILITIES IN IRELAND

Prior to the Industrial Revolution, people with disabilities lived their lives in the community into which they were born. Prosperity and urbanisation in the eighteenth century attracted people from rural areas to centres of high population. As the population grew, so too did the number of 'vagabonds' and 'beggars', giving rise for concern among citizens.

In Dublin in 1773, the authorities responded to this concern by opening the Dublin House of Industry, where those regarded as social 'undesirables' were incarcerated. These institutions (generally known as workhouses) catered for many social problems, but within a very short space of time, the House of Industry had allocated separate space for those with mental health difficulties, then termed 'lunatics' and 'idiots'. This system continued to expand over the next number of decades, and by the time of the Famine, 163 workhouses had been built in Ireland

(Jones and Malcolm 1999: 103). Here, the destitute received meagre food and lodging in return for work done. The idea of difference and practices of segregation continued to grow during the 1850s so that by the close of the nineteenth century, there were 22 district 'lunatic asylums'. Some of these institutions were the forerunners of today's services for people with mental health difficulties, such as St Patrick's Hospital, Dublin (Robins 1986).

In 1869, the Stewart Institution for Idiotic and Imbecile Children was opened in Dublin. Its original aim was to train children with learning disabilities so that by the time they reached 18, they would be able to return to their homes and families. But the children did not return to their homes, and as numbers grew, few vacancies arose. Meanwhile, numbers in the district asylums had swollen, and a suggestion was made that auxiliary asylums be created for 'incurables' – primarily people with learning disabilities.

In 1926, a Catholic order of nuns, the Daughters of Charity, turned the Workhouse School in Cabra into a home and school for children with learning disabilities. Over the next 30 years or so, religious orders opened at least 10 similar types of institutions around Ireland.

During the 1950s, several nondenominational organisations and agencies were founded in Ireland. In 1955, on the initiative of a mother with a son with a learning disability, the first day-service for children with learning disabilities was founded. This association later became St Michael's House. Other organisations had their start in the pioneering work of similar individuals.

A major factor that influenced the structure of these agencies and organisations was the belief that children with disabilities should not have to be 'put away', but instead should receive specialist care and education in purpose-built centres during the day. This welcome progression did not mean that the large institutions were closed down. Rather, the introduction of new organisations and services influenced how institutional care was provided. Changes began to occur for the better within these settings, such as the building of group homes, albeit within the same grounds as the main building.

Despite such improvements, the situation was far from perfect. In most cases, people had to attend centres away from their own neighbourhoods. Children at special schools were not expected to perform to the same level as those in ordinary national schools, limiting their later chances of interacting socially in adult life. Children and young adults were often collected from their homes by ambulance and brought to a centre that may have been known locally as the 'clinic', even though a school might also have been on site. Some agencies even incorporated the word 'clinic' into the official name of the organisation.

The public image projected by most such organisations was that of a benign body that protected and cared for unwell and vulnerable children and adults. But overall, while Western societal attitudes to people with disabilities had generally improved, these same people were still not generally regarded as complete human beings of an equal status to the remainder of society (Collins, B. 2001).

SERVICE RESPONSES TO PEOPLE WITH DISABILITY

Earlier we discussed the medical and social models. Now we return to these concepts to explore further how services responded to the needs of people with disability from the 1950s on in Ireland.

The Traditional/Medical Model

Most organisations developed and operated on the basis of what is now known as the *traditional model* of service provision. In this model, the service was generally self-contained, with little or no outside links. A hierarchical management system operated, with executive management at the top of the organisation (in control of funding and decision-making) and people with disabilities (often referred to as clients, patients or service users) and their families at the bottom of the hierarchy, in receipt of services, but almost always without any influence in relation to real decision-making (see Figure 23.1).

Figure 23.1. The Traditional Service Model

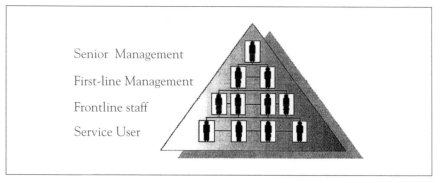

Senior Management

First-line Management

Frontline staff

Service User

Source: O'Brien and O'Brien (1989).

Another significant aspect of the development of services was the medical influence on service delivery approaches. People with disability were viewed as having a 'medical problem' that could only be assisted within a hospital or therapeutic setting. As discussed earlier, this thinking gave rise to what is now referred to as the *medical model*, and the 1980 WHO definition of disability reflected this 'medicalised' thinking.

What is significant about the medical model is that it operates from the belief that the 'disability' can be restored or otherwise treated medically. It operates within the classic understanding of medicine – the science of diagnosing and treating illness and injury and the preservation of health. The medical approach also had the unfortunate tendency of not distinguishing the person from the disability. The person's right to be seen as a person first was lost in descriptions such as 'the cripple', 'an epileptic' or 'the disabled'. In recent times, a rejection of such terms has moved to acknowledging the person first and then the disability, seen, for example, in the term 'person with disability' (NDA 2008).

THE SOCIAL MODEL

A redefinition of disability during the 1980s and 1990s saw a move away from the medical model towards a recognition that disability is 'created' by society. The *social model* recognises that while people may have an 'impairment', they become 'disabled' by a society that actively or passively *excludes* them from full participation. It locates the cause of disability not in the person who experiences the impairment, but in society's response. The response is manifested in the language used to describe the person, the supports put in place to enable him/her to live a full and meaningful life, and how far they are empowered in relation to decisions governing their life. This shift in thinking reflected earlier experiences, particularly in America, of other marginalised groups, such as women and racial minorities, and was driven by people with disability themselves. This change emerged from disability activists who redefined 'disability' and full inclusion in society as a human rights issue.

Reflecting wider international and European influences, in the 1990s people with disabilities in Ireland began to reframe their situation in terms of human rights. A *Strategy for Equality* (Commission on the Status of People with Disabilities 1996: 9) endorsed the change from a medical to a social approach:

> [A] given level of impairment or degree of restriction does not necessarily lead to disadvantage: It is the societal response (in terms of attitudes and expectations as well as the services and facilities made available), which has an important impact on the extent to which impairment or disability lead to disadvantage.

In the late 1980s, John O'Brien, an American activist and writer on disability issues, developed an alternative model of service delivery that embodies the principles of moving from a traditional (medical) to a social model of disability. In his model, the service, rather than 'containing' individuals, acts as a facilitator to ensure that people are linked to and can participate within their own community. The Basic Strategy (Figure 23.2) distinguishes between the person, the service and the community.

Figure 23.2. O'Brien's Basic Strategy

Source: Adapted from O'Brien and O'Brien (1989).

In this model, the person's network of friends and family is recognised as very important. The primary role of the service becomes one of support and safeguarding the individual within his/her own social network and creating and developing new opportunities in the person's own community. The community is seen as a resource and the place the person needs to be connected to, with the support of the service. This type of service has an individual focus, based on individual needs, as opposed to a mass management approach whereby groups of people engage in activities that would normally be undertaken on an individual basis.

O'Brien and O'Brien (1989) describe the 'five valued experiences' they consider all people seek out: relationships, choice, contributing, sharing ordinary places and dignity (Figure 23.3). They propose that all services for people with disability should be designed on the basis of these five valued experiences. When services operate in a way that ensures that service users experience these, they achieve what the O'Briens refer to as the five service accomplishments: community participation, promoting choice, supporting contribution, community presence and encouraging valued social roles. The five valued experiences and the accomplishments resonate for all people as the hallmarks of a fulfilled life.

Figure 23.3. The Five Valued Experiences and Service Accomplishments

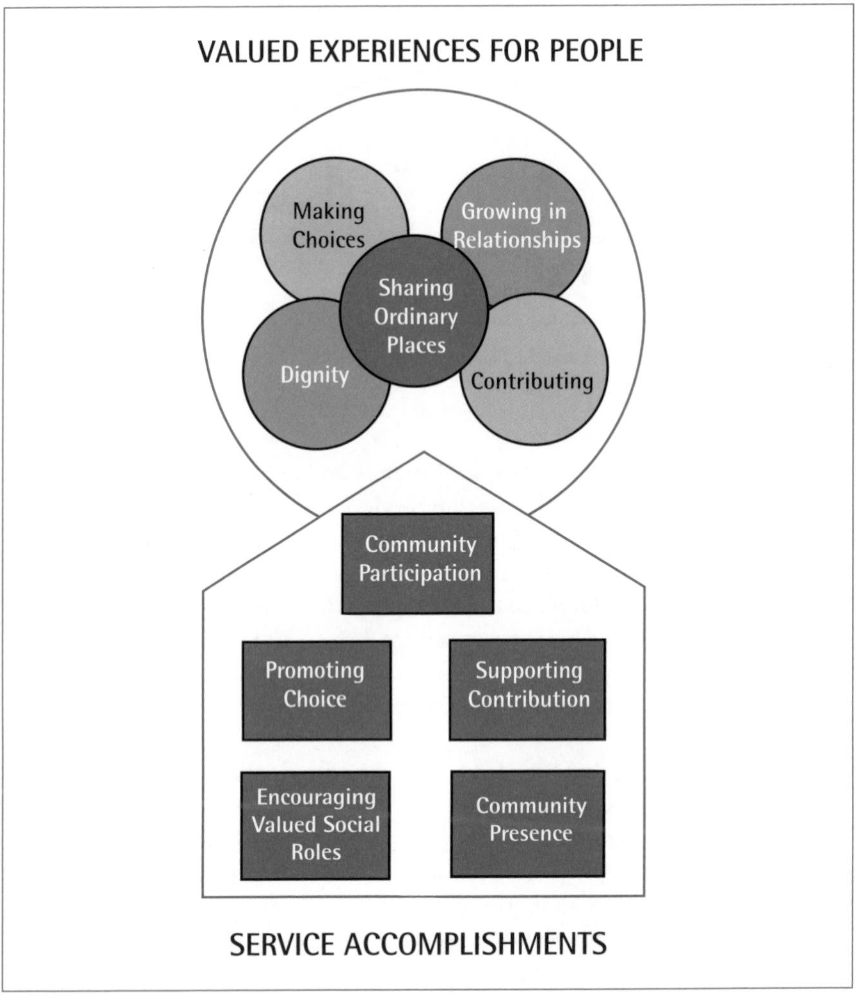

Source: Adapted from O'Brien and O'Brien (1989).

SOCIAL POLICY, LEGISLATION AND DISABILITY IN IRELAND

Box 23.1 outlines some of the major policy documents and items of legislation that have come into effect in Ireland in the last decade or so. A comprehensive review of each is beyond the scope of this chapter and so the list presented here cannot be definitive (see www.fedvol.ie and www.nda.ie for further information), but it does highlight how fast this area has changed and the breadth and depth of some of these changes. The initiation of these changes is attributed to the work of people with disabilities themselves, commencing with *A Strategy for Equality* (Commission on the Status of People with Disabilities 1996).

Box 23.1. Disability-related Policy and Legislation, 1996–2007

1996	*A Strategy for Equality: The Report of the Commission on the Status of People with Disabilities* was the first time that people with disabilities led the way in the development of a major strategy document that would directly affect their lives. It made 404 recommendations calling for the delivery of quality services within a framework of rights, not charity.
1998	The Employment Equality Act outlaws discrimination in employment matters on nine grounds, including disability. The Education Act provides the legal basis for the equal treatment of children in education, including children with disabilities.
2000	The Equal Status Act outlaws certain forms of non-employment-related discrimination, including access to public transport. The Education (Welfare) Act provides a legal basis to allow parents to educate their children in a place other than a recognised school. The Comhairle Act introduced the concept of advocacy into law and social services, but not specifically in relation to disability.
2001	The Mental Health Act established the Mental Health Commission, provided for the protection of people involuntarily admitted to approved hospitals/centres and established an inspectorate of mental health services to offer protection of rights.
2004	The *National Disability Strategy* is a major national strategy focused on delivering institutional, legal and financial reforms targeted at improving the status and quality of lives of people with disabilities in Ireland. The Equality Act changed the basis for determining discrimination on the grounds of disability in the workplace. The Education for Persons with Special Needs Act aims to enhance the rights of children with special educational needs to an appropriate education. Final draft of the *National Standards for Disability Services* developed by the National Disability Authority. Further to the Health Act 2007, these standards now come under the remit of the Health Information and Quality Authority (HIQA). The Comhairle Amendment Bill amends the Comhairle Act 2000 to provide for a personal advocacy service for people with disabilities. This is an element of the National Disability Strategy.
2005	The Disability Act makes provision for the assessment of health and educational need (implemented on a phased basis); the allocation of

resources to meet those needs; appeals process where needs are not being met; access to public buildings, information and services; public sector employment and plans in six sectoral areas.

Six Disability Sectoral Plans are a second strand of the Disability Strategy and set out how services will be improved by each of six government departments to make them more accessible and more open to people with disability.

2006   *From Rhetoric to Rights: Second Shadow Report to the United Nations Committee on the Rights of the Child 2006*, is critical of the government's failure to introduce rights-based legislation in Ireland relating to children, including children with disabilities.

The social partnership agreement Towards 2016 listed a number of priority actions relating to disability. These included progressing training and employment matters for people with disability and public sector employment promoting employment and employment retention of people with disability.

National Disability Survey – 17,000 people interviewed to establish the exact numbers and circumstances of people with disability in Ireland. As of May 2009, the Central Statistics Office (CSO) has not yet published any findings of the survey.

A Vision for Change: Report of the Expert Group on Mental Health Policy sets out a comprehensive policy framework for mental health services in Ireland for the next seven to 10 years. It includes a section on mental health services for people with a disability.

2007   The Health Act 2007 establishes the Health Information and Quality Authority (HIQA), which has statutory responsibility for setting and monitoring standards on safety and quality in health and social and personal services.

The Citizens Information Act amended the Comhairle Act of 2000 to include definitions of disability and social service. It also provided for the setting up of a new personal advocacy service. A new job role, Personal Advocate, was created to deliver this service. Some, but not all, people with disability are entitled to a Personal Advocate.

Quality Framework for Mental Health Services in Ireland outlines a new approach to the way in which statutory services will work with people who experience mental health difficulties. It marks a radical change to how such services are delivered.

The UN Convention on the Protection and Promotion of the Rights and Dignity of Persons with Disabilities. Ireland is one of 126 UN member states to sign up to this convention. At the time of writing, 29 UN countries have ratified the convention – Ireland has not yet done so.

The list of policy and legislative changes is impressive. Undoubtedly, good foundations in terms of legislation, policy and action plans have been laid and there is reason to be optimistic and hopeful. However, the changes are new and the coming years will tell what, if any, difference all of this has made. At the time of writing this chapter, the life situation of many people with disability remains bleak and the statistics are sobering.

Nearly a tenth of people in Ireland have a disability – approximately 9.3 per cent of the population, or 394,000 individuals (Central Statistics Office 2007a). Research has shown that people with disabilities have lower participation in education and far lower participation in the workforce than people without disabilities. This research also revealed that people with disabilities are at twice the risk of experiencing poverty than other citizens (NDA 2005b). A report published by the Equality Authority/NDA in 2007, *Dynamics of Disability and Social Inclusion* (Gannon and Nolan 2007), found that half of those who were ill or disabled had no formal educational qualification, compared to one-fifth of other adults. In terms of social inclusion and participation, people with a chronic illness or disability were much less likely than others to be a member of a club or association, to talk to neighbours most days or to have had an afternoon or evening out for entertainment in the previous fortnight. Commenting in the foreword to this report, Niall Crowley of the Equality Authority notes that it highlights 'the degree to which people are hampered in their daily lives by illness or disability. The more they are hampered the greater the disadvantage. This reflects the disabling nature of society and its institutions' (Gannon and Nolan 2007: 3).

In terms of planning for service provision, for years there was a paucity of information and accurate statistics relating to all disability areas. This has changed: in 1995, the National Intellectual Disability Database (NIDD) was established and it was followed in 2003 by a similar database for physical and sensory disability (NPSDD). Under the remit of the HSE, both databases aim to ensure the availability of accurate information for planning purposes. A Census for Irish Psychiatric Units and Hospitals was undertaken in 2006 (Daly et al. 2006). The Census of Population included a question on disability for the first time ever in 2002 and contained a full section on disability in 2006. In 2006–2007, the Central Statistics Office undertook a major survey on disability. At the time of writing, no information from this survey has been published. Box 23.2 below provides some statistics from the relevant databases, which establish that significant needs in relation to the provision of services still exist.

Box 23.2. Disability Database(s) Information

National Intellectual Disability Database 2007

- 2,430 people without any service or a major element of service (day care or residential or both). These individuals will require services if not immediately, then over the period between 2008–2012.
- 2,181 full-time residential places required, the highest number since the database was established.
- 207 people identified as needing to transfer from living in psychiatric hospitals to more appropriate accommodation.
- 24,898 people with intellectual disability in receipt of services. This represents 97 per cent of the total numbers registered on the database.

Source: Kelly, Kelly and Craig (2007).

National Physical and Sensory Disability Database 2007

- 29,089 people registered on the database, representing 65 per cent of the estimated national target coverage for this database.
- 23,565 people lived with family members.
- 7,551 people require assessment for personal assistance and support services.
- 4,236 people require an alternative or additional service to their existing services.
- 10,623 people requested at least one technical aid or appliance.

Source: O'Donovan and Doyle (2007).

Mental Health: Irish Psychiatric Units and Hospitals Census 2006

- 3,389 people were resident in such units or psychiatric hospitals. This represents a reduction of 83 per cent in the numbers of people resident in psychiatric units and hospitals since 1963.
- Two-thirds of people resident were single. Single males had the highest rate of hospitalisation.
- Over one-third (34 per cent) had a diagnosis of schizophrenia; 7 per cent had a diagnosis of intellectual disability, of which two-thirds had been hospitalised for 10 years or more.

Source: Daly et al. (2006).

While the needs are still significant, changes are evident. In the public sector, the mainstreaming of services includes provision of information and services by Citizens Information Centres, FÁS and government departments to *all* people, including those with and without disabilities. Changes are also evident in service organisations. People with disability and their families/advocates have become more involved in the management of organisations at different levels: at governance level, parents now sit on boards of management; service users and parent councils/representative groups have developed in some organisations; and people with disability sit on interview boards for employing frontline staff.

DISABILITY AND THE SOCIAL CARE PRACTITIONER

This book relates to the practice of social care, so this chapter now moves to focus (briefly) on the role of the social care practitioner in relation to disability and working in the disability area. As with other areas addressed by this book, disability falls under the provisions of the Health and Social Care Professionals Act 2005. Disability services employ numbers of social care practitioners and social care leaders. Social care professionals working in disability services, in addition to the background outlined above, need an understanding of a number of key principles for excellent performance of the role.

In the context of the social model, Hennessy (2002) outlines three primary principles that should govern service delivery in the field of disability:

- *Self-determination*: A process that differs uniquely from person to person according to what each individual determines is necessary and desirable to create a satisfying and personally meaningful life. Self-determination is both person centred and person directed and acknowledges the rights of people with disabilities to take charge of and responsibility for their own lives.
- *Participation*: Concerned with taking part in activities with other people. Community participation suggests active involvement with other community members, not only in ordinary activities, but also in active decision-making that directly affects people's own lives.
- *Empowerment*: Power is given to people with disabilities so that they can directly control their own lives rather than other people fulfilling this role on their behalf. While the concept of empowerment has become quite popular within the human services in recent years, the reality of empowerment has yet to become the norm for the majority of people with disabilities.

The overarching concept within which these principles fit is best described as *advocacy*. Advocacy has many definitions, but in its broadest terms fundamentally relates to human rights.

[A]dvocacy is concerned with getting one's needs, rights, opinions and hopes taken seriously and acted upon. It allows people to participate more fully in society by expressing their own viewpoints, by participating in management and decision-making, and by availing of the rights to which they are entitled. (Commission on the Status of People with Disabilities 1996: 106)

A comprehensive discussion of advocacy and all the types of advocacy would necessitate a chapter of its own (see Forum of People with Disabilities 2001 for an excellent overview). The right to a personal advocate for people with disabilities became enshrined in legislation in Ireland in 2007 in the Citizens Information Act. This followed many years when disability groups sought to have advocacy recognised as a right to which people were entitled. They called for any introduction of advocacy services to be framed within the language of human and constitutional rights (Forum of People with Disabilities 2001: 60). While Ireland now has legislation to protect the delivery of advocacy services, there are limitations in that not all people with disability are entitled to a Personal Advocate. Access will depend on a number of factors, including the degree of difficulty experienced by the person in obtaining a service, the degree of harm experienced if they fail to obtain a service and the availability of advocacy support from other sources. At the time of writing, the introduction of state-supported personal advocacy services had been postponed for budgetary reasons.

Social care professionals most often work within what is called *service-system advocacy*, where the advocacy model and service are based within the service for the person with disability. This type of advocacy is dependent on the service, its staffing and resources. In such a system, the social care practitioner may find him or herself acting to support a person in one or more advocacy types: self-advocacy (where the person with disability advocates on his/her own behalf with support), group advocacy (where a number of people come together to advocate on common issues) or as a direct advocate (representing the decisions and wishes of the person with disability). In some situations, tensions or absolute contradictions can arise between the wishes of the person and the wishes of the service. This is a difficult position for any practitioner to find him or herself in. Ultimately, it must be remembered that 'advocacy' is a rights-based concept and needs to be approached from this standpoint.

Working from the basis of rights brings us to another fundamental aspect of working as a social care professional in services for people with disability. This is the concept of person-centred planning (PCP):

> [A]t the heart of a person-centred approach to planning services lies an appreciation of the person as a unique individual, requiring that all planning is based on supporting each individual to lead his or her life as and how he or she wishes. (National Disability Authority 2004: 11)

Person-centred planning is an approach to planning services that recognises each person as a unique individual, with his/her own wishes as to how they want life to be. It moves away from a focus on the disability to one that sees the person first.

It is about 'citizenship, inclusion in family, community and the mainstream of life. It is about self-determination' (NDA 2004: 12). Research has shown PCP to have a positive impact on the lives of people with learning disabilities. It was associated with benefits in the areas of community involvement, contact with friends and family and exercising choice in life matters (Institute for Health Research 2005). Many service organisations in Ireland would claim to be delivering person-centred services, but as yet there is little evidence from research to support this. To be truly person centred, services need to be clearly and *measurably* operating PCP in line with its key principles (see text box below).

Six Principles of Person-Centred Planning (PCP)

1. Planning is undertaken from the individual's perspective and his or her life – it is not planning from the perspective of the service organisation.
2. The process is creative – asking what is possible rather than limiting an individual to what is available.
3. The process takes into account all resources available to an individual, not just those on offer within the service.
4. PCP requires a serious and genuine commitment and co-operation by all people involved in the process.
5. PCP is an art, not a science – best viewed as an organic, evolving process.
6. The objective of PCP is not the development of a plan – but making a real difference to a person's life.

Source: NDA (2004: 17).

In the context of social care practice, Hennessy (2002) outlines five key priorities.

- *Protection:* Social care practitioners assist in providing protection to people from the risks of ordinary life and also from particular risks a service user's present situation, current difficulties or life circumstances may create. In this protection role, we are also concerned with protection of the community from those whose behaviour may be dangerous and/or who cannot be responsible for their own behaviour.
- *Rehabilitation and habilitation:* The practitioner may be supporting a person or group of people who have suffered or are suffering breakdown, disablement, bereavement, loss, trauma and change through enforced circumstances, usually outside their own control. In rehabilitation work, the concern is with those who have lost a living environment of mutual supports, including family, friends and community.

    In habilitation work, the focus is about enabling those who may never have had certain skills before, for example, supporting someone to live independently for the first time in his or her life.

- *Prevention*: Here the social care practitioner may work to prevent the often drastic and inappropriate reactions to a person's circumstances or condition by institutional responses to their needs, which can often be assessed inaccurately. The practitioner may seek to prevent the collapse of the person's capacity to cope with the normal stress of everyday life.
- *Care*: Social care can be defined as care for those who cannot care for themselves by virtue of their circumstances and/or condition.
- *Quality of life*: These issues are about the service response that enhances and improves the quality of a person's life by helping to provide services that are necessary, chosen, normal, continual and that can be evaluated in terms of the O'Briens' five service accomplishments.

Whatever job is undertaken by a social care practitioner in disability services, the concepts of advocacy and person-centred planning are fundamental, not just as concepts or service approaches, but as an underlying value base that recognises and accepts people with disability to be the same as everyone else and so entitled to self-determination, participation and empowerment.

CONCLUSION

There is no mistaking that disability is a challenging topic. This chapter has outlined how in the last decade or so, the area has been impacted directly by no fewer than 11 Acts of the Oireachtas in addition to a plethora of policy, strategic and planning documents (only some of which this chapter referred to). This perhaps seems less surprising if we view disability as part of the continuum of life that affects all of us in some way or other. Aligned to this is an acceptance that people with disability have the same human and constitutional rights as all other people and that all service provision should operate from this perspective.

One of the most significant changes in disability service provision has been the move from the traditional/medical model to the social model. The social model operates on the principle that people are disabled not by their impairments, but by the failure of society to put supports in place to enable the full participation of all its members. The Acts and policy changes implemented in recent years claim to support the social model, but the extent to which they have actually done so varies. At the time of writing, two items challenge how far we have actually progressed. First, research indicates that a great number of people with disability are significantly worse off than the rest of us in terms of economic wealth and social inclusion. The second is that Ireland has yet to ratify the UN Convention on the Protection and Promotion of the Rights and Dignity of Persons with Disabilities. The legislation and policy changes are new but significant. Time will tell if they can effect change.

And so a new chapter begins in the delivery of services to people with disability in Ireland. Social care practitioners who choose to work in this area are entering at a most challenging and interesting point. They have an opportunity to contribute to fundamental change in attitudes and approaches to how services work with people with disability and their families and advocates. They are in a prime position to work from the principles of empowerment, partnership and equal citizenship, supporting advocacy, person-centred services and the right of all people to live the life of their choosing.

24
Travellers in Ireland and Issues of Social Care

Ashling Jackson

OVERVIEW

This chapter discusses the origins of the Traveller community in Ireland and Traveller culture. Characteristics of the Traveller community are examined, as well as Travellers' ethnic status and the extent of discrimination against Travellers in Ireland. Irish Travellers and minority/dominant group relations are reviewed. Traveller children in care, Traveller perspectives on health, barriers to health services as identified by Travellers and issues of access to education are discussed. Lastly, the chapter concludes by looking at issues for consideration by social care practitioners when working with Traveller groups.

Figure 24.1. 'Ask the Experts'

Source: Pavee Point (2004). Reproduced with kind permission.

WHO ARE THE IRISH TRAVELLERS?

The Equal Status Act 2000 defines Travellers as:

> the community of people who are commonly called Travellers and who are identified (both by themselves and others) as people with a shared history, culture and traditions including, historically, a nomadic way of life on the island of Ireland. (Equal Status Act 2000: 7)

Travellers are often incorrectly considered part of the nomadic Romani, an ethnic group that originated in a region of India, now widespread throughout Europe. However, while both are nomadic, Irish Travellers are native to Ireland. They boast their own culture, customs and traditions, as well as being noted for their musical and storytelling abilities. Irish Travellers are Roman Catholic and speak their own language: Cant, or Gammon.

The historical origins of Irish Travellers remain unclear, with a number of existing theories. Their language and various historical references seem to indicate that they are the remnants of an ancient class of wandering poets, joined by those driven off the land during different times of social and economic upheaval, such as Cromwell's campaign (1649–50), the Battle of the Boyne (1690) and the Battle of Aughrim (1691). Travellers have been seen to be descendants of native chieftains, dispossessed during the English plantations of the seventeenth and eighteenth centuries. They may also be descendants of people left homeless as a result of the potato famines of the nineteenth century. Though the origins of the Traveller community in Ireland are uncertain, that they exist as a discrete group with a separate identity was recognised as far back as 1834, 'when the Travelling community was clearly distinguished from other poor who wandered the land in the report of the Royal Commission on the Poor Laws in that year' (Kendrick 1998: 1).

TRAVELLER CULTURE

'Travellers are an indigenous minority, documented as being part of Irish society for centuries. Travellers have a long shared history and value system which make them a distinct group. They have their own language, customs and traditions' (Pavee Point 2006: 1).

Pavee Point, an Irish national Traveller representative organisation, identifies language, nomadism, music, storytelling and the Traveller economy as among the important features of Traveller culture and heritage. It is here that there is variation with the settled population in Ireland. Being a Traveller is an ascribed status. This means that for an individual to be called a Traveller, he/she must have at least one Traveller parent. One cannot just become a Traveller.

Nomadism

The Commission on Itinerancy (1963) defined a Traveller as a person who habitually wanders from place to place and has no fixed abode. This narrow definition fails to include settled or partially settled Travellers who choose to live in houses as opposed to on campsites or halting sites. However, nomadism is a key component of Traveller culture. Being housed can restrict freedom to travel and result in a range of unanticipated health problems, such as depression (Duggan-Jackson 2000). McCann et al. (1994) noted that some Travellers become physically sick and depressed when they move into houses, and never adjust psychologically to living permanently in one place. It was also pointed out by McCann et al. that just 'as settled people remain settled people when they travel, Travellers remain Travellers, even when they are not travelling. Travellers who are not moving can, and do, retain the mindset of nomads' (McCann et al. 1994: 96).

Music and Storytelling

The tradition of storytelling is used as a way to disseminate information among Travellers. Research into the health needs of Travellers in the Midlands showed that Traveller group interaction is based on storytelling (Duggan-Jackson 2000). Health information is shared through storytelling sessions and health actions suggested. The validity of the health information given out depends on the person recounting the story. This in itself highlights the importance of generalised health awareness among all Travellers in order to reduce information inconsistencies. Word of mouth is a strong and influential method of communication among the Traveller community in Ireland.

TRAVELLER EMPLOYMENT

Table 24.1 shows that 41.2 per cent of Irish Travellers are unemployed, compared to 4.6 per cent of white Irish and 26.6 per cent of those with African or other black background. In Census 2006, of those Travellers who stated the type of work they did, the highest percentages were in manufacturing (9 per cent), construction (9 per cent), wholesale and retail trade (9 per cent) and health and social work (9 per cent). This very high unemployment rate among Travellers indicates non-engagement with mainstream economy employment opportunities. An explanation for this may be that opportunities for economic activity and employment traditionally occupied by Travellers, such as scrap metal recycling, horse-trading and market trading, are diminishing. This type of work means that Travellers can move from place to place and generate an income. The 'Traveller economy' is the term used to describe work the Travellers initiate themselves. The Casual Trading Act 1995 (which prohibits casual trading without a licence and imposes restrictions on casual trading) and the Control of Horse Act 1996 (which provides for the control of horses and the licensing of horses in urban and other areas where horses cause a danger to persons or property or nuisance) have imposed restrictions on Traveller economic activity.

Economic growth in Ireland has also had negative consequences. 'There is less of a market for recycled/second hand goods due to increased spending power nationally' (Irish Traveller Movement 2002: 1). Therefore, while there may be high employment generally in Ireland, the nature of that employment may not suit the lifestyle or traditional work skills of a marginalised group such as Travellers.

Table 24.1. Employment Status by Ethnicity, 2006

| Ethnicity | % of cohort | | | |
	Employed	Unemployed	Not in labour force	Total
White Irish	56.3	4.6	39.1	100.0
White Irish Traveller	13.8	41.2	45.0	100.0
Other white background	71.8	7.6	20.6	100.0
African or other black background	40.7	26.6	32.6	100.0
Chinese	47.8	6.3	45.8	100.0
Other Asian background	62.9	7.8	29.3	100.0
Total aged 15 and over	57.2	5.2	37.6	100.0

Source: Central Statistics Office (2007d: 30); see www.cso.ie.

The Traveller perception of what constitutes employment differs from that of the settled population. In a study conducted in the Health Service Executive (Midlands region), 26 out of the 100 female Traveller research participants specified themselves as being employed outside the home (Duggan-Jackson 2000). When this was explored, it emerged that a Traveller definition of employment was not that typically considered as employment by the dominant population, that is, structured work activities outside the home. In all cases where women attended a training centre, they specified themselves as being in employment (22 out of 26 participants). An allowance is paid to trainees in training centres, but the nature of the allowance is to support training and is not a wage/salary. Therefore, any activity outside of the home that generates an income is defined by Travellers as employment. Only four respondents had 'regular' work outside the training centre – self-employed (1); playschool on halting site (1); local Traveller organisation (2) (Duggan-Jackson 2000: 48).

CHARACTERISTICS OF THE TRAVELLER POPULATION IN IRELAND

Number of Travellers in Ireland

According to the Central Statistics Office (CSO), close to 22,435 Irish Travellers were enumerated in the 2006 census. This represents 0.5 per cent of the Irish population at the time of the 2006 census. Of the towns with a population of 5,000 or more in April 2006, Tuam had the highest proportion of Irish Travellers (7.7 per cent). This was followed by Longford (4.6 per cent), Birr (4 per cent) and Ballinasloe (3.0 per cent) (Central Statistics Office 2007c).

Age Breakdown of Traveller Community

The Traveller community in Ireland has an age structure very different from that of the settled population. According to the 2006 census, two out of every five Travellers were aged less than 15 years, compared with one in five for the population as a whole. There is a very high proportion of Irish Travellers in the 0–14 age group (41.4 per cent), which is twice the overall population rate of 20.4 per cent. Older Travellers, that is, those aged 65 years and over, accounted for just 2.6 per cent of the total Traveller population, compared with 11 per cent for the general population (see Figure 24.2). The distinctive age structure of the Traveller community resulted in a median age of 18, compared with a national figure of 33 (Central Statistics Office 2007c).

Living Conditions

In 2006, 15,195 of the 22,002 Travellers residing in private households lived in permanent accommodation. A further 5,489 lived in temporary accommodation, while 1,318 did not indicate the type of accommodation they occupied. Four out of 10 Travellers who responded to the question therefore lived in temporary accommodation (Central Statistics Office 2007c).

Health

On a number of key indicators, Traveller health status is poorer than that of the settled population. Life expectancy at birth in Ireland was 76.7 years for males and 81.5 years for females in 2004–2006 (Central Statistics Office 2008: 54). The life expectancy of Traveller men is 10 years shorter than for settled men (Combat Poverty Agency 2004: 3). Traveller women have a life expectancy of 12 years less than settled women (Combat Poverty Agency 2004: 3). Infant mortality among the settled population in Ireland was 3.7 births per 1,000 population in 2006 (Institut National D'Études Démographique 2008). However, infant mortality

Figure 24.2. Percentage of Population by Age Group, 2006

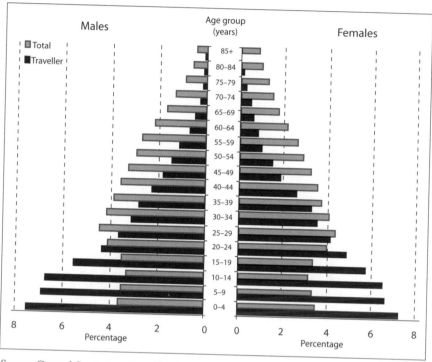

Source: Central Statistics Office (2007c: 28), www.cso.ie.

among Travellers is two and a half times higher than in the settled population (Combat Poverty Agency 2004: 3).

Research shows that children's health is given the highest priority in the Travelling community. Illness in children prompts biomedical treatment much more often than adult illness. There is distinct evidence that Traveller children suffer from a higher incidence of illnesses than other children (especially those of the upper respiratory and lower gastro-intestinal tracts) and of hospitalisations for at least some of those illnesses (Treadwell 1998). Treadwell (1998) points out that there is a gradation in the seriousness of children's health and the necessity to seek biomedical care:

> This gradation is based on different stages of the life cycle. That is, concern and care seeking strategies for illnesses are highest for young children and infants, slightly less for older children and generally fairly low for adults, and is explained by the concept that Traveller children become 'hardier' as they grow older. (Treadwell 1998: 127)

Younger children who are considered more vulnerable, less capable of rational actions and indeed less hardy are given much more personal, individual attention and care than older children. That is not to say that older children do not get any personal attention, but rather the care and attention they receive is predicated upon the concept that they are more mature, more capable and hardier individuals. Traveller parents socialise their children to become independent adults, a gradual and constant process that begins in early childhood.

Marriage

Marriage rates are higher for the Traveller community (56.3 per cent) than for the settled community (49.2 per cent) (Central Statistics Office 2007c). Most notably, Travellers tend to marry younger than the settled population. Some 21.6 per cent of male Travellers aged 15–24 years were married, compared with 1.4 per cent for the same age group in the general male population. The corresponding rates for females were 26 per cent and 2.7 per cent, respectively (Central Statistics Office 2007c). Marriage rates are also higher in the 25–44 year age group for Travellers (63 per cent) than for the settled population (48 per cent) (Central Statistics Office 2007c).

Premarital co-habitation as a sequence of relationship development occurs for both the settled and Traveller communities. However, while 8 per cent of settled households comprise co-habiting couples (including those with children), only 2.7 per cent of Traveller households (including those with children) comprise co-habiting couples (Central Statistics Office 2007c).

TRAVELLERS AS AN ETHNIC GROUP IN IRELAND?

Ethnicity has been defined as 'a shared cultural heritage. Members of an ethnic category have common ancestors, a language or a religion that, together, confer a distinctive social identity' (Macionis and Plummer 2008: 330).

Irish Travellers, although accorded rights as a named group (Travellers) in Irish policy (see Table 24.2), are not formally recognised as a distinct ethnic group within Ireland. As far back as 1963, the Commission on Itinerancy noted:

> Itinerants (or travellers as they prefer themselves to be called) do not constitute a single homogenous group, tribe or community within the nation although the settled population are inclined to regard them as such. Neither do they constitute a separate ethnic group. There is no system of unified authority or government and no individual or group of individuals has any powers or control over the itinerant members of the community. (1963: 37)

Ireland ratified the Convention on the Elimination of All Forms of Racial Discrimination (CERD) in 2000 and submitted its first report in 2004. In CERD, the term 'racial discrimination' is defined as meaning:

> any distinction, exclusion, restriction or preference based on race, colour, descent, or national or ethnic origin which has the purpose or effect of

nullifying or impairing the recognition, enjoyment or exercise, on an equal footing, of human rights and fundamental freedoms in the political, economic, social, cultural or any field of public life. (Office for the High Commissioner for Human Rights 1969: 1)

In the course of its reporting to CERD, the Irish government declared that Irish Travellers 'do not constitute a distinct group from the population as a whole in terms of race, colour, descent or national or ethnic origin' (Government of Ireland 2004: 90). The government insisted that it remained committed to challenging discrimination against Irish Travellers and has defined membership of the Traveller community as a separate ground on which it is unlawful to discriminate under equality legislation (Employment Equality Act 1998; Equal Status Act 2000). This was not meant 'to provide a lesser level of protection to Travellers compared to that afforded to members of ethnic minorities' (Government of Ireland 2004: 90).

Following its consideration of this report, the UN Committee on the Elimination of Racial Discrimination commented on the government's position in its concluding observations as follows:

Recalling its General Recommendation VIII on the principle of self-identification, the Committee expresses concern at the State party's position with regard to the recognition of Travellers as an ethnic group. The Committee is of the view that the recognition of Travellers as an ethnic group has important implications under the Convention. (Committee on the Elimination of Racial Discrimination Ireland 2005: Article 1 and 5)

The Irish government's response to this was:

The Government accepts the right of Travellers to their cultural identity and is committed to applying all the protections afforded to national minorities under relevant international conventions. However, the Government has not concluded that Travellers are ethnically different from the majority of Irish people. The point also needs to be made that the Government is not alone in making this assessment. The 1995 Task Force Report on the Traveller Community, which consisted of Government Departments, civil society and Traveller representatives did not recommend that Travellers should be identified as an ethnic minority. (Committee on the Elimination of Racial Discrimination 2006: 29–30)

Traveller groups such as the Irish Traveller Movement, Pavee Point and local Traveller organisations have been lobbying for years (since the 1980s) for Traveller ethnicity to be recognised.

The Equality Authority is an independent body set up under the Employment Equality Act 1998 and was established on 18 October 1999. The conclusion to the Equality Authority report *Traveller Ethnicity* makes a very clear statement on this issue:

This report validates the position of the Equality Authority in recognizing Travellers as an ethnic group. It is recommended that the Government should now recognise Travellers as an ethnic group and that this recognition should be reflected in all policies, programmes and institutional practices that impact on the Traveller community. (Equality Authority 2006a: 65)

DISCRIMINATION TOWARDS THE TRAVELLER COMMUNITY IN IRELAND

In 2000, a nationwide survey (Behaviour and Attitudes Ireland 2000) examined attitudes to Travellers and minority groups. It indicated that 42 per cent of the population held negative attitudes towards Travellers. Those who were negatively disposed towards Travellers tended to be more prejudiced than the average person and their prejudice tended to be accentuated in the case of Travellers. Similarly, research commissioned by Amnesty International (Lansdowne Market Research Ltd 2001) shows that prejudice towards minority groups focuses specifically on Travellers and that they are least likely to be viewed as a sector of society that is welcome either personally or in the neighbourhood. This view seems to have changed little over time. A public attitudes survey (Milward Brown 2004), published by the government's 'Know Racism' campaign in February 2004, showed that 72 per cent of respondents agreed that the settled community did not want members of the Traveller community living amongst them, while 48 per cent disagreed that Travellers made a positive contribution to Irish society. This research also showed that there is a strong link between non-interaction and negative perceptions about minority ethnic groups in Ireland. This includes Travellers, as well as other ethnic minority groups. Therefore, limited social contact with the Traveller community can lead to negative perceptions about the Traveller community.

In its 2007 *Annual Report*, the Equality Authority reported that the 'Traveller ground' constituted the second highest area of case files under the Equal Status Acts (63 of 328 case files, or 19 per cent). The majority of these cases related to allegations of discrimination in relation to educational establishments and the provision of education. The Traveller ground was also the dominant factor in cases under the Intoxicating Liquor Act, which governs access to licensed premises (Equality Authority 2007). This shows that Travellers continue to experience discrimination on a regular basis in Ireland.

IRISH TRAVELLERS AND MINORITY/DOMINANT GROUP RELATIONS

For sociologists, a *dominant group* is a group in society that has a disproportionate amount of power. Importantly, a minority is not always a numerical minority, for example, the black population of South Africa during the apartheid regime. A *minority group* refers to a group that does not have proportionate access to power. Often, because of physical or cultural characteristics, a *minority group* is singled out from others for unequal treatment. This is the case for Travellers in Ireland.

The relationship between the dominant and minority groups in any society can take the following forms.

- *Segregation:* The practice of physically separating occupants of some social statuses from occupants of others, for example, segregated seating in public venues.
- *Assimilation:* Members of ethnic groups are expected to conform to the culture of the dominant group.
- *Amalgamation:* The process by which two or more previous racial, ethnic or nationality identified groups intermarry and have children.
- *Genocide:* The systematic annihilation of one category of people by another (as in so-called 'ethnic cleansing' or the Holocaust).
- *Pluralism:* A state in which racial and ethnic minorities are distinct but have social parity.

Very often, the relationship between the dominant group in a society and the minority group is reflected in government policy. Indeed, it may even be a result of government policy. Recent government policy within Ireland is more inclusive of the views of Travellers, with increased importance being given to Traveller opinion in the drawing up and implementation of policy that responds to Traveller-identified needs. The *Traveller Health Strategy 2002–2005* is an example of this. Travellers were consulted in the design of the strategy. There is definitely a move away from assimilation towards pluralism at an official government level. This process of change is documented in Table 24.2.

Table 24.2. Sample of Legislation in Ireland Affecting the Traveller Community

1963	Commission on Itinerancy recommended assimilation of Travellers into the settled community.
1983	*Report of the Travelling People Review Body* promoted the integration of Travellers into mainstream society without adequately supporting and promoting their cultural identity.
1988	Housing Act provides the first statutory (government) recognition of Traveller-specific accommodation.
1991	Prohibition of Incitement to Hatred Act. Travellers are named specifically.
1992	Housing (Miscellaneous Provisions) Act. Section 10 of this Act empowers local authorities to remove Travellers who are camped unofficially to an official site anywhere within a five-mile radius of where they are.

1993	Unfair Dismissals (Amendment) Act. Travellers are named specifically.
1994	*Shaping a Healthier Future: A Strategy for Effective Health Care in the 1990s* contained a section on Traveller health and pledged to address the particular health needs of the Traveller population.
1995	*White Paper on Education: Charting our Education Future* called for full participation in school life by Traveller children by means of integration, while at the same time respecting Traveller culture. *The Report of the Task Force on the Travelling Community* made a large number of recommendations covering all aspects of Traveller life and government policy relating to Travellers. It acknowledges the distinct culture and identity of the Traveller community.
1998	Housing (Traveller Accommodation) Act obliges local authorities to meet the current and projected needs of the Traveller community. Sections of the Act give increased powers of eviction to local authorities.
1999	Employment Equality Act outlaws discrimination in employment on several grounds, including membership of the Traveller community.
2001	Housing (Miscellaneous Provisions) Bill. Local authorities were granted additional powers to protect public land from trespass by large numbers of temporary dwellings.
2001–02	Youth Work Act covers the provision of youth services to Travellers and the settled community. It is the first Act regarding youth work.
2000–2004	Equal Status Acts prevent discrimination against Travellers. Travellers are named specifically as one of the groups against which discrimination must not occur.
2002–2005	In *Traveller Health: A National Strategy*, there is now recognition at official level that Travellers are a distinct minority with their own culture and beliefs. Most importantly, they have a right to have their culture recognised in the planning and provision of services.
2005	The National Action Plan against Racism notes that 'racism takes different, sometimes overlapping, forms and impacts on a range of groups in Ireland, including: racism experienced by Travellers' (Department of Justice, Equality and Law Reform 2005: 29). The plan states that 'Irish Travellers are an important part of the existing cultural diversity in Ireland. Travellers are an indigenous Irish community with a shared history, a nomadic way of life and distinct cultural identity' (Department of Justice, Equality and Law Reform 2005: 50).
2007	All Ireland Traveller Health Study launched by the Minister for Health and Children. This health study will develop and extend the information collected in the *Travellers Health Status Study – Vital Statistics of the Travelling People* (Barry et al. 1987) in 1987. However, and very importantly, data collection will be conducted by Traveller peer researchers. The final report is expected in 2010.

SOCIAL CARE AND THE TRAVELLER COMMUNITY

Traveller Children in Care

Traveller children are more likely to experience poverty and may also encounter issues associated with poor living conditions, such as alcohol abuse. As a consequence, they are likely to be identified as being at risk and in need of intervention measures such as community care services.

Traveller children, like settled children, may be taken into care for a variety of reasons. Sometimes a family is unable to look after a child because of problems in the home. In situations where a child needs to be placed into care, the responsibility lies with the local Health Services Executive to provide suitable accommodation. Children can be placed in care for short or long periods of time. A major issue for Travellers has been the placement of Traveller children in the care and the culture of settled people. This can influence the child and may often cause feelings of displacement and isolation.

As far back as 1983, the *Report of the Travelling People Review Body* recognised the specific needs of Traveller children. It stated that 'a small minority of Traveller families have multiple social problems. Many children of alcoholic parents lack adequate care and supervision' (Department of the Environment 1983: 131). It was noted that residential child care in the Dublin area was unsuitable for Travellers. The Travelling People Review Body recommended that Travellers should be provided with an opportunity to train to work with Travellers.

In response to the particular needs of Traveller children, the child care service, which has developed a system of fostering for children who need either temporary or long-term care, provides culture-specific options for Traveller children. These may be offered after an assessment of the child's situation and needs has been carried out by a social worker and other professionals involved with the child's family.

Supporting the cultural identity of the child can be difficult if they are placed without any contact with other Travellers in a residential setting, or with a settled foster family. This has been resolved somewhat by Travellers' Family Care, a voluntary organisation funded by the HSE under Section 10 of the Child Care Act 1991. It provides residential and family support services for Traveller families and their children from the Eastern region. The Shared Rearing Service recruits, trains and supports foster families from the Traveller community for Traveller children from throughout the country who need alternative family care when they cannot remain in their families of origin.

Services provided by Travellers' Family Care also include provision of an emergency and assessment unit in Dublin. This short-term unit offers emergency residential care for young Travellers and support for their families. An assessment service examines how their needs can be best met and an outreach service to the Travelling community is provided, where necessary.

Health Priorities for Travellers

Pavee Point has identified that Travellers are a distinct cultural group with different perceptions of health, disease and health care needs, requiring special consideration in the health service. Duggan-Jackson (2000) suggests that Traveller cognitive processes (ways of thinking and understanding) are communicated either through storytelling or creatively through art and craft. This extends to expressing health concerns and discussing health issues.

The patchwork quilt (Figure 24.3), created by the Primary Health Care Project trainees (Tullamore), epitomises a Traveller definition of health and what key components of primary health care should be. This project was set up as a collaborative initiative between the Health Services Executive (Midlands region), Tullamore Travellers' Movement and FÁS in 1999. Primary health care for Travellers means that they are trained to work within the Traveller community as health care workers, to provide health care advice and to act as an intermediary between Travellers and medical/allied health professionals.

A Traveller definition of health includes female health issues, hygienic living conditions, dental health, nutrition, exercise, immunisation and adequate child/general medical care. It also encompasses the importance of not smoking. Travellers also included depression as something to be overcome if full health status is to be achieved.

Figure 24.3. Traveller Definition of Health and What Key Components of Primary Health Care Should Be

Barriers to Health Services for Travellers

The Department of the Environment (1995) identified three obstacles for Travellers in accessing health services: illiteracy, failure to transfer records of Travellers who are mobile and prejudice on the part of the general public and service providers.

Treadwell (1998) has outlined that, for Travellers, once the health care system is accessed, generally through local family doctors and their practice(s), there are several things that Travellers expect. First, they expect to be seen immediately. If the illness episode has been determined to be serious enough to warrant medical attention, that attention should, they believe, be forthcoming. Travellers expect to attend services when it is convenient for them. Unfortunately, the services are not structured accordingly. Likewise, many Travellers feel that even when appointments are made ahead of time, there is always going to be a queue, and many will go in up to an hour after their appointment. While it may not be unusual to have to wait to see the doctor, even when an appointment is made, doctors have the expectation that patients will arrive on time. As Travellers have different expectations around time and around waiting, serious conflicts can arise. 'This can affect the services Travellers receive and make them frustrated – a situation very often unsatisfactory for both parties' (Treadwell 1998: 115).

This issue of Travellers' perception of time as a contributory factor towards missing appointments or being late was also identified in Bonnar's study (1996) on family planning needs of Travelling women in the Midlands region. Travellers often missed appointments or were late in arriving because of anticipated delays. She also emphasised that barriers exist to good health care for Travellers as a result of the mobility of Travellers, different cultural perceptions of illness and time-keeping, illiteracy, lack of postal services and absence of continuity of care, and medical records (Bonnar 1996).

Education

Localised research in Co. Wexford shows exceptionally low participation by Travellers in education, training and employment. Only 2.9 per cent of secondary-school age Traveller children were attending school in 1997 (Wexford Area Partnership 2000).

The Department of Education and Science *Survey of Traveller Education Provision* (2006) shows that just over 10 per cent of Travellers who enrol in post-primary schools complete their post-primary education. This contrasts with over 82 per cent of students generally (McCoy et al. 2007).

Table 24.3. Highest Level of Education Attained by Equality Ground, 2006

Ground	Primary only or less	Secondary only	Third level or higher	Total	Total
% of category, 000 persons					
Gender					
Male	21.4	50.0	28.7	100.0	1,221.6
Female	19.4	47.8	32.8	100.0	1,244.1
Marital status					
Single	14.9	45.0	40.1	100.0	717.9
Married	19.2	51.6	29.2	100.0	1,434.0
Sperated/divorced	21.7	54.1	24.2	100.0	147.0
Widowed	52.6	37.1	10.3	100.0	166.8
Family statues					
Lone parents	12.7	62.8	24.5	100.0	81.6
Other parents	7.7	57.6	34.7	100.0	743.5
Carers	16.5	51.7	31.8	100.0	139.4
Religion					
Roman Catholic	21.7	49.8	28.5	100.0	2,181.4
Other Christian	13.1	46.0	40.9	100.0	138.9
Other stated religions	8.0	35.1	56.8	100.0	24.5
No religion	6.9	38.6	54.5	100.0	120.9
Age group					
25–44	5.2	51.9	42.9	100.0	1,183.0
45–64	25.3	51.6	23.1	100.0	863.4
65 & over	52.9	34.5	12.6	100.0	419.2
Disability	43.7	39.8	16.5	100.0	296.2
Nationality					
Irish	21.9	48.9	29.3	100.0	2,194.6
UK	8.2	54.5	37.3	100.0	78.7
Other EU	4.3	55.2	40.5	100.0	81.3
Other stated	7.1	36.4	56.4	100.0	61.1
Not stated	37.5	46.9	15.6	100.0	12.6
Ethnicity					
White	20.7	49.2	30.1	100.0	2,363.5
Black or Black Irish	6.7	41.6	51.7	100.0	11.9
Asian or Asian Irish	7.3	27.2	65.5	100.0	19.7
Other including mixed	10.7	47.0	42.4	100.0	19.4
Irish Traveller	83.6	15.5	0.9	100.0	6.3
Total aged 25 & over	20.3	48.9	30.8	100.0	2,465.7

Source: Central Statistics Office (2007d: 11); see www.cso.ie.

When Travellers are compared to all other categories of people dealt with by the Equality Authority, their completion of second-level education is very low at 15.5 per cent. Only 0.9 per cent of Travellers progress to third-level education.

Noonan (1994) concluded that many Traveller parents doubt the relevance of what their children learn in settled schools and parents fear that their children will become alienated from the Traveller culture. However, the Pavee Point Parents and Traveller Education project attempts to redress this. The project was established in 2004 and aims to increase inclusion by providing information on the education system and encouraging Traveller parental involvement in school and parent organisations. There is also an emphasis on raising awareness among settled parents and those working within schools, acknowledging the impact they can have on Traveller access and participation in school and their potential for excluding Travellers.

CONCLUSION

Travellers, though severely marginalised and discriminated against in Irish society, are the experts on their own culture and on what constitutes acceptable care. This may range from family care to residential care, to health care to educational care. These areas all involve social care practitioners to a greater or lesser degree. Consultation with Travellers, as with any group, is essential if a productive relationship for both the practitioner, as the caregiver/service provider, and the Traveller, as the care recipient/service user, is to be ensured.

Consultation can be defined as a process of engaging with a group (Travellers or otherwise) in order to determine the group's needs from the perspective of the members of that group. This can be done informally or through the use of standard research techniques. It also implies regular reassessment of the needs of the group and inclusion of the group's views in all stages of programme design, delivery and implementation. A case study reflecting an excellent model of consultation is outlined below. Here the principles of collaborating together on a formal and informal basis resulted in a process whereby Travellers were enabled to become advocates of their own and their community's health care.

Social care students should start the process of becoming aware of what consultation is and how it should be carried out. This process can be initiated by not assuming one knows what the Traveller experience in Ireland is, or has been, but allowing Travellers to be the experts on themselves. Exposure to the Traveller community and a willingness to get to know the Traveller individual will dispel many preconceptions one may hold. Facilitating Travellers in identifying their own needs, and responding to those needs, will be an instrumental way of working in partnership and collaboration.

The effect of this open-minded approach cannot be overemphasised. Better acceptance of ethnic and cultural differences will lead to a truer multicultural and, eventually, pluralistic Irish society.

'Do not go where the path may lead, go instead where there is no path and leave a trail' (Emerson, cited in Poolos 2006: 6).

Case Study: Primary Health Care Project for Travellers (Tullamore) as a Model of Consultation

Primary health care can be defined as the first level of contact people have with the health services.

Mission Statement of the Primary Health Care Project (Tullamore)

'To support Community Health Workers, to deal with specific Traveller health related issues, in a culturally appropriate way, for both caregiver and care receiver' (Midland Health Board 2004: 3).

Summary of the Project's Aims

* To develop a primary health care project for Travellers in consultation with Travellers, FÁS, the Midland Health Board and Tullamore Travellers Movement.
* To train Traveller women to work as Community Health Workers among Travellers in their locality.

Background to the Project (Midland Health Board)

The Primary Health Care Project in Dublin (partnership between Eastern Regional Health Authority and Pavee Point, 1994) was used as a model to design the project in the Tullamore region. A health needs assessment study was carried out to determine the exact health needs of Travellers, according to Travellers, in the Midland region (Duggan-Jackson 2000). A partnership was also set up between the Tullamore Traveller Movement, the Midland Health Board and FÁS.

Structure of the Project

* Stage One: Capacity Building. This means increasing the capacity (ability) of a community or organisation. The aim is to enable Travellers to begin to think about gaining greater control over social, political, economic and environmental factors affecting their health.

- Stage Two: Pre-training Phase, 1999–2001. The aim is to assist Traveller participants to develop an understanding of health in conjunction with community development and personal development. The focus is:
  - Building ability.
  - Team building.
  - Communication.
  - What primary health care actually is and how community health workers can provide a primary health care service.
  - Emphasis on responding to needs in an area and developing a sense of community.

- Stage Three: Health Intervention Phase, 2001–2003. Trainees are given specific training in particular aspects of health, identified as being important for Traveller health, for example, immunisation, dental health and children's health.

Consultation Process in the Project

- Local Travellers consulted regarding their own health needs.
- Trainees (Traveller women) consulted regarding design of project and cultural appropriateness (mainly achieved through the evaluation of the project and inclusion of Travellers in that evaluation).
- Inclusion of trainees at steering group meetings (management meetings to organise the running of the project).

RESULT: Six Traveller women trained and employed as Community Health Workers in Tullamore.

ACKNOWLEDGEMENT

Travellers employed as Community Health Workers with the Health Service Executive (Midlands Region) in Tullamore kindly commented on and approved the information in this chapter prior to publication. I am grateful to:

- Lily Kavanagh (Community Health Worker)
- Sarah McDonagh (Community Health Worker)
- Bridget McInerney (Community Health Worker)
- Bridget (Pinkie) McInerney (Community Health Worker)
- Mary McInerney (Community Health Worker)
- Maureen Wilson (Community Health Worker)
- Deirdre Kavanagh (Primary Health Care Project Co-ordinator)

All information contained here has therefore been deemed by 'the experts' to be accurate and reflective of current Traveller issues in Ireland.

25

Working with Young People

Maurice Devlin

OVERVIEW

A great deal of social care work is carried out with children and young people. This raises the question of how it relates to other types of service or provision that are concerned with the same or similar age groups. In fact, recent years have seen a proliferation of what might be termed 'youth services', and sometimes the boundaries between the different services are not readily clear, especially to external observers. This chapter will deal specifically with *youth work*, an approach to working with young people that has undergone significant development in Ireland in recent years.

WHAT IS YOUTH WORK?

Like other types of educational, developmental or welfare-based approaches to working with people – what are sometimes collectively called the 'social professions' (see, for example, Banks 2004) – the term 'youth work' is open to contrasting and even sometimes conflicting interpretations. There is still plenty of room for discussion and debate about what youth work is or should be, but if we are seeking a starting point, we need look no further than the legal definition. Youth work, in fact, is unusual among the social professions in that there is actually a law that says what it is. According to the Youth Work Act 2001 (Section 3), youth work is:

> A planned programme of education designed for the purpose of aiding and enhancing the personal and social development of young persons through their voluntary involvement ... which is –
> (a) complementary to their formal, academic and vocational education and training; and
> (b) provided primarily by voluntary organisations.

This definition may be imperfect (for a criticism, see Spence 2007), and it may have the rather technical or instrumental character that legal language typically does, but it nonetheless encapsulates a few key points or principles that would command widespread agreement among people involved in youth work in Ireland today. The first is that youth work is above all else an educational endeavour and it should therefore complement other types of educational provision. Indeed, it is sometimes called 'out-of-school education', but that designation is misleading because it can take place in school buildings in some cases. It is now more common, therefore, to refer to it as 'non-formal' or 'informal' education (terms which will be returned to below).

The second key point is that young people participate in youth work voluntarily: they can take it or leave it, a situation that is markedly different from their relationship with the formal education system. The third point is that youth work is mostly carried out by organisations that are non-statutory or non-governmental as well as non-commercial (they are not businesses). Furthermore, it is in the nature of these voluntary organisations that many – perhaps most – of the adults who work with them do so on an unpaid basis. Throughout its history, Irish youth work has relied enormously on voluntary effort, both individual and institutional. This continues to be the case although, as we will see, recent years have seen the emergence of enhanced roles for the state and for full-time professional staff in the provision of youth work services.

THE EMERGENCE AND DEVELOPMENT OF YOUTH WORK

The key points highlighted above make it immediately clear that contemporary youth work – despite some areas of overlap which we will return to later in this chapter – is different in significant ways from social care work with young people. By definition, the latter's principal focus must be the care of the young person, which is related to their education but is not the same as it; and children and young people do not as a rule volunteer to put themselves in care.

If we look back to their origins, both youth work and social care work (and indeed social work) were part of the broad philanthropic movement of the nineteenth and early twentieth centuries concerned with 'rescuing' (or controlling) needy, destitute and troublesome children and young people, whose numbers and visibility had increased substantially as society industrialised and urbanised. The particular direction that care work took was shaped by its links with the industrial and reformatory school system and with provision for young offenders (Lalor et al. 2007: 290). The direction taken by youth work (and its emergence as a separate area of practice) was due to the fact that the early combination of philanthropy and 'moral panic' (Cohen 2002) gradually merged with other impulses that associated youth not just with the problems of the present, but with the promise of the future and with the potential to defend and promote certain political, cultural or religious values and beliefs.

Social movements involving young people (and largely directed by young people) had been found throughout Europe since the Middle Ages (Zemon Davies 1971). The first voluntary youth groups and organisations in Ireland in the nineteenth and early twentieth centuries – including the various scouting and guiding organisations and the early boys' and girls' clubs – might also be seen as part of a broad youth movement, albeit one with adults exercising key leadership roles, and they were closely associated with other movements of the time concerned with promoting national aspirations or religious ideals (see Figure 25.1 below).

Ireland was certainly not the only country where youth work (and other work with young people) had its origins in voluntary activity, but in Ireland, the emphasis on voluntarism took on a particular character because of the fraught nature of the historical relationship with Britain and the fact that the great majority of the country's population, particularly south of the border after independence, was Roman Catholic. In this context voluntarism was, among other things, an expression of the principle of *subsidiarity*, which was emphasised by Catholic social teaching. According to this principle, the state should only have a secondary ('subsidiary') role in providing for people's care, welfare and education and the primary responsibility should be vested in families, communities and voluntary associations. In Ireland, historically, the Churches set up most such associations and therefore many of the longest-established youth organisations have religious affiliations.

In youth work, therefore, as in other areas of social policy (including formal education at primary and secondary levels and the Irish hospital system), the state's main role in the past has been to fund and support the non-governmental sector to be the main direct provider of services. Thus, almost all the existing youth work services in Ireland are delivered by voluntary organisations. Figure 25.1 lists some of the major youth organisations in Ireland. These were set up, mostly

Figure 25.1. Some Major Voluntary Youth Work Organisations

Catholic Youth Care

Established in 1944 and formerly known as the Catholic Youth Council, CYC operates within the Dublin Catholic archdiocese, supporting voluntary youth clubs and running several youth information centres and also local youth work services in partnership with VECs in Co. Dublin and Co. Wicklow, as well as other youth and community-based projects.

Foróige

Founded in 1952 as Macra na Tuaithe, Foróige has a national network of youth clubs (Foróige clubs) and also runs a number of youth information centres and various types of youth development projects in partnership with, and/or funded by, VECs, Local Drugs Task Forces, the Young People's Facilities and Services Fund, the Department of Justice, Equality and Law Reform and the Health Services Executive (HSE).

Youth Work Ireland

Formerly the National Youth Federation and with a history going back to 1961, Youth Work Ireland is a federal organisation with a membership of 22 local and regional youth services (Donegal Youth Service, Waterford Regional Youth Service, Kerry Diocesan Youth Service and so on). It also hosts the Irish Youth Work Centre at its head office (a library, resource and study centre) and other training and programming services. Its member organisations support youth club work as well as running projects similar to those run by CYC and Foróige.

Ógra Chorcaí

Founded in 1966. Like the other organisations listed above, its work primarily consists of supporting voluntary youth clubs and running special projects for young people in co-operation with various statutory agencies (including Cork city and county VECs, the HSE, Local Drugs Task Force and the Department of Justice, Equality and Law Reform).

Uniformed Organisations

The Boy Scouts and Girl Guides and the Boys' and Girls' Brigades were established in Ireland before independence, initially as part of the British parent movements. After independence, Catholic versions of the scouting and guiding movements were established (1927 and 1928). In 2004, after several years of negotiation, the two separate scouting organisations formally joined together as Scouting Ireland. There are still two guide organisations, the Irish Girl Guides and the Catholic Guides of Ireland.

National Youth Council of Ireland

All the above-named organisations are members of the National Youth Council of Ireland (NYCI, founded 1967), which is recognised under the terms of the Youth Work Act 2001 as the national representative body for the voluntary youth work sector in Ireland. In addition to its representative and lobbying role, the NYCI hosts a number of specialist and support programmes, such as the National Youth Arts Programme, the National Youth Health Programme, the National Youth Development Education Programme and the Child Protection Unit.

For more information and contact details for all these organisations, go to www.youth.ie.

independently of each other, over a period of more than a century. A significant development took place in 1967 when the largest organisations came together to form a representative or umbrella body, the National Youth Council of Ireland (NYCI). The next year, Bobby Molloy, TD was appointed as the first Parliamentary Secretary with responsibility for youth and sport (the role of Parliamentary Secretary was the precursor of what is now known as Minister of State or, informally, Junior Minister), and in 1970, the Department of Education began to distribute the first formal youth service grants to the voluntary sector.

The main exception to the pattern of voluntary (or non-statutory) predominance has been in Dublin, where the City of Dublin Youth Service Board (CDYSB), which is a sub-committee of the City of Dublin Vocational Education Committee (CDVEC), was established on the instructions of the Minister for Education in 1942 in response to the severe problem of youth unemployment in the city at the time. Although this represented direct intervention on the part of the state, the development had the active encouragement of the then Archbishop of Dublin, Dr John Charles McQuaid, and the early focus of the organisation (which was initially called Comhairle le Leas Óige, or Council for the Welfare of Youth) was on the provision of practical skills training for the young unemployed. Over the years, it broadened its range of services to include funding, support and training for youth clubs and volunteer youth leaders and for community-based youth projects employing full-time paid workers, particularly since the 1980s.

The arrangement whereby the Department of Education and Science (as it is now called) disburses grant aid through its Youth Affairs Section to the voluntary youth work sector (and the small statutory sector) has changed relatively little since the outset, although the amount of funding involved has increased enormously, particularly since the introduction of the National Lottery in 1986. There are two main funding lines: the Youth Service Grant Scheme (mostly for what is sometimes called 'mainline youth work') and the Special Projects for Youth (or SPY) scheme. The latter is intended to enable the employment of full-time paid staff to work with disadvantaged young people. The Youth Affairs Section also funds a network of youth information centres and supports a number of other initiatives related to youth work (for example, Gaisce, the President's Award; North–South and international youth exchanges; the national youth arts and health programmes; and the Child Protection Unit for the youth work sector, the last three all based in the NYCI in Montague Street, Dublin). In 2007, the total Youth Affairs budget was more than €50 million, the vast majority of which was drawn from National Lottery proceeds. Even so, funding from the Youth Affairs Section now makes up only a minority of the public monies expended on work with young people. Garda Youth Diversion Projects funded by the Department of Justice, Equality and Law Reform (of which there are more than 100) and work with young people funded by Local Drugs Task Forces and the Young People's Facilities and Services Fund account for a large proportion of youth services provision and practice. In many cases, youth work organisations are in receipt of funding from multiple sources, including those just mentioned, and the fact that different funders will inevitably have different expectations regarding both process and product (or 'outcomes', as it is increasingly called) raises important questions about the interface between youth work as it is now defined in law and other types of youth service.

PRINCIPLES AND PRACTICE: WHAT DO YOUTH WORKERS DO?

We have already seen that according to the vast majority of practitioners and policy makers, youth work rests on a number of key principles.

1. It is primarily concerned with the education and development, personal and social, of young people.
2. It relies on the voluntary engagement of young people: they are not compelled to attend or to take part.
3. As an important part of civil society or what is sometimes called 'associative life' (through which citizens come together to work collaboratively to achieve shared objectives), the role in youth work of voluntary organisations, and individual volunteers, is vital.

We can add a number of other principles to these, reflecting existing policy and practice (for example, Department of Education and Science 2003a: 13–15; National Youth Council of Ireland 2006).

4. Young people are full and active partners in youth work, participating meaningfully in making decisions and in programme planning and implementation.
5. Youth work should aim to empower young people and give them a voice, individually and collectively, and it should uphold and promote the rights of children and young people as citizens (such as those set out in the UN Convention on the Rights of the Child).
6. Youth work should aim for openness and inclusiveness and for the active promotion of equality; no individual young person, and no group of young people, should feel excluded or diminished in a youth work context.
7. Youth work has a community dimension and a social purpose; it has benefits for adults as well as young people; it strengthens social solidarity and contributes to positive social change.
8. Youth work, like all good education, should be experienced as both challenging and enjoyable, both fulfilling and fun, both enriching and uplifting, for young people and for adults.

How do youth workers go about implementing these principles? What do they actually do? The main point to stress relates back to the first principle – that above all else, youth work is *educational*. As the *National Youth Work Development Plan* (Department of Education and Science 2003a: 13) has put it, 'education is by definition a planned, purposeful and conscious process (whereas "learning" may or may not be planned and purposeful, and may or may not be conscious)'. This means that the youth worker should approach any activity or programme, any situation or eventuality – however structured or unstructured and however expected or spontaneous – asking her/himself what opportunities it presents to further the education and development of young people, both individually and collectively.

This is why it makes sense to say that youth work can be educational in both 'non-formal' and 'informal' ways, as mentioned earlier. It is non-formal in that it does not (for the most part) take place in schools or follow a predetermined curriculum, and it is informal in that it rests crucially on a relationship between adults and young people which strives for optimum mutuality, cordiality and conviviality and makes the most of spontaneously arising 'daily life activities' (Youth Service Liaison Forum 2005: 13), seeing these as central to its concerns rather than as distractions from some more 'serious' purpose. In answer to the question 'what do youth workers do?', therefore, an important part of the response is that *how* they do things is at least as important as the things that they do. This is often described in terms of 'process' and 'product' (or 'process' and 'task'). It is not helpful (despite what some earlier writing in youth work would seem to suggest) to see these in terms of a polarity, whereby an emphasis on one must inevitably be at the expense of the other. It is better to see them as different dimensions of the youth worker's role, one enriching the other.

For this to happen, whatever the activity, programme or pursuit being engaged in, it is important that workers and young people have the space and the opportunity (and the support) to reflect consciously and purposefully on what they have learned and what they have yet to learn, and how they might go about doing this. Much theory and practice in youth work (and related areas, like community development and adult education) have been influenced by the idea of learning as a cycle that moves through stages of experience, reflection and conceptualisation and then onto further, enriched experience and experimentation, which begins the cycle again (see Kolb 1984; and for a discussion and critique see Smith 2001). But however the youth worker envisages his or her work with young people, its key purpose is likely to be seen in educational and developmental terms.

As regards the activities and programmes to which youth workers bring the approach just sketched, the range is very wide. Figure 25.2 lists just some of the major possibilities. The important point is that the overall approach to the programme or activity and the principles informing the interaction with young people are consistent with those indicated above. Many of the areas mentioned are themselves associated with specialist ability or professional expertise (for example, outdoor pursuits and sports, information technology, artistic and creative work), and of course many young people avail of learning and leisure opportunities in these fields completely independently of youth work. What makes youth work different, however, is that these and other activities are engaged in not just for their own intrinsic value or interest (although that remains an important reason), but because of their potential to contribute to young people's broader development in both personal and social terms and also to contribute to community and societal development. Many worthwhile and innovative programmes involve youth workers and professionals in other fields working collaboratively, as, for example, in the case of youth arts where youth workers and artists are often jointly involved (Devlin and Healy 2007).

Figure 25.2. Youth Work Activities and Programmes

Activities and programmes in youth work might include, but are not limited to, the following.

1. Recreational and sporting activities and indoor/outdoor pursuits, uniformed and non-uniformed.
2. Creative, artistic and cultural or language-based programmes and activities.
3. Spiritual development programmes and activities.
4. Programmes designed with specific groups of young people in mind, including young women or men, young people with disabilities, young Travellers or young people in other ethnic groups, young asylum-seekers, young LGBT people (lesbian, gay, bisexual and transgender).
5. Issue-based activities (related to, for example, justice and social awareness, the environment, development education).
6. Activities and programmes concerned with welfare and well-being (health promotion, relationships and sexuality, stress management).
7. Intercultural and international awareness activities and exchanges.
8. Programmes and activities focusing on new information and communication technologies (ICTs).

It is also important to note that in keeping with the principles outlined above, and especially those numbered 5 to 7, youth work often focuses on particular groups of young people who share certain identities, circumstances or needs, and in many cases who have collectively been the victims of social inequalities (based on such factors as gender, class, disability, race and ethnicity and sexuality). Such work clearly has an important role to play in addressing the developmental needs of individual young people who may be facing particular difficulties related to their material circumstances, lack of equal opportunities for leisure and socialising, who may be dealing with prejudice and discrimination and the impact this can have on confidence and self-esteem, and so on. However, youth work also has the potential – even the responsibility – to raise awareness in society as a whole of the nature and impact of such inequalities and to involve young people themselves in working to challenge and change them, and not just the young people directly affected. This is not a novel insight. A quarter of a century ago, the National Youth Policy Committee made the point forcefully (NYPC 1984: 116):

> If youth work is to have any impact on the problems facing young people today then it must concern itself with social change. This implies that youth work must have a key role both in enabling young people to analyse society and in motivating and helping them to develop the skills and capacities to become involved in effecting change.

RECENT AND CURRENT POLICY DEVELOPMENTS

The National Youth Policy Committee was appointed in 1983 and issued its final report a year later (NYPC 1984). Its proposal for a comprehensive national youth service with a legislative basis was broadly accepted by the government of the day

Figure 25.3. Youth Work Structures in Ireland, 2009

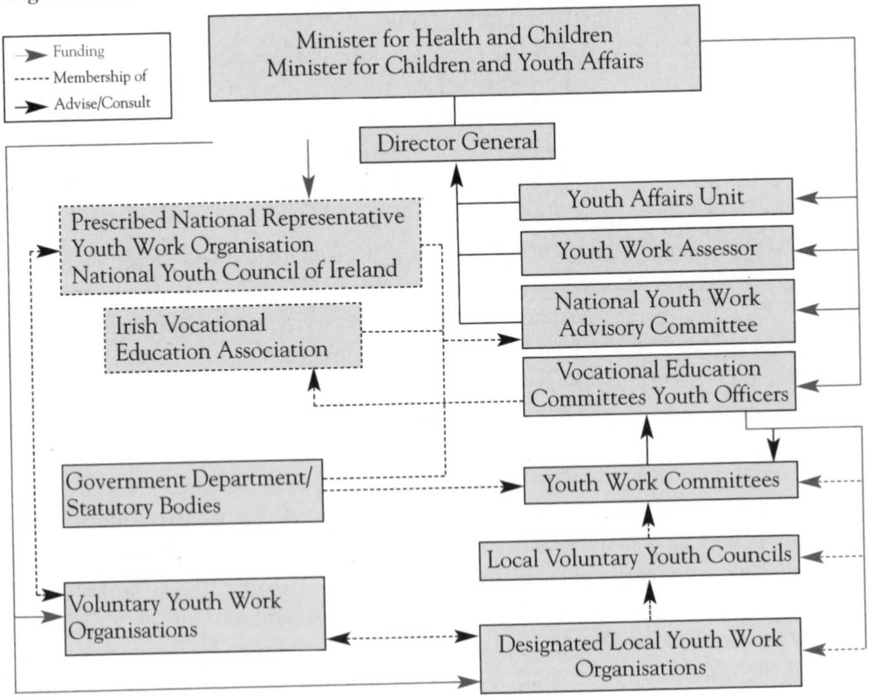

Source: Office of the Minister for Children and Youth Affairs.

Note: This outline does not take account of the integration of the Youth Affairs Section within the Office of the Minister for Children and Youth Affairs (OMCYA), announced in mid-2008.

in a White Paper published in 1985 (Government of Ireland 1985), but a general election and change of government intervened before the national youth policy was implemented, and in the intervening years a similar pattern was repeated several times, whereby political and administrative change delayed or frustrated the execution of youth work plans or policies. The report of the National Youth Policy Committee remained influential, however, and its proposals can clearly be seen to have contributed to the shaping of the current legislative framework, passed as the Youth Work Act in 2001. This was one of the most significant developments in the history of Irish youth work, and along with the *National Youth Work Development Plan 2003–2007* (Department of Education and Science 2003a), it led to the rolling out of a number of important new initiatives and structures. Each of these two instruments will be briefly summarised below, and Figure 25.3 provides an outline of the structures in diagrammatical form (it also takes account of more recent administrative changes referred to later in this section). For a more detailed account, see the chapter on services and policy for young people in Lalor et al. (2007).

As we have already seen, the Youth Work Act 2001 defined youth work as essentially a part of the broader education system. It placed an onus on the Minister for Education to ensure the development and co-ordination of youth work programmes and services at national level, and a similar responsibility on the Vocational Education Committees (VECs) at local level, although as we have seen, it specifies that voluntary organisations will remain the primary direct providers of youth work. Overall, if 'subsidiarity' was a key governing principle of Irish youth work policy and provision in the past (as outlined above), then 'partnership' seems to be the key principle underlying the current youth work legislation, as it does in so much contemporary Irish social policy (Fanning 2006: 14). The main partnership in this case is that between the statutory and voluntary sectors.

Under the terms of the Youth Work Act, a young person is anyone under the age of 25 years, but it specifies that youth work will have particular regard to young people between the ages of 10 and 20 inclusive, and those who are socially or economically disadvantaged. It also raises the issues of access and participation by both young males and females, young people's information needs and the youth work requirements of young Irish speakers.

For the VECs, carrying out their functions under the Youth Work Act involves:

- Providing assistance, including financial assistance, to voluntary youth work organisations.
- Preparing and implementing multi-annual Youth Work Development Plans within their areas (while ensuring co-ordination with other local services for young people).
- Drafting annual youth work budgets and reporting on youth work services to the Minister for Education and Science.

VECs have also been given the responsibility to 'monitor and assess youth work programmes and services' and evaluate the expenditure incurred. To support them in carrying out their functions, the Act provided that each VEC would establish a Youth Work Committee and a Voluntary Youth Council. Although the Youth Work Act was passed in 2001, it was only in 2006 that the VECs secured funding to employ Youth Officers to enable them to begin to fulfil their functions under the Act (other than in the small number of cases where they already had youth work staff), and therefore at the time of writing the structures are just being put in place.

The role of the Youth Work Committee is to advise and make recommendations to the VEC on the performance of its youth work functions. It has a membership of 16 to 20 members, and in keeping with the principle of partnership these comprise in equal proportion persons nominated by the relevant local statutory agencies (for example, local authorities, health services, FÁS, the Gardaí) and nominees of the Voluntary Youth Council for the area.

The Youth Work Committee is a sub-committee of the VEC. In effect and allowing for differences in the detail of their constitution, this means that every VEC has a sub-committee along the lines of the one that has existed in the City of Dublin VEC since 1942 (the City of Dublin Youth Service Board).

The Voluntary Youth Council's role is to act as a forum for voluntary youth work organisations in the VEC area, including the nomination of members to the Youth Work Committee. It also has a role of advising the VEC on matters related to the Youth Work Development Plan. The Voluntary Youth Council has 10 to 20 members, of whom, 'as far as practicable', at least one-fifth should be under 25 years old, and at least three-quarters should be volunteers. This is a reflection of the key role of volunteers and volunteering in Irish youth work, past and present, but some commentators have argued that it is also a reflection of an ambivalence about the role and contribution of paid workers, and an expression of the view that their main function is to support volunteers rather than to play an active part in the development of policy and provision in their own right. This raises a question about whether and to what extent youth work is a profession, to which we will return shortly.

Just as the Youth Work Committees at local level are based on a statutory–voluntary partnership, the Youth Work Act 2001 provided for a National Youth Work Advisory Committee (NYWAC), also built on such a partnership. In fact, NYWAC first came into existence as a result of an earlier Youth Work Act passed in 1997 but not implemented (apart from the establishment of NYWAC itself) due to a change of government after a general election. The later legislation, the Youth Work Act 2001, replicated the role and function of NYWAC, with a slightly expanded membership. It numbers 31 to 33 members, and apart from a small number of ministerial nominees (one to three), consists of:

- Nominees of the various government ministers and statutory organisations with an involvement in the provision of services for young people, including four nominees of the Irish Vocational Education Association (the VEC representative body).

- Nominees of the 'prescribed national representative organisation' for the voluntary sector. The National Youth Council of Ireland was explicitly named in the Act as having that status for the first three years, and at the expiry of that period the status was renewed. The Act provides that the voluntary sector representatives will equal in number the total of all other members, excluding the chairperson.

The role of NYWAC is to advise the minister in relation to the provision of youth work programmes and services, the development and implementation of youth work policies, the co-ordination of youth work with other services for young people, the equitable treatment of young men and women in youth work and the implementation of the detailed provisions of the Youth Work Act at national and VEC level.

The Youth Work Act also provided for the appointment of an Assessor for Youth Work with two principal functions: the assessment and monitoring of youth work programmes and services and the review of certain aspects of the minister's and the VECs' functions. This section of the legislation has not been formally implemented, but an Assessor for Youth Work was nonetheless appointed in the Youth Affairs Section of the Department of Education in 2006, and the development and implementation of a quality standards framework (QSF) for youth work was identified as his first priority. After a process of consultation with the sector, the pilot stage of the QSF commenced early in 2008, involving the voluntary participation of a number of local youth groups and projects, VECs and national youth organisations. In the longer term, it is intended that there will be a 'whole organisation assessment' for youth work, somewhat analogous to the 'whole school evaluation' that takes place in the formal education sector.

It was already mentioned that the National Youth Work Advisory Committee first came into existence in 1997, as a result of the passing of an early version of the youth work legislation. In 1999, NYWAC approved a proposal from the National Youth Council of Ireland (NYCI, which nominates approximately half of NYWAC's members) that it prepare proposals for a National Youth Work Development Plan, to complement and build on the amending legislation then in preparation. The Minister of State for Youth Affairs endorsed the idea, and over the next two years NYWAC engaged in a comprehensive process of research and consultation, resulting in a set of recommendations for a plan that was eventually adopted by the minister and the Department of Education and approved by the government. It was launched in 2003 as the *National Youth Work Development Plan 2003–2007* (Department of Education and Science 2003a).

The development plan was constructed around four broad goals and a number of related actions. The goals were to:

- Facilitate young people and adults to participate more fully in, and to gain optimum benefit from, youth work programmes and services.

- Enhance the contribution of youth work to social inclusion, social cohesion and active citizenship in a rapidly changing national and global context.
- Put in place an improved infrastructure for development, support and co-ordination at national and local level.
- Put in place mechanisms for enhancing professionalism and ensuring quality standards in youth work.

Among the actions that have been implemented since the development plan was adopted are the following.

- Significant increases in funding for the youth work sector in the years immediately after the plan's launch (with a levelling off since then, in common with other sectors).
- An annual development fund providing additional support for local clubs and groups.
- Support for 'single worker projects' to recruit additional staff.
- A major review of funding in the youth work sector (the results of which are under consideration by NYWAC and the DES at the time of writing).
- A revision of the code of good practice on child protection in youth work (Department of Education and Science 2003b) and the establishment of a Child Protection Unit to offer support and training to youth organisations.
- Development of codes and guidelines on various aspects of youth health and welfare.
- Establishment of the North South Education and Training Standards Committee for Youth Work (the NSETS; see next section of this chapter).

The National Youth Work Development Plan also included as 'a priority action' the establishment of a National Youth Work Development Unit to manage and co-ordinate research, pilot innovative methods and approaches to youth work and support the development of good practice. The establishment of the unit was still pending at the time of writing. In 2008, the work plan of the National Youth Work Advisory Committee included a review of the implementation of the Development Plan and the preparation of recommendations to the minister on what steps to take next.

A further important development must be noted here on recent and current policy developments in youth work. In mid-2008, the new Taoiseach, Brian Cowen, reshuffled the Cabinet and the Ministers of State and announced that the Youth Affairs Section of the Department of Education and Science was to be integrated within the Office of the Minister for Children (OMC), to be renamed the Office of the Minister for Children and Youth Affairs (OMCYA). The OMC was established in 2005 and is attached to the Department of Health and Children, but it also serves as a strategic environment within which that department's responsibilities relating to children can be better co-ordinated with early years education (the responsibility of the Department of Education and Science) and the new Youth Justice Service of the Department of Justice, Equality and Law Reform (Lalor et al. 2007: 288). As part of the integration of the Youth Affairs Section (now called the Youth Affairs Unit) within the OMCYA, the responsibilities of the Minister for Education and Science under the Youth Work Act 2001 were reassigned to the Minister for Education and Health by way of what is called a 'transfer order'. These new administrative arrangements are likely to prove as significant in the long run as any initiative documented in the foregoing pages.

PROFESSIONALISM, PROFESSIONALISATION AND TRAINING

Is youth work a profession? The answer is not as straightforward as it might seem (as is also the case in social care; see Chapters 1 and 5). The study of professions is itself the subject of an extensive literature in sociology and applied social sciences (see, for example, Banks 2004; Evetts 2006; Freidson 2001; Macdonald 1995). There has long been an academic debate about the *definition* of professions – which occupations fall under the category of 'profession' and which do not, and on what basis one makes the distinction – but most research in this field now takes the view that a static definitional or categorical approach is of limited value and that it is more helpful to study the *processes* that occupations go through as they change over time. This involves making use of the concept of *professionalisation*.

Youth work has certainly changed enormously over time, and one of the key changes is that the people doing it are now much more likely than they were in the past to be doing it on a full-time paid basis and to have to give an account of themselves to line managers, boards of management and funders. This is itself suggestive of a process of professionalisation. Exact figures are hard to come by, but it is likely that there are now several thousand people in paid youth work positions in Ireland (working directly with young people, rather than in management/supervisory roles). It is also generally recognised that youth work has become an increasingly complex and challenging job and that to be able to do it properly, a substantial process of advanced training and education is necessary. Three third-level institutions in Ireland currently offer professional programmes in this field (NUI Maynooth, University College Cork and Dundalk Institute of Technology), as does the University of Ulster at Jordanstown (and given the increasing number and range of services for young people, it is highly likely that other institutions will begin to offer programmes). Furthermore, these institutions now fall under an all-Ireland framework for the sectoral approval or endorsement of their youth work training programmes, carried out by the North South Education and Training Standards Committee (NSETS), established as part of the National Youth Work Development Plan and referred to above. In turn, NSETS works closely with its counterparts in England, Scotland and Wales, helping to ensure a common approach to training and workforce concerns and enhancing student and worker mobility.

This does not mean that it is legally required that someone needs to possess a particular qualification to do the job of youth work (as is the case in the more established and regulated professions), but in practice, employers are now likely to stipulate that applicants for posts hold a professionally endorsed qualification. Employer interests are represented on the NSETS committee, as are the Departments of Education, both North and South (as well as all the other major stakeholders), meaning that the endorsement process has a wide currency in the sector. This too might be seen as a significant indication of professionalisation.

Possessing an endorsed qualification does not as yet bear any relation to the salary earned by the worker, and different organisations continue to use different pay scales depending on the funding available to them. This was a matter considered by the funding review referred to above (conducted under the National Youth Work Development Plan) and salary arrangements and other aspects of job conditions and career structure for youth workers will hopefully improve in the coming years.

Of course, it remains the case that most of the people who do youth work are volunteers, and they too carry significant responsibilities in their engagement and interaction with young people. Goodwill is not enough to make for successful youth work practice, whether on the part of paid staff or volunteers. This is why youth organisations have provided volunteer training programmes for many years, and consideration is being given within both the NYWAC and the NSETS to the adoption of a co-ordinated approach to training for volunteers throughout Ireland.

The concept of *professionalism*, referring to high standards, responsibility and accountability, need not (and should not) be limited to paid workers:

> Youth work is not just a *vocation*, although almost inevitably the people who do it have a particularly strong sense of personal commitment to the work and to the well-being of young people. It is a *profession*, in the sense that all those who do it, both volunteer and paid, are required and obliged, in the interests of young people and of society as a whole, to carry out their work to the highest possible standards and to be accountable for their actions. (Department of Education and Science 2003a: 14)

CONCLUSION

This chapter has defined youth work, given a brief account of its origins and development, outlined the key youth work principles and practices and the major recent and current youth work policy initiatives. It has also briefly considered the issues of professionalism and professionalisation in youth work. It was made clear early in the chapter that in certain significant respects, youth work and social care work are different, particularly regarding youth work's primary focus on (informal and non-formal) education and the voluntary participation of young people. However, in other respects they have important things in common (for example, their fundamental ethical commitment to the well-being of children and young people and a concern with giving a voice to those they work with; the fact that in practice they have a particular focus on disadvantaged individuals and communities; and the use in certain cases of the same or similar activities and methods). As already suggested, they are both part of what are sometimes termed the 'social professions' (Banks 2004), which also include (at least) community work and social work. As different forms of work with people, all of the social professions are facing particular challenges in this late modern or postmodern era, all the more so in a society such as Ireland which has experienced so much social change on so many fronts, and so rapidly. However, by the same token, involvement in the social professions presents us with a valuable opportunity to make a positive impact on the lives of the individuals we work with, and moreover, to contribute to making society a fairer and better place for children and young people.

26

Exploring the Complexity of Addiction in Ireland

Joe Doyle

OVERVIEW

According to the United Nations Office on Drugs and Crime (UNODC) and the World Health Organization (WHO), there are an estimated 205 million people in the world using illicit drugs, including 25 million who suffer from illicit drug dependence (UNODC, WHO 2008). Ireland, like other countries, has been devastated by the problems associated with illegal drug use over the past 30 years. Lives have been lost, families left to grieve the premature loss of a relative and communities torn apart in the wake of what is known as 'the opiate epidemic'.

The problem use of drugs or alcohol is a complex issue, but its complexity manifests at a number of different levels: its causes, its impacts and its outcomes.

Numerous social and psychological factors interact to bring about the emergence of a drug problem in the individual. Different individuals may use different drugs or combinations of drugs, which in turn may have different effects, depending on the individual characteristics of the user and the context in which they find themselves. Drug users do not exist in isolation, but as part of families, peer groups and communities, each of which is affected by, and in turn affects, the drug user and the pattern and consequences of his/her drug use. Different drug users also respond differently to the wide range of treatments and supports that are actually or potentially available to them, and do so at different times and to different degrees. Finally, there are changes over time in patterns of problem drug use, both by individual users and within society as a whole. This in turn affects the reactions to drug use by services, local communities and by the wider society.

Amidst all this diversity and variation, it is still possible to discern similarities. It is these similarities which enable practitioners to recognise patterns and trends in drug use, to identify particular social groups and individuals who may be at risk of drug-related problems and to devise systematic responses in terms of awareness, education, treatment and rehabilitation. A strategy or service based only on what drug users have in common, and indifferent to their individuality, will be inflexible, unresponsive and ultimately ineffective, as drug users have diverse and multiple needs.

In this chapter, problem drug use/addiction is explained, drug use in an Irish context is reflected upon and policy is explored. Current Irish drug prevalence and trends are commented on and the range and types of drug treatment services are identified. Finally, current developments in Irish drug treatment are illustrated.

PROBLEMATIC DRUG USE/ADDICTION – WHAT DOES IT MEAN?

The problematic use of drugs or alcohol and the associated dangers of addiction is a complex psychosocial problem that is not easily defined or explained within the confines of this chapter. However, an understanding of the difference between problematic use and addiction needs to be understood by the social care practitioner in order to develop appropriate intervention models, whether they be preventative, treatment orientated or rehabilitative in nature. Taking the drugs area as the main example, problem drug use refers to 'the use of illegal and legal substances in a manner that results in physical or mental harm or loss of social well-being for the individual, for other individuals, or for society at large' (Bryan et al. 2000: xi). This broad definition covers the problematic use of alcohol, prescribed drugs and illicit drugs such as cocaine, hash or heroin. In 1994, the WHO developed a lexicon[1] that aims to provide a set of definitions of terms concerning alcohol, tobacco and other drugs. The following terms are useful in this regard:

- *Unsanctioned use*: A drug not approved by society.
- *Hazardous use*: A drug leading to harm or dysfunction.
- *Dysfunctional use*: A drug leading to impaired psychological or social functioning.
- *Harmful use*: A drug that is known to cause tissue damage or psychiatric disorders.

'Addiction' or 'drug dependence', on the other hand, is the term used to describe the altered physical and psychological state which results in disturbed physical and mental functioning when the drug is abruptly discontinued. This implies the repeated use of a substance, despite knowing and experiencing its harmful effects. The WHO (1969) defined addiction as 'a state, psychic and sometimes also physical, resulting from the interaction between a living organism and a drug, characterised by behavioural and other responses that always include a compulsion to take the drug on a continuous or periodic basis in order to experience its physical effects, and sometimes to avoid the discomfort of its absence'. In essence, the individual cannot control the craving to use the substance and needs increasing amounts to achieve the desired effect.

DRUGS AND THE IRISH CONTEXT

During the mid to late 1980s, the drug problem in Ireland was concentrated in Dublin as heroin took root in areas of socio-economic deprivation. In the early

1990s, thousands of young people began to use heroin and some areas of the city were seen as open markets for all kinds of drugs. People injected openly and discarded their injecting equipment in public places. It was a period where there was also growing concern worldwide about Human Immunodeficiency Virus (HIV) and the acknowledgement that this and hepatitis could be contracted through the sharing of needles. Drug-related crime was at an all-time high, and from the communities' perspective, dealers were openly flaunting their wealth while the Gardaí appeared powerless. Many young people were dying as a result of drug overdoses, drug-related suicide and AIDS-related illnesses. Local neighbourhood committees were formed and some drug dealers, who were often addicts themselves, found themselves forcibly evicted from their homes. Thousands of people marched on the Dáil demanding a comprehensive response from government and community leaders insisted that the community be involved in any policy-making.

O'Sullivan and Butler (2004: 1) note that 'health and health care have for many years been at, or close to, the top of political and media agenda in Ireland'. However, until 1996, the individualised medical perspective on the heroin problem dominated the provision of drug services in Ireland. The government at this time established the Ministerial Task Force on Measures to Reduce the Demand for Drugs, which recommended a new spatial approach to the heroin problem based on an inter-sector partnership model (Department of the Taoiseach 1996).

This Ministerial Report departed from the prevailing individualised perspective on the drug problem. It broadly outlined a health promotion approach that contained many similarities to the principles of the Ottawa Charter for Health Promotion (WHO 1986):

> The Charter defines health promotion as the process of enabling people to increase control over, and to improve their health. To reach a state of complete physical, mental and social well-being, an individual or group must be able to identify and to realise aspirations, to satisfy needs, and to change or cope with the environments. Health is, therefore, seen as a resource for everyday life, not the objective of living. Health is a positive concept emphasising social and personal resources, as well as physical capacities. Therefore, health promotion is not just the responsibility of the health sector, but goes beyond healthy life-styles to well-being.

According to Butler (2002: 202), the willingness of the state to adopt an environmental/inter-sectoral approach at the time was influenced by 'the obvious failure of all previous attempts to reduce the demand for drugs in socially deprived urban communities' and the political pressure brought on by community action coupled with the murder of the journalist Veronica Guerin. This realisation, combined with the prevailing partnership approach to social and economic planning from the late 1980s onwards, created a political context for radical change in Irish drug policy. The growing political awareness of the seriousness of the drugs problem led to the creation of community-based Local Drugs Task Forces.[2] These agencies acted (and continue to act) as a co-operative effort between statutory and non-statutory agencies and enabled local communities to respond to the drugs problem. This reinforces the argument for a multifaceted response that takes due consideration of a range of individual needs. To date, communities have been and continue to be involved in this process, services have been developed and legislation has been passed.

In order for the social care practitioner to be best equipped to respond to the ever-evolving drugs problem, it is necessary to be aware of the strategies developed to tackle the problem as well as the prevalence and trends of drug use. Drug data is valuable from a public health perspective to assess needs and to plan and evaluate services/policy.

POLICY CONTEXT

Drug misuse is what the Strategic Management Initiative (SMI)[3] described as a 'cross-cutting' issue, requiring a co-ordinated response across a range of issues and sectors. The structures outlined in Figure 26.1 were established on SMI principles in that they bring together organisations and individuals from various sectors with the goal of developing an integrated response. The establishment of these 'cross-cutting' teams was a relatively new approach. In this context, the social care practitioner should note that these structures are not only attempting to address an extremely complex issue (drug misuse), but are doing so through a team-based approach involving inter-agency and inter-sectoral working.

The National Drugs Strategy (NDS) 2001–2008[4] (Department of Tourism, Sport and Recreation[5] 2001) continues to provide the framework for Ireland's national policy on illicit drugs. The overall objective of this framework is to significantly reduce the harm caused to individuals and society by the misuse of drugs through the concerted focus on supply reduction, prevention, treatment and research. The structures set in place are intended to combine 'top-down' co-ordination of relevant policy issues with 'bottom-up' or community-level participation in the policy process.

The Interdepartmental Group on Drugs (IDG) is involved in monitoring the implementation of the National Drug Strategy. It does this in conjunction with the National Drug Strategy Team (NDST). The two groups are also responsible for reviewing the government's policy on drugs and for making recommendations to the Cabinet Committee on Social Inclusion. The Interdepartmental Group on Drugs is made up of representatives from relevant government departments and keeps the Cabinet Committee on Social Inclusion regularly briefed on the implementation of the National Drug Strategy. The meetings provide an opportunity to review trends in drug misuse and also in the treatment and prevention of drug misuse.

Figure 26.1. Illustration of Ireland's Drug Strategy Co-ordination System

National Drugs Strategy 2001–2008

Cabinet Committee on Social Inclusion

Has overall responsibility for social inclusion measures, meets on a monthly basis and is chaired by An Taoiseach.

National Drug Strategy Team

Meets fortnightly to consider and drive policy relating to the National Drugs Strategy and review and decide upon recommendations from the IDG. The National Drugs Strategy Team (NDST) is a dedicated team consisting of senior civil servants from relevant departments, along with representatives from An Garda Síochána, the HSE, FÁS and the community and voluntary sectors.

Interdepartmental Group on Drugs (IDG)

Meets quarterly to advise the Cabinet Committee on critical matters relating to drugs; to ensure difficulties arising in implementation of the NDS are dealt with; to approve the plans of L/RDTFs; and to evaluate and monitor outcomes. Membership includes Departmental Assistant Secretaries and is chaired by the Minister of State for Drugs (the Department of Community, Rural and Gaeltacht Affairs (Dept. CRAGA), which has been identified as the lead department for the NDS.

Local/Regional Drug Task Forces

LDTFs are sited in areas with a high prevalence of drug problems, while RDTFs cover areas that have no LDTF (based on former Health Board boundaries). Membership includes state agencies and the community/voluntary sectors.

The Cabinet Committee on Social Inclusion also assesses the progress of the various strategies and programmes that have been put in place at national and local level to combat the drug problem.

Ireland's National Drug Strategy 2001–2008 was developed with the co-operation and input of various state agencies and voluntary and community groups[6] working in drug-affected areas throughout the country. All contributors to the strategy were asked to identify any gaps that they saw in the government response to the drug problem and make suggestions and recommendations for the formulation of an improved strategy. The Department of Community, Rural and Gaeltacht Affairs, through the Interdepartmental Group on Drugs and the National Drug Strategy Team, has the responsibility of co-ordinating the implementation of the NDS in partnership with government departments, state agencies and the community and voluntary sectors. Four pillars were pinpointed in the strategy as being 'crucial' in any attempt to address the problem: reduction in the supply of drugs; prevention of drug use (including education and awareness); drug treatment (including rehabilitation and risk reduction); and research.

The National Drug Strategy Mid-Term Review (Department of Community, Rural and Gaeltacht Affairs 2005) recommended rehabilitation as a fifth pillar of the strategy. A working group to develop an integrated rehabilitation provision, chaired by the Department of Community, Rural and Gaeltacht Affairs, delivered its report in May 2007 (Department of Community, Rural and Gaeltacht Affairs 2007).

In September 2006, the new social partnership agreement, Towards 2016 (Department of the Taoiseach 2006), was agreed between the government and the social partners, including trade unions, employers, farming organisations and the community and voluntary sector. The agreement adopts a 'lifecycle framework',[7] which places the individual at the centre of policy development and delivery by assessing the risks facing him/her, and the supports available to him/her to address those risks, at key stages in his/her life. The key lifecycle stages are identified as children, people of working age, older people and people with disabilities. Drug and alcohol misuse is addressed in relation to children and people of working age (Pike 2006). It is important that the social care practitioner takes cognisance of this partnership agreement, as it reflects the emergence of a new social inclusion policy framework[8] in Ireland. While not altering the direction of drug policy, the new framework has changed the way in which the drugs issue is presented.

DRUG USE IN IRELAND

There are a number of routine data sources available in Ireland. These include:

- Drug Treatment Data, obtained from the Central Treatment List and compiled by the Drug Treatment Centre Board.
- National Drug Trends Reporting System, Alcohol and Drug Research Unit (Health Research Board).

- Police arrests and seizures, customs and excise seizures, the Garda National Drugs Unit and the Central Statistics Office.
- Drug-related deaths (Central Statistics Office, National Drug Related Death Index).
- Drug-related morbidity (Hospital Inpatient Enquiry (HIPE), Health Protection Surveillance Centre (HPSC) and National Psychiatric Inpatient Reporting System (NPIRS)).
- Laboratory data (state lab, toxicology labs, forensic science lab; Central Statistics Office).
- Medical Bureau of Road Safety.
- National Focal Point Annual Report.[9]

Non-routine data is also a useful source of information. Examples of this type of data include:

- Prevalence studies that are once off or repeated only every few years.
- Studies of drug users.
- Ethnographic or qualitative types of studies.
- Sociological studies of drug issues, drug use, drug markets and supply.
- National Documentation Centre.

The EU Action Plan on Drugs (2000–2004)[10] called on member states to provide reliable and comparable information on five key epidemiological indicators according to the European Monitoring Centre for Drugs and Drug Addiction's (EMCDDA) recommended technical tools and guidelines.[11] The EMCDDA[12] five key indicators are:

- Prevalence and patterns of drug use among the general population (population surveys).
- Prevalence and patterns of problem drug use (statistical prevalence/incidence estimates and surveys) among drug users.
- Drug-related infectious diseases (prevalence and incidence rates of HIV, hepatitis B and C in injecting drug users).
- Drug-related deaths and mortality of drug users (general population mortality special registers statistics and mortality cohort studies among drug users).
- Demand for drug treatment (statistics from drug treatment centres on clients starting treatment).

DRUG PREVALENCE IN IRELAND

Two National Drug Prevalence[13] Surveys have been carried out by the National Advisory Committee on Drugs (NACD)[14] in Ireland. The first survey was conducted during the period 2002–2003 and the second during 2006–2007. Drug prevalence surveys of the general population are important in that they can shed light on the patterns of drug use, both demographically and geographically, and, if repeated, can track changes over time. They help to increase our understanding of drug use and to formulate and evaluate drug policies. They also enable informed international comparisons, provided countries conduct surveys in a comparable manner. Data[15] from the surveys is presented in 'lifetime use', use during the 'last year' and use during the 'last month'. Tables 26.1 and 26.2 indicate that when comparison is made between the two periods, illegal drug use emerges as a youth phenomenon. Although there is no comparable change in 'last year' and 'last month' drug use since the last survey, the 2006–2007 survey shows young adults (15–34 years) with a 'last year use' of 12 per cent and a 'last month use' of 5 per cent as compared to older adults (35–64 years) with a 'last year use' of 3 per cent (35–64 years) and 'last month use' of 1 per cent of 'any illegal drug'. This is further enhanced by the figures for the lifetime prevalence, which has increased to 31 per cent (15–34 years) compared to 18 per cent (35–64 years) in 2006–2007, with both figures up 5 per cent and 6 per cent, respectively, from the 2002–2003 survey.

Table 26.1. National Drug Prevalence Survey, Young Adults (15–34 Years) versus Older Adults (35–64 Years), 2002–2003

| Drug Type | 2002–2003 | | | | | |
| | Lifetime Use | | Last Year Use | | Last Month Use | |
	Young Adults (15–34) %	Older Adults (35–64) %	Young Adults (15–34) %	Older Adults (35–64) %	Young Adults (15–34) %	Older Adults (35–64) %
Cannabis	24	11	9	2	4	1
Cocaine	5	1	2	0.3	1	0.05
Heroin	0.7	0.3	0.2	–	0.1	–
Amphetamines	5	1	0.8	0.1	0.3	0.05
Ecstasy	7	1	2.3	–	0.6	–
LSD	5	1	0.2	–	0.05	–
Any illegal drug	26	12	10	2	5	1
STDs*	8	16	4	8	2	6
Alcohol	92	88	86	81	75	73

* Sedatives, Tranquillisers, Anti-depressants

Source: Based on figures compiled from the NACD Drug Prevalence Surveys of 2002–2003 and 2006–2007.

Table 26.2. National Drug Prevalence Survey, Young Adults (15–34 Years) versus Older Adults (35–64 Years), 2006–2007

Drug Type	2006–2007					
	Lifetime Use		Last Year Use		Last Month Use	
	Young Adults (15–34) %	Older Adults (35–64) %	Young Adults (15–34) %	Older Adults (35–64) %	Young Adults (15–34) %	Older Adults (35–64) %
Cannabis	27	16	10	3	4	1
Cocaine	8	3	3	0.5	1	0.0
Heroin	0.4	0.4	0.1	0.1	0.0	0.1
Amphetamines	5	2	0.8	0.1	0.2	0.0
Ecstasy	9	2	2	0.2	0.6	0.1
LSD	4	2	0.4	0.0	0.1	0.0
Any illegal drug	31	18	12	3	5	1
STDs	6	15	2.6	6.5	1	4
Alcohol	91	90	86	82	74	73

Source: Based on figures compiled from the NACD Drug Prevalence Surveys of 2002–2003 and 2006–2007.

Table 26.3 below ranks the five most preferred illegal drugs of choice in both prevalence studies and for both age categories.

Table 26.3. Five Most Commonly Used Illegal Drugs, Young Adults (15–34 Years) Compared to Older Adults (35–64 Years) and 2002–2003 Compared to 2006–2007

	All Adults (15–64 years)				Young Adults (15–34 years)			
	Lifetime		Last Year		Lifetime		Last Year	
	2002–3	2006–7	2002–3	2006–7	2002–3	2006–7	2002–3	2006–7
Cannabis	1	1	1	1	1	1	1	1
Magic mushrooms	2	2	4	4	3	3	5	4
Ecstasy	3	3	2	3	2	2	2	3
Amphetamine	4	5	4	5	4	5	4	5
Cocaine	5	4	2	2	5	4	3	2

Source: Based on figures compiled from the NACD Drug Prevalence Surveys of 2002–2003 and 2006–2007.

The NACD Drug Prevalence Survey 02/03 on cannabis use[16] indicates that most people:

- Smoke cannabis via a 'joint', which in itself has health consequences.
- First use cannabis with friends/shared in a group at home and obtain the drug from friends.
- Stop using because friends stop and because of its unpleasant effects.
- Do not want to see cannabis legalised.
- Would accept cannabis available for medicinal purposes and a majority perceive a moderate to great risk of harm.

According to the NACD Drug Prevalence Survey 02/03, cocaine[17] use has increased over the last few years, with 19 per cent of users taking the drug regularly. Of these, 62 per cent have stopped, with the main reasons being its cost, health concerns and 'didn't want to take it any more'. Cocaine was mostly obtained in a friend's house (56 per cent) or bar/disco/club (33 per cent). More people are likely to purchase cocaine from the house of a dealer (9 per cent) than with cannabis (3 per cent), while 69 per cent of young adults have reported it 'easy' or 'fairly easy' to obtain. Fewer people shared the drug with friends. The majority of young adults perceive great risk of harm (83 per cent), though only 61 per cent of those who have used cocaine perceive it to be a great risk of harm. The level of poly-drug use is a concern, as the survey indicates that alcohol is used in combination with most drugs. Ninety-one per cent of cannabis users drank alcohol in the 'last month' and 90 per cent of cocaine users drank alcohol in the 'last month'. Alcohol worsens the ill effects of all illegal substances and many legal ones; for example, when alcohol and cocaine combine in the body, they create cocaethylene, which is toxic.[18]

In summary, the drug prevalence survey reflects changing patterns of drug use, with cocaine growing in popularity and ecstasy and amphetamines losing ground. It also indicates that illegal drug use decreases over one's lifespan, with large reductions from 'lifetime' to 'recent' and 'current' use reflecting an element of experimentation among young people, with fewer people continuing their drug use as they mature.

CURRENT TRENDS IN PROBLEMATIC DRUG USE

The National Drug Treatment Reporting System (NDTRS),[19] operated by the Alcohol and Drug Research Unit of the Health Research Board, requires that a form be completed for each new client coming for first treatment and each previously treated client returning to treatment for problem alcohol or drug use. Agencies/services involved in the provision of treatment are required to complete a detailed paper form in relation to each person presenting for treatment, including personal details, information about their drug use and the kinds of treatment to be provided. Once the treatment has commenced, the agency/service provider sends a version of the form (with the name and address of the person removed) to the Health Research Board, where the details are entered on the computerised database. Typically, forms are returned quarterly. Data that can be extrapolated from this reporting system includes:

- Demographic, social and economic characteristics (gender, age, living with whom, living where, nationality, employment status, age left primary or secondary school, highest education level completed).
- Referral/assessment/treatment data (type of contact with centre, ever previously treated for problem drug or alcohol use).
- Treatment status (new, ever previously for treatment status – new versus previously treated cases).
- Drug use (age of first drug use – excluding drug use, ranked problem substance use in the month preceding the current treatment contact).
- Risk behaviours associated with injecting drug use (injecting past month prior to treatment contact, ever injected, age first injected, ever shared injecting equipment).
- Type of intervention.
- Yearly returns by service provider, therefore information is available on new/repeat clients (in accordance with variables) and numbers of continuous clients at start of each year.

Since 2004, clients who reported alcohol as their main problem drug are included in this reporting system. The NDTRS uses a broad definition of treatment as any activity targeted at people who have problems with substance use, and which aims to improve the psychological, medical and social state of individuals who seek help for their problem substance use, which includes one or more of the following: medication (detoxification, methadone reduction and substitution programmes), medication-free therapy, addiction counselling, psychiatric treatment and/or life skills training, provided in both residential and non-residential settings. The Health Research Board's Trends Series 2 paper (Reynolds et al. 2008) is an analysis of the NDTRS and the Central Treatment List.[20] This paper indicates that between 2001 and 2006:

- 68,754[21] cases were treated for substance misuse, of which 54 per cent received methadone treatment.
- The number of individuals on methadone treatment increased from 4,963 in 2001 to 7,269 by the end of 2006.
- The number of continuous care cases (in essence, those on methadone treatment) increased by 46 per cent.
- The number of previously treated cases increased by 6 per cent per year.
- The number of new cases entering treatment increased by 8 per cent, from 2,108 to 2,278 between 2001 and 2006.

Table 26.4 is an analysis of the socio-economic characteristics of people entering treatment in Ireland, by treatment status, reported to the NDTRS from 2001 to 2006.

Table 26.4. Socio-economic Characteristics of Cases Entering Treatment in Ireland, by Treatment Status, Reported to the National Drug Trends Recording System (NDTRS), 2001 to 2006

Characteristics	2001	2002	2003	2004	2005	2006
	Number (%)					
All cases	4,797	4,948	5,054	4,506	4,877	5,191
Median age (range) in years	24 (16–40)	24 (16–40)	25 (16–40)	25 (16–40)	26 (16–41)	27 (17–42)
Under-18s	440 (9.2%)	497 (10.0%)	526 (10.4%)	415 (9.2%)	404 (8.3%)	363 (7.0%)
Males	3,516 (73.3%)	3,552 (71.8%)	3,577 (70.8%)	3,291 (73.0%)	3,613 (74.1%)	3,983 (76.7%)
Living with parents/family	2,861 (59.6%)	2,871 (58.0%)	2,817 (55.7%)	2,393 (53.1%)	2,536 (52.0%)	2,664 (51.3%)
Homeless	153 (3.2%)	148 (3.0%)	195 (3.9%)	197 (4.4%)	217 (4.4%)	265 (5.1%)
Non-Irish nationals	135 (2.8%)	135 (2.7%)	168 (3.3%)	123 (2.7%)	162 (3.3%)	195 (3.8%)
Early school leavers	937 (19.5%)	895 (18.1%)	974 (19.3%)	892 (19.8%)	986 (20.2%)	1,040 (20.0%)
Still at school	198 (4.1%)	318 (6.4%)	377 (7.5%)	271 (6.0%)	275 (5.6%)	222 (4.3%)
Employed (16–64-year-olds)	1,240 (26.7%)	1,125 (23.8%)	1,080 (22.3%)	956 (22.0%)	1,025 (21.8%)	1,069 (21.2%)
Previously treated cases	2,588	2,721	2,838	2,555	2,760	2,781
Median age (range) in years	25 (18–40)	26 (19–42)	26 (19–41)	27 (19–41)	28 (19–42)	28 (19–43)
Under-18s	80 (3.1%)	81 (3.0%)	86 (3.0%)	64 (2.5%)	72 (2.6%)	72 (2.6%)
Males	1,882 (72.7%)	1,892 (69.5%)	1,953 (68.8%)	1,782 (69.7%)	1,972 (71.4%)	2,093 (75.3%)
Living with parents/family	1,451 (56.1%)	1,441 (53.0%)	1,454 (51.2%)	1,250 (48.9%)	1,291 (46.8%)	1,343 (48.3%)
Homeless	86 (3.3%)	85 (3.1%)	124 (4.4%)	136 (5.3%)	155 (5.6%)	156 (5.6%)
Non-Irish nationals	80 (3.1%)	63 (2.3%)	86 (3.0%)	69 (2.7%)	74 (2.7%)	95 (3.4%)
Early school leavers	578 (22.3%)	587 (21.6%)	617 (21.7%)	599 (23.4%)	685 (24.8%)	660 (23.7%)
Still at school	24 (0.9%)	37 (1.4%)	43 (1.5%)	31 (1.2%)	29 (1.1%)	22 (0.8%)
Employed (16–64-year-olds)	582 (22.7%)	555 (20.7%)	559 (19.9%)	445 (17.5%)	460 (16.8%)	447 (16.2%)
New cases	2,030	2,005	2,097	1,790	1,976	2,228
Median age (range) in years	22 (15–37)	22 (15–38)	22 (15–39)	22 (15–38)	23 (15–39)	24 (15–40)
Under-18s	351 (17.3%)	407 (20.3%)	430 (20.5%)	338 (18.9%)	326 (16.5%)	285 (12.8%)
Males	1,495 (73.6%)	1,497 (74.7%)	1,539 (73.4%)	1,392 (77.8%)	1,542 (78.0%)	1,758 (78.9%)
Living with parents/family	1,344 (66.2%)	1,322 (65.9%)	1,323 (63.1%)	1,065 (59.5%)	1,175 (59.5%)	1,227 (55.1%)
Homeless	51 (2.5%)	48 (2.4%)	62 (3.0%)	52 (2.9%)	54 (2.7%)	103 (4.6%)
Non-Irish nationals	47 (2.3%)	61 (3.0%)	78 (3.7%)	50 (2.8%)	84 (4.3%)	93 (4.2%)
Early school leavers	333 (16.4%)	279 (13.9%)	338 (16.1%)	264 (14.7%)	274 (13.9%)	339 (15.2%)
Still at school	171 (8.4%)	276 (13.8%)	325 (15.5%)	234 (13.1%)	240 (12.1%)	196 (8.8%)
Employed (16–64-year-olds)	615 (32.3%)	522 (28.4%)	501 (26.1%)	487 (29.4%)	542 (29.7%)	590 (28.0%)
Treatment status unknown	179	222	119	161	141	182

Source: Reynolds et al. (2008: 29).

As we can see, the median age of previously treated cases entering treatment increased from 25 to 28 years between 2001 and 2006, while the median age of new cases increased by two years, from 22 to 24 years. Almost 18 per cent of new cases were under 18 years of age, while less than 3 per cent of previously treated cases were in this age group. The proportion of new cases under 18 years decreased noticeably in 2006, which may reflect under-reporting in two HSE regions. There was an increase in the number of male cases entering treatment, most notably among new cases. The proportion of cases that reported living with their parents or family was higher among new cases entering treatment than among previously treated cases, at 62 per cent compared to 51 per cent. Though small, the proportion of cases reporting being homeless and the proportion not born in Ireland both increased steadily during the reporting period. Previously treated cases entering treatment reported a higher incidence of homelessness (5 per cent) than new cases (3 per cent). In 2006, a higher proportion of new cases (4 per cent) than of previously treated cases (3 per cent) reported that they were not born in Ireland. The increase in the proportion of other nationalities seeking treatment may have implications for service provision, in particular counselling and medication-free approaches due to a lack of information to determine the extent of the problem and from the new community perspective barriers to accessing treatment services, including language difficulties. These, as well as cultural and religious differences, need to be taken into consideration when organising treatment facilities. The proportion of cases who reported leaving school early was higher among previously treated cases (23 per cent) than among new cases (15 per cent). The proportion of cases reporting that they were still in school on entry to treatment was higher among new cases (12 per cent) than among previously treated cases (1 per cent). Overall, 19 per cent of previously treated cases aged 16–64 years reported that they were in employment on entry to treatment, in comparison to 29 per cent of new cases. These factors highlight that social exclusion, in the guise of homelessness and insecure accommodation, inadequate education and poor employment skills, is closely associated with problematic drug use.

The trends and characteristics of people being treated for problem drug use and their patterns of drug use are important, as they enable policy-makers, services and health care managers/practitioners to develop appropriate interventions. The evidence suggests that the nature of the drugs problem is changing and becoming more complex, with drugs more widely accessible to young people. Notwithstanding the challenges that this presents to treatment providers, these trends will require a more concerted approach to prevention[22]/early intervention.

DRUG TREATMENT IN IRELAND

Under the Health Act 2004, the Health Service Executive has statutory responsibility for the provision of an integrated range of preventative and therapeutic drug treatment services, including harm reduction interventions, to meet the diverse health and social care needs of service users. It discharges this responsibility in conjunction with the voluntary and community sectors, where appropriate.

On 1 January 2005, the 10 Health Boards managing the health services in Ireland were replaced by a single entity, the Health Service Executive (HSE), which manages Ireland's public health sector (Health Act 2004). The chief executive of the HSE is directly accountable to the Oireachtas for the performance and management of the HSE and the Minister for Health and Children is responsible for legislation and policy.

Through the HSE, primary, community and continued care (PCCC) and hospital networks, the Health Service Executive Addiction Service promotes a drug-free lifestyle, and in partnership with other statutory and voluntary agencies provides prevention, treatment, rehabilitation and aftercare programmes to minimise the harmful effects of drug addiction and prevent the spread of HIV, hepatitis C virus (HCV) and other infections.

The strategic objectives of the Addiction Service, in line with the National Drug Strategy, are to provide the following in conjunction with voluntary agencies where appropriate:

- Education and prevention programmes.
- Services aimed at delivering advice and harm minimisation programmes to problem drug users not in contact with services, including advice on safer drug use, ways of reducing the risks of HIV and hepatitis transmission, advice on safer sex practice and good health.
- Treatment programmes that are service user focused and have as their objective, firstly, the control of addiction followed by the long-term aim of returning the problem drug user to a drug-free lifestyle.
- Aftercare and rehabilitation programmes that assist people in recovery to access education, training or employment opportunities.
- Evaluation of the various service responses to ensure maximum effectiveness.

Conscious of the need to develop a stepped framework for the services outlined above, a working group[23] was established to respond to Action 49[24] of the National Drugs Strategy. Amongst its recommendations was that a four-tier model be adopted based on the tiered model developed in 1996 by the UK Health Advisory Service (HAS) and adapted to an Irish context. This provides a solid framework for a multidisciplinary approach to service delivery that enables the necessary collaboration and co-ordination required to tailor treatment to the needs of young people presenting with problem drug use (see Table 26.5).

Table 26.5. The Four-Tier Model of Adolescent Addiction Treatment

	Specialist Skills	Type of Adolescent Accessing Service	Type of Intervention for Addiction Difficulties	Intervention Delivered By	Examples of Services at This Tier	Intensity and Duration
Tier 1	Specialist skills in neither adolescent mental health nor addiction	Considering or commencing experiment with drugs or alcohol	Basic advice Onward referral	An individual	Teacher, GP, probation officer, youth worker, A&E, nurse, social worker	Low intensity and ongoing
Tier 2	Specialist skills in either adolescent mental health or addiction	Abusing drugs or alcohol and encountering some problems with same	Basic counselling Brief intervention Harm reduction	An individual	Child and family service, addiction service, teen counselling, JLO, Local or Regional Drugs Task Force projects, home school liaison officer, Youthreach, educational psychologist	Low intensity and medium-term duration
Tier 3	Specialist skills in both adolescent mental health and addiction	Substantial problems due to drug or alcohol abuse	Specialist addiction counselling Family therapy Group addiction therapy Substitution treatment	A multi-disciplinary team	The specialist adolescent addiction service	High intensity and short- to medium-term duration (1–6 months)
Tier 4	Specialist skills in both adolescent mental health and addiction	Drugs or alcohol dependence with severe associated problems	Specialist addiction counselling Family therapy Group addiction therapy Substitution treatment	A multi-disciplinary team	Specialist inpatient or day hospital adolescent addiction services	Very high intensity and short duration (2–6 weeks)

Source: Department of Health and Children (2005: 48).

The Report of the HSE Working Group on Residential Treatment and Rehabilitation, Substance Users (Health Service Executive 2007) also promotes the tiered framework and includes the provision of residential specialist treatment using a care planned approach by a multidisciplinary team and more extended rehabilitative care. Other interventions in inpatient settings are assessment, detoxification, psychosocial interventions, support training and shared care to other tiers. Indeed, much of the information on best practice presented in the paper was derived from two UK reports (Health Advisory Service 1996, 2001). For the first time in Irish policy, a framework identifying a multi-level structure, which advocated close co-operation between the four tiers, was documented. This framework has been adapted as a working model for the addiction services generally.

The four tiers of this model of service delivery are as follows.

- *Tier 1:* Generic services provided by teachers, social services, Gardaí, GPs, community and family groups for those at risk of drug use. Generic services would include advice and referral and would be suitable for those commencing experimentation with drugs or alcohol.
- *Tier 2:* Services with specialist expertise in either adolescent mental health or addiction, such as juvenile liaison officers, Local Drug Task Forces, home–school liaison, Youthreach and GPs specialising in addiction and drug treatment centres. The types of service delivered at this level would include drug-related prevention, brief intervention, counselling and harm reduction and would be suitable for those encountering problems as a result of drug or alcohol use.
- *Tier 3:* Services with specialist expertise in both adolescent mental health and addiction. These services would have the capacity to deliver comprehensive child-centred treatments through a multidisciplinary team. This team would provide medical treatment for addiction, psychiatric treatment, child protection, outreach, psychological assessment and interventions and family therapy. These types of services would be suitable for those encountering substantial problems as a result of drug or alcohol use.
- *Tier 4:* Services with specialist expertise in both adolescent mental health or addiction and the capacity to deliver a brief but intensive intervention through an inpatient or day hospital. These types of services would be suitable for those encountering severe problems as a result of drug or alcohol dependence.

From the point of view of a social care practitioner, what is evident from this report is the notion of clients progressing through different tiers depending on their needs and point of contact. The primary principle of this model for adolescents is the premise that the intervention should be at the lowest level appropriate to their circumstances when presenting for treatment.

As a core part of its transformation programme, the HSE has embarked on a reconfiguration of its primary care services with the target of placing clients at the centre of the care continuum (this will obviate the need for clients to move across care groups and thus reduce and simplify their journey). This lifestyle approach places individuals at the centre of service delivery by assessing the risks that face them and the supports available/required at key stages of the lifecycle.

The transformation programme is particularly relevant to clients with social inclusion issues (including addiction) and underpins five key priorities for such clients:

- Improved access.
- Training and quality standards.
- Continuity of care.
- Community involvement and participation.
- Inter-sectoral collaboration.

Another key element of the programme is the assurance that there will an integrated approach taken in providing for the client's journey across HSE services irrespective

Figure 26.2. An Illustration of Potential Routes through Treatment

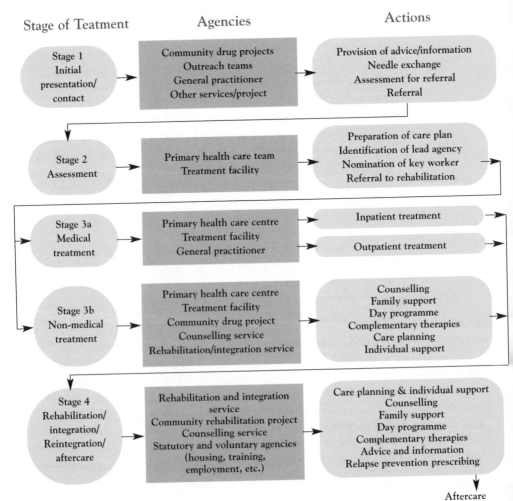

of where this is provided, for example, in a hospital, community or primary care setting. A key element of this will be the commitment that all services utilised by clients with addiction issues, whether provided by the statutory, voluntary or community sector or under the umbrella of a Local/Regional Drug Task Force, are linked in a seamless way to either a primary care team (PCT) or a social care network (SCN).

The effective provision of facilities and services requires not only the provision of resources, but also the development of appropriate strategies for the planning, management and co-ordination of these facilities and services. Figure 26.2 maps out the potential journey for a problem drug user.

As can be seen in Figure 26.2, there is 'multiple agencies' involvement in drug treatment and in the provision of other services relevant to drug users. By planning and delivering services in a co-ordinated manner, there will be a decrease in service duplication, an elimination of gaps in and between services and it will assist client progression by providing a continuum of care. It is envisaged that the four-tier model will provide a framework for this to happen and that PCTs/SCNs will improve the co-ordination of service delivery.

DRUG TREATMENT INTERVENTIONS

Drug addiction is a complex illness. This complexity is compounded by compulsive, at times uncontrollable, craving, seeking and use that persist even in the face of extremely negative and sometimes fatal consequences.

Because addiction has so many dimensions and disrupts so many aspects of an individual's life, treatment for this illness is never simple. Drug treatment must help the individual stop using drugs and maintain a drug-free lifestyle while achieving productive functioning in the family, at work and in society. Effective drug and addiction treatment programmes normally incorporate many components, each directed to a particular aspect of the illness and its consequences.

Drug treatment is defined by the UK National Treatment Agency for Substance Misuse as 'a range of interventions which are intended to remedy an identified drug-related problem or condition relating to a person's physical, psychological or social (including legal) well-being' (National Treatment Agency for Substance Abuse 2002: 3). According to this definition, treatment potentially includes a very wide range of interventions, which include but are not restricted to medical interventions. The main categories of treatment interventions are as follows:

- Advice and information.
- Assessment.
- Health promotion.
- Counselling and support.
- Prescription of medication.
- Day programmes.
- Inpatient treatment.
- Residential treatment.

Each of these categories may include several different approaches to treatment that are scientifically based. Drug treatment can include behavioural therapy (such as counselling, cognitive therapy or psychotherapy), medications or a combination of these. Behavioural therapies offer people strategies for coping with their drug cravings, teach them ways to avoid drugs and prevent relapse and help them deal with relapse if it occurs. Case management and referral to other medical, psychological and social services are crucial components of treatment for many patients. For example, Figure 26.3 identifies the wheel of change model outlined by DiClemente (2003). The model is a useful way of explaining when changes in cognition, emotion and behaviour take place during the drug treatment process. This model builds in the potential for relapse at all stages. Things go wrong and the individual may go back and need to revisit the pre-contemplation stage and move on to fresh contemplation.

Figure 26.3. Wheel of Change: Stages of Change Model

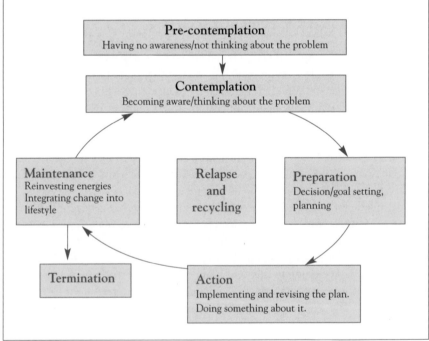

Source: DiClemente (2003: 30).

The reasons for different approaches to treatment relate, fundamentally, to differences in drugs and drug usage on the one hand and differences in the personal and social characteristics of drug users on the other.

Methadone substitute treatment

Methadone substitute treatment is governed by the Protocol for the Prescribing of Methadone, issued by the Department of Health and Children (1998c), and exists within the context of the Methadone Protocol (Statutory Instrument No. 255 of 1988),[25] which provides for a robust and effective framework that allows for the appropriate treatment of opiate-related addiction.

Ward (2002: 19) concludes that 'the accumulated results of nearly four decades of research suggests that methadone maintenance treatment is an effective treatment for opioid dependence, and that its widespread application throughout the world is a good example of an evidence-based intervention for the treatment of drug dependence'. Similar conclusions were reached by qualitative studies that evaluated the effectiveness of methadone treatment, such as the National Treatment Outcome Research Study (NTORS) (Gossop et al. 2003), the Drug Abuse Treatment Outcome Studies (DATOS) (Hubbard et al. 2003) and ROSIE (National Advisory Committee on Drugs 2006c, 2007b). The ROSIE study is the first national, prospective, longitudinal, multi-site drug treatment outcome study in Ireland. The aim of the study was to recruit and follow opiate users entering treatment over a period of time, documenting the changes observed. The study recruited 404 opiate users entering treatment from approximately 54 services provided by 44 agencies and/or organisations and followed them over a three-year period. The main findings of the study indicated the following.

- Strong positive outcomes were observed for mortality rates, drug use, abstinence rates, crimes committed and employment. Mixed results were observed for physical and mental health.
- Positive outcomes from drug treatment were observed at one year and were sustained over a longer time period of three years.
- Involvement in drug treatment has a positive impact not only on the individual, but also on society, and recovery is a long journey for many people.

Methadone as an intervention is but one component of the overall holistic approach to the treatment of heroin misuse. It is important to note that individuals presenting for treatment for opiate-related issues are provided with a full and comprehensive assessment not only in terms of medical but psychosocial needs also. The initial aim of treatment where chaotic drug use is concerned is to reach a degree of stabilisation. Best practice would advocate that on the basis of assessment, a care plan would then be agreed with the individual concerned and interventions required.

There is a range of residential drug treatment centres that provide medical detoxification. These include Cuan Dara and Beaumont Hospital; community-based detoxification services provided by the Peter McVerry Trust and Merchants Quay Ireland; and drug-free residential rehabilitation centres such as Keltoi,

Coolmine House and The Rutland. However, the HSE Working Group[26] on Residential Treatment and Rehabilitation (Substance Abuse) calculated that currently in Ireland, there is a deficit of dedicated beds for medical detoxification, stabilisation, community-based residential detoxification, residential rehabilitation and step-down/halfway house beds (HSE 2007: 48).

CONCLUSION

Addiction interventions are always evolving, as evidenced by the changing use of drugs. This chapter clearly indicates that there is no readily available manual that will allow the social care practitioner to solve problematic drug use. She or he will be an advocate and vital link in the chain of care for the drug user.

The complexity of issues in this area means that each individual must have a custom-built care plan. A lifecycle approach enshrined within Towards 2016 and the HSE transformation programme which places the individual at the centre of the care continuum both speak to this.

The social care practitioner will need to be aware of the national drug strategy, the five pillars contained within it and how to access, network and navigate the four-tier model. The role of the social care practitioner will be key across the pillars in reducing the negative consequences of drug use for the individual, the family, the community and society. This will require social care interventions in prevention, education, treatment and rehabilitation. What is evident is that the social care professional will need initial training in addiction issues as part of his/her undergraduate education and continuing up-skilling as new trends emerge.

EPILOGUE: NATIONAL SUBSTANCE MISUSE STRATEGY 2009–2016 UPDATE

On 31 March 2009, the Government agreed to include alcohol in a National Substance Misuse Strategy, with individual Ministers (Health and Community, Rural and Gaeltacht Affairs) being responsible for the aspects relevant to their respective briefs.

Work on completing the new Drugs Strategy will be finalised by the end of June/early July 2009. This Strategy will then be published as an 'interim' Strategy pending the drafting and finalisation of a National Substance Misuse Strategy (which will include alcohol and will operate until 2016). It is envisaged that the new Strategy will recommend the establishment of an Office of the Minister for Drugs (OMD). The new OMD will incorporate the work and functions that were carried out by the NDST (which ceased to exist at the end of April 2009) and it will also impact on the role of the IDG. For updates, see www.pobail.ie/en/NationalDrugsStrategy.

Homelessness

Mairéad Seymour

OVERVIEW

This chapter examines the issue of homelessness with specific reference to the role of the social care practitioner. The definition, nature and extent of homelessness in Ireland are outlined before an overview of the risk factors and common 'pathways' into homelessness for young people and adults are presented. The social care practitioner is required to respond to the needs of homeless people in line with the vision outlined in national and local homeless policy approaches. It is with this in mind that a detailed overview of homeless policy is provided, stretching from the Housing Act 1998 to the most recent homeless strategy, *The Way Home: A Strategy to Address Adult Homelessness in Ireland 2008–2013*. Key service provision issues are discussed in light of recent policy developments. The chapter concludes with an account of the challenges for social care workers when working with the homeless.

There is limited agreement and much debate about how homelessness is defined, both nationally and internationally. While the image of the unkempt individual huddled under a blanket in a public doorway may be the stereotype, in reality, sleeping rough, or 'rooflessness', is the narrowest definition of homelessness. Homelessness manifests itself in various forms, from families staying in bed and breakfast accommodation or young people staying in homeless hostels, to adults staying involuntary with family or friends because no other accommodation options are available to them. Homelessness is best understood not as a static situation, but as a process whereby 'individuals and households may move between being homeless, poorly housed and adequately/well housed' (Anderson and Tulloch 2000: 3). In recent years, the European Observatory on Homelessness has developed a typology of homelessness and housing exclusion based on the premise that there are three main domains that constitute a home: the physical domain (having an adequate dwelling (or space) over which a person and his/her family can exercise exclusive possession); the social domain (being able to maintain privacy and enjoy relations); and the legal domain (having a legal title to occupation) (FEANTSA 2007). The absence of any of these three domains can be said to define homelessness. The typology outlines four housing situations in a continuum of homelessness: rooflessness, houselessness, insecure housing and inadequate housing (see Table 27.1).

Table 27.1. The European Typology of Homelessness and Housing Exclusion (ETHOS)

Roofless	People living rough.	Living in the streets or public spaces, without a shelter that can be defined as living quarters.
	People in emergency accommodation.	People with no usual place of residence who make use of overnight shelter, low-threshold shelter.
Houseless	People in accommodation for the homeless.	Where the period of stay is intended to be short term.
	People in women's shelters.	Women accommodated due to experience of domestic violence and where the period of stay is intended to be short term.
	People in accommodation for immigrants.	Immigrants in reception or short-term accommodation due to their immigrant status.
	People due to be released from institutions.	No housing available prior to release. Stay longer than needed due to lack of housing. No housing identified (e.g. by 18th birthday).
	People receiving longer-term support (due to homelessness).	Long-stay accommodation with care for formerly homeless people (normally more than one year).
Insecure	People living in insecure accommodation.	Living in conventional housing but not the usual place of residence due to lack of housing. Occupation of dwelling with no legal tenancy; illegal occupation of a dwelling. Occupation of land with no legal rights.
	People living under threat of eviction.	Where orders for eviction are operative. Where mortgagee has legal order to repossess.
	People living under threat of violence.	Where police action is taken to ensure place of safety for victims of domestic violence.
Inadequate	People living in temporary/ non-conventional structures.	Not intended as place of usual residence. Makeshift shelter, shack or shanty. Semi-permanent structure, hut or cabin.
	People living in unfit housing.	Defined as unfit for habitation by national legislation or building regulations.
	People living in extreme overcrowding.	Defined as exceeding national density standard for floor space or useable rooms.

Source: European Federation of National Associations Working with the Homeless (FEANTSA) (2007).

The official legislative definition of homelessness in Ireland is contained in the Housing Act 1988. Under the Act, a person is considered homeless by the relevant local authority if:

(a) There is no accommodation available which in the opinion of the authority he, together with any other person who normally resides with him or who might reasonably be expected to reside with him, can reasonably occupy or remain in occupation of, or

(b) He is living in a hospital, county home, night shelter or other such institution and is so living because he has no accommodation of a kind referred to in paragraph (a) and he is, *in the opinion of the authority*, unable to provide accommodation from his own resources [emphasis added].

The words 'in the opinion of the authority' are noteworthy because they give power to the local authority to decide if an individual is deserving of assistance. Previous research suggests that discretionary judgements by housing officials may be biased against homeless individuals based on their age (Crane and Warnes 2005), gender (Cramer 2005), marital status (Cloke et al. 2007) or the extent to which they have the social skills to communicate their housing needs.

'Youth homelessness' refers to young people less than 18 years old who are out of home independently of their parents/guardians. The definition adopted in the *Youth Homeless Strategy 2001* refers to homeless youth as:

> Those who are sleeping on the streets or in other places not intended for night-time accommodation or not providing safe protection from the elements or those whose usual night-time residence is a public or private shelter, emergency lodging, B&B or such, providing protection from the elements but lacking the other characteristics of a home and/or intended only for a short stay. (Department of Health and Children 2001c: 11)

Young people who look for accommodation from the Out-of-Hours Service[1] and those in insecure and inappropriate accommodation with relatives or friends are also included in this definition.

THE NATURE AND EXTENT OF HOMELESSNESS

Under the Housing Act 1988, local authorities are required to undertake an assessment of housing need at least every three years. In conjunction with this exercise, an assessment of the number of homeless people in each area is also undertaken. Enumeration of the homeless by local authorities is problematic, not least because it is dependant on the manner in which data are recorded and the accuracy of official records (O'Sullivan 2005). In Dublin, the assessment of homelessness is undertaken by the Economic and Social Research Institute (ESRI) on behalf of the Homeless Agency and the data generated provide a more comprehensive analysis of the nature and extent of homelessness based on the scope and robustness of the methodology employed. Despite these strengths, the data do not account for the homeless who neither appear on official records (O'Connor 2008) nor attend homeless services and are therefore unlikely to capture the full extent of homelessness (Edgar et al. 1999).

The first official counts of homelessness under the Housing Act 1988 were undertaken in 1991 and 1993. Thereafter, homeless assessments have been undertaken on a triennial basis. These official data suggest that homelessness increased substantially in the main cities in Ireland, and particularly in Dublin, throughout the 1990s. Between 1999 and 2002, increases in recorded homelessness were modest relative to the preceding years. It is important to note, however, that inconsistent trends have been identified in the data provided by local authorities from assessment to assessment (O'Sullivan 2005). As a result, trends in the extent of homelessness, as reported in the official data, should be interpreted with caution.

Nationally, the most recent available statistics demonstrate a reduction in the number of homeless individuals and households from 5,581 individuals (2,468 households) in 2002 to 3,031 individuals (2,399 households) in 2005.[2] In the greater Dublin area, there has been a reported decrease of almost one-fifth in the number of households reporting homelessness since 2002 (Wafer 2006; Williams and Gorby 2002). The overall reduction in homelessness has been largely attributed to substantial government investment in the homeless sector and the increased provision of social housing in recent years (Department of the Environment, Heritage and Local Government 2005; Government of Ireland 2007a; Harvey 2008; O'Sullivan 2004).

Homelessness in Ireland is predominantly an urban phenomenon (O'Sullivan 2006) and is particularly concentrated in Dublin. The *Counted In 2005* assessment of homelessness in Dublin identified a total 2,015 individuals as homeless (made up of 1,361 households), which represents a substantial proportion of the recorded homeless in Ireland (Wafer 2006). While not directly comparable, national data collected by local authorities in the most recent housing need assessment records 341 homeless households in Cork City, 132 in Limerick City and 81 and 59, respectively, in the cities of Galway and Waterford (Department of the Environment, Heritage and Local Government 2005).

The absence of comprehensive profile data about the homeless population from local authority assessments across the country forces a reliance on the data collected as part of the *Counted In 2005* assessment of homelessness in Dublin. In line with the international literature (Fitzpatrick et al. 2000), adult homelessness was reported more commonly amongst males, who made up two-thirds of the recorded homeless population in Dublin. Single adults are deemed to be of low priority on local authority housing lists. Consequentially, difficulties in accessing social housing may partly explain why three-quarters (77 per cent) of all homeless households consisted of single-person households in 2005 (Wafer 2006). Families with children are prioritised and rental units tend to be configured towards the needs of families with children (Burke 2008), placing most single adults in a disadvantageous position regarding housing access. Despite the priority to house families, a total of 16 per cent (n=220) of homeless households in Dublin contained child dependents and accounted for 463 children, of whom almost three-quarters were 11 years or under. Of these homeless households, almost three-quarters (72 per cent) were recorded as staying in B&B accommodation for some or all of the previous seven days (Wafer 2006). Notwithstanding the development of some alternative accommodation services for families and a reduction in the number of homeless households with children since 2002, it remains the case that homeless children and their parents are forced to share cramped and unsuitable living conditions with detrimental consequences for their social and psychological well-being (Halpenny et al. 2002).

Homeless households rely heavily on emergency accommodation in Dublin. Bed and breakfast accommodation (privately owned but block booked by local authorities for emergency accommodation) was the most commonly reported arrangement (38 per cent), followed by hostel accommodation (22 per cent). Sleeping rough is considered to be the 'most extreme form of homelessness' (Anderson and Christian 2003: 114) and enumerating those who sleep rough within a particular timeframe is difficult, not least because of the extremely transient nature of their existence. Despite these limitations, the *Counted In* data recorded 14 per cent of homeless households, or 185 individuals, as rough sleepers (Wafer 2006). Taken together, the high proportion of the homeless population reporting use of emergency accommodation, or rough sleeping, reflects the dearth of services to assist individuals' move out of homelessness. This results in homeless people spending long periods in emergency homeless services and is particularly significant given that 'the lack of "move-on accommodation" … hinders and sometimes impedes reintegration' (FEANTSA 2005: 26). In turn, reintegration becomes increasingly difficult as homelessness persists (Higgins 2001). It is perhaps unsurprising to find that of the 1,361 recorded homeless households in Dublin, 26 per cent had been homeless between six months and three years, and an additional 34 per cent had been homeless for more than three years (Wafer 2006), illustrating that long-term homelessness (defined as being homeless for six months or more) is not uncommon.

YOUTH HOMELESSNESS

It is difficult to establish an accurate figure of the number of homeless youth given that there is no centralised system for gathering and co-ordinating information from all of the agencies that work with homeless young people (Department of Health and Children 2001c). Furthermore, data are collected only on those youth who access homeless services and do not account for those who remain outside the formal support system (Mayock and Carr 2008).

The official data source on youth homelessness is based on the number of young people who appear to be homeless according to Health Service Executive (HSE) records. In 2004, 495 young people under 18 years old were identified as homeless. Of those, 254 were female, and just under two-thirds (63 per cent) were aged between 16 and 18 years, almost one-quarter (24 per cent) were aged 14 and 15 years and a smaller proportion (13 per cent) were under 14 years.[3] Notwithstanding the caveats associated with officially recorded data, it would seem that youth homelessness has declined since the late 1990s, when 774 were identified as homeless (Department of Health and Children 1999).[4] Since 2004, a youth homeless contact form is completed for all homeless young people who come into contact with statutory and HSE-funded agencies. The total number of contacts made by 495 homeless young people in 2004 was 1,038, illustrating that some individuals had presented as homeless on more than one occasion. A breakdown of current sleeping arrangements was provided for 923 of the total contacts. As demonstrated in Table 27.2, the majority (517) of contacts were generated through the Out-of-Hours Crisis Intervention Service, followed by those in other emergency accommodation arrangements. In total, 30 contacts involved cases of young people sleeping on the streets and a further 26 cases accounted for those staying in accommodation not intended as night-time accommodation or not providing protection against the elements (Department of Health and Children 2004a).

Table 27.2. Total Number of Youth Homeless Contacts by Current Sleeping Arrangement

Out-of-home and sleeping on streets	30
Out-of-home and sleeping in places not intended for night-time accommodation	17
Out-of-home and sleeping in places not providing safe protection from the elements	9
Out-of-home and coming to the attention of the Health Board's out-of-hours service (currently relevant in the ERHA)	517
Out-of-home and sleeping in places that provide protection from the elements but are intended for short stay only, e.g. emergency or temporary lodgings/accommodation provided by the Health Board or a non-statutory organisation	154
Out-of-home and sleeping in places that provide protection from the elements but where the young person is not in a position to remain	140
Out-of-home and sleeping in places that provide protection from the elements but where the Health Board would have concerns regarding the welfare of the young person if he/she remains in this accommodation	43
Other reason not listed above (see summary)	13
TOTAL	**923**

Source: Child Care Interim Dataset (2004).

BECOMING HOMELESS

Structural issues such as poverty and unemployment, coupled with an inability to access appropriate housing, have been consistently forwarded as contributory factors to homelessness. However, as O'Sullivan (2008) argues, structural explanations do not explain why only some households that experience impoverished circumstances become homeless as a result. It is increasingly acknowledged, therefore, that the risk factors associated with homelessness are complex and involve a number of structural, institutional, family and individual issues (see Table 27.3).

Households may experience a range of risk factors in the lead-up to becoming homeless, but a single 'trigger' or event is usually related 'to finally pushing them into homelessness' (Anderson and Tulloch 2000: 50). Triggers range from leaving home after an argument or relationship breakdown, to eviction from accommodation or financial crisis, through to leaving prison or state care (Fitzpatrick et al. 2000; Greater London Authority Research Group 2000).

Care leavers have been identified as being especially vulnerable to homelessness (Fitzpatrick et al. 2000; Kelleher et al. 2000; Mayock and O'Sullivan 2007). Although the link between residential care, foster care and homelessness requires

Table 27.3. Risk Factors for Becoming Homeless

Structural factors	• Shortage of affordable housing. • Low income and poverty.
Institutional factors	• Being in local authority care. • Being in the armed forces.
Family background factors	• Experience of family homelessness in childhood. • Family breakdown and disputes. • Being in reconstituted families with stepparents. • Sexual or physical abuse in childhood or adolescence. • Experiencing premature death of parents or stepparents. • Having parents or stepparents with drug or alcohol problems. • Having a mother aged under 25 at birth of first child.
Individual factors	• Using drink or drugs at an early age. • Getting involved in crime at an early age. • Offending behaviour and/or experience of prison. • Having difficulties at school and lack of qualifications. • Lack of social support networks. • Debts, especially rent or mortgage arrears. • Causing nuisance to neighbours. • Drug or alcohol misuse. • Poor physical or mental health.

Source: Anderson and Tulloch (2000: 48).

further study, Metraux and Culhane (1999: 375) conclude that the relationship between these variables 'appears to manifest itself as a mutually reinforcing cycle'. Efforts to access accommodation are compounded for ex-prisoners by the stigma of their imprisonment, which places them at risk of homelessness, particularly if they have undergone limited preparation for release (Seymour and Costello 2005). Family conflict, relationship difficulties, abuse, substance misuse, mental health problems, criminality and victimisation are all associated with increasing the likelihood of becoming homeless (Anderson et al. 1993; Fitzpatrick et al. 2000; Randall and Brown 1999; Thrane et al. 2006; Wardhaugh 2000).[5] However, it is equally the case that many of these issues occur for the first time, or are exacerbated, as a *consequence* of becoming homeless (Lawless and Corr 2005; Tyler and Johnson 2006). Overall, the evidence suggests that the multiplicity of risk factors associated with homelessness requires a diverse and nuanced health and social care response to meet the needs of the homeless.

ROUTES INTO HOMELESSNESS

Of themselves, risk factors tell us little about the processes by which individuals become homeless. The need for a more sophisticated analysis to explain homeless causation has been advocated (Anderson and Christian 2003) and recent research has focused attention on the process by which factors combine and create *pathways* into homelessness (Mayock and Carr 2008; Mayock and O'Sullivan 2007; Warnes and Crane 2006). Anderson and Tulloch (2000: 18) suggest that pathways fall under three age-related categories: youth pathways (15–24 years), adult pathways (20–50 years) and later life pathways (50+ years).

Youth Pathways

Recent studies of homeless young people in Dublin (Mayock and Veki 2006) and in Cork (Mayock and Carr 2008) identified three different but interrelated pathways into homelessness. Mayock and Carr (2008: 36) explain that 'while typologies [pathways] provide a useful tool for framing and understanding the complex transition to homelessness, not all young people fit neatly into the pathways identified'. In these circumstances, young people were assigned to the group most representative of their life circumstances and experiences. The three common pathways that emerged from a total of 77 biographical interviews across the two studies were having a care history; experiencing household instability and family conflict; and becoming involved in problem behaviour and negative peer association.[6]

- *Care history pathway:* A distinct pathway for one group of young people emanated from their history of state care. Their experiences were characterised by separation from their family, multiple placements, placement breakdown and social isolation. In turn, they sought alternative sources of support, including anti-social peer groups that sometimes led them to drug use and criminal activity (Mayock and O'Sullivan 2007). The combination of failed care placements and a lack of a nurturing environment were identified as placing them at increased risk of homelessness.

- *Household instability and family conflict pathway:* Another group consisted of young people who lived mostly with family or extended family, but their negative experiences at home eventually culminated in them leaving home. The negative experiences described were broadly similar to those in the international literature (Thrane et al. 2006; Tyler and Johnson 2006) and included frequent moves as children, family problems for several years, trauma, conflict related to a stepparent in the home, assault, parental drinking, inconsistent parenting and unfair treatment.

- *Negative peer associations and 'problem' behaviour pathway:* The final group of young people consisted of those who described how risk behaviour, drinking, drug use and negative peers led to them being 'kicked out' of home and to contact with the police. Most of this group also outlined events and circumstances that left them vulnerable, including serious illness or death of a family member, and tension and conflict in the home (Mayock and O'Sullivan 2007).

Adult Pathways

In contrast to youth homelessness, pathways into adult homelessness are more often attributed to a lack of suitable and affordable accommodation at a time of crisis (Pillinger 2007) and financial matters such as mortgage arrears/repossession, rent arrears/abandonment or eviction (Anderson and Tulloch 2000). The breakdown of a marital or other intimate relationship can give rise to additional housing needs as one household breaks into two. Relationship breakdown associated with domestic violence creates a differentiated pathway into homelessness, as does leaving institutional care, long-term hospitalisation or imprisonment. A final pathway relates to homelessness linked to addiction or physical and mental health difficulties.

Distinct causes and pathways into homelessness have been identified amongst the elderly. Crane and Warnes's (2006: 412) study of 131 homeless individuals aged 50 years or over found that there were 'five "packages of reasons" that created distinctive "pathways" into elderly homelessness'. While many of the pathways were common to all adults, the death of a close relative or friend was identified as an age-specific pathway amongst this cohort. Those with dependency needs were particularly vulnerable following the death or infirmity of their carer. Other pathways for the elderly are likely to include retirement from longstanding employment with accommodation, domestic violence and mental health problems, including dementia (Anderson and Tulloch 2000).

These youth and adult pathways clearly indicate that homelessness is an issue that permeates all spheres of social care work across all age groups and settings. As a result, practitioners are likely to have a role to play in responding to or preventing homelessness amongst those at risk, whether their work is based in a community or residential setting or in mainstream or homeless services.

RESPONDING TO HOMELESSNESS: LEGISLATION AND POLICY

Statutory responsibility for assisting the homeless was assigned to the local authorities under the Housing Act 1988. As part of its obligations, local authorities were tasked with developing a priority scheme for letting dwellings to those unable to access accommodation from their own resources. They also had the power to give direct financial and other assistance to homeless people or to fund approved agencies to provide and manage homeless accommodation options. Despite these measures, the Act had limited impact in reducing homelessness in the 1990s. One of the main limitations was that it did not place a statutory duty on local authorities to house the homeless. In addition, implementation of the Act coincided with a declining stock of available local authority housing (O'Sullivan 2005), thus limiting the opportunities to access housing, even for those who were deemed worthy.

Publication of the document *Homelessness: An Integrated Strategy* (Department of the Environment and Local Government 2000) has been described as the first 'semblance of a coherent policy approach to the needs of homeless households ... in the history of the Irish state' (O'Sullivan 2004: 336). The terms of reference of the strategy were 'to develop an integrated response to the many issues which affect homeless people including emergency, transitional and long-term responses as well as issues relating to health, education, employment and home-making' (Department of the Environment and Local Government 2000: 3). Arising from the strategy, each county was tasked with developing a three-year action plan for the delivery of all services to the homeless at local level. Homeless forums were established across the country, consisting of representatives from the local authorities, the HSE (formerly the Health Boards) and the voluntary bodies. Local authorities held responsibility for providing accommodation to homeless people and the Health Boards were tasked with providing health and social care services. In recognition of the extent of homelessness in Dublin, the Homeless Agency (formerly the Homeless Initiative) was established in 2001 as a partnership structure to bring together the voluntary and statutory agencies responsible for planning, funding and delivering homeless services in the local authority areas of Dublin City, Dun Laoghaire/Rathdown, Fingal and South Dublin.[7]

The *Homeless Preventative Strategy 2002* was another noteworthy policy development. It focused attention on the need for early intervention and prevention of homelessness amongst at-risk groups such as those leaving mental health and acute care facilities, adult and young offenders and young people leaving care. Recommendations included the need to develop appropriate policies and procedures to avoid situations whereby individuals become homeless as a result of unplanned releases or discharges from institutional care or custody.

In 2005, the government commissioned a review of the implementation of the *Integrated Strategy* and the *Preventative Strategy* (Fitzpatrick Associates 2006). The review culminated in a report recommending the introduction of a new revised homeless strategy, with the elimination of long-term homelessness as its core objective. It outlined a series of recommendations to prevent homelessness, to improve co-ordination and co-operation across all homeless service agency sectors and to ensure greater consistency in the management of individual homeless cases by adopting a standard case management approach.[8]

The recommendations of the review were accepted by the government and formalised in the *National Action Plan for Social Inclusion 2007–2016* (Government of Ireland 2007a). They also shaped the most recent strategy on homelessness, entitled *The Way Home: A Strategy to Address Adult Homelessness in Ireland 2008–2013* (Department of the Environment, Heritage and Local Government 2008). This strategy is based on an ambitious vision to eliminate long-term homelessness (defined as an individual occupying emergency accommodation for longer than six months) by 2010 and to minimise homelessness through effective preventative policies and services. Underpinning the vision are six strategic aims:

- To prevent homelessness through early intervention with those at risk of homelessness, using mainstream services targeted in areas such as early school-leaving, unemployment, addiction and mental health, amongst others.
- To eliminate the need to sleep rough. This aim is contingent on the availability of emergency and long-term accommodation options.
- To eliminate long-term homelessness. This requires the provision of an adequate supply of long-term housing options in each local area, as well as an appropriate level of community support services for vulnerable households.
- To meet long-term housing needs, focusing on the acquisition of increased housing stock, and greater use of the private, voluntary and co-operative housing sectors and other schemes, including the Rental Accommodation Scheme (RAS).[9]
- To ensure effective services to assist individuals' move out of homelessness and the provision of standards to improve consistency in the quality of homeless services.
- To improve co-ordination of funding arrangements to allow for a more streamlined system of service provision.

Substantial resources will be required to fully implement the strategy and to achieve the goal of eliminating long-term homelessness. It remains to be seen if this can be achieved, particularly in the context of declining economic prosperity and considerable limitations on government finance.

YOUTH HOMELESSNESS POLICY

Under Section 5 of the Child Care Act 1991, the HSE has a statutory responsibility to provide for children aged under 18 years who become homeless. The strategic approach to youth homelessness is set out in the *Youth Homeless Strategy 2001*. The goal of the strategy is to reduce and if possible eliminate youth homelessness through preventative strategies, and where this is not possible to ensure that a comprehensive range of services aimed at reintegrating the child into his/her community are provided as quickly as possible (Department of Health and Children 2001c). The objectives set out to prevent homelessness include the development of multi-agency services and multidisciplinary teams to target young people at risk, and a strengthening of aftercare services for children leaving foster care, residential care, centres for young offenders and other supported accommodation.[10] Where homelessness occurs, the objectives are focused on minimising the impact on the child through the provision of accessible emergency services, the development of a care plan and the appointment of a key worker for the child or young person. This response has the objective of providing accommodation and support services to meet children's health, educational, welfare and recreational needs. The HSE is the lead agency responsible for implementing the strategy and the Child Welfare and Protection Unit at the Office of the Minister for Children and Youth Affairs (OMCYA) monitors the implementation via the Youth Homelessness Strategy Monitoring Committee (YHSMC). In the absence of a review of the *Youth Homelessness Strategy 2001*, other data sources are drawn from when commenting on youth homelessness policy and service provision since the turn of the century.

As mentioned previously, there has been a downward decline in the number of young people recorded as homeless; however, access to key services in the areas of family support, drugs, mental health and appropriate care placements continue to present challenges to the goal of preventing young people from becoming homeless in the first instance (Department of Health and Children 2005; Social Services Inspectorate 2003). The dearth of services further increases the risk of homelessness in already vulnerable young people, particularly those with a history of care or social service involvement. A number of services have been developed to assist homeless youth since the implementation of the strategy, but it remains the case that there is an over-reliance on the use of emergency accommodation and limited opportunities for long-term placements to move young people out of homelessness. The importance of moving young people off the streets at the earliest opportunity is central to minimising the risk of long-term homelessness. Furthermore, it is essential in light of the evidence that suggests young people become quickly immersed in the homeless culture of the streets, including risk behaviour, criminality (Hagan and McCarthy 1997) and its associated dangers, such as exploitation and victimisation (Mayock 2008; Thrane et al. 2006). Finally, if young people remain homeless, they automatically transfer to the adult homeless system at 18 years of age, irrespective of their maturity, vulnerability or other factors.

SERVICES FOR THE HOMELESS

The Homeless Agency co-ordinates the delivery of homeless services in Dublin, and local homeless forums are tasked with the role in areas outside Dublin. The extent to which needs are identified and resources targeted varies considerably from area to area, resulting in a somewhat limited and/or ad hoc approach to the delivery of homeless services in some areas (Fitzpatrick Associates 2006). The majority of homeless services are provided in urban centres in response to the larger numbers of homeless individuals in these locations. It is not possible to establish the extent to which those who become homeless in rural or suburban areas migrate to urban centres to access services; however, in the Irish context, there is at least some tentative data to support the claim (Fitzpatrick Associates 2006; Wafer 2006).

Traditionally, homeless services in Ireland have focused on providing assistance to the homeless to fulfil their basic needs for food, shelter and advice. As a result of substantial government investment in the homeless sector in recent years, there is a much-improved range of services, including accommodation services, day centres, street outreach services, food centres, health services, advice services, drug rehabilitation and resettlement services. There has also been an expansion in the range of specialist services for some sub-groups of the homeless population, such as street drinkers, drug users and those with mental health difficulties (see www.homelessagency.ie for details of the services available).

While all of these basic and specialist services provide a vital level of support, they cannot, of themselves, assist individuals to *move out* of homelessness. In fact, one of the main criticisms of the system is the limited availability of services to help individuals make the transition away from homelessness. There is a dearth of transitional and long-term supported housing options for homeless people, culminating in many spending long periods of time in short-term emergency hostel accommodation (Edgar and Meert 2006). The absence of stable living arrangements adversely impacts on their opportunities to gain employment and frequently affects their ability to address the very issues that may have led them into homelessness in the first place. The result is that many struggle to maintain a level of stability in their lives, becoming trapped in a system of short-term assistance matched with long-term uncertainty.

CHALLENGES FOR SOCIAL CARE PRACTITIONERS

The challenge for social care practitioners in the years ahead will be to develop their practice in line with the policy goals and strategies for preventing and eliminating long-term homelessness amongst adults and young people. Homeless prevention work encompasses a wide range of social care tasks and is not restricted to work with homeless young people or adults. Ensuring that vulnerable individuals and families are supported in a way that diminishes their risk of homelessness, either through direct work with them or by accessing support services on their behalf, are important preventative roles executed by social care practitioners. Preventing homelessness can also entail working with those in state care, acute hospitals or prisons to reduce their vulnerability to homelessness on their return to the community. The challenge for social care practitioners is to work effectively on an individual or collaborative inter-agency basis to minimise the crises that often leave individuals and families without stable housing.

Necessity may bring many homeless people into daily contact with services, but for some, the profoundly negative social and psychological effects of homelessness (Bentley 1997; Vandemark 2007) will impact on their ability or willingness to engage with services (Crane and Warnes 2005). Others may resist the intervention of services because of the stigma associated with being identified as homeless (Cleary et al. 2004; Harter et al. 2005), because of previous negative experiences with homeless services (Hoffman and Coffey 2008) or because they have chosen to manage their homeless existence without service intervention (Osborne 2002).

Some sub-groups of the homeless population, such as young people and those with mental health, substance abuse or related problems, are likely to present additional challenges to practitioners. Homeless young people are required to navigate the pathway to adulthood and experience the challenges associated with it while also coping with the absence of a stable home. In negotiating this pathway, they require support on the one hand and independence on the other (De Winter and Noom 2003), leaving a challenge for service providers 'to strike a balance between recognising and respecting young people's social and cultural worlds, and at the same time, setting rules that help to protect [them]' (Mayock and O'Sullivan 2007: 238).

Working with those with mental health and substance abuse problems is another challenging role that requires a balance between meeting the day-to-day needs associated with being homeless while also having due regard for the difficulties related to the addiction or health-related problems. Challenges reported by practitioners include the need to detect and recognise the signs and symptoms of different drugs, to deal with the multiple needs of homeless drug users, to motivate service users, to address preconceptions about homeless drug users and to have regard for staff and service user safety (Lawless and Corr 2005).

The complexity of factors underlying entry into homelessness requires social care practitioners to advocate for and access a range of services and supports for homeless service users. It is in negotiating this system that social care practitioners may face the greatest challenges. The limited availability of specialist services and long-term accommodation options, as documented above, may limit the extent to which practitioners can fully support homeless individuals. Finally, the heterogeneity of risk factors and pathways into homelessness provides strong evidence of the need to avoid making assumptions about the needs of homeless people or attempting to impose interventions based on these assumptions (Kidd et al. 2007). It is in this context that social care practitioners must be mindful of the incontestable right of homeless individuals to choose or reject intervention and to be accorded respect on the basis of their decision.

CONCLUSION

This chapter set out to provide an overview of homelessness, particularly focusing on the policy and practice issues relevant to the role of the social care practitioner. Homelessness by definition and context is a complex phenomenon that requires careful exploration and analysis. A nuanced understanding of homelessness that recognises the diversity of the profile and needs of the homeless population provides an important baseline from which to develop practice in the area of preventing and responding to homelessness. Homelessness has been the focus of numerous social research agendas, but to date there has been limited evaluation of the effectiveness of services for homeless people (Crane and Warnes 2005; Lawless and Corr 2005) or opportunities for them to be involved in a meaningful way in informing policy and service development and delivery (Anderson and Christian 2003). In practice, as in research, the voice of the service user must remain paramount, particularly when working with some of the most vulnerable and marginalised individuals in society.

Social Care in a Multicultural Society

Celesta McCann James

OVERVIEW

For the first time in recent history, Ireland has become a country of immigration, with movement, relocation and resettlement occurring for thousands of individuals. Although immigration to Ireland is not a new phenomenon, rapidly increasing numbers combined with a perception of 'difference' (for example, in relation to skin colour, clothing or religion) is unprecedented. The 2006 census reveals that 10 per cent of the present population are immigrants (Central Statistics Office 2007b), resulting in definitions and experiences of modern Irish society being challenged and changed.

'Immigrant' is the term generally used to describe those individuals or groups of individuals who come from another country and are granted legal permission to live in a host country. Most definitions of immigrants imply a permanent or semi-permanent residency to a specific country, regulated by state legislation regarding rights to employment, education, health services and so on. In comparison, the term 'migrant' refers to an individual who is primarily motivated by economics and who usually moves within or from their own country with the purpose of seeking employment. Migrants may move to a number of places, doing seasonal work or living temporarily in any given location. The terms 'immigrant' and 'migrant' are used interchangeably in Irish literature, with only minor differentiation, if any, being highlighted (for example, Feldman et al. 2008).

Another term widely associated with this change in Irish demography is 'multiculturalism'. This describes an ideology and subsequent social policies or institutions that imply a recognition and validation of ethnocultural minorities as well as the promotional acceptance of difference, including societal structures that support ethnic organisations and common concerns, such as human rights or fear of racism.

For many Irish citizens previously accustomed to a single, dominant culture, the exposure to different traditions, customs and routines is an unfamiliar reality. New faces, identities and practices appear in shops, local pubs and the media, at recreational facilities, school, work and, sometimes, next door. Among the newcomers are those seeking economic and/or social opportunities, while others come to seek asylum and refuge. Ireland is legally and socially obliged to admit these immigrants as refugees, if and when their case is proven. It also has a political and moral duty to ensure that immigrants have access to appropriate legal, social, health and educational services.

Some political and media speculation has fuelled hostility towards immigrants, portraying them as 'illegal' or 'bogus' non-nationals unworthy of social assistance that is not rightfully theirs, thereby costing the Irish taxpayer unfairly and unjustly (see, for example, Immigration Control Platform 2008). In research on migrants and social resources in the Dublin 15 area, Ní Chonaill (2007) found that while some Irish people view migrants' presence and participation as acceptable when resources are abundant (jobs, housing), views were very different when resources were perceived as scarce (school places). Participants' views in Ní Chonaill's research parallel findings from Balibar (1991) and Lewis (2005) that indicate that refugees and migrants are blamed for scarcity in social resources.

This discourse distracts the focus from the Irish government's failure to plan and provide for adequate public services. Lorenz (1998) notes that perceived misappropriation of taxpayers' money is not limited to existing definitions commonly associated with commercial transactions (such as having paid into insurance funds as a precondition for getting benefits), but through cultural criteria such as not being 'of the same kind'. Yet close inspection of Irish statistics reveals that the majority of immigrants are Irish returning from abroad or Europeans from EU countries, followed by 25,326 from Asia, 24,425 from Africa and a further 45,549 from the rest of Europe and the Americas (Central Statistics Office 2007b).

This chapter focuses on three related aspects of social care practice in Ireland. In order to put the discussion of care provision and multiculturalism into an Irish perspective, modern trends in immigration will first be presented and will include the identification of policy issues and current responses that support or neglect the care needs of immigrants. Having outlined social care provision for immigrants, the chapter will then contextualise key concepts related to a multicultural society: ethnicity, racism and, in particular, institutional oppression. It is acknowledged that any discussion on multiculturalism in Ireland is incomplete without reference to Travellers. Their specific contribution to and participation in Irish society is discussed in Chapter 24. By recognising the effects of oppression on social institutions, this chapter will help to clarify challenges that face the social care profession. Finally, a model for strategic change will be presented that offers an integrated approach to best practice for all those involved in social care practice in a multicultural society.

EMERGING TRENDS IN IMMIGRATION AND CARE PROVISION

Recent years have produced a growing body of research evidence on changing migration patterns in Ireland. In addition to migration between EU countries, specific attention has been given to the upsurge of individuals and minority groups who enter Ireland either as refugees or as asylum seekers. The Office of the Refugee Applications Commissioner (ORAC 2007: 8) defines a refugee as:

> a person who, owing to a well-founded fear of being persecuted for reasons of race, religion, nationality, membership of a particular social group or political opinion, is outside the country of his or her nationality and is unable or, owing to such fear, is unwilling to avail himself or herself of the protection of that country; or who, not having a nationality and being outside of the country of his or her former habitual residence, is unable or, owing to such fear, is unwilling to return to it.

In comparison, an asylum seeker is defined as 'a person who seeks to be recognised as a refugee in accordance with the terms of the 1951 Geneva Convention relating to the status of refugees and the related 1967 Protocol, which provides the foundation for the international protection of refugees' (Office of the Refugee Applications Commissioner 2007: 7). The annual report published by the Office of the Refugee Applications Commissioner (ORAC 2006) states that in 1992 there were 29 applications for asylum in Ireland, but by 2002 this number had risen to 11,632. By 2005, applications had decreased to 4,323 and in 2007 the number of applications was at 3,985 (Kanics 2007). The overall increase has been accompanied by serious economic and social challenges, particularly experienced in the eastern region of the country, where major responsibility for the needs of asylum seekers falls to the Health Service Executive (HSE).

Implications for social care provision therefore coincide with wider political, social and economic concerns, where parity of opportunities is conditional upon social policies and legislation that define entitlements. Government reports show that immigrants are twice as likely to be experiencing consistent poverty and deprivation (Office for Social Inclusion 2007c) and employment, enterprise, education and welfare rights are partly restricted as a result of policies such as the Habitual Residence Condition that restricts new immigrants from access to certain social welfare assistance payments and child benefits (Department of Social and Family Affairs 2008; Nasc 2008).

The need to provide services to a culturally diverse and ethnically hetero-geneous population is unprecedented in Ireland. As a result, contemporary research and debate have focused on social services and inclusion and have challenged public awareness and social policy development (Begley et al. 1999; Fanning 2001; Faughnan 1999; Faughnan and O'Donovan 2002; Feldman et al. 2002; Office for Social Inclusion 2006, 2007a, 2007b, 2007c; Torode et al. 2001; Ward 2001). While some studies have concentrated on the experiences of statutory service workers who respond to the reception needs of asylum seekers and refugees (Faughnan et al. 2002), a renewed discussion has centred on human rights and entitlements for immigrants, focusing on the process of domination and power held by the state and its control over those seeking inclusion and/or citizenship (Bloemraad 2007; Gilroy 1998; Heisler-Schmitter 1992; Lentin 2004, 2007).

On 11 June 2004, the Irish electorate voted to change Article 9 of the Irish Constitution. Following lengthy media and political debates about nationality and citizenship, entitlement to *jus sanguinis* (blood-based) rights took precedence over the *jus solis* (soil-based) citizenship rights formerly granted to anyone born in Ireland. With the stated intent of preventing the 'abuse' of citizenship rules by pregnant asylum seekers, the amendment was adopted by the Irish public, who voted overwhelmingly by a majority of four to one in favour of the amendment. King (2004) argues strongly that the Irish government based its campaign for constitutional change on obscure, inconsistent and inaccurate statistics along with anecdotal evidence that was both uncertain and highly subjective. According to Lentin (2007), the Irish Constitution became a tool in defending the newly defined 'integrity of Irish citizenship'.

In an analysis of racism in Ireland, Lentin (2004, 2007) and Lentin and McVeigh (2006) have argued that the regulation of citizenship is in direct contradiction to the government's supposed commitment to equality, care and interculturalism. Rather than facilitating social, economic and political cohesiveness, the revised constitution has created a 'racist state' where persons born on the island of Ireland no longer have an entitlement to Irish citizenship (Lentin 2007).

UNACCOMPANIED MINORS

Amongst the thousands of individuals, families and groups migrating to Ireland, many are children, accompanied or unaccompanied, seeking refuge and asylum. Of asylum seekers, 3.2 per cent of applications in 2006 were on behalf of children (Mooten 2006). These children are vulnerable and dependent upon a humane and compassionate response from Ireland's social care services. This has prompted research that explores procedures and working relationships between Irish social care professionals and unaccompanied children from ethnic minority backgrounds. The Irish Refugee Council (1999) has argued that for unaccompanied minors, immigration status should not be the state's priority, but rather, their well-being as children should take precedence. Care should also be delivered within the context of the Irish state's obligation to treat all children in its jurisdiction equally (United Nations Committee on the Rights of the Child 2005).

In 1999, the Irish Refugee Council published a report that revealed that there were 32 separated children seeking asylum in Ireland (Irish Refugee Council 1999). According to the Office of the Minister for Children (2006b), the numbers presenting to the HSE were 1,085 in 2001 and 668 in 2005. Of these cases, the majority were reunited with their families, while 32 per cent were taken into care. While we know little about why separated children leave their country of origin, research by Vekic (2003) and Conroy (2004) cites factors such as escaping war and discrimination, parental detention or death, and poverty. Regardless of why children arrive, the UN Convention on the Rights of the Child states that:

[P]arties shall take appropriate measures to ensure that a child who is seeking refugee status … shall, whether unaccompanied or accompanied by his or her parents or by any other person, receive appropriate protection and humanitarian assistance in the enjoyment of applicable rights set forth in the present Convention and in other international human rights or humanitarian instruments to which the said States are Parties. (Article 22(1))

The Parties to this Convention also undertook in Article 22(2) to co-operate with different organisations not only to protect and assist refugee children, but to help trace family members in order to facilitate family reunification. Articles 19, 34, 37(a) and 37(c) of the Convention state that if reunification with family is unsuccessful, the child shall be accorded the same protection as any other child permanently or temporarily deprived of his or her family environment. In Ireland, explicit provisions in the Child Care Act 1991 specify that unaccompanied minors are to be provided for. This includes an obligation under Article 3(2)(a) on the part of the HSE to identify children who are not receiving adequate care and protection. In addition, it is the duty of the HSE, under Article 4(1), to take into care any child who is residing or located in its area requiring care or protection.

Significant concerns arise in relation to social care provision for children who are members of ethnic minority groups and separated from their families. According to Conroy and Fitzgerald (2005), Fanning (2004) and Veale et al. (2003), separated children in care do not automatically benefit from the same services as their Irish counterparts. Older teenagers are placed in hostels rather than residential children's homes and their accommodation and subsequent services are not monitored by the Social Services Inspectorate. Furthermore, the Reception and Integration Agency (2003) outlines its policy of reception and dispersal for children aged 16 or over who are seeking asylum. It states that children who are not reunited with their family are placed in self-catering hostels, where they receive a full supplementary welfare allowance (€124.80 per week) and prepare their own meals. Interim care becomes the responsibility of a social welfare team who work in partnership with hostel staff to access medical and social services for minors, including appointments with the Refugee Legal Service, Office of the Refugee Application Commissioner and Refugee Appeals Tribunal. Children aged six to 14 years of age are placed in residential care, supportive lodgings or in foster care and attempts are made to place very young children in foster care.

As the Child Care Act 1991 does not specifically refer to 'separated children', non-Irish unaccompanied minors seeking refuge or asylum are treated as homeless Irish children for welfare purposes. Care, therefore, is often inappropriate and disordered, as it has not been designed for specific circumstances such as experience of recent trauma, coping with a new and unfamiliar culture, a different language, an unfamiliar educational system or the absence of family and friends. Additionally, social care providers are constrained by a lack of resources, such as training in language and cultural diversity. In response, the Office of the Minister for Children (OMC) published a report in 2006 entitled *Diversity and Equality Guidelines for Childcare Providers* (Office of the Minister for Children 2006a). For those who work in the child care sector, the report provides relevant and practical information regarding steps towards supporting equal and inclusive treatment and encourages the development of services that are inclusive of all children and their families.

OTHER ISSUES RELATED TO CULTURAL DIVERSITY

As crucial as it is to implement practical and effective care for unaccompanied minors, we must not overlook the increasing challenge that faces the profession in providing care for other service user groups. As in the 'Irish' community, ethnic minority groups have members who are disabled, elderly, homeless or socially troubled. Many newcomers enter Ireland as family groups and will present needs to professional care services that are broader than the requirement to assist unaccompanied minors. In many ways, care practitioners are already overstretched and under-resourced – how much more stretched will the profession be when caring for young and heavily pregnant women, or disabled or elderly immigrants who have little English and unfamiliar cultural practices?

Practitioners and service users recognise that language and cultural barriers can limit the provision of effective and meaningful social care. When a service user and worker do not speak the same language, we can expect that cultural understanding may also be absent or at least problematic. The social care profession, therefore, is faced with the challenge of informing its practice with theoretical knowledge, skill-based experience and attitudinal competencies that reflect an inclusive, multicultural Ireland. This is not a challenge that will be easily met, but it can be addressed purposefully and systematically.

O'Loingsigh (2001) maintains that although structural barriers inhibit the active or real participation by ethnic minorities in the education system, intercultural education is an education for both the minorities and the majority community in Irish society. Fundamental instruction in communicative and cultural acquisition could be required as part of the curriculum offered to future care practitioners, a curriculum that explores and applies tolerance, human rights, democracy and respect for difference rather than concerning itself with 'integrating' ethnic minorities into a social care system that makes service users 'more Irish'.

At present, many of the third-level institutions that offer academic qualifications in social care integrate intercultural training throughout their academic programmes. Some offer full modules with cultural diversity as a focus as well as research opportunities for undergraduate and postgraduate students. This is facilitated through regular exposure to and experience with diverse ethnic communities and practices throughout Irish society as well as participation in social care practice placement arrangements outside Ireland.

CURRENT CHALLENGES FACING PROFESSIONAL SOCIAL CARE

As a profession, social care practice is faced with the challenge of providing adequate and appropriate care to vulnerable service users, such as minors, the disabled, older people and those outside of home. For some of these service users, their national and cultural characteristics may be different from those of the dominant Irish culture. Such distinctions do not make physical and social needs less legitimate, nor do they dilute the legal responsibility or social obligations to provide a fair and humane service to all those residing in the state.

By definition, social care services reflect more than physical or material support, thus we are drawn into an ethical and philosophical sphere where cultural uncertainties cause us to examine our beliefs and values. The following questions therefore deserve consideration by all social care practitioners:

- Can society continue to prioritise care on the basis of dominant social and cultural practices?
- Is social care afforded only to those in our society who are 'worthy' members of the dominant culture (such as Irish or EU citizens) or perhaps to those individuals who make 'genuine' contributions through voluntary or paid work?
- Are Irish social services provided or withheld on the basis of nationality, contributions, ethnicity or need?
- Will we develop and deliver social care services that are capable of providing effective support for all residents in Ireland who need care?
- Whose interests are being served in the present provision of social care: state officials', administrators', taxpayers' or those who are users of care services?
- Will the Irish social care profession progress to ensure that ethnic and cultural differences are embraced thoughtfully and sensitively, guaranteeing a truly caring service that is inclusive of all those seeking or dependent on its provision?

Questions such as these are hard to ask, but even more problematic to answer. Responses and solutions are dependent upon complex systems that involve philosophies, politics and practices from a variety of perspectives. Inevitably they involve concepts such as *ethnicity*, *racism* and *oppression*.

ETHNICITY

The term 'ethnicity' derives from the Greek '*ethnos*', meaning 'people' or 'tribe'. Simply defined, ethnicity describes characteristics that relationally connect people together in a manner that negotiates a group identity, be it political, religious, cultural or social. The underlying beliefs and values that support such a bond offer solidarity and a 'sense of belonging', collective membership and shared experiences. According to Smith (1991), ethnic groups may be defined both internally and externally, offering a way of distinguishing 'them' from 'us'. Members of an ethnic group possess cultural solidarity that often extends from generation to generation, making them eligible to access the social, emotional and physical benefits of 'inclusion' within their community. Unity is reinforced when an ethnic group sustains a collective sense of continuity by adopting a specific name, sharing historical memories and/or common ancestry, associating with a specific homeland or differentiating elements of common culture, beliefs and boundaries (Glazer and Moynihan 1975; Jenkins 1996b, 1997).

The issue of ethnicity is inevitably linked with questions of identity and difference. Although not unique, until recently Ireland has been categorised as a monocultural society with social institutions that reinforce sameness. As a result, Irish identity has exhibited specific forms of approved social practices, be they political, economic, religious, educational or familial. This 'institutionalised culture' has informed and influenced individuals and group relationships and has defined dominant values and patterns of behaviour. Similar to sociological norms in other cultures, Ireland's ethnic and other minority communities have been socially stratified, being organised in a subordinate fashion and allowed, at the very most, to be identified as Irish sub-cultures.

RACISM AND INSTITUTIONAL OPPRESSION

'Racism' is a term used by sociologists to denote a belief (or an action based on belief) that one racial category is superior or inferior to another racial category. Racism defines patterns of thought or action that allow individuals or groups to be considered different, often with negative consequences. Whether or not the thought or action intends to inspire discrimination is irrelevant, as racism is seen to exist when a deliberate or unintentional attitude or behaviour disadvantages the social position of a specific racially defined group in society. Ireland has participated in the debate about racism and nationalism, seeking its own clarity as to the implications of 'Irishness' and citizenship. It has sought answers to rapid changes in a society where adjustments are occurring within the traditional understanding of national identity within the economy, family structure, religion and language (Farrell and Watt 2001; Lentin 1998; Royal Irish Academy 2003).

Oppression describes a complex situation that may result from many processes. It is a condition that is relatively stable and may be reflected in the education system, the legal system, the media and social customs. What separates it from other kinds of mistreatment is its systematic nature. By 'systematic', we mean that the mistreatment is part of the social system. It is a structure of inequality in which one group systematically dominates the other by means of interrelated social practices (Frye 1983). Systematic domination is also present when hierarchical controls exist that are not consensual and that involve institutionalised inequality (Moane 1994). Whenever there is systematic domination of the members of one group by the members of another group or by society as a whole, we call it oppression. The presence of ethnic or racial discrimination in society is categorised as oppressive, then, when social structures are organised and operate in a way that maintains discriminating and unequal practices. For example, the social ranking or stratification of particular ethnic groups or communities may disadvantage their access to and equal participation in social services.

Oppression is not a random affair, but is predictable (Knoppers 1993; Van Leeuwen 1993). If we say that individuals or particular groups (such as refugees) are oppressed in Irish society, we should be able to predict the kinds of experiences they are likely to confront. These experiences will be encountered regardless of which individual member is involved. Although oppression can take the form of deliberate and premeditated abuse of vulnerable individuals or groups, it is described more often as camouflaged, operating within socially approved and authorised structures. Difficulty (or unwillingness) to discern the systematic nature of oppression facilitates its continuance and helps to maintain unequal power structures.

Knoppers (1993) claims that oppression is easily reproduced because its features become intertwined in society, where both dominants and subordinates fail to 'see' or 'feel' it in their lives. Moane (1994, 1999) maintains that although patterns of oppression are generally unrecognised, of those signs that are visible, most are viewed as unalterable. This helps to sustain long-standing hierarchical management and social systems. It is therefore understandable that *institutional oppression*, as encountered in the social care system, may be viewed as impenetrable. Although care practitioners may not consciously participate in oppressive behaviour, existing mechanisms that surround and support them facilitate the continuation of discriminating programmes and regimes.

Moane (1994) has identified psychological and social patterns associated with being dominant or subordinate in a hierarchical system. She emphasises the link between oppression and areas of psychological functioning that can be understood only by analysing the social context of individuals' lives. The central feature of this social context is that it is hierarchical, or stratified, so that a select number of people have access to power and resources, while others are deprived of the same. Applying this framework, we can now explore the provision of social care services in Ireland and draw parallels that reveal institutionalised patterns of control that legitimate the domination of dependent and vulnerable minority groups.

THE NATURE OF OPPRESSION

Six indicators of oppression are listed below. Each demonstrates an association between existing social care practice and the institutional oppression of some ethnic minority groups in Ireland. Bear in mind that oppression is predictable, therefore experiences in any of the following categories are likely to apply to most members of discriminated groups, regardless of which individual encounters them.

1. *Physical control* is a primary mechanism of oppression and is reflected in punishment or the threat of it to ensure co-operation. It operates within a hierarchical system that depends on forms of coercion, intimidation, threats, imprisonment or beatings. Asylum seekers are physically controlled through the legal processes of immigration. The Refugee Act 1996, as amended by the Immigration Act 2003, incorporates provisions for asylum seekers under Section 9(10)a. The Act states that the individual must be brought before a judge of the District Court 'as soon as is practicable'. In practice, this would normally be the next sitting of the court. An individual can be committed for ensuing periods of up to 21 days without charge by a judge pending the determination of their application under Section 9(10)(b)(i). This is a recurring obligation if the judge orders the individual's continued detention. Further powers of detention are proposed in the Immigration, Residence and Protection Bill 2008, which allows for detention at every stage of the asylum process. Asylum seekers are by definition, then, subject to absolute physical control. They may additionally be referred to one or more agencies under the Department of Justice, Equality and Law Reform (such as the Asylum Policy Unit, Garda National Immigration Bureau, Office of the Refugee Applications Commissioner or Refugee Appeals Tribunal), the UN High Commissioner for Refugees or non-statutory bodies. Noncompliance with any of these agencies may result in imprisonment.

2. *Economic control* reinforces physical control in that members of the oppressed group are kept powerless by prohibiting paid employment or by locating them in low-paid or low-status jobs. While low-paid, low-status jobs may be a simple reflection of minimal skills, training or education, it can be argued that members of oppressed groups have a higher incidence of poverty and are less secure in their jobs than members of other groups because they regularly experience discrimination and lack of access to education and training. For refugees and asylum seekers, employment is prohibited while status decisions are pending; however, the HSE provides accommodation and 'direct provision' plus €19.10 per week to adults and €9.60 per week per child. Furthermore, lack of state support, language skills and information regarding their entitlements increases the risk of disadvantaged social status and economic control for refugees and asylum seekers in Ireland.

3. *Sexual exploitation* is a further form of oppression, often operating through rape and prostitution. The Irish media has reported cases of young asylum seekers and refugees, often traumatised and vulnerable, left unsupervised while in the care of the HSE. Unaccompanied minors have been housed in mixed-sex hostels, sharing their rooms with adult asylum seekers (*Irish Times*, 1 March, 2000). Even more worrying is the disappearance of minors who have fallen out of the welfare system, and research confirms that some minors are involved in

trafficking or prostitution (Conroy 2004). Statistics indicate that approximately 316 separated children seeking asylum have gone missing from the HSE's care since 2001 and 71 separated children seeking asylum went missing in 2005, with 17 subsequently located (Office of the Minister for Children 2006b). In her report on migrant children, Kanics (2007) states that the likely rate of missing children is, on average, one child each week.

4. *Exclusion* is a further form of oppression that removes authority from the subordinate group by withholding power, either through restrictions or lack of representation. Exclusion can take various forms, and when members of minority ethnic groups are demeaned through physical and economic controls (such as peripheral housing, language barriers, economic and employment restrictions), it is often the case that they are excluded and marginalised socially, emotionally and politically from mainstream Irish society. They are perceived as 'different' and often 'unworthy' of meaningful participation and decision-making. Under-representation by ethnic minorities in social care work renders them less influential over decision-making and service provision to service users. This may apply to input regarding policy change, care planning, cultural and religious practices, medical ethics and educational practices. It should be noted that the Office for Social Inclusion (2007a) has proposed that individuals directly affected by policies should be a part of the group(s) that are creating those policies.

5. *Psychological control* underlies most of the above forms of control. It is maintained by the dominant group controlling the definition of what is 'natural' or 'normal' for members of the oppressed group. 'Irish' ideology and culture are managed through the dominance of influential social systems such as education, the media, religion and language. As part of psychological control, there is a suppression (or erasure) of history and the propagation of stereotypes of inferiority, widely facilitated through prejudice, myths, misinformation and unawareness. As members of minority ethnic groups in Ireland, individuals are subjected to an Irish society that, until recently, has been culturally restricted and purposefully isolated. Social care services reflect this background and consequently provide support (and expect co-operation from service users) that largely operates according to the customs and routines of the dominant culture.

6. *Fragmentation and tokenism* regularly occur in a system that promotes a select few of the subordinate group, thereby creating competition and envy among the subordinates – a situation of divide and conquer. In administrative departments in Irish social care, ethnic representation is minimal. Members from minority ethnic communities may be visible as interpreters or as volunteer workers, but as trained personnel with decision-making authority, they are all but absent.

The above indicators demonstrate how members of some ethnic minority groups are oppressed and subsequently marginalised in Irish society. Whether for reasons of race or ethnic origin, physical or economic control, subjection to sexual exploitation, exclusion from meaningful participation and/or psychological dominance, many are left exposed and vulnerable. Even with the best of intentions, social care providers may fail to 'see' or 'feel' oppressive features that are systematically woven into the fabric of care services. As explained earlier, 'systematic' implies that oppression is part of a larger social system and is marked by interrelated social practices that camouflage an inequitable structure of power differentials. *Intent*, therefore, is not an essential factor and an examination of social care services alone is not sufficient to determine whether social care environments are flawed or inadequate.

While most care practitioners value self-reflective practice and operate with transparency, existing structural forms (for example, legislation and HSE regimes) reinforce the preservation of hierarchical decision-making, enforced authority and management of services. Consequently, members of ethnic minorities who participate in social care services (including asylum seekers and refugees) may internalise their oppression (Ruth 1988), believing they hold an inferior social status and are powerless to change things. They may comply with the status quo and therefore fail to confront the disadvantages and inequalities they are subjected to. As a result, many are pushed towards the most extreme margins of Irish society and are more likely to remain dependent upon inadequate and restricted social services in the future.

A MODEL FOR CHANGE

Irish society is at a crossroads and must choose whether or not it will embrace diversity. It must choose between 'doing care unto them' in a patronising and oppressive manner or implementing care policies that are representative and inclusive. Even though Irish legislation, including the Refugee Act 1996 and the Child Care Act 1991, established legal definitions and procedures for dealing with refugees and asylum seekers, the jury is still out as to whether Irish society will accept ethnic minorities as 'deserving' and 'worthy' social care service users.

An equally demanding test for Irish society will be whether or not to facilitate institutional change at all levels, including the dedicated recruitment of ethnic minority group members as social care practitioners and HSE administrators. In other words, the Irish social care profession is faced with a dilemma: is there to be a reform of care participation and delivery? In order to explain how social care might renegotiate current service provision, four categories of social participants and developments are proposed below, identifying a new model for strategic change.

The Identifier

The first category is made up of the 'identifier'. The identifier is the individual or group that has the authority or resources to ask and answer the following questions:

- Who or what determines and/or defines a given social need or problem?
- On what basis is it drawn into the public arena?
- Who or what sets the standards of what is worthy of disclosure, discussion, treatment, funding or change?

To some extent, EU membership brought Irish social services to account for the management and treatment of ethnic minority groups through relevant European directives and regulations. As a member state, Ireland is obliged to implement EU legislation at a national level for the benefit of Europe at large. A steady increase in immigrant numbers has been identified by Irish social institutions as requiring attention at a number of levels. Government departments and interest groups concerned with justice, education, employment, health, welfare, and so on have provoked debate concerning the legitimacy of traditional Irish social practices and cultural beliefs based on homogeny. As *identifiers*, the European Union, Irish government and special interest groups have contributed to the objectives and organisational structures of social care provision.

The Identified

A second category is the 'identified'. The identified may be a situation, problem, an individual, group, agency or institution. Relevant questions that may be asked regarding the identified include:

- What role, if any, do the identified have in naming a given problem or situation?
- What power relationships exist between the identifier and the identified?
- Are there social structures that serve to advantage, disadvantage or equalise all participants?

Applying these questions to the present discussion, ethnic minorities may have been *identified* as different or not 'belonging' in Ireland. Apart from a small number of token contributors, members from such communities are precluded from naming their care needs or solutions, thereby minimising their participation in social care services. Their existence is acknowledged, but little if any attention is given to ethnic members' own analysis of their circumstances. Although gradually increasing through various agencies such as the Irish Refugee Council, the Centre for Criminal Justice and Human Rights and the Irish Human Rights Commission, research by or about refugees and/or asylum seekers remains insufficient. A lack of qualitative data providing first-hand accounts of their physical and social needs will keep ethnic minority groups on the fringes of meaningful social participation, leaving them instead in inferior positions and disadvantaged within a hierarchical social system.

The Movement

The third category is the 'movement'. Sometimes, movement occurs because the identifier changes; sometimes the identified changes; sometimes they both change; and sometimes neither changes. In order for movement to occur (or not occur), one must observe the following:

- Who or what changes?
- Does change occur as a result of pressure (or lack of pressure) from existing interest groups, social structures and institutions?
- Does change come about as a result of public awareness, dissatisfaction, a sense of justice or economic reality?
- How is change directed?
- What path does change take during the process of movement?
- When is change implemented and by whom or by what?

Although some movement concerning care provision for multicultural service users is occurring, to date most has been reactive rather than as a result of strategic social policy. For example, evidence of a two-tiered accommodation framework in social care was highlighted above, demonstrating that separated children who are members of ethnic minority groups and separated from their families are housed in hostels while most Irish children are placed in residential children's homes that are monitored by the Social Services Inspectorate. Research challenges limited resources, lack of protective legislation, alarmist media coverage and indifferent public opinion regarding perceptions of 'foreigners' gaining access to 'our' social services (Christie 2003; Lentin 2007; Ní Chonaill 2009).

An example of movement was evidenced through the 2004 constitutional amendment that redefined Irish citizenship. The result left multicultural Ireland socially divided, as some voters considered the new definition of 'Irish' as strengthening Irish identity, while others saw the constitutional change as intensifying racism and intolerance (see, for example, Jesuit Centre for Faith and Justice 2004; Lentin 2004). Citizenship prescribes equality between citizens not only in terms of rights, but also in how those rights are realised. Citizenship presumes that individuals will have an opportunity for meaningful participation in the economic and social life of their communities and guarantees, in principle, that citizens can access services without unnecessary restrictions or barriers.

To date, *movement* has been directed at providing minimal services for 'non-Irish' service users who are believed to be draining already limited social care resources. Unaccompanied children from ethnic minority groups are allowed to live in accommodation that would be considered unsuitable for Irish children in care. While language, dietary, religious and other cultural distinctions are integrated in some social care environments, they are less visible in many other settings. Care providers are largely from the dominant Irish culture and few are sufficiently trained or experienced in ethnic or cultural diversity.

The Beneficiary

Last is the 'beneficiary'. The beneficiary is comprised of those individuals or groups who receive assistance or who gain socially, economically, politically or culturally from social change. Clarification of this category requires answers to the following:

- Who or what benefits from movement or lack of movement?
- Is there an economic, social or cultural cost incurred?
- If change occurs, who or what is advantaged or disadvantaged?
- If change does not occur, who benefits from the status quo?

If change does not occur, there may be some short-term savings for the Exchequer, but there are likely to be few social *beneficiaries* and social services will probably be compromised. In order for Irish social care to benefit, a radical shift is needed in the social value of service users as well as standards of provision. All social care service users are entitled to an equality of service provision and are deserving of sensitive, respectful and non-discriminatory care. Inevitable benefits occur when changes focus on empowerment, inclusion and extended agency to minority groups as users and providers of care services. Only when multiculturalism inspires, rather than immobilises, our social care services will we have the potential for meaningful reform.

CONCLUSION

If we seek to provide a care service based on best practice, it must have at its core a regard for cultural diversity and a framework that incorporates the development and inclusion of 'difference'. It must unite service providers, service users, a range of communities and 'traditional Irish' society into an effective and transparent integrated whole. Integration within the social care profession will facilitate all participants with the ability to contribute fully without having to relinquish their cultural identity. According to the Department of Justice, Equality and Law Reform (2000: 9), 'the emphasis of integration policy should be on supporting initiatives which enable the preservation of ethnic, cultural and religious identity of the individual'. Accepting this governmental assertion, it can be argued that an integration policy is not operating equitably if it requires cultural compromise or full assimilation on the part of ethnic minorities.

Recipients of Irish social care services are, by definition, vulnerable and dependent service users who are linked to state care, protection, support, welfare and advocacy. They are entitled, as indicated by government policy, to benefit from 'initiatives which enable the preservation of [their] ethnic, cultural and religious identity' (ibid.). They should not be required or expected to embrace a pre-defined form of Irishness, but should instead be provided with a service that strengthens material, social and emotional supports while respecting and valuing diversity, including cultural traditions and practices.

This chapter has shown that the rise in the numbers of immigrants entering Ireland has been paralleled by complexities associated with service provision to an ethnically diverse population. While attempting to meet its legislative obligations, the Irish state has failed as a social institution in many of the challenges associated with models of best practice in social care (equality of service provision and anti-oppressive practice). It is now time to reform current routines and procedures. We must organise our specialisations to present a service that not only considers the practical challenges of care that faces an increasing number of individuals and groups from diverse backgrounds and experiences, but also philosophically embraces a multicultural Irish society. It is time to eliminate our prejudices and insecurities and replace them with an integrated service that provides support, equal access and full participation in the identification and elimination of institutional oppression. It is our social moment to care.

Endnotes

Chapter 1

1   The report is a useful overview of social care in Ireland in the early years of this decade. In addition to defining the profession, it examined issues of training and education, career structures and implications for management. However, the report is peculiarly anonymous, making sourcing it difficult. The report does not indicate a date or place of publication. The author(s) is not identified, nor are the members of the Joint Committee. It is not available on either the Department of Health and Children or the IMPACT websites (we are grateful to IMPACT for providing a hard copy for our inspection).

Chapter 4

1   Since devolution in the late 1990s, responsibility for service provision in social care has moved to the four national governments of England, Wales, Scotland and Northern Ireland. Much of the general policy direction remains the same across the four nations, but this chapter focuses on the position in England.
2   The title 'care worker' has been retained for convenience; most study informants had a different job title.
3   Social pedagogy is an established field of theory, practice and policy in many Continental European countries that focuses on working with the whole child/person, using relationships and critical reflective practice as the foundations of practice. It is discussed in more detail in Chapter 2 in this volume and in Petrie et al. (2006).

Chapter 11

1   Companion website available at www.evidence.brookscole.com.

Chapter 15

1   In this chapter, we primarily use the term 'interdisciplinary'. However, in social care work, the terms 'multi-agency' and 'inter-professional' are also often used to mean the same approach to working.

Chapter 17

1   Published figures are available in regular 'Review of Adequacy' reports on the HSE website: www.hse.ie.
2   See www.hiqa.ie/functions_ssi_inspect_rep.asp.

3   Reports on the fostering inspections can be found at www.hiqa.ie/
    functions_ssi_inspect_rep_fcs.asp.
4   The standards for special care units can be found at www.hiqa.ie/media/pdfs/
    standards_children_scu.pdf.
5   www.hiqa.ie/functions_ssi_inspect_rep.asp.

Chapter 19

1   See www.equalitytribunal.ie.

Chapter 21

1   A social admission is admission for reasons other than physical disability. The
    reasons for admission are numerous but are related to a person's personal
    circumstances, for example fear for personal safety, isolation or loneliness.
2   Sonas is a multi-sensory communication programme developed by Sr Mary
    Threadgold, a speech and language therapist, that helps to activate the
    potential of older people with impaired communication.
3   It was estimated that in 1982 in the Eastern Health Board, there were 51 such
    facilities (Department of Health 1988: 108), while in 1999 there were
    approximately 156 day centres or clubs for older people (Eastern Health Board
    1999: 37).
4   www.dit.ie/socialscienceslaw/socialsciences/shortcourses/socialcareforolder
    people.

Chapter 22

1   This measures those who are at risk of poverty and who have the following
    difficulties: cannot afford a substantial meal one day per fortnight; having to
    go without heating; debt problems; unable to afford two pairs of shoes; unable
    to afford a weekly roast dinner; unable to afford a meal with fish, chicken, meat
    (or vegetarian equivalent) every second day; unable to afford new clothes; and
    unable to afford a warm waterproof coat.

Chapter 26

1   www.who.int/substance_abuse/terminology/who_ladt/en/.
2   Local Drug Task Forces were originally set up in the following areas:
    Ballyfermot, Ballymun, Blanchardstown, Canal Communities, Clondalkin,
    Cork, Dublin 12, Dublin North-East, Dun Laoghaire/Rathdown, Finglas/
    Cabra, North Inner City, South Inner City and Tallaght. In 2000, another
    Local Drugs Task Force was established in Bray, and by the end of 2003, 10
    Regional Drugs Task Forces were established covering all of the former Health
    Board regions in the state.

3   For further information, see Boyle (1999) for an examination of national and international initiatives to manage 'cross-cutting' issues such as drugs, homelessness and unemployment, which cut across government departments and levels of government.

4   The current National Drugs Strategy is being reviewed, as it reached its conclusion at the end of 2008.

5   Responsibility for the National Drug Strategy transferred to the Department of Community, Rural and Gaeltacht Affairs from the Department of Tourism, Sport and Recreation in June 2002 after the general election.

6   Some of these state agencies include the Health Service Executive, An Garda Síochána, Vocational Educational Committees, the Irish Prison Service, local authorities and government departments.

7   For more information, see National Economic and Social Council (2005).

8   The National Development Plan and the action plan for social inclusion also reflect the emergence of the new social inclusion policy framework in Ireland. For further information, see Government of Ireland (2007a, 2007b).

9   National Focal Points are appointed by European member countries at the national level as primary links/contacts between Europe and the member country. The Drug Misuse Research Division of the Health Research Board is designated as a 'focal point' for the European Monitoring Centre for Drugs and Drug Addiction. It exchanges information requests and deliveries between national and EU level.

10   For more information, see www.emcdda.europa.eu/?nnodeid=1563.

11   For more information, see European Monitoring Centre for Drugs and Drug Addiction (2000).

12   For more information, see www.emcdda.europa.eu/html.cfm/index1365EN.html.

13   The term 'prevalence' refers to the proportion of a population that has used a drug over a particular time period. In general population surveys, prevalence is measured by asking respondents in a representative sample drawn from the population to recall their use of drugs. The three most widely used recall periods are lifetime (ever used a drug), last year (used a drug in the last 12 months) and last month (used a drug in the last 30 days). Provided a sample is representative of the total population, prevalence information obtained from a sample can be used to infer prevalence in the population. For more information, see European Monitoring Centre for Drugs and Drug Addiction (2002).

14   The NACD was established in July 2000 to advise the government in relation to the prevalence, prevention, treatment and consequences of problem drug use in Ireland, based on the committee's analysis and interpretation of research findings and information available to it.

15   The full Drug Prevalence Survey, including detailed methodology, is available on the NACD website in the form of bulletins at www.nacd.ie. EMCDDA guidelines for drug prevalence surveys are available on the EMCDDA website at www.emcdda.eu.int. Also see European Monitoring Centre for Drugs and

Drug Addiction (2004) for a comparative study across the European Union and Norway.

16 See National Advisory Committee on Drugs (2006a).

17 See National Advisory Committee on Drugs (2006b).

18 For more information on poly-drug use, see National Advisory Committee on Drugs (2007a).

19 The National Drug Treatment Reporting System (NDTRS) was established by the Health Research Board in 1990. Initially covering only the greater Dublin area, it was extended nationally in 1995. It is designed to gather information about each incident where someone presents for treatment of drug addiction (and, since 2004, for treatment for alcohol addiction). In 1996, NDTRS data were used to identify a number of local areas with problematic heroin use (Department of the Taoiseach 1996). These areas were later designated as Local Drugs Task Force (LDTF) areas as per footnote 2.

20 The Central Treatment List is an administrative database used to regulate the dispensing of methadone treatment. It is administered by the Drug Treatment Centre Board.

21 It is important to note that the NDTRS collects data on episodes of treatment, rather than the number of individual people treated each year. This means that individuals may appear in the figures more than once if they attend more than one treatment service in a year, and may reappear in subsequent years.

22 For more information, see Morgan (2001).

23 See Department of Health and Children (2005).

24 To develop a protocol, where appropriate, for the treatment of under-18s presenting with serious drug problems, especially in light of the legal and other dilemmas which are posed for professionals involved in the area. In this context, a working group should be established to develop the protocol. The group should also look at issues such as availability of appropriate residential and day treatment programmes, education and training, rehabilitative measures and harm reduction responses for young people.

25 See Department of Health and Children (1998b).

26 The HSE appointed the group to provide a detailed analysis and overview of known current residential treatment services and to advise on the future residential requirements of those affected by drug and alcohol use.

Chapter 27

1 The Out-of-Hours Crisis Intervention Service is an emergency service that provides accommodation to young people when no other option is available and it is not possible for them to return home. To access the service, young people must report to a Garda station after 8:00 p.m. Gardaí have a duty to contact the out-of-hours social worker, who in turn arranges a placement for the young person or facilitates his/her return home.

2 The most recent Housing Needs Assessment took place in March 2008, but this new data was not available at the time of writing.

3   The vast majority of homeless young people under 14 years (58 of 64 cases) were recorded in the Eastern Region Health Authority (Department of Health and Children 2004a).

4   The overall trend is downwards; however, there have been some peaks in the interim years: 588 cases in 2000, 451 cases in 2001, 534 cases in 2002 and 476 cases in 2003 (Department of Health and Children 1999–2004).

5   Research findings based on studies of the homeless population vary considerably in the extent to which the prevalence of risk factors such as alcohol, drugs and mental health issues are identified. This arises mainly because of variances in conceptual, definitional and methodological approaches used in different studies.

6   A fourth pathway, described as 'abusive family situation', was identified in the Cork-based study (Mayock and Carr 2008).

7   To date, the Homeless Agency has produced three action plans: *Shaping the Future 2001–2003* (Higgins 2001), *Making It Home 2004–2006* (Homeless Agency 2004) and *A Key to the Door 2007–2010* (Homeless Agency 2007). These have informed service responses and strategies to address homelessness in Dublin.

8   A standard case management approach involves an assessment of need, the appointment of a case manager/key worker and the development and implementation of an action plan.

9   The Rental Accommodation Scheme (RAS) is a new initiative to cater for the accommodation needs of persons who are in receipt of rent supplement, normally for more than eighteen months, and who have a long-term housing need.

10 National guidelines on leaving care and aftercare were published in 2004 in response to this objective (Youth Homeless Strategy Monitoring Committee 2004).

References

Achenbach, T. (1991), *Integrative Guide for the 1991 CBLC/4-18 and TRF Profiles*. Burlington, VT: University of Vermont Department of Psychiatry.

ACYCP (2007), The North American Certification Project Update. <www.acycp.org>

Adair, J. (1983), *Effective Leadership*. London: Gower.

Adams, R., Dominelli, L. and Payne, M. (2002), *Social Work: Themes, Issues and Critical Debates*. London: Open University Press.

Ahern, B. (2007), Opening address at Evidence-based Policy Making: Getting the Evidence, Using the Evidence and Evaluating the Outcomes, Conference Proceedings. Dublin: National Economic Social Forum (NESF).

Ainsworth, M.D.S., Blehar, M., Waters, E. and Wall, S. (1978), *Patterns of Attachment: A Psychological Study of the Strange Situation*. Hillside, NJ: Lawrence Erlbaum.

Alderson, P. (2000), *Young Children's Rights: Exploring Beliefs, Attitudes, Principles and Practices*. London: Jessica Kingsley Publishers.

Aldridge, M. and Evetts, J. (2003), 'Rethinking the Concept of Professionalism: The Case of Journalism', *British Journal of Sociology*, 54/4, 547–64.

Alimo-Metcalfe, B. and Nyfield, G. (2002), 'Leadership and Organizational Effectiveness', in I. Robertson, M. Callinan and D. Bartram (eds.), *Organizational Effectiveness: The Role of Psychology*. Chichester: Wiley.

Allen, G. and Langford, D. (2008), *Effective Interviewing in Social Work and Social Care – A Practice Guide*. London: Palgrave Macmillan.

American Psychiatric Association (1994), *Diagnostic and Statistical Manual of Mental Disorders, DSM-IV*. Washington, DC: American Psychiatric Association.

Anderson, I. and Christian, J. (2003), 'Causes of Homelessness in the UK: A Dynamic Analysis', *Journal of Community and Applied Social Psychology*, 13, 105–118.

Anderson, I. and Tulloch, D. (2000), *Pathways through Homelessness: A Review of the Research Evidence* (Homeless Task Force Research Series). Edinburgh: Scottish Homes.

Anderson, I., Kemp, P. and Quillars, D. (1993), *Single Homeless People*. London: HMSO.

Anglin, J. (1992), 'How Staff Develop', *FICE Bulletin*, 6, 18–24.

Anglin, J. (2001), 'Child and Youth Care: A Unique Profession', *CYC-Net*, 35/1–3.

Anglin, J. (2002), 'Staffed Group Homes for Children and Youth: Constructing a Theoretical Framework for Understanding', PhD thesis, School of Social Work, University of Leicester.

Appleby, J., Walshe, K. and Ham, C. (1995), *Acting on the Evidence*. Research Paper No. 17. London: National Association for Health Authorities and Trusts.

Askheim, O-P. (1998), *Omsorgspolitiske endringer*. Oslo: Ad Notam Gyldendal.

Baer, D., Wolf, M. and Risley, R. (1987), 'Some Still-Current Dimensions of Applied Behavior Analysis', *Journal of Applied Behavior Analysis*, 20, 313–27.

Baker, J., Lynch, K., Cantillon, S. and Walsh, J. (2004), *Equality: From Theory to Action*. London: Palgrave Macmillan.

Balibar, E. (1991), 'Racism and Crisis', in E. Balibar and I. Wallerstein (eds.), *Race, Nation, Class: Ambiguous Identities*. London: Verso.

Balloch, S., McLean, J. and Fisher, M. (eds.) (1999), *Social Services: Working under Pressure*. Bristol: Policy Press.

Bandura, A. (1965), 'Influence of Models' Reinforcement Contingencies on the Acquisition of Imitated Responses', *Journal of Personality and Social Psychology*, 1, 589–95.

Bandura, A. (1977), *Social Learning Theory*. Englewood Cliffs, NJ: Prentice Hall.

Bandura, A., Ross, D. and Ross, S.A. (1961), 'Transmission of Aggression through Imitation of Aggressive Models', *Journal of Abnormal and Social Psychology*, 63/3, 575–82.

Banks, S. (2004), *Ethics, Accountability and the Social Professions*. London: Palgrave Macmillan.

Banks, S. (2006), *Ethics and Values in Social Work*. Basingstoke: Palgrave.

Banks, S. (2007), 'Between Equity and Empathy: Social Professions and the New Accountability', *Social Work and Society*, 5 (Special issue: Festschrift Walter Lorenz). <www.socwork.net/2007/festschrift/esw/banks>

Barnes, C. (1991), 'Disabled People in Britain and Discrimination: A Case for Anti-Discrimination Legislation', British Council of Organisations of Disabled People. <www.leeds.ac.uk/disability-studies/archiveuk/Barnes/bcodp.pdf>, accessed on 9 September 2008.

Barnes-Holmes, Y., Barnes-Holmes, D., McHugh, L. and Hayes, S.C. (2004), 'Relational Frame Theory: Some Implications for Understanding and Treating Human Psychopathology', *International Journal of Psychology and Psychological Therapy*, 4, 355–75.

Barnes, J. and Connelly, N. (eds.) (1978), *Social Care Research*. London: Policy Studies Institute, Bedford Square Press.

Barry, J., Herity, B. and Solan, J. (1987), *The Traveller Health Status Study: Vital Statistics of Travelling People*. Dublin: The Health Research Board.

Baum, W.M. (2005), *Understanding Behaviorism: Behavior, Culture and Evolution*. Oxford: Blackwell.

Baumrind, D. (1972), 'Socialization and Instrumental Competence in Young Children', in W.W. Hartup (ed.), *The Young Child: Review of Research (Vol. 2)*. Washington, DC: National Association for the Education of Young Children.

Beech, B. and Leather, P. (2006), 'Workplace Violence in the Health Care Sector: A Review of Staff Training and Integration of Training Evaluation Models', *Aggression and Violent Behaviour* 11, 27–43.

Begley, M., Garavan, C., Condon, M., Kelly, I., Holland, K. and Staines, A. (1999), *Asylum in Ireland: A Public Health Perspective*. Dublin: University College Dublin and Congregation of the Holy Ghost.

Behaviour and Attitudes Ireland Ltd (2000), *Attitudes to Travellers and Minority Groups*. Survey prepared for Citizen Traveller by Behaviour and Attitudes Ireland Ltd.

Beker, J. (2001), 'Development of a Professional Identity for the Childcare Worker', *Child and Youth Care Forum*, 30/6, 345–54.

Belbin, R.M. (1993), *Team Roles at Work*. Oxford: Butterworth-Heinemann.

Bentley, A. (1997), 'The Psychological Effects of Homelessness and their Impact on the Development of a Counselling Relationship', *Counselling Psychology Quarterly*, 10/2, 195–210.

Beresford, P. and Trevillion, S. (1995), *Developing Skills for Community Care: A Collaborative Approach*. Aldershot: Ashgate.

Berube, P. (1984), 'Professionalisation of Childcare: A Canadian Example', *Journal of Child and Youth Care*, 2/1, 13–26.

Bessant, J. (2004), 'Risk Technologies and Youth Work Practice', *Youth and Policy*, 83, 60–77.

Bibby, P. (1994), *Personal Safety for Social Workers*. Aldershot: Arena.

Bickenback, J.E. (1992), *Physical Disability and Social Policy*. Toronto: University of Toronto Press.

Biestek, F. (1961), *The Casework Relationship*. London: Allen & Unwin.

Bion, W.R. (1961), *Experiences in Groups*. London: Tavistock.

Bird, H. (1996), 'Epidemiology of Childhood Disorders in a Cross Cultural Context', *Journal of Child Psychology and Psychiatry*, 37/1, 35–49.

Blanz, B., Schmidt, M.H. and Esser, G. (1991), 'Familial Adversities and Child Psychiatric Disorder', *Journal of Child Psychology and Psychiatry*, 32, 393–450.

Bloemraad, I. (2007), 'Citizenship and Pluralism: The Role of Government in a World of Global Migration', *The Fletcher Forum of World Affairs*, 31/1, 169–82.

Blome, W. and Steib, S. (2004), 'Whatever the Problem, the Answer is "Evidence-Based Practice" – Or Is It?', *Child Welfare*, 83/6, 611–15.

Bonnar, C. (1996), *Family Planning Needs of Travelling Women in the Midland Health Board Region*. Midland Health Board: Department of Public Health.

Bowlby, J. (1951), 'Maternal Care and Mental Health', *World Health Organization Monograph* (Serial No. 2).

Bowlby, J. (1969), *Attachment and Loss, Vol. 1: Attachment*. New York: Basic Books.

Bowlby, J. (1973), *Attachment and Loss, Vol. 2: Separation*. New York: Basic Books.

Bowlby, J. (1978), 'Attachment Theory and Its Therapeutic Implications', in S.C. Feinstein and P.L. Giovacchini (eds.), *Adolescent Psychiatry: Developmental and Clinical Studies*. New Jersey: Jason Aronson, pp. 5–33.

Boyle, R. (1999), *The Management of Cross-Cutting Issues, Committee for Public Management Research, Discussion Paper 8*. Dublin: Institute of Public Administration.

Braun, D. (2001), 'Perspectives on Parenting', in P. Foley, J. Roche and S. Tucker (eds.), *Children in Society: Contemporary Theory, Policy and Practice*. Basingstoke: Palgrave.

Braye, S. and Preston-Shoot, M. (1995), *Empowering Practice in Social Care*. Buckinghamshire: Open University Press.

Brechin, A. and Siddell, M. (2000), 'Ways of Knowing', in R. Gomm and C. Davies (eds.), *Using Research in Health and Social Care*. London: Sage Publications.

Brehm, S., Kassin, S. and Fein, S. (1999), *Social Psychology* (4th edn.). New York: Houghton Mifflin Company.

Bronfenbrenner, U. (1979), *The Ecology of Human Development*. Cambridge, MA: Harvard University Press.

Bronfenbrenner, U. and Evans, G.W. (2000), 'Developmental Science in the 21st Century: Emerging Questions, Theoretical Models, Research Designs and Empirical Findings', *Social Development*, 8/1, 115–25.

Brown, B. (1971), *Introduction to Social Administration in Britain*. London: Hutchinson.

Bruner, J.S. (1993), *Child's Talk: Learning to Use Language*. New York: Norton.

Bryan, A., Moran, R., O'Brien, A. and Farrell, E. (2000), *Drug-related Knowledge, Attitudes and Beliefs in Ireland: Report of a Nationwide Survey*. Dublin: Health Research Board.

Bryman, A. (1986), *Leadership and Organisations*. London: Routledge and Kegan Paul.

Bryman, A. (2004), *Social Research Methods* (2nd edn.). Oxford: Oxford University Press.

Bubeck, D. (1995), *Care, Gender and Justice*. London: Clarendon.

Buckley, H., Skehill, C. and O'Sullivan, E. (1997), *Child Protection Practices in Ireland: A Case Study*. Dublin: Oak Tree Press.

Bunreacht na hÉireann/Constitution of Ireland. Dublin: Stationery Office.

Burke, D. (2008), 'A Place to Call Home? Issues in Housing Provision for Homeless Persons', in D. Downey (ed.), *Perspectives on Irish Homelessness, Past, Present and Future*. Dublin: The Homeless Agency, pp. 90–101.

Burmeister, E. (1960), *The Professional Houseparent*. New York: Columbia University Press.

Burnard, P. (1992), *Communicate!* London: Edward Arnold Publishers.

Burns, N. and Grove, S. (1997), *The Practice of Nursing Research: Conduct, Critique and Utilisation.* Philadelphia: Saunders.

Burton, J. (1993), *The Handbook of Residential Care.* London: Routledge.

Butcher, H., Banks, S., Henderson, P. and Robertson, J. (2007), *Critical Community Practice.* Bristol: The Policy Press.

Butler, S. (2002), *Alcohol, Drugs and Health Promotion.* Dublin: Institute of Public Administration.

Byrne, J. (2005), 'Social Care Workers' and Students' Perspectives on Issues Related to Professional Status and Representation of Social Care in Ireland'. Unpublished MA thesis, Waterford Institute of Technology.

Byrne, J. (2008), 'Professional and Personal Development for Social Care Workers', *Curam*, Issue 38, June 2008: Irish Association of Social Care Workers.

Byrne, J. and McHugh, J. (2005), 'Residential Childcare', in P. Share and N. McElwee (eds.), *Applied Social Care: An Introduction for Irish Students.* Dublin: Gill & Macmillan.

Byrne, L. (2000), 'Practice Placement in Social Care Worker Education', unpublished Masters thesis, Cork Institute of Technology.

Cameron, C. and Moss, P. (2007), *Care Work in Europe: Current Understandings and Future Directions.* London: Routledge.

Carr, A. (1999), *The Handbook of Child and Adolescent Clinical Psychology: A Contextual Approach.* London: Routledge.

Carr, A. (ed.) (2000), *What Works with Children and Adolescents.* London: Routledge.

Carr, A. and McNulty, M. (2006), 'Cognitive Behaviour Therapy', in A. Carr and M. McNulty (eds.), *Handbook of Adult Clinical Psychology: An Evidence Based Practice Approach.* London: Routledge.

Case, R. and Okamoto, Y. (1996), 'The Role of Central Conceptual Structures in the Development of Children's Thought', *Monographs of the Society for Research in Child Development*, 61/1–2 (Serial No. 246).

Casey, J. (2005), *A Brief History of Disability.* Dublin: Centre for Independent Living.

Cashdan, S. (1988), *Object Relations Theory: Using the Relationship.* New York: Norton.

Cavanagh, K. and Cree, V. (eds.) (1996), *Working with Men: Feminism and Social Work.* London: Routledge.

CBI (Confederation of British Industry) (2007), *Absence and Labour Turnover Survey.* London: CBI/AXA.

Central Statistics Office (2007a), *2006 Census of Population – Volume 11: Disability, Carers and Voluntary Activities.* Dublin: Central Statistics Office.

Central Statistics Office (2007b), *Annual Report 2006.* Dublin: CSO.

Central Statistics Office (2007c), *Census 2006 Volume 5 Ethnic or Cultural Background (Including Traveller Community).* Dublin: Stationery Office.

Central Statistics Office (2007d), *Equality in Ireland 2007*. Dublin: Stationery Office.

Central Statistics Office (2007e), *EU Survey on Income and Living Conditions*. Dublin: Central Statistics Office.

Central Statistics Office (2007f), *Ageing in Ireland*. Dublin: Stationery Office.

Central Statistics Office (2008), *Measuring Ireland's Progress 2007*. Dublin: Stationery Office.

CERD (Committee on the Elimination of Racial Discrimination) (2005), *Consideration of Reports Submitted by State Parties under Article 9 of the Convention. Concluding Observations of the Committee on the Elimination of Racial Discrimination IRELAND*. Sixty-sixth session 21 February–11 March 2005. CERD/C/IRL/CO/2.

CERD (Committee on the Elimination of Racial Discrimination) (2006), *Comments by the Government of Ireland to the Concluding Observations of the Committee on the Elimination of Racial Discrimination*. CERD/C/IRL/CO/2/Add.1.

Chakrabarti, M. and Hill, M. (2000), *Residential Child Care: International Perspectives on Links with Families and Peers*. London: Jessica Kingsley.

Chappell, D. and Di Martino, V. (2006), *Violence at Work*. Geneva: International Labour Organization.

Charles, G. and Gabor, P. (1988), *Issues in Child and Youth Care Practice in Alberta*. Lethbridge: Lethbridge Community College.

Charles, G. and Gabor, P. (1990), 'An Historical Perspective on Residential Services for Troubled and Troubling Youth in Canada', in G. Charles and S. McIntyre (eds.), *The Best in Care: Recommendations for the Future of Residential Services for Troubled and Troubling Young People in Canada*. Ottawa: Canadian Child Welfare Association.

Charles, G. and Gabor, P. (2006), 'An Historical Perspective on Residential Services for Troubled and Troubling Youth in Canada Revisited', *Relational Child and Youth Care Practice*, 19/4, 17–26.

Chess, S. and Thomas, A. (1995), *Temperament in Clinical Practice*. New York: Guilford.

Child Care (Amendment) 2004 Act. Dublin: Stationery Office.

Child Care Act 1991. Dublin: Stationery Office.

Child Care Act 2001. Dublin: Stationery Office.

Chomsky, N. (1968), *Aspects of the Theory of Syntax*. Cambridge, MA: MIT Press.

Chrisjohn, R. and Young, S. (1997), *The Circle Game: Shadows and Substance in the Indian Residential School Experience in Canada*. Penticton: Theytus.

Christie, A. (1998), '"Balancing Gender" as Men Social Workers', *Irish Social Worker*, 16/3, 4–6.

Christie, A. (ed.) (2001), *Men and Social Work*. London: Palgrave.

Christie, A. (2003), 'Unsettling the "Social" in Social Work: Responses to Asylum Seeking Children in Ireland', *Child and Family Social Work*, 8/3, 223–31.

Christophe, A. and Morton, J. (1998), 'Is Dutch Native English? Linguistic Analysis by 2 Month Olds', *Developmental Science*, 1, 215–19.

Citizens Information Act 2007. Dublin: Stationery Office.

Clark, C. (2005), 'The Deprofessionalisation Thesis, Accountability and Professional Character', *Social Work and Society*, 3/2. <www.socwork.net/2005/2/articles/490/Clark2005.pdf>

Clarke, J. (1993), *A Crisis in Care: Challenges to Social Work*. London: Sage.

Clarke, M. (1998), *Lives in Care: Issues for Policy and Practice in Children's Homes*. Dublin: Mercy Congregation and Children's Research Centre, Trinity College Dublin.

Clarke, M. (2003), *Fit to Practice: The Education of Professionals*. Conference Paper. Cork: 2003 IASCE Conference.

Cleary, A., Corbett, M., Galvin, M. and Wall, J. (2004), *Young Men on the Margins*. Dublin: The Katharine Howard Foundation.

Cloke, P., Johnsen, S. and May, J. (2007), 'The Periphery of Care: Emergency Services for Homeless People in Rural Areas', *Journal of Rural Studies*, 23, 387–401.

Clough, R. (2000), *The Practice of Residential Work*. Basingstoke, Hampshire: Macmillan.

Coakley, J. and Gallagher, M. (2005), *Politics in the Republic of Ireland*. London: Routledge.

Cohen, P., Cohen, J., Kasen, S., Velez, C., Hartmark, C., Johnston, A., Rojas, M., Brook, J. and Streuning, E. (1993), 'An Epidemiological Study of Disorders in Late Childhood and Adolescence – 1. Age- and Gender-Specific Prevalence'. *Journal of Child Psychology and Psychiatry*, 34, 851–67.

Cohen, S. (2002), *Folk Devils and Moral Panics: The Creation of the Mods and Rockers* (3rd edn.). London: Routledge.

Collander-Brown, D. (2005), 'Being with Another as a Professional Practitioner: Uncovering the Nature of Working with Individuals', *Youth and Policy*, 86, 33–47.

Collins, B. (2001), *The Development of Services. Module 1: Introduction to Disability*. Bachelor of Arts in Applied Social Studies (Disability). Dublin: The Open Training College.

Collins, W. (1992), *Reference English Dictionary*. London: Paragon Books.

Collins, J. (2001), *Good to Great*. London: Random House.

Combat Poverty Agency (2004), *Poverty Briefing – Poverty and Health*. <www.cpa.ie/publications/povertybriefings/Briefing15_Poverty&Health_2004.pdf>, accessed on 4 April 2008.

Combat Poverty Agency and Equality Authority (2003), *Poverty and Inequality: Applying an Equality Dimension to Poverty Proofing*. Dublin: CPA and EA.

Comhairle (Amendment) Bill 2004. Dublin: Stationery Office.

Comhairle Act 2000. Dublin: Stationery Office.

Commission on Itinerancy (1963), *Report of the Commission on Itinerancy*. Dublin: Stationery Office.

Commission on the Status of People with Disabilities (1996), *A Strategy for Equality. Report of the Commission on the Status of People with Disabilities*. Dublin: Stationery Office.

Condron, M. (1989), *The Serpent and the Goddess*. San Francisco: HarperCollins.

Conklin, J. (2006), *Dialogue Mapping: Building Shared Understanding of Wicked Problems*. London: Wiley.

Conneely, S. (2005), 'Legal Issues in Social Care', in P. Share and N. McElwee (eds.), *Applied Social Care: An Introduction for Irish Students*. Dublin: Gill & Macmillan.

Connell, P. and Pringle, D. (2004), *Population Ageing in Ireland: Projections 2002–2021*. Dublin: National Council on Ageing and Older People.

Connell, R. (1987), *Gender and Power*. Oxford: Blackwell.

Connell, R. (1995), *Masculinities*. Cambridge: Polity.

Connolly, L. (2002), *The Irish Women's Movement*. Basingstoke: Palgrave.

Connolly, L. and Hourigan, N. (2006), *Social Movements and Ireland*. Manchester: Manchester University Press.

Conroy, P. (2004), *Trafficking in Unaccompanied Minors in Ireland*. Dublin: International Organisation for Migration.

Conroy, P. and Fitzgerald, F. (2005), *Separated Children Seeking Asylum Research Study 2004: Health and Social Education Needs*. Bray: Health Service Executive.

Cooper, C. (1985), *Good Enough Parenting*. London: BAAF.

Cooper, C., Hoel, H. and di Martino, V. (2003), *Preventing Violence and Harassment in the Workplace: Report of the European Foundation for the Improvement of Living and Working Conditions*. <http://eurofound.europa.eu/pubdocs/2002/112/en/1/ef02112en.pdf>

Cooper, J.O., Heron, T.E. and Heward, W.L. (2007), *Applied Behavior Analysis* (2nd edn.). New Jersey: Prentice Hall.

Corry, M. and Tubridy, A. (2001), *Going Mad: Understanding Mental Illness*. Dublin: Newleaf.

Costello, C. (2005), *Professional Identity Crisis: Race, Class, Gender, and Success at Professional Schools*. Nashville, TN: Vanderbilt University Press.

Coughlan, M., Cronin, P. and Ryan, F. (2007) 'Step-by-step Guide to Critiquing Research. Part 1: Quantitative Research', *British Journal of Nursing*, 16/11, 658–663.

Courtney, D. (2003), *Social Care Education and Training: Towards a National Standard, Welcome Address*. Conference Paper. Cork: 2003 IASCE Conference.

Craig, J. (2006), 'Production Values: Building Shared Autonomy', in J. Craig (ed.), *Production Values: Futures for Professionalism*. London: Demos.

Cramer, H. (2005), 'Informal and Gendered Practices in a Homeless Persons Unit', *Housing Studies*, 20/5, 737–51.

Crane, M. and Warnes, A. (2005), 'Responding to the Needs of Older Homeless People: The Effectiveness and Limitations of British Services', *Innovation*, 18/2, 137–52.

Cree, V. (2001), 'Men and Masculinities in Social Work Education', in A. Christie (ed.), *Men and Social Work*. London: Palgrave.

Crimmens, D. (1998), 'Training for Residential Child Care Workers in Europe: Comparing Approaches in the Netherlands, Ireland and the United Kingdom', *Social Work Education*, 17/3, 309–20.

Cross, M.C. and Papadopoulos, L. (2001), *Becoming a Counsellor: A Manual for Personal and Professional Development*. London: Brunner-Routledge.

Crowley, N. (2006), *An Ambition for Equality*. Dublin: Irish Academic Press.

Crowley, R. (2003), *Mental Health: The Neglected Quarter*. Dublin: Amnesty International Ireland.

CSCI (Commission for Social Care Inspection) (2008), *The State of Social Care in England 2006/07*. <www.csci.org.uk/about_us/publications/state_of_social_care_07.aspx>

Cullen, E. (2006), 'Growth and the Celtic Cancer: Unprecedented Growth but for Whose Benefit?', in T. O'Connor and M. Murphy (eds.), *Social Care in Ireland – Theory, Policy and Practice*. Cork: CIT Press.

CYCAA (Child and Youth Care Association of Alberta) (2000), *Certification Manual*. Edmonton: Child and Youth Care Association of Alberta.

Dalrymple, J. and Burke, B. (2007), *Anti-Oppressive Practice: Social Care and the Law*. Oxford: Oxford University Press.

Daly, A., Walsh, D., Ward, M. and Moran, R. (2006), *Irish Psychiatric Units and Hospitals Census 2006*. Dublin: Irish Health Research Board.

Daniel, B., Wassel, S. and Gilligan, R. (1999), *Child Development for Child Care and Protection Workers*. London: Jessica Kingsley.

Darling, N. and Steinberg, L. (1993), 'Parenting Style as Context: An Integrative Model', *Psychological Bulletin*, 113, 487–96.

Davies, H. and Nutley, S. (1999), 'The Rise and Rise of Evidence in Health Care', *Public Money and Management*, 191, 9–16.

Day, D.V., Halpin, S. and Zaccaro, S. (eds.) (2004), *Leader Development for Transforming Organisations: Growing Leaders for Tomorrow*. New Jersey: Lawrence Erlbaum Associates.

DeCasper, A.J. and Fifer, W. (1980), 'Of Human Bonding: Newborns Prefer Their Mothers' Voices', *Science*, 28, 174–6.

de Róiste, Á. (2005), 'Attachment', in P. Share and N. McElwee (eds.), *Applied Social Care: An Introduction for Irish Students*. Dublin: Gill & Macmillan.

De Winter, M. and Noom, M. (2003), 'Someone Who Treats You as an Ordinary Human Being ... Homeless Youth Examine the Quality of Professional Care', *British Journal of Social Work*, 33/3, 325–37.

Degener, T. (2004), *Definition of Disability*. Europe: EU Network of Experts on Disability Discrimination.

Dennehy, T. (2006), 'Winnicott and the Care Worker', in T. O'Connor and M. Murphy (eds.), *Social Care in Ireland: Theory, Policy and Practice*. Cork: CIT Press.

Dent, M. and Whitehead, S. (2002), 'Introduction: Configuring the "New" Professional', in M. Dent and S. Whitehead (eds.), *Managing Professional Identities: Knowledge, Performativity and the 'New' Professional*. London: Routledge.

Department of Community, Rural and Gaeltacht Affairs (2005), *Mid-term Review of the National Drugs Strategy 2001–2008*. Dublin: Stationery Office.

Department of Community, Rural and Gaeltacht Affairs (2007), *Report of the Working Group on Drugs Rehabilitation*. Dublin: Stationery Office.

Department of Education (1970), *Reformatory and Industrial Schools Systems Report* [The Kennedy Report]. Dublin: Stationery Office.

Department of Education and Science (2003a), *National Youth Work Development Plan 2003–2007*. Dublin: Stationery Office.

Department of Education and Science (2003b), *Code of Good Practice: Child Protection Guidelines for the Youth Work Sector (Revised)*. Dublin: Stationery Office.

Department of Education and Science (2006), *Survey of Traveller Education Provision*. Dublin: Department of Education and Science.

Department of Health (1988), *The Years Ahead: A Policy for the Elderly*. Dublin: Stationery Office.

Department of Health (1994), *Shaping a Healthier Future: A Strategy for Effective Health Care in the 1990s*. Dublin: Stationery Office.

Department of Health (1996), *Report on the Inquiry into the Operation of Madonna House*. Dublin: Government Publications Office.

Department of Health (1997), *Survey of Long-stay Units 1995*. Dublin: Stationery Office.

Department of Health and Children (1998a), *Adding Years to Life and Life to Years – Health Promotion Strategy for Older People*. Dublin: Stationery Office.

Department of Health and Children (1998b), *Misuse of Drugs (Supervision of Prescription and Supply of Methadone) Regulations (Statutory Instrument No 225)*. Dublin: Stationery Office.

Department of Health and Children (1998c), *Report of the Methadone Treatment Services Review Group*. Dublin: Stationery Office.

Department of Health and Children (1999), *Children First: National Guidelines on Child Protection and Welfare*. Dublin: Stationery Office.

Department of Health and Children (1999–2004), *Preliminary Analysis of Interim Child Care Data Set 1999–2004*. Dublin: Department of Health and Children. <www.nco.ie>, accessed on 9 September 2008.

Department of Health and Children (2001a), *National Standards for Children's Residential Centres*. Dublin: Stationery Office.

Department of Health and Children (2001b), *Quality and Fairness – A Health System for You: Primary Care Strategy*. Dublin: Stationery Office.

Department of Health and Children (2001c), *Youth Homelessness Strategy*. Dublin: Stationery Office.

Department of Health and Children (2002), *Traveller Health: A National Strategy*. Dublin: Department of Health and Children.

Department of Health and Children (2004a), *Analysis of Child Care Interim Minimum Dataset*. Dublin: Department of Health and Children.

Department of Health and Children (2004b), *Working for Children and Families: Exploring Good Practice*. Dublin: Stationery Office.

Department of Health and Children (2005), *Report of the Working Group on Treatment of Under 18 Year Olds Presenting to Treatment Services with Serious Drug Problems*. Dublin: Stationery Office. <www.dohc.ie/publications/pdf/ drug_treatment_under_18s.pdf?direct=1>, accessed 7 January 2009.

Department of Health and Children (2007), *National Standards for Residential Care Settings for Older People*. Dublin: Stationery Office.

Department of Health and Children (2008), The Nursing Homes Support Scheme Bill 2008. Dublin: Stationery Office.

Department of Justice, Equality and Law Reform (2000), *Integration: A Two Way Process*. Dublin: Official Publications.

Department of Justice, Equality and Law Reform (2005), *National Action Plan against Racism 2005–2008*. Dublin: Department of Justice, Equality and Law Reform.

Department of Social and Family Affairs (2008), *Habitual Residence Condition – Guidelines for Deciding Officers on the determination of Habitual Residence*. <www.welfare.ie/EN/OperationalGuidelines/Pages/habres.aspx#5>, accessed on 14 November 2008.

Department of the Environment (1983), *Report of the Travelling People Review Body*. Dublin: Department of the Environment.

Department of the Environment (1995), *Report of the Task Force on the Travelling Community*. Dublin: Brunswick Press.

Department of the Environment and Local Government (2000), *Homelessness: An Integrated Strategy*. Dublin: Stationery Office.

Department of the Environment, Heritage and Local Government (2005), *Local Authority Housing Needs Assessment*. <www.environ.ie>, accessed on 31 August 2008.

Department of the Environment, Heritage and Local Government (2008), *The Way Forward: A Strategy to Address Adult Homelessness in Ireland 2008–2013*. Dublin: Department of the Environment, Heritage and Local Government.

Department of the Taoiseach (1996), *First Report of the Ministerial Task Force on Measures to Reduce the Demand for Drugs*. Dublin: Stationery Office.

Department of the Taoiseach (2006), *Towards 2016: Ten-Year Framework Social Partnership Agreement 2006–2015*. Dublin: Stationery Office.

Department of Tourism, Sport and Recreation (2001), *Building on Experience: National Drugs Strategy 2001–2008*. Dublin: Stationery Office.

Devlin, M. and Healy, D. (eds.) (2007), 'Work in Progress': Case Studies in Participatory Arts with Young People. Dublin: National Youth Council of Ireland.

Dewe, B., Otto, H-U. and Schnurr, S. (2005), 'Introduction: New Professionalism in Social Work – A Social Work and Society Series', Social Work and Society, 3/1. <www.socwork.net/2005/2>

DiClemente, C.C. (2003), Addiction and Change: How Addictions Develop and Addicted People Recover. New York: Guilford Press.

Dingwall, R. (2008), Essays on Professions. Aldershot: Ashgate.

Disability Act 2005. Dublin: Stationery Office.

Dixon, N. (1994), On the Psychology of Military Incompetence. London: Pimlico.

Dogra, N., Parkin, A., Gale, F. and Frake, C. (2002), A Multidisciplinary Handbook of Child and Adolescent Mental Health for Front-Line Professionals. London: Jessica Kingsley Publishers.

Doherty, D. (1998), 'Adapting Health Management Structures to Achieve Health and Social Gains', in A. Leahy and M. Wiley (eds.), The Irish Health System in the 21st Century. Dublin: Oak Tree Press.

Dominelli, L. (1997), Sociology for Social Work. London: Macmillan.

Dominelli, L. (2002), 'Anti-oppressive Practice in Context', in R. Adams, L. Dominelli and M. Payne (eds.), Social Work: Themes, Issues and Critical Debates (2nd edn.). Basingstoke: Palgrave.

Dominelli, L. (2007), 'The Post-modern "Turn" in Social Work: The Challenges of Identity and Equality', Social Work and Society, 5.

Dondio, P., Barrett, S., Weber, S. and Seigneur, J-M. (2006), Extracting Trust from Domain Analysis: A Case Study on Wikipedia Project. School of Computer Science and Statistics, Distributed System Group, Trinity College, Dublin. <cui.unige.ch/~seigneur/publications/ExtractingTrustfromDomainAnalysisfin alcorrected.pdf>

Dozier, M., Case Stovall, K., Albus, K. and Bates, B. (2001), 'Attachment for Infants in Foster Care: The Role of Caregiver State of Mind', Child Development, 72/5, 1467–77.

Dublin Institute of Technology (2006), Social Care Placement Handbook. Dublin: DIT.

Duggan-Jackson, A. (2000), The Voice of Traveller Women through Research. Department of Public Health: Midland Health Board.

Dunn, J. (1993), Young Children's Close Relationships Beyond Attachment. London: Sage.

Duyvendak, J., Knijn, T. and Kremer, M. (eds.) (2006), Policy, People and the New Professional: De-professionalisation and Re-professionalisation in Care and Welfare. Amsterdam: Amsterdam University Press.

Eastern Regional Health Authority (2001), Review of the Implementation of the Ten Year Action Plan for Services for Older People 1999–2008. Eastern Regional Health Authority, Dublin: Stationery Office.

Eborall, C. (2003), The State of the Social Care Workforce in England. Volume 1 of the First Annual Report of the TOPSS England Workforce Intelligence Unit, 2003. Leeds: TOPSS England.

Edgar, B., Doherty, J. and Mina-Coull, A. (1999), *Services for Homeless People: Innovation and Change in the European Union*. Bristol: The Policy Press.

Edgar, V. and Meert, H. (2006), *Fifth Review of Statistics on Homelessness in Europe*. Brussels: FEANTSA (European Federation of National Organisations Working with the Homeless).

Edmond, T., Megivern, D., Williams, C., Rochman, E. and Howard, M. (2006), 'Integrating Evidence-based Practice and Social Work Field Education', *Journal of Social Work Education*, 42/2, 277–396.

Education (Welfare) Act 2000. Dublin: Stationery Office.

Education Act 1998. Dublin: Stationery Office.

Education for Persons with Special Needs Act 2004. Dublin: Stationery Office.

EHB (1998), *Childcare and Family Support Service in 1998, Review of Adequacy*. Dublin: Eastern Health Board.

EHB (Eastern Health Board) (1999), *Ten Year Action Plan for Services for Older Persons 1999–2008*. Dublin: Stationery Office.

Ehrenreich, B. and English, D. (1974), *Witches, Midwives and Nurses: A History of Women Healers*. London: Compendium.

Emerson, E. (1995), *Challenging Behaviour: Analysis and Intervention in People with Learning Disabilities*. Cambridge: Cambridge University Press.

Emerson, E. (2001), *Challenging Behaviour: Analysis and Intervention in People with Severe Intellectual Disabilities*. Cambridge: Cambridge University Press.

Employment Equality Act 1998. Dublin: Stationery Office.

Enable Ireland (2008), *Family Support Services*. Tralee: Enable Ireland Family Support Services.

Engel, G.L. (1977), 'The Need for a New Medical Model: A Challenge for Biomedicine', *Science*, 196, 129–36.

Equal Status Act 2000. Dublin: Stationery Office.

Equality Authority (2006a), *Traveller Ethnicity: An Equality Authority Report*. Dublin: Equality Authority.

Equality Authority (2006b), *Annual Report*. Dublin: Equality Authority.

Eraut, M. (1994), *Developing Professional Knowledge and Competence*. London: Falmer Press.

Erikson, E.H. (1970), *Childhood and Society*. New York: W.W. Norton.

Erikson, E.H. (1980), *Identity and the Life Cycle*. New York: W.W. Norton.

Eriksson, L. and Markström, A-M. (2003), 'Interpreting the Concept of Social Pedagogy', in A. Gustavsson et al. (eds.), *Perspective and Theories in Social Pedagogy*. Göteborg: Daidalos.

Eron, L.D. (2000), 'A Psychological Perspective', in E.B. Van Hasselt and M. Hersen (eds.), *Aggression and Violence: An Introductory Text*. Boston: Allyn & Bacon.

Esping-Anderen, G. (1990), *The Three Worlds of Welfare Capitalism*. New Jersey: Princeton University Press.

European Anti-Poverty Network Ireland (2008a), *A Handbook on Using a Human Rights-based Approach to Achieve Social Inclusion and Equality*. Dublin: Combat Poverty Agency/European Anti-Poverty Network Ireland.

European Anti-Poverty Network Ireland (2008b), *Poverty in Ireland*. Dublin: Combat Poverty Agency/European Anti-Poverty Network Ireland.

European Monitoring Centre for Drugs and Drug Addiction (2000), *Scientific Report: Treatment Demand Indicator Standard Protocol 2.0*. Lisbon: EMCDDA.

European Monitoring Centre for Drugs and Drug Addiction (2002), *Handbook for Surveys on Drug Use Among the General Population: Final Report*. The Netherlands: EMCDDA.

European Monitoring Centre for Drugs and Drug Addiction (2004), *The State of the Drugs Problem in the European Union and Norway, Annual Report*. Lisbon: European Commission.

Evetts, J. (ed.) (2006), 'Trust and Professionalism in Knowledge Societies', special issue of *Current Sociology*, 54/4.

Expert Group on Mental Health Policy (2006), *A Vision for Change. Report of the Expert Group on Mental Health Policy*. Dublin: Stationery Office.

Fahey, T. and Fitzgerald, J. (1997), *Welfare Implications of Demographic Trends*. Dublin: Oak Tree Press/Combat Poverty Agency.

Fahlberg, V. (1994), *A Child's Journey through Placement* (1st edn.). London: British Association for Adoption and Fostering.

Fanning, B. (2001), *Beyond the Pale: Asylum-Seeking Children and Social Exclusion in Ireland*. Dublin: Irish Refugee Council.

Fanning, B. (2004), 'Asylum Seeker and Migrant Children in Ireland: Racism, Institutional Racism and Social Work', in D. Hayes and B. Humphries (eds.), *Social Work, Immigration and Asylum: Debates and Ethical Dilemmas for Social Work and Social Care Practice*. London: Jessica Kingsley Publishers.

Fanning, B. (2006), 'The New Welfare Economy', in B. Fanning and M. Rush (eds.), *Care and Social Change in the Irish Welfare Economy*. Dublin: University College Dublin Press.

Fanning, B. and Rush, M. (2006), *Care and Social Change in the Irish Welfare Economy*. Dublin: University College Dublin Press.

Farrell, F. and Watt, P. (eds.) (2001), *Responding to Racism in Ireland*. Dublin: Veritas.

Farrelly, T. and O'Doherty, C. (2005), 'The Health and Social Care Professionals Bill (2004) – Implications and Opportunities for the Social Professions in Ireland', *Administration*, 53/1, 80–92.

Faughnan, P. (1999), *Refugees and Asylum Seekers in Ireland: Social Policy Dimensions*. Dublin: Social Science Research Centre, University College Dublin.

Faughnan, P. and O'Donovan, A. (2002), *A Changing Voluntary Sector: Working with New Minority Communities in 2001*. Dublin: Social Science Research Centre, University College Dublin.

Faughnan, P., Humphries, N. and Whelan, S. (2002), *Patching Up the System: The Community Welfare Service and Asylum Seekers*. Dublin: Social Science Research Centre, University College Dublin.

FEANTSA (2005), *Street Homelessness: FEANTSA's Thematic Report 2005*. Brussels: FEANTSA.

FEANTSA (2007), *European Typology of Homelessness and Housing Exclusion*. Brussels: FEANTSA. <www.feantsa.org>, accessed on 31 August 2008.

Feder Kittay, E. (1999), *Love's Labour*. New York: Routledge.

Feldman, A., Frese, C. and Yousif, T. (2002), *Research, Development and Critical Interculturalism: A Study on the Participation of Refugees and Asylum Seekers in Research and Development-based Initiatives*. Dublin: Social Science Research Centre, University College Dublin.

Feldman, A., Gilmartin, M., Loyal, S. and Migge, B. (2008), *Getting On: From Migration to Integration. Chinese, Indian, Lithuanian and Nigerian Migrants' Experiences in Ireland*. Dublin: Immigrant Council of Ireland.

Fenson, L., Dale, P., Resnick, S., Bates, E., Thal, D. and Pethick, S.J. (1994), 'Variability in Early Communicative Development', *Monographs of the Society for Research in Child Development*, 59, 1–73.

Ferguson, H. and Kenny, P. (1995), *On Behalf of the Child: Child Welfare, Child Protection and the Child Care Act 1991*. Dublin: A&A Farmar.

Ferguson, H. and O'Reilly, M. (2001), *Keeping Children Safe: Child Abuse, Child Protection and the Promotion of Welfare*. Dublin: A&A Farmar.

Ferguson, R. (1993), 'Introduction: Child and Youth Care Education: Approaching a New Millennium', *Child and Youth Care Forum*, 22/4, 251–61.

Fewster, G. (1990a), *Being in Child Care: A Journey into Self*. New York: Haworth Press.

Fewster, G. (1990b), 'Growing Together: The Personal Relationship in Child and Youth Care', in J.P. Anglin et al. (eds.), *Perspectives in Professional Child and Youth Care*. London: The Haworth Press.

Fewster, G. (1999), 'Turning Myself Inside Out: My Theory of Me', *Journal of Child and Youth Care*, 13/2, 35–55.

Fielder, F. (1967), *A Theory of Leadership Effectiveness*. New York: McGraw Hill.

Fink, J. (ed.) (2004), *Care: Personal Lives and Social Policy*. Bristol: The Open University/The Policy Press.

Finlay, L. (2000), 'The Challenge of Professional Critical Practice in Health and Social Care', in A. Brechin et al. (eds.), *Critical Social Practice in Health and Social Care*. London: Sage.

Fitzpatrick Associates (2006), *Review of Implementation of Homeless Strategies*. Dublin: Stationery Office.

Fitzpatrick, S., Kemp, P. and Klinker, S. (2000), *Single Homelessness: An Overview of Research in Britain*. Bristol: The Policy Press.

Fivush, R. (2006), 'Scripting Attachment: Generalised Event Representations and Internal Working Models', *Attachment and Human Development*, 8/3, 283–89.

Flick, U., von Kardoff, E. and Steinke, I. (2004), 'What Is Qualitative Research? An Introduction to the Field', in U. Flick, E. von Kardoff and I. Steinke (eds.), *A Companion to Qualitative Research*. London: Sage.

Focus Ireland (1996), *Focus on Residential Child Care in Ireland: 25 Years Since the Kennedy Report*. Dublin: Focus Ireland.

Fodor, J. (1992), 'A Theory of the Child's Theory of Mind', *Cognition*, 44, 286–93.

Forum of People with Disabilities (2001), *Advocacy: A Rights Issue, A Reflection Document*. Dublin: Forum of People with Disabilities.

Foucault, M. (1980), *Power/Knowledge: Selected Interviews and Other Writings 1972–1977*. Brighton: Harvester.

Foucault, M. (1991), *Discipline and Punish: The Birth of the Prison*. Harmondsworth: Penguin.

Fournier, S. and Crey, E. (1997), *Stolen from our Embrace: The Abduction of First Nations Children and the Restoration of Aboriginal Communities*. Toronto: Douglas and McIntyre.

Friedson, E. (1970), *Profession of Medicine: A Study of the Sociology of Applied Knowledge*. New York: Dodd, Mead.

Friedson, E. (1990), 'Professionalisation, Caring, and Nursing'. Paper prepared for the Park Ridge Center, Park Ridge, Illinois. <www.virtualcurriculum.com/N3225/Freidson_Professionalism.html>

Friedson, E. (1994), *Professionalism Reborn: Theory, Prophecy and Policy*. Cambridge: Polity Press.

Friedson, E. (2001), *Professionalism: The Third Logic*. Cambridge: Polity Press.

Friere, P. (1972), *Pedagogy of the Oppressed*. Harmondsworth: Penguin.

Frye, M. (1983), *The Politics of Reality*. Freedom, CA: Crossing Press.

Gaffney, M. and Harmon, C. (2007), 'Overview and Policy Conclusions', in *Evidence-based Policy Making: Getting the Evidence, Using the Evidence and Evaluating the Outcomes, Conference Proceedings*. Dublin: National Economic Social Forum.

Gallagher, C. (2008), *The Community Life of Older People in Ireland*. Oxford: Peter Lang.

Gallagher, C. and Kennedy, K. (2003), 'The Training Implications of a Social Care Approach to Working with Older People', *Irish Journal of Applied Social Studies*, 4/1, 21–35.

Gallagher, C. and O'Toole, J. (1999), 'Towards a Sociological Understanding of Social Care Work in Ireland', *Irish Journal of Social Work Research*, 2/1, 69–86.

Galvin, P. (2002), *The Raggy Boy Trilogy*. Dublin: New Island.

Gannon, B. and Nolan, B. (2007), *Dynamics of Disability and Social Inclusion in Ireland*. Dublin: Equality Authority and National Disability Authority.

Garavan, R., Winder, R. and McGee, H. (2001), *Health and Social Services for Older People* (HeSSOP). Dublin: National Council on Ageing and Older People.

Gardener, A. (2007), 'Beyond Anti-oppressive Practice in Social Work: Best Practical and Ethical Use of Power in Adult Care', in K. Jones, B. Cooper and H. Ferguson (eds.), *Best Practice in Social Work: Critical Perspectives*. London: Palgrave Macmillan.

Garfat, T. (1998), 'The Effective Child and Youth Care Intervention', *Journal of Child and Youth Care*, 12/1–2, 1–168.

Garfat, T. (1999), 'Questions about Self and Relationship', *Journal of Child and Youth Care*, 13/2, iii–vi.

Garfat, T. (2003), 'Some Thoughts on the Process of Becoming Relevant to Social care Practice'. A talk prepared for the Resident Managers' Association Conference. Dundalk: 5–7 November 2003.

Garfat, T. (2004), *A Child and Youth Care Approach to Working with Families*. New York: Haworth Press.

Garfat, T. and Ricks, F. (1995), 'Self-Driven Ethical Decision-Making: A Model for Child and Youth Care', *Child and Youth Care Forum*, 24/6, 393–404.

Garfat, T., McElwee, N. and Charles, G. (2005), 'Self in Social Care', in P. Share and N. McElwee (eds.), *Applied Social Care: An Introduction for Irish Students*. Dublin: Gill & Macmillan.

Gaughan, P. and Gharabaghi, K. (1999), 'The Prospects and Dilemmas of Child and Youth Care as a Professional Discipline', *Journal of Child and Youth Care*, 13/1, 1–18.

Gerstel, N. and Gallagher, S. (2001), 'Men's Caregiving', *Gender and Society*, 15/2, 197–217.

Gibbs, L. (2003), *Evidence-based Practice for the Helping Professions: A Practical Guide with Integrated Multimedia*. Pacific Grove, CA: Brooks/Cole.

Gibbs, L. and Gambrill, E. (2002), 'Evidence-based Practice: Counterarguments to Objections', *Research on Social Work Practice*, 12, 452–76.

Gilchrist, A. (2004), *The Well-Connected Community*. Bristol: The Policy Press.

Gilligan, R. (1991), *Irish Child Care Services: Practice, Policy and Provision*. Dublin: Institute of Public Administration.

Gilligan, R. (2001), *Promoting Resilience: A Resource Guide on Working with Children in the Care System*. London: British Association for Adoption and Fostering.

Gilroy, P. (1998), 'Race Ends Here', *Ethnic and Racial Studies*, 21/5, 838–47.

Glaser, R. (1984), 'Education and Thinking: The Role of Knowledge', *American Psychologist*, 39, 93–104.

Glazer, N. and Moynihan, D. (1975), *Ethnicity: Theory and Experience*, Cambridge, MA: Harvard University Press.

Goebel, B.L. and Brown, D.R. (1981), 'Age Differences in Motivation Related to Maslow's Need Hierarchy', *Developmental Psychology*, 17/6, 809–15.

Goffman, E. (1963), *Stigma: Notes on the Management of Spoiled Identity*. Englewood Cliffs, NJ: Prentice Hall.

Goodbody Economic Consultants (2006), *Report on Government Tax Reliefs*. Dublin: Goodbody Economic Consultants.

Goodin, R., Heady, B., Muffels, R. and Dirven, H-J. (1999), *The Real Worlds of Welfare Capitalism*. Cambridge: Cambridge University Press.

Gossett, M. and Weinman, L.M. (2007), 'Evidence-based Practice and Social Work: An Illustration of the Steps Involved', *Health and Social Work*, 32/2, 147–50.

Gossop, M., Marsden, J., Stewart, D. and Kidd, T. (2003), 'The National Treatment Outcome Research Study (NTORS): 4–5 Year Follow-up Results', *Addiction*, 98, 291–303.

Goswami, U. (2001), 'Cognitive Development: No Stages Please We're British', *British Journal of Psychology*, 92, 257–77.

Gould, C.C. (1995), 'Positive Freedom, Economic Justice, and the Redefinition of Democracy', in J. Howie and G. Schedler (eds.), *Ethical Issues in Contemporary Society*. Carbondale, IL: Southern Illinois University Press.

Government of Ireland (1970), *Reformatory and Industrial Schools System Report* [The Kennedy Report]. Dublin: Stationery Office.

Government of Ireland (1985), *In Partnership with Youth: The National Youth Policy*. Dublin: Stationery Office.

Government of Ireland (2004), *First National Report by Ireland as Required under Article 9 of the Convention on the Legislative, Judicial, Administrative or Other Measures Adopted to Give Effect to the Provisions of the Convention: United Nations International Convention on the Elimination of All Forms of Racial Discrimination*. Dublin: Stationery Office.

Government of Ireland (2007a), *National Action Plan for Social Inclusion 2007–2016*. Dublin: Stationery Office.

Government of Ireland (2007b), *National Development Plan 2007–2013: Transforming Ireland – A Better Quality of Life for All*. Dublin: Stationery Office.

Graham, G. (1995), 'The Roles of the Residential Care Worker', *Journal of the European Association of Training Centres for Socio-Educational Care Work*, 1, 125–53.

Graham, G. (2006), 'Social Care Work with Families in Crisis: Attachment Strategies and Effective Care-Giving through Life-Space Opportunities', in T. O'Connor and M. Murphy (eds.), *Social Care in Ireland: Theory, Policy and Practice*. Cork: CIT Press.

Graham, G. and Megarry, B. (2005), 'The Social Care Portfolio: An Aid to Integrated Learning and Reflection in Social Care Training', *Social Work Education*, 24/7, 769–80.

Greater London Authority Research Group (GLARG) (2000), *Blocking the Fast Track from Prison to Rough Sleeping – A Report to the Rough Sleepers Unit*. London: Greater London Authority Research Group.

Greene, S. (1994), 'Growing Up Irish: Development in Context', *Irish Journal of Psychology*, 15/2–3, 354–71.

Hagan, J. and McCarthy, B. (1997), *Mean Streets: Youth Crime and Homelessness*. New York: Cambridge University Press.

Hallstedt, P. and Högström, M. (2005), *The Recontextualisation of Social Pedagogy: A Study of Three Curricula in the Netherlands, Norway and Ireland*. Published PhD thesis. Malmö: University of Malmö.

Halpenny, A., Keogh, A. and Gilligan, R. (2002), *A Place for Children? Children in Families Living in Emergency Accommodation: The Perceptions of Children, Parents and Professionals*. Dublin: The Homeless Agency and the Children's Research Centre.

Halpern, D. (2005), *Social Capital*. Cambridge: Polity Press.

Hanmer, J. and Statham, D. (eds.) (1999), *Women and Social Work*. London: Macmillan.

Harris, M. (2004), 'First Words', in J. Oates and A. Grayson (eds.), *Cognitive and Language Development in Children*. Milton Keynes: Open University Press.

Harris, M., Barlow-Brown, F. and Chasin, J. (1995), 'The Emergence of Referential Understanding: Pointing and the Comprehension of Object Names', *First Language*, 15, 19–34.

Harris, M., Jones, D. and Grant, J. (1983), 'The Nonverbal Context of Mothers' Speech to Infants', *First Language*, 4, 21–30.

Harrison, P. (2006), *Managing Social Care: A Guide for New Managers*. Dorset: Russell House Publishing.

Harter, L., Berquist, C., Titsworth, B., Novak, D. and Brokaw, T. (2005), 'The Structuring of Invisibility among the Hidden Homeless: The Politics of Space, Stigma, and Identity Construction', *Journal of Applied Communication Research*, 33/4, 305–27.

Harvey, B. (2008), 'Homelessness, the 1988 Housing Act, State Policy and Civil Society', in D. Downey (ed.), *Perspectives on Irish Homelessness, Past, Present and Future*. Dublin: The Homeless Agency, pp. 10–14.

Haslett, D. (2003), *The Role and Future Development of Day Services for Older People in Ireland*. Dublin: National Council on Ageing and Older People, Report no. 74.

Hawkins, P. and Shohet, R. (2000), *Supervision in the Helping Professions* (2nd edn.). Milton Keynes: Open University Press.

Hawkins, P. and Shohet, R. (2007), *Supervision in the Helping Professions* (3rd edn.). Buckingham: Open University Press.

Hayden, G. (1997), *Teaching About Values: A New Approach*. London: Cassell Publications.

Hayes, S., Barnes-Holmes, D. and Roche, B. (2001), *Relational Frame Theory: A Post-Skinnerian Account of Human Language and Cognition*. New York: Plenum.

Health Act 2004. Dublin: Stationery Office.

Health Advisory Service (HAS) UK Report (1996), *The Substance of Young Needs*. London: Her Majesty's Stationery Office.

Health Advisory Service (HAS) UK Report (2001), *The Substance of Young Needs*. London: Her Majesty's Stationery Office. <www.drugs.gov.uk/publication-search/young-people/Health-advisory-service-report?view=Binary>, accessed on 7 January 2009.

Health and Social Care Professional Act 2005. Dublin: Government Publications.

Health Act 2006. Dublin: Stationery Office.

Health (Nursing Homes) Act 1990. Dublin: Stationery Office.

Health Service Executive/Kerry Family Support Team (2007), *Evaluation for the Period September 2006–August 2007*. Kerry: Health Service Executive.

Hearn, J. (1999), 'A Crisis in Masculinity or New Agendas for Men?', in S. Walby (ed.), *New Agendas for Women*. Oxford: Polity.

Heisler-Schmitter, B. (1992), 'The Future of Immigrant Incorporation: Which Models? Which Concepts?', *International Migration Review*, 26/2 (Special Issue: The New Europe and International Migration), 623–45.

Helliwell, J.F. and Putnam, R.D. (2005), 'The Social Context of Well-being', in F. Huppert, N. Baylis and B. Keverne (eds.), *The Science of Well-being*. Oxford: Oxford University Press.

Henderson, J. and Atkinson, D. (eds.) (2003), *Managing Care in Context*. London: Routledge.

Hennessy, S. (2002), 'Assessing Work in the Living Environment', in *Module 14 Creating Living Environments*. Bachelor of Arts in Applied Social Studies (Disability). Dublin: The Open Training College.

Herbert, M. (1981), *Behavioural Treatment of Problem Children*. London: Academic Press.

Herd, P. and Meyer, M. (2002), 'Care Work: Invisible Civic Engagement', *Gender and Society*, 16/5, 665–88.

Hessle, S. (2002), 'What Happens When Social Pedagogy Becomes Part of the Academic Higher Social Work Education Programme?', *European Journal of Social Education*, 3, 1–3.

Heumann, L., McCall, M. and Boldy, D. (2001), *Empowering Frail Elderly People: Opportunities and Impediments in Housing, Health, and Support Service Delivery*. New York: Praeger.

Higgins, M. (2001), *Shaping the Future: An Action Plan on Homelessness in Dublin 2001–2003*. Dublin: The Homeless Agency.

Higham, P. (2006), *Social Work: Introducing Professional Practice*. London: Sage.

Hill, A. (2008) 'Parenting Websites – A New Form of Support', *The Observer*, 30 April.

Hill, M. (2000), 'The Residential Child Care Context', in M. Chakrabarti and M. Hill (eds.), *Residential Child Care – International Perspectives on Links with Families and Peers*. London and Philadelphia: Jessica Kingsley Publishers.

Hillman, J. (1979), *Insearch: Psychology and Religion*. Dallas, TX: Spring Publications.

Hoffman, L. and Coffey, B. (2008), 'Dignity and Indignation: How People Experiencing Homelessness View Services and Providers', *The Social Science Journal*, 45, 207–22.

Holmes, J. (1993), *John Bowlby and Attachment Theory*. London: Routledge.

Homeless Agency (2004), *Making it Home: An Action Plan on Homelessness in Dublin 2004–2006*. Dublin: The Homeless Agency.

Homeless Agency (2007), *A Key to the Door: The Homeless Agency Partnership Action Plan on Homelessness in Dublin 2007–2010*. Dublin: The Homeless Agency.

House of Commons (2001), *Care Trusts and Long Term Care in the Health and Social Care Bill*. Research Paper 01/02. <www.parliament.uk/commons/lib/research/rp2001/rp01-002.pdf>

Houser, J. (2008), *Nursing Research: Reading, Using and Creating Evidence*. London: Jones and Bartlett Publishers.

Howe, D. (1987), *An Introduction to Social Work Theory*. Aldershot: Ashgate.

Howe, D., Schofield, G., Brandon, M. and Hinings, D. (1999), *Attachment Theory, Child Maltreatment and Family Support: A Practice and Assessment Model*. Basingstoke: Palgrave.

Howes, C. and Hamilton, C.E. (1992), 'Children's Relationships with Child Care Teachers: Stability and Concordance with Parental Attachments', *Child Development*, 63, 867–78.

HSA (Health and Safety Authority) (2007), *Summary of Injury, Illness and Fatality Statistics 2005–2006*. Dublin: Health and Safety Authority.

HSE (2006), *Review of Adequacy of Services for Children and Families 2006*. Naas: Health Service Executive.

HSE (Health Service Executive) (2007), *Report of the HSE Working Group on Residential Treatment and Rehabilitation (Substance Users)*. Dublin: Stationery Office. <http://hrbndc.imaxan.ie/attached/3966-42381118.pdf>, accessed on 7 January 2009.

Hubbard, R.L., Craddock, S.G. and Anderson, J. (2003), 'Overview of 5-Year Outcomes in the Drug Abuse Treatment Outcome Studies (DATOS)', *Journal of Substance Abuse Treatment*, 25, 125–34.

Huczynski, A. and Buchanan, D. (2001), *Organisational Behaviour: An Introductory Text*. Harlow: Financial Times/Prentice Hall.

Huesmmann, L.R. (1997), 'Observational Learning of Violent Behaviour: Social and Biosocial Processes', in A. Raine, P.A. Brennan, D.P. Farrington and S.A. Mednick (eds.), *Biosocial Bases of Violence*. New York: Plenum.

Hurley, L. (1992), *The Historical Development of Irish Youth Work 1850–1985*. Dublin: Irish Youth Work Press.

IASCE (Irish Association of Social Care Educators) (2009), *Practice Placement Manual*. Sligo: Big Fish/IASCE.

ILO (International Labour Organization/International Council of Nurses/World Health Organization/Public Services International) (2002), *Framework for Addressing Workplace Violence in the Health Sector*. Geneva: International Labour Office.

Immigration Control Platform (2008), <www.immigrationcontrol.org/>, accessed on 14 November 2008.

Indecon (2006), *Report on Property Based Tax Reliefs*. Dublin: Indecon.

Inglis, T. (1998a), 'Foucault, Bourdieu and the Field of Irish Sexuality', *Irish Journal of Sociology*, 7, 5–28.

Inglis, T. (1998b), *Lessons in Irish Sexuality*. Dublin: University College Dublin Press.

Inglis, T. (2008), 'The Neary Case', in M. Corcoran and P. Share (eds.), *Belongings: Shaping Identity in Modern Ireland*. Irish Sociological Chronicles, Vol. 6 (2005–2006). Dublin: Institute of Public Administration.

Institut National D'Études Démographique (2008), 'Birth and Death Rates (per 1,000 Pop) and Infant Mortality Rate (per 1,000 Live Births)'. <www.ined.fr/en/pop_figures/developed_countries/birth_and_death_rates_infant_mortality_rate/>, accessed on 13 June 2008.

Institute for Health Research (2005), *The Impact of Person Centred Planning*. Lancaster: Institute for Health Research, Lancaster University.

Institute of Technology, Tralee (2006), *IT Tralee Programmatic Review*, Section 5.1.3, 'Personal Development', pp. 13–14.

Inter-departmental Committee on the Care of the Aged (1968), *Care of the Aged Report*. Dublin: Stationery Office.

IRC (Irish Refugee Council) (1999), *Separated Children Seeking Asylum in Ireland: A Report on Legal and Social Conditions*. Dublin: Irish Refugee Council.

Irish Times (1 March 2000), 'Refugee Council is Concerned at Dispersal of Underage Asylum Seekers' by Eithne Donnellan.

Irish Traveller Movement (2002), *International Covenant on Economic, Social and Cultural Rights. Second Report by Ireland 1999. Submission by the Irish Traveller Movement.* <www.itmtrav.com/publications/Subm-ESCR.html>, accessed on 15 May 2008.

Jack, G. and Gill, O. (2003), *The Missing Side of the Triangle*. London: Barnardos.

Jay, D. (1962), *Socialism and the New Society*. London: Longmans.

JCFJ (Jesuit Centre for Faith and Justice) (2004), Statement on the Citizenship Referendum. <www.cfj.ie/content/viw/71/>, accessed on 2 December 2008.

Jenkins, R. (1996a), *Social Identity*. London: Routledge.

Jenkins, R. (1996b), ' "Us" and "Them": Ethnicity, Racism and Ideology', in R. Barot (ed.), *The Racism Problematic: Contemporary Sociological Debates on Race and Ethnicity*. Lampeter, Wales: Edward Mellen Press, pp. 69–88.

Jenkins, R. (1997), *Rethinking Ethnicity: Arguments and Explorations*. London: Sage.

Johns, H. (1996), *Personal Development in Counsellor Training*. London: Sage.

Jones, G. and Malcolm, E. (1999), *Medicine, Disease and the State in Ireland, 1650–1940*. Cork: Cork University Press.

Jordan, B. (2007), *Social Work and Well-being*. Dorset: Russell House Publishing.

Jull, D. (2001), 'Is Child and Youth Care a Profession?', *Journal of Child and Youth Care*, 14/3, 79–88.

Kadushin, A. (1976), *Supervision in Social Work*. New York: Columbia University Press.

Kanics, J. (2007), *Missing Children Should Be Called to Action – Not Indifference!* Dublin: Irish Refugee Council.

Kanter, R.M. (1977), *Men and Women of the Corporation*. New York: Basic Books.

Kazdin, A. (1995), *Conduct Disorders in Childhood and Adolescence*. London: Sage.

Kazenbuch, J. and Smith, D. (1993), *The Discipline of Teams*. Cambridge, MA: Harvard Business Review Press.

Kearney, N. and Skehill, C. (eds.) (2005), *Social Work in Ireland: Historical Perspectives*. Dublin: Institute of Public Administration.

Keating, D. (2004), 'Cognitive and Language Development', in R. Lerner, L. Steinberg and N. Hoboken (eds.), *Handbook of Adolescent Psychology* (2nd edn.). Hoboken, NJ: Wiley & Sons.

Kelleher, K. and Kelleher, P. (1997), *Family Resource Centres*. Dublin: Stationery Office.

Kelleher, P., Kelleher, C. and Corbett, M. (2000), *Left Out on their Own: Young People Leaving Care in Ireland*. Dublin: Oak Tree Press and Focus Ireland.

Kellmer-Pringle, M. (1974), *The Needs of Children*. London: Hutchinson.

Kelly, F., Kelly, C. and Craig, S. (2007), *Annual Report of the National Intellectual Disability Database Committee 2007*. Dublin: Health Research Board.

Kelly, G.A. (1991), *The Psychology of Personal Constructs, Vol. 1 and 2*. London: Routledge.

Kelly, M. (ed.) (1994), *Critique and Power: Recasting the Foucault/Habermas Debate*. Oxford: Blackwell.

Kendrick, D. (1998), *Patrin, the Travellers of Ireland* [online text]. <www.geocities.com/paris/5121/Ireland.htm>, accessed on 19 May 2004.

Kennedy, K. and Gallagher, C. (1997), 'Social Pedagogy in Europe', *Irish Social Worker*, 15/1, 6–8.

Kennefick, D. (1998), 'Managing Social Services', in L. Joyce (ed.), *A Healthier Future*. Dublin: Gill & Macmillan.

Kennefick, P. (2003), 'Training the Person', *European Journal of Social Education FESET*, 4, 91–4.

Kennefick, P. (2006), 'Aspects of Personal Development', in T. O'Connor and M. Murphy (eds.), *Social Care in Ireland: Theory, Policy and Practice*. Cork: CIT Press.

Kenny, M. and McNeela, E. (2006), *Assimilation Policies and Outcomes: Travellers' Experiences*. Dublin: Pavee Point Travellers' Centre.

Kerry Family Support Team (2007), *Annual Report*. HSE South.

Kidd, S., Miner, S., Walker, D. and Davidson, L. (2007), 'Stories of Working with Homeless Youth: On Being "Mind-Boggling" ', *Children and Youth Services Review*, 29, 16–34.

King, D. (2004), *Immigration and Citizenship in Ireland*. Dublin: Children's Rights Alliance.

Kirby, P. (2001), 'Inequality and Poverty in Ireland: Clarifying Social Objectives', in S. Cantillon, C. Corrigan, P. Kirby and J. O'Flynn (eds.), *Rich and Poor: Perspectives on Tackling Inequality in Ireland*. Dublin: CPA/Oak Tree Press.

Kirby, P. (2006), 'The Changing Role of the Irish State: From Welfare to Competition State', in T. O'Connor and M. Murphy (eds.), *Social Care in Ireland*. Cork: CIT Press.

Klaus, M.H. and Kennell, J.H. (1976), *Maternal-Infant Bonding*. St Louis: The Mosby Company.

Knoppers, A. (1993), 'A Critical Theory of Gender Relations', in M. Van Leeuwen (ed.), *After Eden*. Grand Rapids, MI: Eerdmans Publishing Company, pp. 225–58.

Knorth, E., Van den Bergh, P.M. and Verheij, F. (eds.) (2002), *Professionalization and Participation in Child and Youth Care: Challenging Understandings in Theory and Practice*. Aldershot: Ashgate.

Kochanska, G. (2001), 'Emotional Development in Children with Different Attachment Histories: The First Three Years', *Child Development*, 72/2, 474–90.

Kolb, D.A. (1984), *Experiential Learning: Experience as the Source of Learning and Development*. New Jersey: Prentice Hall.

Kosonen, M. (1996), 'Siblings as Providers of Support and Care During Middle Childhood: Children's Perceptions', *Children and Society*, 10/4, 267–79.

Kotter, J. (1990), *A Force for Change: How Leadership Differs from Management*. New York: Free Press.

Kouzes, J. and Posner, B. (1987), *The Leadership Challenge: How to Get Extraordinary Things Done in Organizations*. San Francisco: Jossey-Bass.

Kröger, T. (2001), *Comparative Research on Social Care: The State of the Art*. Brussels: European Commission. <www.uta.fi/laitokset/sospol/soccare/report1.pdf>

Krueger, M. (1998), *Interactive Youth Work Practice*. New York: CWLA Press.

Krueger, M. (1999), 'Presence as Dance in Work with Youth', *Journal of Child and Youth Care*, 13/2, 59–72.

Krueger, M. (2002), 'A Further Review of the Development of the Child and Youth Care Profession in the United States', *Child and Youth Care Forum*, 31/1, 13–26.

Kuhn, D., Amsel, E. and O'Loughlin, M. (1988), *The Development of Scientific Thinking Skills*. San Diego: Academic Press.

Lalor, K., de Róiste, Á. and Devlin, M. (2007), *Young People in Contemporary Ireland*. Dublin: Gill & Macmillan.

Laming, Lord (2003), *The Victoria Climbié Inquiry. Report of an Inquiry by Lord Laming Presented to Parliament by the Secretary of State for Health and the Secretary of State for the Home Department*. London: HMSO.

Lansdowne Market Research Ltd (2001), *Attitudes to Minorities*. Survey prepared for Amnesty International in association with Public Communication Centre. Dublin: Lansdowne Market Research.

Lapsley, D.K. and Narvaez, D. (eds.) (2004), *Moral Development, Self and Identity*. New Jersey: Lawrence Erlbaum Associates.

Laurence, J. (1999), *Argument for Action: Ethics and Professional Conduct*. Aldershot: Ashgate.

Lawless, M. and Corr, C. (2005), *Drug Use among the Homeless Population in Ireland: A Report for the National Advisory Committee on Drugs*. Dublin: Stationery Office.

Layard, R. (2005), *Happiness: Lessons from a New Science*. London: Penguin.

Layder, D. (1993), *New Strategies in Social Research*. Cambridge: Polity.

Layder, D. (2004), *Social and Personal Identity: Understanding Yourself*. London: Sage.

Layte, R., Fahey, T. and Whelan, C. (1999), *Income, Deprivation and Well-being Among Older Irish People*. Dublin: National Council on Ageing and Older People, Report no. 55.

Layte, R., McGee, H., Quail, A., Rundle, K., Cousins, G., Donnelly, C., Mulcahy, F. and Conroy, R. (2006), 'The Irish Study of Sexual Health and Relationships'. Dublin: Department of Health and Children and Crisis Pregnancy Agency.

Leadbetter, C. (2006), 'Production by the Masses: Professionals and Postindustrial Public Services', in J. Craig (ed.), *Production Values: Futures for Professionalism*. London: Demos.

Leadbetter, M. (2002), 'Empowerment and Advocacy', in R. Adams, L. Dominelli and M. Payne (eds.), *Social Work: Themes, Issues and Critical Debates* (2nd edn.). Basingstoke: Palgrave.

Leavy, A. and Kahan, B. (1991), *The Pindown Experience and the Protection of Children. The Report of the Staffordshire Child Care Enquiry*. Stafford: Staffordshire County Council.

Lees, S. (1993), *Sugar and Spice: Sexuality and Adolescent Girls*. London: Penguin.

Lentin, R. (1998), 'Irishness, the 1937 Constitution and Citizenship: A Gender and Ethnicity View', *Irish Journal of Sociology*, 8, 5–24.

Lentin, R. (2004), 'From Racial State to Racist State', *Variant*, 2/20, 7–8.

Lentin, R. (2007), 'Illegal in Ireland, Irish Illegals: Diaspora Nation as a Racial State', *Irish Political Studies*, 22/4, 433–53.

Lentin, R. and McVeigh, R. (2006), *After Optimism? Racism and Globalisation*. Dublin: Metro Éireann Publications.

Lewis, J. (2001), 'What Works in Community Care?', *Managing Community Care*, 9 (February), 3–6.

Lewis, M. (2005), *Asylum: Understanding Public Attitudes*. London: IPPR.

Lewis, M., Feiring, C. and Rosenthal, S. (2000), 'Attachment Over Time', *Child Development*, 71/3, 707–20.

Liberatore, R. (1981), 'Training Child Care Workers: Three Essentials' [online text], <www.cyc-net.org/cyc-online/cycol-0202-liberatore.html>.

Likert, R. (1961), *New Patterns of Management*. New York: McGraw-Hill.

Lindsay, M. (2002), 'Building a Professional Identity: The Challenge for Residential Child and Youth Care', in E. Knorth, P. van den Bergh and F. Verheij (eds.), *Professionalization and Participation in Child and Youth Care*. Aldershot: Ashgate.

Littleton, K., Miell, D. and Faulkner, D. (2004), *Learning to Collaborate, Collaborating to Learn*. New York: Nova Science.

London, M. (2002), *Leadership Development: Paths to Self-insight and Professional Growth*. New Jersey: Lawrence Erlbaum Associates.

Lorenz, W. (1994), *Social Work in a Changing Europe*. London: Routledge.

Lorenz, W. (1998), 'Cultural Diversity as a Challenge for Social Work', *Irish Social Worker*, 16/3 (Summer), 15–17.

Lukes, S. (1974), *Power: A Radical View*. London: Macmillan.

Lynch, K. and McLaughlin, E. (1995), 'Caring Labour and Love Labour', in P. Clancy, S. Drudy, K. Lynch and L. O' Dowd (eds.), *Irish Society: Sociological Perspectives*. Dublin: Institute of Public Administration, pp. 250–92.

Lyon, D. and Glucksman, M. (2008), 'Comparative Configurations of Care Work across Europe', *Sociology*, 42/1, 101–18.

Lyons, D. (2007), 'Just Bring Your Self: Exploring the Training of Self in Social Care Education', unpublished Masters thesis, Dublin Institute of Technology.

Maccoby, E. and Martin, J. (1983), 'Socialization in the Context of the Family: Parent–Child Interaction', in E.M. Hetherington, (ed.), *Handbook of Child Psychology: Socialization, Personality and Social Development (Vol. 4)*. New York: Wiley.

Macdonald, K. (1995), *The Sociology of Professions*. London: Sage.

Macionis, J. and Plummer, K. (2008), *Sociology: A Global Introduction* (4th edn.). London: Pearson/Prentice Hall.

MacKenna, P. (1994), 'Ontario Association of Child and Youth Care Counsellors: Effectiveness and Future Directions', *Journal of Child and Youth Care*, 9/4, 1–10.

MacKenna, P. (1999), 'Self: It All Starts Here', *Journal of Child and Youth Care*, 13/2, 73–90.

Macpherson Report (1999), *The Stephen Lawrence Inquiry: Report of an Inquiry by Sir William Macpherson of Cluny*, Cm 4262–1. London: The Home Office.

Madsen, B. (1995), *Socialpedagogik og samfundsforvandling*. Copenhagen: Socialpedagogisk Bibliotek.

Maier, H. (1990), 'A Developmental Perspective for Child and Youth Care Work', in J.P. Anglin et al. (eds.), *Perspectives in Professional Child and Youth Care*. London: The Haworth Press.

Main, M. (1995), 'Recent Studies in Attachment', in S. Goldberg, R. Muir and J. Kerr (eds.), *Attachment Theory: Social, Developmental, and Clinical Perspectives*. Hillsdale, NJ: The Analytic Press, pp. 467–74.

Main, M. and Solomon, J. (1990), 'Procedures for Identifying Infants as Disorganized/Disoriented during the Ainsworth Strange Situation', in M. Greenberg, D. Cicchetti and E.M. Cummings (eds.), *Attachment in the Preschool Years: Theory, Research and Intervention*. Chicago: University of Chicago Press.

Mansell, J. (1992), *Services for People with Learning Disabilities and Challenging Behaviour or Mental Health Needs* [The Mansell Report]. London: HMSO.

Mareschal, D., Johnson, M.H. and Grayson, A. (2004), 'Brain and Cognitive Development', in J. Oakes and A. Grayson (eds.), *Cognitive and Language Development in Children*. Milton Keynes: The Open University Press.

Marsh, P. and Fisher, M. (2005), *Developing the Evidence Base for Social Work and Social Care Practice*. London: Social Care Institute for Excellence.

Martin, M. and Carr, A. (2007), *The Clonmel Project Report: Mental Health Needs of Children and Adolescents in the South East of Ireland*. Clonmel: Health Service Executive.

Maslow, A. (1970), *Motivation and Personality*. New York: Harper & Row.

Mathiesen, R. (2000), *Socialpedagogisk perspektiv*. Hamar: Sokrates.

Mayock, P. (2008), 'Young People's Pathways through Homelessness: The Offender–Victimisation Nexus', in D. Downey (ed.), *Perspectives on Irish Homelessness, Past, Present and Future*. Dublin: The Homeless Agency, pp. 76–86.

Mayock, P. and Carr, N. (2008), *Not Just Homeless ... A Study of 'Out of Home' Young People in Cork City*. Health Service Executive, South.

Mayock, P. and O'Sullivan, E. (2007), *Lives in Crisis: Homeless Young People in Dublin*. Dublin: The Liffey Press.

Mayock, P. and Veki , K. (2006), *Understanding Youth Homelessness in Dublin City: Key Findings from the First Phase of a Longitudinal Cohort Study*. Dublin: Stationery Office.

McCann, M., O'Siochain, S. and Ruane, J. (1994), *Irish Travellers, Culture and Ethnicity*. Queen's University, Belfast: Institute of Irish Studies.

McCoy, S., Kelly, E. and Watson, D. (2007), *School Leaver's Survey Report*. Dublin: ESRI.

McDonnell, A., Sturmey, P., Oliver, C., Cunningham, J., Hayes, S., Galvin, M., Walshe, C. and Cunningham, C. (2008), 'The Effects of Staff Training on Staff Confidence and Challenging Behaviour in Services for People with Autism Spectrum Disorders', *Research in Autism Spectrum Disorders*, 2/2, 311–19.

McGuinness, C. (1993), *The Report of the Kilkenny Incest Investigation*. Dublin: Stationery Office.

McKay, S. (2007), *Silent People and Other Stories*. Dublin: Combat Poverty Agency.

McLaughlin, E. (2001), 'From Catholic Corporation to Social Partnership', in A. Cochrane et al. (eds.), *Comparing Welfare States*. London: Sage.

McMahan-True, M., Pisani, L. and Oumar, F. (2001), 'Infant Mother Attachment Among the Dogon of Mali', *Child Development*, 72/5, 451–66.

McVerry, P. (2008), 'State Failure of Social Care Clients'. Paper presented to Visiting Speaker Series, Cork Institute of Technology, 2 October 2008.

Means, R., Richards, S. and Smith, R. (2008), *Community Care*. London: Palgrave.

Mearns, D. and Thorne, B. (2007), *Person Centred Counselling in Action*. London: Sage.

Meenan, D. (2002), 'The Phenomenology of Career and Personal Development as Perceived by Residential Child Care Workers in the North Western Health Board', unpublished MBA (Health Services Management) thesis, University College Dublin/Royal College of Surgeons in Ireland.

Mehler, J. and Dupoux, E. (1994), *What Infants Know*. Oxford: Blackwell.

Mental Health Act 2001. Dublin: Stationery Office.

Mental Health Commission (2006), *A Vision for Change*. Dublin: Stationery Office.

Mental Health Foundation (1999), *Bright Futures: Promoting Children and Young People's Mental Health*. London: Mental Health Foundation.

Metraux, S. and Culhane, D. (1999), 'Family Dynamics, Housing, and Recurring Homelessness among Women in New York City Homeless Shelters', *Journal of Family Issues*, 20/3, 371–96.

Midland Health Board (MHB) (2002), *Tapping the Talent: A Report on the Arts in Care Settings for Older People Project*. Age and Opportunity, Midland Health Board and Laois County Council.

Midland Health Board (MHB) (2004), 'Primary Healthcare Programme for Travellers, Annual Report 2003–2004'. Unpublished report.

Miller, T. (2008), ' Implementing Competencies and Their Impact on Social Education', *European Journal of Social Education*, 14/15, 113–20.

Mills, S. (2002), *Clinical Practice and the Law*. Dublin: Butterworths.

Milward Brown IMS (2004), *Research on General Opinions on Racism and Attitudes to Minority Groups*. Dublin: Milward Brown IMS.

Mintzberg, H. (1979), *The Structuring of Organizations*. Englewood Cliffs, NJ: Prentice Hill.

Moane, G. (1994), 'A Psychological Analysis of Colonialism in an Irish Context', *The Irish Journal of Psychology*, 15/2 & 3, 250–65.

Moane, G. (1999), *Gender and Colonialism: A Psychological Analysis of Oppression and Liberation*. London: Macmillan Press Ltd.

Mooten, N. (2006), *Making Children Visible*. Dublin: Irish Refugee Council.

Morgan, M. (2001), *Drug Use Prevention: Overview of Research*. Dublin: National Advisory Committee on Drugs.

Moss, P. and Cameron, C. (2004), 'Does Care Work Have a Future?' *Socialvetenskaplig tidsktift*, 3–4, 223–37.

Mulcahy, W. (2007), 'Perceptions of Social Care Course and Practice: A Study of 3rd and 4th Year Social Care Students in CIT.' Unpublished BA (Hons) dissertation, Department of Social and General Studies, Cork Institute of Technology.

Murgatroyd, S. (1996), *Counselling and Helping*. London: Routledge.

Murphy, C., O'Shea, E., Cooney, A., Shiel, A. and Hodgins, M. (2006), *Improving Quality of Life for Older People in Long Stay Care Settings in Ireland*. Dublin: National Council on Ageing and Older People, Report no. 93.

Nasc [The Irish Immigrant Support Centre] (2008), *Integrating the Future*. Cork: Nasc.

National Advisory Committee on Drugs (NACD) (2006a), *Drug Use in Ireland and Northern Ireland 2002/2003. Drug Prevalence Survey: Cannabis Results*,

Bulletin 3. Dublin: National Advisory Committee on Drugs, Drug and Alcohol Information Research Unit (DAIRU).

National Advisory Committee on Drugs (NACD) (2006b), *Drug Use in Ireland and Northern Ireland 2002/2003. Drug Prevalence Survey: Cocaine Results, Bulletin 4.* Dublin: National Advisory Committee on Drugs, Drug and Alcohol Information Research Unit (DAIRU).

National Advisory Committee on Drugs (NACD) (2006c), *ROSIE Findings 1.* Dublin: National Advisory Committee on Drugs. <http://www.nacd.ie/publications/ROSIEFindings1Final.pdf>, accessed on 7 January 2009.

National Advisory Committee on Drugs (NACD) (2007a), *Drug Use in Ireland and Northern Ireland: 2002/2003 Drug Prevalence Survey: Polydrug Use Results, Bulletin 5.* Dublin: National Advisory Committee on Drugs, Drug and Alcohol Information Research Unit (DAIRU).

National Advisory Committee on Drugs (NACD) (2007b), *ROSIE Findings 7.* Dublin: National Advisory Committee on Drugs. <www.nacd.ie/publications/ROSIE_7_web.pdf>, accessed on 7 January 2009.

National Committee on Volunteering (NVC) (2002), *Tipping the Balance: Report and Recommendations to Government on Supporting and Developing Volunteering in Ireland.* Dublin: National Committee on Volunteering.

National Council on Ageing and Older People (2000), *Framework for Quality in Long-Term Residential Care for Older People in Ireland.* Dublin: National Council on Ageing and Older People, Report no 62.

National Economic and Social Council (2005), *The Developmental Welfare State.* Dublin: NESC.

National Institute for Mental Health (2000), *Treatment of Children with Mental Disorders.* Bethesda, MD: NIMH.

National Treatment Agency for Substance Misuse (2002), *Models of Care for the Treatment of Adult Drug Misusers.* London: National Treatment Agency.

NCEA (National Council for Education Awards) (1992), *Report of the Committee on Caring and Social Studies.* Dublin: NCEA.

NDA (National Disability Authority) (2004), *Guidelines on Person Centred Planning in the Provision of Services for People with Disabilities in Ireland.* Dublin: National Disability Authority.

NDA (National Disability Authority) (2005a), *Disability Agenda*, Issue 2.3 (*Measuring Health and Disability in Europe*). Dublin: National Disability Authority.

NDA (National Disability Authority) (2005b), *How Far towards Equality? Measuring how Equally People with Disabilities Are Included in Irish Society.* Dublin: National Disability Authority.

NDA (National Disability Authority) (2008), 'Appropriate Terms to Use' [online text], <www.nda.ie>.

Neville, H.J., Bavelier, D., Corina, D. et al. (1998), 'Cerebral Organization for Language in Deaf and Hearing Subjects: Biological Constraints and Effects of Experience', *Proceedings of the National Academy of Science*, USA, 95, 922–9.

Ní Chonaill, B. (2007), 'The Impact of Migrants on Resources: A Critical Assessment of the Views of People Working/Living in the Blanchardstown Area', *Translocations*, 2/1, 70–89.

Noonan, P. (1994), *Travelling People in West Belfast*. London: Save the Children.

Norton, D.L. (1995), 'Education for Self-Knowledge and Worthy Living', in J. Howie and G. Schedler (eds.), *Ethical Issues in Contemporary Society*. Carbondale, IL: Southern Illinois University Press.

NWCI (National Women's Council of Ireland) (2003), *Valuing Care Work*. <wwwnwci.ie/publications/published_reports/valuing_care_work_2003>, accessed on 6 April 2008.

NYCI (National Youth Council of Ireland) (2006), *What Is Youth Work?* Information leaflet. Dublin: NYCI.

NYPC (National Youth Policy Committee) (1984), *Final Report*. Dublin: Stationery Office.

O'Brien, G. (2003), *Coming Out: Irish Gay Experiences*. Dublin: Currach.

O'Brien, J. and O'Brien, L.C. (1989), *Framework for Accomplishment*. Georgia: Responsive Systems Associates.

O'Carroll, I. and Collins, E. (eds.) (1995), *Lesbian and Gay Visions of Ireland*. London: Cassells.

O'Carroll, P. (1998), 'Blood', in M. Peillon and E. Slater (eds.), *Encounters with Modern Ireland: A Sociological Chronicle, 1995–1996*. Dublin: Institute of Public Administration.

O'Connor, N. (2008), 'Can We Agree the Number of People Who Are Homeless (And Does It Really Matter)?', in D. Downey (ed.), *Perspectives on Irish Homelessness, Past, Present and Future*. Dublin: The Homeless Agency, pp. 58–63.

O'Connor, P. (1992), 'The Professionalisation of Childcare Work in Ireland: An Unlikely Development', *Children and Society*, 6/3, 250–66.

O'Connor, P. (1998), *Emerging Voices: Women in Contemperory Irish Society*. Dublin: Institute of Public Administration.

O'Connor, P. (2000), 'Ireland: A Man's World?', *The Economic and Social Review*, 31/1, 81–102.

O'Connor, T. (2007), 'Pay Them Some Mind', *Irish Examiner*, 31 October.

O'Connor, T. (2008), 'Towards a Holistic Model for Social Care'. Paper to annual conference of Irish Association of Social Care Educators, Newlands Cross, March.

O'Connor, T. and Murphy, M. (eds.) (2006), *Social Care in Ireland*. Cork: CIT Press.

O'Doherty, C. (2003), 'Shanakill Family Resource Centre: An Evaluation'. Unpublished report for the HSE South.

O'Doherty, C. (2004), 'Towards the Construction of an International Model for the Promotion of Child and Family Welfare Practice: Family Support

Activities of the Irish Health Boards Under the Child Care Act, 1991', unpublished PhD thesis, University College Dublin.

O'Doherty, C. (2006), 'Social Care and Social Capital', in T. O'Connor and M. Murphy (eds.), *Social Care in Ireland: Theory, Policy and Practice*. Cork: CIT Press.

O'Doherty, C. (2007), *A New Agenda for Family Support – Providing Services that Create Social Capital*. Dublin: Blackhall Press.

O'Doherty, C. (2008), 'Critical Social Care Practice'. Paper to annual conference of Irish Association of Social Care Educators, Newlands Cross, March.

O'Doherty, Y., O'Doherty, D. and Walsh, D. (2006), *Family Support Study*. Dublin: Health Research Board.

O'Donovan, M.A. and Doyle, A. (2007) *National Physical and Sensory Disability Database Committee Annual Report 2007*. Dublin: Health Research Board.

O'Farrell, U. (1999), *First Steps in Counselling*. Dublin: Veritas.

O'Higgins, K. (1996), *Disruption, Displacement, Discontinuity? Children in Care and Their Families in Ireland*. Aldershot: Avebury.

O'Leary, P. (2005), 'Case Reports', *Equality News*, Spring edition.

O'Loingsigh, D. (2001), 'Intercultural Education and the School Ethos', in F. Farrell and P. Watt (eds.), *Responding to Racism in Ireland*. Dublin: Veritas.

O'Neill, E. (2004), *Professional Supervision: Myths, Culture and Structures*. Fethard, Co. Tipperary: RMA Publications.

O'Reilly, M. (1993), *With Travellers: A Handbook for Teachers*. Dublin: Blackrock Teachers Centre.

O'Shea, E. (2005), 'The Financing of Long-Term Care in Ireland'. Paper presented to Visiting Speaker Series, Cork Institute of Technology, March.

O'Shea, E. (2006), 'Public Policy for Dependent Older People in Ireland', in E. O'Dell (ed.), *Older People in Modern Ireland: Essays on Law and Policy*. Dublin: First Law.

O'Sullivan, E. (2004), 'Welfare Regimes, Housing and Homelessness in the Republic of Ireland', *European Journal of Housing Policy*, 4/3, 323–43.

O'Sullivan, E. (2005), 'Homelessness', in M. Norris and D. Redmond, *Housing Contemporary Ireland: Policy, Society and Shelter*. Dublin: Institute of Public Administration, pp. 245–67.

O'Sullivan, E. (2006), 'Homelessness in Rural Ireland', in P. Milbourne and P. Cloke, *International Perspectives on Rural Homelessness*. Abingdon: Routledge, pp. 188–207.

O'Sullivan, E. (2008), 'Researching Homelessness in Ireland: Explanations, Themes and Approaches', in D. Downey (ed.), *Perspectives on Irish Homelessness, Past, Present and Future*. Dublin: The Homeless Agency, pp. 16–23.

O'Sullivan, T. and Butler, S. (2004), *Current Issues in Irish Health Management: A Comparative Review*. Dublin: Institute of Public Administration.

O'Toole, F. (2008), 'Inequality Now Official Policy', *The Irish Times*, 15 January.

O'Toole, J. (1998), 'Young Women in Rural Ireland.' Unpublished M.Soc.Sc [Sociology], University College Dublin.

Oakley, A. (1972), *Sex, Gender and Society*. London: Temple Smith.

Obholzer, A. and Roberts, V.Z. (1994), *The Unconscious at Work: Individual and Organizational Stress in the Human Services*. London: Routledge.

Office for National Statistics (2000), *The Mental Health of Children and Adolescents in Great Britain*. London: HMSO.

Office for the High Commissioner for Human Rights (1969), *International Convention on the Elimination of All Forms of Racial Discrimination*. <www.unhchr.ch/html/menu3/b/d_icerd.htm>, accessed on 15 May 2008.

Office of the Minister for Children (2006a), *Diversity and Equality Guidelines for Childcare Providers*. Dublin: OMC.

Office of the Minister for Children (2006b), *Separated Children Seeking Asylum*. Dublin: OMC.

Open University (1975), *Making Sense of Society: Attitudes and Beliefs*. Milton Keynes: Open University Press.

ORAC (Office of the Refugee Applications Commissioner) (2006), *Annual Report*. Dublin: Government Publications.

ORAC (Office of the Refugee Applications Commissioner) (2007), *Annual Report*. Dublin: Government Publications.

Orme, J. (2001), *Gender and Community Care*. London: Palgrave.

Osborne, R. (2002), ' "I May Be Homeless, but I'm Not Helpless": The Costs and Benefits of Identifying with Homelessness', *Self and Identity*, 1, 43–52.

OSI (Office for Social Inclusion) (2006), *National Report for Ireland on Strategies for Social Protection and Social Inclusion*. Dublin: ESRI.

OSI (Office for Social Inclusion) (2007a), *Fourth Meeting of the Social Inclusion Forum: Conference Report*. Dublin: Department of Social and Family Affairs.

OSI (Office for Social Inclusion) (2007b), *Ireland: National Development Plan 2007–2013: Transforming Ireland*. Dublin: Stationery Office.

OSI (Office for Social Inclusion) (2007c), *National Action Plan for Social Inclusion 2007–2016*. Dublin: Stationery Office.

Page, S. (1999), *The Shadow and the Counsellor*. London: Routledge.

Palmer, S. and McMahon, G. (1997), *Client Assessment*. London: Sage.

Parekh, B. (2002), *Rethinking Multiculturalism: Cultural Diversity and Political Theory*. Basingstoke: Palgrave.

Parfitt, T. (2006), 'Bell Tolls for Hemingway's Fake', *The Observer*, 12 February.

Parfitt, W. (2006), *Psychosynthesis: The Elements and Beyond*. Glastonbury: Avalon.

Pavee Point (2004), *Discrimination*. <www.paveepoint.ie/pav_discrimination_a.html>, accessed on 19 May 2008.

Pavee Point (2006), *Traveller Culture*. <www.paveepoint.ie/pav_culture_a.html>, accessed on 20 February 2008.

Pavlov, I.P. (1927), *Conditioned Reflexes: An Investigation of the Physiological Activity of the Cerebral Cortex*. London: Oxford University Press.

Pawson, P., Boaz, A., Grayson, L., Long, A. and Barnes, C. (2003), *Types and Quality of Knowledge in Social Care*. London: Social Care Institute for Excellence.

Payne, M. (1996), *What Is Professional Social Work?* Birmingham: Venture Press.

Pedler, M., Burgoyne, J. and Boydell, T. (2004), *A Manager's Guide to Leadership*. London: McGraw Hill.

Petrie, P., Boddy, J., Cameron, C., Heptinstall, E., McQuail, S., Simon, A. and Wigfall, V. (2005), 'Pedagogy – A Holistic, Personal Approach to Work with Children and Young People Across Services. European Models for Training, Education and Qualification'. Briefing paper, Thomas Coram Research Unit, Institute of Education, University of London. <http://k1.ioe.ac.uk/tcru/Ped_BRIEFING_PAPER.pdf>

Petrie, P., Boddy, J., Cameron, C., Wigfall, V. and Simon, A. (2006), *Working with Children in Care: European Perspectives*. Buckingham: Open University Press.

Phelan, J. (2003), 'Supervision Levels'. Unpublished conference paper presented at the Residential Managers' Conference 2003.

Phelan, M. (1988), 'The Certification of Child and Youth Care Workers', in G. Charles and P. Gabor (eds.), *Issues in Child and Youth Care Practice*. Lethbridge: Lethbridge Community College.

Phillips, A. (1999), *Which Equalites Matter?* Oxford: Polity Press.

Phillipson, C., Bernard, M., Phillips, J. and Ogg, J. (2001), *The Family and Community Life of Older People*. London and New York: Routledge.

Piaget, J. (1959), *The Language and Thought of the Child*. London: Routledge and Kegan Paul (first published 1923).

Pike, B. (2006), 'Politicians and the Drugs Debate', *Drugnet Ireland*, 19 (Autumn), 16–17.

Pillinger, J. (2007), *Homeless Pathways: Developing Effective Strategies to Address Pathways Into, Through and Out of Homelessness*. Dublin: Focus Ireland.

Pinker, S. (1994), *The Language Instinct: The New Science of Language and Mind*. London: Penguin.

Plath, D. (2006), 'Evidence-based Practice: Current Issues and Future Directions', *Australian Social Work*, 59/1, 56–72.

Pollard, K., Sellman, D. and Senior, B. (2005), 'The Need for Interprofessional Working', in G. Barrett et al. (eds.), *Interprofessional Working in Health and Social Care*. London: Palgrave.

Poolos, J. (2006), *Ralph Waldo Emerson: The Father of the American Renaissance*. New York: Rosen Publishing Group.

Punch, M. (1998), *Introduction to Social Research: Qualitative and Quantitative Approaches*. London: Sage.

Quinn, M., Carr, A., Carroll, L. and O'Sullivan, D. (2007), 'Parents Plus Programme. Evaluation of Its Effectiveness for Preschool Children with Developmental Disabilities and Behavioural Problems', *Journal of Applied Research in Intellectual Disabilities*, 22, 345–59.

Quinn, P.C. and Eimas, P.D. (1997), 'A Reexamination of the Perceptual-to-Conceptual Shift in Mental Representations', *Review of General Psychology*. September, 1/3, 271–87.

Quinton, D. (2005), 'Themes from a UK Research Initiative on Supporting Parents', in J. Scott and H. Ward (eds.), *Safeguarding and Promoting the Well-Being of Children, Families and Communities*. London: Jessica Kingsley Publishers.

Raftery, M. and O'Sullivan, E. (1999), *Suffer the Little Children: The Inside Story of Ireland's Industrial Schools*. Dublin: New Island.

Randall, G. and Brown, S. (1999), *Prevention Is Better than Cure*. London: Crisis.

Rappaport, J. (1984), 'Studies in Empowerment', cited in C. Lupton and P. Nixon (1999), *Empowering Practice: A Critical Appraisal of Family Group and Conference Approach*. Bristol: Policy Press.

Reception and Integration Agency (2003), *The Asylum Process: Reception and Dispersal*. Dublin: Department of Justice, Equality and Law Reform.

Residential Forum (1998), *A Golden Opportunity: A Report on Training and Staff Development for People Working in Residential Services for Children and Young People*. London: National Institute for Social Work.

Reynolds, S., Fanagan, S., Bellerose, D. and Long, J. (2008), *Trends in Treated Problem Drug Use in Ireland, 2001 to 2006. HRB Trends Series 2*. Dublin: Health Research Board.

Richards, J. (2003), 'Draft Report of the Review by Mr John Richards of Residential Care Services for Children in the South East Health Board'. Internal SEHB document.

Ricks, F. (1989), 'Self-awareness Model for Education and Training in Child and Youth Care Work', *Journal of Child and Youth Care*, 4/1, 33–41.

Ricks, F. and Charlesworth, J. (2003), *Emergent Practice Planning*. New York: Kluwer Academic/Plenum Publishers.

Ricks, F., Laliberte, P., Savicki, V. and Hare, F. (1991), 'Child and Youth Care Education Consortium: Report on the Consideration of Accreditation for Child and Youth Care Education Programmes', *Journal of Child and Youth Care*, 7/1, 110–17.

Rigg, C. with Richards, S. (2006), *Action Learning, Leadership and Organizational Development in Public Services*. London: Routledge.

Riley, J.C. (2008), *Low Income, Social Growth, and Good Health: A History of Twelve Countries*. Berkley, CA: University of California Press.

Rittel, H. and Webber, M. (1973), 'Dilemmas in a General Theory of Planning', *Policy Sciences*, 4, 155–69.

Robins, J. (1986), *Fools and Mad: A History of the Insane in Ireland*. Dublin: Institute of Public Administration.

Rogers, C.R. (1951), *Client Centred Therapy*. London: Constable & Company.

Rogers, C.R. (1967), *On Becoming a Person: A Therapist's View of Psychotherapy*. London: Constable & Company.

Rogers, N. (1993), *The Creative Connection*. California: Science and Behaviour Books Inc.

Rolfe, G., Freshwater, D. and Jasper, M. (2001), *Critical Reflection for Nursing and the Helping Professions: A User's Guide*. Basingstoke: Palgrave Macmillan.

Rosen, A. (2003), 'Evidence-based Social Work Practice: Challenges and Promise', *Social Work Research*, 27/4, 197–208.

Royal Irish Academy (2003), *Mosaic or Melting Pot? Living with Diversity*. Dublin: European Cultural Foundation and Royal Irish Academy.

RTÉ (2008), Radio Telefis Éireann *Prime Time* documentary 29/04/2008 and subsequent discussion on *Morning Ireland* political and social affairs radio show 30/04/08.

Ruch, G. (2005), 'Relationship-based Practice and Reflective Practice: Holistic Approaches to Contemporary Child-Care Social Work', *Child and Family Social Work*, 10, 111–24.

Ruddle, H., Donoghue, F. and Mulvihill, R. (1997), *The Years Ahead Report: A Review of the Implementation of Its Recommendations*. Dublin: National Council on Ageing and Older People.

Ruth, S. (1988), 'Understanding Oppression and Liberation', *Studies* (Winter), 434–44.

Rutter, M. (1975), *Helping Troubled Children*. Harmondsworth: Penguin Education.

Rutter, M. (1981), *Maternal Deprivation Reassessed*. Harmondsworth: Penguin.

Rutter, M. (1995), 'Clinical Implications of Attachment Concepts: Retrospect and Prospect', *Journal of Child Psychology and Psychiatry*, 36/4, 549–71.

Rutter, M., Tizard, J. and Wightmore, K. (1970), *Education, Health and Behaviour*. London: Longman.

Ryan, A. (1999), *Walls of Silence*. Ireland: Red Lion Press.

Sarantakos, S. (2005), *Social Research*. Basingstoke: Palgrave Macmillan.

Schön, D. (1991a), *The Reflective Practitioner: How Professionals Think in Action* (new edition). Aldershot: Arena.

Schön, D. (1991b), *The Reflective Turn: Case Studies in and on Educational Practice*. New York: Teachers Press, Columbia University.

Scott, A. (2008), 'Confronting Challenge: Enabling Care Home Staff to Understand and Work Effectively with Challenging Behaviours in Dementia. Abstract for Poster Session 111', *European Psychiatry*, 23, 304–409.

Seebohm Report (1968), *Report of the Committee on Local Authority and Allied Personal Social Services*. Cmd 3703. London: HMSO.

Seymour, M. and Costello, L. (2005), *A Study of the Number, Profile and Progression Routes of Homeless Persons before the Court and in Custody*. Dublin: Government of Ireland.

Share, P., Tovey, H. and Corcoran, M. (2007), *A Sociology of Ireland*. Dublin: Gill & Macmillan.

Sheaff, R., Rogers, A., Pickard, S., Marshall, M., Campbell, S., Sibbold, B., Halliwell, S. and Roland, M. (2003), 'A Subtle Governance: "Soft" Medical Leadership in English Primary Care', *Sociology of Health and Illness*, 25/5, 408–28.

Sheppard, M. (2004), *Appraising and Using Social Research in the Human Services: An Introduction for Social Work and Health Professionals*. London: Jessica Kingsley Publishers.

Shor, I. (1992), *Empowering Education: Critical Teaching for Social Change*. Chicago: University of Chicago Press.

Shore, B.A., Iwata, B.A., Vollmer, T.R., Lerman, D.C. and Zarcone, J.R. (1995), 'Pyramidal Staff Training in the Extension of Treatment for Severe Behaviour Disorders'. *Journal of Applied Behaviour Analysis*, 28/3, 323–332.

Simon, A., Owen, C., Moss, P., Petrie, P., Cameron, C., Potts, P. and Wigfall, V. (2008), *Working Together Volume 1. Secondary Analysis of the Labour Force Survey to Map the Numbers and Characteristics of the Occupations Working within Social Care, Childcare, Nursing and Education*. London: DCSF. <www.dfes.gov.uk/research/data/uploadfiles/DCSF-TCRU-01-08.pdf>

Sinclair, I. and Gibbs, I. (1998), *Children's Homes: A Study in Diversity*. Chichester: Wiley.

Sinclair, I., Gibbs, I. and Hicks, L. (2000), *The Management and Effectiveness of the Home Care Service*. York: Social Work Research and Development Unit, University of York.

Skehill, C. (1999), *The Nature of Social Work in Ireland: A Historical Perspective*. Lampeter: Edwin Mellen.

Skehill, C. (2003), 'Social Work in the Republic of Ireland', *Journal of Social Work*, 3/2, 141–59.

Skehill, C. (2005), 'Child Protection and Welfare Social Work in the Republic of Ireland: Continuities and Discontinuities between the Past and the Present', in N. Kearney and C. Skehill (eds.), *Social Work in Ireland: Historical Perspectives*. Dublin: Institute of Public Administration.

Skinner, A. (1994), *Another Kind of Home: A Review of Residential Child Care* (2nd edn.). Scotland: HMSO.

Skinner, B.F. (1953), *Science and Human Behavior*. New York: Macmillan.

Skott-Myhre, H. (2004), 'Radical Youth Work: Creating a Politics of Mutual Liberation for Youth and Adults', *Journal of Child and Youth Care Work*, 19, 89–95.

Skott-Myhre, H. and Skott-Myhre, K. (2007), 'Radical Youth Work: Love and Community', *Relational Child and Youth Care Practice*, 20/3, 48–57.

Smith, A. (1991), *National Identity*. London: Penguin.

Smith, M.K. (2001), 'David A. Kolb on Experiential Learning'. The Encyclopedia of Informal Education [online text], <www.infed.org/b-explrn.htm>.

Snyder, J., McEachern, A., Schrepferman, L., Zettle, R., Johnson, K., Swink, N., McAlpine, C. (2006), 'Rule-governance, Correspondence Training, and Discrimination Learning: A Developmental Analysis of Covert Conduct Problems', *The Journal of Speech and Language Pathology - Applied Behavior Analysis*, 1/1, 43–55.

Social Care Association (SCA) (1991), *Keyworking in Social Care: An Introductory Guide*. London: Social Care Association.

Social Services Inspectorate (2003), *Practice Guidelines on Safeguarding and Child Protection in Children's Residential Centres*. <www.hiqa.ie/media/pdfs/sc_guidance_safeguarding.pdf>

South and Mid-West Community Development Support Agency Ltd (2006), *A Profile of Community Development Projects and Family Resource Centres in the South and Mid-West Regions*. Limerick: SMCWCDA.

Spence, J. (2007), 'What Do Youth Workers Do?: Communicating Youth Work', *Youth Studies Ireland*, 2/2, 3–18.

Spillane, J.P. (2006), *Distributed Leadership*. London: Wiley.

SRSB (2003), *Definition and Usage of High Support in Ireland*. Dublin: Special Residential Services Board.

Stevens, M., Liabo, K. and Roberts, H. (2007), 'A Review of the Research Priorities of Practitioners Working with Children in Social Care', *Child and Family Social Work*, 12, 295–305.

Stirling, C. and McHugh, A. (1997), 'Natural Therapeutic Holding: A Non-aversive Alternative to the Use of Control and Restraint in the Management of Violence for People with Learning Disabilities', *Journal of Advanced Nursing*, 26/2, 304–11.

Stuart, C. (2001), 'Professionalising Child and Youth Care: Continuing the Canadian Journey', *Journal of Child and Youth Care Work*, 15–16, 264–82.

Stuart, C. (2003), 'Musings on the Art and Science of Professionalizing Child and Youth Care', *Relational Child and Youth Care Practice*, 16/1, 15–20.

Stuart, C., Carty, W. and Dean, M. (2007), 'The Role of Competence in Outcomes for Children and Youth: An Approach for Mental Health', *Relational Child and Youth Care Practice*, 20/1, 47–56.

Stuart, C.A. (1999), Youth Who Attempt Suicide: Exploring Their Experience of Relationship', *Journal of Child and Youth Care*, 13/2, 17–34.

Suizzo, M.A. (2000), 'The Socio-emotional and Cultural Contexts of Cognitive Development: Neo-Piagetian Perspectives', *Child Development*, 71/4, 846–9.

Sutton, C. (2000), *Child and Adolescent Behaviour Problems: A Multidisciplinary Approach to Assessment and Intervention*. Leicester: British Psychological Society.

Sutton, P. (1997), 'Reviewing and Evaluating Therapeutic Progress', in S. Palmer and G. McMahon (eds.), *Client Assessment*. London: Sage.

Task Force on Child Care Services (1980), *Final Report to the Minister for Health: Task Force on Child Care Services*. Dublin: Stationery Office.

Tawney, R.H. (1952), *Equality*. London: Allen & Unwin.

Taylor, C. (2002), 'The Dialogical Self', in D. Hiley, J. Bohman and R. Shusterman (eds.), *The Interpretive Turn: Philosophy, Science and Culture*. New York: Cornell University Press.

Thomas, A. and Chess, S. (1977), *Temperament and Development*. New York: Brunner/Mazel.

Thompson, N. (1996), *People Skills: A Guide to Effective Practice in the Human Services*. London: Macmillan Press.

Thompson, N. (1997), *Anti-discriminatory Practice*. Basingstoke: Macmillan.

Thompson, N. (2002a), 'Anti-discriminatory Practice', in M. Davies (ed.), *The Blackwell Companion to Social Work* (2nd edn.). Oxford: Blackwell Publishing.

Thompson, N. (2002b), *People Skills* (2nd edn.). New York: Palgrave Macmillan.

Thompson, N. (2003), *Promoting Equality: Challenging Discrimination and Oppression* (2nd revised edn.). London: Palgrave.

Thompson, N. (2006), *Anti-discriminatory Practice* (4th edn.). Basingstoke: Palgrave.

Thompson, N. (2007), 'Sociological Contexts for Practice', in R. Adams (ed.), *Foundations of Health and Social Care*. Basingstoke: Palgrave.

Thrane, L., Hoyt, D., Whitbeck, L. and Yoder, K. (2006), 'Impact of Family Abuse on Running Away, Deviance, and Street Victimization among Homeless Rural and Urban Youth', *Child Abuse and Neglect*, 30, 1117–28.

Tolmie, A., Thomson, J.A., Foot, H., Whelan, K., Morrison, S. and McLaren, B. (2005), 'The Effects of Adult Guidance and Peer Discussion on the Development of Children's Representations: Evidence from the Training of Pedestrian Skills', *British Journal of Psychology*, 96, 181–204.

Toolan, D. (2006), 'Disability and Discrimination'. Paper presented to Disability and Discrimination Summer School, National University of Ireland, Galway.

Torode, R., Walsh, T. and Woods, M. (2001), *Working with Refugees and Asylum-Seekers*. Dublin: Trinity College.

Treadwell, K. (1998), 'Border Crossings: Negotiating Marginalities and Accommodating Health Issues among Irish Travellers'. MA thesis, NUI Maynooth.

Tremblay, K. and Downey, E. (2004), 'Identifying and Evaluating Research-based Publications: Enhancing Undergraduate Student Critical Skills', *Education*, 124/4, 734–40.

Tripodi, T. (1974), *Uses and Abuses of Social Research in Social Work*. New York: Columbia University Press.

Tsang, N.M. (1993), 'Shifts of Students' Learning Styles on a Social Work Course', *Social Work Education*, 12/1, 62–75.

Tuairim (1966), *Some of Our Children: A Report on the Residential Care of the Deprived Child in Ireland*. London: Tuairim.

Tuckman, B.W. and Jensen, M. (1977), 'Stages of Small Group Development Revisited', *Groups and Organization Studies*, 2, 419–27.

Tunstill, J., Aldgate, J. and Hughes, M. (2007), *Improving Children's Services: Lessons from Family Centres*. London: Jessica Kingsley Publishers.

Tyler, K. and Johnson, K. (2006), 'Pathways In and Out of Substance Use Among Homeless-Emerging Adults', *Journal of Adolescent Research*, 21/2, 133–57.

Ungerson, C. (1997), 'Social Politics and the Commodification of Care', *Social Politics*, 4/3, 362–82.

UNCRC (United Nations Committee on the Rights of the Child) (2005), 'General Comment No. 6: Treatment of Unaccompanied and Separated Children Outside Their Country of Origin'. Geneva: UNCRC.

United Nations (1994), *Guide for a National Action Programme on the International Year of the Family*. New York: United Nations.

United Nations (2007), *The UN Convention on the Protection and Promotion of the Rights and Dignity of Persons with Disabilities*. New York: United Nations.

UNODC, WHO (2008), *Principles of Drug Dependence Treatment: Discussion Paper*. <www.unodc.org/documents/drug-treatment/UNODC-WHO-Principles-of-Drug-Dependence-Treatment-March08.pdf>, accessed on 7 January 2009.

Utting, W. (1991), *Children in the Public Care*. London: HMSO.

Utting, W. (1997), *People Like Us: A Review of the Safeguards for Children Living Away from Home*. London: HMSO.

Van Doccum, N. (2004), 'The Negligent Carer', *Curam*, 33.

Van Ewijk, H. (2008), 'Social Change and Social Professions', *European Journal of Social Education*, 14/15, 9–19.

Van Leeuwen, M. (ed.) (1993), *After Eden*. Michigan: Eerdmans.

Vandemark, L. (2007), 'Promoting the Sense of Self, Place, and Belonging in Displaced Persons: The Example of Homelessness', *Archives of Psychiatric Nursing*, 21/5, 241–8.

Veale, A., Palaudaries, L. and Gibbons, C. (2003), *Separated Children Seeking Asylum in Ireland*. Dublin: Irish Refugee Council.

Vekíc, K. (2003), *Unsettled Hope: Unaccompanied Minors in Ireland: From Understanding to Response*. Dublin: Marino Institute.

Vygotsky, L. (1978), *Thought and Language*. Cambridge, MA: MIT Press (first published 1934).

Wafer, U. (2006), *Counted In 2005*. Dublin: The Homeless Agency.

Walby, S. (1990), *Theorising Patriarchy*. Oxford: Blackwell.

Walsh, K. (2004), 'The Effects of Living in a Nursing Home on the Cognitive, Sensory, and Sensorimotor Abilities of Low-Dependency Older Adults'. A summary report of a Doctor of Philosophy thesis, University of Limerick.

Ward, H. and Rose, W. (2002), *Approaches to Needs Assessment in Children's Services*. London: Jessica Kingsley Publishers.

Ward, J. (2002), 'Justifying Drug Substitution Therapies: The Case of Methadone Maintenance Treatment', in *Debating Public Policies on Drugs and Alcohol*. Addiction Research Centre, Trinity College Dublin, Second Annual Conference, September 2002. <www.ndc.hrb.ie/attached/1767–1692_Debating_Public_Policies_on_Drugs__Alcohol.pdf>

Ward, T. (2001), *Immigration and Residency in Ireland*. Dublin: CDVEC.

Wardhaugh, J. (2000), *Sub City: Young People, Homelessness and Crime*. Aldershot: Ashgate.

Warner, N. (1992), *Choosing with Care: The Warner Report*. London: Department of Health.

Warnes, A. and Crane, M. (2006), 'The Causes of Homelessness among Older People in England', *Housing Studies*, 21/3, 401–21.

Waters, H.S. and Waters, E. (2006), 'The Attachment Working Models Concept: Among Other Things, We Build Script-Like Representations of Secure Base Experiences', *Attachment and Human Development*, 8/3, 185–97.

Watson, J.B. and Rayner, R. (1920), 'Conditioned Emotional Reactions', *Journal of Experimental Psychology*, 3/1, 1–14.

Wayman, S. (2008), 'Mum's the Word for Networking Mammies', *The Irish Times*, 8 April.

Wexford Area Partnership (2000), *Social Inclusion Plan for the Wexford Area 2000–2004*. Wexford: Wexford Area Partnership.

Wheelan, S.A. (1990), *Facilitating Training Groups: A Guide to Leadership and Verbal Intervention Skills*. Westport: Praeger Publishers.

WHO (1969), *Report on the 16th Session, Expert Committee on Drug Dependence*. Geneva: World Health Organization.

WHO (1980), *International Classification of Impairments, Disabilities and Handicaps: A Manual of Classification Relating to the Consequences of Disease*. Geneva: World Health Organization.

WHO (1986), *Ottawa Charter, 1st International Conference on Health Promotion*. Ottawa: Canada.

WHO (1992), *The International Classification of Diseases, ICD-10. Classification of Mental and Behavioural Disorders*. Geneva: World Health Organization.

WHO (2001), *World Health Day. Mental Health: Stop Exclusion – Dare to Care*. Geneva: World Health Organization. <www.who.int/world-health-day/ previous/2001/en>

WHO (2002), *Toward a Common Language for Functioning, Disability and Health*. Geneva: World Health Organization.

Williams, D. and Lalor, K. (2001), 'Obstacles to the Professionalisation of Social Care in Ireland', *Irish Journal of Applied Social Studies*, 2/3, 73–90.

Williams, G. (2000), 'Research Agenda and Social Care in Wales'. Paper delivered at What Works as Evidence for Practice? The Methodological Repertoire in an Applied Discipline Seminar. 27 April 2000, Cardiff.

Williams, J. and Gorby, S. (2002), *Counted In 2002: The Report of the Assessment of Homelessness in Dublin*. Dublin: The Homeless Agency and the Economic Social and Research Institute.

Wilson, R. (2005), 'Wrong Policies to Build Social Capital', *The Irish Times*, 6 September.

Wistow, G. (2005), *SCIE Position Paper 4: Developing Social Care: The Past, the Present and the Future*. London: Social Care Institute of Excellence. <http://www.scie.org.uk/publications/positionpapers/pp04.asp>

Wosket, V. (1999), *The Therapeutic Use of Self: Counselling Practice and Supervision*. London: Routledge.

Wynne, R., Clarkin, N., Cox, T. and Griffiths, A. (1997), *Guidance on the Prevention of Violence at Work*. Luxembourg: European Commission DG-V.

Youth Homeless Strategy Monitoring Committee (2004), *Developing a Leaving Care and Aftercare Policy: Guidelines for Health Boards*. Dublin: National Children's Office.

Youth Service Liaison Forum (2005), *Strategy for the Delivery of Youth Work in Northern Ireland*. Belfast: Department of Education for Northern Ireland.

Zemon Davies, N. (1971), 'The Reasons of Misrule: Youth Groups and Charivaris in Sixteenth-Century France', *Past and Present*, 50, 41–75.

Index

ABA (applied behaviour analysis), 87–8,
    103–4
abandonment, 294
A-B-C (antecedent-behaviour-
    consequence) approach, 204
absenteeism, 220
abuse
    alcohol, 383, 389–90
    drugs see drug addiction
    physical/non-physical, 199
    scandals and inquiries, 62, 100, 183,
        247, 309
    sexual see sexual abuse
    see also violence
academic qualities, 14
Academy of Professional Child and Youth
    Care, 40
acceptance of a person, 235–6
accommodation (cognitive development),
    78
accountability, 60, 69–70, 183, 328
    supervision function, 186–7
Achenbach, T., 264, 266
Active Retirement groups, 312–13
addiction, 382–402
    defining, 383
    drug prevalence surveys, 388–91
    policy, 384–6
    reporting system, 391–4
    treatment, 394–402
Adding Years to Life and Life to Years, 307
ADHD, 202, 264, 266
advocacy, 54, 109, 121, 232, 343–4
    deficiencies in practice, 104
    definitions, 232, 343–4
    people with disabilities, 54, 339, 340,
        343–4
    self-advocacy, 120, 147
    service-system advocacy, 344

affection, 267
affective equality, 119, 120
Age Action Ireland, 104, 106, 117
Age and Opportunity, 314, 315
ageing, 305–7 see also older people
ageism, 280, 282
aggression, 199, 303 see also challenging
    behaviour
Ahern, Bertie, 161
AIDS, 384
Ainsworth, Maria et al., 95, 269
Alberta Association of Services for Child
    and Families, 44
alcohol abuse, 383, 389–90
Aldridge, M. and Evetts, J., 63, 64
Alimo-Metcalfe, B. and Nyfield, G.,
    219–20, 222
Allen, G. and Langford, D., 276–7
Allen and Tynan, 207
altruism, 125, 170–1
amalgamation (ethnic groups), 357
Amnesty International, 356
Anderson, I. and Tulloch, D., 403, 409,
    410, 411
Anglin, J., 11, 17, 37, 38
anxiety, 264, 266
Appleby, J. et al., 151
applied behaviour analysis (ABA), 87–8,
    103–4
Arousal Relaxation Cycle, 270
'Arts for Older People in Care Settings',
    314–15
ASPIRE model, 232
assault, physical, 199
assessment (child psychological problems),
    272–5
assessment model (young people in care),
    229–31
assessment skills, 181

assimilation, 78, 357, 432
Association for Child and Youth Care
    Practice (ACYCP), 39–40, 41
associative life, 371
asylum seekers, 419–23, 427–8
    children, 421–3, 431, 432
    defining, 420
    statistics, 420
    see also multiculturalism
asylums, 333–4
attachment, 94–7, 268–70
Attention Deficit Hyperactivity Disorder
    (ADHD), 202, 264, 266
attitudes, 123
    challenging, 236–7
    non-judgemental, 235–6
authority-based practice, 150
autism, 87–8, 103, 264–5
autonomy of professionals, 62
autonomy, psychosocial theory, 91
avoidance, 96
avoidance learning, 85–6
awareness see self-awareness

'bad worker', fear of being, 124
Baker, J. et al., 111, 112, 113, 114, 117,
    120
Bandura, Albert, 86–7
Banks, Sarah, 9–10, 69, 70, 71, 72, 108,
    381
Barnados, 18, 106, 117, 232
Barnes, C., 277
Barnes, J. and Connolly, N., 46
Beech, B. and Leather, P., 198, 200
befriending clients, 170, 235
behaviourism, 82–6, 87
Belbin, R., 217, 218
beliefs, 123
    challenging, 236–7
belonging, 89, 90
beneficiary, 432
Beresford, P. and Trevillion, S., 100
best practice, 8–9, 121
betrayal, 297
bioecological model, 97–8
Bird, H., 265
Blanz, B. et al., 270
blind spots, 133, 238
Blome, W. and Steib, S., 161

Bonnar, C., 361
Bowlby, John, 94–5, 96, 268
boys' clubs, 35, 36, 368, 369
Braun, D., 322
Braye, S. and Preston-Shoot, M., 102,
    105–6, 203, 285, 286
Brehm, S. et al., 135
Britain, 46–57, 152, 244
Bronfenbrenner, U. and Evans, G.W., 97–8
Brothers of Charity, 18, 284
Brown, B., 47
Bruner, J., 80, 82
Bryan, A. et al., 383
Bryman, A., 154
Bubeck, D., 142
bullying, 199
Burton, J., 299
Butcher, H. et al., 318
Butler, S., 384
Buzan, Tony, 129
Byrne, J., 234, 240, 241
Byrne, L., 128

CABAS (combined applied behavioural
    analysis), 88
Cameron, C. and Moss, P., 53, 54, 55
Campaign for Independent Living, 105
Campbell Collaboration, 157–8
Canada, child and youth care, 34–45, 67
Canadian Outcome Research Institute, 44
cannabis, 391
care, 142–3, 228
    duty of care, 200–1, 205, 232
    paid/unpaid carers, 142, 143
        UK, 52
    replication of work, 53
    see also social care
Care of the Aged report (1968), 307, 308
care orders, 249
care plans, 108, 228, 297–8
    needs assessment, 228–31
Care Trusts, 50
Care Work in Europe study, 54–5
Carr, A., 263, 264–5, 274, 275
    and Martin, M., 266, 275
Catholic Church, 12, 145, 368
Catholic Youth Care (CYC), 368
Central Remedial Clinic, 214
centration, 79

Centre for Independent Living, 284
CERD, 354–5
Chakrabarti, M. and Hill, M., 297
challenging behaviour, 19–20, 177–9,
    196–210, 303
    defining, 201
    duty of care and, 200–1, 205
    managing, 204–10, 303
    physical/non-physical violence, 199
    student placements and, 177–9
    triggers, 178, 295
    use of restraint, 203–4, 209
chaotic parenting, 95–6
Chappell, D. and Di Martino, V., 198
Charles, G. and Gabor, P., 35, 36
child and youth care (CYC), 34–45, 67
Child and Youth Care Forum, 41
childcare
    assessment model, 229–31
    care/placement plans, 228, 297–8
    deficiencies in, 103–4
    immigrant children, 422, 431, 432
    intervention process, 292
    North America, 34–45
    numbers employed in, 18
    placement types statistics, 245, 292–3
    Travellers, 359
    see also foster care; residential childcare
Child Care Act 1991, 12–13, 231, 247,
    248–9, 251, 253, 255, 291, 292,
    326–7, 359, 414, 422, 429
Child Care (Residential Care)
    Regulations, 249, 251, 252, 256, 297
child development theories, 77–98
Child Protection Unit, 378
Children Act 2001, 13, 231, 249, 256
Children First (1999), 10
Children's Act 1908, 12
children's needs, 267
Child Welfare League of America, 44
Child Welfare League of Canada, 44
choice, 100
Chomsky, N., 81
Citizens Information Act 2007, 340, 344
citizenship, 48, 51, 345
    Irish citizenship, 420–1, 425, 431
City of Dublin Youth Service Board
    (CDYSB), 370
Clareville Day Centre, 314

Clarke, J., 102
Clarke, M., 126, 128, 300
classical conditioning, 83–5
client group, 5–8
Clonmel Project, 266
Clough, R., 295
cocaine, 391
Cochrane Collaboration, 157–8
cognitive behaviour therapy, 87
cognitive development, 77–81
co-habitation, 319
Cohen, P. et al., 265
Cohen, S., 367
Collander-Brown, D., 68
Collins, Jim, 223
Combat Poverty Agency, 117
Comhairle Amendment Bill 2004, 339
Commission for Social Care Inspection, 56
Commission on Itinerancy, 350, 354
Commission on the Status of People with
    Disabilities, 13, 117, 331, 336, 339,
    344
Commission on the Status of Women, 118
communication, 181, 301
communities, sustainable, 51
community care, 107, 203, 307, 318
community development, 107
community hospitals, 308, 310–11, 312
community networks, 323
community nursing units, 310–11, 312
Community, Rural and Gaeltacht Affairs,
    Dept of, 387
competencies, 70, 124
    core skills, 181
compulsiveness, 91
conditioning, 83–5
conduct, professional, 238
    student placements, 58–63
Conklin, J., 211
Connell, R., 141
conservative-corporatist welfare state, 21,
    23, 26
Constitution of Ireland, 13, 111, 291, 318
    citizenship amendment, 421, 431
constructivist theory, 77–80
Cooper, C., 198, 200, 267
core competency skills, 181
CORI, 106
Cork Institute of Technology, 129

'correction' movement, 35, 37
Council of Canadian Child and Youth Care Associations (CCYCA), 39–40, 41
counselling skills, 233
Counted In 2005, 406–7
County Homes, 308
Courtney, D., 135
Cowen, Brian, 118, 378
CPD (Continued Professional Development), 14–5, 183, 240–1
    Personal Development programmes, 129–31
    see also self-development
Craig, J., 63–4
Crane, M. and Warnes, A., 411
Cree, V., 144
Criminal Justice Act 2006, 13
Crimmens, D., 64
critical action, 108
critical social education, 107
critically reflective practice, 184, 190, 206, 233, 286–7
Cross, M. and Papadopoulos, L., 131, 135
Crowley, Niall, 280, 281–2, 341
CSI (Crisis Prevention Institute), 204
Cuan Dara, 401
cultural diversity *see* multiculturalism
cultural equality, 118, 120, 278
cultural tools, 80–1
culture, institutionalised, 425, 428
CYC (Catholic Youth Care), 368
CYC (North America), 34–45, 67
CYC-OnLine, 41

Daughters of Charity, 334
Day, D. et al., 132, 135
day-to-day shared life experiences, 8
debriefing, 179, 209–10
'decent work', 198
de-commodification, 26
defining social care, 5–9, 120–1, 228
democratic professional, 72, 108
demystification, 287
Denmark, 52, 54, 56
Dent, M. and Whitehead, S., 69, 70
deprivation, maternal, 95
deprofessionalisation, 71
despair, 93–4

detention schools, 13, 250, 251
development stages of workers, 127
development theories, 77–98
dialogical education, 107
DiClemente, C., 400
difference, 112, 114–15, 118, 280, 425
dignity, 337–8
Dingwall, Robert, 60
diplomas, 15–16, 240
disability, 330–47
    advocacy, 54, 339, 340, 343–4
    defining, 330–3
    disabled people's movements, 105–6, 107–9, 117, 284
    discrimination, 112, 115, 117, 277–83, 284, 333, 339–40
    extent of, 341–2
    history of services, 333–4
    inspection of services, 250
    medical/traditional model, 332, 335–6
    numbers employed in services, 18
    policy and legislation, 333, 338–43
    social care and, 343–6
    social model of, 51, 332, 336–8, 343
Disability Act 2005, 107, 231–2, 333, 339–40
Disability Federation of Ireland, 104, 106, 284
disadvantage, 7
discipline, 271
discipline and emancipation, 30–1
disclosure, 238
discrimination, 110–21, 276–87
    anti-discriminatory approaches, 282–7, 333, 339–40, 354–5
    defining, 280, 354–5
    indirect, 280
    institutional, 118, 277, 278, 356–7, 425–9
    legislation, 280–2, 333, 339, 355, 357–8
    minority/dominant group relations, 356–7, 425–9
    racial discrimination, 354–5, 425–9
    Travellers, 354–7
    types of, 277–81, 354–5
disempowerment, 203, 279
distress, 260, 265
District Court, 249, 250

distrust, 90
Diversity and Equality Guidelines for Childcare Providers, 423
divorce, 319
Dixon, N., 220–1
Dogra, N. et al., 260
domestic violence, 213, 231
Domestic Violence Act 1996, 231
dominant group, 356–7, 425–9
Dominelli, L., 143–4, 282, 283–4
Dondio, P. et al., 157
doubt, 91
drug addiction
    defining, 383
    drug prevalence surveys, 388–91
    policy, 384–6
    reporting system, 391–4
    treatment, 394–402
dual-focus approach, 187–8, 194
Dublin House of Industry, 333
Dublin Institute of Technology, 166
Duggan-Jackson, A., 350, 351, 360, 365
Dundalk Institute of Technology, 129, 316
Durkheim, Émile, 60
duty of care, 200–1, 205, 232

eating disorders, 265
Eborall, C., 52, 56
EBP *see* evidence-based practice
ecological theory, 97–8
education, 372
    equality ground statistics, 362
    informal/non-formal, 367, 372
Education for Persons with Special Needs Act 2004, 339
education of practitioners *see* training
Egan, Gerard, 225
ego integrity, 93–4
elderly *see* older people
emancipation and discipline, 30–1
emergent practice planning, 132–3
Emerson, E., 201
emotional health, 259–60
emotional needs assessment, 229–30
emotional support, 53
empathy, 234, 298
employment in social care, 16, 18–19
Employment Equality Acts 1998–2004, 280, 333, 339, 355

empowerment, 10, 119, 121, 285, 328
    deficiencies in practice, 103, 107
    defining, 203
    disabled people, 343
    older people, 100
    social care workers, 286
    UK, 48–9
    young people, 371
Enable Ireland, 18, 232, 326
enablement, 48–9
Engel, George, 332
entrepreneurial professional, 72
equality, 110–21, 276–87
    difference and, 112, 114–15, 118, 280
    equality of outcomes, 113
    legislation, 280–2, 333, 339, 355
    liberal/radical perspectives, 112–14
Equality Act 2004, 339
Equality Authority, 117, 341, 355–6
Equality Tribunal, 281–2
Equal Status Acts 2000–2004, 232, 280–1, 282, 339, 349, 355
Erikson, Erik, 90–4
Eriksson, L. and Markström, A-M., 29, 67
Esping-Andersen, G., 21, 116
esteem, 89, 90
ethics, 60, 68
ethnicity, 418–33
    challenges facing social care workers, 423–4
    defining, 354, 424–5
    employment status, 351
    immigration and, 418–23, 427–8
    minority/dominant group relations, 356–7, 425–9
    model for change, 429–32
    racism and oppression, 425–9
    see also Travellers
EU (European Union), 430
EU Action Plan on Drugs, 388
European Monitoring Centre for Drugs and Drug Addiction (EMCDDA), 388
European perspectives in social care, 21–33, 46–57
Every Child Matters, 50, 52
evidence-based practice (EBP), 150–62
    critiquing, 155–9
    internet research, 156–9
    sources of social care knowledge, 153–4
exclusion, 93, 336, 428

Fahlberg, V., 268, 269, 293
family and family support work, 318–29
    changing structure of family, 319
    family stress, 270–1
    family well-being, 322–3
    human rights approach, 328–9
    services, 324–7
    training of workers, 327–8
    types of support, 319–20
family resource centres, 324–5
Family Support Agency, 324
Farrell, T. and O'Doherty, C., 64, 66, 67,
    70
FEANTAS, 403–4, 407
feedback, 184, 190
femininity, 138–40
Ferguson, H. and O'Reilly, M., 292
Ferguson, R., 37
Ferry House (Clonmel), 292
Fewster, G., 125, 126, 135
Fielder, F., 222
Fink, J., 142
Focus Ireland, 18, 106
Foróige, 368
Forum of People with Disabilities, 117, 344
foster care, 292, 294
    cost of, 293
    inspections, 249, 251
    statistics, 245, 292, 293
Foucault, Michel, 27, 30, 31, 63
fragmentation, 428
Freedom of Information Act 1997, 183
Freidson, Eliot, 60, 61–2, 63
friendship, befriending clients, 170, 235
Friere, Paulo, 104, 107
From Rhetoric to Rights, 340
functional behavioural assessment (FBA),
    204

Gaffney, M. and Harmon, C., 160–1
Gaisce, 370
Gallagher, C., 313, 314
    and O'Toole, J., 64, 137
Galvin, Paddy, 100
Garda Síochána, 13, 168–9, 250, 388, 427
Gardener, A., 285–6
Garfat, T., 126, 135
gatekeepers, 110, 277, 286
Gaughan, P. and Gharabaghi, K., 37, 38

gay people, 148–9
gender, 62, 137–49
    identity, 138–9
    inequality, 113, 115, 118, 140–1, 279
    male/female workers, 52, 142–4
        North America, 38, 42–3
    sexuality, 145–9
Gender Equality Monitoring Committee,
    118
General Social Care Council, 56
generativity, 93
genocide, 357
genuineness, 234–5, 298
geriatric homes, 308, 310, 312
Germany, 56
Gibbs, L., 157
    and Gambrill, E., 150
Gilchrist, A., 323
Gilligan, R., 297, 299, 300
girls' clubs, 35, 36, 368, 369
Go for Life campaign, 315
goal-directed social education work, 68
Goodin, R. et al., 23
Google, 156
Gossett, M. and Weinman, L., 157
Graham, G., 96
groups, 212–13
    stages of, 215
Guerin, Veronica, 384
guilt, 91

habilitation, 345
Hallstedt, Pelle and Högström, Mats, 21,
    64–5, 67, 68–9
handicap, 331 see also disability
harassment, 280–1
    sexual, 198, 199, 280–1
Harney, Mary, 309
Haslett, D., 312, 313
Hawkins, P. and Shohet, R., 125, 126, 127,
    171, 235, 241
Health Act 2004, 248, 394
Health Act 2007, 248, 249–50, 251, 252
health and safety at work, 197–201
Health and Safety Authority (HSA),
    197–8, 199
Health and Social Care Professionals
    Act 2005, 5, 12, 15, 65, 101,
    240, 343

Health and Social Care Professionals Council, 18
Health Information and Quality Authority (HIQA), 248–58, 339, 340
Health (Nursing Homes) Act 1990, 309
health promotion, definition, 384
Health Service Executive see HSE
Hennessy, S., 343, 345
Herbert, M., 267–8
heroin, 383–4, 389–90
Hessle, Sven, 28–9
hierarchy of needs, 88–90
Higham, P., 48
Higher Education Authority (HEA), 16
Higher Education Training and Awards Council (HETAC), 65
Hill, A., 321
Hillman, J., 125
HIQA, 248–58, 339, 340
history of social care, 12–14, 26, 367
   North America, 34–7
HIV, 384, 395
holistic nature of social care practice, 8, 327
home help, 47, 53–4, 306
   cutbacks, 104
Homeless Agency, 406, 412, 415
homelessness, 403–17
   becoming homeless, 409–12
   definitions and typology, 403–5
   extent of, 406–8
   policy and services, 412–15
   youth, 405, 407–9, 410–11, 414
Homelessness: An Integrated Strategy, 412
Homeless Preventative Strategy, 412–13
Home-Start, 326
homophobia, 280
homosexuality, 148–9
Houser, J., 154
Housing Act 1988, 405–6, 412
Housing (Traveller Accommodation) Act 1998, 358
Howe, D. et al., 269
HSA (Health and Safety Authority), 197–8, 199
HSE (Health Service Executive), 67, 248, 395
   child care, 248, 250, 292
   cutbacks, 103

drug addiction treatment, 394–5, 397–9, 402
family support services, 326–7
older people's services, 306
   cutbacks, 104
Human Rights Commission, 117
humility, 287
Hungary, 54

ICF (International Classification of Functioning, Disability and Health), 332
identity, 92, 280
   construction, 24, 26, 28
   gender identity, 138–9
   Irish identity, 421, 425, 428, 431
immigration, 418–23, 427
   children, 421–3, 431, 432
   see also multiculturalism
Immigration Act 2003, 427
Immigration, Residence and Protection Bill 2008, 427
IMPACT, 65
impairment, 331–2, 336
   psychological development, 262–3
   see also disability
impulsiveness, 91
incident and response plans, 206–7
industrial schools, 13, 66, 110, 367
inequality, 110–21, 276–87
   difference and, 112, 114–15, 118, 280
   equality legislation, 280–2, 333, 339, 355
   ethnic groups, 425–9
   gender, 113, 115, 118, 140–1, 279
   political/economic/cultural, 118
infantilisation, 279
inferiority and industry (psychosocial theory), 91–2
Inglis, T., 145, 146
inhibition, 91
initiative (psychosocial theory), 91
inspection of residential centres
   for children, 247–58
   for older people, 250, 309–10
Institutes of Technology, 15–16, 166
   personal development programmes, 129–31
   Sligo, 26–7, 28, 29, 32
institutional discrimination, 118, 277, 278, 356–7, 425–9

institutional oppression, 425–9
institutional racism, 277, 356–7, 425–9
institutionalisation, 315, 333–4
institutionalised culture, 425, 428
integration, 68, 423, 432
intellectual needs assessment, 230–1
Intercultural Strategy for Youth Work, 213
Interdepartmental Group on Drugs (IDG), 385–7
interdisciplinary teamwork, 13–14, 211–26
    lack of integration, 101–2
internal working model (IWM), 94
International Federation of Social Workers (IFSW), 10
International Labour Organization (ILO), 198, 207, 209
International Leadership Coalition for Professional Child and Youth Care Workers (ILCFPCYCW), 40
internet research, 156–9
intervention skills, 181
intimacy, 92–3
Irish Association of Social Care Educators (IASCE), 16, 65
    definitions of social care, 5, 7
    student placements, 165–6, 172, 173
Irish Association of Social Care Workers (IASCW), 65, 242
Irish Human Rights Commission, 430
Irish identity, 421, 425, 428, 431
Irish Journal of Applied Social Studies, 65
Irish Medical Organisation, 107
Irish National Organisation of the Unemployed (INOU), 117
Irish Nurses Organisation (INO), 109, 242
Irish Refugee Council, 421, 430
Irish Society for the Prevention of Cruelty to Children (ISPCC), 104, 106
Irish Traveller Movement, 117, 232, 284, 355
Irish Youth Justice Service, 250
isolation, 92–3

James, William, 127
Jay, Douglas, 111
Jenkins, R., 122
Johari Window exercise, 238
Johns, H., 132

Joint Committee on Social Care Professionals, 8, 120, 228
Jordan, B., 324, 329
Journal of Child and Youth Care, 41
Jung, Carl, 127, 170
Justice, Equality and Law Reform, Dept of, 292, 427, 432

Kanics, J., 428
Kanter, Rosabeth Moss, 220
Kazdin, A., 271
Kellmer-Pringle, M., 267
Kelly, G., 132
Kendrick, D., 349
Kennedy, K. and Gallagher, C., 12
Kennedy Report (1970), 13, 100, 239
Kennefick, Patricia, 123, 125, 129–30, 233
Kerry Family Support, 327
keyworking, 299–300
Kilkenny incest case, 13
King, D., 421
Kirby, P., 115–16
Klaus, M. and Kennell, J., 268
Knoppers, A., 426
knowledge, 153–4, 159 see also evidence-based practice
Kotter, J., 224
Kouzes, J. and Posner, B., 224
Kröger, T., 46
Krueger, M., 126, 135

Labour Court, 227
language development, 77, 81–2
    milestones, 83
Laurence, J., 238
Lawrence, Stephen, 277
Layder, D., 125, 131–2, 154
Leadbetter, C., 72
leadership, 219–25
    compared to management, 223–4
    theories, 221–3
learning, and supervision, 186, 187
learning, development theories, 77–98
learning theory, 82–7
Leas Cross nursing home, 309
Lentin, R., 421
Lewis, Janet, 159
liberal equality, 112–14
liberal welfare state, 21, 23, 26, 55, 106, 115

Liberatore, R., 128
Likert, R., 222
Lillehammer, 24–6, 29, 32
Limerick Institute of Technology, 129–30
Lindsay, Margaret, 59, 61
Local Drugs Task Forces, 370, 385, 386, 397, 399
Lorenz, W., 29, 419
love, 93
    need for, 89, 90
Lukes, S., 105
lunatic asylums, 333–4
Lyon, D. and Glucksman, M., 142, 143

McCann, M. et al., 350
McCarthy, Justin, 173–5, 177, 181
Maccoby, E. and Martin, J., 271
McDonnell, A., 207, 208
McDowell, Michael, 111
Macionis, J. and Plummer, K., 139, 141, 354
McKenna, Danielle, 175–7, 181
MacKenna, Patti, 123, 128
Macpherson Report (1999), 277
McQuaid, Archbishop John Charles, 370
McVerry, Fr Peter (McVerry Trust), 106, 401
Madsen, Bent, 29, 68, 69
Magdalene laundries, 113
Maier, H., 125
Main, M. and Solomon, J., 269
Malmö University, 27–8, 29
management, compared to leadership, 223–4
Mansell Report (1992), 202, 203
marginalisation, 7, 278
Marsh, P. and Fisher, M., 151, 152
Martin, M. and Carr, A., 266, 275
masculinity, 138–40, 141, 143–4
Maslow, Abraham, 88–90, 228
maternal deprivation, 95
Mathiesen, Roger, 29
Maycock, P. and Carr, N., 410–11
Maycock, P. and O'Sullivan, E., 416
meals on wheels, 306
Mearns, D. and Thorne, B., 234, 235
MEBS (multi-element behaviour support), 204
medical model, 332, 335–6
medical profession, 102

men, as social care workers, 143–4
    in North America, 38, 42–3
mental health, 259–75, 330–47
    anti-discriminatory initiatives, 284, 338–41
    deficiencies in services, 103
    defining, 259–60
    family support services, 326
    history of services, 333–4
    medical/traditional model, 332, 335–6
    numbers in psychiatric units, 342
    policy and legislation, 338–43
    social care and, 343–6
    social model, 51, 332, 336–8, 343
    young people, 259–75
Mental Health Act 2001, 339
Mental Health Coalition, 106
Mental Health Foundation, 259–60
metacognitive understanding, 79
methadone, 401–2
Metraux, S. and Culhane, D., 410
migration, 418–23 see also multiculturalism
mind maps, 129
minority groups, 357 see also multiculturalism; Travellers
Mintzberg, H., 223
mistrust, 90
Moane, G., 426
modelling, 86–7
Molloy, Bobby, 370
mood disorders, 265, 266
morale of staff, 183, 200, 220
Moss, P. and Cameron, C., 142
motherese, 81
motivation, 87
Mountjoy Prison, 292
Mulcahy, W., 102
multiculturalism, 418–33
    challenges facing social care workers, 423–4
    employment status, 351
    immigration, 418–23, 427–8
    minority/dominant group relations, 356–7, 425–9
    model for change, 429–32
    racism and oppression, 425–9
    see also Travellers
multidisciplinary teams, 13–14, 211–26
    lack of integration, 101–2

National Action Plan for Social Inclusion, 413

National Advisory Committee on Drugs (NACD), 388

National Children's Strategy (2000), 292

National Council on Ageing and Older People, 312

National Disability Authority (NDA), 284, 330–1, 344–5

National Disability Strategy, 339

National Disability Survey (2006), 340

National Drugs Strategy, 385–7, 395

National Drug Treatment Reporting System (NDTRS), 391–4

National Intellectual Disability Database (NIDD), 341, 342

National Physical and Sensory Disability Database, 342

National Qualifications Authority of Ireland (NQAI), 15

National Standards for Children's Residential Centres, 182, 246, 251–2, 256

National Standards for Disability Services, 339

National Standards for Foster Care, 249

National Standards for Residential Care Settings for Older People, 309

National Women's Council of Ireland, 117

National Youth Council of Ireland (NYCI), 369, 370, 377

National Youth Health Programme, 214

National Youth Policy Committee, 374–5

National Youth Work Advisory Committee (NYWAC), 376–7, 378, 380

National Youth Work Development Plan, 372, 375, 376, 377–8

Neary case, 62

needs, 88–90, 228
    assessment model (young people), 229–31
    of children, 267

negative reinforcement, 85–6

neo-liberalism, 106, 115

Netherlands, 14, 23–4, 27, 29, 31–2, 52, 54

new social movements (NSMs), 106–8, 117

Ní Chonaill, B., 419

Nijmegen study programme, 23–4, 27, 29, 31–2

Non-violent Crisis Intervention, 204

Noonan, P., 363

normalisation, 25

North America, child and youth care (CYC), 34–45, 67

North American Certification Project (NACP), 39, 40

North American Consortium of Child and Youth Care Education Programmes, 40

Norway, 24–6, 29, 32

NSETS (North South Education and Training Standards Committee), 378, 379, 380

nursing homes, 308–11, 314–17
    abuse scandals, 309
    criticisms of, 315
    inspection of services, 250, 309–10
    statistics, 310

Nursing Homes Support Scheme Bill 2008, 309

Oblates, 36

O'Brien, J. and O'Brien, L., 336–8

observational learning, 86–7

O'Connor, Pat, 64, 140, 141, 145–6

O'Connor, Tom, 102, 121, 137, 142

O'Doherty, C., 104, 108, 318, 326, 327, 325

O'Donnell case, 280

O'Farrell, U., 234, 234, 238

Ógra Chorcaí, 369

older people, 305–17
    community care, 307
    day care services, 312–14, 315–17
    deficiencies in services, 104, 306, 313
    home help, 47, 53–4, 306
        cutbacks, 104
    policy developments, 104, 306, 307–8
    projected population increase, 306
    psychosocial theory, 93–4
    residential care, 308–11, 314–17
        abuse scandals, 309
        criticisms of, 315
        inspection of services, 250, 309–10
        statistics, 310

social care model, 315–16
staff training, 316
UK, 53–4, 55, 56
O'Loingsigh, D., 423
OMCYA (Office for the Minister for
Children and Youth Affairs), 378–9,
414
O'Neill, Des, 309
OPEN (Network of Lone Parents Groups),
117
openness, 287
operant conditioning, 85–6
oppression, 425–9
ORAC (Office of the Refugee Applications
Commissioner), 420, 427
organisational activities, 17
Orme, J., 143
orphanages (North America), 35
O'Shea, E., 100, 306, 308, 310
O'Sullivan, E., 406, 409, 412, 416
O'Sullivan, T. and Butler, S., 384
Ottawa Charter for Health Promotion, 384

Page, S., 128
Parekh, B., 115
parentese, 81
parenting, 321–2
and attachment, 94–7, 268–71
Parents Plus programme, 87
participation, 328, 343
partnership, 7, 285, 375
patriarchy, 140–1
Pavee Point, 117, 284, 349, 355, 360, 363
Pavlov, Ivan, 83–5
pay scales, 18–19
UK, 53
Pedler, Mike et al., 216, 220, 223
peer tutoring, 80, 87
People with Disabilities in Ireland, 106
performativity and institutional reform,
69–71
personal development, 122–36, 233–43
CPD, 14–5, 183, 240–1
Personal Development (PD) programmes,
129–31
'personal social services', 47
person-centred planning (PCP), 344–5
personhood, 100
Petrie, P. et al., 66

Phelan, J., 126
Phillips, A., 114, 119
physical assault, 199
physical needs assessment, 231
Piaget, Jean, 77–80, 81
Pinker, S., 81
placement plans, 228, 297–8
needs assessment, 228–31
placements, student, 165–81
check-list, 171
preparation for, 167–71
professionalism, 169–70
'quality of fit', 167–8
planning skills, 181
Plath, D., 154, 161
pluralism, 357
policy see social policy
Poor Servants of the Mother of God, 311
Positive Interaction Cycle, 270
positive reinforcement, 85–6
poverty, 115–17, 321–2, 341
power, 105
between client and worker, 30–1,
277–8, 285
disempowerment, 203, 279
motives for becoming a social care
worker, 125, 170–1
professionalisation and, 58–63
see also empowerment
prejudice, 278, 279, 286
pressure groups, 105–9, 117, 284
primary care centres, 214
privation, maternal, 95
process groups, 233
professional conduct, 238
placements, 58–63
professional development, 64–6, 233–43
CPD, 14–5, 183, 240–1
Personal Development programmes,
129–31
professionalisation, 5–6, 58–73, 238–43,
379
defining, 58–61
democratic professional, 72, 108
fear of being a 'bad worker', 124
gender dimensions, 62
Irish practice, 64–6, 67, 69–70, 72–3
performativity, 69–71
professional cloak, 126

professionalisation (*continued*)
    professional conduct, 238
    resistances to, 71
    typology of professionalising strategies,
        71–2
projection, 129
promiscuity, 92
prostitution, 427–8
protection, 231–2, 345
Protection for Persons Reporting Child
        Abuse Act 1998, 183
Psychiatric Nurses Association, 280
psychiatric units, 342
psychological development theories, 77–98
psychological problems (young people),
        259–75
    assessment, 272–5
psychosocial theory, 90–4
psychotherapy, 234
Punch, M., 154
punishment, positive/negative, 86

qualifications, 15–16
    UK, 56–7
    unqualified workers, 239
qualities of social care practitioners, 14–15
    core competency skills, 181
    development stages, 127
    unqualified workers, 239
*Quality and Fairness: A Health Strategy for
    You*, 307–8
*Quality Framework for Mental Health
    Services*, 340–1
Quinton, D., 319

racism, 425
    institutional, 277, 356–7, 425–6
    racial discrimination, 354–5, 425–9
    Travellers, 354–7
Raftery, Mary, 100
Rappaport, J., 203
Reception and Integration Agency, 422
reflective practice, 184, 190, 206, 233,
        286–7
reflexive professional, 72
reformatory schools, 13, 66, 110, 367
Refugee Act 1996, 427, 429
refugees, 419–23, 427–8
    children, 421–3, 431, 432

defining, 420
statistics, 420
see also multiculturalism
registration, 240–1
    children's centres, 251
rehabilitation, 345
reinforcement, positive/negative, 85–6
Relational Child and Youth Care Practice, 41
relational frame theory, 87
relationships, 125–6, 233–7, 298–300
    attachment, 94–7, 268–70
    defining, 126
    genuineness in, 234–5, 298
    power in, 30–1, 125, 171
    unconditional acceptance, 235–6
Rental Accommodation Scheme (RAS),
        413
repetition disorders, 264
replication of care given by family, 53
Report on Caring and Social Studies (1992),
        13
research, 150–62
    critiquing, 155–9
    qualitative/quantitative, 154
residential care for elderly, 308–11, 314–17
    abuse scandals, 309
    criticisms of, 315
    inspection of services, 250, 309–10
    statistics, 310
residential childcare, 244–58, 291–304
    aims and objectives, 245–6
    assessment model, 229–31
    attachment theory and, 96–7
    care and placement plans, 228, 297–8
    challenges in, 19–20, 302–3 *see also*
        challenging behaviour
    cost of, 292–3
    designated centres, 249
    high-support and special care units,
        292, 294
    historical development, 12–13, 367
    immigrant children, 422, 431
    inspection, 247–58
    intervention process, 292
    North America, 35–7
    numbers employed in, 18
    reasons for being in care, 293
    staff role, 247–8, 294–302
    staff self-care, 302–3

staff supervision, 182, 302
standards and regulations, 246, 251–2
statistics, 245, 292–3
Travellers, 359
UK, 244
Residential Forum, 298–9
Resident Managers' Association (RMA), 65
resilience, 260
respect, 90, 100, 203, 205
Reynolds, S. et al., 393
Richards, J., 293
Ricks, F., 126, 132
and Charlesworth, J., 132
rights, 285–7, 328
refugees, 421–2
UN Declaration of Human Rights, 111,
328
young people, 292, 421–2
rights-based model, 48, 51, 328–9
Riley, J., 329
risk, 19, 69, 197–200
assessment procedures, 205–6
Rogers, Carl, 234–6, 298
role confusion, 92
role of social care workers, 17–18, 99–100,
171, 228, 231–6
defining, 120–1
development stages, 127
therapeutic, 233–4
UK, 53–5
Rosen, A., 153
ROSIE study, 401
ruthlessness, 91
Rutter, M., 95, 261, 262, 263
Ryle, Gilbert, 159

safety at work, 197–201
Safety, Health and Welfare at Work Act
1989, 183
Safety, Health and Welfare at Work Act
2005, 197
safety needs, 89–90, 267
St Gabriel's nursing home, 311
St Michael's House, 334
St Patrick's Hospital, 334
St Patrick's Institution, 292
Saint Vincent de Paul, 106
salary scales, 18–19
UK, 53

Satir Model, 129
scaffolding, 80
schizophrenia, 265
Schizophrenia Ireland, 326
Schön, Donald, 69, 159, 286
Scott, A., 205, 207
Scouting Ireland, 369
scripts, 95
search engines, 156
security needs, 89–90, 267
felt security, 268–9
Seebohm Report (1968), 47, 55
segregation, 357
self, 122–3
self-actualisation, 88, 89
self-advocacy, 120, 147
self-awareness, 24, 27, 122–36, 233
core skills, 181
hidden self, 127–8
managing challenging behaviour, 206
training, 128–35, 237–8
self-care in residential work, 302–3
self-determination, 343
self-development, 122–36, 233–43
CPD, 14–5, 183, 240–1
stages, 127
training, 128–35, 237–41
self-disclosure, 238
self-management, 63–4
Senior Citizens' clubs, 312–13
service-system advocacy, 344
sex, 138
sexism, 279, 280
sexual abuse
allegations and social care workers, 42–3
consequences of, 178–9
scandals, 62
sexual exploitation (immigrants), 427–8
sexual harassment, 198, 199, 280–1
sexuality, 145–9
shame, 91
shaping, 86
Shaping a Healthier Future, 307, 358
Share, Perry, 108
et al., 138, 141, 145, 148
Sheaff, R. et al., 70
sheltered housing, 308
Sheppard, M., 162
shift-working, 301

Shore, B.A. et al., 207
Simon, A. et al., 48, 52, 56
Simon Community, 106
single-parent families, 319
SIPTU, 65
Skehill, Caroline, 10, 11
skills, core competency skills, 181
Skinner, A., 172
Skinner, B.F., 85–6
Sligo Institute of Technology, 26–7, 28, 29, 32
Smith, A., 425
social capital, 323, 329
social care, 3–20, 66, 99–109, 137, 227–8
    defining, 5–9, 120–1, 228
    different to social work, 9–12, 47–8, 66
    employment of practitioners, 16, 18
        UK, 52–3
    European perspectives, 21–33, 46–57
    historical developments, 12–14, 26, 367
    lack of integration, 101–9
    language of care, 142–3
    profession see professionalisation
    qualities of practitioners, 14–15
        core skills, 181
        development stages, 127
        unqualified workers, 239
    role see role of social care workers
    salary scales, 18–19
    SWOT analysis, 100–1
    training see training
    values and principles, 50–1
Social Care Association, 299
Social Care Institute for Excellence, 56
Social Care Registration Board, 240–1
Social Care Value Based Activities
    Programme for Older People, 316
social change, 99–109
social-constructivist theory, 80–1
social democratic welfare state, 21, 23, 25, 116
social education work, 68
    critical social education, 107
social justice, 116, 327
social model of disability, 51, 332, 336–8, 343
social movements, 106–8, 117, 367–8
social needs assessment, 229
social networks, 323

social pedagogy, 9, 22–3, 66–7, 68
social policy, 21–57, 65, 101–9
    European perspectives, 21–33, 54, 116
    UK, 46–57, 116
    Ireland, 26, 65, 101–9, 212, 307–8, 368
        deficiencies, 101–9, 306, 308, 313
    North America, 34–45, 67
    research and, 160–1
social political discourse, 25
social restriction, 262
Social Services Inspectorate (SSI), 247–58
social skills, 260
social work, 9–12, 102
    different to social care practice, 9–12, 47–8, 66
    United Kingdom, 47–8
socialisation and gender, 139–40
socio-emotional development, 88–94
soft coercion, 70–1
Sonas, 311, 315
Song for a Raggy Boy, 100
Spain, 54
Special Care Orders, 249
Special Care Regulations 2004, 256
special care units, 292, 294
    inspection of, 249, 252
Special Projects for Youth (SPY) scheme, 370
special schools, 292, 334
spiritual needs assessment, 231
Springboard programme, 325–6, 327
stagnation, 93
State see social policy
stereotyping, 278
Stevens, M. et al., 152
Stewart Institution for Idiotic and Imbecile
    Children, 334
stigma, 202
Stirling, C. and McHugh, A., 203
'Strange Situation' procedure, 95–6
Strategic Management Initiative (SMI), 70, 385
Strategy for Equality, 13, 117, 331, 336, 339, 344
Strategy to Address Homelessness in Ireland, 413
stress, 262, 265
    and family adversity, 270–1
stress, work-related, 198–9, 220, 302–3

Stuart, C., 126, 135
student placements *see* placements, student
subsidiarity principle, 368, 375
subvention scheme, 308–9
Suffer the Little Children, 100
supervision, 182–95, 241–2, 302
    dual-focus approach, 187–8, 194
    negative experiences, 185, 189, 241
    skills of effective supervisor, 193–4
    student placements, 165–6, 171–2,
        174–6, 179–80
support of clients, 232, 319–20
support of social care workers, 186, 187,
    302
sustainable communities, 51
Sutton, P., 232
Sweden, 27–8, 29, 52, 54, 116
SWOT analysis, 100–1
systematic domination, 425–9

targeted services, 50
Task Force on the Travelling Community,
    118
Task Force Report on Child Care Services
    (1980), 13
Tawney, R., 113–14
teamwork, 211–26
    dysfunctional teams, 218–19
    formation stages of team, 215
    high-performance teams, 216
    lack of integration, 101–2
    residential childcare, 301
    team characteristics, 212–13
    team roles, 216–18
    interdisciplinary teams, 13–14, 213–14,
        225
temperament, 272
therapy and therapeutic intervention,
    233–4
    therapeutic crisis intervention (TCI),
        99, 204
Thomas, A. and Chess, S., 272
Thompson, N., 125, 135, 233, 276, 277–9,
    283, 286–7
tokenism, 428
Towards 2016, 340, 387
traditional professional, 72
training, 12, 26–7, 101, 239–40
    criticisms of, 102, 104

European examples, 21–33, 47–8
    UK, 52, 56–7
    North America, 38–9
    ongoing *see* CPD; self-development
    placements *see* placements, student
    qualifications, 15–16
    self-awareness training, 128–36, 237–8
    unqualified workers and, 239
    see also Institutes of Technology
trait theory, 221
Tralee Institute of Technology, 130–1
Traveller Health Strategy 2002–2005, 357,
    358
Travellers, 348–65
    advocacy, 232
    age profile and numbers, 352, 353
    children in care, 359
    definition, 349
    discrimination and racism, 354–7
    education, 278, 361–3
    employment, 350–1
    ethnicity and, 354–7
    health, 352–4
        strategies, 357, 358, 360–1, 364–5
    inequality, 110, 117, 118
        initiatives, 284
    legislation affecting, 355, 357–8
Travellers' Family Care, 359
Treadwell, K., 353, 361
Trinity College Dublin, 113
Trinity House School (Dublin), 292
trust, 62
    psychosocial theory, 90
Tsang, N., 128, 135
Tuairim Report (1966), 13
Tuckman, B. and Jensen, M., 215
Tullamore Primary Health Care Project
    (Travellers), 360, 364–5
Tunstill, J. et al., 325
tutors, on placements, 165–6, 173

unconditional positive regard (UPR), 235–6
United Kingdom, 46–57, 152, 244
United Nations
    Convention on the Rights of the Child,
        292, 421–2
    Declaration of Human Rights, 111, 328
    disability convention, 340
    UN Office on Drugs and Crime, 382

United States, 34–45, 67, 105, 265
universal services, 50
unqualified workers, 239
Utting, William, 245

valued experiences, 337–8
values, 123
   challenging, 236–7, 279
values of social care, 50–1
Van Doccum, N., 232
Van Ewijk, H., 67
verbal abuse, 199
vetting of students, 168–9
violence, 196–210
   costs of, 200
   dealing with violent situations, 178,
      204–10
   debriefing after, 179, 209–10
   domestic, 213
   sexual see sexual abuse
   statistics, 197
   student placements, 177–9
   types of physical/non-physical violence,
      199
   use of restraint, 203–4, 209
A Vision for Change, 340
vocation, 59, 61
Vocational Education Committees
   (VECs), 375–6
voluntarism, 368
Voluntary Youth Council, 376
Vygotsky, Lev, 80–1

Walby, S., 140, 141
Walsh, K., 315
Ward, J., 401
Warner Report (1992), 244
Watson, J. and Rayner, R., 85
The Way Home, 403
Weber, Max, 60
welfare nurses, 24–5
welfare state, 112, 115–16
welfarism, 279

wellbeing
   emotional, 259–60
   family wellbeing, 322–3
'wicked problems', 211
Wikipedia, 157
Williams, D. and Lalor, K., 60, 64
Williams, G., 151
willpower, 91
Wistow, G., 50–1
women
   inequality, 113, 115, 118, 140–1, 284
   sexism, 279, 280, 284
   sexuality, 145–9
   as social care workers, 142–4
   women's rights movement, 140
Women's Aid, 232
work, 'decent', 198
workhouses, 47, 333–4
Working for Children and Families, 151
World Health Organisation (WHO), 260,
   265, 331–2, 382, 383
Wynne, R. et al., 198

The Years Ahead: A Policy for the Elderly,
   307, 308, 310, 312
Young Men's Christian Association
   (YMCA), 35, 36
Young Women's Christian Association
   (YWCA), 35, 36
youth homelessness, 405, 407–9, 410–11, 414
Youth Homelessness Strategy, 405, 414
Youth Service Grant Scheme, 370
youth work, 366–81
   definition, 366–7
   history and policy developments,
      367–71, 374–9
   role of youth workers, 371–4
   training and professionalisation, 379–80
   Youth Work Act 2001, 366, 369, 375–7
   Youth Work Committee, 376
   Youth Work Ireland, 369

zone of proximal development (ZPD), 80